104

lonely planet

Sweden

Carolyn Bain
Graeme Cornwallis

D0011328

LONELY PLANET PUBLICATIONS
Melbourne • Oakland • London • Paris

FINLAND

NORWEGIAN SEA

GULF OF BOTHNIA

NORRLAND

LAPPLAND

NORRBOTTEN

VÄSTERBOTTEN

ÅNGERMANLAND

JÄMTLAND

MEDELPAD

JUKKASJÄRVI
This tiny town is home to Sweden's coolest attraction, the stunning Ice Hotel – a unique accommodation experience

INLANDSBANAN
The Inland Railway Line – a 1067km route from Mora to Gällivare via Östersund – is one of the great rail journeys of Scandinavia and an excellent way to see the north

HÖGA KUSTEN
The High Coast is one of the most attractive parts of Sweden's coastline, with striking landscapes of lakes, fjords, islands and tiny fishing villages

KUNGSLEDEN
Sweden's premier hiking trail passes through rugged mountain landscapes including Kebnekaise, the country's highest peak

SAREK NATIONAL PARK
Known as the finest wilderness area in Europe, this rarely visited area is a haven for wildlife and an endurance test even for experienced hikers

Arctic Circle

Rovaniemi

Oulu

Haparanda

Kalix

Luleå

Piteå

Skellefteå

Umeå

Vaasa

Örnsköldsvik

Härnösand

Östersund

Åre

Stjørdal

Trondheim

Mo i Rana

Bodø

Narvik

Karesuando

Jukkasjärvi

Kiruna

▲ Kebnekaise (2111m)

Gällivare

Jokkmokk

Kvikkjokk

Ammarnäs

Sorsele

Storuman

Vilhelmina

Kittelfjäll

Gäddede

Strömsund

Lycksele

Åsele

Pajala

Övertorneå

Överkalix

Boden

E8

E10

E10

E4

E4

E12

E14

45

45

45

Abisko National Park

Sarek National Park

Akkajaure

Hornavan

Över...

Storsjön

E45°

0   60   120km
0   30   60mi

N

NORWEGIAN SEA

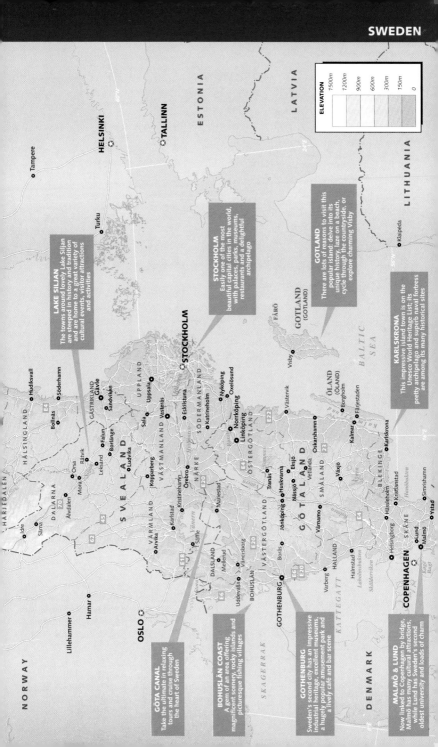

ELEVATION

1500m
1200m
900m
600m
300m
150m
0

STOCKHOLM
Easily one of the most beautiful capital cities in the world, with palaces, parks, museums, restaurants and a delightful archipelago

LAKE SILJAN
The towns around lovely Lake Siljan are steeped in history and tradition and are home to a great variety of cultural events, visitor attractions and activities

GOTLAND
There are lots of reasons to visit this popular island: delve into its unique history, laze on a beach, cycle through the countryside, or explore charming Visby

KARLSKRONA
This impressive island town is on the Unesco World Heritage List; its pretty archipelago and superb naval fortress are among its many historical sites

GÖTA CANAL
Take the ultimate in relaxing tours and cruise through the heart of Sweden

BOHUSLÄN COAST
A gem of an area offering magnificent scenery, rocky islands and picturesque fishing villages

GOTHENBURG
Sweden's second city has an impressive industrial heritage, excellent museums, a hugely popular amusement park and a lively café and bar scene

MALMÖ & LUND
Now linked to Copenhagen by bridge, Malmö has many cultural attractions, while Lund has Sweden's second oldest university and loads of charm

NORWAY

DENMARK

ESTONIA

LATVIA

LITHUANIA

BALTIC SEA

SKAGERRAK

KATTEGATT

HELSINKI

TALLINN

OSLO

COPENHAGEN

STOCKHOLM

GOTLAND
(GOTLAND)

ÖLAND
(ÖLAND)

SVEALAND

GÖTALAND

DALARNA

HÄRJEDALEN

HÄLSINGLAND

GÄSTRIKLAND

UPPLAND

VÄSTMANLAND

SÖDERMANLAND

ÖSTERGÖTLAND

NÄRKE

VÄRMLAND

DALSLAND

BOHUSLÄN

VÄSTERGÖTLAND

HALLAND

SMÅLAND

BLEKINGE

SKÅNE

Tampere
Turku
Hamar
Lillehammer
Idre
Särna
Älvdalen
Mora
Orsa
Rättvik
Leksand
Falun
Borlänge
Ludvika
Hudiksvall
Söderhamn
Bollnäs
Gävle
Sandviken
Sala
Uppsala
Västerås
Eskilstuna
Kopparberg
Örebro
Köping
Karlstad
Arvika
Säffle
Mariestad
Nyköping
Oxelösund
Katrineholm
Norrköping
Linköping
Västervik
Mellerud
Uddevalla
Vänersborg
Borås
GOTHENBURG
Varberg
Halmstad
Tranås
Nässjö
Jönköping
Värnamo
Vetlanda
Eksjö
Huskvarna
Växjö
Oskarshamn
Borgholm
Färjestaden
Kalmar
Karlskrona
Kristianstad
Hässleholm
Helsingborg
Lund
Malmö
Simrishamn
Ystad
Visby
FÅRÖ

Klaipeda

Vänern
Vättern

E4
E20
E6
E18
70
E22
23
E4

Sweden
2nd edition – April 2003
First published – July 2000

Published by
Lonely Planet Publications Pty Ltd ABN. 36 005 607 983
90 Maribyrnong St, Footscray, Victoria 3011, Australia

Lonely Planet Offices
Australia Locked Bag 1, Footscray, Victoria 3011
USA 150 Linden St, Oakland, CA 94607
UK 10a Spring Place, London NW5 3BH
France 1 rue du Dahomey, 75011 Paris

Photographs
Many of the images in this guide are available for licensing from
Lonely Planet Images.
w www.lonelyplanetimages.com

Front cover photograph
A juxtaposition of red and green with a barn roof and grass, Salem,
Sweden.
(© Macduff Everton/CORBIS)

ISBN 1 74059 227 1

Contents – Text

2 Contents – Text

NORRLAND 277

LANGUAGE 315

GLOSSARY 321

INDEX

MAP LEGEND back page

METRIC CONVERSION inside back cover

Contents – Maps

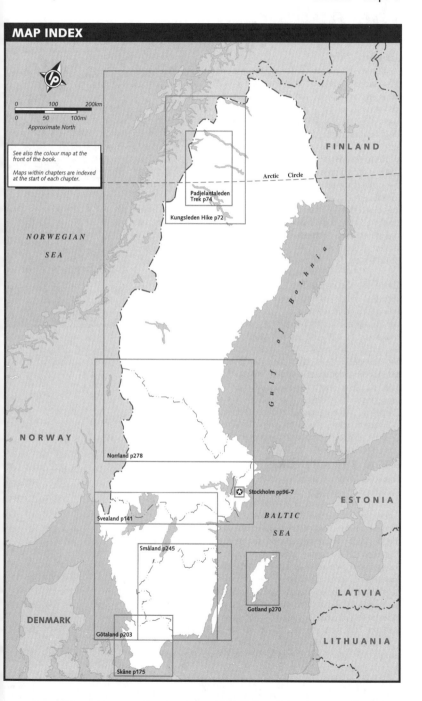

MAP INDEX

NORWEGIAN

SEA

FINLAND

Arctic   Circle

0   100   200km
0   50   100mi
Approximate North

See also the colour map at the
front of the book.

Maps within chapters are indexed
at the start of each chapter.

Padjelantaleden
Trek p74

Kungsleden Hike p72

Gulf

of

Bothnia

NORWAY

Norrland p278

Stockholm pp96-7

ESTONIA

Svealand p141

BALTIC

SEA

Småland p245

Gotland p270

LATVIA

DENMARK

Götaland p203

Skåne p175

LITHUANIA

The Authors

Carolyn Bain

Melbourne-born Carolyn was raised on a diet of ABBA music and the Muppet Chef and first travelled around Scandinavia as a teenager, while living and studying in Denmark. That experience left her with a love of all the best that Scandinavia has to offer – open, egalitarian societies populated by unfairly attractive people, long summer nights and cosy winters, wonderful art and design, pickled fish (or perhaps not…) – and she jumped at the chance to return to Sweden for this project.

After obtaining a degree in languages Carolyn embarked upon the obligatory tour of duty, living, working and travelling in Europe, Africa and North America. Upon her return to Australia she joined Lonely Planet as an editor of its Europe titles, but in time she decided guidebook authors have more fun than editors and joined their illustrious ranks. She has covered other fabulous, far-flung destinations for Lonely Planet, including the Greek Islands, New Zealand and Texas.

Graeme Cornwallis

Born and raised in Edinburgh, Graeme later wandered around Scotland before coming to rest in Glasgow. While studying astronomy at Glasgow University, he developed a passion for peaks – particularly the Scottish Munros – and eventually bagged all 284 summits over 3000ft in Scotland at least once. Graeme has travelled extensively throughout Scandinavia and he has a detailed knowledge of Sweden. He has also travelled widely in Asia, North & South America and the Pacific. Mountaineering successes include trips to the Bolivian Andes, Norway and arctic Greenland; Graeme has also scaled Kebnekaise, the highest peak in Sweden. When he's not hiking, climbing, travelling or writing, Graeme teaches mathematics and physics at home in Glasgow.

FROM THE AUTHOR

Thanks to Graeme Cornwallis, author of the 1st edition of *Sweden*, for advice and assistance, and for sharing some excellent Swedish contacts with me. *Tack så mycket* to Ann-Charlotte Carlsson and Emelie Klein at the Swedish Travel & Tourism Council in London for providing helpful big-picture information, and to Sylvie Kjellin of the Stockholm Information Service for her useful tips on the capital. The wonderful Magnus Welin provided a friendly welcome to Sweden and invaluable assistance for the duration of my research and beyond, for which I'm hugely grateful. I'm also indebted to the helpful staff at tourist offices throughout Sweden who answered all my questions and pointed me in the right direction; other tourist-industry folk also helped greatly – Monica Sansaricq, of the brilliant Ice Hotel, deserves a special thanks for her cheery assistance.

I was fortunate to meet a number of fellow travellers and expats in Sweden who offered further insight into the country; I'm especially grateful to Kieron Hayter for his company and ace driving skills in and around Stockholm, to Kenyan Kim in Helsingborg for fascinating conversation, and to Amy Archer for her fabulous company in and around Uppsala. Kiitos also goes to LP Finland author Paul Harding for a very entertaining few days on the Sweden-Finland border: thanks Paul for enduring Groundhog Day with me and for showing me the humppa! Thanks also for information on the Åland islands.

Jules Bain and John Foley once again gave me free run of their place in London before and after my trip – a mere thank-you is not enough. Big cheers also to the fine folk at Lonely Planet for their patience and for getting this final product on the shelves. Finally, my heartfelt appreciation, as ever, goes to family and friends for their unfailing encouragement and support, and for once again farewelling me and warmly welcoming me home.

This Book

Lonely Planet's 1st guide to Sweden was written by Graeme Cornwallis. This 2nd edition was updated by Carolyn Bain.

From the Publisher

This book was produced in Lonely Planet's Melbourne office. This title was commissioned and developed by Chris Wyness and Amanda Canning. Victoria Harrison coordinated the editing and proofing with assistance from Susannah Farfor, Tony Davidson, Ann Seward, Evan Jones, Kristin Odijk, Rebecca Lalor and Lou McGregor. Emma Koch edited the language chapter. Production of the book was managed by Huw Fowles. Helen Rowley coordinated the cartography with assistance from Chris Thomas and Natasha Vellely. Jacqui Saunders designed the colour wraps and steered the book through the layout stage. The book's cover was designed by James Hardy. Thanks to Nicholas Stebbing and Kate McDonald for their technical support.

Thanks to AB Storstockholms Lokaltrafik and Göteborgs Spårväga for providing their subway and tramway maps.

THANKS
Many thanks to the travellers who used the last edition and wrote to us with helpful hints, advice and interesting anecdotes. Your names appear in the back of this book.

Foreword

ABOUT LONELY PLANET GUIDEBOOKS

The story begins with a classic travel adventure: Tony and Maureen Wheeler's 1972 journey across Europe and Asia to Australia. There was no useful information about the overland trail then, so Tony and Maureen published the first Lonely Planet guidebook to meet a growing need.

From a kitchen table, Lonely Planet has grown to become the largest independent travel publisher in the world, with offices in Melbourne (Australia), Oakland (USA), London (UK) and Paris (France).

Today Lonely Planet guidebooks cover the globe. There is an ever-growing list of books and information in a variety of media. Some things haven't changed. The main aim is still to make it possible for adventurous travellers to get out there – to explore and better understand the world.

At Lonely Planet we believe travellers can make a positive contribution to the countries they visit – if they respect their host communities and spend their money wisely. Since 1986 a percentage of the income from each book has been donated to aid projects and human rights campaigns, and, more recently, to wildlife conservation.

Although inclusion in a guidebook usually implies a recommendation we cannot list every good place. Exclusion does not necessarily imply criticism. In fact there are a number of reasons why we might exclude a place – sometimes it is simply inappropriate to encourage an influx of travellers.

UPDATES & READER FEEDBACK

Things change – prices go up, schedules change, good places go bad and bad places go bankrupt. Nothing stays the same. So, if you find things better or worse, recently opened or long-since closed, please tell us and help make the next edition even more accurate and useful.

Lonely Planet thoroughly updates each guidebook as often as possible – usually every two years, although for some destinations the gap can be longer. Between editions, up-to-date information is available in our free, monthly email bulletin *Comet* (**W** www.lonelyplanet.com/newsletters). You can also check out the *Thorn Tree* bulletin board and *Postcards* section of our website, which carry unverified, but fascinating, reports from travellers.

Tell us about it! We genuinely value your feedback. A well-travelled team at Lonely Planet reads and acknowledges every email and letter we receive and ensures that every morsel of information finds its way to the relevant authors, editors and cartographers.

Everyone who writes to us will find their name listed in the next edition of the appropriate guidebook. The very best contributions will be rewarded with a free guidebook.

We may edit, reproduce and incorporate your comments in Lonely Planet products such as guidebooks, websites and digital products, so let us know if you don't want your comments reproduced or your name acknowledged.

How to contact Lonely Planet:
Online: **e** talk2us@lonelyplanet.com.au, **W** www.lonelyplanet.com
Australia: Locked Bag 1, Footscray, Victoria 3011
UK: 10a Spring Place, London NW5 3BH
USA: 150 Linden St, Oakland, CA 94607

Introduction

Every country has its stereotypes and cliches but, let's face it, who wouldn't want to live up to the image that Sweden has in the outside world? A nation of tall, blonde, attractive types, famously open-minded and nonaggressive (well, at least in the recent past). A country full of athletic folk (think Björn Borg) at the cutting edge of technology (think Ericsson), well cared-for by the state and living very comfortable lives: flash cars parked in the garage (think Volvo and Saab) and houses full of stylish, cleverly designed furniture (think Ikea), with the population spending their long summer days eating meatballs and listening to ABBA (OK, maybe that last bit is taking it too far…). To the casual observer it might well seem that the cliches are pretty spot on. But, as ever, there's a lot more to a country than its stereotypes. Dig even slightly below the glossy surface and you'll find more to be impressed by.

Although Sweden has enjoyed a fairly colourful history, images of Viking warriors ravaging a helpless Europe belong firmly to nostalgia. Those who know the Swedes may well remark on their peace-loving nature; indeed, Sweden hasn't waged war since 1809, when it lost Finland to Russia. Sweden is also the spiritual home of the Nobel Peace Prize and has enjoyed a long-standing tradition of neutrality. As a result, the country has been able to flourish and welcome the many positive foreign influences that have been offered.

Sweden not only accepts a larger number of immigrants per capita than most other European countries, but Swedes enjoy the best ethnic and local cuisines, drink the finest foreign wines, and travel widely to gain first-hand experience of the world at large. You'll find them all over the world – working on aid projects in Africa, selling mobile phones in Shanghai, backpacking through Borneo, modelling in California, or drinking and partying in Ibiza. However, Swedes still tend to think of themselves as observers rather than the ones being observed, and may wonder

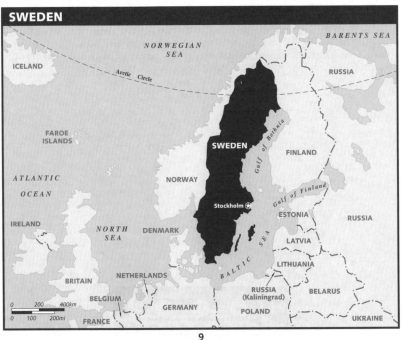

why outsiders have an interest in their country. As a visitor, explaining this will probably be your responsibility.

It would take a lifetime to visit all the major sites of interest around Sweden, Western Europe's third-largest country. With more than 25,000 protected Iron Age graveyards and burial mounds, 1140 prehistoric fortresses, 2500 open-air rune stones, 3000 churches (almost a third of them medieval), thousands of nature reserves, 28 national parks and more than 10,000km of trekking and bicycle paths – not to mention 12 royal castles in the Stockholm area, hundreds of superb museums and 12 Unesco World Heritage Sites – there's plenty to keep the visitor busy.

In the south, Danish influence is reflected in the castles and the impressive architecture of towns and cities such as Helsingborg and Lund. The lovely capital city, Stockholm, enjoys a superb location between Mälaren lake and the Baltic Sea, and the historic ties with France are revealed by some of its stylish architecture. Stockholm's coastal archipelago consists of at least 24,000 islands, and is served by one of the largest antique steamer fleets anywhere in Europe. Another scenic patchwork of fjords and islands stretches along the rocky Skagerrak (North Sea) coastline.

Away from its attractive cities, Sweden is a vast forested and lake-studded country, and the mountainous western border with Norway provides some topographic relief and wonderful outdoor recreational opportunities. It would be difficult to imagine more starkly beautiful landscapes than those of Norrland (northern Sweden), one of the last remaining wilderness areas in Europe. Here, you'll encounter Sami reindeer herders as well as the legendary midnight sun in summer and the aurora borealis (northern lights) in winter. The far north has Kebnekaise (2111m), arctic Scandinavia's highest mountain, and thousands of kilometres of hiking trails through immense protected areas, including Sarek, Padjelanta, Stora Sjöfallet, Abisko and Vadvetjåkka National Parks.

Sweden can be quite expensive, as the Swedish welfare state is costly to maintain. The result of this is immediately apparent to visitors – while the quality of goods and services is generally high and many attractions are free, when you must pay, you can pay dearly. But with the devaluing of the krona in recent years, costs for travellers are not as extortionately high as in the past; at any rate, the simple joys of fresh air, landscape and culture are among the least extravagant and most rewarding of pleasures available to visitors. Your best hope is to tighten your belt, take advantage of discounts, and avoid calculating your expenses in your own currency!

Facts about Sweden

HISTORY
Stone Age
Approximately 10,000 years ago, at the end of the last glacial period of the Ice Age (when the Scandinavian ice sheet had melted), people migrated northwards from central Europe into southern Sweden. At about the same time, it's thought that the ancestors of the Sami people migrated from Siberia and settled in northern areas of the country.

Many thousands of years passed before these nomadic Stone Age hunter-gatherers made more permanent settlements, which involved keeping animals, catching fish and growing crops. Without local sources of flints, most of their tools were made from bone, but imported flints have been found. A typical relic of this period (3000 to 1800 BC) is the *gångrift* (dolmen or passage tomb), usually built using raised stone blocks to form an oval or rectangular passage over which capstones and an earth mound (barrow) was laid. The dead (not normally cremated) were entombed accompanied by grave goods including pottery, amber beads and valuable flint tools.

It's likely that the predominant type during the Stone Age was the same tall, blonde and blue-eyed person still common today, and probably a Germanic language (the ancestral tongue of most modern Scandinavian languages) was spoken.

Bronze & Iron Ages
From 1800 to 500 BC, a period when the climate was relatively warm and favourable, Bronze Age cultures such as the Battle-Axe, Boat-Axe and Funnel-Beaker peoples created *hällristningar* (rock carvings) of ritual and mythological symbols, including the sun, deer and boats. *Hällristningar* are found in many parts of Sweden, including Högsbyn, near Dals Långed, Dalsland and Tanumshede, just off the E6 Hwy between Uddevalla and the Norwegian border.

Boats were significant for use in the travel and trade links across the Baltic Sea, the Skagerrak and the Kattegatt. Relatively few bronze artefacts from this period have been found in Sweden due to a local lack of the necessary metals – these had to be imported from central Europe in exchange for goods such as furs and amber. Other evidence of Bronze Age cultures includes burial customs, which involved mounds, suggesting spiritual and temporal leadership by powerful chieftains.

After 500 BC, the Iron Age, with its cooler climate, brought about technological advances as evidenced by finds of agricultural implements, graves, farm ruins and primitive furnaces. Although trade between southern Sweden and the Mediterranean area was interrupted by Celtic migrations westward across Europe, it was revived during the 3rd and 4th centuries when links developed with the Roman Empire – imports included fabrics, iron implements and pottery. Southern areas of Sweden were partly cleared of trees, and larger boats were built using iron axes. The runic alphabet arrived, probably from a Germanic source, and it was developed over the coming centuries, often being cut as inscriptions in stone slabs known as rune stones.

Migration & Vendel Periods
For around 200 years from the late-4th century; small-scale migrations and periods of warfare ensued in Sweden as local chieftains vied for supremacy. By the 7th century, the Svea people of the Mälaren valley had gained power over surrounding areas by the use of force – and Sweden (Sverige, in Swedish) has been named after them. The era known as the Vendel Period ended in about AD 800, when the Vikings put in an appearance.

Vikings & the Arrival of Christianity
Sweden's greatest impact on world history probably occurred during the Viking Age, commonly thought to have lasted from 800 to 1100, when the prospects of military adventure, trade and an increasingly dense agricultural population at home inspired many Swedes to seek out greener pastures abroad. The word 'Viking', derived from *vik*, which means 'bay' or 'cove', is probably a reference to their anchorages during raids.

It's suspected that the main catalyst for the Viking movement was overpopulation:

The Warrior Swedes & their Customs

The Viking Age was the period when Scandinavians from Sweden, Norway and Denmark made their mark on the rest of Europe. Vikings travelled greater distances than the earlier Roman explorers and established trading posts and an impressive communications network. Vikings settled in North America and Greenland, traded with eastern and southern Asia, fought for the Byzantine Empire and sacked and looted towns in southern Spain, among many other places.

The Vikings were not all warlike, but they were initially all pagans; all Scandinavian Vikings spoke the same language and worshipped the same gods. Burial of the dead usually included some possessions which would be required in the afterlife. In Sweden, it was popular to cremate the dead, then bury the remains in a clay pot under a mound. There are also a few impressive stone ship settings, consisting of upright stones arranged in the plan of a ship, usually with larger prow and stern stones. Viking graves have yielded a large amount of information about their culture.

Rune stones were often erected as memorials, or markers for highways, graveyards or other important sites. Runic inscriptions were also carved on things like metal and bone. Sweden has around 3000 such inscriptions, containing a wealth of information about the Viking world.

Applied art was important for decorative purposes, but some of the most spectacular art appears along with runic inscriptions and usually features dragons, horses or scenes from ancient sagas that bear little or no relevance to the attached runes.

If you're interested in learning more about Viking culture and customs, visit Foteviken on the Falsterbo Peninsula, near Malmö (see the Skåne chapter). This 'living' reconstruction of a late Viking Age village gives you a better impression of Viking life than any textbook!

when polygamy led to an excess of male heirs and too little land to go around. The division of land into ever smaller plots became intolerable for many, causing young men to migrate abroad to seek their fortunes.

Birka, founded around 760 on Björkö (an island in Mälaren lake, 30km west of modern Stockholm), was a powerful Svea centre for around 200 years until it was abandoned. Large numbers of Byzantine and Arab coins have been found and there are also many stone slabs with runic inscriptions in the surrounding area.

From the late 8th century, Svea warriors and traders from Birka assisted the Viking's expansionism in Europe. Their initial hit-and-run raids on European coastlines were followed by major military expeditions, settlement and trade. The Vikings sailed in a new type of vessel that was sturdy enough for ocean crossings, fast and also highly manoeuvrable, with a heavy keel, up to 16 pairs of oars and a large square sail. The sight of a Viking fleet struck terror into the hearts of many people during these unsettled times (but historians tell us that their helmets did *not* have horns!).

The well-travelled Vikings penetrated the Russian heartland and beyond, following the Volga and Dnieper waterways. They set up trading posts, founded Kiev around 900, and even got as far as Constantinople and Baghdad. There's even a possibility that the tsars, the imperial rulers of Russia until 1917, were descendants of Vikings.

Early in the 9th century, the missionary St Ansgar visited Birka and established a church there. Despite this, and attempts by other missionaries, Sweden didn't convert to Christianity until the late 11th century. In rural areas, pagan beliefs hung on among ordinary people for a long time afterwards; conversion was a gradual process due to deeply ingrained beliefs in Viking gods such as Odin, Thor and Freya. Although Iceland and Norway converted to Christianity in 999 and 1024 respectively, worship in the pagan temple at Uppsala in Sweden lasted until around 1090.

Rise of the Swedish State

The wealth and power of the Svea overwhelmed the southern Götar (Gauts) by the early 11th century, allowing a Christian, Olof Skötkonung, to become king of both the Svea and Gauts. This development paved the way for the emergence of the Swedish state. By 1160, King Erik Jedvarsson (the patron saint of Sweden, St Erik) had virtually completed the destruction of the old religious ways and, in 1164, shortly after his death, Sweden's first archbishopric was established in Uppsala, previously a centre for pagan beliefs.

During the 12th and 13th centuries, Finland was Christianised and steadily absorbed by the expanding Swedish state in a series of crusades. However, in 1240, the Russians temporarily halted the eastward expansion by defeating the Swedes in battle near where St Petersburg stands today.

Mälaren had become a freshwater lake due to the continuing rise of the land (freed of its Ice Age burden) and, by the 13th century, it became difficult for boats to enter, forcing a relocation of the capital. While the significance of the main lakeside town of Sigtuna dwindled, Stockholm – previously a small trading centre where Mälaren meets the Baltic – grew steadily in size and importance, especially after 1252 when new defensive walls were built.

Although King Magnus Ladulås organised a form of feudalism in 1280, Sweden avoided its worst excesses during the Middle Ages. In fact, the powers of the privileged aristocracy were held in check by the king, to whom they owed allegiance. A representative council with members from the nobility and the church was set up to advise the king.

Following the death of King Magnus in 1290, the Swedish regent pursued aggressive military policies against Finland and Russia. When Magnus' eldest son, Birger, assumed power in 1302, chaos ensued and Birger was eventually forced into exile in Denmark. The infant grandson of King Haakon V of Norway was elected king of Sweden by the Swedish nobility after the exile of Birger and, when Haakon died without leaving a male heir, the kingdoms of Norway and Sweden were united in 1319.

The increasingly wealthy church ordered extensive construction of monasteries and nunneries in the 13th and 14th centuries. Work began in 1285 on Scandinavia's largest Gothic cathedral in Uppsala, which took 150 years to complete. The great emancipation of slaves took place in 1335, ending another Viking tradition. King Magnus Eriksson instigated a national law code in 1350 that superseded previous provincial laws. Also in 1350, the arrival of the Black Death killed around a third of the Swedish population, subsequently weakening the economy and curtailing the power of both nobility and church. St Birgitta, the mystic, reinvigorated the church with her writings, and she founded an order of nuns at Vadstena on Vättern lake in 1370.

Hanseatic League & the Union of Kalmar

Meanwhile, Danish rule and influence had penetrated the far south of Sweden and the German-run Hanseatic League established walled trading towns such as Visby and maintained a strong presence in early Stockholm. The Hanseatic traders tightened their economic grip on Norway and Sweden throughout the 14th century. However, with the support of the Swedish nobility, the Danish regent Margrethe intervened and joined with Norway and Sweden in the Union of Kalmar, creating one crown for all of Scandinavia (1397).

Erik of Pomerania (Margrethe's nephew) held the throne until 1439 and high taxation to fund wars against the Hanseatic League led to his rule in Sweden becoming deeply unpopular. In Stockholm, the Danes allowed an assembly of four estates (nobility, clergy, merchants and peasants), the forerunner of the modern *riksdag* (parliament).

During the 15th century, there was almost continuous strife, with Danes, Hanseatic traders, Swedish nobility and ordinary Swedish people pulling in various directions. Engelbrekt Engelbrektsson became a national hero after his revolt against the Danes in 1434. Sten Sture, however, rose to greater eminence as 'Guardian of Sweden' in 1470 and he defeated the Danes at the Battle of Brunkenberg (1471) in Stockholm.

Denmark repeatedly attacked Sweden during the last 50 years of the union in an attempt to counter growing Swedish nationalism and unwelcome Swedish links with the Hanseatic League. These policies helped to hasten the end of the union, but the final straw was the brutal 'Stockholm bloodbath' of 1520. After invading Sweden and entering Stockholm without a prolonged siege, Christian II of Denmark gathered 80 of the Swedish nobility and city burghers under an amnesty, then arrested and beheaded all of them, including Sten Sture's son. This barbaric act sparked off a major rebellion under the leadership of the young nobleman Gustav Vasa and, in 1523, Sweden seceded from the union and installed the first Vasa king.

Vasa Dynasty

Gustav I introduced the Reformation to Sweden principally as a fundraising exercise. Church properties were confiscated by the crown and a powerful, centralised nation-state arose with religious control in the hands of Lutheran Protestants. In mainly Catholic Småland, Nils Dacke defied Gustav, but his death in 1543 left a strong throne firmly in control. The following year, parliament was reformed, the first regular standing army in Europe was set up, and a hereditary monarchy was established.

Complexities in the Swedish succession followed the death of Gustav I in 1560; his eldest son, Erik XIV, held the throne for only eight years until being deposed. During this time, Swedish interests on the other side of the Baltic led to the steady absorption of northern Estonia into their growing empire. The Danes tried and failed to reassert sovereignty over Sweden during the Seven Years War (1563–70). Johann III, Gustav's second son, was king from 1568 to 1592, followed by Johann's son Sigismund, who held both Swedish and Polish crowns before returning to Poland in 1599. Gustav's third son, Karl IX, became king but his military ambitions were thwarted by the Poles and Russians. At home he ruled with a heavy hand until the succession of his son, Gustav II Adolf, in 1611.

Gustav II, despite his youth, proved to be a military genius and he concluded the Kalmar War (1611–14) with Denmark and Norway after recapturing parts of southern Sweden. Some years later he consolidated the Swedish grip on the eastern side of the Baltic with an invasion of Latvia, and Riga was besieged and captured.

From the beginning of the Thirty Years' War in 1618, Gustav II supported the German Protestants and he invaded Poland, defeating Sigismund, who still had his eye on the Swedish throne. Gustav II was a pious individual who took his Lutheran Protestantism very seriously and prosecuted his war against Catholic Poland with great vigour. However, in 1632, Gustav II was killed by his Catholic enemies in battle at Lützen in Germany.

Gustav II's daughter, Kristina, was still a child in 1632, and her regent continued her father's warlike policies, defeating the Danes in 1645. In 1654, Kristina abdicated in favour of Karl X Gustav, ending the Vasa dynasty, and she turned her back on her father's beliefs by travelling to Rome and converting to Catholicism.

Peak & Decline of the Swedish Empire

During the harsh winter of 1657, Swedish troops achieved a remarkable success by invading Denmark across the frozen Kattegat, and the last remaining parts of southern Sweden still in Danish hands were handed over on the signing of the Peace of Roskilde. Bohuslän, Härjedalen and Jämtland had also been seized (from Norway), and the empire reached its maximum size when Sweden established a short-lived American colony in what is now Delaware.

The end of the 17th century saw a developing period of scientific and artistic enlightenment in Sweden; Olof Rudbeck achieved widespread fame as a scientific genius with his medical discoveries, including the lymphatic system.

King Karl XII, who ruled the Swedish empire from 1697 to 1718, was an over-enthusiastic military adventurer who spent almost all of his time conducting wars in Norway, Germany, Poland and Russia. He was eventually defeated by Peter the Great at Poltava in 1709, and promptly lost Latvia and Estonia to the clutches of the Russians. Karl XII then lost Poland, leaving him with Finland and little else, but this wasn't to last long. Finland was occupied by Russia from 1714 to 1721 from where they launched attacks on the Swedish coast. The constant fighting had seriously drained the country of resources and turned Sweden from a great regional power to a backwater.

The Great Nordic War with Norway was fought throughout the early 18th century and, in 1716, the Swedes occupied Christiania (formerly Oslo, which was renamed by the Danish king, Christian IV, in honour of himself). Trondheim was besieged by the Swedes in the winter of 1718, but the effort was abandoned after Karl XII was mysteriously shot dead while inspecting his troops, a single event that sealed the fate of Sweden's military might.

Liberalisation of Sweden

Parliamentary power increased at the expense of regal power during the 50 years after Karl XII's death. The days of absolute monarchs leading the country to ruin through interminable wars seemed to be over and the monarchs immediately following Karl XII were little more than heads of state. However, Russia remained a threat and it re-took Finland by force in 1741; it was 'liberated' 10 years later.

The pace of intellectual enlightenment quickened and Sweden produced several celebrated writers, philosophers and scientists. The scientists included Anders Celsius, whose temperature scale now bears his name, Carl Scheele, the discoverer of chlorine, and Carl von Linné, also known as Linnaeus, the great botanist who developed theories about plant reproduction (see the boxed text 'Carl von Linné' in the Svealand chapter). In 1739, the Swedish Academy of Sciences opened in Stockholm, with Linnaeus as one of the founders.

The country developed as a trading nation, and the Swedish East India Company was formed in Gothenburg in 1731. The height of the Little Ice Age (1738–42) brought severe hardship to remote rural areas: crops failed and famine stalked the country. In 1766, the parliament passed the world's first Freedom of the Press Act.

Gustav III (who reigned from 1771 to 1792) curtailed parliamentary powers with a coup in 1772 and reintroduced absolute rule in 1789. However, he greatly appreciated fine arts; French culture was brought to his court and he supported opera with the opening of the Royal Opera House in Stockholm (1782). Among other things, the king opened the Swedish Academy of Literature (1786), which is now known for awarding the annual Nobel Prize for Literature.

Gustav III's foreign policy was less auspicious and he was considered exceptionally lucky to lead Sweden virtually intact through a two-year war with Russia (1788–90). Enemies in the aristocracy finally conspired to assassinate the king, and he was shot in 1792 while at the opera in fancy dress.

Gustav IV Adolf, Gustav III's son, assumed the throne and got drawn into the Napoleonic Wars. He declared war on France, but in 1808 Finland was attacked and occupied by Russia. In 1809, Gustav IV abdicated and Sweden lost Finland permanently on signing a treaty with Russia. Gustav IV's uncle, Karl XIII, took the Swedish throne under a new constitution that ended unrestricted royal power.

The constitution divided legislative powers between king and parliament. The king's advisory council was also responsible to the parliament, which controlled taxation, and an ombudsman was created as a check on the bureaucracy.

Napoleon's Marshal Jean Charles Bernadotte was chosen to fill a gap in the succession in 1810 and, taking the name Carl Johan, became regent to the ailing Karl XIII. Carl Johan changed sides and led Sweden, allied with Britain, Prussia and Russia, into war against France and Denmark.

After Napoleon's defeat, Sweden negotiated with Denmark at the Treaty of Kiel in 1814 to exchange the country's possession of German land (Swedish Pomerania) for Norway. The Norwegians objected and chose a king and constitution, which resulted in Swedish troops occupying most of the country. A compromise in the form of devolved power was reached. The enforcement of the union with Norway was Sweden's last military action.

Industrialisation

The late arrival of industry in Sweden during the second half of the 19th century was based on, among other things, efficient steel making, explosives, the safety match, logging and timber products. Iron-ore mining, then steel manufacture, began to expand and a middle class began to form. Exports to Europe (eg, timber, iron and steel) helped power Sweden's industrial revolution, transforming the country from one of Western Europe's poorest to one of its richest.

From the 1820s onwards, major changes also took place in Sweden due to sweeping agricultural reforms. The old social fabric disappeared as small-scale peasant farms were replaced with larger concerns. With around 90% of Swedes tied to the land, the demands of modernisation and the need for industrial workers made itself felt – and the economy transformed from agricultural to industrial. These changes led to widespread discontent in the countryside and started the population drift into the towns, cities and beyond. Potatoes had become the staple crop for farmers, producing, among other things, *brännvin,* also called schnapps or Swedish vodka.

The Göta Canal, opened in 1832, provided a valuable transport link between the east and west coasts and development of the country accelerated when the main railway across Sweden was completed in 1862. Compulsory primary schooling was introduced by the parliament in 1842, providing a better educated workforce for the new industries. Free trade was adopted in the 1850s and significant 19th-century Swedish inventions, including dynamite (Alfred Nobel) and the safety match (Gustaf Pasch), were carefully exploited by government and industrialists.

In 1866, a limited franchise was introduced for a new and bicameral parliament. However, many poverty-stricken farmers and agricultural workers were unhappy with rural conditions and, in just a few decades, around a million people (a quarter of the population) emigrated, mainly to the USA. Also during the latter years of the 19th century, industrial trade unions developed and soon came into conflict with the government. The Social Democratic Labour Party (Social Democrats for short), founded to support industrial workers in 1889, grew quickly and obtained representation in the parliament in 1896 when Hjalmar Branting was elected to the second chamber.

By 1900, almost one in four Swedes lived in cities and industrial output (based on timber, steel, precision machinery and hardware) was increasing steadily. Conscription was first introduced as a measure against Russia in 1901.

In 1905, an independence referendum was held in Norway and virtually no-one supported continuing the union with Sweden. The Swedish king, Oscar II, was forced to recognise Norwegian sovereignty and the countries then went their separate ways.

Between 1906 and 1909, a system of proportional representation was introduced for elections to the parliament. Men aged over 24 years received the vote in 1909, but moves to cut wages caused 300,000 people to strike two years later. Temperance movements, founded to curb excessive alcohol consumption, profoundly influenced the labour movement and alcohol restrictions later became state policy.

Welfare State

Sweden declared itself neutral in 1912, just before the outbreak of WWI. However, British interference crippled the economy, leading to food shortages and unrest, so consensus was no longer possible and, for the first time, a Social Democrat and Liberal coalition government took control in 1921. Reforms followed quickly and suffrage for all adults aged over 23 years was introduced in the same year, as well as the eight-hour working day. Although Marxist thinking lurked behind some Social Democratic policies, the traditional fear of Russia (and support for Finland's separation) and the liberal tendencies of the 1920s prime minister (*statsminister*), Hjalmar Branting, kept the worst excesses of communism at bay.

The Depression in the early 1930s led to dwindling export prices, soaring unemployment and conflict between the government and workers. After 1932, the Social Democrats dominated politics and after the hardships caused by the Depression, they took the liberal tendencies of Hjalmar Branting and combined with economic intervention policies and other measures to introduce a welfare state.

Swedish neutrality during WWII was somewhat ambiguous to say the least. German troop movements through the north of the country tarnished the image of neutral Sweden, but perhaps the leaders of the country's coalition government were wise in preventing German occupation. As it was, the country was a haven for refugees from Finland, Norway, Denmark and the Baltic states, and many thousands of Jews from various countries escaped persecution and death with a helping hand from Sweden. Downed allied aircrew also escaped the Gestapo by fleeing to Sweden.

After the war and throughout the 1950s and '60s the Social Democrats continued setting up the *folkhemmet,* or welfare state, in coalition with the Agrarian Party, or sometimes with its own small majority in the parliament. Although not as far-reaching as the British model, a national health service was formed, allowing free hospital treatment, and a drive for full employment occurred along with the development of comprehensive social security measures. The standard of living for ordinary Swedes rose rapidly and real poverty was virtually eradicated – lasting monuments to the policies of Tage Erlander, Olof Palme and others.

Modern Sweden

In 1971, the parliament was reconstituted as a single chamber and, three years later, a revised constitution effectively reduced the monarch's status to that of a figurehead. The economic pressures of the 1970s began to cloud Sweden's social goals and it was under Olof Palme that support for social democracy first wavered.

The order of monarch succession was altered in 1980, giving equal status to men and women and allowing Princess Victoria, the eldest child of the current king, to become heir to the throne.

Despite several changes of government during the 1970s and '80s, external forces on the Swedish state continued to mount. The bungled police inquiry into the 1986 assassination of Prime Minister Palme shook ordinary Swedes' confidence in their country, its institutions and its leaders. Although there have been many theories about the still unsolved killing, it seems most likely that foreign intervention and destabilisation lay behind this appalling act. Certainly, the fortunes of the Social Democrats took a turn for the worse, and subsequent corruption and scandals, including Bofors illegally trading in arms, seriously damaged the government.

By late 1992, during the world recession, the country's budgetary problems culminated in frenzied speculation against the Swedish krona. In November of that year Sveriges Riksbank, the central bank, was forced to abandon fixed foreign exchange rates and let the krona float freely; the result was a foregone conclusion and the currency immediately devalued by 20%. Interest rates reached stratospheric levels, unemployment soared to 14% and the government retaliated with tax hikes and punishing cuts to the welfare budget.

The previously relaxed immigration rules were scrapped, reversing the magnanimous approach to asylum seekers. The immigrant population (over 10% of the total population) then proved to be an easy target for xenophobic sections of the community, which blamed them for all the country's woes.

With both economy and national confidence severely shaken, Swedes narrowly voted in favour of joining the European Union (EU), effective from 1 January 1995. Since then, Sweden's welfare state, taxation system and economy have undergone further major reforms and the economy has improved considerably, with falling unemployment and inflation. The country has not yet joined the single European currency and a referendum is likely to be held on the issue in 2003. The widening gap between rich and poor is causing some disquiet and racial tension is increasing, especially since the events of 11 September 2001 in the USA. Perhaps surprisingly, and going against political trends elsewhere in Europe, the Swedes voted to maintain the status quo by re-electing the left-wing Social Democrat Party in September 2002.

GEOGRAPHY

With a surface area of 449,964 sq km, Sweden occupies the eastern part of the Scandinavian peninsula and shares borders with Norway (in the west) and Finland (in the east). At its closest, Denmark is only 4km from the southwest of Sweden, across the Øresund Strait, and the two countries are

LÄN BOUNDARIES

LANDSKAP BOUNDARIES

Map labels: Lappland, Norrbotten, NORRLAND, Västerbotten, Jämtland, Ångermanland, FINLAND, Medelpad, Härjedalen, Hälsingland, NORWAY, Dalarna, Gästrikland, Helsinki, Oslo, SVEALAND, Uppland, Värmland, Västmanland, Stockholm, Tallinn, Dalsland, Närke, Södermanland, ESTONIA, Bohuslän, Östergötland, Västergötland, GÖTTLAND, Götland, LATVIA, Halland, Småland, Öland, Skåne, LITHUANIA, Copenhagen, DENMARK, Blekinge

now connected by bridge and tunnel between Malmö and Copenhagen.

Sweden measures 1574km from north to south, but it averages only 300km in width. The country has a 7000km-long coastline, running from the Skagerrak on the North Sea, to the Gulf of Bothnia at the inner end of the Baltic Sea. In places, particularly in the west and near Stockholm, the coast is cut by fjords (long, narrow sea inlets) and peppered with islands and rocky skerries; the Stockholm archipelago alone boasts an extraordinary 24,000 islands. Sandy beaches can be found in various places along the coast, especially south of Gothenburg.

Around 100,000 inland lakes form 9% of the country's surface area and Vänern is the largest lake in Western Europe at 5585 sq km. The largest island in the Baltic Sea, Gotland, is part of Sweden and covers an area of 3001 sq km. The heavily glaciated Kjölen Mountains, with glaciers still affecting the highest peaks, extend along approximately 800km of the Norwegian border and reach over 2000m above sea level. Kebnekaise (2111m), in the far north, is Sweden's highest mountain. However, most northern areas

have a cover of coniferous forest and lie below 1000m. About 16% of Sweden can be considered mountainous. Along most of the Baltic coastline, and areas south of Stockholm, the land is rather flat (mainly under 200m) with Skåne resembling Denmark. Around 8% of the country is arable (almost entirely in Skåne, Blekinge and Halland), while an astonishing 54% is forest.

Geographical divisions in Sweden are complex. The two kingdoms that united in the 11th century form the southern 40% of the country: Götaland in the south and Svealand in lower central Sweden. Most of the Swedish population live in these two areas, and population densities are generally in the range 15 to 55 persons per sq km (the capital, Stockholm, has 266 persons per sq km). By contrast, the rest of the country, Norrland, is virtually empty, with population densities ranging from three to 16 people per sq km.

The 25 historical regions, or *landskap*, remain as denominators for people's identity and a basis for regional tourist promotion, and are used throughout this book. The 21 counties *(län)* in Sweden form the basis of local government, and these county administrations are responsible for things like regional public transport *(länstrafik)* and regional museums *(länsmuseum)*.

Around 80% of the Swedish population live in settlements of more than 500 people, making Sweden more urbanised than neighbouring Norway. Stockholm is in Svealand and it's the largest city in Sweden; the four largest regional centres are Gothenburg, Malmö, Uppsala and Linköping.

Nearly a sixth of the country lies north of the Arctic Circle, the latitude at which there is at least one full day when the sun never sets and one day when it never rises. For more information on this phenomenon, as well as the polar night, see the boxed text 'Arctic Phenomena' in the Norrland chapter.

GEOLOGY

The pre-Cambrian bedrock of southern and eastern Sweden, part of the Baltic shield, was the original core of the European continent and most of it dates back to more than 2 billion years ago. Much of Sweden's mineral wealth (such as lead, zinc, copper and iron) lies in these rocks, which include granite, gneiss and amphibolite.

From 500 to 370 million years ago, the European and North American continental plates were in collision and an impressive range of peaks called the Caledonian Mountains were thrust up, reaching a height similar to the Himalaya today. These have now been eroded by ice and water to a fraction of their previous size and their exposed roots form the Kjölen Mountains along the border with Norway. Parts of Skåne and the islands of Öland and Gotland consist of flat limestone and sandstone deposits, probably laid down in a shallow sea east of the Caledonian Mountains during the same period.

During the glacial periods of the past two million years, much of the country subsided at least 700m due to an ice sheet up to 2000m thick. The movement of this ice, driven down former river valleys by gravity, created sharp-ridged mountains, widened the valleys, and smoothed coastal rock faces. The bulk of the ice melted away in several stages between 12,000 and 9000 years ago, and Sweden is currently experiencing an interglacial period. As a result, only a few remnant cirque glaciers remain, and most of these are retreating.

Evidence of the ice sheet – large areas of moraine (gravel and boulder heaps previously pushed along by the ice), *åsar* (eskers, winding sand and gravel ridges created by subglacial meltwater rivers) and thick clay deposits (formed from powdered rock deposited by glacial rivers in a marine environment but now on dry land due to post-glacial uplift) is found everywhere in Sweden.

CLIMATE

Most of Sweden has a cool temperate climate with precipitation in all seasons, but the southern quarter of the country has a warm temperate climate. The mountain ranges of Norway and, to a lesser degree, the land masses of Britain and Denmark, shield Sweden from the worst effects of Atlantic low pressure systems and their moisture-laden southwesterly winds, hence yearly precipitation totals are moderate. High pressure systems over Russia bring more stable and sunny conditions with warm weather in summer, cold weather in winter.

Although the west coast is influenced by the warming waters of the Gulf Stream, the east is somewhat colder – the Gulf of Bothnia freezes every winter and the Baltic Sea freezes one or two winters in every 10. Snow

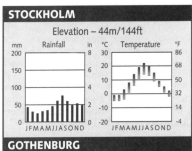

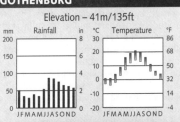

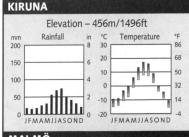

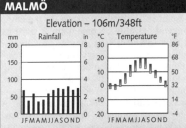

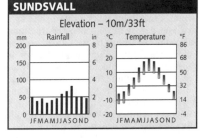

can accumulate to depths of several metres in the north, making for superb skiing, but in the south, where it sometimes rains in winter, snow depths average only 20cm to 40cm. It usually rains in winter in the far south (Skåne). The harsh Lappland winter starts in October and ends in April, and temperatures can plummet as low as -50°C. In January, the average maximum temperature in the south of Sweden is -1°C and in the north, -13°C.

Summer weather throughout Sweden is generally fairly sunny with only occasional rainfall, but August can be wet. The area around Gothenburg and Uddevalla is the wettest in the country (over 700mm annually). The average maximum temperature for July is 18°C in the south and around 14°C in the north. Long hot periods in summer aren't unusual, with unpleasant high humidity, particularly in Stockholm, and temperatures soaring to over 30°C.

Generally, temperature variations between day and night are not great in western coastal districts, but large variations can occur throughout inland northern areas.

ECOLOGY & ENVIRONMENT

Sweden led Europe, as early as 1909, in setting up national parks, and the biggest and best are in Lappland (see the National Parks & Nature Reserves section later in this chapter). Ecological consciousness among Swedes is high and reflected in concern for native animals, clean water and renewable resources. Although concern for the environment has only become popular since the 1970s, Sweden now has a good record when it comes to environmental policies. Industrial and agricultural waste is highly regulated, sewage disposal is advanced and highly efficient, greenhouse gas emissions are only about 1% of the level in the USA, recycling is popular, there's little rubbish along roadsides and general tidiness takes a high priority in urban and rural environments. Stockholm takes pride in the fact that you can swim and fish for trout and salmon in the waters by the city centre.

Overgrazing by Sami reindeer herds is causing serious problems in northern Sweden, and there's little sign of action to tackle this problem. Other ecological issues include acid rain degrading soil, damaging buildings, acidifying waterways and defoliating forests. Nitrogen runoff from farms in

Sweden has also caused severe pollution and eutrophication in the North and Baltic Seas. As a result, algae growth has increased and animal life has decreased. Overfishing of these waters has also become an additional cause for concern.

Recycling

Recycling is highly popular and Swedes strongly support sorting of household waste (eg, paper, glass, plastics, tyres, car batteries and organic matter) for collection. Travellers staying in many hostels and camping grounds will be expected to sort their waste.

Forestry

The percentage of forest cover in Sweden has been rising in the last 150 years and it's now one of the most densely forested countries in Europe. Although no forestry operation can be entirely environmentally sound, overall, Sweden has a highly sustainable forestry policy and any currently visible damage to the forests is mainly due to agricultural clearing and timber overexploitation prior to the 1850s.

In general, forestry operations employ selective cutting to prevent soil erosion and unsightly landscape degradation, and replanting takes place almost immediately.

Energy

Electricity generation always creates environmental problems and the situation in Sweden is no different.

Hydroelectric Power Some 47% of Sweden's electricity generation comes from hydroelectric sources, mainly dams on large northern rivers. Despite being touted as an 'environmentally friendly' resource, there are problems associated with hydroelectricity in Sweden:

- Indigenous Sami people were displaced and their traditional reindeer-herding activities disrupted when valleys were flooded to create artificial lakes
- Landscape scarring is caused by the artificial shorelines of dammed lakes
- Dried-up rivers and waterfalls lie 'downstream' of the dams, including the great waterfall Stora Sjöfallet, now, incongruously, in the national park of the same name
- Unsightly high voltage power lines sweep across remote regions of the country
- Natural fish stocks, including Baltic salmon, have been severely depleted in rivers with hydroelectric schemes

Nuclear Power The contentious issue of nuclear power generation first came to a head as early as 1976, when a coalition government led by Thorbjörn Fälldin's Centre Party took control. The Centre Party's policy of scrapping the country's nuclear power programme was blocked by various forces and Fälldin's government collapsed over the issue just two years later. However, another coalition led by the persistent Fälldin took power in 1979 and a referendum regarding the future of nuclear power in Sweden was held in March 1980. The electorate narrowly voted for the phasing-out of the nuclear programme by 2010. Support for the antinuclear lobby remained high during the 1980s, especially after Sweden was badly affected by fallout from the 1986 Chernobyl disaster in Ukraine (then part of the Soviet Union).

In 1997 the 2010 target was abandoned, because of the high costs involved and the shortage of energy sources to replace the output from the nuclear plants (nuclear power currently provides about 45% of Sweden's electricity generation). At the time of writing, only one nuclear reactor had been closed, and another closure was planned for 2003. Authorities now say that closure of all plants may take up to 40 years.

Environmental Organisations

Naturvårdsverket (☎ 08-698 1000; Ⓦ www.environ.se; Blekholmsterrassen 36, SE-10648 Stockholm), the Swedish environmental protection agency, has an extensive and highly informative website.

Svenska Naturskyddsföreningen (Swedish Society for Nature Conservation; ☎ 08-702 6500; Ⓦ www.snf.se/english.cfm; Åsögatan 115, Box 4625, SE-11691 Stockholm) has around 140,000 members and 274 local branches. It has successfully protected endangered species, including peregrine falcons; it has good Web pages in English on current environmental issues facing Sweden.

Svenska Ekoturismföreningen (Swedish Society of Ecotourism; ☎ 0647-660025; Ⓦ www.ekoturism.org; Box 87, SE-83005 Järpen) promotes environmentally friendly tourism in Sweden.

FLORA & FAUNA

Sweden has many climate zones due to its great range of latitude and altitude, and this is reflected in the diversity of species found in the country. Indigenous wildlife populations are reasonably dense in remote forests, far from human activity.

Flora

Generally, Swedish flora is typical of that in temperate climates, and includes around 250 species of flowering plants. In the mountains along the border with Norway, alpine and arctic flowers predominate. Limey soils are well liked by alpine flowers, especially the large white flowers with eight petals called mountain avens. Some other mountain flowers worth noting include the long stalked mountain sorrel, which is an unusual source of vitamin C; glacier crowfoot; various saxifrages (livelong, mossy, purple, pyramidal and starry); alpine milk-vetch; trailing azalea; diapensia; alpine gentian; forget-me-nots (myosotis); bearded bellflower; wood anemone; alpine fleabane; and alpine aster. Heather grows mainly in low-lying areas, particularly along the Bohuslän coast north of Gothenburg. A wide range of flowers can be found in forest meadows, including daisies, harebells and the violet-coloured crane's bill. The limey soils of Öland and Gotland have an excellent flora, including several rare flowering plants and many varieties of orchid, all of them protected.

The south originally had well mixed woodland, with tree species including conifers, alder, ash, elm, linden, oak, beech, birch, horse chestnut, maple and willow. However, much of this has been replaced by farmland or conifer plantations. The northern forests are dominated by Scots pine, Norway spruce and various firs, but aspen, mountain ash and silver birch can also be seen. Mosses and fungi, including edible mushrooms, grow on the forest floor.

In the mountains, dwarf birch, juniper and willow extend far above the tree line, as high as 1200m (in Sylarna) or 800m (in the far north, eg, Abisko). Between the dwarf trees and the snow line, the main vegetation types are fungi, lichens and mosses, such as reindeer moss. Mountain grasses, including sedges, deer grass and Arctic cotton grow mainly in boggy areas and, high in the mountains, near the summer snow line, you'll find saxifrage and a range of smaller tundra plants.

Hikers will find a profusion of berries, most of which grow low to the ground and ripen between mid-July and early September. The most popular edible varieties are blueberries (huckleberries), which grow on open uplands; blue swamp-loving bilberries; red cranberries; muskeg crowberries; and the lovely amber-coloured cloudberries. The latter, known locally as *hjortron,* grow one per stalk on open swampy ground and are considered a delicacy.

Fauna
Land Mammals Sweden has a good variety of European mammals and visitors have a chance to view species such as lynx and wolverine, which are rare elsewhere.

Rabbits are found in the south of the country, where they've probably escaped from captivity. Arctic hares are mainly found in hilly or mountainous areas along the border with Norway, typically on moors or mountain grassland and sometimes in woodland. Hedgehogs occur south of Örnsköldsvik. Forested and lake-studded areas support a good-sized beaver population. Badgers are found in the river valleys and woods of southern Sweden and otters are found by wooded watercourses and in the sea. Mink also like water and forests, so they're found by rivers and lakes, and in marshland.

Weasels and stoats are endemic in all counties; northern varieties turn white in the winter and are trapped for their fur (ermine). The more solitary wolverine, a larger cousin of the weasel, inhabits high mountain forests and alpine areas near the Norwegian border (see Endangered Species later in this section). Pine martens are found in moderate numbers throughout the Swedish forests.

Red squirrels are ubiquitous in coniferous forests throughout Sweden, and rodents such as the house mouse, brown rat, shrew and vole are prolific in all counties. Some voles, including bank voles, mountain rats and northern water voles, are found as high as 1300m.

Lemmings, which reside in mountain areas along the Norwegian border, stay mainly around 800m altitude in the south, but somewhat lower in the north. They measure up to 10cm and have soft orange/brown and black fur, beady eyes, a short tail and prominent upper incisors. These little creatures are famous for their extraordinary reproductive capacity – every ten years or so, the population explodes, with catastrophic

results including a denuded landscape and vast numbers (in excess of 10,000) of dead lemmings in rivers, lakes and on roads! Hikers encountering lemmings in the mountains may be surprised when these frantic little creatures become enraged and launch incredibly bold attacks with much hissing and squeaking. There's also a forest-dwelling version (wood lemming).

Most Swedish bat species favour the south, but the northern bat flits about the country.

Red deer prefer deciduous woodland and range as far north as the Arctic Circle. The much more common roe deer and elk inhabit a wider range of forests, although they wisely tend to stay clear of people and roads. Even so, elk, which are up to 2m high at the shoulder, are a serious traffic hazard, particularly at night. Elk hunting is popular, but it's strictly regulated. There are around 260,000 reindeer, which roam the fells in large herds, usually above the tree line and sometimes higher than 1400m. They're mostly semi-domesticated and under the watchful eyes of Sami herders.

Musk ox were re-introduced into Dovrefjell National Park (Norway) from Greenland in the late 1940s and herds have wandered into neighbouring areas of Sweden, notably Härjedalen county. Their favoured fodder is grass and moss and, although they appear as lethargic as contented cows, hikers shouldn't approach them since angry adults have a habit of charging anything that annoys them.

As in most places, wolves aren't popular with farmers or reindeer herders and Swedish public opinion is sharply divided on the issue of re-introduction (see Endangered Species later in this section). The red fox is found in most places although numbers are declining due to sarcoptic mange (scabies), while Arctic foxes are found in the mountains along the Norwegian border, mainly above the tree line.

A fascinating forest dweller is the solitary lynx, which belongs to the panther family and is Europe's only large cat. Numbers have increased rapidly in recent years and there are approximately 1000 lynx in Sweden now, but they're notoriously difficult to see because of their nocturnal habits. Lynx inhabit most areas of the country, although there are relatively few in the far south.

Although brown bears were persecuted for centuries, conservation measures have resulted in an increase in numbers to around 1000. They're mostly found in forests in the northern half of the country, but are now moving into new areas farther south.

Marine Mammals The seas around Sweden used to be rich fishing grounds due to ideal summer conditions for the growth of plankton. However, the combination of over-fishing and pollution has caused a serious decline in fish and seal numbers, particularly in the Baltic. About two-thirds of the seal population was wiped out by a virus in 1988, after pollution had weakened their immune systems, and the virus appears to have resurfaced in 2002, killing hundreds of seals in the region. Seal species seen in Swedish waters include grey and common seals and common dolphins may also be observed from time to time.

Fish & Crustaceans The aforementioned ecological problems in the Baltic, and the algal bloom in the Kattegatt (1988), have badly affected many fish species, including herring, the smaller Baltic herring, sprats and Baltic salmon. The latter also faces insensitive hydroelectric developments on many rivers as it swims upstream to spawning grounds (see Ecology & Environment earlier in this chapter).

Sprats and herring are economically important food sources. Among other marine species, cod, haddock, sea trout, whiting, flounder and plaice are reasonably abundant, particularly in the salty waters of the Kattegatt and Skagerrak, but cod numbers are much reduced by overfishing. Pike are fairly common in the brackish waters of the Baltic and are highly sought after by anglers.

Rivers and lakes are also very popular with anglers and catches include Arctic charr, eels, grayling, pike, salmon, trout and zander. Bream, perch, roach and tench are commonly caught in lowland lakes and slow-flowing rivers. In winter, when lakes are frozen, fishing takes place through holes in the ice (see Fishing in the Activities chapter).

Indigenous crayfish were caught in lakes with nets or traps, but overfishing and disease has made them virtually extinct. North American crayfish have been imported from the US and they're breeding successfully. Marine crustaceans such as shrimp, crab, lobster and mussels are also good to eat.

Birds The Swedish lakes, swamps and forests are excellent for ornithologists, but the country attracts so many nesting species and permanent residents, it would be impossible to discuss them all in detail here. The most significant, as well as a few rarer ones, are discussed in this section.

Some of the best bird-watching sites are: Falsterboneset, Getterön (near Varberg); several places on Öland; Tåkern; Hornborgasjön; and the national parks Färnebofjärden, Muddus and Abisko. For more about bird-watching, check out *Where to Watch Birds in Scandinavia* by Gustaf Aulen.

Coastal species include common, little and Arctic terns, various gulls, oystercatchers, cormorants (now nesting in summer), guillemots and razorbills. Arctic skuas can be seen in a few places, notably the Stockholm archipelago and the coast north of Gothenburg.

There are several species of raptor and the most dramatic to watch is the lovely white-tailed sea eagle. Golden eagles are found in the mountains (and the forests in winter); they're easily identified from their immense wing span and characteristic shape. Reasonably common forest raptors include goshawks and sparrowhawks. Honey buzzards nest near the forest edge, however ordinary buzzards can be seen in very varied environments. Rough-legged buzzards winter in southern Sweden and are common when lemming numbers in the north are high. Marsh and hen harriers prefer open ground and are generally only found in the south. A moderate but expanding population of red kites lives in southern Sweden. Peregrine falcons are very rare, but kestrels are commonly seen throughout the country. Hobbies and merlins only breed in the south and north respectively. Both types of gyrfalcon are extremely rare. Ospreys hunt fish and nest near water; they're not particularly common, but they can be seen at Båven lake in Södermanlands Län, and Djurö and Färnebofjärden National Parks.

There are at least seven types of owl: tawny owls, commonly seen in woods, parks and gardens; short-eared owls, found on marshy moors; long-eared owls and pygmy owls, seen mainly in coniferous forests; snowy owls, which like alpine areas; and rare eagle owls, which prefer northern forests.

Especially in southern and south-central Sweden, you'll find the usual variety of

European woodland birds, including wood-cocks, several types of colourful woodpeckers, bullfinches, chaffinches, bramblings, crossbills, yellowhammers, warblers, wood-pigeons, collared doves, nightjars, cuckoos, jays, treecreepers, thrushes, fieldfares and a wide range of tits. Look out for lovely little goldcrests in coniferous forests. A few of the spectacular waxwings breed in Lappland, but in winter they arrive from Russia in large numbers and may be observed in woods, parks and gardens throughout Sweden.

Tree pipits like scattered woodland, but meadow pipits prefer more open ground such as moors, farmland or sand dunes. Black grouse are found in forests, moors and farmland, while hazel grouse mainly lurk in dense woods. The willow grouse prefers treeless moors and tundra, and the bizarre capercaillie, which resembles a large turkey, struts around in coniferous forests. Ptarmigan and snow buntings may be seen above the tree line in the mountains along the Norwegian border, while ring ouzel tend to nest in mountain areas with scattered trees and scrub. Partridges and pheasants are mainly found in fields, but also in marshes. Beautiful kingfishers nest by rivers and lakes in the far south of Sweden and are well worth making an effort to see. Swallows and house martins commonly nest in farm buildings, while the elusive corncrake prefers long grass or fields (agricultural machinery has badly affected numbers). Crows, ravens and jackdaws are common, as are garden variety birds such as blackbirds, magpies, robins, sparrows, starlings. If you're lucky, you might see the brightly coloured golden oriole in woods or parks in the extreme south of Sweden.

Sweden has quite a wide range of wading and water birds, including wood, common and green sandpipers, snipes, curlews, ruffs, whimbrels, redshanks and greenshanks. Black-tailed godwits nest only in the extreme south, while the unusual and beautiful red-necked phalaropes only breed in the northern mountains. Other waders you're likely to encounter are majestic grey herons (in the south only), noisy bitterns (mainly in south-central Sweden), plovers (including dotterel, in the mountains) and turnstones. The most prominent of many species of duck are mallards, eiders, goosanders and red-breasted mergansers. Spectacular horned

and great-crested grebes can be seen by lakes or coasts, mainly in the south and east of Sweden. In marshes, lakes and ponds, you may observe swans and geese, such as whooper and mute swans, bean geese, grey-lags and Canada geese. Dippers may be observed diving into streams. Wagtails are fairly common in marshes and by rivers and streams. Other water birds found in Sweden include cranes, coots, moorhens and the lovely black-throated and red-throated divers, called 'loons' in North America.

See the section on bird-watching in the Activities chapter for information about local ornithological groups.

Endangered Species

Wolves and wolverines are the most endangered mammal species in Sweden and in 1997 and '98 the Swedish Environmental Protection Agency set up various action programmes to increase the populations. Reports that wolves and wolverines have been illegally shot by members of the Sami community can't be easily dismissed and wolverines have also been illegally poached for their fur. A compensation system is in place to reimburse the Sami for any livestock killed, but ingrained prejudice remains high. There are currently around 50 wolves, mainly in Värmland and Dalarna, but numbers are increasing. However, despite protection since 1969, wolverine numbers have remained steady at around 300, with most of them located in Norrbotten and Västerbotten.

Although many marine species have been badly affected by pollution, cod and Norwegian lobster are on the verge of extinction, mainly due to overfishing. It remains to be seen whether the current fishing quotas will help numbers return to anything like a normal level.

Hydroelectric power schemes blocking access to spawning grounds have contributed to the serious decline in the Baltic salmon population. Recent efforts to redress this environmental problem include the creation of National Heritage Rivers in 1993 to put a brake on hydroelectric developments. Disease and overfishing has virtually wiped out the Swedish crayfish in many rivers but they've been replaced with stocks of American crayfish.

National Parks & Nature Reserves

There are now 28 national parks in Sweden (see the boxed text 'Sweden's National Parks'); the first nine were formed by authorisation of the parliament in 1910. Upland districts predominate, forming nearly 90% of the aggregate area of just under 7000 sq km, with the remainder consisting mainly of natural forest, swamp and coastal landscapes. The 'full protection' of national parks from commercial exploitation – apart from traditional Sami reindeer herding in the mountains – didn't save Stora Sjöfallet from hydroelectric development in 1917, and the parliament redrew the park boundaries to exclude the flooded area! Four of the Lappland national parks (Muddus, Padjelanta, Sarek and Stora Sjöfallet), and two nearby nature reserves, received international attention with their Unesco World Heritage Site listing in 1996.

Nature reserves tend to be smaller than national parks, with a current and steadily increasing total of around 2200 (amounting to over 32,000 sq km). Reserves exist for their wildlife, botanical or geological significance. Generally, outdoor activities are permitted, but restrictions may be enforced during the breeding season – visitors should check local regulations.

Four of Sweden's large rivers (Kalixälven, Piteälven, Vindelälven and Torneälven) have been declared National Heritage Rivers in order to protect them from hydroelectric development.

National parks and nature reserves are established by **Naturvårdsverket** (☎ 08-698 1000; ☒ www.environ.se; Blekholmsterrassen 36, SE-10648 Stockholm), the Swedish environmental protection agency. However, they're managed by local government, at both county and municipal levels. The agency provides national park information (in Swedish and English) for visitors in the form of pamphlets, and an excellent book *Nationalparkerna i Sverige* (National Parks in Sweden).

The right of public access to the countryside *(allemansrätten)*, which includes all national parks and nature reserves, dates back to common practices in medieval times, but isn't enshrined in law. See the boxed text 'The Right of Public Access' in the 'Hiking' special section for further details on *allemansrätten*.

NATIONAL PARKS & WORLD HERITAGE SITES

NATIONAL PARKS
1 Vadvetjåkka
2 Abisko
3 Stora Sjöfallet
4 Padjelanta
5 Sarek
6 Pieljekaise
7 Muddus
8 Haparanda Skärgård
9 Björnlandet
10 Skuleskogen
11 Sånfjället
12 Töfsingdalen
13 Fulufjället
14 Hamra
15 Färnebofjärden
16 Ängsö
17 Tyresta
18 Garphyttan
19 Tresticklan
20 Djurö
21 Tivedon
22 Gotska Sandön
23 Blå Jungfrun
24 Norra Kvill
25 Store Mosse
26 Söderåsen
27 Dalby Söderskog
28 Stenshuvud

UNESCO WORLD HERITAGE SITES
A Laponian Area
B Gammelstad Church Village; Luleå
C Höga Kusten (High Coast)
D Kopparberg Copper Mine, Falun
E Engelsberg Ironworks
F Royal Domain of Drottningholm
G Skogskyrkogården, Stockholm
H Birka & Hovgården
I Tanumshede Rock Carvings
J Hanseatic Town of Visby
K Agricultural Landscape of Southern Öland
L Naval Port of Karlskrona

Sweden's National Parks

Northern

Abisko This fabulous national park offers numerous hiking routes and good accessibility. Here you'll find the lovely Lake Torneträsk, the landmark Lapporten pass, and the northern gateway to the famed Kungsleden hiking track.

Haparanda Skärgård A group of several islands in the far north of the Gulf of Bothnia, with sandy beaches, striking dunes, unusual flora and migrant bird life, it's reached by boat from Haparanda.

Muddus This 493-sq-km park, southwest of Gällivare in Lappland, features the lake Muddusjaure and the surrounding ancient forests and muskeg bogs. It also has several deep and impressive gorges, such as the Måskoskårså, and superb bird-watching opportunities.

Padjelanta This park consists mainly of high moorland surrounding the lakes Vastenjaure and Virihaure. It's favoured by grazing reindeer and also hosts a range of Swedish wildlife. Hikers especially enjoy the renowned Akkastugorna–Kvikkjokk trail, Padjelantaleden.

Pieljekaise Just south of the Arctic Circle in western Lappland, this park features moorlands, birch forests, flowering meadows and lakes rich in Arctic char. The Kungsleden hiking trail passes through the park.

Sarek With its wild mountain ranges, glaciers, deep valleys, impressive rivers and vast tracts of birch and willow forest, Sweden's best-loved national park, Sarek, represents the wild essence of the country's far north. There's no access by road, but experienced hikers can reach the park from the Kungsleden route.

Stora Sjöfallet This park, dominated by the lake Akkajaure and lofty Mt Áhkká, has been spoiled by hydroelectric development. It's readily accessible by road.

Vadvetjåkka Sweden's northernmost national park protects a large river delta containing bogs, lakes, limestone caves and a variety of bird species. The easiest access is on foot from Abisko.

Central

Björnlandet In the far south of Lappland and well off the beaten track, this small park includes natural forest, cliffs and boulder fields.

Färnebofjärden This park is noted for its abundant bird life, forests, rare lichens and mosses. There's good road access to the eastern side of the park.

Fulufjället Sweden's newest national park (created in 2002) is in northwestern Dalarna, west of Särna, and contains Njupeskär, the country's highest waterfall at 93m.

Garphyttan This tiny 111-hectare park is easily reached from Örebro. The previously cultivated areas, still traditionally maintained, exhibit fantastic flower displays, particularly in spring.

Hamra This park in the far north of Dalarna measures only 800m by 400m, but it's a protected area of virgin coniferous forest. Access is by a minor road off national road No 45.

GOVERNMENT & POLITICS

Government

Sweden is a constitutional hereditary monarchy but the monarch, as head of state, only has ceremonial duties and doesn't participate in government. The monarchy, headed by King Carl XVI Gustaf and Queen Silvia of the House of Bernadotte, does however provide a sense of national identity and is widely respected throughout the country. Carl XVI Gustaf has held the throne since 1973 and his eldest child, Princess Victoria, is first in line of succession (the successor is the first-born child, regardless of gender). It's possible to learn a lot more about Sweden's royal family on the Internet at its website W www.royalcourt.se.

Democratic general elections using proportional representation are held every four years, on the third Sunday in September, for the 349 seats in the parliament. Parties must achieve at least 4% of the vote to obtain representation. There are 29 constituencies for parliamentary elections and 310 fixed constituency seats; the remaining 'adjustment seats' are allocated to parties depending on their share of the vote. A majority in the parliament must vote for a prime minister, who then chooses a cabinet (regeringen) that will hold executive power. In the 2002 general election, the Social Democrat Party's share of the vote was the largest (39.8%), resulting in 144 seats; the prime minister, Göran Persson, is the party leader

Sweden's National Parks

Skuleskogen This hilly coastal area in Ångermanland has untouched forest, deep valleys, several good hiking trails and great views out to sea. There are also Bronze Age graves and the rare grey woodpecker has been observed. Access is from the nearby E4 Hwy.

Sånfjället Protected from reindeer grazing, Sånfjället in Härjedalen has natural mountain moorland and extensive views. Road and footpath access is possible from several sides.

Tresticklan Another area of natural coniferous forest, Tresticklan has small rift valleys and fine bird life. Access is by road from Ed, in Dalsland.

Tyresta Stockholm's own national park, Tyresta is an extensive forest area with huge 300-year-old pines and interesting rock formations. There is easy access from the city by car or bus.

Töfsingdalen This remote area in northern Dalarna must be approached on foot. It's exceptionally wild, with virtually impenetrable boulder fields and pine forest, but great views from the hill Hovden.

Ängsö This is a tiny island in the northern Stockholm archipelago that is noted for wonderful meadows, deciduous forest, bird life and spring flowers. Boat access is from Furusund.

Southern

Blå Jungfrun A wonderful island with smooth granite slabs, caves, a labyrinth, woods and great views. Boat access is from Oskarshamn.

Dalby Söderskog Located in densely-populated Skåne, this forest is a haven of peace for people and wildlife. Take a bus from Lund.

Djurö An archipelago of 30 islands in Lake Vänern, Djurö has lots of bird life and deer. The submerged reefs are a hazard for boats. Access is by private boat only.

Gotska Sandön The beautiful sandy isle of Gotska Sandön, north of Gotland, features dunes, dying pine forest and varied flora and fauna, including unusual beetles. Boats run from Nynäshamn and Fårösund.

Norra Kvill Another tiny park, just 114 hectares, Norra Kvill in Småland is noted for its ancient coniferous forest, excellent flora and gigantic boulders. The park is just northwest of Vimmerby.

Söderåsen This new park, east of Helsingborg and easily reached by road, contains deep fissure valleys, lush forests and flowing watercourses, and offers pleasant hiking trails and cycling paths.

Stenshuvud This is a small coastal national park in eastern Skåne with a great combination of beaches, forest and moorland. It's noted for its abundant wildlife and is easily reached by road; buses run from Simrishamn.

Store Mosse Dominated by extensive bogs with sand dunes, this park is noted for its bird life and great views from several hills. A road runs through the park.

Tiveden The wild hills, forests and lakes of this area include extensive boulder fields, beaches and excellent viewpoints. Minor roads and trails pass through the park and access is from road No 49.

---

and his deputy, or *vice statsminister,* is Lena Hjelm-Wallén.

Parliamentary business is usually carried out in a nonpartisan atmosphere by the wide range of standing committees elected by the Riksdag, which include representatives of union, business and cooperative movements.

All citizens over the age of 18 are eligible to vote in both local and national elections, and voter turnout is quite high (80% in the 2002 election). Women are well represented in the parliament and currently hold 157 seats or 45%, among the highest percentage in the world.

The elected councils of the 21 counties, each one convened by a cabinet-appointed governor, can levy taxes and are responsible for the administration of regional services such as public transport and health. At municipal level, the 289 *kommuner* (municipalities) take care of most of the education system and provide housing, roads, water supplies and other local infrastructure.

Regarding foreign relations, Sweden was a founding member of the League of Nations in 1920 and the United Nations in 1946. The policy of nonalignment has kept the country out of NATO, but Sweden has taken part in several international peacekeeping missions.

For further details on the **Sveriges Riksdag** *(Swedish Parliament;* W *www.riksdagen .se),* check out its website.

Politics

Sweden isn't noted for political extremes (the conservative parties are fairly moderate by European standards) but there has always been some support for the far left. Members of the parliament are under no obligation to follow party views as each member has a personal mandate from the voters; however, it's uncommon for a member to deviate from the general party line on an issue.

In the 2002 general election, the following parties achieved representation: the left-wing, egalitarian Social Democrats (144 seats); the right-of-centre Moderate Party (55 seats), supporters of the market economy; the Liberal Party (48 seats), promoting a policy of integration of immigrants and winning the biggest increase in votes; the right-of-centre Christian Democrats (33 seats), which promotes Christian values; the Left Party (30 seats), known as the Communist Party before 1990; the Centre Party (22 seats), formerly the Agrarian Party, now supporting decentralisation; and the Green Party (17 seats), the environmentalists who first entered the parliament in 1988. At the time of writing, Prime Minister Persson was keen to govern as a minority administration without a formal coalition, but this may lead to a good deal of instability. In the past the Social Democrats formed an alliance with the Left and Green parties, but after the 2002 election the Greens were pushing for stronger representation in the cabinet in order to continue their support.

For party information and details of the election results, see the **Sveriges Riksdag** (Swedish Parliament; W www.riksdagen.se) website.

ECONOMY

Despite being a small country, Sweden has a strong industrial base, typified by internationally known companies such as Volvo, Ericsson, Saab and ABB. The country's fortunes depend, to a large extent, on the success of its international trade; in 2000, exports amounted to 47% of the Gross Domestic Product (GDP).

Unemployment, which reached 14% in the early 1990s, has fallen to 4.1% (at the time of writing), inflation is low (2%) and the krona has regained some of its strength. The recent increases in employment are almost entirely due to the private sector. The GDP, which

rose at rates approaching 5% per annum in the 1960s, lost its momentum in 1990 and went into reverse, losing 5% between 1990 and 1993. Since 1994, annual growth has varied between 1% and 4%, mainly due to a still weak krona, lower employee payrolls and a substantial increase in exports. In 2001, the Swedish GDP was over US$210 billion, or around US$23,600 per inhabitant.

Although Sweden remains one of the wealthiest countries in the world, its tightly regulated and highly socialised 'economic model' is now viewed far more critically at home and abroad than before.

Agriculture & Industry

The mainstays of timber and mining are still important to industry, but the iron-ore mines of Kiruna and Gällivare in Lappland are not as crucial as they once were. Over half the country is forested and nearly half of this is in the hands of government or forestry companies. Most pulp and paper mills are found in the northern half of Sweden, near their wood supplies. About 8% of Sweden is farmland, mostly in the south of the country and, although only 3.3% of the workforce is engaged in agriculture, fishing and forestry, the country is self-sufficient in food.

Its engineering and high-technology industries include the manufacture of motor vehicles (Volvo and Saab) and aircraft (Saab), the nuclear power industry, arms manufacture (Bofors), telecommunications (Ericsson) and pharmaceuticals (Astra). Sweden is also home to the Ikea furniture empire and Tetra Pak, which developed the ubiquitous food and drink cartons. Swedish companies carry out large research and development programmes, mainly because they've expanded internationally and employ large numbers of people outside the country. In recent years Saab has been taken over by General Motors and Volvo by Ford: further blows to Swedish interests. Adding to the current climate, the national business flagship, Ericsson, has relocated some of its administrative and management personnel to a new European office in London and cut its workforce significantly at home and abroad.

Industry and construction suffered grievously during the recession of the early 1990s and many thousands of employees lost their jobs, contributing to the huge increase in unemployment. Subsequent improvement in the economy has allowed many of these people to go back to work.

Services

More than 3.1 million people work in services, with an astonishing 27.7% of the total labour market working for government agencies, with a further 43.4% working for private services. Sweden's enormous public sector (one of the largest in the world) gives a high level of employment to women, but only about 60% of them work full-time.

Taxation

The notorious Swedish taxation system used to set taxes that ranked among the highest in the world. In 1970, the rate of national income tax was 45% but, after a major revision of the tax system in the early 1990s (which was designed to lower rates and broaden the tax base), by 2001 this had dropped to 20% on all income between Skr252,000 and Skr390,400 and 25% on all income over Skr390,400.

Other taxes include local income tax (between 26% and 35% of income, depending on municipality), capital income tax (30%), value added tax on almost all goods and services (25% basic rate), and corporate tax (28%). The total tax revenue in 2000 as a percentage of GDP was a very high 52% (compared with figures of under 30% in the USA and Australia).

There are also indirect taxes on alcohol, tobacco, motor vehicles, fuel and energy. Although the tax burden is still high, taxpayers benefit through high quality public services and the welfare system.

POPULATION & PEOPLE

As of March 2002, Sweden's population was 8,914,336, representing 21.7 persons per sq km, one of the lowest population densities in Europe. The largest cities are Stockholm with 756,305 residents, Gothenburg with 472,203, Malmö with 262,995, Uppsala with 191,495 and Linköping with 134,254 (figures dated 31 March 2002). There's just a sprinkling of towns in Norrland and only Umeå has over 100,000 people.

Life expectancies are very high: for men it's 77.4 years and for women it's 82 years. Sweden has one of the oldest populations on earth, with more than 17% being over 65. The birth rate has been slowly decreasing – it is currently just under 1%, but the death rate is virtually constant at 1.06%. Immigration usually slightly exceeds emigration, so there is a small overall increase in population in most years (0.02% in 2001).

Nordic

Most of Sweden's population is considered to be of Nordic stock. These people are thought to have descended from central and northern European tribes who migrated northward after the end of the last Ice Age around 10,000 years ago, and modern Nordic peoples are in fact the indigenous peoples of southern and central Scandinavia. The 'Nordic type' is generally characterised by a tall sturdy frame, fair hair and blue eyes (although plenty of Nordic individuals do have darker features).

Sami

Sweden's approximately 17,000 indigenous Sami people (formerly known as Lapps) make up a significant ethnic minority. This hardy, formerly nomadic people have for centuries occupied northern Scandinavia and northwestern Russia, living mainly from their large herds of domestic reindeer. The total population of around 60,000 Sami still forms ethnic minorities in four countries – Norway, Sweden, Finland and Russia. In Sweden, they're mainly found in the mountain areas along the Norwegian border, northwards of mid-Dalarna. The Sami people themselves refer to their country as Sápmi, or Samiland.

In 1989, a cabinet-appointed commission of inquiry reported that the Sami people should be formally confirmed as an indigenous ethnic minority within the Swedish Constitution. The commission proposed the following: amendments to the Reindeer Husbandry Law (1971) to strengthen the Sami people's legal position; new laws designed to protect Sami land and water rights (such as hunting and fishing) and promote Sami institutions and culture; and the formation of an elected agency, Sameting, to further Sami interests. Only the latter has come into force – the rest were rejected by the Riksdag. With the resultant weakening of the Sami legal position, many observers view Sami developments as regressive rather than progressive steps and the ineffectual Sameting has come under heavy criticism in recent years.

SAMI CULTURAL AREA & DIALECTS

Dialects
1 South
2 Ume
3 Pite
4 Lule
5 North
6 Inari
7 Skolt
8 Kildin
9 Ter

History The oldest written reference to the Sami was penned by the Roman historian Tacitus, who described the 'Fenni' as a hunting people of the far north in the year AD 98. Chinese sources around AD 500 mention people using 'deer' for transport in the area. In 555, the Greek Procopius referred to Scandinavia as Thule, the farthest north, and its peoples as *skridfinns,* who hunted, herded reindeer and travelled about on skis. The late-9th-century trader Ottar, who 'lived further north than any other Norseman', served in the court of English King Alfred the Great and wrote extensively about his native country and its indigenous peoples. The medieval Icelandic sagas confirm trading between Nordic and Sami people. Sami traditions are also highlighted in the 1673 book, *Lapponia,* by Johannes Schefferus.

From the earliest times, the Sami lived by hunting and trapping in small communities or bands known as *siida,* each occupying their own designated territory. While 17th and 18th century colonisation of the north by Nordic farmers presented conflicts with this system, many of the newcomers found the Sami way of life better suited to the local conditions and adopted their dress, diet, customs and traditions.

Most early writings about the Sami tended to characterise them as pagans, and although churches were established on their lands as early as the 12th century, the first real missions didn't arrive until around 1610 when the first *lappkapell* (Sami chapels) were founded. Efforts concentrated mainly on eradicating the practice of Shamanism and *noaidi* (Sami spiritual leaders) were persecuted. Use of the Sami language was discouraged and efforts were made to coerce Sami children into school to learn Swedish. Subsequent missionary efforts, however, reversed the repressive religious policy and concentrated on translating the Bible into the Sami language. The Lutheran catechism was available in North Sami as early as 1728, thanks to the efforts of the missionary Morten Lund.

In the 18th and 19th centuries, permanent and mobile schools were set up by the Lutheran Church of Sweden to educate Sami children in their own language. However, from 1913 to 1930 the emphasis changed to providing a basic education in Swedish – apparently to enable young Sami to enter mainstream Swedish society, if they chose to do so. Nowadays, Sami education is available in government-run Sami schools or regular compulsory nine-year municipal schools, providing identical schooling to that received by Swedish children, but taking into account the Sami linguistic and cultural heritage. Recent improvements in Sami schooling include the establishment of teacher training programmes for Sami-speaking teachers at the college in Luleå. As for higher education, there has been a professor of the Sami language at Umeå University since 1974, and the language is also taught at the University of Uppsala.

Generally speaking, the Sami in Sweden do not enjoy the same rights as Sami people in Norway and Finland and reasons for this include hydroelectric developments and mining activities on traditional Sami land, which are of great importance to the Swedish establishment and economy. The Sami language only has the status of a 'regional official language', which means that school children receive part of their education in the Sami language, and that people have the right to use the Sami language when in contact with authorities, hospitals, official agencies etc, but only in certain (northern) regions.

Reindeer-herding techniques have undergone significant modernisation in recent years, with snowmobiles and helicopters commonly used. However, even when processing and transport are included, reindeer are not significant earners of capital and the meat is very expensive to produce. In addition to reindeer herding, modern Sami engage in forestry, agriculture, trade, small industry, tourism and the production of handicrafts, as well as most other trades and professions in Swedish society.

Religions Historically, the Sami religious traditions were characterised mainly by a relationship to nature and its inherent god-like archetypes. At sites of special power, particularly at prominent rock formations, people made offerings to their gods and ancestors to ensure success in hunting or other endeavours. Intervention and healing were effected by shamanic specialists, who used drums and small figures to launch themselves onto out-of-body journeys to the ends of the earth in search of answers. Interestingly, as with nearly all indigenous peoples in the northern hemisphere, the bear, as the most powerful creature in nature, was considered a sacred animal.

Historically, another crucial element in the religious tradition was the singing of the *yoik* (also spelt *joik*), or 'song of the plains'. Each person had their own melody or song, which conveyed not their personality or experiences, but rather their spiritual essence. So powerful and significant was this personal mantra, that the early Christian missionaries considered it a threat to their efforts and banned it as sinful. Nowadays most Sami profess Christianity, and there's no sign of interest in the old religion in Sweden.

Political Organisations The first central permanent Sami political organisation in Sweden, was founded in 1950. The **National Union of the Swedish Sami People** (Svenska Samernas Riksförbund) draws members from Sami villages, and other organisations. In addition to the elected Sami agency (parliament), which convenes in various places (but most often in Kiruna) and is elected by direct ballot, the Swedish Sami people also belong to the Sámiráddi (Sami Council), which has fostered cooperation between political organisations in Norway, Sweden and Finland since 1956 and now includes the Sami of Russia. The Sami also participate in the World Council of Indigenous Peoples (WCIP), which encourages solidarity and promotes information exchanges between indigenous peoples in the various member countries. The Nordic Sami Institute at Kautokeino in Norway, established in 1974 and funded by the Nordic Council of Ministers, seeks to promote Sami language, culture and education, as well as to promote research, economic activities and environmental protection.

In 1980, the Nordic-Sami Political programme adopted the following principles at a meeting in Tromsø (Norway):

We, the Sami, are one people whose fellowship must not be divided by national boundaries.
We have our own history, tradition, culture and language. We have inherited from our forebears a right to territories, water and our own economic activities.
We have an inalienable right to preserve and develop our own economic activities and our communities, in accordance with our own circumstances and we will together safeguard our territories, natural resources and national heritage for future generations.

An informative but rather angry treatise on Sami culture is the English-language booklet *The Saami – People of the Sun & Wind,* which is published by Ájtte, the Swedish Mountain and Saami Museum, in Jokkmokk. It does a good job of describing Sami traditions in all four countries of the Sápmi region, and is available at tourist shops around the area.

Other

About 30,000 Finnish-language speakers form a substantial native ethnic minority in the northeast, mostly in the area by the river Torneälven, where it forms the border with Finland. There are more than 160,000 citizens of other Nordic countries living in Sweden (including around 100,000 Finns and 33,000 Norwegians).

Most immigrants have come from other European countries, with large numbers in recent years from Eastern Europe (including 21,000 from Yugoslavia and 20,000 from Bosnia-Hercegovina). Currently the largest non-European ethnic group is made up of Middle Eastern citizens, who number over 100,000. Middle Eastern countries with the highest representation in Sweden are Iraq

(36,000 citizens), Turkey and Iran (around 14,000 each). Other countries with a sizeable presence include the Poland (15,000), Chile (10,000) and Somalia (10,000). There are also an estimated 25,000 Roma (Gypsies).

Immigration from outside the EU is now strictly regulated, but statistics reveal that 20% of Swedes are either foreign-born or have at least one non-Swedish parent.

EDUCATION

From the age of about six, every child in Sweden faces nine years of compulsory education at comprehensive school *(grundskolan)*. Depending on interest and ability, most pupils (some 98%) then move on to the three-year upper secondary school *(gymnasieskolan)*, where they can study academic courses specifically designed for university entrance, or take a variety of vocational courses. Sweden has one of the lowest rates in Europe of school leavers departing without a certificate.

Universities, and a variety of other higher education institutions, attract around 30% of young Swedes within five years of their completion of upper secondary school, but most students study short courses rather than completing a three-year degree. There are universities in Uppsala (founded in 1477), Lund (1668), Stockholm (1878), Gothenburg (1887), Umeå, Linköping, Karlstad, Växjö, Örebro and Luleå, plus about 20 small and medium-sized university colleges.

Education, books and lunches provided in the municipality-run schools are free of charge. Teaching at the mainly state-run higher education institutions is free and students can obtain loans on very good terms. A basic student grant (for students under 20 it's dependent on parental income) is available to all and is usually worth around Skr1500 per month.

SCIENCE & PHILOSOPHY

Sweden has consistently produced outstanding scientists and early explorers in scientific fields include the remarkably skilled Olof Rudbeck (1630–1702), who discovered the human lymphatic system, and Anders Celsius (1701–44), the astronomer and mathematician who invented the temperature scale that bears his name. The great botanist and physician Carl von Linné (1707–78), pioneered plant taxonomy under Latin classifications which are still used today (see the boxed text in the Svealand chapter). Carl Wilhelm Scheele (1742–86), a chemist, was the first to separate air into oxygen and nitrogen, and he discovered chlorine, molybdenum and the stages of oxidisation. Jöns Jacob Berzelius (1779–1848), also a chemist, determined the first table of atomic weights in 1818, developed the system of denoting elements by one or two letters, and discovered selenium, silicon and thorium. The spectrometry studies by the outstanding physicist Anders Jonas Ångström (1814–74) led to his identification of spectral lines for nearly 100 elements, and the determination of their wavelengths. The unit of measurement he introduced for small wavelengths (one ten-thousand millionth of a metre), the angstrom, was named in his honour.

The Swedish Academy of Sciences in Stockholm, founded in 1739, has fostered cooperation between individual scientists and remains a prestigious body to this day.

Although Sweden has not been well known for philosophical thinkers, there are a few, including Emanuel Swedenborg (1688–1722), who was partly educated in England (1710–13). There's a Swedenborg Society in London.

ARTS

For many years, the arts in Sweden have been best represented by literature, but in more recent times modern music has risen in significance and some well-known pop groups have gained international stardom.

Dance

Ballet is reasonably popular in Sweden and the Royal Swedish Ballet, founded in Stockholm by King Gustav III in 1773, is the fourth oldest ballet company in the world. The company has a good reputation for the quality of its productions, including classical and modern ballets. Aficionados should also seek out the Cullberg Ballet, a leading dance company in the field of modern dance since it was established by pioneering dancer and choreographer Birgit Cullberg in 1967.

In Stockholm, there's the House of Dance, the Dance Museum, the Stockholm Cultural Centre (the principal venue for guest appearances in the capital) and the Dance Centre, which arranges festivals and encourages people to get involved. Ballet and modern

Swedish Inventions

Swedes have helped human development with a wide range of inventions, and Sweden boasts a large number of inventors for a country with such a small population.

In the late 1880s, Frans Wilhelm Lindqvist patented the paraffin (kerosene) stove and, in partnership with his brother, set up the Primus factory, which manufactured around 50 million stoves over the next 100 years or so. These were sold worldwide and were greatly enjoyed by campers.

Victor Hasselblad (1906–78) took six years to develop his single lens reflex (SLR) camera, which had interchangeable lenses and film reels. The camera was first shown in New York in 1948, and caused quite a stir. Hasselblad cameras were used by astronauts when exploring the moon and many photographers aspire to own and use one of these precision instruments.

The Tetra Pak food-storage system, invented by Erik Wallenberg, was developed in 1951. One of its successors, Tetra Brik (1969), is now used worldwide for storing liquids such as milk and fruit juice.

Leif Lundblad (born 1938) patented the automatic transaction machine (ATM) for dispensing bank notes in 1978 and his company has been one of modern Sweden's successes.

Other notable Swedish inventors include Gustaf Erik Pasch (1788–1862), who patented the safety match in 1844; John Ericsson (1803–89), the inventor of screw propellers for ships; Nils Gustav Dalén (1869–1937), the developer of automatic marine beacons and winner of the Nobel Prize for physics in 1912; and Johan Petter Johansson (1853–1943), the designer of the adjustable wrench and other important inventions. Sven Wingquist (1876–1953) created the modern ball bearing, and although the zipper was invented by an American designer, Swede Gideon Sundbäck's design (patented in 1913) made it user-friendly.

Probably the most internationally-known Swedish inventor is Alfred Nobel (1833–96), who discovered dynamite, and whose will founded the Nobel Institute in 1901 (see the boxed text 'Alfred Nobel' in the Stockholm chapter).

---

dance aren't restricted to Stockholm and they can also be seen at the Gothenburg Opera and the Dance Station in Malmö, with other smaller-scale productions around the country.

Folk dancing goes hand-in-hand with folk music and the best time to enjoy this is at Midsummer.

Music

The popularity of music in Sweden is highlighted by the facts that Swedes buy more recorded music per capita than any other nationality, and the country is the third-largest exporter of music in the world (after the US and UK). There are around 600,000 choral singers in Sweden and some 120 music festivals are staged annually, ranging from medieval and baroque to folk, jazz and rock. Some choruses are internationally known, as are some home-grown pop groups.

The **Swedish Music Information Centre** (W *www.mic.stim.se*) is a good place to start for those looking for more information on the topic. For more details on music festivals, including those mentioned below, see the boxed text 'Festivals & Concerts' in the Facts for the Visitor chapter.

Classical Although Sweden has never produced a classical composer to match Norway's Edvard Grieg, there has been no shortage of contenders. One of the earliest was the serious Emil Sjögren (1853–1918). He was followed by the Wagnerian Wilhelm Peterson-Berger (1867–1942) and Hugo Alfvén (1872–1960), one of Sweden's greatest symphonists.

Opera flourished after the opening of the Royal Opera House, known as Operan, in Stockholm (1782) and, since 1922, many other venues have appeared, including the Drottningholm Court Theatre in Stockholm, Göteborgs Operan in Gothenburg, the Malmö City Theatre, Dalhalla near Rättvik, the Norrland Opera in Umeå and the Folkoperan in Stockholm, which brings the audience into close contact with the singers. Renowned Swedish opera performers have included Jenny Lind (1820–87), known as the 'Swedish nightingale', and Birgit Nilsson (1918–).

Folk Interest in Swedish folk music really took off in the 1970s and '80s, thanks mainly to the Falun Folk Music Festival. It's considered to be the fastest-growing area in Swedish music, with folk rock and other avant garde variants becoing increasingly popular. Traditional Swedish folk music revolves around the triple-beat *polska*, originally a Polish dance, and instruments played include the fiddle, accordion, harp, violin and (more rarely) the bagpipe. Ethnic-minority folk music includes the Sami *yoik* (see Population & People earlier in this chapter) and a wide range of styles brought to Sweden by immigrants from around the world.

Jazz Between the 1920s and '60s, jazz was all the rave and the country produced a series of artistes who excelled on the guitar, saxophone and clarinet. The pianist, Jan Johansson (1931–68), succeeded in blending jazz and folk in a peculiar Swedish fashion. The rise of jazz rock during the 1970s and '80s, and a good selection of young vocalists in the '90s has ensured the place of jazz as an important music genre. Both Stockholm and Umeå host popular annual jazz festivals.

Pop & Rock After the Beatles visited Sweden in 1963, the pop scene exploded in their wake and over 100 new bands were formed in a few weeks. During this era, the space-age Spotnicks, from Gothenburg, became internationally renowned.

ABBA is the best-known Swedish pop group from the 1970s (see the boxed text). After winning the Eurovision Song Contest in 1974 with the song 'Waterloo', they went on to achieve huge international success.

Thank You for the Music

If asked to name Sweden's most famous exports, the pop group ABBA would top many people's list. Indeed, around the globe there are probably thousands of people who couldn't easily pinpoint Sweden on a world map but who could tell you the names of the four band members plus recite the chorus to 'Dancing Queen' without much prompting.

During the 1970s ABBA, consisting of two couples, was founded and became one of the most successful popular music acts of the decade and beyond (even Nelson Mandela once declared ABBA his favourite pop group). The individual members were all show-business veterans in their native Sweden, and their wholesome image, perfectly constructed pop songs and strong melodies took the world by storm. ABBA, an acronym of their names (Agnetha, Björn, Benny and Anni-Frid – more commonly known as Frida), was used by their manager Stig Anderson for convenience, but when a newspaper competition came up with the same result, the decision was made and ABBA was born. There was already a Swedish canned-fish company with the same name, but when Stig asked them if they would mind lending their name to a popular music group, fortunately they didn't object.

ABBA won the Eurovision Song Contest in 1974 with 'Waterloo', topping the charts in several countries and reaching the top five in several others, including the USA. They went from success to success – ABBA toured the world, made a film and recorded hit after hit. ABBA's last year together was 1982 and by then the fairytale was over and both couples had divorced but, in the words of one of their songs, 'the music still goes on'. The 1990s saw something of an ABBA revival, with successful cover versions of ABBA anthems, ABBA tribute bands attracting huge crowds, the group's elevation to the status of gay icons, and popular movies such as *Muriel's Wedding* and *The Adventures of Priscilla – Queen of the Desert* featuring ABBA music and impersonations. In 1992 the compilation album *ABBA Gold* became the group's biggest seller ever, topping charts the world over (to date it has sold a staggering 22 million copies). Despite this revival success, sadly no reunion is on the cards. Agnetha, and to a lesser extent Frida, have retired from public life, while Benny and Björn have concentrated on other ventures, including writing successful musicals.

On 6 April 1999, 25 years to the day after winning the Eurovision Song Contest, Benny and Björn's musical, *Mamma Mia!*, featuring nearly 30 of ABBA's legendary songs, received its world premiere in London. Since then it has won awards and packed in audiences in Toronto, Melbourne, on Broadway and throughout the US. In late 2002 it will open in Hamburg and Tokyo. For more information, visit the musical's official site Ⓦ www.mamma-mia.com. There are hundreds of ABBA websites on the Internet; a good place to start is Ⓦ www.abbasite.com.

In the late '70s, anarchic punk groups such as Ebba Grön arose to challenge the accepted order and, in 1986, the long-haired rock group Europe achieved a number-one hit around the world with 'The Final Countdown'. In the late 1980s and into the '90s, more mainstream pop acts such as Roxette, Ace of Base and the Cardigans held international attention, and the pop and rock music industry has expanded to form one of Sweden's most successful exports. The latest Swedish band to hit the big time is punk rockers The Hives, out of Fagersta, north of Västerås. Other bands in the international limelight include Lambretta and Millencolin.

There are a number of popular rock-music festivals staged annually in summer, including those at Hultsfred, Arvika and Sölvesborg.

Literature

The best known members of Sweden's artistic community have been writers, chiefly the influential dramatist and author August Strindberg (1849–1912) and the widely translated children's writer Astrid Lindgren (1907–2002). (See the boxed texts in the Stockholm and Småland chapters respectively.) Strindberg's *Röda Rummet* (The Red Room) was completed in 1879 and is considered by many as the first modern Swedish novel. Lindgren's well-known fantasy characters, especially Pippi Longstocking and her pet monkey Herr Nilsson, have an enduring fascination for children – highlighted by the popularity of Astrid Lindgrens Värld (a theme park in Vimmerby, about 100km east of Jönkjöping). Lindgren's book *Pippi Longstocking* was first published in English in 1950.

Selma Lagerlöf (1858–1940) was also an early literary giant. Two of her best-known works are *Gösta Berlings Saga* (1891) and *Nils Holgerssons underbara resa genom Sverige* (The Wonderful Adventures of Nils; 1906–7); the latter was very popular in schools and has great character portrayals. Despite her opposition to the Swedish establishment, Lagerlöf became the Nobel Laureate in Literature in 1909. This accolade has also been awarded to five other Swedes (two jointly) in the years since. In 1951 it went to Pär Lagerkvist (1891–1974), from Växjö (Småland), whose works include lyric poetry, dramas (including *The Hangman*, 1935), and novels, such as *Barabbad* (1950).

Albert Engström (1869–1940) from Eksjö in Småland was an accomplished author who wrote witty stories about the gap between rich and poor, and drunks who had consumed too much aquavit. Engström is also known for his amusing sketches.

During WWII, some Swedish writers bravely opposed the Nazis, including Eyvind Johnson (1900–76) with his *Krilon* trilogy, completed in 1943, and the famous poet and novelist Karin Boye (1900–41), whose novel *Kallocain* was published in 1940.

Vilhelm Moberg (1898–1973), a representative of 20th-century proletarian literature and controversial social critic, won international acclaim with *Utvandrarna* (The Emigrants; 1949) and *Nybyggarna* (The Settlers; 1956). Moberg's books concentrated primarily on rural society and history, and several of his books dealing with the 19th-century emigrations to America were adapted for the cinema.

Twentieth-century poetry tended to dwell on political and social issues, such as the Vietnam War, apartheid in Southern Africa, and social conditioning at home. Some of the better-known Swedish poets include Karin Boye; Göran Sonnevi (1939–), writer of the famous *Om kriget i Vietnam* (On the War in Vietnam; 1965); Sonja Åkesson (1926–77), a social critic with an interest in women's issues; and the recently popular Kristina Lugn and Bodil Malmsten.

Sven Delblanc (1931–92) was a highly admired writer, active from the early '60s; his successful *Hedeby* series is set in rural parts of Södermanland. More recently, the powerful imagination of Göran Tunström (1937–) is reflected in *Juloratoriet* (The Christmas Oratorio; 1983), which was made into a film, and *Skimmer* (Shimmering; 1996), set in Iceland during Viking times. Other recent authors of note include Torgny Lindgren (1938–), who writes 'fantasy novels' such as *Hummelhonung* (Bumble-bee Honey; 1995), Robert Kangas (1951–), a prize-winning author of bleak but realistic novels, and Inger Edelfeldt (1956–), whose psychological stories delve into the minds of weak and disturbed people.

However, to the Swedish soul, the Gustavian balladry of Carl Michael Bellman is perhaps the dearest. Bellman was born in

Stockholm in 1740 and he completed one of his best-known writings, *Fredmans Epistlar* (Fredman's Epistles), when he was only 30 years of age. Greek themes, with references to drunken revelry and Bacchus, the Greek and Roman god of wine, are strong features in this work. Evert Taube (1890–1976), sailor, author, composer and painter, is known as the modern successor of Bellman.

Architecture

While many Swedish towns and cities contain faceless office blocks and flats dating from the 1960s and '70s, there's a wide variety of architectural gems around the country.

Early Structures Apart from the elaborate graves, such as Mysinge hög on Öland, little survives of Bronze Age buildings in Sweden. Also on Öland, there are several large Iron Age relics including Ismantorp, a fortified village with limestone walls and nine gates, and Eketorp, a reconstructed circular-plan, 3rd-century fort.

Romanesque & Gothic There are some excellent examples of Romanesque church architecture throughout Sweden, primarily constructed in sandstone and limestone, and characterised by archways and barrel-vaulted ceilings. One of the finest is Lund Cathedral, consecrated in 1145 and still dominating the city centre with its two imposing square towers.

Gothic styles from the 13th and 14th centuries mainly used brick rather than stone. Some fine examples can be seen at the Mariakyrkan in Sigtuna (completed in 1237) and Uppsala Cathedral, which was consecrated in 1435.

Gotland is the best place in Sweden to see ecclesiastical Gothic architecture, with around 100 medieval churches on the island, and there's also the virtually intact stone-built, 13th-century Visby town wall, complete with 40 towers.

Renaissance, Baroque & Rococo During and after the Reformation, monasteries and churches were plundered by the crown and wonderful royal palaces and castles were constructed (or rebuilt) instead, such as Gustav Vasa's Kalmar Slott (castle) in Kalmar and Gripsholm Slott, 50km west of Stockholm, which has one of the best Renaissance interiors in Sweden. Construction of the old fortress town of Kristianstad was ordered in Renaissance style by the Danish king, Christian IV, in 1614 and many of the buildings are still standing today.

Magnificently ornate baroque architecture arrived in Sweden (mainly from Italy) during the 1640s while Queen Kristina held the throne. Kalmar Cathedral, designed in 1660, the adjacent Kalmar Rådhus and Drottningholm palace (1662) just outside Stockholm were all designed by the court architect Nicodemus Tessin the Elder, and Drottningholm has been placed on Unesco's World Heritage List. Nicodemus Tessin the Younger designed the vast 'new' Kungliga Slott (Royal Palace) in Stockholm after the previous palace was gutted by fire in 1697, but it wasn't completed until 1754 and most of the interior is 18th-century rococo.

Highly ornamented, asymmetrical rococo designs of mainly French origin are prevalent in many grandiose 18th-century buildings. Towards the end of that century, neoclassical designs became quite popular, especially with the king, Gustav III.

Neoclassical, Neo-Renaissance & Neo-gothic Architecture of the 19th century known as the Carl Johan style clearly reflects the king's French neoclassical interests. Later in the century, neogothic and neo-Renaissance architectural designs appeared, including the Helsingborg Rådhus (town hall), a fairly outlandish red-brick structure with peculiar towers and turrets.

Romanticism, Art Nouveau & Functionalism The late 19th century and early 20th century saw a rise in romanticism, a particularly Swedish style mainly using wood and brick, which produced such wonders as the Stockholm Rådhus (1916) and Stadshus (City Hall; completed in 1923), and the extraordinary Tjolöholm Slott, 35km south of Gothenburg. Many of the excellent Art Nouveau buildings in Gothenburg itself were built around the same time.

From the 1930s to the '80s, functionalism and the so-called international style took over, with their emphasis on steel, concrete and glass. Flat roofs and huge windows, hopelessly inadequate in Sweden, were eventually abandoned by architects. Although some buildings from this period are quite attractive, ghastly ranks of apartment blocks are an unpleasant reminder of the unacceptable face of Swedish socialism: conformity. More recently, as in many European towns and cities, restoration of older buildings has become popular.

Painting

Interest in 19th- and 20th-century Swedish art has risen in recent years and sales at auction have fetched extraordinarily high sums of money. There are substantial art collections at many art galleries and museums throughout the country.

Carl Larsson, Nils Kreuger and others were leaders of an artistic revolution in the 1880s and some of the best 19th-century oil paintings were painted by Larsson in a warm Art Nouveau style. Anders Zorn's portraits of famous Swedes and August Strindberg's surprisingly modern landscapes have also come to the attention of the art world. The nature paintings of Bruno Liljefors are well regarded and consequently sell for high prices at auction. Eugéne Jansson's vivid Stockholm landscapes indicate influence from the Norwegian painter, Edvard Munch.

Although there was an initially cautious approach to Cubism, some artists embraced the concepts of surrealist and abstract art, albeit with their own Swedish style, such as the rather bizarre 'dreamland' paintings of Stellan Mörner. Otto Carlsund was the driving force behind early abstract art in Sweden, which strongly impinged on the public conscience during the Stockholm exhibition of 1930 but didn't really become established until after WWII. Olle Baertling's post-war geometrical styles still sell well at auction.

Considerably more radical art movements in the 1960s and '70s were influenced by diverse sources including far left-wing politics, popular culture, minimalism and pop art. The intriguing paintings by Jan Håfström remind observers how close many Swedes are to nature and the vaguely disturbing *Will you be profitable, my little one?* by Peter Tillberg is clearly an attack on 1970s society and schooling.

More recently, women artists have become increasingly significant and the modern art scene developed with a renewed interest in paint.

Peter Dahl, Norwegian-born but living in Stockholm, is noted for his paintings of Bellman ballads.

Society and the environment continue to play an important part in the psyche of many Swedish artists.

Sculpture

Carl Milles (1875–1955) is Sweden's greatest sculptor and indeed one of the 20th century's most eminent artists in this field. He once worked as Rodin's assistant and his home in Lidingö, on the outskirts of Stockholm, is now an open-air museum, known as Millesgården.

Cinema

Sweden led the way in the silent-film era of the 1920s with such masterpieces as *Körkarlen* (The Phantom Carriage), adapted from a novel by Selma Lagerlöf and directed by Mauritz Stiller. However, the 'Golden Age' was short-lived, as Stiller and others (including the actress Greta Garbo) emigrated to Hollywood.

After WWII, Swedish film makers produced more artistic movies that went down well with foreign audiences at film festivals throughout Europe. The highly acclaimed Ingmar Bergman directed many excellent films from the late 1940s up to 1982. Many of Astrid Lindgren's books were made into films that were (and still are) shown worldwide and the actress Ingrid Bergman won Academy Awards for her roles in several films. However, as in many other countries, the growing power of television in the 1960s caused cinema audiences to dwindle. Government intervention to save the industry caused increasing politicisation, but failed to halt the decline. By the 1990s, the trend had reversed and the film industry was rejuvenated with new blood and new styles, including close cooperation with television (terrestrial, satellite and cable) and video.

Sweden has been incorrectly branded as the world's major source of blue movies, but finger-pointers would be wise to take a closer look at activities in some nearby countries first. Sweden actually has the world's oldest film censorship board (formed in 1911) and it can ban, cut, and set minimum ages for any film that is screened in Sweden.

Theatre

King Gustav III founded the Royal Dramatic Theatre, known as Dramaten, in Stockholm in 1773, and interest in theatre and opera blossomed. Greta Garbo attended the drama school of the Royal Dramatic Theatre in 1922, and Ingmar Bergman made his directorial debut here in 1951.

With the arrival of social democracy, functional-style theatres were built in various towns around the country, particularly from the 1920s to the '50s, to encourage an appreciation among ordinary people. Currently, about 30% of government funding for the arts goes to theatre, but there's still a struggle in the face of intense competition from other pursuits, such as mime, dance and music.

SOCIETY & CONDUCT

Swedes are generally decent, law-abiding and serious, but they're well known for boisterous drinking sessions, especially when they travel to countries where booze is cheaper. They are also a patriotic bunch, and proud of their country's history. Sweden's reputation as a social reformer, albeit sometimes misunderstood, is justified. After having sold (as a neutral country) weapons to the rest of the world during WWII, Sweden decided to save the world from all other evils, including capitalism. This institutionalised niceness saved refugees from developing countries, built the most comprehensive welfare state in the world, established equality among workers, liberated women and made life easier for the old and disabled. Just when other nations were starting to tire of this over-zealous, self-appointed 'moral guardian' of the world, political and economic factors in the late 1980s forced Swedes to fundamentally re-assess themselves.

Still, Sweden regulates, taxes and subsidises every step from cradle to grave. Even queuing is infallibly ordered: press a button for your own numbered ticket, then wait until it comes up on a digital display, even if you only want to buy a bottle of wine! All this is just *lagom* (satisfactorily acceptable) to Swedes who have created one of the cleanest, most comfortable and stylish societies anywhere – an almost perfect destination for travellers, if only you can afford it!

Although the strong rural traditions are not forgotten (the summer cottage is almost *de rigueur* – there are 600,000 second homes), modern Sweden is becoming increasingly urban. Late-model Volvos and Saabs are everywhere, and mobile phone ownership is sky-high. Its small population also has an impressive presence in world music charts and international sporting arenas.

Traditional Culture

Traditional culture is best showcased at annual events like Midsummer celebrations. See Public Holidays & Special Events in the Facts for the Visitor chapter for a rundown on annual Swedish festivities and how these are celebrated.

Styles of traditional folk dress, known as *folkdräkt*, vary around the country and may be different in adjacent communities. The national version, which can be worn everywhere, was designed in the 20th century. Women wear a white hat, yellow skirt and blue sleeveless vest with white flowers on top of a white blouse. Men wear a simpler costume of knee-length trousers (breeches), white shirt, vest and wide-brimmed hat. *Folkdräkt* comes out of the cupboard on national day, and for Midsummer, weddings, feasts, birthdays and church visits.

Social Graces

Most Swedes have few customs that differ from those of European descent. There are of course also the ethnic-minority immigrants with Islamic and other customs.

The traditional handshake is used liberally in both business and social circles when greeting friends or meeting strangers. In the latter case, the customary introductions will include your full names. *Var så god* (pronounced roughly vahsh-o-**goot**), is commonly said throughout Sweden and this phrase carries all sorts of expressions of goodwill, including both 'Welcome', and 'Please', as well as 'Pleased to meet you', 'I'm happy to serve you', 'Thanks' and 'You're welcome'. There's no equivalent in English, but it roughly approximates the all-purpose German *bitte* or *aloha* in Hawaiian.

If you're an informal guest in a Swedish home, particularly in the countryside, it's not uncommon to remove your shoes before entering the living area. It's customary to present your host with a small gift of sweets or flowers and avoid sipping your drink before he or she makes the toast, *Skål*, which you should answer in return. This traditional ritual is most frequently accompanied by direct eye contact with whoever offered the toast, symbolising respect and absence of guile. Don't toast the hostess if there are more than eight people at the table.

Treatment of Animals

Animals are reasonably well treated in Sweden, but hunting is still a popular activity. Some rare species such as wolverines and wolves have been (and still are) persecuted by farmers and Sami herders. Hunting methods using traps were prohibited in the 19th century and the modern technique uses high-powered rifles.

To learn more about the situation in Sweden, contact **Svenska Djurskyddsföreningen** *(Swedish Society for the Protection of Animals;* ☎ *08-783 0368;* W *www.djurskydd.org; Erik Dahlbergsgatan 28, Box 10081, SE-10055 Stockholm).* The website is in Swedish only. For more general information, **People for the Ethical Treatment of Animals** (W *www .peta.org/liv/travel-help.html)* has good information for travellers.

RELIGION

Christianity arrived fairly late in Sweden (see History earlier in this chapter) and is now most heavily influenced by the German Protestant reformer Martin Luther, who viewed the scriptures as the sole authority of God and advocated that only by grace can humankind be saved from its savage nature. Luther's doctrines were adopted in 1527.

According to the Swedish constitution, Swedish people have the right to practise any religion they choose. Complete separation of church and state took place in 2000 and Evangelical Lutheranism is no longer the official religion. Since 1994 citizens do not legally acquire a religion at birth but voluntarily become members of a faith. About 10% of Swedes regularly attend church services, but church marriages, funerals and communions are still popular.

These days, about 85% (7.5 million) of the country's population are members of the Church of Sweden, which is a denomination of Protestant Evangelical Lutheranism headed by the Archbishop of Uppsala. Despite controversy and substantial resistance in some quarters, women can be ordained as priests.

Other religious groups with sizeable representation in Sweden include Roman Catholics (166,000 members); the Orthodox Churches of the Finns, Greeks, Russians and Serbs (around 98,500 members); and Pentecostals (91,000 members). The country also has around 250,000 Muslims and 18,000 Jews, together with approximately 3000 to 4000 Buddhists and the same number of Hindus. For information on Sami religions, see Population & People earlier in this chapter.

Facts for the Visitor

HIGHLIGHTS

Highlights for visitors to Sweden range from spectacular mountain scenery in Lappland to picturesque historic towns, especially in the country's south. The following list covers just some of them:

Bohuslän Coast

This area has some of Sweden's most impressive landscapes, with large areas of exposed rock slab smoothed by Ice Age glaciers. The picturesque village of Åstol, perched on a tiny rocky islet, is well worth visiting. You'll also find a Unesco World Heritage Site at Tanumshede, with 3000-year-old rock carvings etched into the slabs.

Castles

Sweden has hundreds of castles, royal palaces and castle-like manor houses, especially around Stockholm and in the region of Skåne. Visitors can enjoy Drottningholm near Stockholm, the royal residence with its lovely gardens and wonderful old court theatre; castles such as Skokloster or Gripsholm, both by Lake Mälaren; formidable fortresses such as Kalmar and Örebro castles; and impressive ruins like those at Borgholm on Öland.

Churches

Around 3000 churches were built during the last 900 years in Sweden. There are 92 medieval churches in Gotland, 240 in Skåne and more than 130 in the Stockholm-Uppsala region. Entry to almost all churches is free. Some fine examples of cathedral (domkyrka) styles include Lund (Romanesque), Uppsala (Gothic) and Kalmar (baroque).

Historic Towns

Sweden's historic towns, many of them dating back to early medieval times, include Lund, the oldest town in Sweden, still centred around its 12th-century cathedral; Visby and its astonishing 13th-century town wall; and Kristianstad, with its beautiful 17th-century Renaissance architecture. Sigtuna is the oldest remaining town in Sweden, and other fine examples include Ystad, Kalmar and Karlskrona.

Hostels

One of country's nicest surprises is the extensive network of well-equipped hostels, offering reasonably priced accommodation in old ships, train carriages, former prisons, schools, farms, manor houses, on off-shore islands and other novel spots. Most are pleasantly decorated, spotlessly clean and have excellent facilities. The only downside is their restricted opening hours.

Ice Hotel

Built anew every winter from ice taken from the frozen local river, the hotel structure is breathtakingly beautiful and wonderfully unique, not to mention cold. This incredible complex, in Jukkasjärvi outside of Kiruna in the country's far north, nicely takes advantage of the Arctic weather extremes, but there are attractions here year-round.

Islands

The Baltic islands of Gotland and Öland are different from the mainland, and this is reflected in the unusual raukar rock formations and the flora. The islands are big summer centres for Swedes – cycling, camping and cabin holidays are popular. Some 24,000 islands off Stockholm and many more around the long Swedish coastline provide endless opportunities for exploration.

Lake Siljan & Around

This area is noted for its lovely scenery and events ranging from huge Midsummer celebrations and fast-and-furious ice hockey to operas performed in a deep quarry. You can visit an excellent selection of museums, including the former homes of some of Sweden's greatest artists, a copper mine, and a bear park.

Laponia World Heritage Area

For the best mountain scenery, travel north of the Arctic Circle to the magnificent Kebnekaise region and the national parks Sarek and Stora Sjöfallet. The valleys from Abisko to Kebnekaise offer superb trekking, but Sarek is the place to go for a much more serious wilderness, wildlife or mountaineering experience.

Stockholm & the Archipelago

Stockholm's slogan 'Beauty on Water' is perfectly justified – the city's setting must rank among the loveliest in the world. There's also a great range of cafés and restaurants, museums to satisfy most interests, and a rocky archipelago of scenic islands, rustic villages and old steamships puffing to-and-fro.

SUGGESTED ITINERARIES

To get the most out of your stay in Sweden, you might like to consider the following:

Two Days

Depending on your point of entry into the country, either visit Stockholm and its environs or travel by train between Helsingborg and Malmö via Lund.

One Week

Spend three days in Stockholm and Uppsala, two or three days around Gothenburg and the Bohuslän Coast, then continue south to Malmö.

Alternatively, explore the Stockholm region more thoroughly, including Birka and a couple of days in the archipelago, before heading to Uppsala via Sigtuna.

Two Weeks
As above, but include a trip northwards to the Lake Siljan region, or add Kristianstad, Karlskrona, Kalmar and Öland to a tour of the south. Alternatively, explore Gotland by bicycle or rented car for several days.

One Month
Traverse the country from Malmö to Abisko, taking in all of the above, plus Småland, the Inlandsbanan railway north of Mora (Siljan), and include hiking on Kungsleden around Kvikkjokk, Kebnekaise and Abisko.

Two Months
Explore the country thoroughly and include stops at smaller towns, visit the more remote national parks and the Jämtland mountains, and follow the Baltic Coast and the great northern rivers.

PLANNING

Careful planning is crucial for any trip to Sweden – you don't want to find most things closed because you've arrived in May, several weeks before the season has started. If you're on a limited budget, detailed advance planning will save time and money and may enable you to stay longer than anticipated.

When to Go

Despite its northern location in Europe, Sweden isn't as cold as you might expect. The south has a year-round temperate climate and summer can be quite warm in the north. See the Climate section in the Facts about Sweden chapter for further details. Sweden is at its best during summer and autumn (late May to September), but hikers and campers may wish to avoid the peak of the mosquito season (June and July).

Due to the country's high latitude, daylight hours are long in summer. Malmö gets 17½ hours of daylight around midsummer and Sundsvall has constant light during the second half of June, but you have to travel north of the Arctic Circle to experience the true 'midnight sun' – in Kiruna, the sun remains above the horizon for 45 days, from 31 May to 14 July.

However, deciding when to go should also be influenced by the following factors: from late June (Midsummer) to mid-August, most hotels offer discounts of up to 50%; seasonal tourist offices, museums, youth hostels and camping grounds are open (although prices at most camping grounds and some hostels increase during this period); and buses run more frequently. However, most Swedes also take their holidays in this period, so finding accommodation in areas favoured by the locals (eg, Gotland and Öland) may prove difficult.

Winter sports enthusiasts can enjoy a visit any time from December to March or April. At 69° north latitude, there's an average 'day' of only four twilight hours in December, with the sun never above the horizon, and fairly short daylight hours even in the south. Travel in winter is somewhat restricted and should be better planned, but there are good opportunities for activities like skiing, or dog-sledge and snowmobile safaris. The big cities are in full swing all year, but the smaller towns almost go into hibernation when the temperatures begin to drop (the notable exceptions being popular ski resort towns like Åre, and Jukkasjärvi, home to the Ice Hotel). Some readers have reported their frustration at finding many attractions closed outside of the peak summer months. As one reader wrote:

'You are here at the wrong time of year' is the phrase winter visitors to Sweden hear most often.

Maps

Tourist offices, libraries and places to stay usually stock free local town plans.

The best maps of Sweden are published and updated regularly by Kartförlaget, the sales branch of the national mapping agency, Lantmäteriet. Maps can be bought at most tourist offices, bookshops and some youth hostels, service stations and general stores.

Motorists planning an extensive tour should get *Motormännens Sverige Atlas* (Kartförlaget; Skr270), with 27 pages of town plans and 169 pages of detailed coverage at 1:250,000 (as far north as Sundsvall) and 1:400,000 for the remainder.

The best tourist road maps are those of Kartförlaget's *Vägkartan* series, at a scale of 1:100,000, available from larger bookshops. Also useful, especially for hikers, are the *Fjällkartan* mountain series (1:100,000, with 20m contour interval); these are usually priced from Skr80 to Skr110 apiece and are available at larger bookshops, outdoor equipment stores and mountain stations operated by **Svenska Turistföreningen** *(STF; ☎ 08-463 2100;* e *info@stfturist.se,* w *www.merav sverige.nu; Box 25, SE-10120 Stockholm).*

To get your maps in advance, contact **Lantmäteriet** *(☎ 026-633000;* w *www.lant materiet.se; SE-80182 Gävle);* its website has a good mail-order service, with information in English. The following shops also sell a range of Swedish maps by mail order.

Kartbutiken (☎ 08-202303, w www.kartbutiken .se) Kungsgatan 74, SE-11122 Stockholm, Sweden

The Map Shop (☎ 0800 085 4080, w www.the mapshop.co.uk) 15 High St, Upton-upon-Severn, Worcs, WR8 0HJ, UK

Omni Resources (☎ 336-227 8300, w www.omni map.com) 1004 S Mebane St, PO Box 2096, Burlington, NC 27216-2096, USA

Map Land (☎ 03-9670 4383, w www.mapland .com.au) 372 Little Bourke St, Melbourne, Vic 3000, Australia

What to Bring

Swedes normally dress fairly casually but, if you're staying in luxurious hotels and dining in fine restaurants, bring an alternative to T-shirts and jeans. In summer, a wide-brimmed hat is essential, while winter visitors will need lots of warm clothing, good boots, a scarf, hat and gloves. Sunglasses are strongly recommended – even in winter, in order to protect your eyes from glare off snowy surfaces. Outdoor enthusiasts need to be equipped for all weather, preferably using a layer system so that clothes can be removed easily to prevent overheating (or added, if it turns chilly). Strong hiking boots, waterproof garments and a woolly jersey (sweater) will be needed for a visit to the mountains. Budget travellers and mountain hikers going into remote areas should carry a tent, a cooking stove and a warm sleeping bag (even in summer). Hostellers and cabin users can save money by bringing their own sleeping sheets and towels. Rucksacks (backpacks) can be more convenient than suitcases.

RESPONSIBLE TOURISM

Facilities for tourists are well developed throughout most of Sweden, and locals and visitors alike seem intent on doing the right thing for the environment. However, a few problems have arisen due to some travellers abusing public access (see the boxed text 'The Right of Public Access' in the 'Hiking'

special section). Be sensible: don't exploit the land or the people; don't leave rubbish in huts and keep camping areas clean; take advantage of the excellent recycling facilities common in Sweden. Many hostels have environmentally friendly rubbish collection policies whereby you can sort your waste by type (eg, paper, aluminium, glass, plastic). Supermarkets also give refunds when you return plastic or aluminium drink containers.

TOURIST OFFICES
Local Tourist Offices

Most towns in Sweden have centrally located tourist offices *(turistbyrå)* that provide free street plans and information on accommodation, attractions, activities and transport. Brochures for other areas in Sweden are often available. Ask for the handy booklet that lists addresses and phone numbers for most tourist offices in the country; the website of **Swedish Tourism Associated** *(*w *www.turism.se)* also has this information.

Most tourist offices are open long hours daily in summer; during the off-season (mid-August to mid-June) a few close down, while others have short opening hours – they may close by 4pm, and not open at all at weekends. However, public libraries or large hotels are good alternative places for information.

Tourist Offices Abroad

The official website for the **Swedish Travel and Tourism Council** *(*w *www.visit-sweden .com)* contains loads of excellent information in many languages, and you can request for brochures and information packs to be sent to you.

The following tourist offices can assist with inquiries and provide tourist promotional material. In countries without a designated tourist office, a good starting point for information is the Swedish embassy (see Embassies & Consulates later in this chapter for contact details).

France (☎ 01-53 43 26 27, e servinfo@suede -tourisme.fr) Office Suédois du Tourisme et des Voyages, 18 boulevarde Malesherbes, F-75008 Paris

Germany (☎ 040-32 55 13 55, e info@swetour ism.de) Schweden-Werbung für Reisen und Touristik, Lilienstrasse 19, DE-20095 Hamburg

UK (☎ 020-7870 5600, ☎ 0800 3080 3080, e info@swetourism.org.uk) Swedish Travel &

Tourism Council, 5 Upper Montagu St, London W1H 2AG
USA (☎ 212-885 9700, ⓔ info@gosweden.org) Swedish Travel & Tourism Council, PO Box 4649, Grand Central Station, New York NY 10163-4649

VISAS & DOCUMENTS
Passport
Your passport must be valid for the intended length of your stay in Sweden. Carry your passport at all times and guard it carefully.

Visas
Citizens of European Union (EU) countries can enter Sweden with a passport or a national identification card (passports are recommended) and stay up to three months. Nationals of Nordic countries (Denmark, Norway, Finland and Iceland) can stay and work indefinitely but nationals of other countries require residence permits *(uppehållstillstånd)* for stays of between three months and five years; there is no fee for this permit for EU citizens.

Non-EU passport holders from Australia, New Zealand, Canada and the US can enter and stay in Sweden without a visa for up to three months. Australian and New Zealand passport holders aged between 18 and 30 can also qualify for a one-year working-holiday visa (the application fee is Skr1000).

Citizens of South Africa and many other African, Asian and some Eastern European countries require tourist visas for entry. These are only available in advance from Swedish embassies (allow two months); the cost is Skr225/275 for permits allowing a maximum 30/90 days. Visa extensions aren't easily obtainable.

Non-EU citizens can also obtain residence permits, but these must be applied for before entering Sweden. An interview by consular officials at your nearest Swedish embassy is required – allow up to eight months for this process. Foreign students are granted residence permits if they can prove acceptance by a Swedish educational institution and are able to guarantee that they can support themselves financially.

Migrationsverket (☎ 011-156000; ⓔ *migrationsverket@migrationsverket.se*, ⓦ *www.migrationsverket.se; SE-60170 Norrköping*) is the Swedish migration board and it handles all applications for visas and work or residency permits. A minimum of six weeks (allow eight) is needed to process an application, and you may have to send your passport to have it stamped, plus provide a number of personal details.

Travel Insurance
You should seriously consider taking out travel insurance that covers not only medical expenses, personal liability, theft or luggage loss but also cancellation or delays in your travel arrangements (due to illness, ticket loss, industrial action, etc).

A standard insurer may offer better deals than companies selling only travel insurance. Note that some policies specifically exclude 'dangerous activities' such as motorcycling, skiing, mountaineering, scuba diving or even hiking. Also check whether the policy covers ambulances and an emergency flight home.

Paying for airline tickets with a credit card often provides limited travel accident insurance, and you may be able to reclaim the payment if the operator doesn't deliver. A policy that pays doctors or hospitals directly may be preferable to one where you pay on the spot and claim later. If you have to claim later, make sure you keep all documentation. Some policies ask you to phone (reverse charges) an emergency number so that an immediate assessment of the problem can be made.

In Sweden, EU citizens pay a fee for all medical treatment (including emergency admissions), but showing an E111 form will make matters much easier. Inquire about the E111 at your social security office, travel agent or local post office well in advance. Travel insurance is still advisable, however; it allows treatment flexibility and will also cover ambulance and repatriation costs.

Driving Licence & Permits
Short-term visitors can hire or drive their own car using their own driving licence. Ask your automobile association for a letter of introduction, which entitles you to services offered by affiliated organisations in Sweden, usually free of charge, such as touring maps and information, help with breakdowns, technical and legal advice etc. See the Getting Around chapter for more details.

Hostel & Student Cards
A Hostelling International (HI) card means discounts on STF hostel, mountain-station

and mountain-cabin rates (eg, non-members pay an additional Skr45 for a bed in a hostel). You can join the STF at hostels and many tourist offices while in Sweden (membership costs Skr275 for adults, Skr100 for those aged 16 to 25, free for children, Skr375 for families).

The most useful student card is the International Student Identity Card (ISIC), a plastic ID-style card with your photograph, which provides discounts on many forms of transport (including some airlines, international ferries and local public transport) and on admission to museums, sights, theatres and cinemas. Children under 16 and seniors normally receive similar discounts.

Copies

While the risk of theft in Sweden is low, it's wise to carry photocopies of all important documents (passport data page and visa page, credit cards, travel insurance policy, air/bus/train tickets, driving licence etc). Leave one copy with someone at home and keep another with you, separate from the originals.

EMBASSIES & CONSULATES
Swedish Embassies & Consulates

The following are some of the Swedish embassies around the world. A complete list of Swedish missions abroad is available in English on the Internet at W www.utrikes .regeringen.se/addresser.

Australia (☎ 02-6270 2700, W www.embassyof sweden.org.au) 5 Turrana St, Yarralumla ACT 2600

Canada (☎ 613-241 8553, W www.swedish embassy.ca) 377 Dalhousie St, Ottawa K1N 9N8

Denmark (☎ 33 36 03 70, W www.sverigesambas sad.dk) Sankt Annæ Plads 15A, DK-1250 Copenhagen K

Finland (☎ 09-6877 660, W www.sverige.fi) Pohjoisesplanadi 7B, 00170 Helsinki

France (☎ 01-44 18 88 00, W www.amb-suede .fr) 17 rue Barbet-de-Jouy, F-75007 Paris

Germany (☎ 030-505 060, W www.schweden .org) Rauchstrasse 1, 107 87 Berlin

Ireland (☎ 01-671 5822, W www.swedishem bassy.ie) 13-17 Dawson St, Dublin 2

Netherlands (☎ 070-412 0200, W www.sweden embnl.org) Burg. Van Karnebeeklaan 6A, 2508 Den Haag

New Zealand (☎ 04-499 9895) Vogel Building, 13th Floor, Aitken St, Wellington

Norway (☎ 24 11 42 00, W www.sverigesambas sad.no) Nobelsgate 16, NO-0244 Oslo

UK (☎ 020-7917 6400, W www.swedish-embassy .org.uk) 11 Montagu Place, London W1H 2AL

USA (☎ 202-467 2600, W www.swedish -embassy.org) 1501 M St NW, Suite 900, Washington DC 20005-1702

Embassies & Consulates in Sweden

The diplomatic missions listed here are in Stockholm; some neighbouring countries have additional consulates in Gothenburg, Malmö and Helsingborg.

Australia (☎ 08-613 2900) 11th floor, Sergels Torg 12

Canada (☎ 08-453 3000) Tegelbacken 4

Denmark (☎ 08-406 7500) Jakobs Torg 1

Finland (☎ 08-676 6700) Gärdesgatan 9-11

France (☎ 08-459 5300) Kommendörsgatan 13

Germany (☎ 08-670 1500) Skarpögatan 9

Ireland (☎ 08-661 8005) Östermalmsgatan 97

Netherlands (☎ 08-556 93300) Götgatan 16A

New Zealand (☎ 08-660 0460) Nybrogatan 34

Norway (☎ 08-665 6340) Skarpögatan 4

UK (☎ 08-671 9000) Skarpögatan 6-8

USA (☎ 08-783 5300) Dag Hammarskjöldsväg 31

CUSTOMS

Duty-free goods can only be brought into Sweden from non-EU countries and Åland. Duty-free alcohol allowances for travellers from outside the EU are: 1L of spirits or 2L of fortified wine, 2L of wine and 32L of strong beer. The tobacco allowance is 200 cigarettes, 50 cigars or 250g of smoking tobacco.

The limits on goods brought into Sweden with 'tax paid for personal use' from another EU country are more generous: 2L of spirits or 6L of fortified wine, 26L of wine and 32L of strong beer; plus 400 cigarettes, 100 cigars or 550g of tobacco.

Tobacco products and alcoholic drinks can only be brought into Sweden duty-free by those over 18 and 20 respectively.

Going through customs rarely involves any hassles, but rules on illegal drugs are strictly enforced; you may be searched on arrival, especially if you're travelling from Denmark. Live plants and animal products (meat, dairy etc), from outside the EU, and all animals, syringes and weapons must be declared to customs on arrival. For the latest regulations, contact **Swedish Customs** (☎ 0771-232323; W www.tullverket.se).

MONEY
Currency

The Swedish krona (plural: kronor) is usually represented as Skr (preceding the amount) in northern Europe, and in this book, and SEK (preceding the amount) in international money markets; within Sweden it's just kr (after the amount). One Swedish krona equals 100 öre. Coins come in denominations of 50 öre and Skr1, 5 and 10, while notes are in denominations of Skr20, 50, 100, 500 and 1000.

It is expected that Sweden will adopt the euro some time in the not-too-distant future, dependent on the outcome of a referendum.

Exchange Rates

The following exchange rates prevailed at the time of writing.

country	unit		kronor
Australia	A$1	=	Skr5.12
Canada	C$1	=	Skr5.83
Denmark	Dkr1	=	Skr1.22
Eurozone	€1	=	Skr9.08
New Zealand	NZ$1	=	Skr4.53
Norway	Nkr1	=	Skr1.25
UK	UK£1	=	Skr14.19
USA	US$1	=	Skr9.17

Exchanging Money

Travellers Cheques Banks around the country exchange major foreign currencies and accept international brands of travellers cheques, however they may charge up to a rather steep Skr60 per travellers cheque (which means you're better off with higher denomination cheques), so shop around and compare service fees and exchange rates.

You're better off heading for dedicated currency-exchange businesses like Forex and X-Change. Forex offices, found in major towns and cities and many points of arrival and departure (eg, airports and international ferry terminals), offer good exchange rates and charge a service fee of Skr15 per cheque. There are fewer branches of X-Change, but they offer good deals (Skr10 per cheque, with a maximum charge of Skr50).

ATMs With an ATM card from your home bank, Swedish ATMs will allow access to cash in your account. 'Bankomat' ATMs are found adjacent to many banks and around busy public places such as shopping centres. They accept major credit cards as well as Plus

and Cirrus cards. Note that many ATMs in Sweden will not accept PINs of more than four digits; if your PIN is longer than this, just enter the first four and you should be able to access your account.

Credit & Debit Cards Visa, MasterCard, American Express and Diners Club cards are widely accepted. You're better off using a credit card since exchange rates are better and transaction fees are avoided. Credit cards can be used to buy train tickets but are not accepted on domestic ferries, apart from on sailings to Gotland. Electronic debit cards can be used in most shops.

If your card is lost or stolen in Sweden, report it to one of the following appropriate agencies.

American Express	☎ 08-429 5600
Diners Club	☎ 08-146878
MasterCard	☎ 020 791324
Visa	☎ 020 793146

Costs

Sweden is fairly expensive and you can easily spend your money quickly, so it pays to plan your trip carefully. It's worth remembering that you have to pay for a wide range of things, such as parking, tap water in some restaurants, and public toilets.

The cheapest way to visit Sweden is to camp in the woods for free, eat supermarket food and hitchhike – this will cost under Skr100 per day. If you stay in commercial camping grounds and prepare your own meals you can squeak by on around Skr200 per person per day. Staying in hostels, making your own breakfast, eating the daily special at lunchtime in a restaurant, and picking up supermarket items for dinner will probably cost you Skr300 per day. During the low-price summer period, if you stay in a mid-range hotel (which usually includes a huge buffet breakfast), eat a daily special for lunch and have an evening meal at a moderately priced restaurant, you can expect to spend Skr500 per person per day if you're doubling up and Skr800 if you're travelling alone.

Day trips, museums, entertainment, alcohol, snacks and so on will further erode even the most careful budgets, but Stockholm, Gothenburg and Malmö all sell tourist cards offering substantial savings on admission costs, parking and local transport. Reasonably

Conserving Your Kronor

High prices mean that travellers on a budget may struggle to do and see it all in Sweden. The accrued costs of transport, food, accommodation and attractions, coupled with simple things like luggage storage (up to Skr70 at lockers in some cities), a cup of coffee (Skr20) or a beer (Skr40 to Skr50) mean that money disappears quickly.

However, don't be put off – Sweden *can* be inexpensive. With a tent you can sleep for free in forests, or bring sheets and an HI membership card, and you'll pay Skr80 to Skr200 per night in the 300-plus STF hostels, which generally offering a very high standard of accommodation. Students with an ISIC card (and often seniors) are eligible for discounts in museums, theatres and cinemas. Big cities offer excellent hotel packages that come with free entry to most attractions and public transport, and most hotels offer heavily reduced prices at weekends, throughout the year and in summer.

Stuff yourself at the breakfast buffet for about Skr45 (included in the price at most hotels), or choose a lunch special *(dagens rätt)* offered by numerous restaurants instead of dining a la carte in the evening. Other inexpensive options include takeaway pizzas and kebabs, and taking advantage of the good kitchen facilities at hostels and camping grounds. You may need to avoid alcohol to keep to a budget – boozing here is definitely for the wealthy.

Avoid overpriced tourist traps and look for any of the free 30,000-odd historical or natural attractions.

To save money on transport, buy daily or weekly passes rather than one-way bus tickets. Or get a rail pass to get from A to B and then set about exploring towns and regions on foot or by bike.

priced hotel packages are also available. You'll still have to add travelling costs but a rail pass and an itinerary that sticks to the railway lines will be relatively inexpensive. Adding bus or air travel, or a trip to the far north, will increase your costs.

If there are a few of you, sharing car rental for a weekend in order to see some out-of-the-way places is worth considering (some petrol stations offer small cars for as little as Skr200 per day). That said, petrol prices are high (and more expensive in the far north). Self-service pumps that take banknotes or credit cards are slightly cheaper, though many won't accept foreign credit cards.

Tipping & Bargaining

Service charges and tips are usually included in restaurant bills and taxi fares; a common practice is to round up a restaurant bill to the nearest Skr10. There's certainly no problem if you want to reward good service with an extra tip (or round up the taxi fare, particularly if there's luggage).

Bargaining isn't customary, but you can get 'walk-in' prices at some hotels and *stugby* (chalet parks).

Taxes & Refunds

Value-added tax *(mervärdeskatt,* known locally as *moms),* is normally included in marked prices for goods and services, including books, food, transport, meals and accommodation. The amount varies but it can be as high as 25%.

At shops that display the sign 'Tax Free Shopping', non-EU citizens making single purchases of goods exceeding Skr200 (including *moms*) are eligible for a VAT refund of 15% to 18% of the purchase price. Show your passport and ask the shop for a 'Global Refund Cheque', which should be presented along with your unopened purchases (within three months) at your departure point from the country (before you check in), to get export validation. You can then cash your cheque at any of the refund points, which are found at international airports and harbours. The *Tax Free Shopping Guide to Sweden* is available from tourist offices free of charge, or call ☎ 020 741741 for more information.

POST & COMMUNICATIONS
Post

The Swedish postal service, **Posten** *(☎ 020 232221;* Ⓦ *www.posten.se)* operates an efficient network. General information is available on its website or you can call for customer service.

Postal Rates Mailing letters or postcards up to 20g within Sweden costs Skr5, Skr8 to elsewhere in Europe, and Skr10 beyond Europe. The *ekonomibrev* (economy post) option takes longer to reach its destination and costs marginally less (Skr4.50, Skr7 and Skr8, respectively). Air mail will take a week to reach most parts of North America, perhaps a little longer to Australia and New Zealand.

A package weighing 2kg costs Skr160/ 220 by air mail within/outside Europe. The *ekonomibrev* option here is roughly Skr30 cheaper, but postage time may take up to a month.

Sending & Receiving Mail At the time of writing, Posten was undergoing big changes, including moving to new premises all over the country. Service outlets of Posten are opening in some 3000 new venues, mostly in food stores and petrol stations, and will therefore be open for longer hours (many from 9am to 9pm daily). These outlets will offer all that most travellers will need, eg, stamps *(frimärken)*, letters *(brev)* and package *(paket)* service. You can also buy stamps from many tourist offices, convenience stores, tobacconists, bookshops and newsagents. Look out for the yellow post symbol on a pale blue background, which indicates that some postal facilities are offered.

Receiving poste restante mail under the new postal system will be slightly more difficult for travellers. As many of the large, old-style post offices have closed or relocated, there is no central 'holding place' in most towns. The person sending you mail will need to specify which post outlet you will be collecting from, with a specific address and postal code.

Telephone

Swedish phone numbers have area codes followed by varying numbers of digits. Numbers beginning with ☎ 020 or ☎ 0200 are toll-free, although not from either public telephones or when called from abroad, and ☎ 010 or ☎ 070 are mobile codes. The toll-free general emergency number is ☎ 112. In addition to the **Yellow Pages** (Ⓦ *www.gulasi dorna.se)*, Telia phone books include green pages (for community services) and blue pages (for regional services, including health and medical care).

For directory assistance, dial ☎ 118118 (for numbers within Sweden) or ☎ 118119

(international), but note that these services aren't free.

Telia, the state-owned telephone company, has a deteriorating and dwindling network of public telephones. They can usually be found at train stations in larger cities, but are pretty tough to find elsewhere. Those that do exist will usually accept credit cards as well as phonecards. Many are out of order, virtually none accept coins. It's not possible to receive return international calls.

It's worth considering bringing your mobile phone from your home country and buying a Swedish SIM card, which gives you a Swedish mobile number. Both Vodafone and Comviq offer starter packages (Skr350), which include a local SIM card and Skr250 worth of prepaid calls; you can then purchase top-ups at many stores, including petrol stations. Your mobile may be locked onto your local network in your home country, so ask your home network for advice before going abroad.

For international calls dial ☎ 00 followed by the country code and the local area code. Calls to Sweden from abroad require the country code ☎ 46 followed by the area code and telephone number (omitting the first zero in the area code).

Costs Telia phonecards *(telefonkort)* for public phones cost Skr35, Skr60 and Skr100 (for 30, 60 and 120 units, respectively) and can be bought from Telia phone shops, tobacconists, kiosks and newsagents. International telephone calls can be made with the Telia Travel Card; a call to the UK/USA/Australia costs the equivalent of Skr3/4.50/7.50 per minute with a 50-unit card (Skr75, available from Telia shops). You can also buy a wide range of phone cards from tobacconists that give cheap rates for calls abroad. International collect calls cannot be made from pay phones.

Home Country Direct For collect calls, contact your home operator on the following numbers.

Australia
Telstra	☎ 020 799061
Optus	☎ 020 799161)
Canada	
Canada Direct	☎ 020 799015
New Zealand	
New Zealand Telecom	☎ 020 799064

UK

British Telecom	☎ 020 795144
Cable & Wireless	☎ 020 799044

USA

AT&T	☎ 020 795611
MCI	☎ 020 795922
Sprint	☎ 020 799011

ekno Communication Service

Lonely Planet's ekno global communication service provides low-cost international calls – for local calls you're better off with a local phonecard. Ekno also offers free messaging services, email, travel information and an on-line travel vault, where you can securely store all your important documents. You can join online at Ⓦ www.ekno.lonelyplanet.com, where you will find the local-access numbers for the 24-hour customer service centre. Once you have joined, always check the ekno website for the latest access numbers for each country and updates on new features.

Fax

With the popularity of email and text messaging, the fax is not a very common form of communication in Sweden, and is difficult for on-the-road travellers to access. Many post offices used to offer a fax service but don't any longer, so your best bet is to ask at the local tourist office or your place of accommodation. Faxes can still be received at most hotels for free and you can send a fax for a moderate charge.

Email & Internet Access

Email and Internet services are very popular in Sweden, and most tourism-oriented businesses have websites and email addresses.

Internet cafés typically charge around Skr1 per online minute, or Skr50 per hour. However, facilities to log on can be rare outside big cities, largely due to the fact that most Swedes have Internet access at home. Many Internet cafés, where they do exist, are more like amusement arcades than traveller hangouts, full of young guys playing computer games. We have listed Internet cafés for most larger towns, but be aware that these open and close at random. Check out Ⓦ www.net cafeguide.com and Ⓦ www.cybercafes.com for comprehensive lists of facilities.

Many tourist offices now offer a computer terminal for visitor use (sometimes for free). Nearly all public libraries offer free Internet access, but often the half-hour or hour slots are fully booked days in advance by locals, and email facilities may occasionally be blocked.

DIGITAL RESOURCES

The World Wide Web is a rich resource for travellers. You can research your trip, hunt down bargain air fares, book hotels, check on weather conditions or chat with locals and other travellers about the best places to visit (or avoid!). The Lonely Planet website (Ⓦ www.lonelyplanet.com) is a great place to start your online explorations.

Most Swedish organisations have their own websites, and many of these have pages in English (look for a British flag or some other icon).

The following websites are some of the most helpful with lots of information available in English.

General Tourist Information
 Ⓦ www.visit-sweden.com
 Ⓦ www.sweden.se
 Ⓦ www.sverigeturism.se
 Ⓦ www.cityguide.se
Yellow Pages
 Ⓦ www.gulasidorna.se
Swedish Environmental Protection Agency
 Ⓦ www.naturvardsverket.se
Swedish Touring Club
 Ⓦ www.meravsverige.nu
Swedish Institute
 Ⓦ www.si.se
Virtual Sweden
 Ⓦ www.sweden.se

To get information on most towns in Sweden, simply type in 'www.' followed by the name of the town, followed by '.se'; when you are at the official site, look for a British flag or click on 'turist' or 'turism'.

Many other useful websites are provided in relevant sections throughout this book.

BOOKS

Most books are published in different editions by different publishers in different countries. As a result, a book might be a hardcover rarity in one country while it's readily available in paperback in another. Fortunately, bookshops and libraries search by title or author, so your local bookshop or library is best placed to advise you on the availability of the following recommendations.

It's a good idea to bring books from home, as English-language books are expensive in Sweden. That said, there's a great range of general books on the country, with emphasis on the arts and literature, at the Sweden Bookshop in Stockholm (inside Sweden House, also home to the main tourist office).

Lonely Planet

If you're planning a big trip around northern Europe, check out Lonely Planet's *Scandinavian Europe,* which covers Denmark, the Faroe Islands, Finland, Greenland, Iceland and Norway, as well as Sweden. Lonely Planet also offers separate, detailed guidebooks to *Denmark; Finland; Iceland, Greenland & the Faroe Islands;* and *Norway.* To facilitate communication throughout the region, pick up Lonely Planet's *Scandinavian Europe phrasebook,* which includes sections on Swedish, Danish, Finnish, Icelandic and Norwegian.

Lonely Planet also produces a *Stockholm* city guide.

Pictorial Guides

Sweden, by Lars Nordström & Chad Ehlers, is a coffee-table book aimed at Americans with Swedish ancestry. An even more lavish production is *Sweden's National Parks,* by Peter Hanneberg, Rolf Löfgren et al, which describes each national park in detail and is illustrated with superb photographs. In a similar vein is *True North: The Grand Landscapes of Sweden*, with text by Per Wästberg and Tommy Hammarström and stunning images by some of Sweden's top nature photographers.

English-language coverage of hiking and climbing in the Swedish mountains is limited to *Scandinavian Mountains,* by Peter Lennon. The Swedish sections aren't very detailed but they're better than nothing. STF publishes a range of guidebooks about outdoor activities, but they're available in Swedish only.

For an interesting and accurate guide to Swedish cultural behaviour, read *Culture Shock! Sweden: A Guide to Customs and Etiquette,* by Charlotte Rosen Svensson, and *Modern-Day Vikings: A Practical Guide to Interacting With the Swedes,* by Christina Johansson Robinowitz and Lisa Werner Carr.

Travel

Very few good travel books about Sweden have been published in English. Mary Wollstonecraft's *A Short Residence in Sweden, Norway & Denmark* records her journey to Scandinavia in 1795 in search of happiness – it's a classic of early English Romanticism, and well worth a read. A hilarious but rather over-the-top account of Bill Bryson's more recent journeys in Sweden is given in two chapters of his book *Neither Here Nor There.*

History & Politics

To get a handle on the country, try *A Journey Through Swedish History,* by Herman Lindqvist. *Sweden: The Nation's History,* by Franklin D Scott, is a weighty tome that delves into the country's history in great detail.

The **Swedish Institute** (W *www.si.se)* publishes several books on history and politics. *A History of Sweden,* by Lars O Lagerqvist, describes the development of the country from the Stone Age to the present day. Carin Orrling's *Vikings* details the life and times of the Vikings, presenting them not just as murderous brigands, but as traders and seafarers, often with highly developed artistic skills. There's no shortage of other books about the Vikings, but they tend to cover all of Europe rather than just Sweden. *The Vikings,* by Else Roesdahl, and *The Penguin Historical Atlas of the Vikings,* by John Haywood, are both fine resources. *The Long Ships*, by Frans Bengtsson, a translation of the classic swashbuckling Viking novel *Röde Orm* (Red Snake), has been highly recommended by readers.

In *Swedish Exodus,* Lars Ljungmark covers the late-19th and early 20th-century mass emigration of Swedes to the US, and its consequences.

General

Country Review: Sweden, edited by Robert Kelly et al, covers many topics including geography, demography, economics, politics and the environment. *Spotlight on Sweden,* by Hans-Ingvar Johnsson (Swedish Institute), describes modern Swedish society with reference to its history. *Swedish Mentality,* by Åke Daun, will help you understand the Swedes themselves.

If you're interested in Swedish festivals, try *Sweden (Festivals of the World),* by

Monica Rabe, or *Maypoles, Crayfish and Lucia – Swedish Holidays and Traditions,* by Jan-Öjvind Swahn (Swedish Institute). *A Taste for all Seasons,* by Helena Dahlbäck Lutteman and Ingegerd Råman (Swedish Institute), blends Swedish cuisine and design and describes foods eaten throughout the year. *Favorite Swedish Recipes,* by Sam Erik et al, is recommended for its mouthwatering descriptions of smörgåsbord and special meals.

Great Royal Palaces of Sweden, by Göran Alm, is a fine coffee-table book with good photos and discussion on royal architecture and the royal families from Vasa to Bernadotte. For an easily understood, practical guide to Swedish interior design using relatively simple and inexpensive methods, consult *Creating the Look: Swedish Style,* by Katrin Cargill. *Swedish Folk Art,* by Barbro Klein, and *The Decorative Arts of Sweden,* by Iona Plath, may also be of interest.

The Swedish Institute publishes the following useful contemporary guides: *A Guide to Swedish Architecture* (Rasmus Waern et al); *Film in Sweden,* (Maaret Koskinen and Francesco Bono); *Theatre in Sweden* (Claes Englund and Leif Janzon); *Art in Sweden* (Sören Engblom); *Swedish Design* (Denise Hag-strömer); *Literature in Sweden* (Magnus Florin et al); and *Music in Sweden* (Göran Bergendahl et al).

Most fiction set in Sweden has been written by Swedes and some has been translated into English; see Literature in the Facts about Sweden chapter.

NEWSPAPERS & MAGAZINES

Domestic newspapers, including the Gothenburg and Stockholm dailies and evening tabloids, are only published in Swedish, however a wide variety of high-priced English-language imports is available. The *International Herald-Tribune, Guardian in Europe,* London dailies, and English-language magazines such as *Time* and *Newsweek* are sold at major transport terminals, Press Stop, Interpress, Pressbyrån, and at tobacconists – often even in small towns. A good, free option for accessing news in English (and a number of other languages) is to head to the local libraries, which often have a reading area stocked with up-to-date newspapers from around the world.

On the Internet, **Sweden Globe** (W *www .swedentimes.com*) has English-language articles on Sweden and related topics.

RADIO & TV

Radio Sweden International (W *www.sr .se/rs*), the overseas network, broadcasts programmes nationally on 1179kHz (FM 89.6 in Stockholm), to Europe on 1179kHz, as well as to North America and Asia/Australia under various other frequencies. Check its Internet site for a full list of frequencies and current programme schedules.

National Swedish Radio (Sveriges Radio) has four main channels. Channel P2 (96.2 FM in Stockholm) is good for classical and opera. For pop and rock, try youth station P3 (99.3 FM in Stockholm but variable around the country) and the wide range of local commercial stations.

The national TV channels TV1 and TV2 don't have advertising, but usually aren't particularly interesting to foreigners. TV3 and TV5 are commercial satellite or cable channels (not available nationally) with a lot of English-language shows and films. The commercial channel TV4 has good quality broadcasting in Swedish and English. Foreign-made programmes and films are always shown in their original language, with Swedish subtitles. Hotels may also have Euro News, Sky News, BBC World, CNN or EuroSport (all in English).

VIDEO SYSTEMS

When buying videos, remember that Sweden (like most of Europe and the UK) uses the PAL system, which is very expensive to convert to NTSC or Secam.

PHOTOGRAPHY & VIDEO
Film & Equipment

Although print and slide film are readily available in towns and cities, prices are fairly high, so you may want to bring your own film and develop your photos or slides back in your own country. You can sort through bargain bins for 24-shot rolls for under Skr30 at photo stores, but generally expect to pay around Skr50/65 for a 24/36-exposure film. Fuji Velvia 36-shot slide film costs Skr110. Prices for print processing vary widely, but it usually costs around Skr100/130 for 24/36 shots over three days (more expensive if you want one-hour processing) and slide processing costs around Skr40 (36 exposures, excluding mounts). You'll pay Skr50 for a 90-minute video film (Sony 8mm).

Expert, a chain of electrical goods shops, sells a wide range of film, including slide film, and camera equipment can be bought or repaired here. Repairs will require sending your equipment away; new equipment isn't cheap but a wide range is available.

Technical Tips
The clear northern light and glare from water, ice and snow may require use of a UV filter (or skylight filter) and a lens shade. ISO 100 film is sufficient for most purposes. In winter, most cameras don't work below -20°C.

Restrictions
Photography and video is prohibited at many tourist sites, mainly to protect fragile artwork. Photographing military establishments is forbidden.

Photographing People
It's wise to ask permission first when a person is the main subject of a photograph. This is especially important in Sami areas, where you may meet resistance to photography.

TIME
Sweden is one hour ahead of GMT/UTC and in the same time zone as Norway, Denmark and most of Western Europe. When it's noon in Sweden, it's 11am in London, 1pm in Helsinki, 6am in New York and Toronto, 3am in Los Angeles, 9pm in Sydney and 11pm in Auckland. Sweden has daylight-saving time: the clocks go forward an hour on the last Sunday in March and back an hour on the last Sunday in October.

Timetables and business hours are quoted using the 24-hour clock, and dates are often given by week number (1 to 52).

ELECTRICITY
Electricity in Sweden is supplied at 220 volts AC, 50Hz; round continental-style two-pin plugs are standard.

WEIGHTS & MEASURES
Sweden uses the metric system; to convert between metric and Imperial units, see the table at the back of the book. Some shops quote prices followed by '/hg', which means per 100g. Decimals are separated from whole numbers by a comma, and thousands are indicated by points. You'll commonly see or hear the Swedish word *mil*, which Swedes may translate into English as 'mile'. However, note that the Swedish *mil* equals 10km.

LAUNDRY
The coin-operated laundrette is virtually nonexistent in Sweden. A *snabbtvätt* (quick wash), where you leave clothes for laundering, isn't available everywhere, may actually take several days and tends to be extremely expensive (up to Skr200). Most hotels offer a laundry service (usually similarly expensive). Thankfully, many hostels and camping grounds have laundry facilities costing around Skr50 for wash and dry. It's also a good idea to carry soap powder or a bar of clothes soap for doing your own laundry in basins.

TOILETS
Public toilets in parks, shopping malls, museums, libraries, and bus or train stations are rarely free in Sweden; some churches and most tourist offices have free toilets. Except at larger train stations (where there's an attendant), pay toilets are coin operated, and usually cost Skr5.

HEALTH
You're unlikely to encounter serious health problems in Sweden. Travel health depends on your predeparture preparations, your daily health care while travelling and how you handle any medical problem that does develop. In reality, few travellers experience anything more than an upset stomach.

There's no general practitioner service in Sweden but pharmacies *(apotek)* sell nonprescription (and prescription) medicines as well as give advice on how to deal with everyday ailments and conditions. *Nattapotek* are 24-hour pharmacies found in major cities.

For emergencies and casualty services, go to a local medical centre *(vårdcentral)* or a hospital *(sjukhus* or *lasarett),* where duty doctors are standing by. There are centres in all districts and main towns, listed by area under municipality *(kommun)* in the local telephone directory. EU citizens with an E111 form are charged around Skr120 to consult a doctor and up to Skr300 for a visit to casualty. Hospital stays cost Skr90 per day (free for patients under 16 years). Non-EU citizens should have adequate travel insurance or be prepared to face high costs, although some countries (such as Australia) have reciprocal health-care agreements with Sweden.

Dentists *(tandläkare)* charge around Skr700 for an hour's treatment.

For general emergencies, including the ambulance service, call ☎ 112.

Pre-departure Planning

Before departure, organise a visit to your dentist to get your teeth in order and obtain travel insurance with good medical cover (see Travel Insurance under Visas & Documents, earlier in this chapter).

Immunisations aren't necessary for travel to Sweden, unless you've been travelling somewhere where yellow fever is prevalent. Ensure that your normal childhood vaccines (against measles, mumps, rubella, diphtheria, tetanus and polio) are up to date. You may also want to have a hepatitis vaccination, as exposure can occur anywhere.

If you wear glasses or contact lenses take a spare set and a copy of your optical prescription. If you require a particular medication, carry a legible copy of your prescription from your doctor. Most medications are available in Sweden, but brand names may be different from your country, so you'll also need the generic name.

Basic Rules

Food Stomach upsets are as possible in Sweden as anywhere else. Occasionally, cooked meats displayed on buffet tables may cause problems. Also, take care with shellfish (cooked mussels that haven't opened properly aren't safe to eat), unidentified berries and mushrooms.

Water Tap water is safe to drink in Sweden, but drinking from streams may be unwise due to farms, old mine workings and wild animals. The clearest-looking stream water may contain giardia and other parasites. The simplest way of purifying water is to boil it vigorously, but you can also use a total water filter, which takes out all parasites, bacteria and viruses.

If you don't have a filter and cannot boil water it should be treated chemically after straining out any dirt. Chlorine tablets will kill many pathogens, but not some parasites like giardia and amoebic cysts. Iodine is more effective in purifying water and is available in liquid and tablet form. Follow the directions carefully and remember that too much iodine can be harmful.

Environmental Hazards

Hypothermia This condition occurs when the body loses heat faster than it can produce it and the core temperature of the body falls. It's surprisingly easy to progress from very cold to dangerously cold due to a combination of wind, wet clothing, fatigue and hunger, even if the air temperature is above freezing. It's best to dress in layers; silk, wool and some of the new artificial fibres are all good insulating materials. A hat is important, as a lot of heat is lost through the head. A strong, waterproof outer layer (and a space blanket for emergencies) is essential. Carry basic supplies, including food containing simple sugars to generate heat quickly, and fluid to drink.

The symptoms of hypothermia are exhaustion, numb skin (particularly toes and fingers), shivering, slurred speech, irrational or violent behaviour, lethargy, stumbling, dizzy spells, muscle cramps and violent bursts of energy. Irrationality may take the form of sufferers claiming they are warm and trying to take off their clothes.

To treat mild hypothermia, first get the person out of the wind and/or rain, remove their clothing if it's wet and replace it with dry, warm clothing. Give them hot liquids (not alcohol) and some high-kilojoule, easily digestible food. Do not rub victims: instead, allow them to slowly warm themselves. This should be enough to treat the early stages of hypothermia. The early recognition and treatment of mild hypothermia is the only way to prevent severe hypothermia, which is a critical condition.

Sunburn In high northern latitudes you can get sunburnt surprisingly quickly, even through cloud, and especially when there's complete snow cover. Use sunscreen, a hat, and a barrier cream for your nose and lips. Calamine lotion or commercial after-sun preparations are good for mild sunburn. Protect your eyes with good quality sunglasses, particularly if you'll be near water, sand or snow.

Infectious Diseases

Diarrhoea Simple things such as a change of water, food or climate can all cause a mild bout of diarrhoea, and a few rushed toilet trips with no other symptoms do not indicate a major problem.

Dehydration is the main danger with any diarrhoea, particularly in children or the elderly. Under all circumstances fluid replacement (at least equal to the volume being lost) is the most important thing to remember. With severe diarrhoea a rehydrating solution is preferable to replace minerals and salts lost. Commercially available oral rehydration salts (ORS) are very useful; add them to boiled or bottled water. In an emergency you can make up a solution of six teaspoons of sugar and a half teaspoon of salt to a litre of boiled water.

Gut-paralysing drugs such as liperamide or diphenoxylate can be used to bring relief from the symptoms, although they do not actually cure the problem. Only use these drugs if you do not have access to toilets, eg, if you *must* travel. Do not use these drugs for children under 12 or if the person has a high fever or is severely dehydrated.

Giardiasis Stomach cramps, nausea, a bloated stomach, watery foul-smelling diarrhoea and frequent gas are all symptoms of giardiasis, which can occur several weeks after you have been exposed to the parasite. The symptoms may disappear for a few days and then return: this can go on for several weeks.

Cuts, Bites & Stings

Bee and wasp stings are usually painful rather than dangerous, but people who are allergic to them can experience severe breathing difficulties and will require urgent medical care.

Mosquitoes, blackflies and deerflies are common from mid-June to the end of July and fly swarms in northern areas are horrific. To avoid bites, completely cover yourself with clothes and a mosquito head net. Any exposed areas of skin, including lower legs (and even underneath trousers), should be treated with a powerful insect repellent such as 100% DEET (frequent application of DEET isn't recommended). Calamine lotion, a sting relief spray or ice packs will reduce any pain and swelling.

WOMEN TRAVELLERS

Scandinavia in general is one of the safest places to travel in all of Europe, but common sense is still the best guide to dealing with potentially dangerous situations like hitching or walking alone at night.

Sexual equality is very well emphasised in Sweden and there should be no question of discrimination. Solo female travellers are unlikely to face the sort of harassment received in parts of southern Europe. Some hostels offer segregated dorms, and women-only compartments are a possibility in 2nd-class rail sleeping sections. Some Stockholm taxi firms offer night-time discounts for women.

Recommended reading is the *Handbook for Women Travellers* by M & G Moss, published by Judy Piatkus Books (London). A good website for women travellers is ⓦ www.journeywoman.com.

GAY & LESBIAN TRAVELLERS

Sweden is a famously liberal country and allows gay and lesbian couples to form 'registered partnerships' that grant general marriage rights, with a few exceptions (eg, no access to church weddings). In 2002 the Swedish parliament voted in favour of allowing gay couples to adopt, and it is envisaged that lesbians will soon have legal access to artificial insemination services.

The national organisation for gay and lesbian rights is **Riksförbundet för Sexuellt Likaberättigande** *(RFSL; ☎ 08-736 0213; Box 350, SE-10126 Stockholm)*. It's based at Sveavägen 59 in Stockholm, where there's also a bookshop, restaurant and nightclub. Gay bars and nightclubs in the big cities are mentioned in this book, but ask local RFSL societies or your home organisation for up-to-date information. The *Spartacus International Gay Guide*, published by Bruno Gmünder Verlag (Berlin), is an excellent international directory of gay entertainment venues, but it's best used in conjunction with more up-to-date listings in local papers; as elsewhere, gay venues in the region can change with the speed of summer.

Another good source of local information is the free, monthly magazine QX. You can pick it up at many clubs, stores and restaurants in Stockholm, Gothenborg, Malmö and Copenhagen, in Denmark. The magazine's website ⓦ www.qx.se has excellent information and recommendations in English.

One of the capital's biggest parties is the annual **Stockholm Pride** (W *www.stockholm pride.org*), a five-day festival celebrating gay culture, held between late July and early August. It's staged mainly in Tantolunden (western Södermalm). The extensive programme covers art, debate, health, literature, music, spirituality and sport. Another festival of interest is **Åre Gaydays** (W *www.skistar .com*), held annualy in January at the Åre ski resort. The 2000-odd partygoers tend to focus more on the 'apres ski' than the skiing itself!

DISABLED TRAVELLERS

Sweden is one of the easiest countries to travel around in a wheelchair. People with disabilities will find special transport services with adapted facilities, ranging from trains to taxis, but contact the operator in advance for the best service. Public toilets and some hotel rooms have facilities for disabled people, some street crossings have ramps for wheelchairs and audio signals for visually impaired people, and some grocery stores are accessible to people in wheelchairs. For further information, contact the national association for the disabled, **De Handikappades Riksförbund** (☎ 08-685 8000; W *www.dhr.se; Katrinebergsvägen 6, Box 47305, SE-10074 Stockholm)*. **Hotels in Sweden** (W *www.hotelsinsweden.net)* indicates hotel facilities.

Contact the 'travel officer' at your national support organisation; they may be able to put you in touch with tour companies that specialise in disabled travel. Other helpful organisations include the following.

Holiday Care (☎ 01293-774 943, W www.holi daycare.org.uk) 2nd Floor, Imperial Buildings, Victoria Rd, Horley, Surrey RH6 7PZ, UK
Royal Association for Disability & Rehabilitation (Radar; ☎ 020-7250 3222, W www.radar.org .uk) 12 City Forum, 250 City Rd, London, EC1V 8AF, UK
Society for Accessible Travel and Hospitality (☎ 212-447 7284) 347 5th Ave, Suite 610, New York, NY 10016)

SENIOR TRAVELLERS

Seniors normally get discounts on entry to museums and other sights, cinema and theatre tickets, and air tickets and other transport. No special card is required, but show your passport if asked for proof of age (the minimum qualifying age is generally 60 or 65). Some hotels have senior discount schemes (eg, the Radisson SAS chain offers 25% off standard rates to those aged 65 and over). See the Train section in the Getting Around chapter for information about senior discounts on Scanrail passes.

In your home country, you may already be entitled to all sorts of interesting travel packages and discounts (on car hire, for instance) through organisations and travel agents that cater for senior travellers. Start hunting at your local senior citizens advice bureau or larger seniors' organisations, such as the **American Association of Retired Persons** (AARP; W *www.aarp.org)* in the USA or **Age Concern England** (W *www.ace.org.uk)* in the UK.

TRAVEL WITH CHILDREN

Successful travel with young children requires planning and effort. Don't try to overdo things; even for adults, packing too much into the time available can cause problems. Make sure the activities include the kids as well – balance an afternoon checking out Stockholm's museums with a few hours at Junibacken, Skansen or Gröna Lund Tivoli. If the kids have helped to work out where you're going, chances are they'll still be interested when you arrive. Lonely Planet's *Travel with Children*, by Cathy Lanigan, is a useful source of information.

Swedes treat children very well, and many towns have attractions and museums specifically for the younger set, such as Astrid Lindgrens Värld in Vimmerby. Domestic tourism is largely organised around children's interests: many museums have a kids section with toys, hands-on displays and activities, and there are also numerous public parks for kids, plus theme parks, water parks and so on. Long-distance ferries and trains, hotels and even some restaurants may have play areas for children. Most attractions allow free admission for young children up to about seven years of age and half-price (or substantially discounted) admission for those up to 16 or so. Hotels and other accommodation options often have 'family rooms' that accommodate up to two adults and two children for little more than the price of a regular double. Summer is very much a time for family vacations and in some areas cabins and camping grounds may be fully booked at this time.

Car rental firms hire out children's safety seats at a nominal cost, but it's essential that you book them in advance. Highchairs and cots (cribs) are standard in many restaurants and hotels. Swedish supermarkets offer a relatively wide choice of baby food, infant formulas, soy and cow's milk, disposable nappies (diapers) etc.

DANGERS & ANNOYANCES
Theft & Drunkenness
Sweden is generally safe, but petty crime is on the increase. In Stockholm, Gothenburg, Malmö and Linköping, ask locally for the latest advice on areas to avoid before wandering around at night. Beware of pickpockets and bag-snatchers in crowded public places. Report any thefts to the police and get a statement, otherwise your travel insurance company will not pay out.

Drunks are an unpleasant feature of many Swedish towns and cities, particularly late on Friday and Saturday nights, when you should stay alert.

Road Hazards
Motorists should be extremely cautious of elk, especially around dawn or dusk and if you see the sign 'viltstängsel upphör', which means that elk may cross the road. About 40 people die every year due to collisions with elk. In the north, wayward reindeer are a problem at all times and you'd be wise to stop when you see one, even if it's on the side of the road. Be on the lookout for black plastic bags tied to roadside trees or posts – this is a sign from local Sami that they have reindeer herds in the area.

Opening Hours & Queuing
It's difficult for foreigners to understand why some tourist offices are open Monday to Friday only (when there are fewer tourists around), museums may open at 11am and close by 4pm (even in July), and hostels (and some hotels) only have reception for two or three hours in the afternoon. This makes booking accommodation ahead of arrival essential, thus taking the spontaneity out of travelling. Don't even think of going to a liquor store in the evening or for most of the weekend – it will be closed.

Queuing by number is a national pastime in Sweden, so you'll need to remember to visit the ticket machine first when you enter

shops, post offices, liquor stores, offices, police stations etc. Don't miss your turn, or you'll have to go back to the end of the queue.

BUSINESS HOURS
Businesses and government offices are open from 8.30am or 9am to 5pm Monday to Friday, although they can close at 3pm in summer. Banks usually open at 9.30am and close at 3pm, but some city branches open from 9am to 5pm or 6pm. Most museums have short opening hours (even in July and August) and many tourist offices may close at 4pm and/or not open at all at weekends from mid-August to mid-June. See individual destinations for details.

Normal shopping hours are from 9am to 6pm weekdays and 9am to between 1pm and 4pm on Saturday, but city department stores are open longer (until 8pm or 10pm) and sometimes also on Sunday (noon to 4pm). Shops often close early on the afternoon before a public holiday. Some supermarkets in large towns will stay open until 7pm or 9pm. Stockholm has convenience stores, such as 7-Eleven, which are open 24 hours. In restaurants, lunch often begins at 11.30am and is over by 2pm.

Systembolaget, the state-owned alcohol stores, are usually only open from 10am to 6pm Monday to Friday, and from 10am to 2pm Saturday, but some have extended hours on Thursday and Friday evenings.

The hours which may be of most interest to travellers are those of the hostels. Frustratingly, many hostels, especially those belonging to the STF network, are closed between 10am and 5pm. See Hostels in the Accommodation section later in this chapter for information.

Summer is used in this book to refer to the period from mid-June to mid-August. Discounted summer prices are offered at this time.

PUBLIC HOLIDAYS & SPECIAL EVENTS
There's a concentration of public holidays in spring and early summer; Midsummer, in particular, brings life almost to a halt for three days. Transport and other services are reduced, so read your timetables carefully, and plan ahead: some food stores are open, as are larger tourist offices (usually with reduced

hours), but not all attractions. Some hotels close between Christmas and New Year, and it's not uncommon for restaurants in larger cities to close during July and early August (when their owners join the holidaying throngs at beach or lakeside areas).

Many businesses will close early the day before and all day after official public holidays, including the following.

Nyårsdag (New Year's Day) 1 January
Trettondedag Jul (Epiphany) 6 January
Långfredag, Påsk, Annandag Påsk (Good Friday, Easter Sunday & Monday) March/April
Första Maj (Labour Day) 1 May
Kristi Himmelsfärds dag (Ascension Day) May/June
Pingst, Annandag Pingst (Whit Sunday & Monday) late May or early June
Midsommardag (Midsummer's Day) first Saturday after 21 June
Alla Helgons dag (All Saints' Day) Saturday, late October or early November
Juldag (Christmas Day) 25 December
Annandag Jul (Boxing Day) 26 December

Note also that **Midsommarafton** (Midsummer's Eve), **Julafton** (24 December) and **Nyårsafton** (31 December) are not official holidays, but are generally nonworking days for most of the population.

Valborgsmässoafton (Walpurgis Night), on 30 April, celebrates the arrival of spring with bonfires and choral singers bursting into song. Upper-secondary-school leavers wearing white caps are a common sight; these festivities have developed from a mixture of traditional bonfires on the eve of May Day, and student celebrations at Lund and Uppsala, which together have caught the popular imagination.

Första Maj (May Day) is traditionally a workers marching day in the industrial towns and cities; it has been observed with labour-movement events, brass bands and marches annually since 1890.

National Day is 6 June (Gustav Vasa was elected King of Sweden on 6 June 1523) but, surprisingly, it isn't a public holiday. This is one of several days in the year when the distinctive Swedish flag (blue, with a yellow cross) is unfurled and hauled aloft at countless flagpoles around the country.

Midsommardag (Midsummer's Day) is *the* festival of the year. Decorating and raising the Midsummer pole and dancing around

it are traditional activities on Midsummer's Eve in towns and villages throughout the countryside. The poles have two large wreaths on either side – it's likely that this is a fertility symbol from pre-Christian times. For the folk touch, the Dalarna region is a good place to celebrate, but folk costumes, singing, music, dancing, pickled herring (washed down with *snaps*), strawberries and cream, and beer drinking, are common almost everywhere.

At the other end of summer, **crayfish parties** in August celebrate the end of the season. In autumn, *surströmming* (strong-smelling fermented Baltic herring) parties take place in the north – while in the south there are eel parties where nothing but eels and *snaps* are served.

Luciadagen (Lucia Festival), on 13 December, is also popular. Oddly, it seems to merge the folk tradition of the longest night and the story of St Lucia of Syracuse. A choir in white, led by Lucia (who wears a crown of candles), leads the singing, and *glögg*, a hot alcoholic punch, is drunk. Many towns host popular **Christmas markets** in December. **Christmas Eve** is the main day of celebration during this season; it's the night of the *smörgåsbord* and the arrival of *jultomten*, the Christmas gnome carrying a sack of gifts.

If you're in Stockholm for Valborgsmässoafton, Midsommardag, Luciadagen, Christmas or New Year's Eve, a great place in which to participate in the festivities is the open-air museum, **Skansen**, on Djurgården.

Nearly all Swedish towns and cities have special festivals and summer concerts, mainly between May and September. The main ones are covered in this book. Music, dance, eating, drinking, competitions and fun for children are regular features of these events, which can last for up to a week. See the 'Festivals & Concerts' boxed text later in this chapter for more information.

WORK

Most foreigners require a work permit for paid employment prior to their arrival in Sweden. Non-EU citizens need to apply for a work permit (and residence permit for stays over three months), enclosing confirmation of the job offer, completed forms (available from Swedish diplomatic posts or over the Internet), a passport photo and passport. Processing takes one to three months; there's an application fee (for most non-EU applicants) of Skr1000. EU citizens only need to apply for a residence permit (free) within three months of arrival if they find work, then they can remain in Sweden for the duration of their employment (or up to five years). Australians and New Zealanders aged 18 to 30 years can now qualify for a one-year working holiday visa. Full application details are available online through **Migrationsverket** (W www.migrationsverket.se), the Swedish migration board.

Despite low unemployment in Sweden (4%), work permits are only granted if there's a shortage of Swedes (or citizens from EU countries) with certain skills, such as those needed in technical manufacturing areas. Speaking Swedish may be essential for the job. Few organisations are looking for builders or people with social services or care skills, and service work opportunities are minimal. Students enrolled in Sweden can take summer jobs, but such work isn't offered to travelling students.

Helpful information is available online from the **Swedish National Labour Market Administration** (AMV; W www.ams.se).

ACCOMMODATION
Camping
Sweden has hundreds of camping grounds and a free English-language guide with maps is available. Some camping grounds are open all year, but the best time for tent camping is from May to August. Many sites also have cabins or chalets (stugor). Visit W www .camping.se for plenty of useful information.

Camping prices vary with season and services, from Skr80 for a small site at a basic ground, to Skr200 for a family-sized site at a ground with the highest standards and lots of facilities. Most camping grounds have kitchens and laundry amenities, however many are extremely popular family holiday spots and have the works – swimming pool, minigolf, bike and canoe rental, restaurant, store etc. If you're a solo hiker or cyclist, you might be able to get a cheaper site (around Skr80) at some grounds, otherwise you'll pay the full rate. You should also ask about reduced rates for short overnight stays (ie, if you arrive in the evening and leave before 9am the following day).

You must have the Svenskt Campingkort (Swedish Camping Card) to stay at most Swedish camping grounds. Apply at least one month before your journey to **Sveriges Campingvärdars Riksförbund** (fax 0522-642430; e adm@scr.se; Box 255, SE-45117 Uddevalla). If this isn't possible, you'll be given a temporary card on arrival. The card itself is free; the annual stamp you need on your card costs Skr90 and is obtainable at the first camping ground you visit.

Primus and Sievert supply propane gas for camping stoves and containers are available at petrol stations. T-sprit Röd (methylated spirit; denatured alcohol) for Trangia stoves can be bought at petrol stations. Fotogen (paraffin; kerosene) is sold at paint shops such as Fargtema and Spektrum.

See the 'Hiking' special section for information on free camping in Sweden.

Hostels
Sweden has well over 450 hostels (vandrarhem) and some 320 are 'official' hostels affiliated with **Svenska Turistföreningen** (STF; ☎ 08-463 2100; e info@stfturist.se, W www.meravsverige.nu; Box 25, SE-10120 Stockholm), part of Hostelling International. STF produces a free detailed guide to its hostels, but the text is in Swedish only (although the symbols are generally easy to understand). All hostel details are available in English on its website.

About half of STF's hostels are open year-round; many others open from May to September, and some open only from mid-June to mid-August (usually these summer-only hostels are found in school buildings, which are only available for use when the students are on holidays).

Holders of HI cards can stay at any STF hostels for between Skr80 and Skr200 and children under 16 pay about half price. Nonmembers can pay Skr45 extra or join up at hostels (membership costs Skr275 for adults, Skr100 for those aged 16 to 25, free for children, Skr375 for families). In this book we quote prices at STF hostels for members.

Facilities are generally excellent and all STF hostels have kitchen facilities. Breakfast may be available for Skr40 to Skr65 extra (if you reserve it the previous day). Sleeping bags are allowed if you have a sheet and pillowcase to cover the mattress and pillow; otherwise you can hire sheets for Skr50 per stay (it's recommended that you take your own). The principle is that you should clean up after yourself, but some hostels push optional 'cleaning fees' of up to Skr100!

Around 150 hostels belong to STF's 'rival', **Sveriges Vandrarhem i Förening** *(SVIF;* ☎ *0413-553 450;* e *info@svif.se; Box 9, SE-45043 Smögen).* No membership is required and rates are similar to those of STF hostels. Breakfast is sometimes available for Skr40 to Skr60; most SVIF hostels have kitchens, but you sometimes need your own utensils. Pick up the free guide at tourist offices or SVIF hostels.

Look out for other hostels that are not affiliated with either STF or SVIF. These can often be found at farmhouses or even hotels, where budget rooms are available if you bring your own linen.

Hostels in Sweden are virtually impossible to enter outside reception opening times, and these hours are generally frustratingly short, except in Stockholm and Gothenburg. For most of the day the doors are firmly locked; the secret is to phone and make a reservation during reception hours (generally between 5pm and 7pm, occasionally also between 8am and 10am); you'll be given instructions on how to get in. Cancellation of bookings is only accepted before 6pm the previous day, otherwise you'll be charged for one overnight.

If you're travelling in winter, check that the hostel is open at Christmas and New Year. In June, July and August you can expect longer reception hours but a reservation is still strongly recommended as many hostels in popular areas may be full. Be aware that hostels are very popular with locals and, especially outside of the major cities, they are not necessarily places where you'll meet fellow backpackers from around the world. Numerous hostels are booked out by local school groups in May; in summer, Swedish families use them for holiday accommodation, and year-round you'll find many retired locals taking advantage of the cheap rates.

Cabins & Chalets

Daily rates for *stugor* (cabins and chalets, often found at camping grounds or in the countryside) offer good value for small groups and families. They range in both facilities and price (Skr200 to Skr800). A *stugby* is a small 'village' of cabins and chalets. The cheapest cabins are simple, with bunk beds and little else (you share the bathroom and kitchen facilities with campers or other cabin users). Chalets are usually fully equipped with their own kitchen, bathroom and even living room with TV. Bring your own linen and clean the cabin yourself to save cleaning fees of around Skr400.

Contact the local or regional tourist offices for listings of cabins, chalets and holiday houses, which can be rented by the week – they're very popular with Swedes in summer. Rates for these vary from Skr700 to Skr5000 (most are around Skr2000) and depend on the season. Also check out the website W www.stuga.nu.

Mountain Huts & Lodges

Most mountain huts and lodges in Sweden are owned by STF (see the earlier section on hostels) and are known as *fjällstugor* and *fjällstationer* respectively. There are about 45 huts and nine mountain lodges, usually spaced at 15km to 25km intervals, primarily in the Lappland region. Reception hours are usually quite long since staff members are always on site. Basic provisions are sold at many huts and all lodges, and many lodges offer hiking equipment for hire.

STF huts have cooking and toilet facilities (none have showers, but some offer saunas). Bring your own sleeping bag. Huts are staffed during March and April and also from late June to early or mid-September. You can't book a bed in advance, but no-one is ever turned away (although in peak summer this may mean you sleep on a mattress on the floor). Charges for STF or HI members vary depending on the season, and range from Skr160 to Skr220 (children Skr50), with the highest charges on northern Kungsleden. Nonmembers pay Skr50 extra. You can also pitch a tent in the mountains, but if you camp near STF huts you are requested to pay a service charge (Skr45/75 for members/nonmembers), which gives you access to any services the hut may offer (eg, kitchen and bathroom facilities).

At the excellent STF mountain lodges, accommodation standards range from hostel (with cooking facilities) to hotel (with full- or half-board options), and overnight prices range from Skr150 to around Skr700. There are often guided activities on offer for guests, plus a restaurant and shop.

Private Rooms, B&Bs & Farmhouse Accommodation

Beds in private rooms offer good value, with singles/doubles averaging Skr150/250. Private rooms aren't available everywhere; they must be booked through tourist offices in some areas. In other areas, the tourist offices hand out lists. Along the highways (mainly in the south), you'll see some 'Rum' or 'Rum & frukost' signs, indicating inexpensive informal accommodation (*frukost* means that breakfast is included) from around Skr100 to Skr250 per person. Kitchen facilities are often available and those who bring their own sheets or sleeping bags may get a discount. Pensions and guesthouses in the Skr250 to Skr400 range are fairly rare and breakfast may cost extra.

The organisation **Bo på Lantgård** (☎ 0534-1207; e bopalantgard@lrf.se, w *www.bopa lantgard.org*) publishes an annual booklet on farmhouse accommodation (B&B and self-catering), available free from any tourist office. Prices average about Skr250 per person in a double room; singles pay a supplement of around Skr50 to Skr75. Prices for self-catering range from Skr300 to Skr800 per night, depending on time of year, facilities and number of beds.

Hotels

There are few really cheap hotels in Sweden. However, almost all hotels offer good-value weekend and summer (mid-June to mid-August) rates, often below Skr700 for a quite luxurious double – about 40% to 50% lower than during the rest of the year. Rates usually include a breakfast buffet. Be aware that prices are sometimes expressed as 'per person'. An extra bed may be included for little or no extra cost at many hotels. Ask your nearest Swedish tourist office for the free booklet *Hotels in Sweden* or visit its website w www.hotelsinsweden.net.

There's usually an independent, budget hotel or guesthouse even in the smaller towns; the majority of these have shared facilities (and many hotels offer cheaper rooms with either private or shared facilities). You should also inquire at hostels – many offer single and double rooms for not much more than the cost of a dorm bed, and some have good-value en-suite rooms of hotel standard.

Of particular interest to travellers on a budget are the two cheapest hotel chains,

Formule 1 (w *www.hotelformule1.com*) and Ibis (w *www.ibishotel.com*), both with flat rates for rooms. Formule 1 hotels are only found in four Swedish cities (Stockholm, Gothenburg, Malmö and Jönköping). Its small and bland but functional rooms with shared facilities cost under Skr300 and can sleep up to three people. Ibis hotels offer simple but adequate rooms with private facilities; the room rates are normally around Skr550 to Skr650. Breakfast is additional at both chains.

Many mid-range and top-end hotels in Sweden are members of chains; the following are the most common.

Choice	w www.choicehotels.se
Countryside	w www.countrysidehotels.se
Ditt Hotell	w www.ditthotell.se
Elite	w www.elite.se
First	w www.firsthotels.com
Radisson SAS	w www.radisson.com
Scandic	w www.scandic-hotels.com
Sweden Hotels	w www.swedenhotels.se

Radisson SAS and Elite are probably the most luxurious of the chains, but all have high standards. Countryside Hotels are another top-end choice; these range from castles and mansions to monasteries and spas and they've all got great character. Most chains have discount schemes such as coupons, hotel passes or cheques, and even offer free nights for 'frequent stayers'.

See the sections on Stockholm, Gothenburg and Malmö (in the Stockholm chapter) for details on good-value accommodation packages, which usually include a hotel room, free or discounted entry to the main sight, free parking and free public transport. A range of hotels is normally offered to suit most budgets; contact tourist offices in these cities for details.

FOOD

Sweden may not be one of the world's cheapest places to eat, but the quality of the food is generally high.

Meals

Breakfast The day begins with *frukost* (breakfast) and the initial fruit juice is usually followed by cereal such as cornflakes or muesli, taken with *filmjölk* (cultured milk) or fruit-flavoured yoghurt. Winter alternatives are hot-oat or rice porridge, bacon, sausages, meatballs and scrambled eggs. There's usually a buffet of several types of bread, pastries, rye bread, crispbread and/or rolls, with *pålägg* (toppings) including butter, sliced cheese, sliced meat and spicy sausage or salami, liver pate, pickled herring, sliced cucumber and pepper, jam and marmalade. Coffee is the main breakfast drink, but tea is usually available.

Breakfast at restaurants is normally only available to residents of the attached hotel or hostel.

Lunch In restaurants, look for the daily special *(dagens rätt)*, usually only available from 11.30am to 2pm weekdays. It offers great value (most restaurants charge between Skr50 and Skr65) and normally includes a main course (meat or fish), salad, drink, bread and butter, and coffee.

Alternatively, look for takeaways offering burgers, pizzas or kebabs (see the following Dinner section). Bakeries, cafés and coffee shops offer open sandwiches, filled baguettes, pies, quiches, baked potatoes, salads etc, for around Skr25 to Skr55. *Konditori* are old-fashioned bakery-cafés where you can get a pastry or a *smörgås* (sandwich) from Sk25, but there are also many modern, stylish cafés where you can do some good people watching over pricier Italian coffees, gourmet salads and filled bagels and ciabattas.

Dinner You can count on spending at least Skr120 for a main course in a good restaurant; quality gourmet restaurants have main courses from around Skr200 or even Skr300. Desserts usually range from Skr40 to Skr70, and choice may be limited. Italian and Asian restaurants are generally cheaper – pasta and rice dishes are often priced around Skr90 to Skr110.

Drinks in restaurants can be expensive: a soft drink is at least Skr18, light beer is around Skr25, full-strength beer from Skr40 to Skr50 and a glass of wine from Skr35 to Skr70. *Ful-lständiga rättigheter* means fully licensed. Due to strict licensing laws, most pubs and bars serve a good range of meals too; chains such as Harry's and O'Leary's are popular. Many of the new, stylish coffee shops (eg, Wayne's Coffee) stay open of an evening and are popular for light meals.

Budget-conscious travellers may want to avoid the expensive *middag* (dinner) menus

in restaurants, and opt for self-catering or takeaways. *Falukorv* or just *korv* is a fairly bland pale-coloured pork sausage which is best fried but can be boiled; these are similar to hot dogs and are available from many fast-food kiosks. The cheapest places to eat dinner are hamburger bars (Sibylla is a reputable local chain), McDonald's (a Big Mac, medium fries and medium drink costs Skr45) and the ubiquitous pizza, kebab and felafel outlets. In many towns, there may be dozens of pizza outlets; pizzas range from Skr35 to Skr55, and *avhämtning* (takeaways) are cheaper than eating-in. Vegetarian pizzas also appear on menus and are usually slightly cheaper than meat-based pizzas.

Pure vegetarian restaurants do exist but are not common; there will usually be at least one vegetarian main-course option on restaurant menus, but meat, game and poultry dishes are the mainstay of Swedish menus. Fillets of beef, pork, reindeer and elk are usually served with a sauce and vegetables. There's usually at least one lamb and one chicken dish on offer. Look out for cheaper menu categories like *husmanskost* (homely Swedish fare), *smårätt* (small dishes) or *lätt och gott* (light meals). You may find traditional meals like *köttbullar och potatis* (meatballs and potatoes), *lövbiff & strips* (thinly sliced fried meat and chips) and *pytt i panna* ('Swedish hash', a mix of diced sausage, beef or pork fried up with onion and potato and served with sliced beetroot and a fried egg) ranging from Skr50 to Skr100. Meatballs and potatoes are commonly served with lingonberry jam.

Fish can be prepared in a variety of ways, but frying and grilling are popular (eg, fried fillet of whitefish, fried char, and grilled salmon and trout). Gravadlax (which is marinated salmon), smoked eel and herring, pickled and fermented herring, caviar, crayfish and shrimps are all considered delicacies, but the stinky *surströmming* (fermented herring) is definitely an acquired taste. There's a huge variety of pickled herring(sold in jars) to be found in Swedish supermarkets. Fish dishes are often used as appetisers (starters) in Swedish restaurant meals.

Some traditional Swedish foods are associated with certain times of year (see the Public Holidays & Special Events section earlier in this chapter for details).

Swedish Smörgåsbord

The best-known Swedish food tradition is the smörgåsbord buffet, which generally includes a large range of hot and cold dishes, followed by a choice of desserts and coffee.

Potatoes are a strong feature and are eaten along with meat stews or sliced meat freshly cut from steaming joints; grilled or baked trout, char or salmon; or herring, either pickled or in mustard or lemon sauce. The potatoes may be boiled, baked, or sliced with onion and anchovy, then oven-baked with lots of cream. Another great smörgåsbord favourite is gravadlax (salmon marinated in sugar and salt) and potatoes stewed with dill. A full range of other vegetables is normally available, usually boiled, but sometimes prepared in more interesting ways.

There's usually a selection of types of bread, including sweet dark rye bread, tasty *tunnbröd* (thin barley crispbread) and *knäckebröd*, a hard bread made from wheat or rye. The best desserts are fresh strawberries or blueberries and cream, *spettekaka* (Skåne meringue), and warm cloudberry jam with ice cream.

The *julbord* (Christmas smörgåsbord), includes *lutfisk* – this is dried ling or saithe that has been soaked for several days in lye to make it gelatinous. It's then stewed in white sauce and served with boiled potatoes, ground pepper and mustard. Sweet rice pudding with cinnamon is often served for dessert.

Self-Catering

Making your own meals is easy enough if you're hostelling or staying in camping grounds with good facilities. In supermarkets, both the item price and comparative price per kilogram have to be shown by law. Plastic carrier bags will usually cost Skr1 or Skr2 at the cashier.

Supermarkets are easily found in Swedish towns and villages. The main chains ICA and Konsum are found almost everywhere, except in small villages. Hemköp supermarkets are less numerous and are often inside Åhléns department stores. Rimi is another good chain. A loaf of bread *(bröd)* will cost you from Skr 15 to Skr18 and milk *(mjölk)* costs Skr6.50 per litre. The selection of fresh vegetables and fruit might seem limited in small supermarkets, but tends to be better at produce markets (these are commonly found on a town's main square).

Svensk Lantmat has a network of small, rural farm shops selling fresh produce. You can visit local strawberry fields – look for common roadside signs saying 'jordgubbar' (strawberries), and indicating 'självplock', which means that you are allowed to pick them yourself. You can also buy fresh produce directly from growers at dairy farms or market gardens – some of the more exotic places, such as fish- and eel-smoking houses, are outings in themselves. The brochure put out by **Bo på Lantgård** (☎ 0534-1207; [W] www.bopalantgard.org) lists these farm stores.

DRINKS

Coffee is Sweden's unofficial national drink, but tea is also generally available. Expect to pay around Skr15 for a cup of filtered coffee at an older-style café (ask for a *påtår* – free refill). In the cool coffee shops like Wayne's Coffee, a large cappuccino could set you back around Skr25.

Soft drinks, including international brands, are popular but expensive; Skr12 to Skr15 is the norm for 330mL, but it's cheaper when bought in larger bottles from supermarkets. Bottles and aluminium cans can then be recycled – supermarket disposal machines give Skr0.50 to Skr1 per item.

Saft (concentrated fruit juice) is commonly made from lingonberries and blueberries. Tap water is drinkable everywhere so you may want to carry a water bottle and refill it regularly. Mineral water is available in supermarkets for around Skr5 per 330mL bottle, but the price rises steeply to around Skr20 in expensive restaurants.

Alcoholic Drinks

We advise taking advantage of your duty-free allowance for Sweden because alcohol is expensive. You must be aged 20 or over to purchase alcohol in Sweden.

Beers are ranked by alcohol content, and the stronger the beer, the higher its price. Good-value light beers (*lättöl*, less than 2.25%) and 'folk' beers (*folköl*, 2.25% to 3.5%) account for about two-thirds of all beer sold in Sweden and can be bought in supermarkets. Medium-strength beer (*mellanöl,* 3.5% to 4.5%) and strong beer (*starköl,* over 4.5%) can only be bought at outlets of the state-owned alcohol store, Systembolaget, or ordered through its agents in remote places. Swedes generally drink strong beer on special occasions. Sweden's largest breweries, including Spendrups, Pripps, Kopparbergs, Falcon and Åbro, produce a wide range of drinks from cider to light and dark lagers, porter and stout. Pear cider is usually less than 2.25% and may even be alcohol free.

Wines and spirits can only be bought at Systembolaget, where prices are kept high as a matter of policy (see the boxed text). Vin & Sprit (V&S) produce some fruit wines and *glögg* (mulled wine). Sweden produces its own spirit, *brännvin, snaps* or *aquavit* (vodka), which is a fiery and strongly flavoured drink that's usually distilled from potatoes.

Pressure from the EU may force Sweden to relax its strict alcohol laws, but in the meantime Swedes go over the border to Denmark, the Åland islands or Finland to stock up (you can still buy duty-free products on the Åland islands).

ENTERTAINMENT
Bars & Clubs
Due to strict licensing regulations, bars in Sweden are attached to restaurants and a real 'pub' atmosphere is rare. There's live music in some places and entry may be free. Pubs and restaurants usually charge around Skr40 to Skr50 for the standard 500mL *storstark* (strong beer), although the cheaper 330mL bottle is common. A glass of wine is unlikely to be below Skr40.

Discos and nightclubs usually admit no-one aged under 20, although the minimum age limit for men may be 23 or even 25. Drinking at these places is an expensive option. Cover charges range from Skr60 to Skr150 and cloakrooms charge around Skr20. In the cities, there's dancing (often with live music) most nights of the week but in small towns the action is usually on Friday and Saturday only.

Cinema & Theatre
Cinemas are found in most towns and cities, but in smaller towns the cinema may be closed for several weeks in summer, or it may only open a few days each week. Cinema tickets usually cost Skr70 to Skr80 (possibly cheaper early in the week) and there are usually student and senior discounts. Foreign films are almost always screened in the original language (usually English) with Swedish subtitles.

Theatre tickets cost anything from Skr100 to Skr500; prices depend on your seat position, the length of performance, and various other factors. Performances are usually in Swedish and many theatres close in summer. Operas are performed in their

Systembolaget

As a visitor to Sweden, you may be left scratching your head at the official attitude to alcohol, the difficulties in buying wine, beer or something stronger, and the strange phenomenon of Systembolaget.

Firstly, in order to make some sense of this, it's worth knowing that the goal of Swedish alcohol policy, as stipulated by the Swedish parliament, is to reduce alcohol consumption and therefore alcohol-related illness. Limiting private profit from alcohol sales is an integral part of the Swedish alcohol policy since private profit and competition increase both sales and the negative effects of too much alcohol consumption. Sweden, along with the majority of the Nordic countries, most Canadian provinces and 18 US states, operates a government monopoly on the sale of alcohol.

The Swedish Alcohol Retailing Monopoly, Systembolaget, a wholly state-owned company, is responsible for selling strong beer, wine and spirits to the general public (low-alcohol beer is available at supermarkets). The monopoly has more than 400 stores and nearly 600 local agencies throughout Sweden.

Systembolaget doesn't favour any particular brand nor does it promote Swedish products over imported brands; as a result, the choice available from the company's catalogue is impressive. Most stores, however, have their products behind locked glass cabinets; the self-service concept is about to be slowly phased in.

Festivals & Concerts

There's a staggering number of festivals staged regularly in Sweden. Almost every town has at least one; the warm summer months are a particularly popular time, with everyone taking advantage of the long daylight hours. Visitors should also look out for outdoor summer concerts and theatre productions staged at wonderfully atmospheric venues like Dalhalla in Rättvik or many of the country's fine castles. While some street festivals and concerts are free, others have admission prices (often quite high).

The following is just a small sample of the wide variety of events on offer. Visit W www.musik festivaler.se or W home.swipnet.se/gretchen for details of many more of the music festivals held throughout the country.

Large, annual, three-day summer rock festivals are held around **Hultsfred** (W *www.rockparty.se)* in mid-June, **Arvika** (W *www.galaxen.se)* in mid-July, and **Sölvesborg** (W *www.swedenrock.com)* in early June. Towns hosting large rock concerts in their central areas include Sundsvall (early July), Östersund (late July) and Skellefteå (late June); see town websites for information.

Jazz, opera and folk music events are also popular: Well-respected jazz festivals are held in **Stockholm** (W *www.svd.se/jazz)* in mid-July and **Umeå** (W *www.botniamusik.se/jazz)* in late October. The Lake Siljan area is busy with events: **Musik vid Siljan** (W *www.musikvidsiljan.se)* is a week-long event in early July with something to suit most tastes, including chamber, jazz and traditional folk music; the stunning Dalhalla venue in Rättvik hosts an **opera festival** (W *www.dalhalla.se)* in early August and Falun has a popular folk and **world-music festival** (W *www.falufolk.com)* in mid-July.

Other popular annual events include **Stockholm Pride** (W *www.stockholmpride.org)*, a gay and lesbian festival held in the capital in early August, and **Medeltidsveckan** (*Medieval Week;* W *www .medeltidsveckan.se)*, staged in Visby on Gotland, also in early August. Big winter events in the north of the country include the **Kiruna Snow Festival** (W *www.kirunasnowfestival.com)* in late January, Europe's largest snow festival featuring snow-sculpting competitions and reindeer-sled racing, with Sami traditions also emphasised. Another event highlighting Sami culture is the **Jokkmokk Winter Market** (W *www.jokkmokksmarknad.com)* in early February, celebrating its 400th anniversary in 2004.

---

original language (which is usually Italian) or in Swedish.

SPECTATOR SPORTS

Many Swedes enjoy competitive sports and even local fixtures attract large crowds. Some highly popular spectator sports, such as bandy, handball and trotting, aren't very well known outside Scandinavia and parts of North America.

Football

Football (soccer) is currently the most popular sporting activity in Sweden; there are 3320 clubs and over one million members. Women's football is strongly represented and it's available at around 1300 clubs. The domestic season is generally from April to early November. Matches are usually held on weekend afternoons or Monday evenings and admission costs upwards of Skr100. The national arena is Råsunda Stadium in Solna, a suburb in Stockholm's northwest, with a capacity for 37,000 spectators.

Internationally, Swedish football has quite a good record. The national team is currently ranked 20th in the world by FIFA and in 2002, Sweden made it into the second round (the final 16) of the World Cup, losing to Senegal in the second round.

Ice Hockey

There are amateur ice-hockey teams in most Swedish communities and the national premier league, the Elitserien, has 12 professional teams; there are a number of lower divisions. Matches take place from autumn to late spring, and up to four times weekly in Stockholm, primarily at the Globen arena. Admission start at around Skr100.

The national ice-hockey team last won the World Championship in April 1998, when it beat Finland in the final, and was placed third in the same competition in 1999, 2001 and 2002. In 2002, the World Championship was held in Gothenburg, with games also being played at Karlstad and Jonköping.

Skiing

Alpine skiing competitions are held annually, particularly in Åre (Jämtland), where events include the Ladies World Cup competitions in late February or early March, and Skutskjutet, the world's greatest downhill ski race (with up to 3000 competitors), in late April or early May. **Vasaloppet** (W *www.vasaloppet.se)*, the world's biggest nordic (cross-country) ski race, takes place on the first Sunday in March, when 15,000 competitors follow a 90km route. For further details, see the sections on Sälen and Mora (Dalarna) or check out its website.

For more about skiing, see the Activities chapter.

Other

Tennis is regarded as a participation sport rather than a spectator sport, and it's very popular. Swedish men have excelled at tennis, including Björn Borg, Mats Wilander and Stefan Edberg (who have all now retired). Borg won the Wimbledon championships in England five times in a row. Currently, Thomas Enqvist is holding media attention. Golf is a similarly popular sport in Sweden, more participatory than spectator, and there are more than 400 courses throughout the country. Annika Sörenstam, ranked as one of the game's leading female players, hails from Sweden.

Bandy, though similar to ice hockey, is played on an outdoor pitch the size of a football field and teams are the same size as in football. The sport is very popular in northern Sweden, but potential spectators may be put off by the fact that they must stand outside in the cold.

Sailing is very popular, around Stockholm in particular, where almost half the population owns a yacht. Races, held every summer, attract crowds of onlookers.

SHOPPING

There's no shortage of examples of the gorgeous furniture and interior design for which Sweden is famous, especially in Stockholm and the larger cities. Head to **DesignTorget** (W *www.designtorget.se)*, which showcase the work (usually quite affordable) of both established and new designers, and pick up some of the funky smaller pieces. There are branches in Stockholm, Gothenburg and Malmö.

Souvenirs, handicrafts or quality Swedish products in glass, wood, amber, pewter or silver are relatively expensive, but tend to be a lot cheaper when bought directly from the manufacturer. Items may also be inconvenient to cart around for the duration of your visit; some places will organise shipping for you. Among the best souvenirs are glassware (such as bowls, jugs, vases and ornaments) from the Glasriket factories, Swedish painted wooden horses from Dalarna (see the Mora section in the Svealand chapter), wooden toys, and amber and silver jewellery. Some foodstuffs, such as cloudberry jam and pickled herring, are also well worth taking home. Sale prices in shops are advertised with the word *rea;* for discounts or special offers look for *lågpris, extrapris, rabatt* or *fynd.*

Handicrafts carrying the round token *Svensk slöjd,* or the hammer and shuttle emblem, are endorsed by Svenska Hemslöjdsföreningarnas Riksförbund, the national handicrafts organisation whose symbol is found on affiliated handicraft shops. Look out for signs reading *hemslöjd,* indicating handicraft sales outlets.

If you're interested in Sami handicrafts, which are usually quite expensive, look for the *Duodji* label (it is a round coloured token of authenticity) and, if possible, go to a Sami village and make your purchase there. Be careful of some town shops that may have fakes on the shelves. Some typical Sami handicrafts include ornately carved sheath knives, cups, bowls, textiles and jewellery. Reindeer bone, wood (birch), reindeer hide and tin are commonly used materials.

Activities

Sweden is ideal for outdoor activities since the country has thousands of square kilometres of forest with hiking (see the special section 'Hiking') and cycling tracks, vast numbers of lakes connected by mighty rivers, and a range of alpine mountains in the north and northwest. Information about most outdoor activities is available on the Internet, but unfortunately it's mostly in Swedish. If you can't read Swedish, contact the national organisations for the particular sport you're interested in (listed under individual sports in this section), and you'll usually get a good response. Regional and local tourist offices are also good places for general information and staff at outdoor stores are usually very familiar with what activities are available in the surrounding areas, and can point you in the right direction.

If you don't have the necessary skills in particular activities, or don't wish to travel alone, consider joining an organised tour. For details, see the Organised Tours section in the Getting Around chapter and check individual destinations in this book. You'll also find information at tourist offices, which supply the booklet *Active Holidays in Sweden*.

Svenska Turistföreningen *(Swedish Touring Association, STF;* ☎ *020 292929;* e *info@ stfturist.se,* w *www.meravsverige.nu; Box 25, SE-10120 Stockholm),* is one of Sweden's largest tour operators, but unfortunately most of its publications are in Swedish only. STF staff are generally happy to answer questions and provide information in English over the phone or via email.

MOUNTAINEERING & ROCK CLIMBING

Mountaineers head for Sylarna, Helagsfjället, Sarek National Park and the Kebnekaise region.

The complete traverse of Sylarna involves rock climbing up to grade 3. The ridge traverse of Sarektjåhkkå (2089m) in Sarek, the second highest mountain in Sweden, is about grade 4. There are lots of other glacier and rock routes in Sarek. The Kebnekaise area has many fine climbing routes (grades 2 to 6), including the north wall of Kaskasapakte (2043m), and the steep ridges of Knivkammen (1878m) and Vaktposten (1852m). Ice climbing in the northern regions is excellent, if you can put up with all the darkness and the cold!

For qualified guides, contact **Svenska Bergsguideorganisation** *(Swedish Mountain Guide Association;* ☎ *08-645 1520;* w *www3 .utsidan.se/sbo; Älgstigen 34, SE-13467 Ingarö).* The website is in Swedish only but under 'medlemmar' there's a list of guides and their contact details.

Rock climbers can practise on the cliffs around Stockholm and Gothenburg – there are 34 climbing areas with around 1000 routes around Gothenburg, and some 200 cliffs around the capital. Other popular spots are Bohuslän, the Kulla Peninsula (north of Helsingborg), and a newly developed bouldering area, Kjugekull, a few kilometres northeast of Kristianstad. You'll find good climbing walls in Stockholm, Gothenburg, Uppsala, Skellefteå and Linköping.

The only English-language guidebook covering mountaineering in Sweden is Peter Lennon's *Scandinavian Mountains*. For further information, you can also try the helpful **Svenska Klätterförbundet** *(Swedish Climbing Federation;* ☎ *08-618 8270;* e *kansliet@klat terforbundet.com; Lagerlöfsgatan 8, SE-11260 Stockholm).*

CYCLING

Sweden is a flat country that's ideal for cycling, with Skåne and Gotland particularly recommended. Cycling is an excellent way to look for points of interest such as prehistoric sites, rune stones, parish churches and quiet spots for free camping. The cycling season is from May to September in the south, and July and August in the north.

You can cycle on all roads except motorways (green sign, with two lanes and a bridge) and roads for motor vehicles only (green sign with a car symbol). Highways often have a hard shoulder, which keeps cyclists well clear of motor vehicles. Secondary roads are better for cyclists; they're mostly quiet and reasonably safe by European standards.

You can take a bicycle on some *länstrafik* trains and most regional buses (free, or up to Skr50). On Malmö region's Pågatåg^en trains, a bike costs the price of a child's ticket. Long-distance buses usually don't accept bicycles, and nor does Sveriges Järnäg (SJ). Bikes are transported free on some ferries, including Vägverket routes.

One-gear bike hire is free in some towns, but multi-gear bikes can cost up to a pricey Skr200/800 per day/week. If you want to buy second-hand, try the bicycle workshops in university towns first.

Some country areas, towns and cities have special cycle routes – contact the local tourist office for information and maps. Kustlinjen (591km) runs from Öregrund (Uppland) southwards along the Baltic coast to Västervik, and Skånespåret (800km) is a fine network of cycle routes. The well-signposted 2600km-long Sverigeleden extends from Helsingborg to Karesuando and links points of interest with suitable roads (mostly with an asphalt surface) and bicycle paths. Brochures and Swedish-text guidebooks including maps are available from **Svenska Cykelsällskapet** (Swedish Cycling Association; ☎ 08-751 6204; e info@svenska-cykelsallskapet.se; Box 6006, SE-16406 Kista).

BikeTour Sweden (☎ 0411-42000; e info@ biketoursweden.se; Södra Industrigatan 6, SE-27430 Skurup) offers self-guided or guided cycling tours in Skåne. Prices range from around Skr700 for a day's outing, to Skr3925 for a week, including accommodation.

An unusual cycling activity, the *dressin* or inspection-trolley ride, is offered on several disused railway lines around the country. Trips cost around Skr200/1200 per day/week.

For further information on cycling, contact your local cycle-touring club.

SKIING

Lift passes and equipment hire are reasonably priced, resorts are well run and facilities are of a high standard. After the spring solstice (21 March), daylight lasts longer than in the Swiss Alps, so you'll get more skiing time out of your pass.

Cross-country (nordic) skiing opportunities vary depending on the snow depth and temperatures, but the northwest usually has plenty of snow from December to April (although not a lot of daylight in December and January). Kungsleden and other long-distance tracks provide great skiing. Practically all town areas (except those in the far south) have marked and often illuminated skiing tracks.

The large ski resorts cater mainly for downhill (alpine and telemark) skiing and snowboarding, but there's also scope for cross-country. For reviews of the Swedish ski fields in English, visit W www.goski.com and W www.thealps.com. **SkiStar** (W www .skistar.com) manages two large resorts, Sälen and Åre, and has good information on its website.

The southernmost large resort in Sweden, Sälen (Dalarna), appeals particularly to families and young party types. Idre, a little further north, is also good for skiers with young families. There's a good ski school here and the resort is quieter than Sälen. The main party place for young skiers, Åre in Jämtland, is great for long, downhill runs (over 1000m descent) and cross-country routes. The nearby ski areas at Duved and Storlien are also good, and less crowded. Further north, in Lappland, Hemavan is fairly busy with spring skiers. Riksgränsen (at the border with Norway on the E10 Kiruna–Narvik road) is the world's northernmost ski resort and offers interesting options, including heli-skiing and alpine ski touring, from mid-February until late June. Downhill runs at Riksgränsen aren't suitable for beginners.

Take the usual precautions: don't leave marked cross-country or downhill routes without emergency food, a good map, local advice, and proper equipment including a bivouac bag. Temperatures of -30°C or lower (including wind-chill factors) are possible, so check the daily forecasts. Police and tourist offices have information on local warnings. In mountain ski resorts, where there's a risk of avalanche *(lavin)*, susceptible areas are marked by yellow, multilingual signs and buried-skier symbols. Make sure your travel insurance covers skiing.

SKATING

Whenever the ice is thick enough, Stockholm's lake and canal system is exploited by skating enthusiasts seeking the longest possible 'run'. Tour skating is now very popular and experienced skaters can manage over 100km per day on Lake Mälaren. When the Baltic Sea freezes (once or twice every ten years), fantastic tours of Stockholm's archipelago are possible, but you should never skate alone. The skating season usually lasts from December to March. **Stockholms Skridskoseglarklubb** (Stockholm's Ice Skate

Sailing Club; W *www.sssk.se)* has some information in English on its website, but its services are for members only.

For those not up to the rigours of tour skating, head to the small ice-skating rink that's constructed every winter in Kungsträdgården in central Stockholm. It's open daily and floodlit of an evening; skate hire is available.

DOG-SLEDGING & SNOWMOBILE SAFARIS

Organised tours with Siberian huskies pulling your sledge are fairly popular in Lappland, as are excursions on snowmobiles. They're usually expensive, but operators mentioned in this book offer value for money. Trips range from an hour to several days (with accommodation and food included). For further details, see the Norrland chapter.

BIRD-WATCHING

This activity is quite popular in Sweden and there are bird-watchers' towers and nature reserves all over the country. See the Fauna section in the Facts about Sweden chapter for details of Sweden's bird life and where the best bird-watching sites are. For further information, contact **Sveriges Ornitologiska Förening** *(Swedish Ornithological Society;* ☎ *08-612 2530;* e *info@sofnet.org,* W *www.sofnet.org; Ekhagsvägen 3, SE-10405 Stockholm).*

FISHING

There are national and local restrictions on fishing many of the inland waters, especially concerning salmon, trout and eel; before dropping a line, check with local tourist offices or local councils. You generally need a permit, but free fishing is allowed on parts of Vänern, Vättern, Hjälmaren and Storsjön Lakes and most of the coastline. Local permits for the waters of a *kommun* (municipality) can be bought from tourist offices and sports or camping shops and typically cost Skr50/280 per day/week. For fishing maps and advice on the best locations, ask the local tourist office.

Summer is the best fishing time with bait or flies for most species, but trout and pike fishing in southern Sweden is better in spring or autumn and salmon fishing is best in late summer. Ice fishing is popular in winter. For good general information about fishing in Sweden, visit W www.top10fishing.se, or

contact **Sportfiskeförbundet** *(Angling Federation;* ☎ *08-704 4480;* e *hk@sportfiskarna.se; Strömkarlsvägen 62, SE-16762 Bromma).*

GOLF

Golf is incredibly popular in Sweden – about one in 20 Swedes plays the game. There are more than 400 golf courses to choose from and many hotel chains offer golf packages. Golf is particularly popular in the south, where courses are often surrounded by the typical rolling farmlands of the region, but things are decidedly more unusual in the north – Björkliden, near Abisko, is home to Sweden's northernmost course (240km above the Arctic Circle), and at the Green Line golf course at Haparanda, on Sweden's border with Finland, playing a round means crossing the border four times.

For more information, contact **Svenska Golfförbundet** *(Swedish Golf Federation;* ☎ *08-755 8439;* e *info@sgf.golf.se; Box 84, Kevingestrand 20, SE-18211 Danderyd).*

CANOEING & KAYAKING

Sweden's superb wilderness lakes and white-water rivers are a real paradise for canoeists and kayakers (but canoeing is more popular than kayaking). The national canoeing body is **Svenska Kanotförbundet** *(☎ 08-605 6000;* e *kanot@rf.se; Idrottens Hus, SE-12387 Farsta).* It provides general advice and produces *Kanotvåg,* a free, annual brochure listing the 75 approved canoe centres that hire out canoes (from Skr140/500 per day/week) throughout the country.

According to the right of common access, canoeists may paddle or moor virtually anywhere provided they respect the basic privacy of dwellings and avoid sensitive nesting areas within nature reserves. More good information is available on the Internet at W www.kanotguiden.com.

RAFTING

White-water rafting in rubber boats isn't a big activity since most rivers have very low gradients. However, localities offering the activity include: Arvidsjaur, on the river Piteälven; Haparanda, on Torneälven; Järpen in Jämtland (one of the best places for rafting in Sweden); and Vindeln, on Vindelälven. You can also go slow-water rafting, especially on the river Klarälven in Värmland. Local companies organise rafting trips that last from an hour to a week and supply fully-qualified guides. See the relevant sections in this book.

BOATING & SAILING

Boating and sailing are popular in Sweden and it seems as if half the population takes to the water in summer. Lake and canal routes offer pleasant sailing in spring and summer (the canals are generally open for limited seasons) but boat hire and lock fees can be expensive. The main canals are the Göta Canal (which crosses the country), the Kinda Canal and the Dalsland Canal. Some simple guest harbours are free, but ones with good facilities average Skr100 per night.

The 7000km-long coastline (including all bays and fjords) is a paradise for boats and yachts, but watch out for the few restricted military areas off the east coast. The *skärgård* (archipelago) areas total over 60,000 islands and provide an exciting setting for sailing or motor boats.

A useful guide is the free, annual *Gästhamnsguiden*, which is published by **Svenska Kryssarklubben** *(Swedish Cruising Club; ☎ 08-448 2880; e info@sxk.se; August-endalsvägen 54, Box 1189, SE-13127 Nacka Strand)*. The guide contains details of some 500 guest harbours throughout the country and their facilities, prices, services etc. It's also available from larger tourist offices and most of the guest harbours listed.

Svenska Sjöfartsverket *(Swedish Maritime Administration; ☎ 011-191000; w www.sjofartsverket.se; Huvudkontoret, SE-60178 Norrköping)* can send you information on harbour handbooks and sea charts. For charts you can also try **Kartbutiken** *(☎ 08-202303; w www.kartbutiken.se; Kungsgatan 74, SE-11122 Stockholm)*.

TRACING YOUR ANCESTORS

Between 1850 and 1930 around 1.2 million Swedes emigrated to the USA and Canada and nowadays many of their 12 million descendants are returning to the old country to find their roots.

Detailed parish records of births, deaths and marriages have been kept in Sweden from 1686 and now there are *landsarkivet* (regional archives) around the country. The national archive is **Riksarkivet** *(☎ 08-737 6350; w www.ra.se; Box 12541, Fyrverkarbacken 13-17, SE-10229 Stockholm)*.

SVAR *(☎ 0623-72500; e info@svar.ra.se; Rafnasil kulturområde, Box 160, SE-88040 Ramsele)* is a research centre which holds most records from the late 17th century until 1928. You can either pay the staff here to research for you (Skr180 per half hour) or you can visit in person and do it yourself.

Utvandrarnas Hus (Emigrant House) is a very good museum in Växjö (Småland) with information and displays on the mass departure (see the Småland chapter). Attached to the museum is **Svenska Emigrantinstitutet** *(Swedish Emigrant Institute; ☎ 0470-21020; e info@svenskaemigrantinstitutet.g.se, w www.svenskaemigrantinstitutet.g.se; Box 201, SE-35104 Växjö)*. The institute also has a research centre and you can visit and use their extensive facilities (Skr150/200 for a half/full day). Staff can also conduct research for you (US$60).

Also worth checking out is *Tracing Your Swedish Ancestry*, by Nils William Olsson, a do-it-yourself genealogical guide (40 pages) available free from the **Consulate-General of Sweden** *(w www.swedeninfo.org/tracing.htm)* in New York . This address also has some good links to other useful websites.

HIKING

Hiking is a popular activity in Sweden and there are thousands of kilometres of marked trails throughout the country. The European Long Distance Footpaths Nos 1 and 6 run from Varberg to Grövelsjön (1200km) and from Malmö to Norrtälje (1400km), respectively. Nordkalottleden runs for 450km from Sulitjelma to Kautokeino (both in Norway), but passes through Sweden for most of its route. Finnskogleden is a 240km-long route along the border between Norway and the Värmland region in Sweden. The Arctic Trail (800km) is a joint development of Sweden, Norway and Finland and is entirely above the Arctic Circle; it begins near Kautokeino in Norway and ends in Abisko, Sweden. The most popular route is Kungsleden, now running from Sälen in Dalarna to Treriksröset, but the most popular sections are in Lappland (see later in this section).

Many counties also have a network of easy walking trails connecting sites of interest rather than a long-distance through route, such as Skåneleden, which totals 950km. Most hikers restrict themselves to day hikes in these areas, but long-distance hiking with a tent is still possible.

The popular multiday routes during the short snow-free season are found in the mountains and forests near the Norwegian border. The best hiking time is between late June and mid-September, but conditions are better after early August, when the mosquitoes have gone. Overnight facilities such as huts and lodges, are provided by the Svenska Turistföreningen (STF) in popular areas (see Accommodation in the Facts for the Visitor chapter for details). All STF lodges sell up-to-date maps, but it's a good idea to buy them in advance.

Mountain trails in Sweden are marked with cairns (piles of stones), possibly with some red paint. Marked trails have bridges across all but the smallest streams and wet or fragile areas are crossed on duckboards. Avoid following winter routes (marked by regular poles with red crosses) since they often cross lakes or marshes!

Equipment

Hikers should be well equipped and must be prepared for snow in the mountains, even in summer months. Prolonged bad weather in the northwest isn't uncommon – Sarek and Sylarna are the most notorious areas. In

Inset & bottom: Hiking the Skåneleden Trail in early Spring. (Photos by Anders Blomqvist)

The Right of Public Access

The right of public access to the countryside *(allemansrätten)*, which includes national parks and nature reserves, dates back to common practices in medieval times, but isn't enshrined in law. Full details can be found on the website of the **Swedish Environmental Protection Authority** *(Natur Vårds Verket;* W *www.environ.se)*.

You're allowed to walk, ski, boat or swim on private land as long as you stay at least 70m from houses and keep out of gardens, fenced areas and cultivated land. You can camp for more than one night in the same place and you may pick berries and mushrooms, provided they're not protected species.

Don't leave any rubbish or take live wood, bark, leaves, bushes or nuts. Fires with fallen wood are allowed where safe, but not on bare rocks. Use a bucket of water to douse a campfire even if you think that it's out. Cars and motorcycles may not be driven across open land or on private roads; look out for the sign 'ej motorfordon' (no motor vehicles). Dogs must be kept on leads from 1 March to 20 August. Close all gates and don't disturb farm animals, nesting birds and reindeer.

If you have a car or bicycle, look for free camping sites around unsealed forest tracks leading from secondary country roads. Make sure your spot is at least 50m from the track and not visible from any house, building or sealed road. Dry pine forests are your best bet. Bring drinking water and food, although running creek water can normally be used for washing (don't pollute the water with soap or food waste).

summer, at the very least, you'll need good boots, waterproof jacket and trousers, several layers of warm clothing (including spare clothing, especially socks), a warm hat, a sun hat, mosquito repellent, a water bottle, maps, compass, mosquito head net (optional) and a sleeping bag. You can carry your own food, but basic supplies are often available at huts and most lodges serve meals. If you're going off the main routes (or camping generally), you'll also need a tent, a stove, your own food, cutlery and a bowl. A torch (flashlight) isn't really needed in June or July, unless you're intending midnight strolls in the south.

Equipment can usually be hired from the STF, but don't rely on this. If you need to replace gear, try the small STF shops at their lodges or the nationwide chain **Naturkompaniet** (W *www.naturkompaniet.se)*. Its website is in Swedish only, but if you click 'butiker' you'll find a list of all stores and contact details.

Information

Information in English about hiking in Sweden is scarce – the best source is **Svenska Turistföreningen** *(Swedish Touring Club, STF;* ☎ *08-463 2100;* e *info@stfturist.se,* W *www.meravsverige.nu; Box 25, SE-10120 Stockholm)*. Most of its website and publications are in Swedish only, but if you email or telephone you'll usually be able to receive advice in English.

Local and regional tourist offices, which often sell booklets and hiking maps, are usually helpful. You can also direct inquiries to **Svenska Gång-och Vandrarförbundet** *(Swedish Walking Association, SGVF;* ☎ *031-726 6000;* e *svenskgang@vsif.o.se; Kvibergsvägen 5, SE-41582 Gothenburg)*.

DAY HIKES

Apart from the day hikes mentioned here, numerous other short walks are described throughout this book.

Kebnekaise

The hike to the top of Sweden's highest mountain is one of the best in the country and the views of the surrounding peaks and glaciers are incredible on a clear day. In July and August, the marked trail up the southern flanks of Kebnekaise is usually snow-free and no technical equipment is required to reach the southern top, the highest point (2111m). To get to the northern top (2097m) from the southern top involves an airy traverse of a knife-edge ice ridge with a rope, ice axe and crampons. The map Fjällkartan BD6 (Abisko-Kebnekaise) covers the route, but there's also the very detailed Fjällkartan Kebnekaise at 1:20,000 scale (maps cost around Skr100 each and are available from Kartförlaget).

The trip involves 1900m of ascent and descent, so you'll need to be fit. Allow 12 hours, and an extra 1½ hours if you include the north top.

Sylarna

This magnificent 1743m-high mountain is easily climbed from STF's Sylarna lodge (see the Jämtland section later). You'll need a copy of Fjällkartan map Z6 (Storlien-Vålådalen-Ljung).

The route is clearly marked with cairns and goes almost due west from the lodge. After crossing the stream, which tastes like lemonade (STF has placed a cup on a post for passing hikers to use for a taste!), go up a broad, bouldery flank to a top at 1600m, which is on the main ridge and about 700m north of the summit. Head southwards, descending a little, then scramble upwards and follow a short ridge to the summit, which is just in Norway.

Allow six or seven hours (return) from Sylarna lodge.

KUNGSLEDEN

Kungsleden, meaning 'The King's Trail', is Sweden's most important waymarked hiking and skiing route. Most hikers visit the part that runs for 450km from Abisko in the north to Hemavan in the south. The route is normally split into five mostly easy or moderate sections, four of them taking four days to a week to complete. The fifth section has a gap of 188km in STF's hut network, between Kvikkjokk and Ammarnäs. The most popular section is the northern one, from Abisko to Nikkaluokta.

Abisko to Nikkaluokta

72km to Singi, 86km to Kebnekaise Fjällstation; 105km to Nikkaluokta; 7-8 days; Fjällkartan map BD6

This section of Kungsleden is usually followed from north to south. It includes a 33km-long trail from Singi to Nikkaluokta which isn't part of Kungsleden, but it allows an easy exit from the area. An alternative (and much more challenging) start is from Riksgränsen on the Norway-Sweden border; the 30km route from there to STF's Unna Allakas is very rocky in places and you'll need to camp en route.

The STF has mountain lodges at Abisko and Kebnekaise, and there are also five STF huts at 12km to 20km intervals along Kungsleden. Most of the

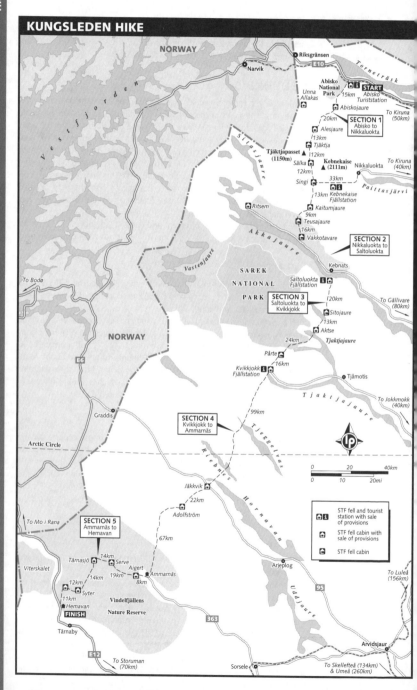

KUNGSLEDEN HIKE

NORWAY

Riksgränsen

E10

Narvik

Torneträsk

Abisko
National
Park

15km

START
Abisko
Turiststation

To Kiruna
(50km)

Unna
Allakas

Abiskojaure

20km

SECTION 1
Abisko to
Nikkaluokta

Alesjaure

13km

Tjäktja

12km

Tjäktjapasset ▲
(1150m)

Sälka

Kebnekaise
▲ (2111m)

Nikkaluokta

To Kiruna
(40km)

12km

Singi

33km

Paittasjärvi

Kebnekaise
Fjällstation

13km

Kaitumjaure

9km

Teusajaure

16km

Ritsem

Akkajaure

Vakkotavare

SECTION 2
Nikkaluokta to
Saltoluokta

Kebnats

Vastenjaure

SAREK

NATIONAL

Saltoluokta
Fjällstation

To Gällivare
(80km)

To Bodø

PARK

SECTION 3
Saltoluokta to
Kvikkjokk

20km

Sitojaure

13km

Aktse

Tjaktjaure

NORWAY

E6

24km

Pårte

16km

Kvikkjokk
Fjällstation

Tjåmotis

To Jokkmokk
(40km)

Graddis

Tjaktjajaure

SECTION 4
Kvikkjokk to
Ammarnäs

99km

Tjeggelvas

Arctic Circle

Riebnes

0   20   40km

0   10   20mi

Jäkkvik

Hornavan

22km

Adolfström

STF fell and tourist
station with sale
of provisions

To Mo i Rana

SECTION 5
Ammarnäs to
Hemavan

67km

STF fell cabin with
sale of provisions

Tärnasjö

14km

Serve

Aigert

STF fell cabin

Viterskalet

14km

19km

Ammarnäs

Arjeplog

To Luleå
(156km)

12km

Syter

8km

11km

Hemavan

Vindelfjällens

Uddjaure

FINISH

Nature Reserve

95

Tärnaby

363

Arvidsjaur

E12

To Storuman
(70km)

Sorsele

To Skellefteå (134km)
& Umeå (260km)

trail passes through spectacular alpine scenery and your highest point will be Tjäktjapasset (1150m). Many people stop at STF's Kebnekaise Fjallstation for a couple of nights and some attempt the ascent of Kebnekaise (Sweden's highest mountain) from there – see Day Hikes earlier for details.

Public transport is available at Abisko, with rail connections to Narvik (Norway), or east to Kiruna and beyond. There are two buses that run daily between Abisko and Kiruna (Skr87), and also a twice-daily bus service that runs between Nikkaluokta and Kiruna (Skr64).

Nikkaluokta to Saltoluokta

71km from Nikkaluokta to Vakkotavare, 38km from Singi; 5 days; Fjällartan map BD8

Apart from the busy paths between Nikkaluokta and Singi (see the previous section), this is a fairly quiet part of Kungsleden. The scenery south of Singi is more rounded and less dramatic than the landscape around Kebnekaise.

STF has mountain lodges at Kebnekaise and Saltoluokta, and regular huts along the trail. You may have to row yourself 1km across lake Teusajaure, but there's an STF boat service (Skr50) in the peak season. Everyone takes the bus along the road from Vakkotavare to Kebnats (Skr31), where there's an STF ferry (Skr85/55 nonmembers/members) across the lake to Saltoluokta Fjällstation, the STF lodge. For more about Saltoluokta, see the Gällivare section in the Norrland chapter.

There's a twice-daily bus service from Ritsem to Gällivare via Vakkotavare and Kebnats.

Saltoluokta to Kvikkjokk

73km; 4 days; Fjällkartan map BD10

Although this section of Kungsleden is relatively uninteresting, there are excellent side trips from Aktse into Sarek National Park, the wildest part of Sweden. Saltoluokta to Kvikkjokk can be completed in four days, but allow six days to include trips into Sarek.

STF has a lodge at Saltoluokta, huts at Sitojaure, Aktse and Pårte, and another lodge in Kvikkjokk.

Sami families run the boat services across the lakes at Sitojaure and Aktse (Skr80 for each trip). Kvikkjokk has a twice-daily bus service to Jokkmokk and Murjek train station.

Kvikkjokk to Ammarnäs

188km; 2 weeks; Fjällkartan maps BD14 (north) & BD16 (south)

There are only a few locally-run huts along this section of Kungsleden, so you'll need a tent. The more interesting northern part, Kvikkjokk to Jäkkvik (99km), can be completed in five or six days.

Boat services for lake crossings are available at Kvikkjokk, Vuonatjviken (Lake Riebnes) and Saudal (Hornavan). Buses run six days per week (not Saturday) from Skellefteå to Bodø (Norway) via Jäkkvik, and one to four times daily from Sorsele to Ammarnäs.

Ammarnäs to Hemavan

78km; 4-5 days; Fjällkartan map AC2

Most of the southernmost section of Kungsleden runs through Vindelfjällens Nature Reserve. The trail is mostly easy, but with a long initial climb.

The STF has hostels at Ammarnäs and Hemavan and five huts en route which all sell provisions.

The Umeå to Hemavan bus runs three or four times daily (only once on Sunday), and continues to Mo i Rana (Norway) once daily.

PADJELANTALEDEN

139km; 8-14 days; Fjällkartan maps BD10 & BD7

The entire Padjelantaleden trail can be hiked in eight days (not allowing any days off), but 10 to 14 days is recommended – it's generally an easy route, with long sections of duckboards, and all rivers are bridged. The southern section from Kvikkjokk to Staloluokta is the most popular hike (four or five days). At the northern end (by lake Akkajaure), you can start at either STF hut, Vaisaluokta or Akka (the latter route is easier). Most of the trail lies in Padjelanta National Park, and all huts in the park are owned by Naturvårdsverket, the Swedish environmental protection agency, and maintained by the local county authorities; make inquiries at local tourist offices.

STF runs the Såmmarlappa, Tarrekaise and Njunjes huts at the southern end of the trail, and the hostel at Kvikkjokk. You can buy provisions at Staloluokta, Såmmarlappa, Tarrekaise and Kvikkjokk.

PADJELANTALEDEN HIKE

To reach the northern end of the trail, take the bus from Gällivare to Ritsem (three times daily) and connect there with the STF ferry to Vaisaluokta and Änonjálme (1.5km north of the Akka STF hut), which runs from Midsummer to early September, one to three times daily (Skr155/125 for nonmembers/members). For details of boats from the end of Padjelantaleden to Kvikkjokk (up to three times daily from July to mid-September), call ☎ 0971-21012. Helicopters (☎ 21040 or ☎ 21068) serve Staloluokta from Ritsem or Kvikkjokk daily from Midsummer up until early August (Skr700 per flight).

JÄMTLAND

The mountainous part of western Jämtland is one of Sweden's most popular hiking areas. There's a good network of easy to moderate hiking trails served by STF lodges and huts, and many route combinations are possible. The most popular route is the 'Jämtland Triangle' (47km), which takes a minimum of three days, but you should allow an extra day for the ascent of Sylarna (see the earlier Day Hikes section). The hike runs between STF's Storulvån, Sylarna and Blåhammaren lodges. Sylarna and Blåhammaren don't have road access and Sylarna only has self-catering; meals at Blåhammaren are excellent. The section from Sylarna to Blåhammaren is very marshy and can be quite difficult in wet conditions. Fjällkartan map Z6 covers the area.

See the Storlien & Around section in the Norrland chapter for public transport details.

Getting There & Away

Your first step when heading for Sweden is to get to Europe, and in these days of intense airline competition, you'll find plenty of cheap deals to European 'gateway' cities, particularly London, Paris, Frankfurt, Berlin, Copenhagen and Stockholm.

Although very few travellers approach Sweden from the east, via Russia, this classic overland route offers some adventurous options. Lonely Planet's *Trans-Siberian Railway* guide has all the details. Another option is to arrive via the Baltic countries or Finland, by ferry.

AIR

You're unlikely to find a cheap direct flight to Sweden from outside Europe, but many European airlines will sell an inexpensive flight to Stockholm via their hub. Flights to Copenhagen airport, just across the Öresund bridge from Sweden, may be cheaper than flights to Malmö.

In Stockholm, you'll find inexpensive deals to/from Delhi, Tokyo, Hong Kong and Bangkok and cheap last-minute seats on charter flights are occasionally advertised (mainly in the daily newspapers).

Remember to reconfirm your onward or return bookings by the specified time (at least 72 hours before departure on international flights). Otherwise there's a risk that you'll turn up at the airport only to find you've missed your flight because it was rescheduled, or that you've been reclassified as a 'no show' and 'bumped'.

Airports & Airlines

Scandinavian Airlines System (SAS), British Airways, KLM, Air France, Lufthansa, Finnair and Icelandair all link **Stockholm Arlanda airport** (☎ *08-797 6000;* Ⓦ *www.lfv.se*) with major European and North American cities. Gothenburg, Malmö and a few other minor airports also have direct international flights. Getting between airports and city centres usually isn't a problem in Sweden thanks to good transport networks.

Tickets

SAS flies daily between London (Heathrow) and Stockholm Arlanda and between

London (Heathrow) and Gothenburg. You can also fly directly to Stockholm from Dublin, and from Manchester (daily except Saturday). SAS also offers numerous daily direct services between Stockholm and various European capitals (including Amsterdam, Brussels, Copenhagen, Helsinki, Moscow, Oslo, Paris and Reykjavík), but many are routed via Copenhagen or Frankfurt. The airline's North American hub is New York City's Newark Airport, with daily flights to/ from Stockholm. There are also daily direct flights between Chicago and Stockholm. SAS flies directly between Stockholm and Bangkok four times weekly, with connections to/from Australia.

Other airlines, including Ryanair, Skyways, City Airlines and Goodjet, connect Swedish cities with European capitals and the major business centres – see The UK and Continental Europe sections later in this chapter for more information and contact details.

World aviation has never been so competitive, making air travel better value than ever. But you have to research the options carefully to make sure you get the best deal. The Internet is an increasingly useful resource for checking air fares.

Full-time students and people under 26 years (under 30 in some countries) have access to better deals than other travellers. You have to show a document proving your date of birth or a valid International Student Identity Card (ISIC) when buying your ticket and boarding the plane.

Generally, there is nothing to be gained by buying a ticket direct from the airline. Discounted tickets are released to selected travel agents and specialist discount agencies, and these are usually the cheapest deals going.

One exception to this rule is the expanding number of 'no-frills' carriers, which mostly sell onto direct to travellers. Unlike the 'full-service' airlines, no-frills carriers often make one-way tickets available at around half the return fare, meaning that it is easy to put together an open-jaw ticket when you fly to one place but leave from another.

The other exception is booking on the Internet. Many airlines, both full-service and no-frills, offer some excellent fares to Web surfers. They may sell seats by auction or simply cut prices to reflect the reduced cost of electronic selling.

Many travel agencies around the world have websites, which can make the Internet a quick and easy way to compare prices. There is also an increasing number of on-line agents that operate only on the Internet.

On-line ticket sales work well if you are doing a simple one-way or return trip on specified dates. However, on-line super-fast fare generators are no substitute for a travel agent who knows all about special deals, has strategies for avoiding layovers and can offer advice on everything from which airline has the best vegetarian food to the best travel insurance to bundle with your ticket.

You may find the cheapest flights are advertised by obscure agencies. Most such firms are honest and solvent, but there are some rogue fly-by-night outfits around. Paying by credit card generally offers protection, as most card issuers provide refunds if you can prove you didn't get what you paid for. Similar protection can be obtained by buying a ticket from a bonded agent, such as one that's covered by the Air Travel Organiser's Licence (ATOL) scheme in the UK. Agents who accept only cash should hand over the tickets straight away and not tell you to 'come back tomorrow'. After you've made a booking or paid your deposit, call the airline and confirm that the booking was made. It's generally not advisable to send money (even

cheques) through the post unless the agent is very well established – some travellers have reported being ripped off by fly-by-night mail-order ticket agents.

If you purchase a ticket and later want to make changes to your route or get a refund, you need to contact the original travel agent. Airlines issue refunds only to the purchaser of a ticket – usually the travel agent who bought the ticket on your behalf. Also many travellers change their routes halfway through their trips, so think carefully before you buy a ticket that is not easily refunded.

Travellers with Special Needs
If they're warned early enough, airlines can often make special arrangements for travellers such as wheelchair assistance at airports or vegetarian meals on the flight. Children under two years travel for 10% of the standard fare (or free on some airlines) as long as they don't occupy a seat. They don't get a baggage allowance. 'Skycots', baby food and nappies should be provided by the airline if requested in advance. Children aged between two and 12 can usually occupy a seat for half to two-thirds of the full fare, and do get a baggage allowance.

The disability-friendly website Ⓦ www .allgohere.com has an airline directory that provides information on the facilities offered by various airlines.

Departure Tax
Sweden levies a departure tax of Skr95, but this should almost always be included in the price of your airline ticket.

The USA
The North Atlantic is the world's busiest long-haul air corridor and the flight options are bewildering. Larger newspapers such as the *New York Times, Chicago Tribune, San Francisco Examiner* and *Los Angeles Times* all produce weekly travel sections in which you'll find any number of travel agents' ads for air fares to Europe.

Thanks to the large ethnic Swedish population in Minnesota, North Dakota, Wisconsin, you may find small local agencies in those areas specialising in travel to Scandinavia and offering good-value charter flights. Check local telephone directories and newspapers. Otherwise, you should be able to fly return from New York or Boston to

Copenhagen, Oslo or Stockholm for around US$500 in the low season and US$1000 in the high season. With most tickets you can usually travel 'open jaws', allowing you to land in one city (Copenhagen, for example) and return from another (such as Stockholm) at no extra cost.

Icelandair (☎ 800 223 5500; W *www.icelandair.net*) flies from Baltimore-Washington, Boston, New York, Minneapolis and Orlando via Reykjavík to many European destinations including Stockholm, Copenhagen, Helsinki and Oslo. It often offers some of the best deals and also allows a free three-day stopover in Reykjavík on all its transatlantic flights (not applicable to tickets purchased on the Internet), making it a great way to spend a few days in Iceland. Accommodation, food and surface transport costs are extra.

On the other hand, if you're planning on flying within Scandinavia, **SAS** (☎ 800 221 2350; W *www.scandinavian.net*) offers its Scandinavian Air Pass to passengers on transatlantic flights (see the Air section in the Getting Around chapter). SAS has direct daily flights between Stockholm Arlanda and both Chicago (O'Hare) and New York (Newark) airports.

Airhitch (e *airhitch@airhitch.org*, W *www.airhitch.org*) specialises in Internet sales of stand-by fares to Europe for US$210/278 (including tax) one way from the East/West Coast, but the destinations are by region (not a specific city or country), so you'll need to be flexible.

Discount Travel Agencies Discount travel agents in the USA are known as consolidators (but you won't see a sign on the door saying Consolidator). San Francisco is the ticket consolidator capital of America, although some good deals can be found in Los Angeles, New York and other big cities. Consolidators can be found through the *Yellow Pages* or the major daily newspapers.

Council Travel (☎ 800 226 8624; W *www.counciltravel.com*), America's largest student travel organisation, became part of Usit World in 2001 and has around 70 offices nationwide. Call or check the website for details of your nearest office. **STA Travel** (☎ 800 781 4040; W *www.statravel.com*) has offices in Boston, Chicago, Miami, New York, Philadelphia, San Francisco and other major cities. Call the toll-free number for

office locations or visit its website. **Ticket Planet** (W *www.ticketplanet.com*) is a leading ticket consolidator in the USA and is recommended.

Canada

Canadian discount air-ticket sellers are also known as consolidators but their ticket prices tend to be about 10% higher than those sold in the USA.

The *Globe & Mail*, *Toronto Star*, *Montreal Gazette* and *Vancouver Sun* carry ads for travel agencies and are a good place to look for cheap fares.

Travel CUTS (☎ 1 866 246 9762; W *www.travelcuts.com*), Canada's national student travel agency, has offices in all major Canadian cities.

The UK

If you're looking for a cheap way into or out of Scandinavia, London is Europe's major centre for discount fares. In fact, you can often find air fares from London that either match or beat surface alternatives in terms of cost. Currently, one no-frills airlines offers cheap direct flights to Sweden, while another can get you to Copenhagen, from where you can easily get a train (25 minutes) across the bridge to Malmö. **Ryanair** (☎ 0870 156 9569; W *www.ryanair.com*) flies from London to Stockholm (100km south at Skavsta Airport near Nyköping), Gothenburg, Malmö and Västerås. Return fares start at under UK£100 including tax but, if you're lucky, you may get a promotional return fare for under UK£40. **Go** (☎ 0870 607 6543; W *www.go-fly.com*) flies from London (Stansted) to Copenhagen, with fares starting at around UK£70 return.

Other commercial airlines, including **SAS** (UK ☎ 0845 60 727 727, Sweden ☎ 020 72772; W *www.scandinavian.net*), offer return flights from London to Stockholm starting at around UK£120. **British Airways** (UK ☎ 08457 733 377, Sweden ☎ 0200 770098) flies daily direct between London Heathrow and Stockholm, and between Manchester and Gothenburg. **Finnair** (UK ☎ 08702 414 411, Sweden ☎ 020 781100) also has regular daily fights from London to Stockholm.

Skyways (Sweden ☎ 08-509 0505; W *www.skyways.se*) flies daily between Stockholm Arlanda airport and Manchester, and **City Airline** (UK ☎ 08703 308 800, Sweden ☎ 0200

25050; W *www.cityairline.com)* connects Gothenburg and Linköping with London (Gatwick) and Manchester. From May to September, **Malmö Aviation** *(☎ 040-302155;* W *www.malmoaviation.se)* has weekly flights between Gothenburg and Dublin, and Malmö and Glasgow.

Discount air travel is big business in London. Advertisements for many travel agencies appear in the travel sections of the weekend broadsheet newspapers, in *Time Out,* the *Evening Standard* and in the free magazine *TNT.*

For students or travellers under 26 years, the most popular travel agency in the UK is **STA Travel** *(☎ 08701 600 599;* W *www.statravel.co.uk; 86 Old Brompton Rd, London SW7)*, which has branches throughout the country. STA Travel sells tickets to all travellers but caters especially to young people and students.

Other travel agencies include **Trailfinders** *(☎ 020-7938 3939; 194 Kensington High St, London, W8 7RG)*; **Bridge the World** *(☎ 020-7734 7447;* W *www.bridgetheworld.com; 4 Regent Place, London, W1B 5EA)*; and **Ebookers** *(☎ 08700 107 000;* W *www.ebookers.com)*.

Continental Europe

Although London is the travel discount capital of Europe, there are also several other cities where you will find a range of good deals, particularly Amsterdam, Athens and Berlin. Generally, there is not much variation in air fares for departures from the main European cities. All the major airlines are usually offering some sort of deal, and travel agents generally have a number of deals on offer, so shop around.

SAS can connect you with all major Scandinavian cities and other European capitals and holiday or business centres. **Finnair** connects Stockholm with a number of Finnish cities, including Helsinki (around 15 flights per day), Tampere, Turku and Vaasa. **Skyways** has flights from regional centres like Kalmar, Karlstad, Linköping and Örebro to Copenhagen, and also between Örebro and Oslo, and Stockholm Arlanda and Vaasa in Finland.

GoodJet *(☎ 031-708 9000;* W *www.goodjet.com)* is a new Swedish budget airline offering cheap flights from Stockholm, Gothenburg and Malmö to Paris and Nice (and Alicante in summer). There's a range of fares on the website, and often good bargains.

Across Europe many travel agencies have ties with STA Travel, from which cheap tickets can be purchased and STA-issued tickets can be altered (usually for a US$25 fee). STA and other discount outlets in important transport hubs include the following.

Alternativ Tours *(☎* 030-881 2089, W www.alternativ-tours.de) Wilmersdorferstrasse 94, D-10629 Berlin

Isyts *(☎* 01-0322 1267, e isyts@travelling.gr) 11 Nikis St, First Floor, Syntagma Square, 10557 Athens

Kilroy Travels *(☎* 020-524 5100, W www.kilroytravels.com) Singel 413-415, NL-1012 WP Amsterdam

My Travel *(☎* 0180-393333, W www.mytravel.nl) Kleinpolderlaan 4, Postbus 281, NL-2910 AG Nieuwerkerk aan den IJssel

OTU Voyages *(☎* 01-44 41 38 50, W www.otu.fr) 39 Ave Georges Bernanos, F-75005 Paris

SSR Travel *(☎* 01-297 1111, W www.statravel.ch, W www.ssr.ch) Ankerstrasse 112, 8026 Zürich

STA Travel *(☎* 030-310 0040, W www.statravel.de) Hardenbergstrasse 9, D-10623 Berlin

Voyages Wasteels *(☎* 0803 88 70 04, W www.wasteels.fr) 11 rue Dupuytren, F-75006 Paris

Australia

Cheap flights from Australia to Europe are usually via Southeast Asian capitals, with stopovers in Kuala Lumpur, Singapore or Bangkok, but flights via New Zealand and the US are only marginally dearer. If a long stopover between connections is necessary, transit accommodation may be included in the price of the ticket. If it's at your own expense, it may be worth considering a more expensive ticket.

Quite a few travel offices specialise in selling discount air tickets. Some travel agents, particularly smaller ones, advertise cheap air fares in the travel sections of weekend newspapers, such as the *Age* in Melbourne and the *Sydney Morning Herald.*

Two well-known agents for cheap fares are STA Travel and Flight Centre. **STA Travel** *(☎ 03-8417 6911,* ☎ *1300 733 035;* W *www.statravel.com.au; 260 Hoddle St, Abbotsford, Vic 3067)* has offices in all major cities and on many university campuses. You can also call **Flight Centre** *(☎ 131 133;* W *www.flightcentre.com.au)* for its locations; it has dozens of offices throughout Australia. For more details, check the website.

From Australia, flights to Stockholm require a couple of stopovers on the way, usually at Singapore or Bangkok and another European city. In the low season, expect to pay around A$1650 for a return fare with Air France/Qantas or KLM. Air France/Qantas and Cathay Pacific have high-season return fares starting from around A$2350.

New Zealand

Round-the-World (RTW) fares for travel to or from New Zealand are usually the best value, often cheaper than a return ticket. Depending on the airline, you may fly across Asia, with stopovers in India, Bangkok or Singapore, or across the USA, with stopovers in Honolulu or one of the Pacific Islands.

The *New Zealand Herald* has a travel section in which travel agents advertise fares. **Flight Centre** (☎ 0800 243544; ⓦ *www.flight centre.co.nz*) has a large **central office** *(Shop 3B, 205-225 Queen St)* in Auckland at the National Bank Towers, and there are many other branches throughout the country. **STA Travel** (☎ 0800 874 773; ⓦ *www.statravel .co.nz*) has a **main office** *(☎ 09-309 0458; Shop 2B, 182 Queen St)* in Auckland; there are also other offices in Auckland and other towns and cities in New Zealand.

From New Zealand, Lufthansa offers some of the best deals for travel to Scandinavia. Low season return fares to Stockholm start from around NZ$2300/2700 in low/ high season.

Africa

Nairobi and Johannesburg are the best places in Africa to buy tickets to Europe, thanks to the strong competition between their many bucket shops.

Some major airlines have offices in Nairobi, which is a good place to determine the standard fare before doing the rounds of the travel agencies. Getting several quotes is a good idea since prices always change. One of the best agencies in Nairobi (and the best for budget travellers) is **Flight Centres** *(☎ 02-210024;* ⓔ *fcswwat@arcc.or.ke; Lakhamshi House, Biashara St)*.

From South Africa, Air Namibia and South African Airlines offer particularly cheap return youth fares to London. **Rennies Travel** *(☎ 011-833 1441;* ⓦ *www.rennies travel.co.za; Unitas Building, 42 Marshall St, Johannesbury)* has a comprehensive network of agencies throughout South Africa and is also the agent for Thomas Cook. **STA Travel** *(☎ 021-418 4689;* ⓦ *www.statravel.co.za; 31 Riebeeck St, Cape Town)* also has offices throughout the country. This international organisation has taken over the student/ budget travel agency business in Southern Africa.

Asia

Most Asian countries offer fairly competitive air-fare deals with Bangkok, Singapore and Hong Kong the best places to shop around for discount tickets. Hong Kong's travel market can be unpredictable, but some excellent bargains are available if you are lucky.

Lauda Air *(*ⓦ *www.laudaair.com)* flies to Vienna from Bangkok. **STA Travel** has branches in Bangkok, Kuala Lumpur, Manila, Singapore, Taipei and Tokyo. Mumbai and Delhi are India's air transport hubs but tickets are slightly cheaper in Delhi. Aeroflot and LOT offer inexpensive deals from India to Europe.

LAND

Direct access to Sweden by land is possible from Norway, Finland and Denmark. Train and bus journeys are also possible from the Continent – these vehicles go directly to ferries and if you sleep, you won't even notice the sea journey! If you're driving include ferry fares in your budget.

The new Öresund toll bridge linking Copenhagen with Malmö was officially opened in July 2000, creating a major direct rail/road link between Denmark and Continental Europe.

Border Crossings

Customs and immigration posts on border crossings between Sweden and Denmark, Finland or Norway are usually deserted, so passports are rarely checked. There are many minor roads between Sweden and Norway without any border formalities at all.

Transport Operators

Contact details for the major transport operators providing services across Swedish borders are listed here.

Eurolines (☎ 020 987377, 🔲 www.eurolines.com) Long-distance express buses throughout Europe. Main offices in Sweden are at Busstop, Cityterminalen in Stockholm; and Kyrkogatan 40, Gothenburg.

Säfflebussen (☎ 020 1600 600, 🔲 www.safflebussen.se) Long-distance buses within Sweden and to Oslo in Norway and Copenhagen in Denmark.

Swebus Express (☎ 0200 218218, 🔲 www.swebusexpress.se) Long-distance buses within Sweden and to Oslo in Norway.

Sveriges Järnväg (SJ, ☎ 0771-757575, 🔲 www.sj.se) Trains lines in the southern part of the country, and to Copenhagen.

Tågkompaniet (☎ 020 444111, 🔲 www.tagkompaniet.se) Trains in the north of the country, and to Narvik (Norway).

Other operators and their contact details are listed in the appropriate sections following. Prices listed are for one-way fares.

Norway

Bus Five times daily **Säfflebussen** runs between Stockholm and Oslo (from Skr250, 7½ hours) via Örebro and Karlstad, and five times daily between Gothenburg and Oslo (from Skr150, four hours). **Swebus Express** runs three times daily on the Stockholm–Oslo route and six times daily between Gothenburg and Oslo, charging similar prices. **Nor-Way Bussekspress** (Oslo ☎ 47-8154 4444; 🔲 www.nor-way.no) also has three daily services between Stockholm and Oslo, and a few buses between Oslo and Denmark/Continental Europe pass through Gothenburg and/or Malmö, however its fares are much more expensive than those of the Swedish operators (eg, Nkr370 Oslo–Stockholm).

In the north, once daily buses from Umeå to Mo i Rana (Skr210, eight hours) and from Skellefteå to Bodø (Skr400, nine hours, not Saturday) are run by **Länstrafiken i Västerbotten** (☎ 020 910019; 🔲 www.lanstrafikeniac.se) and **Länstrafiken i Norrbotten** (☎ 020 470047; 🔲 www.ltnbd.se), respectively. Länstrafiken run buses in a number of counties to within a few kilometres of the Norwegian border.

Train The main rail links run from Stockholm to Oslo, from Gothenburg to Oslo, from Stockholm to Östersund and Storlien (Norwegian trains continue to Trondheim), and from Luleå to Kiruna and Narvik.

Two or three daily trains run between Stockholm and Oslo (Skr535, six hours). Daily train services link Stockholm and Trondheim (from Skr590, 12 hours). Other lines link Stockholm to Narvik (Skr600 including couchette, from 18 hours), and Helsingborg to Oslo (Skr500, seven hours), via Gothenburg (Skr345, four hours). Taking X2000 high-speed trains for all or part of these journeys will increase the prices quoted here.

Car & Motorcycle The main highways between Sweden and Norway are the E6 from Gothenburg to Oslo, the E18 from Stockholm to Oslo, the E14 from Sundsvall to Trondheim, the E12 from Umeå to Mo i Rana, and the E10 from Kiruna to Bjerkvik. Many secondary roads also cross the border. Border-crossing points and formalities range from nonexistent to hardly noticeable.

Denmark

Bus Five days per week, **Eurolines** runs buses between Stockholm and Copenhagen (Skr433/482 low/high season, nine hours) and daily between Gothenburg and Copenhagen (Skr180/260, 4½ hours). **Säfflebussen** buses also regularly connect the same cities for much the same prices (slightly cheaper on the daily Stockholm–Copenhagen route).

Train There are trains running every 20 minutes between Copenhagen and Malmö (Skr70, 35 minutes) via the Öresund bridge, and connecting with many towns in Skåne. Trains usually stop at Copenhagen Airport. Around 10 daily trains run between Copenhagen and Stockholm (Skr600, from five hours), via Norrköping, Linköping, Lund and Malmö. A further five or six services operate between Copenhagen and Gothenburg via Halmstad, Helsingborg, Lund and Malmö. There are trains every hour or two connecting Copenhagen, Kristianstad and Karlskrona. Taking X2000 high-speed trains for all or part of these journeys will increase the price.

Car & Motorcycle You can now drive across the Öresund toll bridge on the E20 motorway from Copenhagen to Malmö. The tolls at Lernacken (on the Swedish side) certainly reflect the expense of building the bridge. A car up to 6m long will cost Skr275

(Dkr220) to cross the bridge and a motorcycle will cost Skr150 (Dkr120).

Finland

Bus Although there are seven crossing points along the river border between Sweden and Finland, only one is used by bus services. Frequent buses run from Haparanda to Tornio (Skr10, 10 minutes) and on to Kemi (Skr45, 45 minutes). Regular buses link Boden and Luleå with Haparanda, and Tornio/Kemi with Oulu (Finland). **Tapanis Buss** (☎ 0922-12955; W www.tapanis.se) runs express coaches from Stockholm to Tornio via Haparanda twice a week via the E4 Hwy (Skr450, 15 hours). The company's website is in Swedish only.

Länstrafiken i Norrbotten (☎ 020 470047; W www.ltnbd.se) operates buses as far as Karesuando, and from here it's only a few minutes walk across the bridge to Kaaresuvanto (Finland). There are also regular regional services that run from Haparanda to Övertorneå (some continue to Pello, Pajala and Kiruna) – you can walk across the border at Övertorneå or Pello and pick up a Finnish bus to Muonio, with onward connections from there to Kaaresuvanto and Tromsø (Norway).

Train It's only possible to reach Boden or Luleå in northern Sweden by train – from there it's necessary to continue by bus (bus services from Boden or Luleå to Haparanda and Kemi are free for those with rail passes).

Car & Motorcycle The main highways between Sweden and Finland are the E4 from Umeå to Kemi and No 45 from Gällivare to Kaaresuvanto; five other minor roads cross the border.

Germany

Bus There are six **Eurolines** (W www.euro lines.com) services a week between Stockholm and Hamburg (Skr818, 15 to 16 hours). The Gothenburg–Berlin route costs from Skr549 one way (13 to 16 hours, daily), while the Stockholm–Berlin route costs from Skr818 (18 to 20 hours, three weekly).

Train Hamburg is the central European gateway for Scandinavia, with several direct trains daily to Copenhagen and a few on to Stockholm. The ferry between Germany and Denmark (Puttgarden to Rødby Havn) is included in the ticket price.

There are direct overnight trains running every day between Berlin and Malmö via the Trelleborg–Sassnitz ferry. The journey takes nine hours and a couchette/bed costs Skr800/1135. See W www.berlin-night-express.com for details.

The UK

Bus Fans of long and arduous journeys can bus it between London and Stockholm in 30 to 35 hours, but you may have to change buses three times. **Eurolines** (W www.euro lines.com) operates this service one to four times weekly, all year, via Amsterdam and Hamburg and reservations are compulsory. The one-way/return fare is from Skr1624/2524 (UK£95/152), so it may well be cheaper to fly! Eurolines also runs buses from London to Gothenburg (from Skr1433/UK£83 one-way, 25 hours) five times weekly.

Train Travelling by train from the UK to Sweden can be more expensive than flying, but at least you can stop en route. The Channel Tunnel makes land travel possible between Britain and Continental Europe. From Brussels, you can connect to Hamburg, which is the main gateway to Scandinavia.

From London, a return 2nd-class train trip will cost around UK£300 to Copenhagen and around UK£400 to Stockholm or Oslo, but these prices include couchettes and a five-day ScanRail pass. For reservations and tickets, contact **Deutsche Bahn UK** (☎ 08702 435 363).

SEA

Forget travelling to Sweden by ship, unless by 'ship' you mean one of the many ferry services operating in the Baltic and North Seas. There is just a handful of ships that still carry passengers across the Atlantic; they don't sail often and are very expensive, even compared with full-fare air tickets.

For ferry bookings, children, students and seniors usually receive discounted rate; many rail-pass holders will also get reduced fares. If you're a family or small group transporting your own car on the ferries, ask about *bilpaket* (car package) rates, which includes a ticket for your car and often up to five passengers. It is generally cheaper to travel from Sunday to Thursday, and on day crossings (where both day and night services are offered). You'll invariably pay more to travel at busy times like weekends (especially overnight cruises on Friday or Saturday) and during the peak season (mid-June to mid-August).

Ferry

Ferry connections between Sweden and Denmark, Estonia, Finland, Germany, Latvia, Lithuania, Norway, Poland and the UK provide straightforward links, especially for anyone bringing their own vehicle. Note that in most cases, the quoted fares for cars (usually up to 6m long) also include up to five passengers. Most lines offer substantial discounts for seniors, students and children, and cruises and other special deals may be available – always ask when booking.

If you're travelling by international ferry from Estonia, Finland (via Åland), Latvia, Lithuania, Norway or Poland, consider purchasing your maximum duty-free alcohol allowance on the boat, as alcohol (particularly spirits) is expensive in Sweden. Even if you don't drink, it will make a welcome gift for Swedish friends.

Denmark There are numerous ferries between Denmark and Sweden, although all boats between Malmö and Copenhagen ceased in 2002; the opening of the new bridge and the excellent train connections between the two cities saw ferry passenger numbers drop dramatically. For the same reasons the ferry service between Landskrona and Copenhagen has also ceased.

The quickest and most frequent services connecting the two countries are between Helsingør and Helsingborg, with three operators plying the route (crossing time is around 20 minutes). **Scandlines** (☎ 042-186300; W www.scandines.se) runs a 24-hour service, with a crossing every 20 to 30 minutes (Skr22; bicycles free; cars with up to nine passengers Skr275). **Sundsbussarna** (☎ 042-216060; W www.sundsbussarne.dk/se) has regular passenger-only ferries to Helsingør from around 7am to 8pm daily (Skr22, bikes Skr11). The frequent, 24-hour **HH-Ferries** (☎ 042-198000; W www.hhferries.se) service to Helsingør is the cheapest, both for individual passengers (Skr18; although the price can be as low as Skr9 on weekdays outside of summer) and cars

(Skr245, with up to five passengers). Those websites are only in Swedish and Danish.

There are also frequent services between Sweden and Jutland, all operated by **Stena Line** (☎ 031-704 0000; W www.stenaline.se). Ticket prices vary with season, but it's always cheaper to travel Monday to Thursday. There's a regular ferry between Gothenburg and Frederikshavn five to seven times daily; the crossing takes a little over three hours (Skr100 to Skr170; bicycles Skr50 to Skr120; cars with up to five passengers Skr595 to Skr995). There is also a fast ferry operating on this route up to three times daily; it covers the journey in only two hours (Skr140 to Skr195; bicycles Skr75 to Skr145; cars Skr745 to Skr1145). Finally, three or four crossings sail daily between Grenå and Varberg, taking around four hours (Skr100 to Skr140; bicycles Skr50 to Skr75; cars Skr595 to Skr795).

The Ystad to Rønne (Bornholm) ferry is run by **BornholmsTrafikken** (☎ 0411-558700; W www.bornholmferries.dk). There are both conventional (two hours) and fast (80 minutes) services, two to nine times daily. Prices are from Skr182 to Skr234; bikes Skr52; cars Skr260 to Skr409, including two passengers.

Estonia Between Sweden and Estonia, **Tallink** (☎ 08-666 6001; W www.tallink.ee) plies two routes. The Stockholm–Tallinn ferry operates every second day (overnight, 15 hours). Tickets are from Skr300 to Skr385 (cabin berths from Skr180); bicycles cost Skr120 and cars cost from Skr400 to Skr500. The Kapellskär–Paldiski service operates daily, and the crossing takes nine to 10 hours. Tickets cost from Skr175 to Skr265 (cabin berths from Skr150); bikes cost Skr90 and cars cost Skr360.

V-V Line (☎ 0490-258080; W www.vv lines.com) connects Paldiski and Västervik a few times a week. This is more a service for freight than for passengers; tickets are much more expensive than Tallink at Skr1000 for foot passengers; transporting a car also costs Skr1000 (this price includes the driver's fare). The crossing takes 16 to 17 hours.

Finland Daily services throughout the year are available on Stockholm–Turku and Stockholm–Helsinki routes, all via the Åland islands (these islands are exempt from the abolition of duty-free within the EU, making them a popular outing for Swedes, who go there to buy cheap alcohol). There are also inexpensive connections to the Åland islands from Kapellskär and Grisslehamn, north of Stockholm. Further north, there are connections from both Umeå and Härnösand to Vaasa. Note that Helsinki is called Helsingfors in Swedish, and Turku is known as Åbo.

Silja Line (☎ 08-222140; **W** www.silja.com) sails daily (overnight) from Stockholm to Helsinki (around 15 hours) and to Turku (day and night crossings; 11 hours). In low season (September to early May), the ferry on the Turku route arrives at and departs from tiny Kapellskär, about 90km northeast of Stockholm, and there are connecting buses operated by Silja Line (Skr50). All ships call briefly at Mariehamn in Åland. Note that there's a lower age limit of 18, unless travelling with parents.

Tickets on the Stockholm–Helsinki route include cabin berths and cost from Skr333 per person in a basic, four-berth cabin (more expensive for travel from Thursday to Saturday, and in peak season). Cars up to 6m long cost Skr265 (excluding passengers), or from Skr727, including up to five passengers; bicycles cost Skr75. Breakfast on board costs Skr60; the buffet dinner is Skr207.

On the Stockholm–Turku crossings, day passage costs from Skr161, night passage from Skr200 (again, it's more expensive to travel from Thursday to Saturday, and in peak season). Cars, excluding passengers, cost Skr190/245 by day/night (or from Skr414/497 with up to five passengers), and bicycles cost Skr75. You can sail with Silja Line to Mariehamn (Skr99 one-way or return, and Skr99/45 per car/bicycle, six hours) but they can only return you to Sweden.

Viking Line (☎ 08-452 4000; **W** www .vikingline.fi) operates daily on the same routes as Silja Line (also all via Åland), but in high season it offers passage to Turku from both Stockholm and Kapellskär. There are age restrictions on all services – a minimum age of 20 years from Sunday to Thursday, 23 years on Friday and Saturday crossings. Tickets for the overnight ferry from Stockholm to Helsinki start at Skr270 (more expensive from Thursday to Saturday), and a berth in a cabin start at Skr220 (double this price for crossings on Thursday and Saturday nights, triple on Friday). Cars (passengers not included) start at Skr193; transporting a bike

costs Skr37. Breakfast is Skr58.50, the dinner buffet is Skr171. For sailings from Stockholm to Turku, a ticket costs from Skr130/158 per day/night crossing; cabins on the night-time crossing cost from Skr164 per person. Transporting a car costs Skr166/193 per day/night trip, and a bike costs Skr37. Trips from Kapellskär to Turku are slightly cheaper than from Stockholm, but you may have to factor in the cost of the connecting bus, operated by Viking Line (Skr55). To travel from Kapellskär to Åland costs just Skr50 (return journey included).

There are two companies operating ferries between Umeå and Vaasa in Finland. **RG Line** (☎ 090-185200; **W** www.rgline.com) is the more passenger friendly of the two. Its boats depart at least five times a week (more frequently in high season); the journey takes four hours. Passenger tickets cost Skr360; to transport a car/bicycle costs Skr360/45, or the 'car package' is Skr1155 and includes passage for a car and up to four people. There are bus connections from Umeå's town centre to the dock. **Botnia Link** (☎ 0611-550555, **W** www.botnialink.se) is the second ferry company, used primarily by freight trucks. It is slightly cheaper, however: tickets cost Skr310 and transporting a car is Skr310; there are four crossings a week. Botnia Link also offers a service four times weekly between Härnösand and Vaasa; again, this is popular with freight trucks. The crossing takes seven to eight hours; tickets cost Skr490 (cars Skr310).

A few companies offer cheap overnight cruises from Stockholm to the Åland islands. **Birka Cruises** (☎ 08-714 5520; **W** www.birka cruises.com) offers passenger-only 22-hour trips to Mariehamn in Åland and return. The return price is from Skr410, including cabin accommodation, dinner and breakfast. **Ånedin-Linjen** (☎ 08-456 2200; **W** www .anedinlinjen.com) runs a passenger ferry from Stockholm to Mariehamn six days a week (six hours). Fares start at Skr50 (couchette) and rise to Skr695 for a luxury suite. The website is in Swedish only.

The quickest and cheapest ferry to the Åland islands departs from Grisslehamn, about 100km north of Stockholm. The **Eckerö Linjen** (☎ 0175-25800; **W** www.eckero linjen.fi) ferry departs up to five times daily from Grisslehamn and arrive two hours later at Eckerö (Åland). One-way and return tickets cost just Skr50/80 in winter/summer (cars Skr50/70, bicycles free). Eckerö Linjen runs regular bus connections from Uppsala and Stockholm to Grisslehamn.

Germany Overnight sailings between Gothenburg and Kiel are run by **Stena Line** (☎ 031-704 0000; W www.stenaline.se), departing daily at 7.30pm from each port. The journey time is 13 to 14 hours; passenger fares are from Skr310/610 in the low/high season, and cars (including driver) are from Skr640/1440. Cabin reservation is compulsory and charges start at Skr180 per person. Some days are cheaper to travel than others (although this varies with season) – inquire when making bookings.

Trelleborg is the main gateway with more than a dozen ferries arriving daily. **Scandlines** (☎ 042-816100; W www.scandlines.se) sails between Trelleborg and Sassnitz five times daily in each direction. The journey takes 3½ hours and fares are Skr70/90 in the low/high season. Transporting a car costs Skr730/880, including up to nine passengers, and a passenger with a bicycle pays Skr105/135. Scandlines also operates a ferry between Trelleborg and Rostock, two or three times daily, which take around six hours. Passenger fares are Skr150/195 low/ high season, a car with up to nine people costs Skr795/1130, and a passenger with bicycle pays Skr150/195.

TT-Line (☎ 0410-56200; W www.ttline .com) runs boats from Trelleborg to Rostock and Travemünde. It has regular and high-speed ferries on the Trelleborg–Rostock route (the regular ferry takes 5½ hours, the catamaran takes 2½ hours); the sailing time to Travemünde is around seven hours. Tickets on all crossings range from Skr270 to Skr380, bikes are Skr50. A car and driver cost from Skr860 to Skr1550, or including up to five passengers the cost is Skr990 to Skr1750. Cabins are available on night crossings (from Skr195 per person).

Latvia There is a **Riga Sea Line** (☎ 08-545 88158; W www.rigasealine.lv) ferry operating between Nynäshamn and Riga (eight hours, every second day), with connecting buses to/from Stockholm. Tickets cost from Skr672; car tickets cost Skr616.

V-V Line (☎ 0490-258080; W www.vv lines.com) connects Nynäshamn and Ventspils

daily except Monday. This is more a service for freight than for passengers; passenger tickets start at Skr800; a car (plus driver) costs Skr1000. The crossing takes approximately 10 hours.

Lithuania There's a daily ferry run by **Lisco Line** (☎ 0454-33680; W www.shipping.lt) between Karlshamn and Klaipėda (17 hours). Passenger fares start at Skr570 (cabin berths cost from Skr810); cars cost Skr660.

Norway There's a daily overnight **DFDS Seaways** (☎ 042-266000; W www.dfdssea ways.com) ferry between Copenhagen and Oslo, via Helsingborg. Fares between Helsingborg and Oslo (14 hours) range from Skr625 to Skr1025, according to the season and day of the week; bike fare is Skr75; cars are charged Skr350. **DFDS Seaways** (☎ 031-650650) also sails from Gothenburg to Kristiansand, three days a week (from seven hours). Passenger fares cost from Skr150 to Skr400, and a car costs from Skr350 to Skr450.

A **Color Line** (☎ 0526-62000; W www.col orline.com) ferry between Strömstad (Sweden) and Sandefjord (Norway) sails two to six times daily year-round (two hours). Tickets cost Skr130/160 in the low/high season (rail passes get 50% discount); bicycles cost Skr27/35 and cars Skr135/175.

Poland Between Ystad and Swinoujscie **Polferries** (☎ 040-121700; W www.polferries .se) sails daily, taking nine hours overnight (from Swinoujscie to Ystad) or seven hours by day (in the reverse direction). One-way passenger fares are Skr450/520 in low/high season; cabin places range from Skr60 to Skr350. You'll pay Skr720/840 in low/high season for a car (including driver) or Skr1190/1350 for a car with five people. Bicycles travel free. The same company sails overnight between Nynäshamn and Gdańsk three times a week (daily from May to September), the journey takes around 18 hours. Passenger fares are Skr470/540 in low/high season; cabin berths range from Skr90 to Skr425. You'll pay Skr910/990 in low/high season for a car (plus driver) or Skr1550/1690 for a car with five people. Again, bicycles travel free.

Unity Line (☎ 0411-556900; W www.unity line.pl) also has daily crossings between

Ystad and Swinoujscie, with crossings taking around eight hours. Fares are identical to those of Polferries.

Stena Line (☎ 031-704 0000; W *www.stena line.se*) sails between Karlskrona and Gdynia once or twice daily year-round. Crossings take around 10 hours and adult fares are from Skr335 to Skr395 depending on season and time of travel. Overnight reclining chairs cost Skr70 and cabins cost from Skr550 to Skr1090 per room (with two, four or six beds); these are obligatory on night crossings. Car fares (including the driver) range from Skr675 to Skr895, or Skr895 to Skr1295 (including five passengers).

The UK There are two **DFDS Seaways** (UK ☎ 08705-333000, Gothenburg ☎ 031-650650; W *www.dfdsseaways.com*) crossings per week between Gothenburg and Newcastle via Kristiansand (Norway). Departures from Newcastle are on Monday and Friday, and from Gothenburg on Thursday and Sunday. The trip takes 25 hours. The cheapest cabin tickets (four-berth, with shared facilities) start at UK£64 one-way in winter, and rise to UK£134 from mid-June to mid-August. Other more luxurious cabins are available, the nicest with fares from UK£144/214 per person in low/high season. Cars cost from UK£45 to UK£65 each way, but check out the 'all-in-a-car' deal: it may work out cheaper. Bicycles are shipped free.

If you're heading from the UK to Malmö, you could use DFDS Seaways' crossing from Harwich to Esbjerg, then drive across Denmark; see its website for details.

Transatlantic Passenger Ships & Freighters

Regular, long-distance passenger ships disappeared with the advent of cheap air travel and were replaced by a small number of luxury cruise ships. Transatlantic passenger ships only go to the UK, so onward transport is required to reach Sweden. Cunard Line's **QE II** (US ☎ 800 728 6273, UK ☎ 0800 052 3840) sails between New York and Southampton around nine times a year each way, taking five nights/six days per trip. The cost of a one-way crossing starts at around US$1800, but they also offer return and 'fly one-way' deals (including a Concorde flight). In July, it does a circuit around the Arctic region, including Nordkapp (North Cape) in

Norway. Most travel agents can provide details.

A more adventurous (but not necessarily cheaper) alternative is to travel as a paying passenger on a freighter. These are far more numerous than cruise ships, and there are many more routes to chose from. With just a little bit of homework, you'll be able to sail to Europe from just about anywhere else in the world, with stopovers at exotic little-known ports. The book *Travel by Cargo Ship* (Cadogan, London, 1995) covers this subject.

Passenger freighters typically carry six to 12 passengers (more than 12 would require a doctor on board) and, although they're less luxurious than dedicated cruise ships, they provide a real taste of life at sea. Schedules tend to be flexible and costs vary, but normally hover around US$100 a day; vehicles can often be included for an additional charge.

ORGANISED TOURS

If you're short of time or have a specialised interest, it may be worth looking into an organised tour. Several reputable operators offer affordable itineraries, concentrating either on Scandinavia in general or Sweden in particular. The US and UK pages of the official website for the **Swedish Travel and Tourism Council** (W *www.visit-sweden.com*) lists a large number of tour operators, with links to their home pages.

North America
Borton Overseas (☎ 800 843 0602, W www .bortonoverseas.com) 5412 Lyndale Ave S, Minneapolis, MN 55419. Borton is run by a Norwegian and offers an array of trips to Scandinavia, ranging form city breaks to cruises or active holidays (cycling, trekking etc).

Brekke Tours (☎ 800 437 5302, W www.brekke tours.com) 802 N 43rd St, Grand Forks, ND 58203. Brekke caters mainly to North Americans of Scandinavian descent. It offers a 12-day coach tour taking in Copenhagen, Oslo, Bergen, Dalarna and Stockholm from US$3395, including airfares from the US. There are a number of other escorted or independent tours available.

Nordic Saga (☎ 800 848 6449, W www.nordic saga.com) 303 5th Avenue S, Edmonds, WA 98020. There's a wide range of activities and vacations on offer here, including ski packages, cycling in Gotland (four days from US$359) and trips to see the Vasaloppet ski race.

Nordique Tours Norvista (☎ 800 995 7997, W www.nordiquetours.com) This company offers a selection of upmarket itineraries, independent or escorted, to various parts of Sweden, including Gotland, the Göta Canal and Glasriket. The self-drive, eight-day 'Swedish Countryside and Manor Houses' tour costs from US$1299 per person, including car hire.

Scantours (☎ 800 223 7226,  www.scantours .com) Scantours can arrange a plethora of tours, offering both escorted journeys or help with independent travel arrangements. Trips include cycling holidays and canal cruises, plus packages like three days in Dalarna (from US$365) and four days exploring the Lake Mälaren region (from US$470).

The UK

Arctic Experience (☎ 01737-214214, W www.arc tic-experience.co.uk) 29 Nork Way, Banstead, Surrey, SM7 1PB. This friendly agency is one of the most popular British tour operators to northern Scandinavia. It offers dog-sledging tours in Lappland (UK£1240 per week) and a wide range of winter activities, including snowmobile safaris based around the Ice Hotel in Jukkasjärvi.

Deep Forest (☎ 0870-757 2533, W www.deep -forest.co.uk) Mustill's Lane, Over, Cambridge CB4 5PW. Deep Forest provides a great range of adventure trips to Sweden (fishing, canoeing, trekking), plus city breaks to Stockholm and Gothenburg and holidays with a cultural theme (eg, Viking heritage or modern Swedish design).

Go Fishing Worldwide (☎ 020-8742 1556, W www.go-fishing-worldwide.com) 2 Oxford House, 24 Oxford Rd N, London, W4 4DH. This flexible company arranges fishing tours to various places, with prices between UK£475 and UK£1030 per person per week. It also offers weekend dog-sledging tours around Lycksele (Lappland) for UK£760, or a winter week in Kiruna, including an overnight dog-sledging tour, for UK£1305.

Scantours (☎ 020-7839 2927, W www.scantours uk.com) 47 Whitcomb St, London WC2H 7DH. Scantours offers a range of options in Sweden and Scandinavia, including eight days on Gotland (from UK£680, including flights from the UK) or nine days touring Dalarna and Lappland from UK£795.

Australia

Bentours (☎ 02-9241 1353, W www.bentours .com.au) Level 7, 189 Kent St, Sydney 2000. Bentours is an Australian agency specialising exclusively in Scandinavian travel. Offers assistance with air fares, ferry tickets and rail passes, as well as cycling and canal tours.

Getting Around

Although Sweden takes time and money to travel through, public transport is well organised with 24 different *länstrafik* (regional networks). Heavily subsidised, the networks offer some of the best bargains in Sweden. The general confusion of so many operators is partly solved by the Tågplus system, where one ticket is valid on trains and buses.

Bus, train and ferry information is available at Ⓦ www.tagplus.se. The three-part *Rikstidtabellen* directory gives timetables for all domestic ferry and train services, and *länstrafik* buses; buy it at railway stations or large newsagents for Skr80. Handier local timetables are available free or at nominal cost from tourist offices or the operators.

National air and train networks have discount schemes available, but the CSN and SFS student discount cards are only for those studying in Sweden. International Student Identification Cards (ISIC) will get discounts with some operators – it pays to ask.

AIR

Sweden's half-dozen domestic airlines mostly use Stockholm Arlanda as a hub, but there are some 20-odd regional **airports** (Ⓦ www.lfv.se). **SAS** (☎ 020 727000; Ⓦ www .scandinavian.net) has daily domestic flights from Malmö in the south to Kiruna in the north, but **Skyways** (☎ 020 959500; Ⓦ www .skyways.se) runs a larger network. **Malmö Aviation** (☎ 020 550010; Ⓦ www.malmoavi ation.se) also flies between a few major cities (eg, Gothenburg, Malmö, Stockholm and Umeå). **GoodJet** (☎ 031-708 9000; Ⓦ www .goodjet.com) is a new Swedish budget airline offering cheap flights between Stockholm, Gothenburg and Malmö.

Flying domestic is quite expensive, but substantial discounts are available, such as those for Internet bookings, student and youth fares, off-peak travel, return tickets booked at least seven days in advance or low-price tickets for accompanying family members and seniors. It's worth asking about stand-by fares; Malmö Aviation and SAS offer stand-by tickets for travellers under 26; these are good value at only Skr280 per flight (from Stockholm).

Visitors who fly SAS to Sweden from Continental Europe, North America or Asia can buy tickets on a Visit Scandinavia Air Pass, allowing one-way travel on direct flights between any two Scandinavian cities serviced by SAS, Skyways and other operators. Using the pass, domestic flights within Sweden cost €69 each (with the exception of the Stockholm–Kiruna route, which costs €122). International flights between Sweden, Denmark, Norway and Finland cost €80. You can buy up to eight tickets and they're valid for three months; they can be purchased after arriving in Sweden if you have a return SAS international ticket. For the latest information, call SAS or check their website.

BUS

You can travel by bus in Sweden on any of the 24 *länstrafik* networks, or on national long-distance routes.

Regional Networks

Länstrafik is usually complemented by the regional train system, and one ticket is valid on any bus, local or regional. Rules vary but transfers are usually free within one to four hours. Most counties are divided into zones; travel within one zone will cost from Skr13 to Skr17. Every time you enter a new zone, the price increases, but there's usually a maximum fare. Fares on local buses and trains are often identical.

Timetables explain the various discount schemes. There are usually good-value daily or weekly passes and many regions have 30-day passes for longer stays, or a special card for summer travel (usually valid from Midsummer to mid-August). The *värdekort* (value card), which you can 'top up' at any time, is also good: you pay, say, Skr200 for over Skr250 worth of travel. Always ask how the regional discount pass works as you may have to run the ticket through a machine, press buttons, tell the driver where you want to go, get your ticket stamped or something else.

In remote areas, taxis may have an arrangement with the county council to provide a reduced-fare taxi trip to your final destination. These fares are only valid when arranged in advance (they cannot be bought from the taxi departure point). Ask the regional bus company for details.

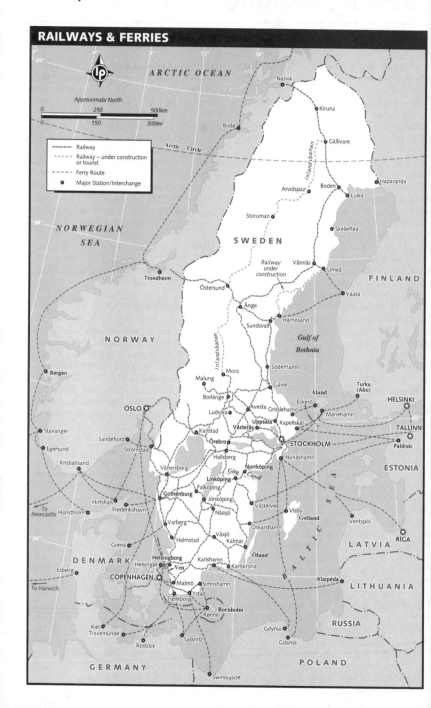

Express Buses

Swebus Express (☎ 0200 218218; W www.swebusexpress.se) has the largest 'national network' of express buses, but they only serve the southern half of the country (as far north as Mora in Dalarna). Fares for 'long' journeys (over 100km) are 30% cheaper if you travel between Monday and Thursday.

Svenska Buss (☎ 0771-676767; W www.svenskabuss.se) and the cheaper **Säfflebussen** (☎ 020 1600 600; W www.saffle-bussen.se) also connect many southern towns and cities with Stockholm. North of Gävle, regular connections with Stockholm are provided by several smaller operators, including **Ybuss** (☎ 0200 334444; W www.ybuss.se) from Sundsvall, Östersund and Umeå.

Most of the above websites are in Swedish only, but it shouldn't be too difficult to navigate them. Clicking on 'turlista' or 'tidtabell' should bring up routes and timetables, 'priser' or 'prislista' will give you prices. If you're a student or senior, it's worth asking about fare discounts, however most bus companies will only give student prices to holders of Swedish student cards (the exception is Swebus Express, where you can get an ISIC discount). Only Swebus Express doesn't require advance reservations – it always guarantees a seat.

TRAIN

Sweden has an extensive railway network and trains are certainly the fastest way to get around, although travellers should be aware that many destinations in the northern half of the country cannot be reached by train alone.

There are a few train operators in Sweden, although the national network of **Sveriges Järnväg** (SJ; ☎ 0771-757575; W www.sj.se) covers most main lines, especially in the southern part of the country. Its flag carriers are the X2000 fast trains running at speeds of up to 200km/h, with services from Stockholm to Falun, Gävle, Gothenburg, Jönköping, Karlstad, Malmö, Sundsvall, Växjö and Copenhagen. **Tågkompaniet** (☎ 020 444111; W www.tagkompaniet.se) operates overnight trains from Gothenburg and Stockholm north to Boden, Kiruna, Luleå and Narvik, and the lines north of Hänösand. The overnight trains have excellent facilities, including a dining car, cinema and even a glass-topped viewing car. (From June 2003, Tågkompaniet's services will be under the new management of Connex Transport, and travellers should expect some changes after the takeover.) In addition to these two major operators, several counties run small regional train networks.

Full-price, 2nd-class tickets are expensive, but there is a wide array of discounts offered, especially for booking a week or so in advance (ask for the *förköpsbiljet*), or at the last minute (for youth and pensioner fares). Students (with a Swedish CSN or SFS student card if aged over 26) and people aged under 26 get a 30% discount on the standard adult fare. All SJ ticket prices are reduced in summer, from late June to mid-August. X2000 tickets include a seat reservation. SJ trains don't allow bicycles to be taken on trains (they can be sent as unaccompanied luggage with an affiliated freight company for about Skr375).

In summer, almost 25 different tourist trains offer special rail experiences. The most notable is **Inlandsbanan** (☎ 063-194409; W www.inlandsbanan.se), a 1067km route from Mora to Gällivare and one of the great rail journeys in Scandinavia. Travel on this line is slow (the train travels at a speed of 50km/h) and it takes seven hours from Mora to Östersund (Skr240) and 15 hours from Östersund to Gällivare (Skr485). A special card allows two weeks' unlimited travel on the route for Skr950.

Station luggage lockers usually cost between Skr20 and Skr30 for 24 hours. Check that the station building will be open when you want to collect.

Train Passes

The Sweden Rail Pass, Eurodomino tickets and the international passes Inter-Rail, Eurail and ScanRail are accepted on SJ services and most other operators, such as regional trains (they often cooperate closely with SJ).

ScanRail (W www.scanrail.com) has a flexible rail pass covering travel in Denmark, Finland, Norway and Sweden. There are three versions: for travel on any five days within a two-month period, the pass costs UK£189/139 for 1st/2nd-class travel (UK£142/105 for travellers under 26); for travel on any 10 days within a two-month period, the pass costs UK£252/187 for 1st/2nd class (UK£189/140 for under 26s); for unlimited travel during 21 consecutive days, the cost of the pass is UK£291/216 for 1st/2nd class (UK£219/162 for those under 26).

If you're aged 60 or over, then you're eligible for the ScanRail Senior pass, which will allow 1st/2nd-class travel over five days in a two-month period for UK£169/123, 10 days in a two-month period for UK£225/166 and 21 consecutive days for UK£259/192.

It's best to buy your ScanRail pass outside Scandinavia – otherwise, you'll face restrictions. Obtaining rail passes in Sweden isn't entirely convenient, but they can be arranged in advance through **Sweden Booking** (☎ 0498-203380; W www.sweden booking.com) for a Skr115 fee.

ScanRail passes are valid on trains that are run by Linx (Copenhagen–Oslo, Oslo–Stockholm) and Tågkompaniet (Narvik–Stockholm–Gothenburg); state railways in Denmark (DSB), Finland (VR), Norway (NSB) and Sweden (SJ); and Swedish *länstrafik* trains; but not Stockholm Local (SL) trains. The pass also includes free travel on buses between Luleå/Boden and Haparanda, and on the Helsingør–Helsingborg (Scandlines) and Trelleborg–Sassnitz (SJ/DFO) boat services.

There's a 50% discount available to pass holders on the following ferry services.

route	operator
Rønne–Ystad	BornholmsTrafikken
Frederikshavn–	
Gothenburg	Stena Line
Grenå–Varberg	Stena Line
Stockholm–Helsinki	Viking or Silja Line
Stockholm–Turku	Viking or Silja Line
Travemünde–Trelleborg	TT Line
Rostock–Trelleborg	TT Line
Nynäshamn–Visby	Destination Gotland
Oskarshamn–Visby	Destination Gotland
Sandefjord–Strömstad	Color Scandi Line

The Mora-Gällivare Inlandsbanan gives a 25% discount on a two-week unlimited travel ticket (not on individual tickets).

X2000 trains require all rail-pass holders to pay a supplement of Skr50 (including the obligatory seat reservation). Seating reservations are also required for Tågkompaniet trains. The reservation supplements for non-X2000 (ie, InterCity) trains (Skr50) aren't obligatory, and there are no supplements for regional *länstrafik* trains.

CAR & MOTORCYCLE

Sweden has good roads and the excellent E-class motorways don't usually have traffic jams. There are no toll roads or bridges in Sweden (with the exception of the bridge from Malmö to Copenhagen). You will only need to bring a recognised full driving licence, even for car rental. If bringing your own car, you'll also need your vehicle registration documents.

Automatic ticket machines for street parking *(billetautomat)* are common and usually cost from Skr5 to Skr10 per hour during the day, but may well be free evenings and at weekends. It's worth getting a local to explain the wording and symbols on parking signs: 'avgift' means that payment is required; the 24-hour clock is used, and often days of the week are specified. In small and medium-sized towns, a sign that says 'skiva' indicates that parking is free for a specified amount of time (usually two hours), so long as you display a *skiva* on your dashboard. It's a cardboard clock used to indicate what time you parked the car, so inspectors know that you haven't overstayed your welcome! In towns where such a system used, you can often pick up a *skiva* at the local tourist office Cities have multistorey car parks *(P-hus)* that charge between Skr15 and Skr40 per hour.

Petrol costs around about Skr9.50/L. If your vehicle happens to breaks down, telephone the 24-hour towing service **Larmtjäns** (☎ 020 910040). Insurance Green Cards are recommended.

In the north, privately owned reindeer and wild elk (moose) are serious road hazards particularly around dawn and dusk. Look ou for black plastic bags tied to roadside trees o poles – this is a sign from local Sami peopl that they have reindeer herds grazing in the area. Report all incidents to police – failure to do so is an offence. Sandboxes on many roads may be a help in mud or snow. Bewar of trams in Gothenburg and Norrköping.

The Swedish national motoring associa tion is **Motormännens Riksförbund** (☎ 020 211111, ☎ 08-690 3800; W www.moto mannen.se; Sveavägen 159, SE-10435 Stock holm). Its website is in Swedish only.

Road Rules

Basic road rules conform to EU standards using international road signs. In Sweden you drive on and give way to the right (interestingly, Sweden drove on the left unti 1967). Headlights should be dipped bu must be on at all times when driving. Use c

Road Distances (km)

	Gävle	Gothenburg	Halmstad	Helsingborg	Jönköping	Kalmar	Karlstad	Kiruna	Linköping	Luleå	Malmö	Skellefteå	Stockholm	Sundsvall	Umeå	Uppsala	Växjö	Örebro	Östersund
Gävle	---																		
Gothenburg	514	---																	
Halmstad	590	145	---																
Helsingborg	672	227	82	---															
Jönköping	431	149	162	241	---														
Kalmar	536	346	248	262	209	---													
Karlstad	322	245	385	467	234	431	---												
Kiruna	1078	1577	1653	1735	1494	1603	1353	---											
Linköping	333	278	291	369	129	225	212	1400	---										
Luleå	752	1251	1327	1409	1168	1277	1041	333	1074	---									
Malmö	701	281	136	60	271	284	504	1764	398	1438	---								
Skellefteå	619	1118	1194	1276	1035	1144	908	460	941	133	1305	---							
Stockholm	173	478	497	575	335	411	313	1251	207	925	604	792	---						
Sundsvall	221	720	796	878	637	746	510	858	543	532	907	399	394	---					
Umeå	490	989	1065	1147	906	1015	779	589	812	262	1176	129	663	270	---				
Uppsala	102	455	531	612	372	447	289	1180	244	854	641	721	72	323	592	---			
Växjö	540	238	139	182	124	109	358	1603	217	1277	205	1144	424	746	1015	461	---		
Örebro	231	283	359	441	200	338	117	1294	113	968	470	835	197	437	706	172	309	---	
Östersund	379	775	869	951	717	874	538	815	659	582	987	464	552	186	365	481	839	546	---

seat belts is compulsory, and children under seven years old should be in the appropriate harness or child seat, if fitted.

The blood-alcohol limit is a stringent 0.02%. The maximum permitted speed on motorways and remote highways is 110km/h; in built-up areas 50km/h; on narrow rural roads 70km/h, and on highways 90km/h. The speed limit for cars towing caravans is 80km/h. Police use hand-held radar equipment to detect speeding and can impose on-the-spot fines of up to Skr1200.

On many highways broken lines define wide-paved edges, and a vehicle being overtaken is expected to move into this area to allow faster traffic to pass safely.

Rental

To rent a car you normally have to be at least 18 (sometimes 25) years of age, need to show a recognised licence (in some cases, an international driving permit), and may be required to pay by credit card.

The international rental chains are expensive, starting at around Skr600 per day with unlimited kilometres and third-party insurance for smaller models (typically a Renault Clio or Ford Fiesta), but there are some reasonable deals to be found if you shop around. Fly-drive packages can bring some savings, and weekend or summer packages may also be offered at discount rates. All the major firms (eg, Avis, Hertz, Europcar) have desks at Stockholm Arlanda airport and offices in most major cities. **Mabi Hyrbilar** (☎ 020 1101000; W www.mabi rent.se) is a national company with branches in many major cities and competitive rates. Prices for a small car are Skr170 per day plus Skr1.70 per kilometre, or Skr495 including 300km. For weekly rentals, prices start at Skr2195, including 1500km.

Cars can be hired from larger petrol stations at better rates (look out for signs saying 'biluthyrning' or 'hyrbilar'), but must be returned to the hiring point. **Statoil** (☎ 020 252525; W www.statoil.se/biluthyrn ing) charges from Skr150 per day plus Skr1.50 per kilometre. **OK-Q8** (☎ 020 850850; W www .okq8.se) has small cars from Skr295 per day, including an allowance of 100km. Both websites listed here are in Swedish only but price lists (*priser* or *prislista*) should be fairly self-explanatory.

Purchase

The used-car columns of *Dagens Nyheter* are best and if you understand Swedish you can check out its website (W www.dn.se). However, anything under Skr20,000 will be at least 10 years old and well used.

BICYCLE

Cycling is an excellent way to see Sweden – see the Activities chapter for details.

HITCHING

Hitching is never entirely safe in any country, and we don't recommend it. Travellers who decide to hitch should understand that they are taking a small but potentially serious risk. People who do choose to hitch will be safer if they travel in pairs and let someone know where they are planning to go.

Additionally, hitching isn't popular in Sweden, and the consensus is that you'll have less luck getting lifts than in other countries. However, the main highways (E4, E6, E10 and E22) aren't too bad and very long lifts are possible. Remember, it's prohibited to hitch on motorways.

BOAT

The national road authority, Vägverket, operates dozens of car ferries, but many are being replaced with bridges. They're part of the road network and are free.

An extensive boat network opens up the attractive Stockholm archipelago, and boat services on Lake Mälaren, west of Stockholm, are busy in summer. Gotland is served by regular ferries from Nynäshamn and Oskarshamn, Ven is served from Landskrona, and there are summer services to many other small islands off the Baltic and Gulf of Bothnia coasts. Boat passes, valid for 16 days (Skr385), are available for the Stockholm archipelago, and the quaint fishing villages off the west coast can normally be reached by boat with a regional transport pass – inquire at the Gothenburg tourist office.

The canals provide cross-country routes linking the main lakes. The longest cruises, on the historic Göta Canal from Söder-köping (south of Stockholm) to Gothenburg, run from mid-May to mid-September, take at least four days and include the lakes between. **Rederiaktiebolaget Göta Kanal** *(☎ 031-806315;* W *www.gotacanal.se)* operates three ships over the whole distance at fares of around Skr9500/13,600 per single/double, including full board and guided excursions. There are a number of companies that offer shorter, cheaper trips on sections of the canal – the tourist offices in this area can help.

LOCAL TRANSPORT

In Sweden, local transport is always linked with the regional *länstrafik* – rules and prices for city buses may differ slightly from long-distance transport, but a regional pass is valid both in the city and on the rural routes. There's usually a flat fare of around Skr15 in towns, and large cities operate a zone system. Tickets may be sold in strips (two tickets per zone, for instance), but it usually works out cheaper to get a day card or other travel pass.

Stockholm has an extensive underground metro system, and Gothenburg and Norrköping run tram networks. Gothenburg also has a city ferry service.

Beware of getting ripped off in taxis. You should be OK if the cab has a meter for measuring short fares, but for longer journeys (ie, to airports) and in many smaller towns, you should agree to a fare beforehand. In Stockholm, flag fall is around Skr32, then Skr7 per km.; most taxis in the capital will take you to Arlanda airport for between Skr350 and Skr450.

ORGANISED TOURS

There are many small tour companies around the country and recommended tours appear throughout this book. The largest tour operator of interest is **Svenska Turistföreningen** *(STF;* ☎ *020 292929;* e *info@stfturist.se,* W *www.meravsverige.nu; Box 25, SE-10120 Stockholm)*, which offers scores of events and tours around the country every season, mostly based on outdoor activities (from an afternoon of kayaking to a week-long hike in the northern mountains). Contact STF directly for information on these events – its brochure and website are in Swedish only.

Another helpful company is **Sweden Booking** *(☎ 0498-203380;* W *www.sweden booking.com; Östervåg 3A, SE-62145 Visby)* which can help organise rail tickets as well as interesting package trips, eg, a traditional Christmas in Dalarna (four days, Skr670) or canoeing in Värmland (four days, Skr150 including rental of camping equipment).

Stockholm

☎ 08 • pop 755,000

Stockholm is, without doubt, one of the most beautiful capital cities in the world, and right now it's an extremely hip destination, famed for its innovative design, fashion and music scenes. Gamla Stan (Old Town) is particularly lovely, especially in summer, but there re dozens more delights in this fair city.

Gamla Stan and some neighbouring areas re built on islands, surrounded by many channels and extensive areas of open water. The 24,000 rocky islands of the *skärgård* (archipelago) protect the urban islands from the open seas. The city waterways are utilised by all manner of craft, from yachts to ferries to luxury cruise liners. Stockholm's location, where the Mälaren lake empties into the sea, is ideal for trade and maritime connections as it allows freighters loaded with goods to berth near the city centre. Parts of the city are industrialised and, in stark contrast to the city centre's splendour, some bleak suburbs seem to be of Kafkaesque and Stalinist inspiration.

Around 1.8 million people live in Greater Stockholm and over 15% of them are immigrants, making for a lively and cosmopolitan atmosphere. Tourists can enjoy a wide range of international cuisine in the ethnic restaurants (from Polish to Japanese) or experience the best in traditional Swedish cooking.

The capital is best seen from the water but strolling through the parklands of Djurgården or the cobblestone alleys of Gamla Stan is also enjoyable. Many of the 70-plus museums contain world-class treasures and you can see a selection of what Sweden has to offer at Skansen, the open-air museum. Stockholm is a royal capital, with 10 royal castles in and around the city, including the largest palace in the world that's still in use, as well as the World Heritage–listed Drottningholm.

Stockholm has the best selection of budget accommodation in Scandinavia and, although it isn't really cheap, it's all clean and comfortable. The city hotels seem to compete on service and luxury, so they tend to have high prices, but good summer discounts bring them into the price range of many travellers. It's wise to make reservations (especially for hostels) well in advance, since

Highlights

- Going on a cruise around the capital and discovering just how accurate Stockholm's slogan 'Beauty on Water' really is

- Getting a sense of the city's history by strolling through the medieval streets of Gamla Stan

- Discovering the multitude of excellent museums, theatres, shops, restaurants, cafés and bars

- Cycling or walking around Djurgården and visiting its outstanding museums, including the Vasamuseet and Skansen

- Island hopping in Stockholm's archipelago, with some 24,000 islands to choose from

- Escaping to the good swimming spots and appealing restaurants of Fjäderholmarna, tiny islands only 25 minutes from the city

- Exploring the quaint streets of pretty Sigtuna, Sweden's oldest town

Around Stockholm p129

Stockholm pp96-7
Inner Stockholm p102
Stockholm Metro p127

SVEALAND

finding a bed in Stockholm can be difficult at the height of summer.

HISTORY

Swedish political power had been centred around Mälaren lake for centuries, but it was forced to move to the lake's outlet when the rising land made navigation for large boats between the sea and lake impractical. Sweden's most important chieftain in the mid-13th century, Birger Jarl, ordered the construction of a fort on one of the strategically placed islets, where the fresh water entered the sea, and traffic on the waterways was controlled using timber stocks arranged as a fence, or boom. Stockholm, meaning 'tree-trunk islet', may well be named after this boom.

The oldest record of the city consists of two letters dating from 1252. Within a hundred years, Stockholm was the largest city in Sweden, dominated by an impregnable castle (which was never taken by force) and surrounded by a defensive wall. During the period of the Kalmar Union, the king's governor directed affairs from the castle. The city was periodically ravaged by fire until timber buildings with turf roofs were replaced with brick structures. By the late 15th century, the population was around 6000 and Stockholm had become a significant commercial centre. Shipping copper and iron to continental Europe was a lucrative trade that was dominated by German merchants.

In 1471, the Danish king, Christian I, besieged Stockholm while attempting to quell the rebellious Sten Sture, but his 5000-strong army was routed by the Swedes just outside the city walls at the Battle of Brunkeberg (the fighting took place between what is now Vasagatan, Kungsgatan and Sergels Torg). Even after the Danish retreat to Copenhagen, trouble between unionists and separatists continued. Things escalated in 1520 when city burghers, bishops and nobility agreed to meet Danish King Christian II in Stockholm, and he arrested them all at a banquet. After a quick trial, the Swedes were found guilty of burning down the archbishop's castle near Sigtuna, and 82 men were beheaded the following day at Stortorget (the main square by the castle). This ghastly event became known as the Stockholm Blood Bath: heavy rain caused rivers of blood from the bodies to pour down steep alleys descending from the square.

A major rebellion followed and Gustav Vasa finally entered the city in 1523 after a two-year siege. The new king then ruled the city with a heavy hand – the role of commerce dwindled and the church was extinguished entirely as royal power grew and the city revolved around the court. Gustav's son Erik XIV (and later kings) racked up taxation on the burghers to fund wars, but some did well from arms manufacturing and the city's importance as a military headquarters increased. At the end of the 16th century, Stockholm's population was 9000, but this expanded in the following century to 60,000 as the Swedish empire reached its greatest extent.

In the 17th century, town planners laid out a street grid beyond the medieval city centre and Stockholm was proclaimed the capital of Sweden in 1634. Famine wiped out 100,000 people across Sweden during the harsh winter of 1696 and starving hordes descended on the capital. Also the old royal castle (Tre Kronor) burned down, in 1697. In 1710 plague arrived and the death rate soared to 1200 per day – from a population of only 50,000! After the death of King Karl XII, the country (and the capital) went into stagnation.

In the 18th century, Swedish science and arts blossomed, allowing the creation of institutions and fine buildings. Another period of stagnation followed the assassination of King Gustav III; promised 19th-century reforms never arrived and bloody street riots were common.

From the 1860s, further town planning created many of the wide avenues and apartment blocks still seen today. The city rapidly industrialised and expanded – by 1915 was home to 364,000 people. In 1912, the Olympic Games were held in Stockholm.

The next major transformation of the city started in the 1960s, when large 'new towns' sprung up around the outskirts, and extensive areas of 'slums' were flattened to make way for concrete office blocks, motorways and other unsightly developments. The financial and construction boom of the 1980s helped make the city a very expensive place. Once that bubble burst due to the 1990s recession the devalued krona actually helped Stockholm: Swedish tourism grew, and foreign tourists arrived in ever-increasing numbers. The easing of licensing restrictions on bars and restaurants, such as hours during which alcohol could be sold, the type of alcohol sold and the age of clientele, caused a huge increase in the number of licensed premises and helped create the lively Stockholm you see today.

ORIENTATION

Stockholm is built on islands, except for the modern centre (Norrmalm), focused the ugly square known as Sergels Torg. This business and shopping hub is linked by a network of subways to Centralstationen (the central train station) in the west; these subways also link with the metro (*tunnelbanan* or T) stations. The large, busy tourist office is in the eastern part of Norrmalm; the popular park Kungsträdgården is almost next door.

The triangular island Stadsholmen and its neighbouring islets accommodate Gamla Stan (Old Town), separated from Norrmalm by the narrow channels of Norrström near the royal palace, but connected by several bridges. To the west of this is Mälaren lake (see the Around Stockholm map).

On the south side of Stadsholmen the main bridge Centralbron and the Slussen interchange connect with the southern part of the city, Södermalm, and its spine Götgatan. From its top end the giant stadium Globen (which looks like a golf ball) is the southern landmark, although you'll cross water again at Skanstull before reaching it.

To the east of Gamla Stan is the pleasant island Skeppsholmen and its little neighbour, Kastellholmen. Farther east along Strandvägen and past the pleasure-boat berths at Nybroviken you can cross to Djurgården, with its impressive collection of museums.

Mälaren, the lake lying west of Gamla Stan, contains a host of other islands. Also in the city's west, the E4 motorway crosses Stora Essingen, Lilla Essingen and Kungsholmen on its way north; yet another series of bridges connects Långholmen with the western tip of Södermalm and the southern side of Kungsholmen.

Maps
The free *What's On Stockholm* tourist booklet has good maps but the folded *Stockholms officiella turistkarta* (Skr20) covers a larger area; both are usually available from tourist offices and hotels. If you're heading for the suburbs, detailed maps can be purchased from tourist offices or map shops. The best available street atlas, *Atlas över Stor-Stockholm* (Kartförlaget; Skr180), covers all of greater Stockholm.

INFORMATION
Tourist Offices
The capital's main tourist office is located in **Sweden House** (Sverigehuset; ☎ 789 2490; info@stoinfo.se; Hamngatan 27; open

8am-7pm Mon-Fri, 9am-5pm Sat & Sun June-Aug, 9am-6pm Mon-Fri, 10am-3pm Sat & Sun Sept-May), by Kungsträdgården. It has lots of good brochures and can help book hotel rooms, theatre and concert tickets, and packages such as boat trips to the archipelago. Also in Sweden House is a Forex currency-exchange counter; a travel agency specialising in the Finnish province of Åland; and Sweden Bookshop, upstairs, has information in English about Swedish life and culture, provided by the Swedish Institute.

Perhaps more convenient for arriving travellers is the busy information office of **Hotellcentralen** *(☎ 789 2490; Centralstationen; open 9am-6pm daily; 8am-8pm daily in summer)*, inside the main train station. In addition to obtaining tourist information, you can reserve hotel rooms and hostel beds (for a fee), buy the Stockholm Package, Stockholm Card or SL Tourist Card, book sightseeing tours and buy maps, books and souvenirs.

Tourist information for disabled travellers is available on ☎ 5506 4130.

Publications & Websites
There are a number of useful publications for visitors to the capital – the best overall guide is the monthly *What's On Stockholm* (available free from tourist offices and most hotels). There are also two separate accommodation guides in English – one for camping, the other for hotels and hostels.

Ask the tourist office for the *Stockholm Teater Guide*. The free weekly paper *Nöjesguiden* (in Swedish) concentrates on the contemporary music, entertainment and pub scene; even if you don't speak Swedish, you'll probably be able to understand many of the listings.

Excellent tourist information is available in English (and many other languages) at Ⓦ www.stockholmtown.com. If you can read Swedish, try Ⓦ www.alltomstockholm .se, which has loads of information on events, restaurants, sports etc.

Discounts
All transport and most sightseeing needs are covered by the **Stockholm Card**, available from tourist offices, some camping grounds and hostels, SL information centres and the larger museums. It costs Skr220/380/540 for 24/48/72 hours (Skr60/120/180 for accompanying children under 18, maximum

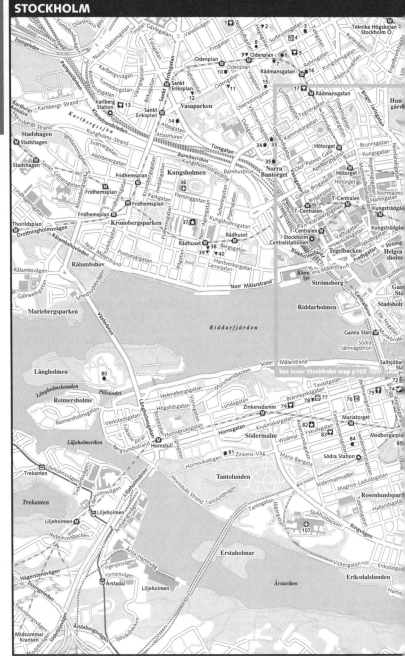

STOCKHOLM

Teknika Högskolan
Stockholm Ö

Essingeleden
Tomtebodavägen
Doktor som gen
Torsgatan
Gävlegatan
Vanadisvägen
Norra Stationsgatan
Freigatan
Odenplan
Odenplan
Rådmansgatan
Rehnsgatan
Kungstensgatan
Karlavägen

Norra Stationsgatan
Pampasparken
Karlbergsvägen
Sankt
Eriksplan
Sankt
Eriksgatan
Odengatan
Birkagatan
Observatoriegatan
Rådmansgatan
Birger Jarlsgatan
Hun
gård

Karlbergs-Strand
Karlberg
Station
Karlbergs
Kanalen
Karlbergs Strand
Tomtebogatan
Vikingagatan
Sankt
Eriksplan
Vasaparken
Drottninggatan
Tegnérgatan
Dalagatan

Klarastrandsleden
Karlbergssjön
Kungsholms-Strand
Atlasgatan
Atlasmuren
Kammakargatan
Dobelnsgatan
Hötorget
Brunnsgatan
Kungsgatan

Stadshagen
Stadshagen
Stadshagen
Igeldammsgatan
Svarvargatan
Alströmergatan
Torsgatan
Norra
Bantorget
Olof Palmes Gata
Apelbergsgatan
Hötorget
Hötorget
Normalms
Hamngatan

Sankt Göransgatan
Fridhemsplan
Kungsholmen
Barnhusviken
Barnhusbron
Gamla Brogatan
Bryggargatan
T-Centralen
Kungsträdgå

Fleminggatan
Flemingatan
Kungsholmsstranden
Scheelegatan
Pipersgatan
Terminalslingan
Klarabergsgatan
T-Centralen
Hamngatan

Fridhemsplan
Kronobergsparken
Kronobergsgatan
Norr Agnegatan
Kungsholmsgatan
Klarabergsviadukten
T-Centralen
Stockholm
Centralstationen
Vattugatan
Herkulesgatan
Kungsträdgå

Thorildsplan
Drottningholmsvägen
Rålambshovsleden
Norr Mälarstrand
Pontonjärgatan
Rådhuset
Rådhuset
Bergsgatan
Hantverkargatan
Garvargatan
Tegelbacken
Fredsgatan
Jakobsgatan
Strömg
Helgea
sholm

Rålambsvägen
Smedsuddsvägen
Norr Mälarstrand
Pilgatan
Klara
Sjö
Klara Mälarströ
Strömsborg

Gjörwellsvägen
Mariebergsparken
Västerbron
Riddarfjärden
Riddarholmen
Stadsholm

Mälarstrand
Söder Mälarstrand
See Inner Stockholm map p102
Gamla Stan
Södra
Järnvägsbron
Saltsjöba
Sta

Långholmen
Långholmskanalen
Reimersholme
Reimersholmsgatan
Påls undet
Heleneborgsgatan
Högalidsgatan
Lundagatan
Hornsbruksgatan
Hornsgatan
Zinkensdamm
Brännkyrkagatan
Tavastgatan
Mariatorget
Södermalm
Medborgarpla

Liljeholmsviken
Verkstadsgatan
Eriksson garan
Bergsundsstrand
Hornstull
Krukmakargatan
Wollmar Yxkullsgatan
Swedenborgsgatan
Södra Station

Trekanten
Lövholmsvägen
Zinkens Väg
Hornsviksstigen
Maria Bangata
Tantolunden
Magnus Ladulåsgatan
Södermalmsallen

Trekanten
Liljeholmsbron
Liljeholmen
Hornstulls Strand
Tantolundsvägen
Tantogatan
Rosenlundspar
Hallandsga

Liljeholmen
Nybohovsbacken
Årstängsvägen
Sjukhusbacken
Ringvägen

Hägerstensvägen
Essingeleden
Ingenjörsvägen
Förmansvägen
Årsta-Hamnväg
Årstadal
Liljeholmen
Erstaholmar
Årstaviken
Eriksdalslunden

Midsommar
Kransen
Årstabergsvägen
Sjöviksbacken

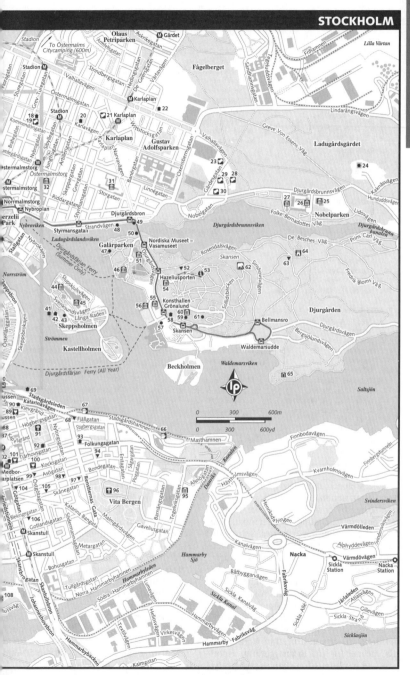

STOCKHOLM

PLACES TO STAY
3 Oden Pensionat
10 Hotell Gustav Vasa; Tvättomat
14 Wasa Park Hotell
16 Hostel Bed & Breakfast
18 A&Be Hotell
20 Östra Reals Vandrarhem
22 Backpackers Inn
33 Hotell Bema
34 Hostel Mitt i City
35 Good Night Hotell Danielsson
41 Vandrarhem af Chapman
42 Vandrarhem Skeppsholmen
58 Scandic Hotel Hasselbacken
69 Gustaf af Klint
73 Hotel Anno 1647
80 Vandrarhem Långholmen;
   Hotell Långholmen; Fängelsemuseum
81 Vandrarhem Zinkensdamm;
   Hotell Zinkensdamm
84 Hotel Tre Små Rum
90 Scandic Sjöfartshotellet
92 Columbus Hotell
93 Hotel Söders Höjder
102 Scandic Hotel Malmen

PLACES TO EAT
2 Haga Restaurang & Delikatess
9 Tranan
11 Le Bistrot de Wasahof;
   Musslan
12 Narknoi
38 Il Caffé Gli Angelini
39 Mamas & Tapas
40 Indian Curry House
52 Wärdshuset Ulla Windbladh
63 Rosendals Trädgårdskafe
68 Hermans
71 Nystekt Strömming
78 Vivo Supermarket
85 Söderhallarna

86 Fenix
87 Waynes Coffee; Press Stop;
   Design Torget
88 Creperie Fyra Knop
94 Zucchero
97 Sonjas Grek
98 Café String
99 Östgöta Källaren
104 Kebab Kungen
105 Koh Phangan
106 Pelikan

MUSEUMS
25 Etnografiska Museet
26 Tekniska Museet; Telemuseum
27 Sjöhistoriska Museet
31 Historiska Museet
32 Armémuseum
44 Östasiatiska Museet
45 Arkitekturmuseet; Moderna
   Museet
46 Vasamuseet
51 Nordiska Museet
54 Biologiskamuseet
55 Liljevalchs Konsthall;
   Blå Porten
60 Tobaks & Tändsticksmuseum
72 Stockholms Stadsmuseum
76 Leksaksmuseet
95 Spårvägsmuseet

ENTERTAINMENT
1 Cliff Barnes
5 La Habana
13 Bagpipers Inn; Boomerang
   BBQ Bar & Steakhouse
17 Tip Top; RFSL
77 Folkoperan
79 Häcktet
83 Side Track
89 Mosebacke Etablissement
99 Soldaten Svejk

100 Kvarnen
103 Bio Palatset

OTHER
4 Nine
6 Stadsbiblioteket
7 Internationella Bibliotek
8 Leksakspalatset
15 Jones Antikvariat
19 French Embassy
21 Irish Embassy
23 Finnish Embassy
24 Kaknästornet TV Tower
28 British Embassy; Norwegian
   Embassy
29 German Embassy
30 US Embassy
36 Sankt Eriks Sjukhus
37 Police Station
43 Svensk Form Design Center
47 Junibacken
48 Rent a Bike
49 Tvillingarnas Sjökrog
50 Sjöcafe
53 Skogens Hus
55 Aquaria Vattenmuseum
57 Gröna Lund Tivoli
59 Skansen Main Entrance
61 Skansen Aquarium
62 Skansen Zoo
64 Rosendals Slott
65 Prins Eugens Waldemarsudde
66 Viking Line Terminal
67 Birka Cruises Terminal
70 Slussen Bus Terminal
74 Netherlands Embassy
75 Maria Magdalena Kyrka
82 Police Station
91 Katarina Kyrka
96 Sofia Kyrka
107 Södersjukhuset
108 Eriksdalsbadet

two children per adult). It gives free entry to over 70 attractions, free city parking, free sightseeing by boat and free travel on public transport (including the Katarinahissen lift, but excluding local ferries, some city buses and airport buses). To get maximum value, use two 24-hour cards over three days (with a rest day in between) and be sure to note opening hours: Skansen remains open until late, whereas royal palaces are only open until 3pm or 4pm.

Students and seniors get discounted admission to most museums and sights without the card, so you'll need to work out if it's cheaper for you to just get a transport pass and pay admission charges separately.

Stockholm à la Carte is a cut-price package that includes a hotel room and the Stockholm Card. It's available weekends year-round and also throughout the summer (mid-June to mid-August) and costs from Skr450 per person, depending on the standard of accommodation (prices for central hotels start at around Skr600). Travel agents in other Scandinavian capitals or major Swedish cities can help with arrangements, otherwise contact **Destination Stockholm** (☎ 663 0080; ⓔ info@destination-stockholm.com, ⓦ www.destination-stockholm.com). The website has lots of good information and lists details of the 50-odd hotels involved in the scheme.

Money

The exchange company **Forex** has about a dozen branches in the capital and charges Skr15 per travellers cheque. Handy locations are at Stockholm Arlanda airport (Terminal 2); inside Centralstationen (open 7am to 9pm daily) and also opposite it at Vasagatan 14; and inside Sweden House.

There are ATMs all over town, including a few at Centralstationen, usually with long queues. You can also exchange money at the banks for up to Skr60 per transaction. You'll find banks around Sergels Torg and along Hamngatan.

There's also an **American Express** (☎ 411 0540; Norrlandsgatan 21) office in town.

Post & Communications

The always-busy Centralstationen **post office** (open 7am-10pm Mon-Fri, 10am-7pm Sat & Sun) keeps the longest hours. You can now buy stamps and send letters at a number of city locations, including newsagents and some supermarkets – keep an eye out for the Swedish postal symbol (yellow on a blue background) to indicate that postal services are performed at that location.

Email & Internet Access

Some hostels have a computer or two and offer Internet access to guests. Otherwise, there are a few reasonable Internet cafés around town.

Access IT (☎ 5083 1489; Sergels Torg; open 10am-7pm Tues-Fri, 11am-5pm Sat & Sun), in the basement at Kulturhuset, is a central cybercafe where 30 minutes online costs Skr20. **Ice** (☎ 248000; Vasagatan 42; open noon-midnight daily), close to Central-stationen, charges Skr30/50 for 30/60 minutes online.

Over at the northern side of town, **Nine** (☎ 612 9919; Odengatan 44; open 10am-midnight/1am daily) charges roughly Skr45 per hour – and there is also an excellent café here too.

At the main city library, **Stadsbiblioteket** (☎ 5083 1100; Sveavägen 73), free 'drop-in' computers are available 10am to 7pm daily (maximum 15 minutes online; email is accessible). The nearby **Internationella Bibliotek** (☎ 5083 1288; Odengatan 59) has drop-in spots available for a maximum of 30 minutes; you can also book a one-hour slot (Skr15).

Travel Agencies

STA (☎ 5452 6666; Kungsgatan 30) and the nearby **Kilroy Travels** (☎ 0771-545769; Kungsgatan 4) both specialise in discount youth and student flights.

Svenska Turistföreningen (STF; ☎ 020 292929) doesn't have a drop-in sales office, but you can make telephone bookings for tour packages.

Bookshops

Sweden Bookshop (☎ 789 2131; Sverigehuset, Hamngatan 27) has the broadest selection of books in English. For English-language newspapers and paperbacks go to **Pressbyrån** (Centralstationen). For both special-interest and international magazines, try **Press Stop** at a few of the locations around town, including Drottninggatan 35, Götgatan 31 and also Kungsgatan 14.

The widest ranges of maps are found at **Kartbutiken** (☎ 202303; Kungsgatan 74) and **Kartcentrum** (☎ 411 1697; Vasagatan 16) (both near Centralstationen). Lonely Planet guidebooks are stocked at both locations.

For books and maps you can also try **Akademibokhandeln** (☎ 613 6100; Mäster Samuelsgatan 32).

Second-hand books (including paperbacks in English) can be found at **Jones Antikvariat** (☎ 307697; Norrtullsgatan 3).

Libraries

Kulturhuset (☎ 5083 1508; Sergels Torg; open 11am-7pm Tues-Fri, 11am-5pm Sat & Sun) has a reading room with international periodicals and newspapers as well as books in various languages.

The main city library, **Stadsbiblioteket** (☎ 5083 1130; Sveavägen 73; open 9am-9pm Mon-Thur, 9am-7pm Fri, 11am-5pm Sat & Sun, shorter hours in summer), is just north of the city centre. It's worth a visit if you're into architecture – it's the best example of Stockholm's 1920s neoclassicist style.

Universities

Stockholm University (W www.su.se; metro T-Universitetet) was founded as a private institution as late as 1877; up until then, students had to go to Uppsala or Lund to further their studies. The university was taken over by the government in 1960 and it is now the largest in the country, with 34,000 students.

Most of the university is located 3.5km north of the city centre in Frescati district.

Laundry

Laundry options are limited and it's best to find a hotel or hostel with facilities or a washing service. The so-called *snabbtvätt* (quick-wash) services in the telephone directory are not all that fast, taking a week or longer. A handy laundrette in the city area is **Tvättomat** *(☎ 346480; Västmannagatan 61; metro T-Odenplan; open 8.30am-6.30pm Mon-Fri, 9am-3pm Sat)*, by Hotell Gustav Vasa. It charges Skr67 per machine load to wash and dry if you do it yourself; last orders are accepted two hours before closing.

Left Luggage

There are three sizes of left-luggage boxes at Centralstationen, costing from Skr20 to Skr70 for 24 hours. Similar facilities exist at the neighbouring bus station and at major ferry terminals.

If you have a lost-property inquiry, ask for 'tillvaratagna effekter'.

Camping & Outdoor Gear

This branch of **Naturkompaniet** *(☎ 24 1996; Kungsgatan 26)* sells a wide selection of outdoor equipment; there are other stores around the city.

Emergency & Medical Services

The toll-free **emergency number** for the fire service, police and ambulance is ☎ 112. For 24-hour medical advice call ☎ 644 9200.

CW Scheele *(☎ 454 8130; Klarabergsgatan 64)* is a central 24-hour pharmacy. In the suburbs, seek the nearest medical centre *(vårdcentral)* listed in the blue pages of the telephone directory. The hospital **Södersjukhuset** *(☎ 616 1000; Ringvägen 52)*, in Södermalm, handles casualties from the central city area.

Emergency dental treatment is available at **Sankt Eriks Sjukhus**, *(☎ 654 1117 Flemminggatan 22; open 8am-9pm)*. Contact the **duty dentist** *(☎ 672 3100)* for advice after 8.30pm.

There are two 24-hour **police stations** *(☎ 401 0100; Torkel Knutssonsgatan 20, Södermalm • ☎ 401 0300; Kungsholmsgatan 37, Kungsholmen)*.

In the case of vehicle breakdowns, contact **Larmtjänst** *(☎ 783 7000)*.

Dangers & Annoyances

Some parts of the city aren't particularly safe late at night and visitors should steer clear of night buses at weekends. It might be a good idea to avoid areas such as Sergels Torg, Medborgarplatsen (Södermalm) and Fridhemsplan (Kungsholmen), especially when the bars empty at 1am.

WALKING TOUR

Most of central Stockholm's sights can be visited on a walking tour, which will take you a good couple of hours. Better still, spend a whole day exploring the medieval heart of the city, Gamla Stan – but it's best to visit when the teeming coach parties aren't there.

Starting from Centralstationen, cross Vasagatan and enter the side street Klara Vattugränd. Turn left onto Klara V Kyrkogatan, past the church **Klara kyrka** (where you can get information on all of Stockholm's churches), then turn right onto Klarabergsgatan. This is one of Stockholm's main modern shopping streets and it's lined with designer shops, expensive boutiques and department stores such as **Åhléns**.

Follow Klarabergsgatan to **Sergels Torg**, where you'll see ghastly sculpture, fountains and possibly a demonstration in the open-air basement arena of **Kulturhuset**, which hosts regular art exhibitions. Continue a short way along Hamngatan before turning right at the tourist office **Sweden House**, into the pleasant **Kungsträdgården**. This park, originally the kitchen garden for the Royal Palace, is now a popular spot for relaxing in the sun. The 17th-century church **Sankt Jakobs kyrka** has an ornate pulpit and is worth a quick look.

Walk through the park to its southern end at **Karl XII:s Torg**, where there's a statue of the warmongering king, Karl XII. On your right is **Operan**, the Royal Opera House (opened in 1896) and across the road you'll see the narrow strait **Norrström**, the freshwater outflow from Mälaren lake. Continue along the water-front, past Operan and **Gustav Adolfs Torg**, to the grandiose **Sophia Albertina Palace** (which houses the Foreign Ministry), then turn left and cross the Riksbron bridge. Continue across the islet **Helgeandsholmen** (Island of the Holy Spirit), between the two parts of Sweden's parliament building, **Riksdags-huset** (see the Helgeandsholmen section later in this

Practical Information

Almost all of the roughly 70 museums and other major attractions in and around Stockholm can be visited for free with the Stockholm Card. Children under 16 are generally admitted for half price and small children can enter for free, if accompanied by a paying adult. Not all museums offer student discounts.

Most museums open daily during the peak summer holiday season (from Midsummer to mid-August), and some open daily from the start of June to the end of August; most are closed on Monday during the rest of the year. Opening hours vary according to season; hours are listed in the brochure accompanying your Stockholm Card, or in the *What's On Stockholm* brochure.

We have listed all the major museums in the capital, but there are many more special-interest museums worth visiting. A useful website for pre-trip research is W www.stockholmsmuseer.com; the website itself is in Swedish but has a drop-down menu with links to all museum homepages (and most of these have information in English).

chapter). After crossing over the short Stallbron bridge, you'll arrive on **Stadsholmen** (City Island), which is home to the medieval core of Stockholm.

Cross Mynttorget and follow Västerlånggatan for one block, then turn left (east) into Storkyrkobrinken to reach **Storkyrkan**, the city's cathedral and oldest building. Facing the cathedral across the cobbled square is **Kungliga Slottet**, the 'new' Royal Palace (see the Gamla Stan section later, for more about the cathedral and palace). Källargränd leads southwards to the square **Stortorget**, where the Stockholm Bloodbath took place in 1520. Three sides of the square are formed by quaint tenements painted in different colours; on the fourth side of the square there's **Börsen**, the Stock Exchange and Swedish Academy building, now home to the excellent museum detailing the history of the Nobel prizes and their recipients.

The narrow streets of the eastern half of Gamla Stan still wind along their medieval 14th-century lines and are linked by a fantasy of lanes, arches and many stairways. Head east along Köpmangatan to the small square

Köpmantorget, and the statue of St George and the Dragon. Turn right into **Österlånggatan** and follow it past antique shops, art galleries, handicraft outlets and **Den Gyldene Freden**, which has been serving food since 1722, until you reach **Järntorget**, where metals were bought and sold in days long past. From there, keep right and turn into Västerlånggatan, looking out for **Mårten Trotzigs Gränd** by No 81: this is Stockholm's narrowest lane, at less than 1m wide. Follow Prästgatan to the lavishly decorated German church, **Tyska kyrkan**.

Västerlånggatan is lined with shops and boutiques selling tourist tat and attracts dense crowds, so follow the quieter parallel street Stora Nygatan. On reaching Riddarhustorget, turn left (southwest) and cross the short Riddarholmsbron bridge to **Riddarholmen** (Knight Island). The large former church **Riddarholmskyrkan**, has an amazing modern spire (see the following Gamla Stan section). Beyond Riddarholmskyrkan, you'll come to the far side of the island, with great views across the lake to the impressive **Stadshuset** (Town Hall) and the eastern end of **Kungsholmen** (King's Island) – see the Central Stockholm section later.

Retrace your steps to Riddarhustorget, then turn left (northwest), cross over Vasabron and continue along Vasagatan back to Centralstationen.

GAMLA STAN

The oldest part of Stockholm is also its most attractive, containing old houses, vaulted cellar restaurants and the royal palace. Allow a day to explore Gamla Stan; include touristy Västerlånggatan, but don't miss the parallel alleys or quiet squares.

The city emerged in the 13th century and adopted the trade and, partly, the accents of its German Hanseatic guests. It continued to grow with Sweden's power until the 17th century, when the castle of Tre Kronor, the symbol of that power, burned to the ground.

Kungliga Slottet

The 'new' Royal Palace, Kungliga Slottet (☎ 402 6130; W www.royalcourt.se; Slottsbacken; adult/child each attraction Skr70/35, combined ticket Skr110/65; most attractions open 10am-4pm daily mid-May–Aug, noon-3pm Tues-Sun Sept–mid-May) is one of Stockholm's highlights; it was constructed

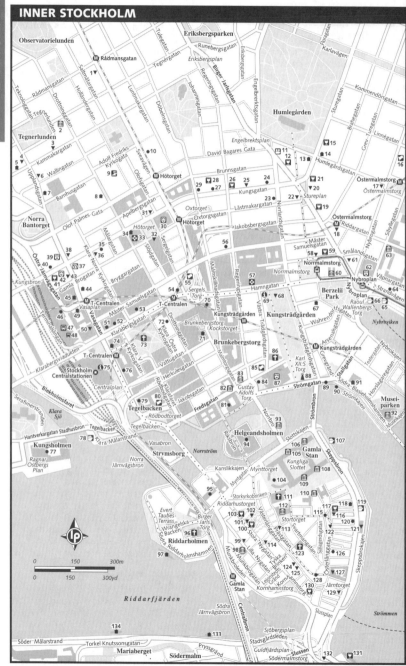

INNER STOCKHOLM

PLACES TO STAY
5 Oden Pensionat
7 City Backpackers
8 Queen's Hotel
13 Scandic Hotel Anglais
14 Lydmar Hotel
34 Rica City Hotel Kungsgatan
44 Central Hotel
45 Nordic Hotel Light
49 Nordic Hotel Sea; Ice Bar
67 Berns Hotel
71 Scandic Hotel Sergel Plaza
74 Scandic Hotel Continental
91 Grand Hôtel Stockholm;
   Franska Matsalen; Verandan
97 Mälardrottningen
118 First Hotel Reisen
133 Mälaren Den Röda Båten
134 M/S Rygerfjord

PLACES TO EAT
1 Souperb
3 Sabai Sabai
4 Carinas Pizzeria
6 Spice House
17 Östermalmshallen;
   Örtagården
18 Sturekatten
20 Sturehof
22 East
25 Waynes Coffee; Press Stop
31 Kungshallen
32 Hötorshallen;
   Filmstaden Sergel
36 Vetekatten
38 Kebab House
43 Waynes Coffee
50 Waynes Coffee
58 Birger Jarlspassagen Cafes
61 Riche
68 Friday's American
   Bar & Café
99 Leijontornet
101 Hermitage
102 Gåsgränd 4; Kebab Stall
113 Chokladkoppen
114 Siam Thai
116 Pontus in the Greenhouse
121 Gamla Stans Bryggeri
122 Grill Ruby; Bistro Ruby
124 Café Art
125 Michelangelo
127 Den Gyldene Freden
129 Zum Franziskaner

132 Gondolen; Katarinahissen;
   Köket

MUSEUMS
2 Strindbergsmuseet
60 Hallwylska Museet
63 Musikmuseet
82 Medelhavsmuseet
83 Dansmuseet
92 Nationalmuseum
93 Medeltidsmuseet
98 Postmuseum
105 Museum Tre Kronor
106 Gustav III:s Antikmuseum
108 Livrustkammaren
109 Skattkammaren &
   Slottskyrkan
110 Kungliga Myntkabinettet
112 Börsen; Nobelmuseet

ENTERTAINMENT
11 Biograf Sture
12 Spy Bar
15 Kharma
19 Bull & Bear Inn
21 Sturecompagniet
26 The Loft
28 Glenn Miller Café
30 Konserthuset
39 Vasateatern
41 Jazzclub Fasching
42 Oscars Teatern
59 Dubliner
62 Dramaten
87 Operan; Operakällaren;
   Café Opera; Bakfickan
100 Wirströms
103 Stampen
117 Mandus
130 Engelen
131 Lady Patricia

OTHER
9 Centralbadet
10 Svensk Hemslöjd
16 New Zealand Embassy
23 American Express
24 Kilroy Travels
27 Naturkompaniet
29 STA Travel
33 PUB Department Store
35 Svenskt Hantverk
37 Ice
40 Kartbutiken

46 Arlanda Express Terminal
47 Cityterminalen
   (Bus Station, Airport Buses)
48 Busstop Ticket Office
51 CW Scheele
52 Systembolaget
53 Åhléns Department Store;
   Hemköp Supermarket
54 Hennes & Mauritz
55 Australian Embassy
56 Akademibokhandeln
57 NK Department Store
64 Svenskt Tenn
65 Strömma Kanalbolaget Boats
66 Djurgården Boats
69 Sweden House; Sweden
   Bookshop; Forex
70 Kulturhuset; Design Torget;
   Access IT; Stockholms
   Stadsteatern
72 Press Stop
73 Klara Kyrka
75 Hotellcentralen; Forex; Post
   Office; Pressbyrån
76 Statoil Car Hire; Forex;
   Kartcentrum
77 Stadshuset; Stadshuskällaren
78 Lake Mälaren Boats (Boats to
   Drottningholm & Birka)
79 AVIS
80 Canadian Embassy
81 Sophia Albertina Palace
84 City Sightseeing
   (Tour Departures)
85 Danish Embassy
86 Sankt Jakobs Kyrka
88 Karl XII Statue
89 Stockholm Sightseeing
   Office
90 Waxholmsbolaget Office
   & Boat Dock
94 Riksdagshuset
95 Riddarhuset
96 Riddarholmskyrkan
104 Royal Apartments Entrance
107 Svea Viking Boat
111 Storkyrkan
115 Köpmantorget;
   St George Statue
119 Ånedin-Linjen Boat Terminal
120 Cinderella Båtarna Office
123 Tyska Kyrkan
126 Ice Gallery
128 Mårten Trotzigs Gränd

on the site of the 'old' royal castle, Tre Kronor, which burned down in 1697. The north wing of the castle survived and was incorporated into the new palace, but its medieval designs are now concealed by a baroque exterior. The new palace, designed by the court architect Nicodemus Tessin the Younger, wasn't completed until 57 years later and, with 608 rooms, it's the world's largest royal castle still used for its original purpose.

The excellent **state apartments**, including the Hall of State and the Apartments of the Royal Orders of Chivalry, are both open to the public (except during state functions), with two floors of royal pomp, 18th- and 19th-century furnishings and portraits of pale princes and princesses. Look out for Queen Kristina's silver throne in the Hall of State. The delightful baroque and rococo designs found throughout the rooms are very impressive.

At **Skattkammaren** (Royal Treasury) the Swedish regalia, crowns, sceptres, orbs and keys are displayed, by the southern entrance to the palace near **Slottskyrkan** (Royal Chapel). **Gustav III:s Antikmuseum** displays the Mediterranean treasures (particularly sculpture) acquired by that eccentric monarch. **Museum Tre Kronor** is in the palace basement and features the foundations of 13th-century defensive walls and exhibits rescued from the medieval castle during the fire of 1697.

The **Changing of the Guard** takes place in the outer courtyard at 12.15pm Monday to Saturday, and 1.15pm Sunday and public holidays.

Livrustkammaren

Livrustkammaren *(Royal Armoury; ☎ 5195 5544; Slottsbakken 3; adult/child Skr65/20; open 10am-5pm daily June-Aug, 11am-5pm Tues-Sun Sept-May)* is part of the palace complex but it can be visited separately. Its displays cover 500 years of royal history and there's a large collection of royal memorabilia, including armour, five colourful carriages, ceremonial costumes and Gustav II Adolf's stuffed horse. It's also worth looking out for the costume Gustav III was wearing when he was assassinated at the opera in 1792.

Kungliga Myntkabinettet

Kungliga Myntkabinettet *(Royal Coin Cabinet; ☎ 5195 5304; Slottsbacken 6; adult/child Skr45/12; open 10am-4pm Tues-Sun)* is just across from the Royal Palace. Here you'll find displays of coins (including Viking silver) and banknotes covering the history of money over the last 2600 years. You'll see the world's oldest coin (from 625 BC), the world's largest coin (a Swedish copper plate weighing 19.7kg) and the world's first banknote (issued in Sweden in 1661).

Storkyrkan & Riddarholmskyrkan

Stockholm's cathedral, Storkyrkan *(☎ 723 3009; adult/child Skr20/free mid-May–Aug,*

admission free Sept–mid-May; open 9am-6pm daily mid-May–Aug, 9am-4pm daily Sept–mid-May) is next to the Royal Palace; Sweden's monarchs used to be crowned here. The brick-built cathedral dates back to the late 13th century (it's the city's oldest building and was consecrated in 1306), but the exterior is baroque. The ancient and ornate interior contains a life-size statue of St George and his horse confronting the mythical dragon, sculpted by the German sculptor Berndt Notke in 1494. You'll also see the two large royal box pews with crown-shaped canopies and the silver altar. Temporary exhibitions are held in the cathedral in summer.

Riddarholmskyrkan *(☎ 402 6130; adult/ child Skr20/10; open 10am-4pm daily mid-May–Aug, noon-3pm Sat & Sun Sept, closed rest of year)*, on the nearby island Riddarholmen, was built by Franciscan monks in the late 13th century. It's no longer a church but has been the royal necropolis since the burial of Magnus Ladulås in 1290 and is home to the armourial glory of the Serafim knightly order. Look for the marble sarcophagus of Gustav II, Sweden's mightiest monarch, and the massed wall-plates displaying the arms of the knights.

Riddarhuset

Until 1865, the Swedish parliament met in the 17th-century Riddarhuset *(House of Nobility; ☎ 723 3990; Riddarhustorget 10; adult/ child Skr40/10; open 11.30am-12.30pm Mon-Fri)*. There are 2325 coats of arms belonging to Sweden's nobility on display and downstairs in the Chancery there's a unique collection of heraldic porcelain.

Postmuseum

The Postmuseum *(☎ 781 1755; Lilla Nygatan 6; adult/child Skr50/free; open 11am-4pm Tues-Sun)*, housed in a 17th-century building, describes the history of Sweden's postal service and there are displays of Swedish stamps from 1855 to the present day. The philatelic library has 51,000 books on stamps and postal history. There's also a miniature post office for children, a café and a shop.

Nobelmuseet

The excellent new Nobelmuseet *(☎ 232506; Stortorget; adult/child Skr50/20; open 10am-6pm daily mid-May–mid-Sept, closed Mon*

Alfred Nobel

Alfred Nobel (1833–96), Swedish chemist, engineer and industrialist, patented a detonator for highly unstable nitroglycerine in 1862. Four years later he made the remarkable discovery that kieselguhr could absorb nitroglycerine safely, but remain an explosive substance. This became known as dynamite and Nobel's factories increased their output 6000-fold over the next 30 years.

As a very wealthy industrialist, Nobel's will created the annual Nobel Prizes (from 1901) in physics, chemistry, medicine/physiology, literature and peace, to be awarded to those who had benefited mankind the most in the preceding year. A sixth prize, for economics, was added in 1969.

rest of year), in the Börsen building (the old Stock Exchange), presents the history of the Nobel Prizes and their recipients.

Ice Gallery

For something completely different, call in at the Ice Gallery (☎ 790 5500; *Österlånggatan 41; adult/child Skr50/25; open 11am-5pm daily*). This small exhibition space has some great ice sculptures, and is kept at about -7°C (warm clothing is provided for visitors), giving guests an idea of conditions at the unique Ice Hotel in northern Sweden (see the boxed text in the Norrland chapter).

Helgeandsholmen

This little island, in the middle of Norrström, is home to the **Riksdaghuset** (*Swedish Parliament;* ☎ 786 4000; ⓦ www.riksdagen.se; *admission free*). The parliament building consists of two parts; the older front section (facing downstream) dates from the early 20th century, but the other, more modern, part contains the current debating chamber. There are free guided tours in English at 12.30pm and 2pm weekdays from late June to August; the rest of the year, they're at 1.30pm on weekends. You can also visit the public gallery and listen to a riveting debate in Swedish.

Medeltidsmuseet (*Medieval Museum;* ☎ 5083 1790; *Strömparterren; adult/child Skr40/5; open 11am-4pm Thur-Mon, 11am-6pm Tues & Wed July & Aug, 11am-6pm*

Tues-Sun Sept-June) is at the other end of the island. Ancient foundations were discovered here when an underground car park for the Riksdag was being constructed and you can now get a taste of medieval Stockholm by exploring faithful, on-site reconstructions of houses, sheds and workshops.

CENTRAL STOCKHOLM
Stadshuset

It looks more like a large church, but the size of Stadshuset (*Town Hall;* ☎ 5082 9058; *Hantverkargatan 1; tours adult/child Skr50/free)* is deceptive because it has two internal courtyards. The dominant brown-brick square tower of Stadshuset is topped with a golden spire and the symbol of Swedish power, the three royal crowns. Inside the building, you'll find the beautiful mosaic-lined **Gyllene salen** (Golden Hall), Prins Eugen's own fresco re-creation of the lake view from the gallery, and the hall where the annual Nobel Prize banquet is held.

Entry is by daily tour only, but these may be interrupted from time to time by preparations for special events. Tours are run at 10am, 11am, noon, 2pm and 3pm daily from June to August, and at 10am and noon daily the rest of year. Climb the **tower** (*adult/child Skr15/free; open 10am-4.30pm daily May-Sept)* for a good view of Gamla Stan.

Medelhavsmuseet

The collections in Medelhavsmuseet (*Museum of Mediterranean Antiquities;* ☎ 5195 5380; *Fredsgatan 2; adult/child Skr50/free; open 11am-8pm Tues, 11am-4pm Wed-Fri, noon-5pm Sat & Sun)* include Egyptian, Greek, Cypriot and Roman artefacts. There are also displays of Islamic art.

Hallwylska Museet

Completed in 1898, Hallwylska Museet (*The Hallwyl Collection;* ☎ 5195 5599; *Hamngatan 4; adult/child Skr65/30)* was once a private palace. Wilhelmina von Hallwyl collected items as diverse as kitchen utensils, Chinese pottery, 17th-century paintings, silverware, sculpture and jewellery. In 1920, she and her husband donated their entire house (including contents) to the nation. The baroque-style great drawing room is particularly impressive and includes a rare, playable grand piano.

This delightful museum has guided tours in English at 1pm daily from late June to mid-August; the rest of the year, English tours are only at 1pm on Sunday (but you could join one of the more regular tours in Swedish).

Nationalmuseum

Sweden's largest art museum, Nationalmuseum (☎ 5195 4300; W www.nationalmu seum.se; Södra Blasieholmshamnen; adult/child Skr75/free; open 11am-8pm Tues, 11am-5pm Wed-Sun) houses the national collection of painting, sculpture, drawings, decorative arts and graphics, ranging from the Middle Ages to the 20th century. Some of the art became state property on the death of Gustav III in 1792, making this one of the earliest public museums in the world. There are around 16,000 items of painting and sculpture on display, including magnificent works by artists such as Goya, Rembrandt and Rubens. There are also around 30,000 items of decorative artwork, including porcelain, furniture, glassware, silverware and late-medieval tapestries.

The museum hosts other types of exhibitions, including design, and there's also an excellent museum shop.

Skeppsholmen

Across the bridge from Nationalmuseum, Östasiatiska Museet (Museum of Far Eastern Antiquities; ☎ 5195 5750; adult/child Skr50/free; open noon-8pm Tues, noon-5pm Wed-Sun) displays ancient and contemporary ceramics, paintings and sculpture. The museum has one of the best collections of Chinese art, stoneware and porcelain in the world (mainly from the Song, Ming and Qing dynasties).

Also on Skeppsholmen are the striking new **Moderna Museet** (Modern Museum; ☎ 5195 5200; Exercisplan 4; W www.modern amuseet.se) and the adjoining **Arkitekturmuseet** (Museum of Architecture; ☎ 5872 7000; Exercisplan 4; W www.arkitekturmu seet.se). Moderna Museet houses a fine collection of modern art, including paintings, sculpture, videos and photographs. Arkitekturmuseet is in an extraordinary building and has displays on Swedish and international architecture, with a permanent exhibition covering 1000 years of Swedish architecture and an archive of 2.5 million documents, photographs, plans, drawings and models.

At the time of writing, both museums were closed for renovations. Parts of their collections are displayed elsewhere in the city: check with tourist offices for details.

Svensk Form Design Center (☎ 463 3134; Holmamiralens väg 2; adult/child Skr20/free; open noon-7pm Tues-Thur, noon-5pm Sat & Sun) has good exhibitions on design, plus a shop and café.

Vin & Sprithistoriska Museet

The Vin & Sprithistoriska Museet (Wine & Spirits Museum; ☎ 744 7070; Dalagatan 100; adult/child Skr40/free; open 10am-7pm Tues, 10am-4pm Wed-Fri, noon-4pm Sat & Sun) sounds eccentric but might explain the weird story behind brännvin or snaps and the birth of the conservative Swedish alcohol policy. It's in Vasastaden, north of the centre. Take bus No 69 from Sergels Torg or walk from T-Odenplan metro station.

Strindbergsmuseet

Strindbergsmuseet (☎ 411 5354; Drottninggatan 85; adult/child Skr40/free; open noon-4pm Tues-Sun) is in the preserved apartment where the writer August Strindberg (1849–1912) spent his final four years. You'll see the dining room, bedroom, study and his interesting library.

Musikmuseet

Musikmuseet (☎ 5195 5490; Sibyllegatan 2; adult/child Skr40/20; open 11am-4pm Tues-Sun) is well presented. You can handle and play some of the museum's musical instruments and see original ABBA paraphernalia from the 1970s.

Armémuseum

Armémuseum (☎ 788 9560; Riddargatan 13; adult/child Skr60/30; open 11am-8pm Tues, 11am-4pm Wed-Sun) has vivid displays of Swedish military history from the Vikings to the present, with some rather graphic depictions.

Historiska Museet

The national historical collection is at Historiska Museet (☎ 5195 5600; W www.his toriska.se; Narvavägen 13; metro T-Karlaplan; adult/child Skr60/free; open 11am-5pm daily mid-May–mid-Sept, closed Mon rest of year). It covers 10,000 years of Swedish history and culture (up to 1520), including some

August Strindberg

August Strindberg was born in Stockholm in 1849. His mother's death when he was 13, was an important event in the life of the tortured genius, who was hailed as the 'writer of the people' towards the end of his chaotic life.

Strindberg periodically studied theology and medicine at Uppsala University from 1867 to 1872, but left without a degree. He then worked as a librarian and journalist prior to becoming a productive author, writing novels, plays, poetry, and over 7000 letters. He was also a talented painter of moody scenes.

His breakthrough as a writer came in 1879 with the publication of his novel *The Red Room*. In 1884, Strindberg became notorious after the publication of *Marriage*, a collection of short stories that led to his trial (and acquittal) for blasphemy in the City Court of Stockholm. Much of his work deals with radical approaches to social issues, which didn't go down well with the Swedish establishment.

Strindberg married three times. His first marriage, to Siri von Essen (married 1877, divorced 1891), produced four children. During his stay in central Europe (1892 to 1899), he led an 'artist life' with the likes of Edvard Munch and Gaughin, and had a short-lived marriage to an Austrian woman, Frida Uhl (married 1893, separated 1894, dissolved 1897), which led to the birth of a daughter. As his instability deepened, Strindberg took an interest in the occult, but the crisis was over upon publication of *Inferno* (1897), an accurate description of his own emotional shambles. After returning to Stockholm in 1899, he married Norwegian Harriet Bosse in 1901 (divorced 1904) and had yet another daughter.

In 1912, Strindberg was awarded an 'Anti-Nobel Prize' (funded by ordinary people from around Sweden) as compensation for not receiving the Nobel Prize for Literature. Although the conservative Swedish Academy basically ignored his work, Strindberg was appreciated by many Swedes and his death, in 1912, was seen as the loss of the country's greatest writer.

archaeological finds from the Viking town, Birka. Don't miss the incredible **Gold Room** in the basement, with its rare treasures. The most astonishing artefact is the 5th-century seven-ringed gold collar with 458 carved figures, weighing 823g. It was found in Västergötland in the 19th century and was probably used by pagan priests in ritualistic ceremonies. Also, look out for the medieval triptychs and altar screens on the 1st floor.

DJURGÅRDEN

The royal park of Djurgården is a 'must see' for visitors to Stockholm. The main attractions are Skansen and the extraordinary Vasa Museum, but there are many other interesting places to visit in the park.

Take bus No 47 from Centralstationen or the Djurgården ferry services from Nybroplan or Slussen (frequent in summer), or take the vintage tram from Norrmalmstorg. You can rent bikes by the bridge (see Getting Around, later in this chapter), and this is by far the best way to explore the area. Parking is limited during the week and prohibited on summer weekends, when Djurgårdsvägen is closed to traffic.

Skansen

The world's first open-air museum, Skansen (☎ 442 8000; W www.skansen.se; adult Skr30-60, child Skr20-30, depending on time of year; open 10am-8pm May, 10am-10pm June-Aug, 10am-5pm Sept, 10am-4pm Oct-Apr) was founded in 1891 by Artur Hazelius to let visitors see how Swedes lived in previous times. Today, around 150 traditional houses and other exhibits from all over Sweden occupy this attractive hill top. It's a spectacular 'Sweden in miniature' and you could spend all day here, wandering between the zoo, the handicraft precinct, the open-air museum or the daily activities that take place on Skansen's stages, including folk dancing in summer. A map and an excellent booklet in English are available to guide you around.

The Town Quarters, mostly consisting of buildings from Södermalm, are inhabited by staff in period costume. The buildings here include a pharmacy, bakery, bank, café, many types of workshop, summer houses and Hazelius' mansion. There are also 46 buildings from rural areas around Sweden, including a Sami camp, farmsteads representing several regions, a manor house and a school.

Trace the unhealthy history of smoking at the **Tobaks & Tändsticksmuseum** (*Tobacco & Matchstick Museum; ☎ 442 8026; open 11am-5pm daily May-Sept; closed Mon rest of year*) or visit the more ecologically oriented **Skogens Hus** (Forestry Information Centre). The **Skansen Aquarium** (*☎ 442 8039; adult/child Skr60/30, open 10am-4pm Mon-Fri, 10am-5pm Sat & Sun Sept-May, 10am-6pm June & Aug, 10am-8pm July*) is also a must – en route to the fish (including piranhas) you'll walk among the lemurs and see pygmy marmosets, the smallest monkeys in the world.

There are several places to eat around Skansen, from cafés to full-blown restaurants. You can get up the hill by **bergbanan** (*mountain railway; tickets Skr20, child under 6 years free; open daily in summer, Sat & Sun rest of year*).

If you're in Stockholm for any of the country's major celebrations (eg, Walpurgis Night, Midsummer's Eve, Lucia Festival, Christmas), Skansen is the place to see how Swedes celebrate. See Public Holidays & Special Events in the Facts for the Visitor chapter for more information on these events.

Nordiska Museet

Nordiska Museet (*National Museum of Cultural History; ☎ 5195 6000; w www.nordm .se; Djurgårdsvägen 6-16; adults/child Skr60/ free; open 11am-5pm daily late-June–Aug, 11am-5pm Tues-Sun Sept–late-June*) was also founded by Artur Hazelius. The museum is the second-largest indoor space in Sweden and it's housed in an enormous, eclectic, Renaissance-style castle. There are notable temporary exhibitions and endless Swedish collections from 1520 to the present day, with a total of 1.5 million items. Information is available in English, either in leaflet form, on the exhibit information plaques, or from free CD players that have several hours of English commentary.

Of greatest interest is the superb **Sami exhibition** in the basement. Look out for the extraordinary 1767 drawing of a rather cool-looking reindeer being castrated by a Sami using his teeth! The permanent **Strindberg painting exhibition** indicates the depth of this man's tortured soul and the intriguing 'small object exhibition' includes a duchess'

silver-lined toilet paper! Other exhibitions include fashion from the 17th to 20th centuries, the table exhibition (running continuously since 1955), Swedish traditions and national costume, and furniture.

Vasamuseet

Behind Nordiska Museet on the western shore of Djurgården, the acclaimed Vasamuseet (*☎ 5195 4800; w www.vasamuseet.se; adult/child Skr70/10; open 9.30am-7pm daily June-Aug, 10am-5pm daily Sept-May*) allows you to simultaneously look into the lives of 17th-century sailors while appreciating brilliant achievements in marine archaeology. You'll need around 1½ hours to appreciate this amazing place.

On 10 August 1628, the top-heavy flagship *Vasa* overturned and went straight to the bottom of the Saltsjön within minutes of being launched. Tour guides will explain the extraordinary and controversial 300-year story of its death and resurrection. After being raised in 1961, the incredible wooden sculptures on the ship were pieced together like a giant jigsaw and almost all of what you see today is original.

On the entrance level, there's a model of the ship at scale 1:10 and a cinema that shows a 25-minute film, covering topics not included in the exhibitions (it's screened in English at 11.30am and 1.30pm daily in summer). There are three other levels of exhibits, including temporary exhibitions, displays of artefacts salvaged from *Vasa*, on naval warfare and 17th-century sailing and navigation, and sculpture.

The bookshop is worth a visit and there's also a **restaurant**. Guided tours are in English hourly from 10.30am in summer, and at least twice daily the rest of the year.

Just outside the museum, there is a walkway leading to two more modern ships: both the icebreaker **Sankt Erik** as well as the lightship **Finngrundet** (*adult/child Skr35/15; open noon-5pm daily June-Aug, to 7pm July–mid-Aug*).

Junibacken

Junibacken (*☎ 5872 3000; adult/child Skr95/ 70; open 10am-5pm daily June-Aug, 10am-5pm Tues-Sun Sept-May*) recreates the fantasy scenes of Astrid Lindgren's childrens books, which should stir the imaginations of children and the memories of adults familiar with her characters. You'll go on a 10-minute train journey past miniature landscapes, fly over Stockholm, observing Swedish historical scenes and traditions, and pass through houses. It's a very professional and rather unusual form of entertainment.

Gröna Lund Tivoli

The crowded Gröna Lund Tivoli (☎ 5875 0100; W www.gronalund.com; admission Skr50; open noon-11pm Sat-Thur, noon-midnight Fri & Sat, May–mid-Sept; noon-11pm most days mid-June–mid-Aug) fun park has more than 25 rides, ranging from the easy circus carousel to the terrifying Free Fall, where you drop from a height of 80m in six seconds. There are lots of places to eat and drink in the park, but whether you could keep it down is another matter. The Åkbandet day pass (Skr220) gives unlimited rides; alternatively, individual rides range from Skr10 to Skr40. Big-name concerts are often staged here in summer.

Admission is free for Stockholm Card or 72-hour SL Tourist Card holders.

Other Things to See & Do

Beyond Djurgården's big and famous drawcards, there are plenty of little gems.

Prins Eugens Waldemarsudde (☎ 5458 3700; Prins Eugens väg 6; adult/child Skr70/free; open 11am-5pm Tues-Sun) is located at the southern tip of Djurgården. It was once the private palace of the painter prince who preferred art to royal pleasures and it holds his large collection of Nordic art. The buildings, art galleries and the old windmill are surrounded by picturesque gardens.

On the northern side of Djurgården, **Rosendals Slott** (☎ 402 6130; Rosendalsvägen; tours adult/child Skr50/25) was built as a palace for Karl XIV Johan in the 1820s, and features sumptuous, typically royal, furnishings. Admission is by guided tour only: tours start on the hour from noon to 3pm daily (except Monday) from June until August. While you're out this way, be sure to stop in the delightful café, which is set among trees and greenhouses, and is very popular with the locals.

Thielska Galleriet (☎ 662 5884; Sjötullsbacken; bus No 69 from Centralstationen; adult/child Skr50/30; open noon-4pm Mon-Sat, 1pm-4pm Sun), found at the east end of Djurgården, has a notable collection of late

19th- and early 20th-century Nordic art (including Anders Zorn and Carl Larsson).

Liljevalchs Konsthall (☎ 5083 1330; Djurgårdsvägen 60; adult/child Skr50/free; open 11am-5pm Wed & Fri-Sun, 11am-8pm Tues & Thur) is a marvellous gallery which covers 20th-century international art and craft.

Other minor museums around Djurgården include **Biologiska Museet** (Museum of Biology; ☎ 442 8215; Hazeliusporten) and the **Aquaria Vattenmuseum** (☎ 660 4940; Falkenbergsgatan 2), yet another aquarium.

LADUGÅRDSGÄRDET

North of Djurgården, in among the vast parkland, are more fine museums and attractions. Ladugårdsgärdet is part of the 27-sq-km **Ekoparken** (W www.ekoparken.com), the world's first national park within a city. Ekoparken is 14km long and stretches far into the northern suburbs of Stockholm.

Take bus No 69 from Centralstationen or Sergels Torg for the attractions covered in this section.

Museums

Sjöhistoriska Museet (National Maritime Museum; ☎ 5195 4900; Djurgårdsbrunnsvägen 24; adult/child Skr50/20; open 10am-5pm daily) has an exhibit of maritime memorabilia and over 1500 model ships. Displays also cover Swedish shipbuilding, sailors and life on board.

Tekniska Museet (Museum of Science & Technology; ☎ 450 5600; Museivägen 7; combined entry adult/child Skr60/20; open 10am-5pm Mon-Fri, 11am-5pm Sat & Sun) is just around the corner from the maritime museum and has exhaustive exhibits on Swedish inventions and their applications. **Telemuseum** (☎ 670 8100) is in the complex and covers everything you wanted to know about telecommunications and LM Ericsson.

Etnografiska Museet (National Museum of Ethnography; ☎ 5195 5000; Djurgårdsbrunnsvägen 34; adult/child Skr50/free; open 11am-5pm Tues & Thur-Sun, 11am-8pm Wed) is concerned with non-European races and cultures and has interesting temporary exhibitions.

Kaknästornet

About 500m from the museums is the 155m Kaknästornet (Kaknä Tower; ☎ 667 2180; open 9am-10pm daily May-Aug, 10am-9pm daily Sept-Apr), the automatic operations centre for radio and TV broadcasting in Sweden. It opened in 1967 and is still the tallest building in the city. There's a tourist office on the ground floor and an **observation deck** (adult/ child Skr25/15) and restaurant near the top. There are guided tours at 2pm and 4pm.

NORTHERN SUBURBS

The areas just north of the city centre are noted for their green and open spaces. Several large parks, spanning from Djurgården in the south, form Ekoparken, the first such protected city area in the world. The Haga Park is particularly pleasant for walks and bicycle tours.

Millesgården

Among the popular attractions is beautiful Millesgården (☎ 446 7594; Carl Milles väg 2, Lidingö island; adult/child Skr75/20, open 10am-5pm daily May-Sept, 10am-5pm Tues-Wed, Sat & Sun Oct-Apr), which was sculptor Carl Milles' home and studio. The gardens feature an outdoor sculpture collection with items from ancient Greece, Rome, medieval times and the Renaissance. There are also temporary exhibitions, a museum shop and a café. Take the metro to Ropsten, then bus No 207.

Naturhistoriska Riksmuseet & Cosmonova

The extensive Naturhistoriska Riksmuseet (National Museum of Natural History; ☎ 5195 4040; w www.nrm.se; Frescativägen 40; metro T-Universitetet; adult/child Skr65/40; open 10am-7pm daily Apr–mid-Aug, 10am-7pm Tues-Sun mid-Aug–Mar) was founded by Carl von Linné in 1739. It's now Sweden's largest museum and includes all the usual stuff – dinosaurs, marine life and the fauna of the polar regions.

Just next door to Naturhistoriska Riksmuseet, Cosmonova (☎ 5195 5130; adult/child Skr75/50) is a combined planetarium and Imax theatre. The diverse topics covered include Everest, Alaska, the oceans and outer space. Cosmonova screens films on the hour and advance reservations are recommended.

A combined entry ticket to the museum and Cosmonova costs only Skr120/80 per adult/child.

Hagaparken

To reach Hagaparken, take bus No 515 from Odenplan to Haga Norra. A few minutes' walk from the bus stop brings you to the amazing, brightly coloured **Koppartälten** (Copper Tent; open daily), built in 1787 as a stable and barracks for Gustav III's personal guard. It now contains a café, restaurant and **Haga Parkmuseum** (admission free), with displays about the park, its pavilions and the royal palace, Haga slott (not open to the public).

Gustav III:s Paviljong (Gustav III's Pavilion; ☎ 402 6130) is open to visitors only by guided tour; these run hourly from noon to 3pm Tuesday to Sunday from June to August and cost Skr50/25 per adult/child. The royal pavilion is a superb example of late neoclassical style; the furnishings and decor reflect Gustav III's interest in all things Roman after his Italian tour in 1782.

Fjärilshuset (Butterfly House; ☎ 730 3981; adult/child Skr60/25; open variable hours Tues-Sat) has an artificial tropical environment with free-flying birds and butterflies.

Ulriksdals Slott

Farther north is the yellow-painted royal palace, Ulriksdal Slott (☎ 402 6130; Ulriksdals Park; metro T-Bergshamra, then bus No 503). This large, early-17th-century building was home to King Gustaf VI Adolf and his family until 1973. Several of their attractive apartments, including the drawing room, which dates from 1923 are open to the public. The Orangery contains Swedish sculpture and Mediterranean plants. Queen Kristina's coronation carriage is also on show here.

Guided tours run hourly between noon and 3pm Tuesday to Sunday from June to August and cost Skr50/25 per adult/child.

SÖDERMALM

Mostly residential, Södermalm has more character than other parts of Stockholm. Head to the northern cliffs for evening walks among the old houses, and good views. Interesting neighbourhoods are around the **Katarina kyrka**, in the park near **Sofia kyrka**, around the **'Puckeln Shop District'** (Hornsgatan) and on Lotsgatan and Fjällgatan, not far from the Viking Line terminal.

You'll get great views from **Katarinahissen** (☎ 743 1395; Slussen; adult/child

Skr5/free; open 7.30am-10pm Mon-Sat, 10am-10pm Sun), a lift dating from the 1930s that takes you up 38m to the heights of Slussen (see Inner Stockholm map). At the top is one of the city's best restaurants, **Gondolen** (see Places to Eat).

Museums

Stockholms Stadsmuseum *(☎ 5083 1600; Slussen; adult/child Skr50/10; open 11am-5pm Tues-Sun Sept-May, 11am-7pm Tues-Sun June-Aug)* is housed in the late-17th-century palace of Nicodemus Tessin the Elder, in Ryssgården. Exhibits cover the history of the city and its people, and it's worth a visit once you develop a romantic attachment to Stockholm.

Leksaksmuseet *(Toy Museum; ☎ 641 6100; Mariatorget; adult/child Skr45/25; open 10am-4pm Tues-Fri, noon-4pm Sat & Sun year-round, 10am-4pm Mon mid-June–mid-Aug)*, behind the Maria Magdalene kyrka, is an oversized fantasy nursery full of everything you probably ever wanted as a child (and may still hanker after as an adult!), including dolls, model railways, planes and cars. Children will enjoy themselves in the playroom and at the children's theatre.

Spårvägsmuseet *(Transport Museum; ☎ 462 5531; Tegelviksgatan 22; adult/child Skr20/10; open 10am-5pm Mon-Fri, 11am-4pm Sat & Sun)*, in the Söderhallen transport depot, near the Viking Line terminal, has around 40 vehicles, including horse-drawn carriages, Stockholm metro trains, vintage trams and buses. Admission is free with the SL Tourist Card.

LÅNGHOLMEN

This small island in the Mälaren lake once housed a prison and **Långholmens Fängelsemuseum** *(Prison Museum; ☎ 668 0500; adult/child Skr25/10; open 11am-4pm daily)* is in one of the cells – the rest of the building has been converted into a quirky hotel and STF hostel (see Places to Stay). The displays here cover 250 years of prison history.

To get to Långholmen, take the metro to Hornstull, then walk along Långholmsgatan. There are some very pleasant picnic and bathing spots on the island.

SOUTHERN SUBURBS

One of Stockholm's more unusual attractions is **Skogskyrkogården** *(Söckenvagen;*

metro to T-Skogskyrkogården; admission free), a cemetery in a peaceful pine woodland setting. Surprisingly, the cemetery is World Heritage–listed in recognition of its unique design and the harmony of function and landscape. The area is dominated by a large granite cross, and there are a number of chapels scattered throughout; this is also where Greta Garbo is buried. It's a pleasant place for a walk.

FJÄDERHOLMARNA

These tiny, delightful islands (Feather Islands) offer an easy escape from the city. They're just 25 minutes away by boat and a favourite swimming spot for locals. As they're located on the eastern side of Djurgården, take one of the boats (adult/child Skr75/35 return) that leave from either Nybroplan (half-hourly) or from Slussen (hourly) between May and early September. There are a couple of craft shops and restaurants here and the last boats leave the islands at around midnight, making them a perfect spot to enjoy the long daylight hours.

ACTIVITIES

Stockholm offers a great variety of activities for everyone and the tourist offices can provide details. Many people head for the coast and the islands of the archipelago (with good swimming spots) or organise picnics in the parks and gardens. Summer sees both locals and visitors taking advantage of the good weather and long daylight hours.

Hiking trips around the city are fairly limited, but the parks offer some good walks – the most popular area for short walks is Djurgården. Climbers have better options, with around 150 cliffs within 40 minutes' drive of the city. There's also Sweden's largest indoor climbing centre, **Klätterverket** *(☎ 641 1048; Marcusplatsen 17, Nacka; admission Skr80)*, with around 1000 sq metres of artificial climbing.

Cycling is best in the parks and away from the busy central streets and arterial roads, but some streets have special cycle lanes (often shared with pedestrians). Tourist offices can supply maps of cycle routes. See Bicycle in the Getting Around section for further information.

There are indoor and open-air pools plus a gym at **Eriksdalsbadet** *(☎ 5084 0250; Hammarby slussväg 8; open daily; entry adult/child*

Skr65/30) in the far south of Södermalm. If you want a relaxing swim in an extraordinary Art Nouveau bathing salon, try **Centralbadet** (☎ 242400; *Drottninggatan 88)*, built in 1904. The entrance price of Skr90 includes access to the pool, saunas and gym. Treatments, such as massage, are available for an additional fee.

From **Sjöcafe** (☎ 660 5757), by the bridge leading to Djurgården, you can rent bikes, in-line skates, kayaks, canoes and rowboats. Opposite is **Tvillingarnas Sjökrog** (☎ 663 3739; *Strandvägskajen 27;* W *www.tvillingar nas.com)*, where you can rent sailing and motorboats in various sizes from April to September. Small boats are available from around Skr350 per hour; larger boats can be rented for a day, weekend or week. You can even rent a 40-foot sailing boat (with or without a skipper).

ORGANISED TOURS

Stockholm Sightseeing (☎ 587 14020; W *www.stockholmsightseeing.com)* operates frequent cruises between early April and mid-December around the central bridges and canals from Strömkajen (near the Grand Hotel), Nybroplan or Stadshusbron. There are one-hour tours from Skr90 to Skr110, but the two-hour 'Under the Bridges of Stockholm' (Skr150) covers more territory and passes under 15 bridges and through two locks. Some of the one-hour tours are free for Stockholm Card holders. The company runs a guided four-hour tour from Stadshusbron to Drottningholm Palace, departing at 11am and 1pm, from early June to mid-August (Skr280).

The land-based sister operation is **City Sightseeing** (☎ 587 14030; W *www.citysight seeing.com)*, which runs daily tours of the city departing from Gustav Adolfs Torg between April and early October. Coach tours of the city (Skr170-280, 1½ to three-hour), and walking tours around Gamla Stan or Haga Park (Skr80, 1½ hours, daily). There are also combo trips offering sightseeing by coach and boat.

It's possible to take a one-hour, English-language guided walk through Gamla Stan with an authorised guide (Skr50). In summer these tours start at 7.30pm on Monday, Wednesday and Thursday; from September to May they commence at 1.30pm on Saturday and Sunday. Meet at the Obelisk at Slottsbacken, outside the royal palace; no reservation is needed. To go back even further in time, take a cruise in a great old wooden ship done up to resemble a Viking longboat. From Midsummer to the end of August, the **Svea Viking** (☎ 202223; W *www .sveaviking.se)* runs regular 1½ hour sightseeing cruises (adult/child Skr150/50) of the city's waterways and out into the archipelago. You can't miss the ship, as it's moored outside the Royal Palace.

An incredible way to appreciate Stockholm's beauty is from a hot-air balloon, which is possible from May to September and costs Skr1695 per person. Contact **City Ballong** (☎ 345464; W *www.cityballong.se)* for further details.

SPECIAL EVENTS

There are many festivals, concerts and other happenings on Sergels Torg and Kungsträdgården throughout the summer, and the major museums exhibit temporary exhibitions on a grand scale. *What's on Stockholm* lists daily events.

The biggest events in Stockholm are those celebrated throughout the country, eg, Midsummer, Walpurgis Night, Lucia Festival, Christmas and New Year's Eve. See Public Holidays & Special Events in the Facts for the Visitor chapter for information on these traditional celebrations, and if you're in Stockholm at the right time, head to Skansen to participate in festivities.

There are good cultural festivals in the capital, including the **Stockholm Jazz Festival** (W *www.svd.se/jazz)* in mid-July and the **Stockholm International Film Festival** (W *www.filmfestivalen.se)* in mid- to late November.

Sporting events include the **Lidingöloppet** (W *www.lidingoloppet.se)*, the world's largest cross-country running race with between 25,000 and 30,000 participants, held in late September or early November in Lidingö on Stockholm's outskirts. Other events include the **Stockholm Open** (W *www.stockholm open.se)* tennis tournament, in October, and the **Stockholm Marathon** (W *www.marathon .se)*, in June.

Two more festivals of interest are the **Stockholm Pride** (W *www.stockholmpride.org)*, a big gay and lesbian event that's held annually in early August, and **Restaurangernas Dag** (early June) when Stockholm's restaurants move into

Visiting Åland

There are more than enough attractions in Stockholm to keep tourists busy for weeks, but visitors to the capital with some time on their hands might be interested in taking advantage of the many boat services between Sweden and Åland (popular with local day-trippers). Technically Finnish, the Åland islands (population 25,400) are unique and autonomous, with their own flag and culture. A number of Swedish dialects are spoken, and few Ålanders speak Finnish. This situation goes back to a League of Nations decision in 1921 after a Swedish-Finnish dispute over sovereignty. Åland took its own flag in 1954 and has issued stamps (prized by collectors) since 1984. Both the euro and Swedish krona are legal tender here.

Although Åland joined the EU along with Finland in 1995, it was granted a number exemptions, including duty-free tax laws which allowed the essential ferry services between the islands and mainland Finland and Sweden to continue operating profitably.

The islands are popular for summer cycling and camping holidays; there are medieval parish churches, ruins and fishing villages to explore. The capital and (only town) of Åland is **Mariehamn**, in the south of the main island group. In summer, Mariehamn is crowded with tourists but it still manages to retain its village flavour and the marinas at the harbours are quite pretty when loaded up with gleaming sailing boats. The main pedestrian street, Torggatan, is a colourful and crowded hive of activity, and there are some fine museums – enough to allow a leisurely day's exploration. Åland's most striking attraction is the medieval castle, **Kastelholm**, in Sund 20km northeast of Mariehamn. You can only visit on guided tours, which run frequently (in English) from June to August.

For more information on Åland, drop into Sweden House (Hamngatan 27, Stockholm); there's a travel agency here, specialising in the islands, whose staff can help to plan your visit.

The main companies operating between Sweden and Åland (and on to Finland) are Viking Line and Silja Line, while Eckerö Linjen, Ånedin Linjen and Birka Cruises operate only between Åland and Sweden. See the Getting There & Away chapter for more details on these ferry services. Once on the islands, you can take your wheels almost anywhere around the island group using the bridges or the network of car and bicycle ferries.

---

central Kungsträdgården and offer food, drinks and entertainment.

PLACES TO STAY
Camping

Open only from late June to mid-August, **Östermalms Citycamping** (☎ 102903; *Östermalms Idrottsplats, Fiskartorpsvägen 2; tent or camper van site per person Skr60*) is a cheap and very central option with reasonable facilities (but no shade for camper vans). To get here, take the metro to T-Stadion then walk 600m, or take bus No 55.

Bredäng Camping (☎ 977071; ⓔ *bredang camping@telia.com; Stora Sällskapets väg; tent sites Skr165/180 low/high season, 4-bed cabins Skr450, dorm beds from Skr140kr, doubles/ triples Skr380/450; open mid-Apr–late Oct)* is 10km southwest of the city centre in a pleasant lakeside location. It's well equipped and there's a hostel here too. Take the metro to T-Bredäng, then walk 700m. If you're driving, it's well signposted from the E4/E20 motorway.

Ängby Camping (☎ 370420; ⓔ *reserva tion@angbycamping.se; Blackebergsvägen 24, Bromma; tent sites Skr140; cabins from Skr400; open year-round)*, about 10km west of Stockholm, by an inlet of Mälaren lake, is a forested camping ground with good facilties and friendly staff. Take the metro to T-Ängbyplan, then walk 600m.

Hostels

Stockholm has both HI-affiliated STF hostels (where a membership card yields a Skr45 discount) and independent hostels (no membership cards required). The choice includes four boat hostels, one in an old prison and some central options; two hostels are open in summer only and accommodation is in school classrooms! Most hostels fill up during the late afternoon in summer so arrive early or book in advance. May is also a very busy time for hostels, with many Swedish school groups visiting the capital. For a Skr20 fee, tourist offices in the city centre can assist in getting a bed – or you can buy a phonecard and start dialling. All hostels listed here are open year-round unless otherwise specified; many have options for single, double or family rooms, and a few have 24-hour reception (a rarity elsewhere in Sweden). Generally, you'll pay extra to use the hostel's linen; bring your own sleeping sheet to save around Skr50 per night. Breakfast is available at many places, usually costing around Skr45.

Skeppsholmen Most travellers head first to Skeppsholmen, just east of the city centre (take bus No 65 from Centralstationen, or just walk).

The popular STF boat hostel **Vandrarhem af Chapman** (☎ 463 2266; e info@chap man.stfturist.se; dorm beds Skr120-150; twin rooms Skr360) has done plenty of travelling of its own but it's now a big anchored hostel swaying gently in sight of the city centre. It's a good idea to book in advance for a bed on board. The bunks are below the decks; breakfast is Skr55. On dry land beside the boat hostel, and with the same reception (open 24-hours) and prices, is the larger **Vandrarhem Skeppsholmen**, with kitchen and laundry facilities. Note that from August 2004, the boat hostel will be closed for an estimated nine months while it undergoes a complete renovation. The land-based hostel here will be open as usual during this time.

City Centre & Vasastaden The closest hostel to Centralstationen is **City Backpackers** (☎ 206920; e info@citybackpackers.se; Upplandsgatan 2A; dorm beds Skr170-200, doubles Skr490). It's a good choice for the clean rooms, friendly staff and excellent facilities, including a kitchen, sauna, laundry and Internet access. A bit further north, **Hostel Mitt i City** (☎ 217 630; e reserva tions@stockholm.mail.telia.com; Västmanna-gatan 13; dorm beds from Skr175, singles/doubles Skr395/590) occupies a few floors of an old apartment building. Rates include breakfast, but there's no kitchen.

Near T-Rådmansgatan, north of the city centre, **Hostel Bed & Breakfast** (☎ 152838; e hostelbedandbreakfast@chello.se; Rehns-gatan 21; dorm beds Skr150-175, singles/doubles Skr325/430) is a pleasant, informal basement hostel with a kitchen and laundry, plus cheap breakfast (Skr25). There's a large summer annexe here filled with beds (Skr100), but it's not for those who like their privacy!

Östermalm Part of the STF hostel network, **Backpackers Inn** (☎ 660 7515; e back packersinn@telia.com; Banérgatan 56; metro T-Karlaplan; beds Skr110-150; open late-June–mid-Aug) has 300 beds in a school building. There are no kitchen facilities, but breakfast is available for Skr50.

Nearby, the SVIF (Sveriges Vandrarhem i Förening) **Östra Reals Vandrarhem** (☎ 664 1114; Karlavägen 79; dorm beds Skr125-150; open mid-June–mid-Aug) is also in an old school; there are kitchen facilities here (and no bunks!).

Södermalm & Långholmen There are a fair number of hostels in and around Södermalm, a good 15-minute walk from the Viking Line boats and Centralstationen.

The ship hostel **Gustaf af Klint** (☎ 640 4077; Stadsgårdskajen 153; dorm beds Skr130, doubles Skr360) has beds in pretty, down-at-heel rooms. There's no kitchen here for self-caterers. West of the railway lines, the red-painted **Mälaren den Röda Båten** (☎ 644 4385; e info@icts.se; Söder Malärstrand, Kaj-plats 6; dorm beds Skr185, hostel singles/doubles Skr400/450, hotel singles/doubles from Skr665/775) is probably the cosiest of Stockholm's floating hostels with very comfortable hotel-standard cabins, and a good summer **restaurant**. A bit further west is the rather unhelpful **M/S Rygerfjord** (☎ 840830; e hotell@rygerfjord.se; Söder Malärstrand Kajplats 14; dorm beds Skr180-195, private cabins from Skr625), with a hostel and hotel-style cabins, plus a **restaurant**.

In the west end of Södermalm, near T-Zinkendamm, the well-equipped STF **Vandrarhem Zinkensdamm** (☎ 616 8100; e mail@zinkensdamm.com; Zinkens väg 20; dorm beds Skr155-200, hotel singles/doubles Skr1095/1395, discounted to Skr705/1095) is a large, attractive complex in a quiet location by Tantolunden park. There are reasonably priced hotel rooms here too.

The small pretty island of Långholmen (off the northwestern corner of Södermalm) is home to STF **Vandrarhem Långholmen** (☎ 668 0510; e vandrarhem@langholmen .com; dorm beds from Skr175, hotel singles/doubles Skr1095/1395, discounted to Skr795/1095). In this former prison, there are dorm beds in former cells (booking is essential) and slightly roomier hotel-standard rooms.

Other Areas If things get desperate, there are more than 20 other hostels around the county that can be reached by SL buses, trains or archipelago boats within an hour or so. There are also a number of summer camping grounds, which usually offer cheap cabin accommodation. Some options are mentioned in the Around Stockholm section.

Klubbensborg (☎ 646 1255; *Klubbensborgsvägen 27; beds from Skr150, singles/ doubles Skr300/600)* is a pleasant SVIF hostel in a gorgeous lakeside setting southwest of the city centre. There are several buildings that date from the 17th century, plus a kitchen, laundry, café and summer camping area. The downside is that it's a meandering 1km walk from the closest metro station (T-Mälarhöjden).

Solna Vandrarhem & Motelcamp (☎ 5148 1550; e *info@solna-vandrarhem.se; Enköpingsvägen 16; dorm beds Skr150, singles/ doubles/triples Skr225/308/510)* is worth trying when the city hostels are full. This 400-bed hostel in the northwestern suburbs, has beds in prefabricated lodges with new kitchens and TV rooms. There's also a restaurant here, and a camping ground. Take the metro to T-Solna, then bus No 505, which stops directly out the front.

Private Rooms
A number of agencies, including **Bed & Breakfast Service** (☎ 660 6654; e *info@bed breakfast.a.se,* W *www.bedbreakfast.a.se)*, and **Bed & Breakfast Agency** (☎ 643 8028; e *info@bba.nu,* W *www.bba.nu)* can arrange good-value apartment accommodation or B&B from around Skr200 per person per night.

Budget Hotels
Hotel Formule 1 (☎ 744 2044; *Mikrofonvägen 30; metro T-Telefonplan; rooms Skr290)* offers perhaps the best value in Stockholm, with very cheap rooms that accommodate up to three people. Rooms are hardly inspiring, facilities are shared, and it's 4km southwest of town, but who can argue at that price?

Hotels
Hotellcentralen (☎ 789 2490; *Centralstationen; open 9am-6pm daily, 8am-8pm daily in summer)* at Centralstationen, can usually find suitable accommodation for a Skr50 fee. The handy booklet *Hotels and Youth Hostels in Stockholm,* available free from tourist offices, lists most hotels and their room rates.

Most Stockholm hotels offer discount rates on weekends (Friday, Saturday and often Sunday night) and in summer (from Midsummer to mid-August). Discounts can be up to 50% off the normal price, making some hotels surprisingly affordable. Almost all hotel prices include breakfast.

Check also the listings under Hostels, earlier in this section. The hostels in Södermalm and Långholmen offer hotel rooms as well as dorm beds. Most hotels have their own website.

If city hotels are full, or if you want free parking, try a suburban hotel – they usually have good public-transport connections.

City Centre & Vasastaden Just north of the centre, **Hotell Bema** (☎ 232 675; *Upplandsgatan 13; singles/doubles Skr820/890, reduced to Skr590/690)* is a small and friendly hotel opposite Tegnérlunden Park. The modern, good-value rooms have all the required facilties.

Good Night Hotell Danielsson (☎ 411 1065; *Västmannagatan 5; singles/doubles Skr600/800, discounted to Skr550/750)* is a simple, cheap-and-cheerful, old-fashioned place with clean and affordable rooms.

Hotell Gustav Vasa (☎ 343801; e *gustav .vasa@wineasy.se; Västmannagatan 61; singles/ doubles from Skr725/1000)* is another small family business.

The welcoming people who run **Oden Pensionat** (☎ 796 9600; e *info@pensionat.nu; Kammakargatan 62 • Odengatan 38; singles/ doubles with shared facilities from Skr680/750, with private facilities Skr930/1025)* must be doing well – a third branch of this affordable pension has just opened, north of Centralstationen. The rooms with private facilities are larger than those without. Reasonable summer discounts apply.

Queen's Hotel (☎ 249460; e *queens hotel@queenshotel.se; Drottninggatan 71A; singles/doubles with shared facilities Skr650/ 750),* is a pleasant place in the middle of town. It has comfortable rooms with either shared or private facilities, in an early-20th-century building (with marble staircases and an antique lift) on the pedestrian mall.

Wasa Park Hotell (☎ 5454 5300; *Sankt Eriksplan 1; singles/doubles from Skr525/625, discounted to Skr495/595*), northwest of the central business district, is functional and another affordable option.

There's no shortage of hotels in the area immediately surrounding Centralstationen; most are in the mid-to-upper price bracket but offer good weekend and summer prices.

Scandic Hotel Continental (☎ 5173 4200; e *continental@scandic-hotels.com; Vasagatan; singles/doubles from Skr1650/2100, discounted to Skr650/750*) is opposite Centralstationen, near Klara kyrka, and offers the regular high standards of the Scandic chain.

Central Hotel (☎ 5662 0800; e *bokning@centralhotel.se; Vasagatan 38; singles/doubles from Skr1575/1775, discounted to Skr795/1095*) caters primarily to the business traveller, but it has comfortable small rooms, a good location and decent summer discounts, plus a pleasant glass-roofed breakfast area.

Nordic Hotels (☎ 5056 3000; e *info@nordichotels.se; Vasaplan; singles/doubles from Skr1500/2400*), two 'design hotels' definitely out to impress, are new and supercool. Nordic Hotel Light and Nordic Hotel Sea feature sleek black-and-white decor and nautical blues and greens, respectively. Regular prices are steep, but summer prices are reasonable (up to 50% discount).

Scandic Hotel Sergel Plaza (☎ 5172 6300; e *sergel.plaza@scandic-hotels.com; Brunkebergstorg 9; singles/doubles from Skr1780/2670, discounted to Skr590/790*) is a fine establishment in the centre of the action. It's just behind Kultuhuset, off Sergels Torg, and comes complete with ornate modern decor and live piano music.

Rica City Hotel Kungsgatan (☎ 723 7220; e *info.kungsgatan@rica.se; Kungsgatan 47; singles/doubles Skr1595/1845, discounted to Skr890/1220*) is right up your alley if you're in town to shop. It offers very comfortable rooms in the same block as the PUB department store (where Greta Garbo started her working career).

Berns Hotel (☎ 5663 2200; e *hotel.berns@berns.se; Näckströmsgatan 8; singles/doubles from Skr2050/2550, discounted to Skr1100/1500*) is chic. It's just off Kungsträdgården, and is a superb example of 19th-century architecture. This extremely elegant and upmarket hotel has a great bar and restaurant. The writer August Strindberg named his novel *Rödarummet* after what's now the breakfast dining room.

Grand Hotel Stockholm (☎ 679 3500; e *info@grandhotel.se; Södra Blasieholmshamnen 8; singles/doubles from Skr2095/3295, discounted to Skr1300/1900*), is another five-star luxury option, that offers impeccable service and some of the city's most sumptuous lodgings. It's an impressive stone building with a copper roof and good views of the Royal Palace; if you can afford the extra money, ask for a room with harbour views. The restaurants and bars here are also first-rate.

Östermalm This quiet, residential neighbourhood is home to a few good accommodation options. **A&Be Hotell** (☎ 660 2100; *Grev Turegatan 50; singles/doubles from Skr490/690*) is small and pretty and offers good value.

Scandic Hotel Anglais (☎ 5173 4000; e *anglais@scandic-hotels.com; Humlegårdsgatan 23; singles/doubles from Skr900/2030, discounted to Skr690/1350*) offers well-appointed rooms with a great breakfast, and economy single rooms that offer reasonable value. **Lydmar Hotel** (☎ 5661 1300; e *info@lydmar.se; Sturegatan 10; singles/doubles from Skr1950/2300, discounted to Skr1280/1520*), frequented by the seriously hip, is a 'concept hotel'. It's stylishly decorated with well-equipped rooms, but you won't need to spend too much time in your room when so much is going on downstairs. The very cool **Lobby Bar & Restaurant** often has art exhibitions and live music (primarily jazz and soul), plus an interesting crowd. You'll have to negotiate all this to find the check-in desk!

Gamla Stan This atmospheric part of town has a few quality options, but budget travellers will be disappointed by the prices!

First Hotel Reisen (☎ 223260; e *reisen@firsthotels.com; Skeppsbron 12; singles/doubles Skr1892/2462, discounted to Skr1252/1402*), on the waterfront, is a luxurious hotel just a few blocks from the Royal Palace. It has an extraordinary swimming pool in an old cellar, with brick archways and ceiling. The rooms are atmospheric and have traditional furnishings.

At one time the world's largest motor yacht, **Mälardrottningen** (☎ 5451 8780; e *reception@malardrottningen.se; Riddarholmen;*

singles/doubles cabins from Skr1050/1180, discounted to Skr870/980) offers accommodation in very well-appointed cabins, each with en suite. The cosy vessel was launched in 1924 and previously owned by American heiress Barbara Hutton (it was a gift from her father for her 18th birthday!). There's also a good **restaurant** on deck.

Djurgården There's only one hotel on this pretty green island. **Scandic Hotel Hasselbacken** (☎ 5173 4300; e hasselbacken@scandic-hotels.com; Hazeliusbacken 20; singles/doubles Skr1510/2160, discounted to Skr1098/1398) is in the heart of the area's fine attractions, away from the hustle and bustle of the city. Facilities are of the usual high standard.

Södermalm The highly recommended **Columbus Hotell** (☎ 503 11200; e columbus@columbus.se; Tjärhovsgatan 11; budget singles/doubles/triples Skr595/795/995, standard singles/doubles from Skr1195/1495, discounted to Skr895/1195) is in a quiet part of Södermalm near T-Medborgarplatsen, set around a cobblestone courtyard, by a pretty park. As well as the budget rooms (which have TV, telephone and shared bathroom facilities), there are classy hotel-standard rooms. All prices include breakfast.

Hotel Tre Små Rum (☎ 641 2371; e info@tresmarum.se; Högbergsgatan 81; rooms with shared facilities Skr695) is a cute place in Söder, near T-Mariatorget. It started off with three small rooms, as the name suggests, but has grown to seven. There's one tiny single room, so even if you're travelling solo, ask for a double (the price is the same).

Hotel Söders Höjder (☎ 615 2135; Rentstiernas gata 15; singles/doubles with shared facilities from Skr795/895), not far from the great city views found at Fjällgatan, is another small, good-value place.

Hotel Anno 1647 (☎ 442 1680; e hotell@anno1647.se; Mariagränd 3; singles/doubles Skr1595/1895, discounted to Skr995/1295) is a historic hotel with labyrinthine hallways and a range of comfortable, well-equipped rooms.

There are two high-standard Scandic Hotels in the area. **Scandic Sjöfartshotellet** (☎ 5173 4900; e sjofart@scandic-hotels.com; Katarinavägen 26; singles/doubles from Skr1100/1400, discounted to Skr790/890) is just a few minutes' walk from Gamla Stan and has a charming nautical atmosphere. Large **Scandic Hotel Malmen** (☎ 5173 4700; e malmen@scandic-hotels.com; Götgatan 49-51; singles/doubles Skr1600/1900, discounted to Skr950/1150) is well located in the heart of the action at Medborgarplatsen.

PLACES TO EAT
Stockholm has thousands of restaurants, ranging from inexpensive lunch cafeterias to gourmet establishments with outrageously fine decor. The city also has some of the finest dining halls in Scandinavia.

Very few restaurants will accept orders after 10pm, although they may stay open until midnight or 1am. Many places are closed on Sunday – it's a good idea to phone ahead to check.

Gamla Stan
Tourists, not surprisingly, love Gamla Stan, and many dine along Västerlånggatan in places like **Michelangelo** (☎ 215099; Västerlånggatan 62; snacks & meals Skr40-160), with pizza and pasta from around Skr80 and great classical decor, or drink their coffee in the stylish vaults of **Café Art** (☎ 411 7661), next door.

Check out the restaurants on nearby Stora Nygatan.

The cosy basement restaurant **Siam Thai** (☎ 200233; Stora Nygatan 25; mains Skr125-185), has a good range of favourite Thai rice, curry and noodle dishes and a weekday lunch offer for Skr75.

Hermitage (☎ 411 9500; Stora Nygatan 11; dinner Skr70) is a welcoming vegetarian restaurant that's well worth a visit. The hearty *dagens rätt* (daily special, usually available only at lunch) costs Skr60

Gåsgränd 4 (☎ 247144; Gåsgränd 4; dinner mains Skr155-205), around the corner from Hermitage, is an attractive restaurant-café with outdoor seating on the lovely square. A neighbouring **kebab stall** has cheap fast-food options.

Chokoladkoppen (☎ 203170; Stortorget; cakes & snacks Skr30-70) plays great tunes and offers wonderful cake selections, plus outdoor seating on bustling Stortorget – what better way to spend a sunny afternoon? This gay-friendly place is pricey but excellent hot chocolate drinks are Skr25.

Locals frequent long-established restaurants such as **Zum Franziskaner** (☎ 411 8330;

Skeppsbron 44; lunch Skr70, dagens rätt Skr70, dinner mains Skr100-300), which was founded in 1421 by German monks and claims to be the oldest restaurant in the city. It still serves German and Austrian beers, as well as hearty, good-value 'Franziskaner classics' such as sausages and schnitzel. Although the current building dates from 1906, it has the appearance of a museum inside.

Gamla Stans Bryggeri *(☎ 4112913; Tullhus 2, Skeppsbron; mains Skr100-250)* is a huge waterside restaurant with its own brewery and a wide-ranging menu to cater to most tastes.

Den Gyldene Freden *(☎ 249760; Österlånggatan 51; mains Skr282-375; open Mon-Sat)* is a total Swedish classic. It is a deluxe establishment that attracts Stockholm's high fliers and has been doing so since it opened in 1722. The à la carte mains may well hurt the wallet, but there are usually cheaper *husmanskost* (traditional home-cooking) dishes on offer as well, priced from around Skr100 to Skr200.

There are several more excellent, though rather pricey, restaurants on and around Österlånggatan. **Pontus in the Greenhouse** *(☎ 238500; Österlånggatan 17; bar menu Skr140-195, fine dining from Skr350)* next to the St George monument, has a great reputation.

Leijontornet *(☎ 142355; Lilla Nygatan 5; lunch from Skr75, dinner mains Skr235-265)* is one of the finest restaurants in the neighbourhood. The dining room includes the foundations of a 14th-century tower; its brick-vaulted ceilings and candlelight add to the atmosphere of romance and history. The bar menu offers a few tapas plates (three for Skr125) should you just want to linger over a drink.

For something a little more modern, **Grill Ruby** *(☎ 206015; Österlånggatan 14; light meals Skr80-140, mains Skr150-250)* and the neighbouring **Bistro Ruby** *(☎ 205776, Österlånggatan 14; meals Skr80-250)* play along a *Paris, Texas* theme. Grill Ruby is a relaxed, American-style place with lots of meat and fish dishes from the grill, plus a good bar menu of light meals such as burgers, burritos or salads. Bistro Ruby is low-lit and intimate, with a French-influenced menu and prices similar to those of its neighbours.

City

Head to the stalls along the eastern edge of Kungsträdgården for a range of fast food, including hot dogs, burgers and baked potatoes, and lots of ice-cream options in summer. **Friday's American Bar & Café** *(☎ 100626; Kungsträdgården; dishes Skr130-220)* is super central in the middle of a bustling park and is a popular drinking spot. It has a long, American-style menu with salads, snacks, burgers, Tex-Mex and pasta.

Souperb *(☎ 673 2301; Sveavägen 92)* is a small store with a clever name. It serves up really great soups (including seafood, green chicken curry or tomato and basil) for around Skr55, including bread. **Kebab House** *(cnr Vasagatan & Kungsgatan)* is perfect for night owls and quite close to Centralstationen. It offers kebabs and burgers until 5am nightly.

Next to the Dubliner pub on Smålandsgatan you'll find the entrance to **Birger Jarlspassagen**, a great little arcade full of cool cafés. **Waynes Coffee** *(☎ 245970; Vasagatan 7; lunch buffet Skr60)* has great café fare and a Skr60 lunch buffet of appealing salads. Look out for other central branches of this stylish café chain that's spreading its way through the country, bringing muffins, paninis, bagels, salads and good coffee to the masses. Other branches include Kungsgatan 14 and Drottninggatan 31.

Vetekatten *(☎ 218454; Kungsgatan 55)* is one of the city's most traditional cafés, with an assortment of inviting rooms and lovely cakes and pastries. Its cosy, grandmotherly decor stands in stark contrast to the modern lines of Waynes and its ilk. **Sturekatten** *(☎ 611 1612; Riddargatan 4)* just east of the centre, also has a great old-world ambience.

Upplandsgatan, close by a few of the hostels and budget hotels, has a couple of good eateries. **Spice House** *(☎ 141032; Upplandsgatan 6; dishes Skr65-150)* serves authentic Indian fare. **Sabai Sabai** *(☎ 790 0913; Kammarkagatan 44; dishes Skr85-170)* is a Thai restaurant with fab food and over-the-top decor. **Carinas Pizzeria** *(☎ 212687; Upplandsgatan 9B; pizza Skr35-55)* has a cheap lunch special – pizza for just Skr29.

Birger Jarlsgatan and Stureplan have many upmarket places. **Riche** *(☎ 5450 3560; Birger Jarlsgatan 4; mains Skr120-270)*, with a glass-fronted veranda, should be seen for its stylish decor alone. Nearby **Sturehof**

(☎ 440 5730; Stureplan 2; mains Skr100-170) offers great people-watching from its outdoor tables. The menu includes simple, reasonably priced Swedish fare (eg, herring, sausages), plus more upmarket dishes like grilled tuna and entrecôte steak. **East** (☎ 611 4959; Stureplan 13; dishes Skr90-250) is a cool, pricey place with an extensive menu offering the best of Asian cuisines including Thai, Vietnamese, Chinese, Malaysian and Japanese.

Franska Matsalen (☎ 679 3584; Grand Hotel Stockholm, Södra Blasieholmshamnen 8; set menus from Skr825-1300, à la carte mains Skr300-500; open Mon-Fri), the 'French dining room', is one of the very best restaurants in town. The excruciatingly expensive menus, influenced by French styles, are magnificent. Less likely to break the bank is **Verandan** (☎ 679 3586; Grand Hotel Stockholm, Södra Blasieholmshamnen 8; breakfast Skr185, mains Skr105-300, buffet Skr315). Here you can enjoy a huge smörgåsbord breakfast, with 124 hot and cold dishes to choose from! There's also a plentiful, traditional buffet on offer at lunch (May to September) and dinner (year-round). It includes all the Swedish dishes you would expect – come hungry! You can also make à la carte selections (from pasta or hamburger to fillet of veal or reindeer).

Super-posh **Operakällaren** (☎ 676 5800; Jakobs Torg 10; mains 350-420), within the Opera House, is one of the most upmarket options in the city – indeed in the entire country. The century-old place has fantastic decor which has to be seen to be believed, and a gourmet menu printed in French, plus an outstanding wine list and super-attentive service. The six-course 'Menu Dégustation' costs a mere Skr1200! **Bakfickan** (☎ 676 5808; mains Skr100-200), also within the Opera House complex, is a *much* more cas-ual option. It's an intimate place with great Art Nouveau decor and well-prepared homely fare.

Vasastaden

For beautifully presented fish and shellfish dishes, head to **Le Bistrot de Wasahof** (☎ 323440; Dalagatan 46; mains Skr140-220), commonly referred to just as 'Wasahof'. As well as superb food, there's magnificent service and a great bistro atmosphere, so you'll need to reserve a table in advance. The seafood platters are exceptional, but there are choices for thse who aren't seafood lovers.

Musslan (☎ 346410; Dalagatan 46; dishes Skr100-220), next door to Wasahof, has the same kitchen and more great food (with the same emphasis on seafood), but draws the younger crowd.

Tranan (☎ 5272 8100; Karlbergsvägen 14; dishes Skr95-275) is a simple, stylish place on Odenplan. Formerly an old beer hall, it's now usually crowded with locals enjoying one of the best neighbourhood restaurants in Stockholm, and enjoying meals from a comprehensive menu of both simple Swedish fare and more expensive international dishes. Downstairs is a popular bar that attracts the hip young crowd.

Haga Restaurang & Delikatess (☎ 319695; Hagagatan 18; meals Skr90-180) is a friendly, cosy, Italian-style family restaurant serving very good pizza and pasta for under Skr100, plus more substantial meals and appealing antipasto platters.

Narknoi (☎ 307070; Odengatan 94; mains Skr115-175), an unpretentious place with excellent Thai food, is another good choice.

Södermalm

Kebab Kungen (☎ 641 0630; Götgatan 60; open until 5am nightly) is a good spot for a quick, cheap fix. Kebabs and felafels start at just Skr25.

The **Nystekt Strömming** (Södermalmstorg) van outside the metro station T-Slussen is another fast-food alternative, but with a much more Swedish slant. Here you'll get some of the best fried herring in Stockholm.

Hermans (☎ 643 9480; Fjällgatan 23A; lunch/dinner buffet Skr65/95) is Södermalm's place for budget vegetarian fare. The food is good and very reasonably priced, but you'll probably be more impressed with the million-dollar view of the city. **Creperie Fyra Knop** (☎ 640 7727; Svartensgatan 4; crepes Skr44-74) is an excellent choice of an evening. It's a cosy and intimate place serving excellent crepes with a variety of fillings, both savoury and sweet.

Södermalm is home to some great restaurants and cafés. There are many fine choices on Götgatan, including busy **Fenix** (☎ 640 4506; Götgatan 40; mains Skr70-200), a restaurant-bar serving a range of beers and a variety of dishes, such as tortillas, sushi, salad and Asian meals.

Sonjas Grek (☎ 702 2229; *Bondegatan 54; mains Skr100-170*), is a popular evening restaurant. It serves good Greek food, with all the regular favourites.

Koh Phangan (☎ 642 6865; *Skånegatan 57; dishes from Skr120*), with its wonderfully tacky tropical decor, is one of the area's hippest restaurants, as the wait for a table might suggest.

Cool **Café String** (☎ 714 8514; *Nytorgsgatan 38; dishes around Skr55*) looks like a second-hand shop and almost everything is for sale – you can even buy your cup or chair. There's good café fare here.

You can pick up a magazine at the Press Stop next door to **Waynes Coffee** (☎ 644 4590; *Götgatan 31*) before relaxing over a coffee and bagel.

Zucchero (☎ 644 2287; *Borgmästargatan 7; pasta dishes from Skr65*), a 1950s-style Italian restaurant, has kitsch decor and decent pasta.

Pelikan (☎ 5560 9090; *Blekingegatan 40; mains Skr90-220*) is a well-established place in a lovely old Art Deco building, where one room is done up like a German beer hall. Traditional Swedish fare is served, and there's usually a daily special for as little as Skr70.

Östgöta Källaren (☎ 643 2240; *Östgötagatan 41; small mains Skr45-90, mains Skr105-165*) is a highly regarded neighbourhood restaurant-bar serving small mains and salads, and more substantial mains like fish and shellfish casserole or cajun chicken.

Gondolen (☎ 641 7090; *Stadsgården 6; mains Skr250-300*) is top of the heap both figuratively and literally. Considered one of Stockholm's finest restaurants, it's at the top of the Katarinahissen at Slussen, with spectacular views of the city and a menu to match. Gourmet main courses feature lobster, duck breast and prime veal; the two-course set menu is Skr320; three courses cost Skr395. There's also an annexe, **Köket**, with a lower-priced bistro menu (meals around Skr165).

Kungsholmen

Over on Kungsholmen, the popular budget restaurants are around Scheelegatan.

Indian Curry House (☎ 650 2024; *Scheelegatan 6; dishes from Skr60*) is small and friendly, and serves very good, and very well-priced, Indian dishes.

Mamas & Tapas (☎ 653 5390; *Scheelegatan 3; mains Skr65-150*) is a colourful, bustling place serving Spanish fare. Make a meal from the huge range of small tapas dishes (including chorizo, grilled octopus and lots of vegie options) priced at Skr30 each.

The small, charming, Italian-style **Il Caffé Gli Angelini** (☎ 652 3004; *Bergsgatan 9*) is the pick of the area's cafés.

Stadshuskällaren (☎ 5063 2200; *Stadshuset; Hantverkargatan 1; weekday lunches Skr115, dinner mains Skr140-270*), in the Town Hall, is very chic and has interesting paintings on the vaulted ceilings. You might not be a Nobel Prize winner, but you can eat like one here: order the most recent Nobel Prize banquet menu for Skr1285, including drinks!

Djurgården

With so many places on the touristy island of Djurgården, you won't go hungry. The restaurant-bars on either side of the bridge to Djurgården, **Tvillingarnas Sjökrog** (☎ 660 3714) and **Sjöcafé** (☎ 660 5757) do a roaring trade on fine summer days. Tvillingarnas especially is a local summer favourite, but go to either for reasonably priced bar food (meals around Skr100), long leisurely drinks and good people watching.

Wärdshuset Ulla Winbladh (☎ 663 0571; *Rosendalsvägen 8; mains Skr170-300, dagens rätt Skr80*) is an old villa dating from 1897, serving fine food in a pretty garden setting.

For an alfresco coffee break, you can try **Blå Porten** (☎ 662 7162; *Djurgårdsvägen 64*), with its great garden patio, behind Liljevachs Konsthall (gallery), or the charming **Rosendals Trädgårdskafe** (☎ 5458 1270; *Rosendalsterassen 12; open daily May-Aug*), in a delightful garden setting.

Market Halls

The colourful market halls are excellent places to sample both local and exotic treats.

Hötorgshallen (*Hötorget*), below the Filmstaden cinema, has many Mediterranean food stalls (eg, Greek, Italian and Spanish) and good specialist shops.

Kungshallen (*Hötorget*) has an enormous selection of food stalls where you can eat anything from Tex-Mex to Indian at very reasonable prices.

Östermalmshallen (*Östermalmstorg*) is a beautiful market hall and a fine example of Stockholm's late-19th-century architectural heritage. It has some very fine fish restaurants, and if you go upstairs you will find **Örtagården** (☎ 662 1728; lunch buffet Skr75, dinner buffet Skr110), which serves excellent vegetarian food at very reasonable prices in a classy setting.

Söderhallarna (Medborgarplatsen) is more modern and includes cafés, restaurants, delis, a cheese shop and a pub.

Fast Food
The cheapest snacks are found at the numerous **gatukök** (literally 'street kitchen') outlets, which serve burgers, hot dogs and sausages. The main gatukök and hamburger-restaurant chains are all over town, including Sibylla, Burger King and McDonald's, and there are countless places serving cheap pizzas and kebabs. There are also several 24-hour **7-Eleven** shops that serve coffee, sandwiches and snacks.

Self-Catering
Head to Hötorget for the excellent street market, held daily. Inquire about the location of the nearest supernmarket at your hostel. The handiest central supermarket is **Hemköp** (Klarabergsgatan 50; open daily), in the Åhlens department store. There's a large **Vivo** supermarket (cnr Horngatan & Torkel Knutssonsgatan) in Södermalm.

Systembolaget (main store, Klarabergsgatan 62), the state-owned alcohol company, has many shops around the city, but they're all closed in the evening and for most of the weekend.

ENTERTAINMENT
Stockholm's lively pub and club scene has boomed in recent years, thanks mainly to an easing of licensing restrictions, but note that many clubs are closed from Midsummer to mid-August, when Stockholmers head out of the city on vacation. The minimum age for entry varies – for most bars and clubs it's 21 years but can be 23 or even higher.

Stockholm nightlife centres around neighbourhoods that offer several pubs and bars conveniently within walking distance (and most places serve meals). In Södermalm, check the Götgatan, Östgötagatan and Skån-egatan area. In Kungsholmen, go to Scheelegatan and Fridhemsplan, and in the northern centre (Vasastaden) try the Tegnérgatan and Rörstrandsgatan areas. For the fashionable nightclubs and late-night

bars frequented by the city's hip, beautiful people, head to Stureplan and its surrounding areas.

Pubs
In the city centre, the lively **Dubliner** (☎ 679 7707; Smålandsgatan 8) has typical pub food and the inevitable Guinness on tap.

The Loft (☎ 411 1991; Regeringsgatan 66) is another great Irish pub with restaurant-quality food.

Bull & Bear Inn (☎ 611 1000; Birger Jarlsgatan 16) is very English and serves good beer, but also has around 120 whiskies. Pub grub here is mostly under Skr100.

On and around Rörstrandsgatan are a few pubs. **Bagpiper's Inn** (☎ 311855; Rörstrandgatan 21) is Scottish themed, with an enthusiastic display of tartan.

Boomerang BBQ & Steakhouse (☎ 330 411; Rörstrandsgatan 23), next door to Bagpiper's, is an Australian-style pub with Australian beer and pricey food.

In Södermalm, **Soldaten Svejk** (☎ 641 3366; Östgötagatan 35) is a genuine Czech pub and restaurant offering a range of great beers at reasonable prices, to wash down the simple and solid Czech fare from the kitchen.

Kvarnen (☎ 643 0380; Tjärhovsgatan 4) is another popular drinking spot, with queues on weekends; plan to get here reasonably early.

Cliff Barnes (☎ 318070; Nortullsgatan 45), named after the loser from the Dallas TV soapie, is very popular. It's tucked away from the centre but is well worth seeking out for a great atmosphere.

Wirströms (☎ 212874; Stora Nygatan 13), on Gamla Stan, is an Irish-style pub packed with locals and expats.

On a balmy summer evening, you could do a lot worse than to take a relaxing drink at one of the restaurant-bars on either side of the bridge leading across to Djurgården, **Tvillingarnas Sjökrog** and **Sjöcafé**.

Bars & Clubs
It seems that almost every decent restaurant and pub in Stockholm has a cool bar attached, and many cafés bring in a DJ of an evening and, voila, another groovy bar is born. A number of places have high entry charges (Skr50 to Skr100 is not uncommon for the big-name clubs).

Drinks on Ice

Head to the unique **Ice Bar** (☎ 5056 3000; Nordic Hotel Sea, Vasaplan; open from 3pm daily) for a taste of life at the Ice Hotel (see the Norrland chapter for more information on this unique attraction, outside of Kiruna). For an entry fee of Skr125 you get to play inside a bar filled with ice sculptures where the temperature is a constant -5°C (warm clothing – a stylish silver cape – and boots are provided). You also receive a drink (alcoholic or otherwise) to imbibe from a glass made of ice – be warned, the vodka cocktails are dangerous!

Stockholm's premier nightclub playground can be found in the area around Stureplan and Biblioteksgatan, but do be warned that the stylish crowds here are impeccably dressed and well cashed up, so you'll need to look the part if you want to get in and blend in.

Sturecompagniet (☎ 611 7800; Sturegatan 4) is a huge club with several rooms over three floors playing different styles of music.

Spy Bar (☎ 5450 3704; Birger Jarlsgatan 20; admission Skr50-100), nearby, is super cool and probably the sleekest club in town.

Kharma (☎ 662 0465; Sturegatan 10) is another hip spot drawing the crowds.

Café Opera (☎ 676 5807; Operahuset, Karl XII:s Torg), part of the Operahus complex, is another chic club, famous in its heyday for attracting big-name celebrities but nowadays drawing a mixed crowd.

La Habana (☎ 166465; Sveavägen 108) is a funky, atmospheric Cuban resturant and bar featuring cigars, rum, and lots of salsa-ing downstairs.

Gay & Lesbian Venues
The gay scene is well established in Stockholm, although Sweden's famous openmindedness means that nonheteros are welcome in almost all bars and clubs. There is no real 'gay district', although Södermalm is where a large section of the gay population live. The tourist office publishes a brochure listing popular gay venues, but probably the best source of local information is the free, monthly magazine *QX*, found at many clubs, stores and restaurants around town. Its website (W www.qx.se) may be more useful.

RFSL (☎ 736 0212; W www.rfsl.se; Sveavägen 59), the national organisation for gay and lesbian rights, has good information. There's also a gay bookshop, restaurant and nightclub, **Tip Top** (☎ 329800) in the same building.

Some popular gay restaurant-bars are **Mandus** (☎ 206055; Österlånggatan 7), in Gamla Stan; **Side Track** (☎ 641 1688; Wollmar Yxkullsgatan 7), in Södermalm; and **Häcktet** (☎ 845910; Hornsgatan 82), on Wednesday and Friday evenings. **Lady Patricia** (☎ 743 0570; Stadsgårdskajen 152) is a rather fabulous nightclub on board a ship with a unique history. It is moored near Slussen and also has a restaurant on board; Sunday night is gay night.

Live Music Venues
Live jazz is extremely popular in the capital and there are a number of venues that showcase it, and an annual jazz festival (held in mid-July). All these clubs have admission charges, and these will vary depending on what's featuring on the night. **Glenn Miller Café** (☎ 100322; Brunnsgatan 21) is small and intimate, with live jazz a few nights a week.

Jazzclub Fasching (☎ 5348 2960; Kungsgatan 63) is one of Stockholm's main jazz venues, attracting performers from around the world as well as excellent local talent. Salsa and soul sometimes feature here too.

Stampen (☎ 205793; Stora Nygatan 5), in Gamla Stan, has live jazz music nightly. Not too far away, **Engelen** (☎ 5055 6000; Kornhamnstorg 59B) is a pub that features live bands (primarily rock) every night.

Mosebacke Etablissement (☎ 5560 9890; Mosebacketorg 3) in Söderhamn is an excellent bar, nightclub and concert venue, featuring all sorts of music and performers. The outdoor bar here offers a great view of the city. Summer sees a lot of outdoor concerts at places like **Gröna Lund Tivoli**.

Cinemas
There are countless cinemas around the city; check the local newspapers for details. The 10-screen **Bio-Palatset** (☎ 644 3100; Medborgarplatsen) and **Filmstaden Sergel** (☎ 5626 0000; Hötorget) screen Hollywood films daily.

Biograf Sture (☎ 678 8548; Birger Jarlsgatan 41) has alternative films, and afternoons are devoted to various themes. Remember that many of these films will not be in English and will only have Swedish subtitles.

Concerts & Theatre

Stockholm is a theatre city, with outstanding dance, opera and music performances; for an overview, pick up the free *Teater Guide* from tourist offices. Ticket sales are handled by the tourist office at Sweden House, or you can buy direct from **Biljett-Direkt** (☎ *0771-707070;* W *www.ticnet.se)*. Tickets generally aren't cheap and they're often sold out, especially for Saturday shows, but you can occasionally get good-value last-minute deals. Operas are usually performed in their original language, while theatre performances are invariably in Swedish.

Konserthuset (☎ *5066 7788;* W *www.konserthuset.se; Hötorget; tickets Skr50-350)* features classical concerts and other musical events, including the Royal Philharmonic Orchestra.

Operan (☎ *248240;* W *www.operan.se; Gustav Adolfs Torg; tickets Skr135-460)*, the Royal Opera, is the place to go for opera and classical ballet. It also has some bargain tickets in seats with poor views for as little as Skr40, and occasional lunchtime concerts for Skr140 (including lunch). **Folkoperan** (☎ *616 0750;* W *www.folkoperan.se; Hornsgatan 72; tickets Skr250-390)* stages unconventional productions of opera and modern ballet that bring the audience close to the stage.

Dramaten (☎ *667 0680;* W *www.dramaten.se; Nybroplan; tickets Skr175-280)*, the Royal Theatre, stages a range of plays in a fantastic Art Nouveau environment. **Stockholms Stadsteatern** (☎ *5062 0100; Kulturhuset, Sergels Torg; tickets around Skr200)* has regular performances and guest appearances by foreign theatre companies.

The classic **Oscars Teatern** (☎ *205000; Kungsgatan 64)* runs Broadway-style musicals. **Vasateatern** (☎ *102363; Vasagatan 19)*, around the corner, sometimes stages plays in English.

Drottningholms Slottsteater (☎ *660 8225;* W *www.drottningholmsslottsteater.dtm.se; Drottningholm; tickets Skr165-600)* is a beautiful, small 18th-century theatre at the royal palace. It stages opera and ballet productions in summer that are well worth attending; see Drottningholm in the Around Stockholm section for more on this unique theatre.

Globen (☎ *0771-310000;* W *www.globen.se; Globentorget 2; metro T-Globen)* is the big white spherical building (it looks like a giant golf ball) just south of Södermalm. Its arenas stage regular big-name pop and rock concerts, as well as sporting events and trade fairs.

SPECTATOR SPORTS

To really see Swedish sports fans in action, head along to an ice hockey game. Contact **Globen** (☎ *0771-310000)* for details; matches take place here up to three times a week from October to April (tickets cost from Skr100 to Skr160). There are regular football fixtures here too, and at **Stadion** (☎ *5082 8362; Lindigövägen 1; metro T-Stadion)* and **Råsunda Stadion** (☎ *735 0953; Solnavägen 51; metro T-Solna Centrum)*, in the city's northwest. The domestic season is generally from April to early November.

SHOPPING

There's no shortage of examples of gorgeous Swedish design in Stockholm, but souvenirs, handicrafts or quality Swedish products in glass, wood or pewter are relatively expensive, and some are not terribly easy to cart around or send home. If you're planning to spend up, see the Taxes & Refunds section in the Facts for the Visitor chapter for details on tax-free shopping for travellers.

If you're not heading into the countryside, buy your souvenirs in the big department stores, such as **NK** (☎ *762 8000; Hamngatan)*, **Åhléns** (☎ *676 6000; Klara-bergsgatan 50)* and **PUB** (☎ *402 1611; Drottninggatan 72-6)*. It's better to avoid the shops in Gamla Stan – there's a lot of junk there. Instead, head for **Svensk Helmslöjd** (☎ *232115; Sveavägen 44)* and **Svenskt Hantverk** (☎ *214726; Kungsgatan 55)*, which both specialise in traditional handicrafts.

Venture along to **DesignTorget** (☎ *5083 1520;* W *www.designtorget.se; Basement, Kulturhuset, Sergels Torg • ☎ 462 3520; Götgatan 31, Södermalm)*, which showcase the works (usually quite affordable) of both established and new designers, and pick up some of the funky smaller pieces. There's a very central branch in the basement of Kulturhuset, and one at Götgatan 31, among the cool stores of Södermalm – this branch also showcases young clothing designers. For more mainstream clothing choices, **Hennes**

& Mauritz (H&M; ☎ 796 5446; Sergels Torg) is a great, reasonably priced Swedish clothing store that's now found throughout Europe and almost everywhere in Sweden.

Visit the deluxe **Svenskt Tenn** (☎ 670 1600; Strandvägen 5) and be careful not to drool over the beautiful furniture and interior design pieces!

GETTING THERE & AWAY
Air

The main airport in Stockholm, **Stockholm Arlanda** (☎ 797 6000; W www.lfv.se), is 45km north of the city centre and can be reached from central Stockholm by both bus and express train (see the following Getting Around section).

Bromma airport (☎ 797 6874) is 8km west of Stockholm and is used for some domestic flights. **Skavsta airport** (☎ 0155-280400), 100km south of Stockholm, near Nyköping is also for domestic flights and some low-cost carriers, including Ryanair.

Skyways (☎ 020 959500; W www.sky ways.se) has a comprehensive network of domestic flights (you can fly to nearly 20 destinations in Sweden from Arlanda and/or Bromma Airports), and the **SAS** (☎ 020 727727) network is more extensive, with 27 Swedish destinations from Arlanda. **Malmö Aviation** (☎ 040-302155; W www.malmoavi ation.se) has flights to Gothenburg, Malmö and Umeå from Bromma airport.

International air services to Copenhagen, Oslo, Helsinki, and a host of other European cities including Amsterdam, Brussels, Berlin, Dublin, Frankfurt, Geneva, Hamburg, London, Madrid, Manchester, Milan, Moscow, Munich, Paris, Reykjavík, Riga, St Petersburg and Tallinn are run by **SAS**. The airline also flies directly to Chicago, New York and Bangkok. **Finnair** (☎ 020 781100) flies from Stockholm to Turku, Vasa and Tampere and there are around 15 flights per day to Helsinki.

British Airways (☎ 020 781144), **Air France** (☎ 679 8855), **KLM** (☎ 593 62430) and **Lufthansa** (☎ 020 228800) have regular European services. Most of the airlines no longer have offices in Stockholm's city centre; it's best to contact them by phone.

Bus

Most long-distance buses arrive at and also depart from Cityterminalen, next to the

Centralstationen. Here you'll find the **Busstop ticket office** (☎ 440 8570; Cityterminalen; open 9am-5.30pm Mon-Fri), which represents the big concerns such as Eurolines, Svenska Buss and Y-Bussen, along with many of the direct buses to the north.

Swebus Express (☎ 0200 218218; W www .swebusexpress.se; 2nd level, Cityterminalen; open daily) runs three times daily to Malmö (Skr435, 9¼ hours) via Jönköping (Skr275, five hours). Daily Swebus Express services run to Gothenburg (Skr350, seven hours), Norrköping (Skr175, two hours), Kalmar (Skr320, six hours), Mora (Skr185, 4¼ hours), Örebro (Skr175, three hours) and Oslo (Skr370, eight hours). There are also direct runs to Gävle (Skr165, 2½ hours), Uppsala (Skr50, one hour) and Västerås (Skr75, 1¾ hours).

Buses to Malmö, Filipstad, Kalmar, Karlskrona, Eksjö, Växjö and Gothenburg are operated by **Svenska Buss** (☎ 0771-676767; W www.svenskabuss.se; Cityterminalen) but not all services run daily.

Säfflebussen (☎ 020 1600 600; W www .safflebussen.se; Cityterminalen) has a less extensive network – destinations include Malung, Örebro, Karlstad, Oslo, Gothenburg, Helsingborg and Copenhagen.

Ybuss (☎ 020 0334 444; W www.ybuss.se; Cityterminalen) runs services to Sundsvall, Östersund and Umeå. **Tapanis Buss** (☎ 0922-12955; W www.tapanis.se; Cityterminalen) runs express coaches from Stockholm to Tornio in Finland along the E4 highway via Haparanda twice weekly.

You'll also find a number of companies running buses from many provincial towns directly to Stockholm. See the relevant destination chapters for details.

Train

Stockholm is the hub for national train services run by **Sveriges Järnväg** (SJ; ☎ 0771-757575; W www.sj.se). and **Tågkompaniet** (☎ 020 444111; W www.tagkompaniet.se).

Centralstationen (Stockholm C; open 5am-midnight daily) is the central train station. At the domestic **ticket office** (open 7.30am-8pm Mon-Fri, 8.30am-6pm Sat, 9.30am-7pm Sun) there are special ticket windows, where you can purchase international train tickets, between 10am and 6pm, Monday to Friday. If your train departs outside these times, you can buy a ticket from the ticket collector on the train.

Direct SJ trains to/from Copenhagen, Oslo and Storlien (for Trondheim) arrive and depart from the Centralstationen, as do the overnight Tågkompaniet trains from Gothenburg (via Stockholm and Boden) to Kiruna and Narvik; the Arlanda Express; and the SL *pendeltåg* commuter services that run to/from Nynäshamn, Södertälje and Märsta. Other SL local rail lines (Roslagsbanan and Saltsjöbanan) run from Stockholm Östrastationen (T-Tekniska högskolan) and Slussen, respectively.

Regular, direct SJ services from Stockholm include: Gävle (Skr238, 1½ hours); Gothenburg (Skr518, five hours); Karlstad (Skr390, three hours); Linköping (Skr266, 2¼ hours); Malmö (Skr551, six hours); Mora (Skr266, four hours); Norrköping (Skr214, 1¾ hours); Örebro (Skr243, two hours); Östersund (Skr499, about six hours); Sundsvall (Skr399, four hours); and Uppsala (Skr81, 40 minutes). All fares are for one-way 2nd-class adult tickets on InterCity trains; X2000 express trains will cost more to travel on, and the journey will often be considerably shorter. Buying your ticket in advance will reduce the fares listed here.

SJ runs some overnight trains, including Stockholm to Malmö, Östersund, Storlien and Trondheim; there are also overnight trains run by Tågkompaniet and Boden and Kiruna in the north.

In the basement at Centralstationen, you'll find small/medium/large lockers costing Skr20/30/70 for 24 hours, toilets for Skr5, and showers (next to the toilets) for Skr25. These facilities are open 5am to midnight, daily. There's also a registered luggage office, open daily, and a **lost property office** (☎ 762 2550; open 10am-6pm Mon-Fri).

Follow the signs to find your way to the local metro (T-bana) network; the underground station here is called T-Centralen.

Car & Motorcycle
The E4 motorway passes through the city, just west of the centre, on its way from Helsingborg to Haparanda. The E20 motorway from Stockholm to Gothenburg via Örebro follows the E4 as far as Södertälje. The E18 from Kapellskär to Oslo runs from east to west and passes just north of the city centre.

For car hire close to Centralstationen, contact **Statoil** (☎ 202064; Vasagatan 16), or **Avis** (☎ 202060; Vasagatan 10B).

Boat
Schedules and fares for international ferry links are given in the Getting There & Away chapter.

Silja Line (☎ 222140; W www.silja.com) ferries depart for Helsinki and Turku from Värtahamnen. To get there, walk from T-Gärdet (about 500m), take bus No 76 from T-Ropsten or take Silja Line's connecting bus from Cityterminalen (Skr20).

Viking Line (☎ 452 4000; W www.viking line.fi) ferries run to Turku and Helsinki from the terminal at Tegelvikshamn on Södermalm. There's a connecting bus from Cityterminalen (Skr20), or else walk 1.5km from T-Slussen.

Tallink (☎ 666 6001; W www.tallink.ee) ferries to Tallinn (Estonia) sail from Tallinnterminalen at Frihamnen; take a connecting bus from Cityterminalen (Skr20), or town bus No 1.

Birka Cruises (☎ 714 5520) ferries to Mariehamn depart from Stadsgårdsterminalen (T-Slussen), while **Ånedin-Linjen** (☎ 456 2200) boats to Mariehamn leave from the quay at Tullhus 1 on Skeppsbron in Gamla Stan.

See Utö and Vaxholm sectiions in Around Stockholm for other boat connections.

GETTING AROUND
To/From the Airports
The **Arlanda Express** (☎ 5888 9000) train from Centralstationen takes only 20 minutes to reach Arlanda; trains run every 15 minutes from about 5am to midnight and cost Skr160. The same trip in a taxi costs from Skr350 to Skr450, but agree on the fare first and don't use any taxi without a contact telephone number displayed. **Taxi Stockholm** (☎ 150000). and **Taxi Kurir** (☎ 300000) are reputable operators.

The cheaper option is the **Flygbuss** service between Arlanda airport and Cityterminalen. Buses leave every 10 or 15 minutes (Skr80, 40 minutes). If you're using Bromma airport, the bus from Cityterminalen costs Skr60 and takes 20 minutes; to Skavsta costs Skr100 and takes 80 minutes. Call ☎ 600 1000 for bus departure times to/from all airports.

Public Transport

Storstockholms Lokaltrafik *(SL;* w *www.sl.se)* runs all *tunnelbana* (T or T-bana) metro trains, local trains and buses within the entire Stockholm county. At T-Centralen there are SL information offices in the basement of the station hall (open until 11.15pm daily) and at the Sergels Torg entrance. Both offices issue timetables and sell the SL Tourist Card and Stockholm Card. You can also call ☎ 600 1000 for schedule and travel information from 7am to 9pm weekdays, and 8am to 9pm on weekends.

The Stockholm Card (see Discounts in the Information section earlier) covers travel on all SL trains and buses in greater Stockholm. The 24-hour (Skr80) and 72-hour (Skr150) SL Tourist Cards differ from the Stockholm Card in that they only give free entry to a few attractions. However they're a much cheaper alternative if you just want transport. The 72-hour SL Tourist Card is especially good value, if you use the third afternoon for transport to either end of the county – you can reach the ferry terminals in Grisslehamn, Kapellskär or Nynä-shamn, as well as all of the archipelago harbours. If you want to explore the county in more detail, bring a passport photo and get yourself a 30-day SL pass (Skr500). Children (aged seven to 18) and seniors can get discounted tickets for about 60% of the adult fare.

On Stockholm's public transport system the minimum fare costs two coupons, and each additional zone costs another coupon (up to five coupons for four or five zones). Coupons are available individually for Skr10, or a better idea is to buy a 10/20-coupon discount ticket for Skr60/110. Coupons are valid for an hour and must be stamped at the start of the journey. Travelling without a valid ticket is a bad idea – the fine is Skr600. Coupons can be bought at metro stations, SL railway stations, SL information offices, and from bus drivers. The SL Tourist Card and other period tickets can also be bought from tourist offices and Pressbyrån kiosks.

International rail passes (eg, Scanrail, Interrail) aren't valid on SL trains.

Bus While the bus timetables and route maps are complicated, they're worth studying as there are some useful connections to suburban attractions. Ask **SL** *(*☎ *600 1000)* or any tourist office for the handy inner-city route map *Innerstadsbussar*.

Inner-city buses radiate from Sergels Torg, Odenplan, Fridhemsplan (on Kungsholmen) and Slussen. Bus No 47 runs from Sergels Torg to Djurgården and bus No 69 runs from Centralstationen and Sergels Torg to the Ladugårdsgärdet museums and Kaknästornet. Useful buses for hostellers include bus No 65, which goes from Centralstationen to Skeppsholmen, and bus No 43, which runs from Regeringsgatan to Södermalm.

Inner-city night buses run from around 1am to 5pm nightly on a few routes. Most operate from Centralstationen, Sergels Torg, Slussen, Odenplan and Fridhemsplan to the suburbs.

Check where the regional bus hub is for each outlying area. Islands of the Ekerö municipality (including Drottningholm palace) are served by bus Nos 301 to 323 from T-Brommaplan. Buses to Vaxholm (No 670) and the Åland ferries (No 637 to Grisslehamn and Nos 640/631 to Kapellskär) depart from T-Tekniska Högskolan. Odenplan is the hub for buses to the northern suburbs, including Haga Park.

Train Local *pendeltåg* trains are useful for connections to Nynäshamn (for ferries to Gotland), to Märsta (for buses to Sigtuna and the short hop to Arlanda Airport) and Södertälje. There are also services to Nockeby from T-Alvik; Lidingö from T-Ropsten; Kårsta, Österskär and Näsbypark from T-Tekniska Högskolan; and to Saltsjöbaden from T-Slussen.

Tram The historical **No 7 tram** *(*☎ *660 7700)* runs between Norrmalmstorg and Skansen, passing most attractions on Djurgården. Separate fees apply for those with a Stockholm Card (adult/child Skr20/10), but the SL Tourist Card is valid.

The new Tvårbanan tram line started running in June 2000 and crosses the southwestern side of the city from Alvik to Gullmarsplan. In mid-2002 it was extended east from Gullmarsplan to Sickla Udde. It's shown as the yellow route on public transport maps and is of little interest to tourists.

Metro The most useful mode of transport in Stockholm is the *tunnelbana*, which converges on T-Centralen, connected by an underground walkway to Centralstationen.

STOCKHOLM METRO

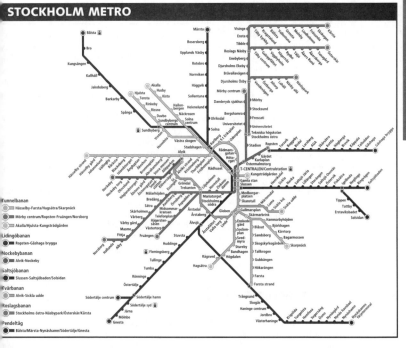

There are three main through lines with branches – check the approaching train is actually going your way before boarding. (See the Stockholm Metro map for route details.)

The 'blue' and 'green' lines serve the Kungsholmen (T-Fridhemsplan) and the 'red' and 'green' lines serve Södermalm and places farther south. The 'blue' line has a comprehensive collection of modern art decorating the underground stations.

Car & Motorcycle

Driving in central Stockholm is not recommended. Small one-way streets, congested bridges and limited parking all present problems; note that Djurgårdsvägen is closed near Skansen at night, on summer weekends and some holidays. Don't attempt to drive through the narrow streets of Gamla Stan.

Parking is a major problem, but there are *P-hus* (parking stations) in the city that charge up to Skr50 per hour (the fixed evening rate is usually more reasonable).

If you have a car, one of the best options is to stay on the outskirts of town and catch public transport into the centre.

Taxi

There's usually no problem finding a taxi but they're expensive so check for a meter or arrange the fare before getting in. Flagfall is Skr35, then it's around Skr7 per km. At night, women should ask about tjejtaxa, a discount rate offered by some operators. Reputable firms are **Taxi Stockholm** (☎ 150000), **Taxi 020** (☎ 020 939393) and **Taxi Kurir** (☎ 300000).

Boat

Djurgårdsfärjan city ferry services connect Gröna Lund Tivoli on Djurgården with Nybroplan and Slussen as frequently as every 10 minutes in summer (considerably less frequently in the low season); a single trip costs Skr20 (free with the SL Tourist Card).

Bicycle

Stockholm has a wide network of bicycle paths, and in summer you won't regret bringing a bicycle with you or hiring one to get around. The tourist offices have maps for sale, but they're not usually necessary.

The top day trips are: Djurgården; a loop going from Gamla Stan to Södermalm,

Art on the Move

The artwork now featured in 90 of Stockholm's metro stations along 110km of track is considered to be the longest art exhibition in the world. Originally presented in 1955 as a motion designed to improve the aesthetics of bleak metro stations, around 140 artists have now contributed paintings, engravings, reliefs, sculptures and mosaics to the metro art project. Displays well worth a look include the metro stations at **Kungstädgården** (classical pieces, ferns and dripping water), **Fridhemsplan** (terracotta sculpture and wall of tiles celebrating Carl von Linné) and **Östermalmstorg** (decoration with the themes of the womens, peace and environmental movements). For more information about metro arts at all the stations, pick up the free *Art in the Stockholm Metro* booklet from tourist offices or SL information offices. There's also excellent information on its website at **W** www.sl.se/international (click on 'Art & Design').

Långholmen and Kungsholmen (on lakeside paths); Drottningholm (return by steamer); Haga Park; and the adjoining Ulriksdal Park. Some long-distance routes are marked all the way from central Stockholm: Nynäsleden to Nynäshamn joins Sommarleden near Västerhaninge and swings west to Södertälje. Roslagsleden leads to Norrtälje (linking Blåleden and Vaxholm). Upplandsleden leads to Märsta north of Stockholm and you can ride to Uppsala via Sigtuna. Sörmlandsleden leads to Södertälje, south of Stockholm.

Bicycles can be carried free on SL local trains, except during peak hour (6am to 9am and 3pm to 6pm weekdays), and they are not allowed in Centralstationen or the metro, although you'll see some daring souls from time to time.

Sjöcafe (☎ 660 5757), by the bridge across to Djurgården, rents out bikes for Skr60/250 per hour/day (with options for longer rentals). They also rent out in-line skates (Skr60/200 per hour/day), which is another good way of getting around.

Just across the water, **Rent a Bike** (☎ 660 7959; Strandvägen, Kajplats 24) also rents bikes from around Skr190 per day. It's open from May to September.

Around Stockholm

You can explore the county of greater Stockholm with the SL Tourist Card or monthly passes that allow unlimited travel on all buses and local trains. Free timetables are available from the SL office in Centralstationen or the SL terminals at Slussen or Östrastationen.

The delightful islands of the Stockholm archipelago are within easy reach of the city. Ferry services aren't expensive and there's a travel pass available if you want to tour around the islands for a while. On warm and sunny summer days, you could easily believe you're in the south of France rather than in the northern reaches of Europe.

EKERÖ DISTRICT
☎ 08 • pop 22,600

Some 20km west of Stockholm and surprisingly rural, the Ekerö district (**W** www.ekero turism.se) consists of several large islands in Mälaren lake, two Unesco World Heritage Sites and a dozen medieval churches.

Drottningholm

The royal residence and parks of Drottningholm on Lovön are popular attractions and easy to visit from the capital. If you're not short of time you can cycle out to the palace. Otherwise, take the metro to T-Brommaplan and change to bus Nos 301 to 323. If you're driving, there are few road signs for Drottningholm, so get hold of a decent map. The car park is second on the left after crossing Drottningholmsbron.

The most pleasant way to get to the palace is by boat. **Strömma Kanalbolaget** (☎ 5871 4000; **W** www.strommakanalbolaget.com, has frequent boats departing from Stadshusbron (Stockholm) daily between May and mid-September, and weekends between mid-September and the end of October (one way/return Skr70/100). For Skr180 you get a return trip on the boat, plus entry to the palace and Kina Slott.

It certainly can be an expensive day out if you wish to see everything at the World Heritage royal residence and parks – it's a good idea to use the Stockholm Card here.

Drottningholms Slott The Renaissance-inspired main palace (☎ 402 6280; **W** www .royalcourt.se; adult/child Skr60/30; open

A replica of the Royal Crown on the bridge to Skeppsholmen, Stockholm

Royal Guard, Stockholm

The face of Swedish patriotism

An old café in Sigtuna, Stockholm

WAYNE WALTON

Ferry passengers feed the locals on Stockholm harbour

JON DAVISON

The entrance to the Gröna Lund Tivoli fun park in Stockholm

DAVID RYAN

The 18th-century Royal Palace in Stockholm was built on the ruins of Tre Kronor, the old castle

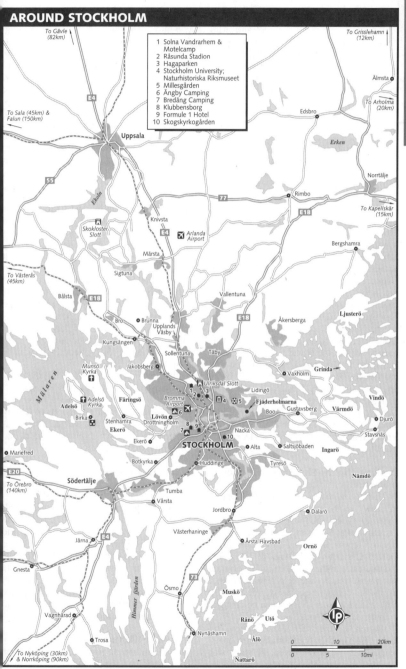

AROUND STOCKHOLM

1 Solna Vandrarhem & Motelcamp
2 Råsunda Stadion
3 Hagaparken
4 Stockholm University; Naturhistoriska Riksmuseet
5 Millesgården
6 Ängby Camping
7 Bredäng Camping
8 Klubbensborg
9 Formule 1 Hotel
10 Skogskyrkogården

10am-4.30pm daily May-Aug, noon-3.30pm Sept, noon-3.30pm Sat & Sun Oct-Apr), with geometric baroque gardens, was designed by the great architect Nicodemius Tessin the Elder and construction began in 1662, about the same time as Versailles. Currently, the palace is home to the Swedish royal family, and you can either walk around the wings open to the public on your own or take a one-hour guided tour (no additional charge; English tours at 11am, noon, 1pm and 3pm daily from June to August, reduced schedules at other times of the year).

The **Lower North Corps de Garde** was originally a guard room but it's now replete with gilt-leather wall hangings, which used to feature in many palace rooms during the 17th century. The **Karl X Gustav Gallery**, in baroque style, depicts the militaristic endeavours of this monarch but the ceiling shows battle scenes from classical times. The highly ornamented **State Bedchamber of Hedvig Eleonora** is the most expensive baroque interior in Sweden and it's decorated with paintings that feature the childhood of Karl XI. The painted ceiling shows Karl X and his queen, Hedvig Eleonora. Although Lovisa Ulrika's collection of over 2000 books has been moved to the Royal Library in Stockholm, the library here is still a bright and impressive room, complete with most of its original 18th-century fittings. The elaborate staircase, with statues at every turn, was the work of both Nicodemius Tessin the Elder and the Younger. Circular **Drottningholms Slottskyrka** *(admission free)*, the palace chapel, wasn't completed until the late 1720s.

Drottningholms Slottsteater & Teater-museum Slottsteater *(Court Theatre; ☎ 759 0406; ⓦ www.drottningholmsslottsteater.dtm .se; tours adult/child Skr60/free)* was completed in 1766 on the instructions of Queen Lovisa Ulrika. This is an extraordinary place because it was untouched from the time of Gustav III's death (1792) until 1922. It's the oldest theatre in the world still in its original state; performances are held here in summer using 18th-century machinery, such as ropes, pulleys and wagons. Scenes can be changed in under seven seconds.

Illusion was the order of the day here and there's fake marble, fake curtains and papier-mâché viewing boxes. Even the stage was designed to create illusions regarding size.

The interesting guided tour will also take you into other rooms in the same building. You'll see hand-painted 18th-century wallpaper and an Italian-style room *(salon de dejeuner)* with fake three-dimensional wall effects and a ceiling that resembles the sky.

There are regular performances in the theatre every summer – see Concerts & Theatre in the Entertainment section.

Tours in English run every hour from 12.30pm to 4.30pm daily in May. From June to August they run every hour from 11.30am to 4.30pm daily, and in September tours start at 1.30pm, 2.30pm and 3.30pm daily. Tours are also available in French and German.

Kina Slott At the far end of the gardens there's Kina Slott *(☎ 402 6270; adult/child Skr50/25; open 11am-4.30pm daily May-Aug, noon-3.30pm daily Sept)*, a lavishly decorated Chinese pavilion that was built by King Adolf Fredrik as a birthday gift to Queen Lovisa Ulrika (1753). It was restored between 1989 and 1996 and is now in its original condition. There's a **café** on the premises serving good waffles, and the admission price includes a guided tour, which run at 11am, noon, 2pm and 3pm daily from June to August (the schedule is reduced from May to September).

On the slope below Kina Slott, the striking **Guards' Tent** *(admission free; open noon-4pm daily June–mid-Aug)* was erected in 1781 as quarters for the dragoons of Gustav III, but it's not really a tent at all. The building now has displays about the gardens and Drottningholm's Royal Guard.

Places to Eat Bring a picnic with you and enjoy it in the gardens, or dine in one of the two restaurants by the palace. **Drottningholms Paviljongen** *(☎ 759 0425; light meals Skr35-100, mains Skr120-185)*, close to the boat dock, has lots of outdoor seating and light meals such as sandwiches and salads or heartier mains. **Drottningholms Wärdshus** *(☎ 759 0308; mains Skr185-230)*, opposite the palace grounds, is a little more upmarket and offers an extensive menu, with simple *husmanskost* dishes, such as meatballs, from Skr95 and fancier meat and fish mains.

Ekerö & Munsö

These long and narrow islands in Mälaren lake are joined together and have a main road running most of their length; the free car ferry to Adelsö departs from the northern end of Munsö.

The two churches of Ekerö and Munsö date from the 12th century. **Munsö kyrka** is an interesting structure with a round tower and a narrow steeple.

Skytteholms Kursgård & Pensionat (☎ 5602 3600; e skytteholm@amica.se; Ekerö; singles/ doubles Skr1300/1600) is a lovely country estate by the water and adjacent to a popular golf course. It's 3km off the main road (signposted), and offers summer B&B deals from as little as Skr345 per person. There's also a **restaurant** here.

Frequent bus Nos 311 and 312 run out this way from T-Brommaplan metro station in Stockholm.

Adelsö

The medieval church **Adelsö kyrka**, which dates from the late 12th century, has a 14th-century sacristy but the distinctive square tower is somewhat younger. Restored in 1832, the interior of the church contains a late-12th-century font and a 14th-century crucifix. Just across the road, **Hovgården** features burial mounds (associated with nearby Birka and part of the Unesco World Heritage Site) and a spectacular **rune stone** with complex intertwined designs.

The hostel **Adelsögården** (☎ 383359; beds from Skr165; open mid-June–early Sept) is just south of the ferry pier. There's a kitchen and a restaurant, and bikes and canoes can be hired. A walking trail from the hostel leads, via some prehistoric sites, to the church.

SL bus No 312 runs nine times daily (five times on Saturday and Sunday) to Adelsö kyrka from T-Brommaplan metro station via the medieval Ekerö and Munsö churches. Free car ferries run quite frequently between Adelsö and Munsö.

Birka

The Viking trading centre of Birka (☎ 5605 1445; w www.raa.se/birka; open 11am-6pm daily May-Sept), on Björkö in Mälaren lake, is now a Unesco World Heritage Site. It was founded around 760 with the intention of expanding and controlling trade in the region. The village attracted merchants and craft workers, and the population grew to about AD 700. A large defensive fort with thick drystone ramparts was constructed next to

the village. In 830, the Benedictine monk Ansgar was sent to Birka by the Holy Roman Emperor to convert the heathen Vikings to Christianity and he lived in Birka for 18 months. Birka was abandoned in the late 10th century when Sigtuna took over the role of commercial centre.

The village site is surrounded by a vast graveyard. It's the largest Viking Age cemetery in Scandinavia, with around 3000 graves. Most people were cremated, then mounds of earth were piled over the remains, but some Christian coffins and chambered tombs have been found. The fort and harbour have also been excavated. A cross to the memory of St Ansgar can be seen on top of a nearby hill.

The **Birka Museum** is excellent. Exhibits include finds from the excavations (which are still proceeding), copies of the most magnificent objects, and an interesting model showing the village as it was in Viking times. Entry is usually included in your ferry ticket.

Cruises to Birka run from early May to late September; the return trip on Strömma Kanalbolaget's *Victoria* from Stadshusbron, Stockholm, is a full day's outing (Skr220). A visit to the museum and a guided tour in English of the settlement's burial mounds and fortifications are included in the cruise price. Call ☎ 5871 4000 for details. From May to September there are also daily boats from Adelsö (Hovgården) to Birka (Skr70, including museum entry), and in July and August there are boats from Rastaholm on Ekerö (Skr140); call ☎ 711 1457 for details on these boats.

Summer cruises to Birka depart from many other places around Mälaren, including Mariefred, Södertälje, Strängnäs and Västerås.

VAXHOLM
☎ 08 • pop 9500

Vaxholm, about 35km northeast of the city by road, is the gateway to the central and northern reaches of Stockholm's archipelago, and thus swarms with tourists in summer. Despite this, it's a pleasant place with several attractions and a relaxed atmosphere, and it's well worth a visit.

There's a **tourist office** (☎ 5413 1480; e infp@visitvaxholm.com, w www.vaxholm .se; open 10am-6pm Mon-Fri, 10am-4pm Sat & Sun June-Aug, 10am-3pm Mon-Fri, 10am-2pm Sat & Sun Sept-May) inside the *rådhus* (town hall), off Hamngatan; the *rådhus* was rebuilt in 1925 with an onion dome on its roof. You'll find a bank, supermarkets and other services on Hamngatan, the main street.

The town was founded in 1647 and has many quaint summerhouses, which were fashionable in the 19th century. The oldest buildings are in the Norrhamn area, a few minutes' walk north of the town hall, but there's interesting architecture along Hamngatan too, plus lots of galleries, boutiques and souvenir shops.

The construction of **Vaxholm Kastell** *(Citadel; ☎ 541 72157; admission Skr40; open noon-4pm daily mid-June–mid-Aug)*, a fortress on an islet just east of the town, was originally ordered by Gustav Vasa in 1544, but most of the current structure dates from 1863. The fortress was attacked by the Danes in 1612 and the Russian navy in 1719. Nowadays, it's home to the National Museum of Coastal Defence. The ferry across to the island departs regularly from Söderhamn (the bustling harbour) and the admission price is included in the fare.

The **Hembygdsgård** *(☎ 5413 1720; Trädgårdsgatan 19; admission free; open 11am-4pm Sat & Sun May-Aug)* has the finest old houses in Norrhamn. The **fiskarebostad** is an excellent example of a late-19th-century fisherman's house, with a typical Swedish fireplace. The café here is open daily from May to mid-September.

Places to Stay & Eat

Vaxholms Camping *(☎ 5413 0101; Eriksövägen; tent sites Skr110, cabins from Skr350; open May-Sept)* is 3km west of the town centre. It's a sizeable camping ground, with good swimming spots.

By an old castle 5km southwest of Vaxholm, **Bogesund Vandrarhem** *(☎ 5413 2240; dorm beds Skr150)* is a pleasant, well-equipped STF hostel located in peaceful countryside. Bus No 671 stops on the main road about 500m from the hostel. Closer to town, **Rum i Backen** *(☎ 314021; Kungsgatan 14; B&B per person from Skr300)* offers bed and breakfast in the summer months.

Waxholms Hotell *(☎ 5413 0150; e info@waxholmshotell.se; Hamngatan 2; singles/doubles from Skr1200/1315, discounted to Skr840/945)*, just opposite the harbourfront, is a mixture of Art Nouveau and modern styles. Discounted rooms are available here on weekends year-round and in July. This grand place is in the centre of the action, and there are restaurants on the premises, including **Kabyssen** *(meals Skr100-200)*, with a popular outdoor terrace.

There are loads more restaurants on the waterfront. **Moby Dick** *(☎ 5413 0705; Söderhamnsplan 1; meals Skr72-150)* has an extensive menu offering pizza, pasta, salad and more. **Gröna Längan** *(☎ 5413 2536; Hamngatan 16)* is a pretty, old-fashioned café that serves sandwiches and cakes.

Getting There & Away

Bus No 670 from the metro station T-Tekniska Högskolan in Stockholm runs regularly to the town.

Waxholmsbolaget *(☎ 679 5830; W www.waxholmsbolaget.se)* boats sail frequently between Vaxholm and Strömkajen in Stockholm (Skr55, 50 minutes). **Strömma Kanalbolaget** *(☎ 5871 4000; W www.strommakanalbolaget.com)* sails between Strandvägen and Vaxholm three times daily from mid-June to mid-August (one way/return Skr70/125), and once daily the rest of the year (no services in December and January).

STOCKHOLM ARCHIPELAGO
☎ 08

Depending on which source you read, the archipelago around Stockholm has anything between 14,000 and 100,000 islands, although the general consensus is 24,000. Whatever the number, a summer visit to one is highly recommended. Summer cottages on rocky islets are popular among wealthy Stockholmers, and regular boats offer great opportunities for outings.

For information on cabin and chalet rental in the archipelago, contact **Destination Stockholms Skärgård** *(☎ 5424 8100; e dess.skarg@dess.se; W www.dess.se; Lillström, SE-18497 Ljusterö)*.

The biggest boat operator in the archipelago is **Waxholmsbolaget** *(☎ 679 5830; W www.waxholmsbolaget.se)*. Timetables and information are available from its offices outside the Grand Hotel on Strömkajen in Stockholm, and at the harbour in Vaxholm. It has detailed timetables, which divide the archipelago into three areas. *Norra Skärgården* is the northern section (north from Ljusterö to Arholma); *Mellersta Skärgården* is the middle section, taking in Vaxholm, Ingmarsö, Stora Kalholmen, Finnhamn, Möja and Sandhamn; and *Södra Skärgården* is the southern section, with boats south to Nämdö, Ornö and Utö.

Waxholmbolaget's Båtluffarkortet pass (Skr385), valid for 16 days, gives unlimited rides on its services plus a handy island map. It costs an additional Skr25 (Skr7 with Båtluffarkortet) per trip to take a bicycle on the ferries, but bikes can be hired on many islands. Waxholmsbolaget's vintage steamers S/S *Storskär* and S/S *Norrskär* sail daily from Strömkajen and Vaxholm to the islands and restaurant service is available on board.

It's worth checking out what **Cinderella Båtarna** (☎ 587 14050; Ⓦ *www.cinderella batarna.com; Skeppsbron)* has to offer. Its boats, *Cinderella I* and *Cinderella II*, also go to many of the most interesting islands from Skeppsbron in Stockholm.

If your time is short, a recommended tour is the **Thousand Island Cruise** offered by **Stromma Kanabolaget** (☎ 5871 4000; Ⓦ *www .strommakanalbolaget.com; Nybrokajen)*, running daily between late June and mid-August. The full day's excursion departs from Stockholm's Nybrokajen at 9.30am and returns at 8.30pm; the cost of Skr625 includes lunch, dinner and guided tours ashore – the boat pulls in to a number of interesting islands, and there are several opportunities for swimming.

The website Ⓦ www.skargardsstiftel sen.se has excellent information about the archipelago.

Arholma

Arholma is one of the most interesting islands in the far north of the archipelago. Everything was burnt down during a Russian invasion in 1719. The **lighthouse** was rebuilt in the 19th century and it's a well-known landmark. The island became a popular resort in the early 20th century. It's noted for its traditional village and chapel, and it offers fine sandy beaches and good swimming from the rocks.

Arholma has a summer café, a shop, a simple camping ground and bike rental. **Vandrarhem Arholma** (☎ 0176-56018; beds Skr110; open year-round) is a pleasant STF hostel in a renovated barn; advance booking is essential.

You can take bus No 640 from Stockholm Tekniska Högskolan to Norrtälje, then No 636 to Simpnäs (two to six daily), followed by a 20-minute ferry crossing to the island (Skr30). **Blidösundsbolaget** (☎ 411 7113) sails directly from Strömkajen to Arholma (Skr105, four to five hours, daily). Båtluffarkortet is valid.

Ängsö

This island, 15km south of Norrtälje, was declared a national park as early as 1909, despite being only 1.5km long and 600m wide. Ängsö is characterised by meadows, virgin woodland and magnificent displays of wild flowers (especially in spring). You may also see ospreys, sea eagles and great crested grebes.

You can't stay overnight in the park, but there are boat trips (from Furusund) and guided walks. Contact **Norrtälje tourist office** (☎ 0176-71990) for current details. Bus No 621 runs every hour or two (fewer at weekends) from T-Danderyds sjukhus (Stockholm) to Norrtälje and bus No 632/634 runs three or four times daily from Norrtälje to Furusund; alternatively, there are boats from Stockholm and Vaxholm to Furusund (Skr90).

Siaröfortet

The tiny island Kyrkogårdsön, in the important sea lane just north of Ljusterö (40km due northeast of Stockholm), may be only 400m long but it's one of the most fascinating islands in the archipelago.

After the outbreak of WWI, the military authorities decided that the Vaxholm Kastell wasn't good enough and, in 1916, construction of a new fort began on Kyrkogårdsön. This powerful defence facility, Siaröfortet, was never used in anger. Renovated in 1996, it's now open as a **museum** (admission free) and a visit is highly recommended. You'll see two impressive 15.2cm cannons (incidentally, they're trained on passing Viking Line ferries!), the officers mess, kitchen, sleeping quarters and tunnels. There are no fixed opening times; contact the STF hostel to arrange a tour.

STF Vandrarhem Siaröfortet (☎ 5424 2149; beds Skr155; open May-Sept) is an excellent STF hostel in the old soldiers' barracks. Canoe hire and breakfast are available; advance booking is recommended.

Waxholmsbolaget ferries to Siaröfortet depart from Strömkajen in Stockholm and sail to Siaröfortet via Vaxholm once or twice daily. The journey takes 1½ hours from Stockholm, or 50 minutes from Vaxholm (Skr90 and Skr80 respectively).

Finnhamn

This 900m-long island, northeast of Stockholm, has rocky cliffs and a small beach with good swimming opportunities. Finnhamn is fairly trendy, attracting wealthy visitors from Stockholm and beyond. However, you can wild camp in the woods.

Vandrarhem Finnhamn (☎ 5424 6212; e inof@finnhamn.nu; dorm beds Skr180; open year-round) is an STF hostel in a large converted warehouse and boats are available to hire. It's the largest hostel in the archipelago; advance booking is essential. The **Finnhamn Café** (☎ 5424 6404) serves good meals, and has a lovely view.

You can sail with **Waxholmsbolaget** (☎ 679 5830) from Stockholm (Strömkajen) to Finnhamn via Vaxholm up to five times daily (Skr95, two hours). **Cinderella Båtarna** (☎ 5871 4050) also sails here daily from Strandvägen in Stockholm (Skr115).

Stora Kalholmen

Measuring only 700m-long by 300m-wide, this rocky islet just south of Finnhamn offers some excellent swimming. The rustic **STF hostel** (☎ 5424 6023; beds Skr130; open early-June–mid-Aug) is nicely located, but it doesn't have electricity or a flush toilet. There is a gas cooker and a sauna, and canoe hire is available. Meals are only available for large groups, so bring your own grub.

Sailings with **Cinderella Båtarna** (☎ 587 14050) from Strandvägen (via Vaxholm and Finnhamn) run one to three times daily (Skr115, 2½ hours).

Sandön

Sandön is 2.5km long and has superb sandy beaches that are reminiscent of the Mediterranean on a sunny day. Sandhamn is the northern settlement on the island but the best beaches are at Trovill, near the southern tip. The wooden houses and narrow alleys of Sandhamn are worth exploring too. However, the island is a popular destination for partygoers and wealthy sailors – many regattas start or finish here. As a result of this, the place is rather expensive and it is best visited just as a day trip. Camping is prohibited.

Sandhamns Värdshus (☎ 5715 3051; singles/doubles Skr720/880) first opened in 1672 and still serves good food. Popular **Dykarbaren** (☎ 5715 3554; mains around Skr140) is a fashionable restaurant-bar just 50m from the quay, with lunch specials from Skr75.

Waxholmsbolaget (☎ 679 5830) sails from Strömkajen to Sandhamn via Vaxholm one to three or four times daily (Skr95, two hours). **Cinderella Båtarna** (☎ 5871 4050) do the same run regularly from Strändvägen (Skr115). It's also possible to take bus No 433 from Slussen to Stavsnäs, then sail from there (Skr55, 40 to 50 minutes, six to eight times daily).

Strömma Kanalbolaget (☎ 5871 4000) runs tours from Nybroplan to Sandhamn daily between mid-June and mid-August (one way/return Skr110/200), departing at 10am and returning at 6pm (with two hours at Sandhamn). The price includes a one-hour guided walking tour around Sandhamn.

Utö

Utö is a fairly large, delightful island in the southern section of the archipelago – it's 13km long and up to 4km wide. The reasonable road and track network make it popular with cyclists.

You can get a reasonable sketch map of the island from the **tourist office** (☎ 5015 7410; open 10am-4pm Mon-Fri Apr-Sept), in a small cabin by the guest harbour at Gruvbryggan, also known as Gruvbyn (the northernmost village). When the tourist office is closed, ask at the värdshus, which is just up the hill.

Things to See & Do Most of the sights are at the northern end of the island, near Gruvbryggan. The most unusual thing to see is Sweden's oldest iron mine, which opened in 1150 but closed in 1879. The three pits are now flooded – the deepest is Nyköpingsgruvan (215m). The **mining museum** (opposite the värdshus) keeps variable hours, so check locally. The well-preserved, 18th-century miners' houses on Lurgatan are worth a look, and the **windmill** (open 11am-3pm daily) is fun. The best **sandy beach** is on the north coast, about 10 minutes' walk from the värdshus, in the direction of Kroka. To see the **glaciated rock slabs** on the east coast, walk for about 20 minutes through the pine forest towards Rävstavik.

STOCKHOLM

Places to Stay & Eat Open from May to September, the **STF hostel** (☎ *5042 0315;* [e] *receptionen@uto-vardshus.se; Gruvbyggan; dorm beds Skr200)*, associated with the nearby *värdshus*, is in a former summer house. Reception and meals are at the *värdshus*.

Utö Värdshus (☎ *5042 0300;* [e] *reception en@uto-vardshus.se; 2-person chalets with breakfast per person low/high season Skr795/ 995, doubles from Skr1200/1400)* is the only hotel on the island and overcharges accordingly. However, facilities are good with the added bonus of the on-site **restaurant** that's considered the best in the archipelago. Lunch specials are Skr79, à la carte dinner mains are around Skr200. There are also a couple of popular summer bars here.

You may prefer to try the more reasonable café **Dannekrogen** (☎ *5015 7079)*, near the Gruvbryggan harbour, or even the **bakery** and **supermarket**.

Getting There & Around The easiest way to reach Utö is to take the *pendeltåg* (commuter train) from Stockholm Centralstationen to Västerhaninge, then bus No 846 to Årsta Havsbad. From there, Waxholmsbolaget ferries connect up to a dozen times a day with Utö (Skr55, 45 minutes), but make sure you know whether your boat stops at Spränga or Gruvbryggan first. You can also sail directly from Strömkajen to Utö (Gruvbryggan is always the first stop) with Waxholmsbolaget, once or twice daily (Skr95, 3½ hours).

Ask at the **guest harbour** (☎ *5015 7410)* about bike hire (Skr70 per day).

GRISSLEHAMN
☎ 0175

The quickest and cheapest ferry to Finland departs from this small settlement, about 100km from Stockholm in the northern part of its *län* (county). There's not much to the place beyond the ferry quay, but it is a pretty spot; the small **tourist office** (☎ *33102; open daily mid-June–mid-Aug)* is by the quay. If you've got some time on your hands, artist **Albert Engström's home, museum and studio** (combined entry Skr60; open noon-5pm daily mid-June–mid-Aug)* are worth a look.

If you need to stay overnight, **Pensionat Solgården** (☎ *30019; singles/doubles from Skr350/550)* is a small, simple pension set in a pretty garden. **Hotell Havsbaden** (☎ *30930;* [e] *info@hotell-havsbaden.se; singles/doubles*

Skr925/1300, discounted to Skr550/1100) is an attractive, upmarket place with good views and an excellent restaurant.

For details of the **Eckerö Linjen** (☎ *25800;* [w] *www.eckerolinjen.fi)* ferries to Eckerö on Åland (see the Getting There & Away chapter). SL tickets apply on bus No 637, which runs four to nine times daily between Grisslehamn and Norrtälje; this journey takes about an hour. Bus Nos 640 and 644 from T-Tekniska Högskolan (Stockholm) to Norrtälje connect with this service.

KAPELLSKÄR
☎ 0176

Kapellskär is so tiny it can't really even be described as a village – there's little to it except for a camping ground, hostel and large ferry terminal. The only reason to visit is to arrive or depart on a ferry; there are connections to Finland and Estonia from Kapellskär; see the Getting There & Away chapter for details.

If you are stuck here, there's an **STF hostel** (☎ *44169; Riddersholm; beds Skr110-120; open year-round)* off the E18, 2km west of the ferry terminal; you'll need to book in advance if you plan to stay outside of the peak summer season (mid-June to mid-August). Bring your own food.

Viking Line's direct bus from Stockholm Cityterminalen to meet the ferries costs Skr55, but if you have an SL pass, take bus No 640 or 644 from T-Tekniska Högskolan to Norrtälje and change to No 631, which runs every two hours or so (infrequently at weekends).

NYNÄSHAMN
☎ 08 • pop 24,300

Nynäshamn is about 50km south of Stockholm. From its humble beginnings as a small fishing village, by the early 20th century Nynäshamn had developed into a thriving spa town and the most important ferry terminal for Gotland. There are also regular ferries to Gdansk (Poland) and Riga (Lativa).

The **tourist office** (☎ *520 14590;* [w] *www .nynashamn.se/turism; Järnvägsgatan 2; open 9am-6pm Mon-Fri, 10am-3pm Sat & Sun June-Aug, 9am-4pm Mon-Fri rest of year)* is close to train and ferry terminals. The town centre, with all services, is nearby, on Centralgatan.

Find out about the cultural history of the area in the **Nynäshamn Hembygdsgård**

(☎ 5201 0050; Strandvägen; admission free; open noon-4pm Sun June-Aug), south of the town centre and near Nynäs Havsbad train station.

Places to Stay & Eat

Nickstabadets Camping *(☎ 5201 2780; Nickstabadsvägen; tent sites Skr120, cabins from Skr235; open mid-May–mid-Sept)* lies about 1km west of the ferry terminal and has good facilities and a small beach. **Nickstagården** *(☎ 5201 2780; Nickstabadsvägen; beds Skr140; open year-round)* is a pretty basic STF hostel at Nickstabadets Camping.

Skärgårdshotellet *(☎ 5201 1120; Kaptensgatan 2; singles/doubles Skr845/1095, discounted to Skr530/650)* is a more pleasant option; it's just across from the ferry terminal and offers comfortable rooms. Summer prices are good value.

There are a few eating options along Centralgatan, but easily the nicest area for dining is down by the fishing harbour. You'll find something to suit most budgets, including grill bars, bakeries, cafés, ice cream kiosks, fish smokehouses and restaurants. **Nynäs Rökeri** *(☎ 5201 0026; snacks & meals Skr30-75)* serves great seafood sandwiches from Skr30, plus smoked fish with potato salad for around Skr60. Nearby is upmarket **Restaurang Kroken** *(☎ 5201 5520; lunch Skr65, meals Skr140-200)*, which is a good fish restaurant in a traditional boathouse.

Getting There & Away

The ferry terminal is the main gateway to Gotland and there are also boats to Gotska Sandön and Fårösund in summer – see the Gotland chapter for details. For details about ferries to Poland and Latvia, see the Getting There & Away chapter.

Regular local trains run from Stockholm to Nynäshamn once or twice hourly. Bicycles and SL tickets are accepted, but not international rail passes. Buses arrive/depart from outside the train station.

TYRESTA NATIONAL PARK

The 4900-hectare Tyresta National Park, established in 1993, is noted for its virgin forest, which includes 300-year-old pine trees. The park lies only 20km southeast of Stockholm, which is the only European capital with virgin forest so close to it. Tyresta is a beautiful area, with rocky outcrops, small lakes, marshes, and also a wide variety of birdlife.

At the southwestern edge of the park is **Nationalparkernas Hus** *(National Parks Visitors Centre; ☎ 08-745 3394; adult/child Skr20/ free; open Tues-Sun)*. Here you can discover all of Sweden's national parks (28 at the time of research) through exhibitions and slide shows, but be sure to check out the centre itself – it is built in the shape of Sweden (with all 41 corners!). There are even 'lakes' on the floor, indicated by different stones.

Ask for the national park leaflet in English and the *Tyresta Nationalpark och Naturreservat* leaflet in Swedish, which includes an excellent topographical map at 1:25,000 scale. From the visitors centre there are various trails into the park. *Sörmlandsleden* track cuts across 6km of the park on its way to central Stockholm.

Access to the park is easy. Take the *pendeltåg* to Haninge centrum (also called Handen station) on the Nynäshamn line, then change to bus No 807 or 834. Some buses run all the way to the park, others stop at Svartbäcken (2km west of Tyresta village).

SIGTUNA

☎ 08 • pop 35,500

About 40km northwest of Stockholm is Sigtuna, founded around AD 980 and the most pleasant and important historical town near the city. It's also the oldest surviving town in Sweden and Stora gatan is probably Sweden's oldest main street. Around 1000, Olof Skötkonung ordered the minting of Sweden's first coins in the town. There are about 150 runic inscriptions in the area, most dating from the early 11th century and located beside ancient roads. Sigtuna has many quaint streets and wooden buildings still following the medieval town plan but, apart from the church, the original buildings didn't survive the devastating late-medieval town fires.

The friendly **tourist office** *(☎ 5925 0020; e turism@sigtuna.se; Stora gatan 33; open 10am-6pm Mon-Sat, 11am-5pm Sun Jun-Aug, 10am-5pm Mon-Fri, 11am or noon-3pm Sat & Sun rest of year)* is in an 18th-century wooden house, Drakegården. There are banks and supermarkets nearby, also on Stora gatan.

Things to See

During medieval times, there were seven stone-built churches in Sigtuna, but most have now disappeared. The ruins of the churches of **St Per** and **St Lars** can be seen off Prästgatan. **St Olof church** was built in the early 12th century, but became ruinous by the 17th century. The adjacent **Maria-kyrkan** *(open 9am-4pm daily Sept-May, 9am-8pm daily June-Aug)* is the oldest brick building in the area – it was a Dominican monastery church from around 1250, but became the parish church in 1529 after the monastery was demolished by Gustav Vasa. There are restored medieval paintings inside and free summer concerts are held weekly.

Sigtuna Museum *(☎ 5978 3870; Stora gatan 55; adult/child Skr30/free; open noon-4pm Tues-Sun Sept-May, noon-4pm daily June-Aug)* looks after several attractions in the town, all of them on Stora gatan and near the tourist office. **Lundströmska gården** *(adult/child Skr10/5; open noon-4pm daily June-Aug, noon-4pm Sat & Sun Sept)* is an early 20th-century, middle-class home and adjacent general store, complete with period furnishings and goods. **Sigtuna rådhus** *(admission free; open noon-4pm daily June-Aug, noon-4pm Sat & Sun Sept)*, the smallest town hall in Scandinavia, dates from 1744 and was designed by the mayor himself. It's on the town square opposite the tourist office. The main museum building has displays of gold jewellery, runes, coins and loot brought home from abroad.

The magnificent private palace **Steninge Slott** *(☎ 5925 9500)*, 7km east of Sigtuna, dates from 1705 and was designed by Nicodemus Tessin the Younger. On the guided palace tour (Skr50; noon and 2pm daily in summer), you'll see luxuriously ornate interiors; in the beautiful grounds there is also the excellent **Cultural Centre** *(admission free; open daily year-round)*. In a converted stone barn dating from the 1870s, you'll find an art gallery, glassworks, candle-making area, café and restaurant.

Another palace, **Rosersbergs Slott** *(☎ 5903 5039; tours adult/child Skr50/25; open 1am-3pm daily mid-May–Aug; tours on the hour)*, is on Mälaren lake about 9km southeast of Sigtuna. It was constructed in the 1630s and used as a royal residence from 1762 to 1860; the interior has excellent furnishings from the Empire period (1790–1820) and Queen Hedvig Elisabeth Charlotta's conversation room is quite extraordinary.

Skokloster Slott *(☎ 018-386077; tours adult/child Skr65/20)*, around 11km due northwest of Sigtuna (26km by road), is an exceptionally fine whitewashed baroque palace. It was built between 1654 and 1671 and has impressive stucco ceilings and collections of furniture, textiles, art and arms. There's a small café at the palace. Guided tours run daily from April to October; it's a good idea to call in advance to check times. From June to August there are tours every hour from 11am to 4pm daily. In May these run from noon to 3pm daily. In April, September and October tours run at 1pm on weekdays and at noon, 1pm, 2pm and 3pm on weekends.

Skoklosterspelen is a popular medieval festival held at Skokloster Slott. It lasts five days in mid-July and includes around 350 performances (eg, tournaments, exhibitions, concerts, 18th-century activities).

The nearby **motor museum** *(☎ 018-386106; adult/child Skr40/10; open noon-4pm daily May-Sept)*, adjacent to the *wärdshus* opposite the palace, has a good collection of vintage cars and motorcycles.

Places to Stay & Eat

Unfortunately Sigtuna's summer hostel had closed at the time of writing; check if it has reopened at the tourist office. Alternative accommodation is quite pricey (although summer rates are more reasonable).

Sigtuna Stiftelsen Gästhem *(☎ 5925 8900; Manfred Björkquists allé 2-4; singles/doubles Skr800/1300, discounted to Skr500/600)* is a pretty place run by a Christian foundation. **Stora Brännbo** *(☎ 5925 7500; Stora Brännbovägen 2-6; singles/doubles from Skr950/1200, discounted to Skr450/650)* is a large hotel and conference centre just north of the town centre.

The pick of the town's lodgings is the central, newly renovated **Sigtuna Stadshotell** *(☎ 5925 0100; e info@sigtunastadshotell.se; Stora Nygatan 3; singles/doubles Skr1600/2150, discounted to Skr1150/1550)*. The decor is all pale, sleek and very stylish, and the upmarket restaurant and bar areas have lovely lake views.

There are a number of excellent cafés and restaurants to choose from. **Tant Brunn Kaffestuga** *(☎ 5925 0934; Laurentii gränd)*, in a small alley off Stora gatan, is a delightful 17th-century café set around a pretty courtyard. It's well worth seeking out for its home-baked bread and pastries.

Farbror Blå Café & Kök (☎ *5925 6050; Stora torget 14; mains Skr100-145*) is a central café, adjacent to the town hall, that does a variety of dishes, including chicken quesadilla, Caesar salad and burgers, as well as cheaper snacks.

Båt Huset Krog & Bar (☎ *5925 6780; Kallbadhusviken; mains Skr175-240*) is a classy wooden restaurant (with a bar) that floats on the lake.

Getting There & Around

Travel connections are easy from Stockholm. Take a local train to Märsta, from where there are frequent buses to Sigtuna (No 570 or 575). Bus No 883 runs every hour or two from Uppsala to Sigtuna. To get to Rosersbergs Slott, take the SL *pendeltåg* train to Rosersberg, then walk the final 2km to the palace (signposted). For Skokloster, take an hourly SJ train to Bålsta, then the infrequent bus No 894.

Strömma Kanalbolaget (☎ *5871 4000;* W *www.strommakanalbolaget.com*) offers full-day cruises four times a week from late June to mid-August between Stockholm and Uppsala via Sigtuna and Skokloster. The price (Skr550) includes lunch, dinner and guided tours; you get 1¼ hours in Sigtuna and 1¾ hours at Skokloster.

Café Vafflan (☎ *5925 0800*) at the harbour rents out boats and fishing gear; the tourist office can arrange bike rental.

MARIEFRED
☎ 0159

Tiny, lakeside Mariefred is a pretty little village with an impressive attraction. **Gripsholm Slott** (☎ *10194; adult/child Skr60/30; open 10am-4pm daily mid-May–mid-Sept, noon-3pm Sat & Sun mid-Sept–mid-May*) is the epitome of castles with its round towers, spires and drawbridge. It contains some of the state portrait collection, which dates from the 16th century and you can explore the well-decorated rooms.

Originally built in the 1370s, Gripsholm Slott passed into crown hands by the early 15th century. In 1526, Gustav Vasa took over and ordered the demolition of the adjacent monastery. A new castle with walls up to 5m thick was built at Gripsholm using materials from the monastery, but

extensions, conversions and repairs continued for years. The oldest 'untouched' room is Karl IX's bedchamber, dating from the 1570s. The castle was abandoned in 1715, but it was renovated and extended during the reign of Gustav III (especially between 1773 and 1785). The moat was filled in and, in 1730 and 1827, two 11th-century **rune stones** were found. These stones stand by the access road and are well worth a look; one has a Christian cross, while the other describes an expedition against the Saracens. The castle was restored again in the 1890s, the moat was cleared and the drawbridge rebuilt.

You can also visit nearby **Grafikens Hus** (☎ *23160; adult/child Skr50/free; open 11am-5pm daily May-Aug, 11am-5pm Tues-Sun Sept-Apr*), which is a centre for contemporary graphic art and printmaking.

Visit the **tourist office** (☎ *29790;* e *malar turism@strangnas.se,* W *www.mariefred.se; open daily June-Aug, Mon-Fri Sept-May*) and pick up a map and notes (in English) for a self-guided walking tour of the idyllic village centre, with cobblestone streets and many 18th-century buildings.

Places to Stay & Eat

STF Vandrarhem Mariefred (☎ *36700;* e *re ceptionen.gripsholm@redcross.se; beds Skr190; open mid-June–mid-Aug*) is a new hostel with excellent facilities, only 500m west of the castle in lovely grounds. It's a Red Cross educational centre for most of the year; during summer break the student lodgings are turned into hostel accommodation.

Mariefreds Camping (☎ *13250;* e *marie fredscamping@telia.com; tent sites low/high season Skr100/120; cabins from Skr300*), beside the lake and 2km east of the town centre, offers budget accommodation from May to mid-September.

Gripsholms Värdshus & Hotell (☎ *34750;* e *info@gripshols-vardshus.se; Kyrkogatan 1; singles/doubles from Skr1600/2190*) opened in 1609 and is Sweden's oldest inn. This charming and elegant place has 45 individually furnished rooms, full of antiques, and many rooms have great views of the castle. There is also a highly regarded **restaurant** here, with a beautiful setting and main courses for around Skr250.

Gripsholms Slottscafe (☎ *10023; meals Skr65-160*), in the gardens by the castle, is a good place for coffee ad cake, or for light meals such as quiche, salad or sandwiches. Nearby, **Gripsholms Grill & Pizzeria**, serves the usual fast-food selections for around Skr50.

Getting There & Away

Mariefred isn't on the main railway line – the nearest station is at Läggesta, 3km west, with hourly trains from Stockholm. A **museum railway** (☎ *21006; one way/return tickets Skr36/48*) from Läggesta to Mariefred runs on weekends from mid-May to September (daily from Midsummer to mid-August), hourly during the day. Bus No 304 runs hourly from Läggesta to Mariefred.

The steamship S/S Mariefred (☎ 08-669 8850) departs from Stadshusbron (Stockholm) for Mariefred, daily from mid-June to mid-August, and weekends only from mid-May to mid-June and mid-August to mid-September (one way/return Skr150/240, 3½ hours). A round-trip ticket from Stockholm including an SJ train, the museum railway, admission to the castle and *S/S Mariefred* costs around Skr350 one way.

Svealand

This is the region where Sweden was born. Viking rune stones, graveyards and forts are reminders of the time when Mälaren lake was an arm of the Baltic Sea, offering safe harbours and links to Finland and Russia. Ultimately, the kingdom of the Svea became synonymous with the rest of country, which became known as Svea Rike or Sverige.

In the northwest of the region amid some picturesque lake and forest scenery, lies Dalarna (sometimes called Dalecarlia in English), a county of rich folk culture, conservative attitudes and beautiful landscapes.

Orientation & Information

Svealand consists of six regions *(landskaps)* and seven counties *(län)*. In the east, there's the regions of Uppland and Södermanland (also called Sörmland), in the middle of the country there's Västmanland and Närke, while the west has Värmland and Dalarna. This book has dealt with the county of Stockholms Län in a separate chapter. The county of Uppsala Län consists of most of the rest of Uppland, Södermanlands Län consists of most of Södermanland and Västmanlands Län takes in the east of Västmanland. Örebro Län consists of the rest of Västmanland and all of Närke. Värmlands Län and Dalarnas Län are the same as their respective regions.

The southern part of the region is dominated by extensive lakes with several large towns on their shores. Further west and north, the forests become denser. Dalarna, around Lake Siljan, has the twin branches of the Dalälven (river) and some lovely lake and forest scenery. The hilly district where Dalarna borders Norway has become popular for travel and winter sports.

Regional Tourist Offices

Each county has a regional tourist office. Visitors can contact the following agencies for more detailed information on the area.

Länsturismen i Örebro Län (☎ 019-602 7000, ⓔ erk.jonsson@orebroll.se, ⓦ www.orebroll .se/turism) Eklundavägen 9-15, Box 1613, SE-70116 Örebro

Sörmlands Turism (☎ 0155-245900, ⓔ info@ sormlandsturism.se, ⓦ www.sormland.se /turism) Brunnsgatan 29, SE-61188 Nyköping

Highlights

- Wandering around the pre-Viking burial mounds at the ancient site of Gamla Uppsala

- Enjoying a performance at the amazing Dalhalla amphitheatre near Rättvik

- Exploring the bowels of the earth in the copper mine at Falun

- Participating in a Midsummer festival at Rättvik or Leksand in Dalarna

- Watching the lynx, bears and wolves at Grönklitt bear park in Orsa

- Hiking or skiing in the mountains along the Norwegian border

- Rafting down the peaceful Klarälven River

Turistinformation Dalarna (☎ 023-64004, ⓔ dalarna.tourist@welcome.falun.se, ⓦ www.dalarna.se) Trotzgatan 10-12, SE-79183 Falun

Uppsala Tourism (☎ 018-274800, ⓔ info@ uppsalatourism.se, ⓦ www.res.till.uppland.nu) Fyris Torg 8, SE-75310 Uppsala

Värmlands Turistråd (☎ 054-222550, ⓔ info@varmland.org, ⓦ www.varmland.org) Tage Erlandergatan 10B, SE-65220 Karlstad

WestmannaTurism (☎ 021-103800, ⓔ info@vastmanland.se, ⓦ www.vastman land.se) Stora Gatan 40, SE-72187 Västerås

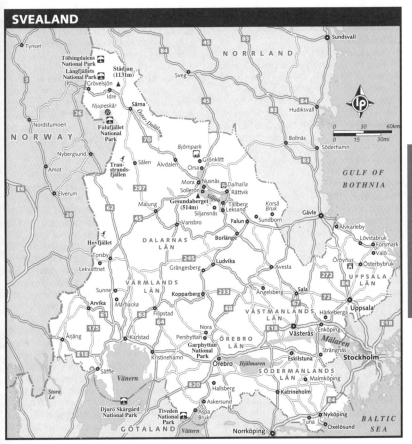

SVEALAND

SVEALAND

Getting Around

Express buses connect major towns in southern areas – for the west and north of the region, you'll need to use *länstrafiken* (regional network) services.

The following companies provide regional transport links. If you're planning to spend a reasonable amount of time in any of these counties, it's worth inquiring about value or rebate cards, monthly passes or a *sommarkort*, offering discount travel in the peak summer period (ie, from Midsummer to mid-August). Check also the respective websites for routes, schedules, fares and passes; these websites don't always have information in English, but if you call the telephone numbers listed you'll usually reach someone who can help you in English.

Dalatrafik (☎ 020 232425,
Ⓦ www.dalatrafik.se)
Länstrafiken Örebro (☎ 020 224000,
Ⓦ www.lanstrafiken.se)
Länstrafiken Sörmland (☎ 020 224000,
Ⓦ www.lanstrafiken.se)
Upplands Lokaltrafik (☎ 020 114 1414,
Ⓦ www.upplandslokaltrafik.se)
Västmanlands Lokaltrafik (☎ 0200 255075,
Ⓦ www.vl.se)
Värmlandstrafik (☎ 020 225580,
Ⓦ www.kollplatsen.com)

There are SJ trains runing along both sides of Mälaren lake. Hallsberg is a major junction and trains continue west to Karlstad and Oslo. There are good services from Stockholm to Uppsala and Mora, and many other destinations.

Uppland

UPPSALA

☎ 018 ● pop 191,100

Uppsala is the fourth-largest city in Sweden, and one of its oldest. Gamla (Old) Uppsala flourished as early as the 6th century. The cathedral was consecrated in 1435 after 175 years of building and the castle was first built in the 1540s, although today's edifice belongs to the 18th century. The city depends on the sprawling university (Scandinavia's oldest), which was founded in 1477.

Information

The **tourist office** (☎ 727 4800; e tb@upp salatourism.se, w www.uppsalatourism.se; Fyristorg 8; open 10am-6pm Mon-Fri, 10am-3pm Sat, also noon-4pm Sun June-Aug) is central and helpful. Ask about Uppsala Kortet, a newly introduced card (24/48/72 hours for Skr75/125/150) that gives free or discounted admission to many of the town's museums and sights, as well as free local bus travel and free parking.

Information about Uppsala's **university** is available online at w www.uu.se, with excellent information in a number of languages plus many useful links. Students in search of information can go to the **student union** (☎ 480 3100; w www.uppsalastudent kar.nu; Övre Slottsgatan 7).

Forex (Fyristorg) is next to the main tourist office. Head to Stora Torget for banks and ATMs. There is a **post office** on Bäverns Gränd, but a number of central newsagencies also provide postal services.

Akademibokhandeln Lundequistska (cnr Bredgränd & Dragarbrunnsgatan), an excellent bookshop, is upstairs in the Forum Gallerian. For newspapers and magazines, go to **Press Stop** (Drottninggatan 2), or **Pressbyrån**, at the train station.

The **public library** (Svartbäcksgatan 17; open 11am-7pm Mon-Fri, 11am-3pm Sat year-round, also 1pm-4pm Sun Sept-Apr) offers free Internet access, but expect long waits. If the wait's too long, pop across the road to **Ink & Art** (Svärtbacksgatan 14; open Mon-Sat), a copy shop that also has public computers (Skr1 per minute). A third option is the **Internet café** (cnr Fyristorg & Drottninggatan; open Mon-Sat) inside the Upsala Nya Tidning newspaper office; it's right by the tourist office and charges Skr10 for 15 minutes online.

STA Travel (☎ 020 611010; Sankt Olofs-gatan 11) is a central travel agency.

If you can read Swedish, a good website is w www.uppsala.com.

Medical & Emergency Services

For emergencies, go to the **police** (☎ 168500; Salagatan 18). If you're after a pharmacy, **Apoteket Kronan** (Svartbäcksgatan 8) is open until 11pm daily. For emergency treatment go to the **university medical centre** (☎ 611 0000; Sjukhusvägen).

Gamla Uppsala

Uppsala began at the three great **grave mounds** (direct bus No 2 from Stora Torget; admission free; open 24hr) at Gamla Uppsala, 4km north of the modern city. The mounds, said to be the graves of legendary pre-Viking kings Aun, Egils and Adils, are part of a larger cemetery that includes about 300 smaller mounds and **boat graves**, dating from around 500 to 1100. Important chieftains were often buried in their boats, along with all necessary provisions for their final journey.

A new **historical centre** (☎ 239300; adult/child Skr50/30; open 11am-5pm daily May-Aug; noon-3pm Sun Sept-April) has good information on the area plus exhibits of ancient artefacts excavated from Gamla Uppsala and the nearby archaeological sites. Helpful information on the site is available online at w www.raa.se/olduppsala.

Gamla Uppsala was the site of a great heathen temple where human and animal sacrifices took place, but Thor, Odin and the other Viking gods were displaced when Christianity arrived in 1090. From 1164, the archbishop of Uppsala had his seat in a cathedral on the site of the present **church** (open 9am-6pm daily Apr-Sept; 9am-4pm daily Oct-Mar). By the 15th century, the church had been enlarged and painted with frescoes.

Next to the flat-topped mound **Tingshögen** is the **Odinsborg Inn** (☎ 323525; buffet Skr150), known for the horns of mead and Viking feasts at its restaurant, although daintier refreshments (sandwiches, cake, coffee) are offered during summer at the downstairs café. The **Disagården** (☎ 169180; admission free; open 10am-5pm daily mid-May–Aug) farm-museum-village consists of about 20 timber houses and is a few minutes

UPPSALA

PLACES TO STAY
2 Basic Hotel
3 Scandic Hotel Uplandia
19 Hotel Svava

PLACES TO EAT
5 East West; Atlantis World Kitchen
10 Ofvandahl's
11 Saluhallen; Svenssons Äkanten
13 Kung Krål
20 Amazing Thai
21 Hemköp Supermarket
23 Hambergs Fisk
24 Domtrappkällaren

33 Eko Caféet
37 Saffet's; O'Connor's
38 Waynes Coffee

ENTERTAINMENT
9 Svenssons Krog
15 O'Learys
16 Royal Cinema
17 Katalin
30 William's
32 Fredmans; Escobar
43 Birger Jarl Kök & Bar

MUSEUMS
1 Linnémuseet
12 Upplands Museum
26 Gustavianum Museum

44 Carolina Rediviva
46 Vasa Vignettes
47 Uppsala Slott; Uppsala Konstmuseum

OTHER
4 Airport Bus
6 Public Library
7 Ink & Art
8 STA Travel
14 Apoteket Kronan
18 Bus Station
22 City Buses
25 Domkyrkan
27 Rune Stones
28 University Main Building

29 Student Union
31 Trefaldighets Kyrka
34 Tourist Office; Forex
35 Internet Café
36 Press Stop
39 Akademibokhandeln Lundequistska; Forum Gallerian Shopping Complex
40 Systembolaget
41 Post Office
42 Boats to Skokloster & Stockholm
45 Orangery
48 University Medical Centre

SVEALAND

Everyday Gods

Some of the greatest gods of the Nordic world, Tyr, Odin, Thor and Frigg, live on in the English language as the days of the week – Tuesday, Wednesday, Thursday and Friday, respectively.

The one-handed Tyr was the god of justice, including war-treaties, contracts and oaths. The principal myth regarding Tyr involves the giant wolf, Fenrir. The gods decided Fenrir had to be chained up, but nothing could hold him. Dwarfs made an unbreakable chain and the gods challenged Fenrir to break it. He was suspicious, but agreed on condition that one of the gods place his hand in his mouth. Tyr was the only one to agree. The gods succeeded in fettering Fenrir, but he retaliated by biting off Tyr's right hand.

The most eminent of the Nordic gods was the one-eyed Odin (the father of most of the other gods), whose eight-legged flying horse, Sleipnir, had runes etched on its teeth. As a god of war, Odin sent his 12 Valkyries (battlemaidens) to select 'heroic dead' killed in battle to join him in everlasting feasting at the palace of Valhalla. Odin carried a spear called Gungnir, which never missed when thrown, and his bow could fire 10 arrows at once. Odin was also the god of poets, a magician and master of runes. Odin's great wisdom had been granted in exchange for his missing eye, but he also gained wisdom from his two ravens Hugin and Munin, who flew daily in search of knowledge.

Frigg was Odin's wife, and she's also known as a fertility goddess and the goddess of marriage.

Thor is usually depicted as an immensely strong god who protected humans from the malevolent giants with the assistance of his magic hammer Mjolnir, which returned to its thrower like a boomerang. Thor represented thunder and the hammer was the thunderbolt. Thor's greatest enemy was the evil snake Jörmungand and it was believed they were destined to kill each other at Ragnarök, the end of the world, when the wolf Fenrir would devour Odin. At Ragnarök, the other gods and humans would also die in cataclysmic battle, the sky would collapse in raging fire and the earth would subside into the sea.

GRAEME CORNWALLIS

---

from the church. Regular guided tours of the village cost Skr30.

Uppsala Slott

Construction of this castle (☎ 272485; admission & tour adult/child Skr60/15; open daily June-Aug) was ordered by Gustav Vasa in the 1550s; it features the state hall where kings were enthroned (and a queen abdicated). On display in the cathedral are the clothes worn by Nils Sture (who was murdered in the castle in 1567) at the time he died. Nils was stabbed by the crazed King Erik XIV, but others finished him (and his two sons, Erik and Svante) off. The clothes are the only example of 16th-century Swedish high fashion still in existence. The castle burnt down in 1702, but was rebuilt and took on its present form in 1757. Entry is by guided tour only (in English at 1pm and 3pm).

Vasa Vignettes (☎ 270000; adult/child Skr40/15; open noon-4pm Mon-Fri, 11am-5pm Sat & Sun May-Aug) is a waxworks museum set in the death-stained dungeons and illustrates the past intrigues of the castle.

The southern wing of Uppsala Slott also houses the **Uppsala Konstmuseum** (☎ 727 0000; adult/child Skr30/free; open noon-4pm Wed-Fri, 11am-5pm Sat & Sun), whose works of art span five centuries.

Wiks Slott

This remarkable brick building, with an unusual clock tower and a magnificent park, is one of Sweden's best preserved medieval castles and dates from the 15th century. The interior was reconstructed in the 1650s and again in the 1860s. Guided tours of the castle (☎ *561000; adult/child Skr30/20*) are available at 1pm and 3pm from Midsummer until the end of August, and B&B is also available during this time (see Places to Stay). The castle is about 20km southwest of the city centre, next to an arm of Mälaren lake; there are five buses (No 847) daily.

Other Attractions

The Gothic **Domkyrkan** (*cathedral; admission free; open 8am-6pm daily*) dominates the city just as some of those buried here dominated their country: St Erik, Gustav Vasa and Carl von Linné, who established the system of scientific names for species. The **treasury** (☎ *187201; adult/child Skr30/free; open daily May-Sept; Tues-Sun Oct-Apr*) in the north tower holds Gustav Vasa's sword and a great display of medieval clothing, including archbishops' vestments, dated from 1200 onwards. The nearby **Trefaldighets Kyrka** isn't outwardly as impressive, but has beautiful painted ceilings.

The **Gustavianum Museum** (☎ *471 7571; Akademigatan 3; adult/child Skr40/free; open 11am-4pm Tues-Sun*) has exhibits about the university and the history of science, an excellent antiquities collection and an old 'anatomical theatre'. **Upplands Museum** (☎ *169100; Sankt Eriks Torg 10; adult/child Skr30/free; open noon-5pm Tues-Sun*), in an 18th-century mill, houses county collections from the Middle Ages.

Carolina Rediviva (☎ *471 3900; Dag Hammarskjöldsväg 1; adult/child Skr20/free; open daily mid-May–mid-Sept, closed Sun rest of year*), the old university library, has a display hall with maps and historical and scientific literature, the pride of which is the surviving half of the *Codex Argentus*, written with silver ink on purple vellum in the now extinct Gothic language in 520.

The excellent **Botanical Gardens** (*open 7am-9pm May-Aug; 7am-7pm Sept-Apr*), including the 200-year-old **Orangery** and a tropical **greenhouse** (*adult/child Skr20/free*), are below the castle hill. The gardens shouldn't to be confused with the **Linnémuseet** (☎ *136540; Svartbäcksgatan 27; adult/child Skr25/free; open noon-4pm Tues-Sun June–mid-Sept*) and its **garden** (☎ *109490; adult/*

child *Skr20/free; open 9am-9pm daily May-Aug, 9am-7pm daily Sept*). The museum keeps memorabilia of Linné's work in Uppsala, and the garden (Sweden's oldest botanical garden), with more than 1300 species, was designed according to an 18th-century plan.

Take sandwiches and sit by the main **Uppsala University** building (imposing enough to demand a glance inside) and absorb the ambience of an historic university. On the lawn at the front are nine typical Uppland **rune stones**.

On 30 April students gather dressed in white to celebrate the Walpurgis Festival in procession and song. There are a number of traditions on this day, including a student boat race on the river at 10am and a run down Carolinabacken at 3pm.

There are a number of smaller, special-interest museums in town, many attached to university departments and keeping complex hours. Inquire at the tourist office for the likes of the Medicinhistoriska Museet (Museum of Medical History), Psykiatrihistoriska Museet (Psychiatric Museum) or Evolutionsmuseet (Museum of Evolution).

Activities

You can ride the steam train **Lennakatten** (☎ *130500*) on a narrow-gauge museum railway 33km into the Uppland countryside on Sunday, up to seven times daily from June to August (Skr100 return). There are also tours on Thursday, Friday and Saturday in July. The trains depart from the Uppsala Östra museum station behind the main station.

Strömma Kanalbolaget (☎ *121230*; ⓦ *www.strommakanalbolaget.com*) offers full-day cruises four times a week from late June to mid-August between Uppsala and Stockholm via the baroque castle of Skokloster and the pretty village of Sigtuna (see Around Stockholm in the Stockholm chapter). The price (Skr550) includes lunch, dinner and guided tours; you get about 1¼ hours in Sigtuna, 1¾ hours at Skokloster. The old steamer departs from Islandsbron by Östra Ågatan at 10am, getting into Stockholm at 7pm. You then need to find your way back to Uppsala by train or bus.

Alternatively, if you don't wish to go on to Stockholm, take a boat cruise to Skokloster on **M/S Kung Carl Gustaf** (☎ *144800*), which sails daily except Monday from late May to mid-August (weekends to late August).

Carl von Linné

Carl von Linné (1707–78), often known in English as Carolus Linnaeus, is known for his classification of minerals, plants and animals, as described in his work *Systema Naturae*. Linnaeus journeyed throughout Sweden to make his observations – his most famous journeys were to Lappland (1732), Dalarna (1734) and Skåne (1749). His pupils and colleagues also gathered information worldwide, from Australia (with Cook's expedition) to Central Asia and South America. Linnaeus insisted on hard physical evidence before drawing any conclusions and his methods were thereafter absorbed by all the natural sciences. His theories of plant reproduction still hold today.

In 1739 Linnaeus was one of the founders of the Swedish Academy of Sciences in Stockholm. Among other achievements, he took Celsius' temperature scale and turned it upside down, giving us 0°C for freezing point and 100°C for boiling point, rather than the other way around.

Tours leave Islandsbron at 11.30am and return at 5.15pm and allow 1¾ hours at Skokloster. The return trip costs Skr120; the return plus a guided tour of Skokloster costs Skr185. A buffet lunch is available on board for Skr85. An evening river cruise is also offered from May to August, including buffet dinner and entertainment, for Skr370.

If you feel like a peaceful walk, **Erikleden** is a 6km 'pilgrims path' between the cathedral and the church at Gamla Uppsala. Ask at the tourist office for more information.

Places to Stay

Well-equipped **Fyrishov Camping** (☎ 274960; e stugbycamping@fyrishov.se; Idrottsgatan 2; bus No 4, 6, 20, 24, 25, 50 or 54; tent sites from Skr115, 4-bed cabins from Skr350; open year-round) is 2km north of the city and nicely located by the river at Fyrisfjädern.

The pleasant, well-equipped STF hostel **Sunnersta Herrgård** (☎ 324220; Sunnerstavägen 24; bus No 20 or 50; dorm beds Skr180; open year-round) is located in a manor house some 6km south of the city centre. Here it's possible to rent boats, canoes and bikes. There's a second, summer STF hostel **Vandraren** (☎ 104300; e info@vandraren.com;

Vattholmavägen; bus No 2, 20, 24 or 54; dorm beds Skr165, singles/doubles Skr190/370; open mid-June–mid-Aug), 2km north of the city. It's a student residence for the rest of the year and facilities, including a private bathroom for each room, are excellent.

Uppsala Room Agency (☎ 109533; e uppsala.rumsformedling@swipnet.se; singles/doubles from Skr250/350) will book private rooms in town.

Wiks Slott (☎ 561000; bus No 847; B&B singles/doubles Skr365/630; open late June–Aug), 20km southwest of the city, is an atmospheric castle set in beautiful grounds, offering good-value B&B in summer only.

A 15-minute bus ride from Stora Torget is **Hotell Årsta Gård** (☎ 253500; Jordgubbsgatan 14; bus No 7 or 52; singles/doubles Skr525/675, discounted to Skr425/675), a small, family-run place.

The clean and central **Samariterhemmets Gästhem** (☎ 103400; Samaritergränd 2; singles/doubles Skr450/690, with bath Skr540/790, prices discounted by around Skr70) is an inviting guesthouse run by a Christian community, with excellent old-style rooms.

Central **Basic Hotel** (☎ 480 5000; e reception@basichotel.com; Kungsgatan 27; singles/doubles from Skr690/790, both discounted to Skr600) has excellent rooms with their own self-catering facilities. This is a good place for families or small groups: four-bed rooms cost Skr760 year-round.

Scandic Hotel Uplandia (☎ 495 2600; e uplandia@scandic-hotels.com; Dragarbrunnsgatan 32; singles/doubles from Skr1261/1584, discounted to Skr640/790) is centrally located and recently refurbished, with modern rooms and all the mod cons. Similar in style, service and price is **Scandic Hotel Uppsala Nord** (☎ 495 2300; e uppsala@scandic-hotel.com; Gamla Uppsalagatan 50; singles/doubles Skr1029/1322), about 2.5km from the city centre on the road to Gamla Uppsala.

Hotel Svava (☎ 130030; e info.svava@swedenhotels.se; Bangårdsgatan 24; singles/doubles Skr1295/1535, discounted to Skr735/900), right opposite the train station, is very comfortable and has all the facilities of a top-end business-style hotel.

Places to Eat

Domtrappkällaren (☎ 130955; Fyristorg; lunch from Skr80, dinner mains Skr170-290), previously a prison, is now a quality restaurant with an atmospheric (and expensive) cellar, or a less interesting upstairs section, where lunch is served.

Hambergs Fisk *(☎ 710050; Fyristorg; lunch from Skr80, à la carte mains Skr130-240)*, next to the tourist office, is an excellent seafood restaurant, especially popular at lunchtime.

East West *(☎ 681890; Dragarbrunnsgatan 25; dishes Skr58-179)* claims to be a 'united world bistro', with a great range of casual bar-style food to meet all tastes – burgers, salad, pasta, tortillas. Sharing the same kitchen is the neighbouring **Atlantis World Kitchen** *(mains Skr100-190)*, a slightly more sophisticated place with a similarly diverse menu, and an emphasis on seafood (eg, crab-filled cannelloni, bouillabaisse, grilled pike, perch).

Kung Krål *(☎ 125090; Gamla Torget; lunch Skr75, mains Skr89-159)*, in the heart of town, is just the place for good Swedish and international dishes in appealing surrounds – with steak, pasta, reindeer, salads, salmon and seafood dishes on the extensive menu.

Amazing Thai *(☎ 153010; Bredgränd 14; lunch buffet Skr60, à la carte dishes Skr75-139)* is a popular lunch spot due to its great-value buffet. The evening menu features a good selection of noodles, vegetarian and seafood dishes, and curries.

Ofvandahl's *(☎ 134204; Sysslomansgatan 3-5; cakes & snacks from Skr25)* is a classy café full of old-world charm. Some of the best coffee in town and Italian-style food such as pasta and panini can be found at funky **Eko Caféet** *(☎ 121845; Drottninggatan 5; meals Skr40-65)*, with retro, mismatched furniture. Serving similar café fare, the sleek **Waynes Coffee** *(☎ 710012; Smedsgränd 4; meals Skr40-65)* has a contrasting decor. It has stylish surrounds, with outdoor tables and a large window opening onto the street.

There are several eateries on the pedestrian mall and Stora Torget. For fast food, **Saffet's** *(Stora Torget)* has the works – burgers, enchiladas, tacos, baked potatoes, fish and chips, kebabs – all for Skr50 or less.

If you're self-catering, there's a central **Hemköp supermarket** *(Stora Torget)*. The indoor produce market, **Saluhallen** *(open Mon-Sat)*, is between the cathedral and the river at Sankt Eriks torg (it's being rebuilt after a fire and should have reopened by the time you read this).

For alcohol, pay a visit to **Systembolaget** *(Dragarbrunnsgatan 50)*, on the 1st floor of the Svava shopping centre.

Entertainment

In the evenings, local students converge on the *krog* (pub) restaurants. The cool **Svenssons Krog** *(☎ 553310; Sysslomansgatan 15)* is very popular, as is the sister venue **Svenssons Åkanten**, an outdoor, riverside restaurant and bar by Saluhallen.

Birger Jarl Kök & Bar *(☎ 711734; Nedre Slottsgatan 3)* is another favourite spot, a great place for an outdoor drink on a warm evening.

O'Learys *(☎ 132030; Påvel Snickares Gränd)* is an American-style sports bar. **William's** *(☎ 140920; Övre Slottsgatan 7)*, in the university quarter, is an English pub with an adjacent Indian restaurant (lunch buffet Skr50). **O'Connor's** *(☎ 144010; Stora Torget 1)*, upstairs from Saffet's, is a friendly Irish pub and restaurant (good pub meals from Skr50). There's also live music nightly, and a selection of over 85 beers.

The excellent **Katalin** *(☎ 140680; Godsmagasinet; Östra Station)* is in a former warehouse behind the train station. It hosts regular live jazz and blues, with occasional live rock and pop bands. There's a good restaurant here too.

Fredmans *(☎ 124212; Drottninggatan 12)* also has pub food and live music; next door is **Escobar** *(☎ 140040)*, a popular bar and nightclub.

Royal Cinema *(☎ 135007; Dragarbrunnsgatan 44)* is a large cinema screening Hollywood films regularly.

Getting There & Away

The bus station is outside the train station. Bus No 801 departs at least twice an hour for nearby Arlanda airport (Skr80) from outside Scandic Hotel Uplandia. **Swebus Express** *(☎ 0200 218218; Ⓦ www.swebusexpress.se)* runs regularly to Stockholm (Skr50), Gävle (Skr120), Västerås (Skr75), Sala (Skr95), Örebro (Skr165) and Falun (Skr205). **Svenska Buss** *(☎ 0771-6767676; Ⓦ www.svenskabuss.se)* also operates services a few times a week west to Västerås, Örebro and Karlstad.

There are frequent SJ trains from Stockholm (Skr81, 40 minutes). All SJ services to/from Gävle, Östersund and Mora also stop in Uppsala. SL coupons take you (and your bicycle) only as far as Märsta from Stockholm.

For car hire, contact **Statoil** (☎ 209100; Gamla Uppsalagatan 48), next to the Scandic Hotel Uppsala Nord.

Getting Around

A local bus ticket costs from Skr20 and gives unlimited travel for two hours – just enough for a visit to Gamla Uppsala. Catch a city bus from Stora Torget or outside Scandic Hotel Uplandia. **Upplands Lokaltrafik** (☎ 020 114 1414) runs traffic within the city and county.

You can hire a bicycle at Fyrishov Camping or either of the STF hostels (or inquire at the tourist office). Regional buses of Upplands Lokaltrafik take bicycles for Skr20 but local trains don't.

NORTHERN UPPLAND

The northern part of Uppland is known for its ironworks and mines, which are up to 500 years old. Some of the ironworks were owned, run and staffed by Dutch and Walloon (Belgian) immigrants, and very fine mansions were built from the profits. A visit to one of these mansions, restored ironworks or mine workings is certainly worthwhile. Ask any tourist office for the free booklet *Vallonbruk in Uppland*. Good information is available on the Internet at Ⓦ www.vallon bruken.nu.

To reach Lövstabruk or Forsmark, take bus No 811 from Uppsala to Östhammar, then change to bus No 832 (four to eight daily). Bus No 823 runs hourly from Uppsala to Österbybruk.

Österbybruk
☎ 0295

Österbybruk is a large village with all facilities (bank, supermarkets etc) 45km north of Uppsala. There's a summer **tourist office** (☎ 21492; open noon-4pm Sat & Sun May; 11am-5pm daily June-Aug) here, which can deal with inquiries about the attractions of the area and the somewhat irregular hours they keep.

The pleasant area around the tourist office includes the mansion **Österbybruk Herrgård**, which has summer art exhibitions, workers' homes and an iron forge. Two types of tours are offered; one takes in the grounds of ironworks, the other takes

you into the forge and explains its original workings. Both tours are given daily in summer (mid-June to mid-August) and cost Skr40/free per adult/child.

About 2.5km west, there's the old 100m-deep **Dannemora Gruvor**, once a mine and now a lake; tours of the mine buildings run at noon and 2pm daily from late June to early August (adult/child Skr45/free). Some 10km further west, the impressive 15th-century castle **Örbyhus Slott** (☎ 21492) is where mad King Erik XIV was imprisoned. The king was murdered here with a poisoned bowl of pea soup. Guided tours (adult/child Skr45/ 15) run at 1pm and 3pm Tuesday to Sunday from late June to early August.

There is a small **STF hostel** (☎ 21570; Storrymningsvägen 4; beds Skr140; open June-Oct) near the Dannemora mine. Another option is **Wärdshuset Gammel Tammen** (☎ 21200; ⓔ gammeltammen@swipnet.se; singles/doubles Skr745/950, discounted to Skr595/850), a lovely old inn by the ironworks estate. It has pleasant accommodation in lovely old rooms, plus a good **restaurant**, with light meals priced around Skr70 and mains for around Skr150.

Karins Stallcafe (☎ 40148) is by the Gammel Tammen and serves lunches and snacks. In the town itself, a few minutes up the road, there is a bakery, supermarket, pizzerias and grill bars.

Lövstabruk
☎ 0294

Tiny Lövstabruk (also known as Leufsta Bruk), 24km due north of Österbybruk, is an excellent example of a mansion with associated factories. In 1627 the Dutchman Louis de Geer came to Lövstabruk and the mansion was built for his grandson, Charles de Geer, around 1700. The house and its factories were destroyed by a Russian attack in 1719, but everything was rebuilt and iron production continued until 1926. From mid-June to mid-August, guided tours of the mansion (at noon and 3pm daily) and the factory area (1pm daily) cost Skr35.

There's a small **tourist office** (☎ 31070; open daily mid-June–mid-Sept) next to the church.

Wärdshuset Leufsta (☎ 31122; singles/ doubles from Skr500/600) has comfortable accommodation directly opposite the mansion; some rooms are inside a beautiful

16th-century house. There's also a fine restaurant here.

Forsmark & Valö
☎ 0173

The beautiful surroundings of the Forsmarksbruk estate are ideal for photographers, with a church, manor house, workshops, English gardens and other items of interest around a pretty, central pond. The **statue** of Neptune in the middle of the pond dates from 1792. There's also a very interesting **bruksmuseum** (adult/child Skr20/free; open noon-4pm daily June–mid-Aug), with old carriages, sleeping quarters and a factory office.

Lovely old **Forsmark Wärdshus** (☎ 50100; singles/doubles Skr600/750) offers both accommodation and meals in a picturesque setting. There's also a **tourist office** (☎ 50015), open daily from mid-June to mid-August.

Most of the **Valö Kyrka**, on a minor road 10km south of Forsmark, dates from 1280, and it contains 44 excellent, albeit slightly faded, biblical-scene ceiling paintings from the 1520s.

Södermanland

NYKÖPING
☎ 0155 • pop 49,300

You could easily spend a pleasant, relaxing summer day or two in Nyköping, checking out its low-key attractions. There's a **tourist office** (☎ 248200; e information@nykoping se, w www.nykoping.se; Stora Torget; open 8am-7pm Mon-Fri, 10am-5pm Sat, 11am-3pm Sun mid-June–mid-Aug; 8am-5pm Mon-Fri rest of year) inside the rather ugly town hall on the main square. The current street grid was created after the town went up in flames in 1665; banks, supermarkets and other services can be found on Västra Storgatan, running west from Stora Torget.

Things to See & Do

The scenic castle **Nyköpingshus** (admission free; open 24hr) is beside the river and you can walk through its grounds at any time. The first Swedish parliament was held here in 1285. You can also visit the **attractions** (☎ 247002; adult/child Skr20/free; open noon-4pm daily July; noon-4pm Tues-Sun Aug-June) at the castle: **Kungstornet**, the whitewashed four-storey castle tower, **Gamla Residenset**,

the old governor's residence, and the neighbouring **Konsthallen**, with interesting art exhibitions and a collection of 19th-century boathouses.

By Stora Torget, there's the old **rådhus**, and **St Nicolai Kyrka** has the usual ecclesiastical furnishings. Also of interest are the two **rune stones** and the 700 Bronze Age **rock carvings** in Släbroparken, beside the river and about 2.5km northwest of town.

Take a walk along the river – 'Sweden's longest museum', so the publicity goes, and if you fancy a longer hike, the 1000km-long **Sörmlandsleden** passes through the town. This is a path that can take you around the entire county, should you so desire. You can also explore the nearby **archipelago**; inquire at the tourist office.

Places to Stay & Eat

The nearest camping ground, beachside **Strandstuviken Camping** (☎ 97810; tent sites Skr130, cabins from Skr345; open May-Sept), is a good 8km southeast of town. There's no public transport out here, so it's really only an option for those with their own wheels.

Nyköpings Vandrarhem (☎ 211810; Brunnsgatan 2; dorm beds Skr150) is an 18th-century wooden SVIF hostel, located just outside the castle grounds. It's a small and friendly place with good facilities.

Comfort Hotel Kompaniet (☎ 288020; Folkungavägen 1; singles/doubles Skr225/ 1415, discounted to Skr775/850), just south of the town centre and near the harbour, has stylishly decorated rooms in a riverside building that was once home to a furniture factory. All prices include a dinner buffet, making the discounted rates particularly good value.

Charming **Café Hellmans** (☎ 210525; Västra Trädgårdsgatan 24; breakfast buffet Skr50, lunch buffet Skr60) is the nicest place in town for lunch. As well as the good-value buffets, there are bagels and subs from Skr30, good coffee and excellent cakes to enjoy in the summer courtyard.

There are a number of pizzerias along Västra Storgatan, but if you're in town on a warm evening, head down to the harbour restaurants for a meal and drink. Casual **Lotsen** (☎ 21203; Skeppsbron; meals Skr68-148) has good simple meals like pizza, pasta, meatballs or burgers for under Skr100, or more upmarket mains like salmon or beef fillet for up to Skr150.

Getting There & Around
Nyköping's **Skavsta airport** (☎ 280400), 8km northwest of town, has flights to/from the UK with Ryanair – see the Getting There & Away chapter. Airport buses meet most flights and run to/from Stockholm (Skr100, 80 minutes). Local bus No 715 runs from Nyköping to Skavsta (Skr15); Alternatively, catch a local **taxi** (☎ 217500).

The bus and train stations are 800m apart on the western side of the central grid. Nyköping is on the regular **Swebus Express** (☎ 0200 218218; W www.swebusexpress.se) routes Stockholm–Norrköping–Jönköping–Gothenburg/Malmö, and also Stockholm–Norrköping–Kalmar. To get to Eskilstuna, take local bus No 701 or 801. SJ trains run every hour or two to Norrköping (Skr65, 40 minutes), Linköping (Skr119, one hour) and Stockholm (Skr162, one hour). Most X2000 services don't stop in Nyköping.

The tourist office has bikes for rent.

ESKILSTUNA
☎ 016 • pop 89,100
Eskilstuna, a large town just south of Mälaren lake, is an old industrial centre and major employers include the Volvo Construction Equipment Group and IBM. It was previously known as the murder capital of Sweden, but strong police action has reduced the crime rate quite significantly in recent years. There are a number of things to see, including one of the most extraordinary rock carvings in Sweden. The river Eskilstuna-ån, which drains Hjälmaren lake, runs through the town centre.

The **tourist office** (☎ 107000; e info@tur ism.eskilstuna.se, W www.turism.eskilstuna.se; Nygatan 15; open 9am-6pm Mon-Fri, 10am-3pm Sat, 11am-3pm Sun June-Aug; 9am-5pm Mon-Fri Sept-May) dispenses helpful information. You'll find most services around Fristadstorget and the pedestrianised part of Kungsgatan. The central **public library** (Rademachergatan) has free Internet access.

Sigurdsristningen
Situated near Sundbyholms Slott and Mälaren lake, 12km northeast of the town centre, this 3m-long Viking Age rock carving (bus No 225; admission free; open 24hr) will leave a lasting impression on you. It was carved into the bedrock around the year 1000 and shows the hero Sigurd (from the Sigurd Fafnesbane saga) killing a huge snake (or dragon). Sigurd's horse Grani and the headless smith Regin are also shown. The runes inscribed within the body of the snake tell of Sigrid, who paid for a nearby bridge in memory of her husband Holmger (the abutments can still be seen).

Other Attractions
There are many renovated factory buildings from the late 19th and early 20th centuries in the central area, and there are pleasant parks next to the river.

Faktorimuseet, on the island Strömsholmen, describes Eskilstuna's industrial and cultural heritage and has operational steam engines. The adjacent **Vapentekniska Museet** covers the history of firearms, and is full of guns of all shapes, ages and sizes. Nearby, the **Rademacher Forges** (Rademachergatan), now a museum, are the only remnants of Eskilstuna's ironworking past. **Konstmuseet**, in a riverside park south of the bus station, has an extensive collection of art from the 17th century to the present day. The open-air museum **Sörmlandsgården** in the Djurgården Park about 1km east of the town centre, features mid-19th-century farm life. All these museums come under the umbrella **Eskilstuna Museer** (☎ 102854; admission free; open 11am-4pm Tues-Sun). All share the same opening hours, with a few variations.

Parken Zoo (☎ 100101; adult/child Skr110/70; bus No 103 or 124; open 10am-6pm daily late June–mid-Aug, shorter hours May & early Sept), 1.5km west of the town centre, has a wide range of mammals, a **reptile house** (adult/child Skr20/10 extra) and an adjacent **amusement park** (rides additional). All these charges make for a very expensive day out – and it costs an outrageous Skr25 extra for parking!

In **Torshälla**, 6km north of the town centre, **Brandt Contemporary Glass** (☎ 355230; Klockberget; admission Skr20; open noon-5pm or 6pm Tues-Sun), just behind the church, is a contemporary glass workshop and gallery exhibiting vases and sculptures. The old wooden houses and pretty riverside areas in Torshälla are worth a look; the **Ebelingmuséet** (☎ 356069; admission free, open noon-4pm Wed-Sun) has bizarre steel sculptures. Take bus No 102 from Eskilstuna to Torshälla.

Places to Stay & Eat

Vilsta Camping (☎ 136227; *tent sites Skr115, cabins from Skr280*) is a large ground 2km south of the town centre.

The local **STF Hostel** (☎ 513080; e vilsta .sporthotell@swipnet.se; *bus No 105 from Fristadstorget; dorm beds Skr140, singles/ doubles Skr495/690; open year-round*) is adjacent to Vilsta Camping and has very good facilities – all rooms have en suite and TV.

There are a number of mid-range and up-market hotels in town; among the cheapest is central **City Hotell** (☎ 108850; e info@city hotell.com; *Drottninggatan 15; singles/doubles from Skr899/1155, discounted to Skr575/750*), with comfortable if unremarkable rooms.

Sundbyholms Slott (☎ 428400; e info@ sundbyholms-slott.se; *singles/doubles from Skr1379/2310, discounted to Skr890/1230*), not far from the Sigurd carvings, is an atmospheric 17th-century manor by Mälaren lake. Luxurious accommodation is offered in a number of buildings in the beautiful grounds. There's also a top-quality **restaurant** (*mains Skr200-240*) here.

The classy **Restaurang Tingsgården** (☎ 516620; *Rådhustorget 2; mains Skr115-230*), in the old part of town, has an intimate dining room inside a wonderful old wooden house, or if the weather's good you can sit out on a large deck over the river. There's an extensive menu of both Swedish and international dishes, from gravadlax and potatoes to veal fillet.

Restaurang Akropolis (☎ 149074; *Fristadstorget 1; lunch Skr60, dinner mains Skr80-200*) has a good menu of Greek dishes, including moussaka, souvlaki and lots of grilled meats.

Pesto (☎ 511118; *Rademachergatan 17; meals Skr50-60*) is a cool little lunch spot, with fashionable takeaway or eat-in café fare such as wraps, noodles, panini and salads.

Getting There & Away

The bus station is 500m east of the train station, beside the river. Local bus Nos 701 and 801 go to Malmköping and Nyköping. **Swebus Express** (☎ 0200 218218; w www.swebus express.se) operates up to six buses daily on its Stockholm–Eskilstuna–Örebro route, but trains are best for destinations like Örebro

(Skr124, every two hours), Västerås (Skr81, hourly) and Stockholm (Skr138, hourly).

Västmanland

VÄSTERÅS
☎ 021 • pop 127,800

Both an old and modern city, Västerås (the sixth-largest city in Sweden) is a centre for Asea Brown Boweri (ABB) industrial technology. Ignore the heavy industry and sprawling suburbs and head for the old town centre and wooden buildings along the Svartån river. You can relax on the shores of Mälaren lake or visit several historical sites nearby.

Information

The **tourist office** (☎ 103830; e info@vast manland.se, w www.vastmanland.se; *Stora Gatan 40; open 9am-7pm Mon-Fri, 9am-3pm Sat, 10am-2pm Sun mid-June–mid-Aug; 9.30am-6pm weekdays, 10am-3pm Sat rest of year*) can help with visitor inquiries for the town and region.

There's a **Forex** (*Stora Gatan 18; open Mon-Sat*) exchange office, and banks and ATMs, as well as most other services visitors will require, along Stora Gatan. The **public library** (*Biskopsgatan 2*) is opposite the cathedral and offers Internet access.

Things to See

Västmanlands Länsmuseum (☎ 156100; *Slottsgatan; admission free; open noon-4pm Tues-Sun*), in Västerås Slottet (manor house), has a strong general historical collection including Iron Age gold jewellery, but it diverts into peculiarities such as dolls houses.

The nearby **Konstmuseum** (☎ 161300; *Fiskartorget; admission free; open 10am-5pm Tues-Fri, 11am-4pm Sat, noon-4pm Sun*) has temporary exhibitions of Swedish painters and the permanent collections also get an occasional airing. There's a café in the vaulted cellar, and a lovely park behind the museum.

The fine late-14th-century brick-built **Domkyrkan** (*Biskopsgatan; open 8am-7pm Mon-Fri, 9.30am-5pm Sat & Sun June-Aug; 8am-5pm Mon-Fri, 9.30am-5pm Sat & Sun rest of year*) has carved floor slabs, six altar pieces and the marble sarcophagus of King Erik XIV.

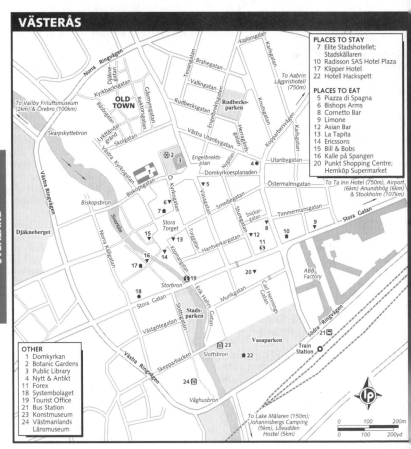

VÄSTERÅS

PLACES TO STAY
7 Elite Stadshotellet;
   Stadskällaren
10 Radisson SAS Hotel Plaza
17 Klipper Hotel
22 Hotell Hackspett

PLACES TO EAT
5 Piazza di Spagna
6 Bishops Arms
8 Cornetto Bar
9 Limone
12 Asian Bar
13 La Tapita
14 Ericssons
15 Bill & Bobs
16 Kalle på Spangen
20 Punkt Shopping Centre;
   Hemköp Supermarket

OTHER
1 Domkyrkan
2 Botanic Gardens
3 Public Library
4 Nytt & Antikt
11 Forex
18 Systembolaget
19 Tourist Office
21 Bus Station
23 Konstmuseum
24 Västmanlands
   Länsmuseum

Vallby Friluftsmuseum (☎ 161670; admission free; open 8am-10pm daily June-Aug), off Vallbyleden near the E18 interchange 2km northwest of the city, is an extensive open-air collection assembled by the county museum. Among the 40-odd buildings, there's an interesting farmyard and craft workshops, but the highlight is the large **Anunds Hus** (bus No 12 or 92 from Vasagatan; admission Skr20), a reconstructed Viking-era house.

The city is surrounded by ancient pre-Christian sites, and the most interesting and extensive is the excellent **Anundshög** (admission free; open 24hr), the largest tumulus in Sweden, 6km northeast of the city. It has a full complement of prehistoric curiosities, such as mounds, stone ship settings (see the boxed text 'The Warrior Swedes & Their

Customs' in the Facts about Sweden chapter) and a large 11th-century rune stone. The two main stone ship settings date from around the 1st century, and the row of stones beside the modern road presumably mark the ancient royal ceremonial road Eriksgata. The area is part of the Badelunda Ridge, which includes the 13th-century **Badelunda Church** (1km north) and the 16m-wide **Tibble Labyrinth** (1km south). Ask the tourist office for the handy map *Badelunda Forntids Bygd*. Take bus No 12 or 92 to the Bjurhovda terminus, then walk 2km east.

Places to Stay

Västerås is no paradise for budget travellers, but you could visit the sights in half a day and catch a train somewhere else for the night. The closest camping ground is **Johannisbergs Camping** (☎ *140279; bus No 25; tent sites/cabins from Skr80/250*), 5km south of the city. Not far from there is the STF hostel **Lövudden** (☎ *185230;* e *info@lovudden.nu; dorm beds Skr150, hotel singles/ doubles Skr550/825, discounted to Skr390/ 625; open year-round*), off Johannisbergsvägen. It's a pleasant lakeside place with both hostel and hotel accommodation.

The only other cheapish possibilities are **Aabrin Lågprishotell** (☎ *143980; Kopparbergsvägen 47; singles/doubles Skr545/605, discounted to Skr375/475*), by the E18, or **Ta Inn Hotel** (☎ *139600; Ängsgärdgatan19; singles/doubles Skr695/850, discounted to Skr395/550*). Both have liveable rooms but are in totally uninspiring locations, each about 1km from the city centre.

Klipper Hotel (☎ *410000; Kungsgatan 4; singles/doubles from Skr595/1190, discounted to Skr595/695*) is a reasonably priced central choice. It's an attractive older-style hotel in the old part of the city, offering comfortable, smallish rooms.

Elite Stadshotellet (☎ *102800;* e *info@ vasteras.elite.se; Stora Torget; singles/doubles Skr1095/1295, discounted to Skr595/795*) is a well-appointed hotel on the main square, surrounded by restaurants and bars. It's housed in a lovely Art Nouveau building from 1907, and has a highly regarded restaurant and an English-style pub.

You can't miss the 25-storey **Radisson SAS Hotel Plaza** (☎ *101010;* e *mailbox@ vasterasplaza.se; Karlsgatan 9A; singles/doubles from Skr1235/1435, discounted to Skr635/ 795*), the most impressive hotel in the city, known as the 'glass skyscraper'. It has all the expected mod cons, plus restaurants and a 'Sky Bar' on the 24th floor.

Places to Eat
On the main square is **La Tapita** (☎ *121044; Stora Torget 3; mains Skr100-185*), a cool Spanish-themed tapas bar and restaurant. You can get tasty paella (Skr125 per person), or choose from a wide array of tapas dishes (Skr25 to Skr60).

Stadskällaren (☎ *102800; Stora Torget; mains Skr150-280*) is good for splurge dinners; it's in the atmospheric cellar of the Stadshotellet. The nearby English-style pub, the **Bishops Arms** (☎ *102850; Östra Kyrkogatan*),

Arty Alternative Lodgings

In addition to Västerås' normal, run-of-the-mill hotels, there are two unique accommodation possibilities in and around town, created by local artist Mikael Genberg and worth investigating if you like your lodgings with a twist.

The **Hotell Hackspett**, or Woodpecker Hotel, is a fabulous treehouse in the midde of Vasaparken, behind the Konstmuseum. The cabin sleeps only one person and is 13m above the ground in an old oak tree; guests (and breakfast) are hoisted up in a basket! The second of Genberg's fascinating creations is the **Utter Inn**, a small, red floating cabin in the middle of Mälaren lake and only accessible by boat. The bedroom is downstairs – 3m below the surface, with glass viewing panels to watch the marine life outside. There's room for two people, and a canoe is provided to use for transportation or to get out and explore the lake.

Accommodation in the treehouse or lake cabin costs Skr500 per person per night if you bring your own food and bed linen, or the 'deluxe package' is Skr800 per person – linen is supplied and you will be delivered food in the evening and breakfast in the morning. For bookings, contact Mikael Genberg directly (☎ *830023,* e *info@mikaelgenberg.com*) or contact the Västerås tourist office. Genberg also has a website (w *www.mikaelgenberg .com*); it's in Swedish only but there are pictures to give you an idea of his creations.

has lots of beers to choose from and serves pub meals.

Limone (☎ *417560, Stora Gatan 4; dishes Skr95-180*) is an elegant, upmarket Italian restaurant with stylish decor and impressive menu items, including linguini with crayfish, shrimp and mussels, or grilled veal wrapped in Parma ham.

Bill & Bobs (☎ *419921; Stora Torget 5; meals Skr80-200*) is a casual place on the main square, attracting a diverse crowd who come to enjoy al fresco drinks or its fine meals, including light dishes under Skr100, or mains like Thai chicken or gorgonzola-stuffed beef fillets.

Reasonably priced restaurants along Vasagatan include **Piazza di Spagna** (☎ *124210; meals Skr63-202*) at No 26, a popular Italian place with good pizza and pasta dishes for less than Skr100, catering to vegetarians and meat-lovers alike, plus there are more expensive meat and fish dishes.

Asian Bar (☎ *186068; Sturegatan 10; lunch Skr45-75)* is worth stopping by for its fresh sushi.

Cornetto Bar *(☎ 419955; Kopparbergsvägen 23; meals Skr40-60)* has a good café-style menu of salads, pasta, wraps and ciabattas.

Kalle på Spangen *(☎ 129129; Kunsgatan 2; meals Skr30-50)*, by the river, is a cute place serving café fare such as coffee, sandwiches, salads and cakes, and all the furniture is for sale.

The **Hemköp supermarket** is in the Punkt shopping centre on Stora Gatan. **Ericssons** *(Stora Torg)* is an excellent delicatessen for stocking up on picnic supplies. For alcohol, visit **Systembolaget** *(Stora Gatan 48)*.

Getting There & Around

The **airport** *(☎ 805600)* is 6km east of the city centre and is connected by bus (No 41); budget carrier **Ryanair** flies here from the UK (see the Getting There & Away chapter for more details). **SAS** flies regularly to Copenhagen, Gothenburg and Malmö (mainly on weekdays).

The bus and train stations are adjacent, on the southern edge of the central Västerås area. Regional buses (Nos 65 and 69) and trains run to Sala (Skr72), and **Swebus Express** *(☎ 0200 218218; W www.swebus express.se)* runs daily to Uppsala, Stockholm and Örebro. **Svenska Buss** *(☎ 0771-676767; W www.svenskabuss.se)* also runs to Stockholm and Uppsala.

Västerås is accessible by hourly trains from Stockholm (Skr133). Trains to Örebro (Skr133), Uppsala (Skr124) and Eskilstuna (Skr81) are also frequent.

Call **Taxi Västerås** *(☎ 185000)* to help you get around or hire a bicycle at **Nytt & Antikt** *(☎ 121210; Kopparbergvägen 29A)*, behind the First Express Hotel, for Skr100 per day.

SALA

☎ 0224 • pop 21,500

The sleepy town of Sala, 120km from Stockholm, is worth a visit. The silver mine here was considered the treasury of Sweden in the 16th and 17th centuries and its importance changed the face of the town. Channels and ponds, the source of power for the mines, weave through and around the town centre.

The **tourist office** *(☎ 55202; e turist byran@sala.se, W www.sala.se/turism; cnr Brunnsgatan & Norrbygatan; open 10am-5pm Mon-Fri, 10am-2pm Sat)* is just off Stora Torget. Though the town centre is small, the free town map is useful if you want to use the walking paths.

Things to See & Do

A stroll along **Gröna Gången** (Green Walk) takes you southwest through the parks to the **Mellandammen** pond at Sofielund.

About 1km further south there is **Sala Silvergruva** *(☎ 19541; open 11am-5pm daily May-Aug, Sat & Sun Sept-Apr)*, the old silver mine area that was worked from the 15th century. The extensive area includes chimneys, holes, channels, mine heads, spoil heaps, touristy shops and a café. There are several different mine tours; the tour down to the 60m level costs Skr80/40 per adult/child (wear warm clothing); the price includes entry to the **museum** and the information centre, with a superb working **model mine**. Have a wander around the **museum village**, whose centrepiece is the **Drottning Christinas Schakt** mine head. Both village and mine are off the Västerås road, and public transport connections are not particularly good; take the Silverlinjen bus from the train station to Styrars, then you can walk the remaining 500m.

In town, next to the main park around the pond **Ekebydamm**, is **Väsby Kungsgård** *(☎ 10637; adult/child Skr20/free; open 1pm-4pm Mon-Fri year-round, also Sun June-Aug)*, a 16th-century royal farm where Gustav II Adolf possibly met his mistress. Excitement for the traveller is limited to the beautifully preserved interiors and the comprehensive weapons collection of the sort wielded by the mighty Swedish armies of the 17th century.

Aguélimuseet *(☎ 13820; Norra Esplanaden 7; admission Skr40; open 11am-4pm Tues-Sun)* houses a large, impressive collection by local artist Ivan Aguéli. Entry is via the town library.

The houses and courtyard **Norrmanska Gården** *(Norrbygatan)* were built in 1736; the area is now home to the tourist office, shops and a café.

Places to Stay & Eat

STF Vandrarhem & Camping Sofielund *(☎ 12730; tent sites from Skr50, dorm beds*

Skr115; open Feb–mid-Nov) is next to the Mellandammen pond, west of the centre of town (500m off Fagerstavägen). It's a large, pleasant complex and offers basic camping from mid-May to September. It's a 25-minute walk along Gröna Gången from the bus station, or take the Silverlinjen bus to the water tower and walk the rest of the way.

Friendly **Hotell Svea** (☎ 10510; Vasbygatan 19; singles/doubles with shared facilities Skr495/595) is handy to transport and the town centre (it's located diagonally right from the train and bus station). Rooms are clean and comfortable.

Norrmanska Café & Bar (☎ 17473; Brunnsgatan 26; lunch Skr55, dinner Skr70-150) is easily the nicest place in town for a bite. There's a great array of lunch meals, including pasta, panini, baked potatoes and salads. It's a popular evening spot too, with a decent dinner menu of pasta, meat and fish dishes. If you're out sightseeing, **Värdshuset Gruvcaféet** (☎ 19545; lunch Skr75), at the mine, does a good lunch special.

Getting There & Around

The regional train or bus No 65 or 69 from Västerås is convenient, and the regional bus network (No 848) or Swebus Express will take you to/from Uppsala. Sala is on the main Stockholm to Mora rail line (via Uppsala), with daily trains roughly every two hours.

Ask about bike hire at the tourist office (Skr50 per day).

ÄNGELSBERG
☎ 0233

Some 40km west of Sala is this wee village, where the main object of interest is **Engelsberg Bruk**, an ironworks dating from the 17th and 18th centuries and comprising a mansion and park, workers' homes and industrial buildings. The very rare timber-clad **blast furnace** (from 1779) and the **forge** are still in working order. The site features on Unesco's World Heritage List and is ranked as one of the most important examples from early industrial times. Guided tours (Skr30) run daily from mid-June to mid-August, and less frequently from May to mid-June and mid-August to mid-September; contact ☎ 13100 for details.

Regional trains run roughly ever hour from Västerås to Ängelsberg (50 minutes);

from the train station it's a 1.5km walk north to the site.

Nya Servering (☎ 30018) is not far from the train station in the village of Ängelsberg and serves food from 11am to 8pm daily. There's a good view from here across to the island Barrön on Åmänningen lake, where the world's oldest-surviving **oil refinery** is located – it was opened in 1875 and closed in 1902.

NORA
☎ 0587 • pop 10,500

Nora is a very likeable lakeside town and there are several interesting things to see, not least the 18th-century buildings and cobbled streets. The helpful **tourist office** (☎ 81120; e nora.turistbyra@nora.se, w www.nora.se; Stationshuset; open 10am-4pm daily May, 10am-6pm daily June & Aug, 9am-7pm daily July, 10am-noon & 1pm-3pm Mon-Fri Sept-Apr) is at the train station, by the lake. It takes bookings for local guided tours (all conducted from June to August) – there are 11 walks offered with differing themes (eg, architecture, shopping) or at various attractions (some of them are only available in Swedish). The guided **town walk** is available in English and costs Skr50/25 per adult/child; alternatively, buy the brochure (Skr10) from the tourist office for self-guided walks.

Trips on the **museum railway** (adult/child return Skr50/25) can take you 10km south-east to Järle or 2.5km west to the excellent old mining village at **Pershyttan**, where there's a guided tour daily at 2pm. The train operates to a complex timetable that includes regular weekend trips from Midsummer to mid-August, and also from Tuesday to Friday in July.

The manor house **Göthlinska Gården**, just off the main square, built in 1739, is now a museum featuring furniture, decor and accoutrements from the 17th century onwards; guided tours (adult/child Skr45/25) are held at 1pm daily from mid-June to the end of August.

Nora Museum (☎ 311420; Torget 2, Gyttorp; adult/child Skr40/free; open 10am-6pm June-Aug), 4km west of town, covers local cultural history and has a good display of model ships.

Boat trips to the family-friendly island Alntorpsö depart regularly from 9am to 6pm daily from mid-May to early September. A walk around the island takes about an hour, and there are swimming spots, a café and kiosk, mini-golf and a children's theatre. Return trips cost Skr15/5 per adult/child and depart from near the train station.

Places to Stay & Eat
The STF hostel **Nora Tåghem** (☎ 14676; dorm beds Skr110; open May–mid-Sept) is a wonderful and friendly place next to the train station and tourist office, with accommodation (somewhat cramped, it must be said) in converted railway carriages from the 1930s. There's a café here, offering breakfast, sandwiches and snacks throughout the day.

The charming, old-style **Lilla Hotellet** (☎ 15400; Rådstugugatan 14; singles/doubles Skr400/600) has large, pleasant rooms (some with shared facilities).

You can't miss the elegant **Nora Stadshotell** (☎ 311435; Rådstugugatan 21; singles/doubles Skr795/980, discounted to Skr525/690), on the main square smack in the middle of town. At its restaurant you'll find good-value lunch deals (Skr60), plus light meals from Skr60 and mains from Skr120.

While in Nora, don't miss **Strandstugan** (☎ 13722; Storgatan 1; snacks Skr30-40), a delightful café set in pretty gardens down by the lake, where you can get coffee, sandwiches, cakes and other home-baked goods.

Head to **Nora Glass** (Storgatan 11) to try some incredible ice cream – the town is renowned for it. Self-caterers will find a **supermarket** on Prästgatan.

Getting There & Around
Länstrafiken Örebro buses run regularly to Örebro (Skr50) and various other destinations in the region.

Ask at the tourist office about bike rental.

Närke

ÖREBRO
☎ 019 • pop 125,000

The most photogenic castle in Sweden stands beside the river at the centre of Örebro, an attractive city and a pleasant place to spend a day or two, especially when the weather's fine. The wealth of Örebro was built on a prosperous textile industry, and it became a university city in 1998. Most of the city was rebuilt after a devastating fire in 1854.

Information
The busy **tourist office** (☎ 212121; e dest nation@orebro.se, W www.orebro.se/turism, open 9am-7pm Mon-Fri, 10am-5pm Sat & Sun June-Aug; 9am-5pm Mon-Fri, 11am-3pm Sat & Sun Sept-May) is inside the castle.

Banks can be found along Drottninggatan, south of the castle. The **library** (Näbbtorgsgatan) is south of the town centre and has Internet access, as does **Video Biljard**, the video store on Järntorget (30/60 minutes Skr20/35).

Things to See & Do
The once-powerful **Slottet** (☎ 212121; adult/child Skr45/free; open daily year-round) is a magnificent edifice that has been restored for use as the county governor's headquarters. Although originally constructed in the late 13th century, most of what you see today was built 300 years later. The admission price includes a tour (in English at noon and 2pm daily from Midsummer to mid-August); buy tickets at the tourist office.

Right outside the castle is **Länsmuseum & Konsthall** (☎ 168020; Engelbrektsgatan 3; adult/child Skr20/free; open 11am-5pm daily), the combined regional and art museums, with local art and cultural history.

A pleasant stroll east of the castle along the river will take you through Stadsparken. Here, the delightful **Stadsträdgården** greenhouse precinct has a café and, further east, there's the excellent **Wadköping** museum village, which has craft workshops, a bakery and period buildings. You can wander around here at any time, but the shops, exhibitions, café and museums are open 11am to 4pm or 5pm Thursday to Sunday year-round.

The **Biologiska Museet** (☎ 216504; adult/child Skr20/10; open 11am-2pm daily mid-June–mid-Aug), in the Karolinska Skolan off Fredsgatan, covers a variety of wildlife, including elk, bears and even has a stuffed polar bear in its collection.

The commercial centre and some grand buildings are around Stortorget, including the 13th-century church **St Nikolai Kyrka** (open 10am-5pm Mon-Fri, 11am-3pm Sat).

You can see Lake Hjälmaren from the **Svampen** (☎ 611 3735; Dallbygatan 4; bus No 16; admission free; open daily), a water tower, north of the city centre. Built in 1958, it was the first of Sweden's modern

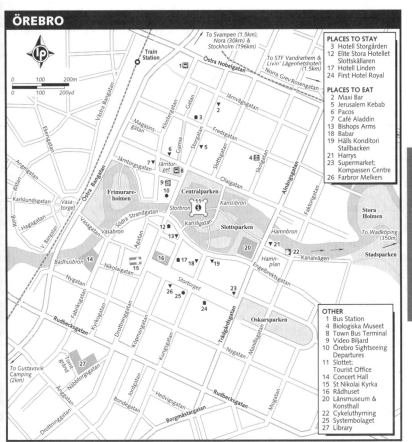

ÖREBRO

PLACES TO STAY
3 Hotell Storgården
12 Elite Stora Hotellet
    Slottskällaren
17 Hotell Linden
24 First Hotel Royal

PLACES TO EAT
2 Maxi Bar
5 Jerusalem Kebab
6 Pacos
7 Café Aladdin
13 Bishops Arms
18 Babar
19 Hälls Konditori
    Stallbacken
21 Harrys
23 Supermarket;
    Kompassen Centre
26 Farbror Melkers

OTHER
1 Bus Station
4 Biologiska Museet
8 Town Bus Terminal
9 Video Biljard
10 Örebro Sightseeing
    Departures
11 Slottet;
    Tourist Office
14 Concert Hall
15 St Nikolai Kyrka
16 Rådhuset
20 Länsmuseum &
    Konsthall
22 Cykeluthyrning
25 Systembolaget
27 Library

'mushroom' water towers and now functions as a lookout; there's a café at the top.

Örebro Sightseeing (☎ 102710) does guided boat tours through the city and surrounds for Skr160 (May to August), departing from Teaterplan, by Storbron, not far from the castle. **Arboga Rederi** (☎ 107191) offers a number of lengthier cruises; evening trips on Lake Hjälmaren (Skr220, including dinner) are popular. There is also a two-day cruise to Stockholm (Skr1500).

Places to Stay

Gustavsvik Camping (☎ 196950; e camping@gustavsvik.com; bus No 11; low/high season tent sites Skr165/205, cabins from Skr430/700) is 2km south of the city centre. It's a huge well-equipped, family-oriented

place with pools, mini-golf and a café. You can rent bikes too (Skr50 per day).

The very good **STF Vandrarhem** (☎ 310240; e vandrarhem@hepa.se; Fanjun-karevägen 5; bus No 16 or 31; dorm beds from Skr120) is quite well hidden, some 1.6km northeast of the train station. The hostel management also owns a new complex of well-equipped apartments next door: **Livin' Lägenhetshotell** (apartments Skr500). Each apartment has a fully equipped kitchen, bathroom and living area. The hostel rents bikes and inline skates.

Central **Hotell Linden** (☎ 611 8711; Köpmangatan 5; singles/doubles from Skr350/450, discounted to Skr250/320) is just off the main square and has comfortable, reasonably priced rooms with shared facilities.

Hotell Storgården (☎ 120200; Fredsgatan 11; singles/doubles from Skr590/690, discounted to Skr295/395) is similarly central and inexpensive, especially in summer. Rooms have private facilities.

First Hotel Royal (☎ 166200; e orebro .royal@firsthotels.se; Stortorget 12; singles/ doubles from Skr1142/1392, discounted to Skr702/852) is an upmarket hotel on the main central square.

The pick of the town's hotels is classy **Elite Stora Hotellet** (☎ 156900; e storahotel let.orebro@elite.se; Drottninggatan 1; singles/ doubles from Skr995/1295, discounted to Skr595/750), right by the castle and offering sumptuous rooms with all mod cons, plus a quality **restaurant** and an English-style **pub** on the premises.

Places to Eat

Upmarket **Slottskällaren** (☎ 156960; Drottninggatan 1; lunch Skr69, mains Skr105-210), at Stora Hotellet, offers fine dining and some good vegetarian selections, plus a great view of the castle. The **Bishops Arms** (☎ 156920) also part of the hotel, has a pleasant outdoor drinking area plus pub meals under Skr100.

Trendy **Babar** (☎ 101900; Kungsgatan 4; meals Skr85-180) is a popular restaurant and bar that appeals to the town's young, fashionable set; another popular nightspot is by the river at **Harrys** (☎ 108989; Hamnplan; mains Skr80-150), which offers a comprehensive menu of snacks and meals in a pub environment.

Bright and appealing **Pacos** (☎ 101046; Olaigatan 13A; lunch Skr49-69; dinner mains Skr100-150), on Järntorget, offers mainly Tex-Mex dishes, but at it's lunchtime pizza buffet you can eat all you want for Skr69.

Hälls Konditori Stallbacken (☎ 611 0766; Engelbrektsgatan 12) is a classic old-style café with a cobbled courtyard (check out the strange bronze horse), serving meals such as salads, quiche, sandwiches and cakes for under Skr50. A stylish alternative is **Farbror Melkers** (☎ 611 8199; Stortorget 6), a central café with the usual good coffee and light meals in modern surrounds.

For cheap eats head to excellent **Café Aladdin** (☎ 183530; Klostergatan 11), on the slightly grungy Järntorget, which offers a wide range of pizza, pasta and baked spuds for under Skr40; **Maxi Bar** (☎ 122803;

Storgatan 22) offers similar fare at similarly cheap prices. **Jerusalem Kebab** (Storgatan) is nearby, with kebabs from Skr25.

There's a **supermarket** in the Kompassen centre on Stortorget, and **Systembolaget** (Stortorget 10) is nearby.

Getting There & Away

You're well placed to go almost anywhere in southern Sweden from Örebro by long-distance buses, which leave from opposite the train station. From here, **Swebus Express** (☎ 0200 218218; w www.swebusexpress.se) has connections in all directions: to Norrköping; Karlstad and Oslo; Mariestad and Gothenburg; Västerås and Uppsala; and Eskilstuna and Stockholm.

Train connections are also good. Direct SJ trains run to/from Stockholm (Skr243, two hours) every hour, some via Västerås (Skr133), others via Eskilstuna (Skr124). To get to Gothenburg, take a train to Hallsberg and change there. Other trains run daily to Gävle and Borlänge (where you can change trains for Falun and Mora).

Getting Around

Town buses leave from Järntorget and cost Skr13. **Cykeluthyrning** (☎ 211909), at the Hamnplan boat terminal, rents bikes from May to September from Skr50 per day. For a taxi, call **Taxi Kurir** (☎ 123030).

ASKERSUND

☎ 0583 • pop 11,500

This pleasant and quiet little town at the northern end of Lake Vättern is often overlooked by travellers, but it's a good place to relax. The **tourist office** (☎ 81088; e turist byran@askersund.se, w www.askersund.se; Lilla Bergsgatan 12A; open 10am-7pm daily mid-June–mid-Aug, shorter hours rest of year) is on the main square. Ask for the free information on walking and cycling routes around the lake, and guided or self-guided tours. Askersund has banks and most other tourist facilities. The town's website is in Swedish only.

Tiveden National Park

This wild area is about 33km south of Askersund. The park is noted for its ancient virgin forests, which are very rare in southern Sweden. The landscape is impressive, with lots of bare bedrock, extensive boulderfields and a scattering of lakes. Three-toed woodpeckers can be found in the woods. There's an information centre in the southeastern part of the park (2km from the entrance). The entrance is 5km off the main road (the turnoff is at Bocksjö, on road No 49). There's no public transport to the park.

Other Attractions

The lavishly appointed **Stjernsund Manor** (☎ 10004), with four-poster beds and other 19th-century furniture, is next to the lake 5km south of town; guided tours (adult/child Skr40/20) are held at 11am, noon, 2pm, 3pm and 4pm daily from mid-May to August (see the information on M/S *Wettervik* later in this entry for information on how to get there). There's a lovely café out by the manor.

Hembygdsgård (admission free; exhibitions open noon-3pm Mon-Fri June-Aug) has wooden houses that survived the 1776 town fire and you can wander around the area freely.

The old shoe shop **Skoaffären** (Storgatan) has appeared on a postage stamp. It was built around 1800 and is still in business.

There's a small **boat museum** (☎ 485510; adult/child Skr10/free; open daily mid-June–mid-Aug) at the harbour with old boats, motors and model ships.

The **S/S Motala Express**, launched in 1895, puffs around the northern part of the lake (but not to Motala!). An extensive programme of tours runs, including lunch and dinner cruises, from mid-May to early September. Fares vary depending on the cruise, but start at Skr165. The **M/S Wettervik** makes regular trips from the harbour, departing at 1.30pm and 3pm on weekdays from early July to early August (Skr75). A nice afternoon excursion is to take the first tour, get off at Stjernsund Manor and return on the second tour. Book these tours at the tourist office.

Places to Stay & Eat

Husabergs Udde Camping (☎ 711435; tent sites Skr100, cabins from Skr250) is a large, lakeside camping ground with all facilities, 2km south of town. You can rent equipment for lots of activities, including canoes, rowing boats, windsurfing gear and bikes.

The tourist office can arrange **private rooms** in the area.

Café Garvaregården (☎ 10445; Sundsgatan; singles/doubles Skr480/600) is an absolute gem; it offers B&B accommodation in a charming 18th-century house, plus simple **café** fare in inviting rooms or a flower-filled courtyard.

Hotel Norra Vättern (☎ 12010; ℮ info .norravattern@swedenhotels.se; Klockarbacken; singles/doubles Skr945/1145, discounted to Skr790/790), near the bridge into town, is an unattractive, modern hotel with pleasant rooms off extremely long corridors! There's a **restaurant** here too.

If you can afford to splurge, **Aspa Herrgård** (☎ 50210; ℮ aspa@edbergs.com; rooms per person from Skr1290, 2-night weekend packages including meals from Skr2200, rooms per person from Skr745 June-Aug), located 17km south of town on road No 49, is the place to go. It's a luxurious boutique hotel in a manor house in a beautiful countryside setting; there's also an exclusive **restaurant** here.

Pizzeria Italia (☎ 711530; Sundsbrogatan 8; pizzas from Skr55) has reasonably priced pizza and pasta dishes.

Asiatisk Restaurang (☎ 12828; mains from Skr79), at the harbour, is good for Asian meals. There are also a couple of **kiosks** to be found down at the harbour, which sell snacks.

Next to the bridge you'll come across **Wärdshuset Sundsgården** (☎ 10088; Sundsbrogatan 1; lunch Skr60, meals Skr55-165), a charming old place with a large waterside deck and a selection of good-value light meals (baked potatoes, pasta, salads) under Skr100.

Getting There & Around

Swebus Express (☎ 0200 218218; ⓦ www .swebusexpress.se) runs to Örebro (Skr60, 40 minutes) up to four times daily, or in the other direction to Karlsborg, Lidköping, Trollhättan and Uddevalla.

Länstrafiken bus Nos 708 and 841 each run four times on weekdays to Örebro, and bus No 704 runs frequently to the main-line train station at Hallsberg.

You can ask about bike and boat hire at **Husabergs Udde Camping** (☎ 711435). Boat hire (with engine) and canoe hire cost Skr250 and Skr150 per day, respectively, from **Sportfiskeforum** (☎ 070 259 4899), which is in the little red hut next to the church on the way into town.

SVEALAND

Värmland

KARLSTAD

☎ 054 • pop 80,800

The port of Karlstad is on Vänern, Sweden's largest lake, and it's the gateway to outdoor experiences in the county of Värmland. The town itself has an excellent location on an island in the Klarälven river delta, but the suburbs have spread onto the mainland. There's a university here and some 10,000 students, resulting in a good restaurant and bar scene.

The helpful **tourist office** (☎ 222140; Ⓦ www.karlstad.se; Carlstads Conference Center, Tage Erlandergatan 10; open 10am-7pm Mon-Fri, 10am-6pm Sat, 11am-4pm Sun June-Aug; 10am- 5pm Mon-Fri Sept-May) has details on both town and county, including the many activities in and on the region's forests, lakes and rivers.

Banks and ATMs can be found along Storgatan. The **library** (Västra Torggatan 26) has Internet access, as does **Bogart Nöjesbutik** (Östra Torggatan 6), a central video store charging Skr35 for an hour online.

Things to See & Do

Värmlands Museum (☎ 143100; adult/child Skr40/free; open 10am-5pm daily mid-June–mid-Aug, 8.30am-5pm Tues-Sun rest of year) is out on the point Sandgrundsudden, where the river bifurcates. Its displays cover the local history and culture from the Stone Age to current times, including local music, the river, forests and textiles.

On the eastern river branch, the stone bridge **Gamla Stenbron**, completed in 1811 and 168m long, is the longest stone bridge in Sweden. On the western river branch, the **Almen district** is the only area to survive the town fire of 1865 and, just across the river, there's a **statue** of the famous Swedish writer Selma Lagerlöf.

The **cathedral** (open 10am-7pm daily June-Aug, 10am-4pm daily rest of year), completed in 1730, replaced an earlier structure that was destroyed by fire. The **old town prison** (Karlbergsgatan 3), opened in 1847 and closed in 1968, has now been transformed into a hotel. There's a small but interesting – and slightly creepy – **museum** (open 7am-11pm daily) in the basement, with original cells, prisoners' letters and a hacksaw found in the post (yes, really!).

Mariebergsskogen (☎ 296990; admission free; bus No 1 or 31; open 7am-10pm daily year-round) is a leisure park next to the water in the southwestern part of town. It combines amusements with an open-air museum, a Naturum and an animal park. There's a wind-powered sawmill, a water mill, a bird-watching tower where you can view the delta, a beach, mini-golf, cafés and a theatre. You can also enjoy rides at the **amusement park** (☎ 152108; open May-Aug) here; individual attractions charge admission.

There are regular **boat cruises** (☎ 219943) on Lake Vänern from late June to mid-August. Two-hour cruises depart from the harbour (behind the train station) and cost Skr80/50 per adult/child.

Places to Stay

Skutbergets Camping (☎ 535139; bus No 18; low/high season tent sites Skr90/110, cabins from Skr320/430) is a large, well-equipped lakeside ground 7km west of the town.

The **STF hostel** (☎ 566840; Ⓔ karlstad vandrarhem@swipnet.se; bus No 11 or 32; dorm beds Skr130) is off the E18 highway at Ulleberg, 3km southwest of Karlstad's centre. It has good facilities and is open year-round.

There are a number of central hotels opposite the train station, including simple **Hotell Freden** (☎ 216582; Ⓔ info@fredenho tel.com; Fredsgatan 1; singles/doubles Skr480/580, discounted to Skr380/480), a pleasant place with comfortable rooms and shared facilities.

Ibis Hotel (☎ 172830; Västra Torggatan 20; rooms Skr690, discounted to Skr515) also has comfortable, good-value rooms, although they're a little bland and formulaic.

The elegant **Elite Stadshotellet** (☎ 293000; Ⓔ stadshotellet@karlstad.elite.se; Kungsgatan 22; singles/doubles from Skr1140/1395, discounted to Skr595/725) is another good, upmarket choice, with excellent facilities and a lovely riverside location.

Friendly, modern **Comfort Hotel Bilan** (☎ 100300; Ⓔ bilan@comforthotels.se; Karlbergsgatan 3; singles/doubles from Skr1195/1445, discounted to Skr765/845), in the old jail, offers large, bright and cleverly decorated rooms. The added bonus here is that prices include an evening buffet, making summer and weekend rates a particularly good deal.

The fully restored 13th-century Örebro Slottet, Svealand

Popular winter pastime, Svealand

The mounds of the pre-Viking kings, Svealand

Calm waters for kayakers, Svealand

Lovstabrük manor, Svealand

Pershyttan museum, Svealand

Badelunda Church in Västerås, Svealand

A field of flowering lupins surrounds a traditional farm building in Svealand

Places to Eat
Head to the main square, Stora Torget, and its surrounds for good eating and drinking options, most with outdoor seating in the summer.

Valfrids Krog (☎ 183040; Östra Torggatan; mains Skr109-189) is a relaxed place for a drink or meal, with light, tapas-style snacks around Skr40, or good main meals of salmon, chicken and the like – something to cater to most tastes.

The very smooth **Umami Lounge** (☎ 210054; Västra Torggatan 10; meals Skr60-200) is a fashionable place with an extensive menu of both light and hearty meals, including sushi and tapas selections, a club sandwich, grilled salmon and beef medallions. It transforms into a cool bar of an evening.

Don't be fooled by the name – **Kebab House** (☎ 1500815; Västra Torggatan 9; meals form Skr50) is a cut above the regular fast-food places and serves good-value pizza, ke-babs, pasta and salads. Vegies will love its neighbour, **Gröna Trädgården** (☎ 190255; 1st floor Västra Torrgatan 9; meals Skr60-90), which offers mainly vegetarian selections and an excellent buffet lunch for Skr55.

Somewhat out of the way is the inviting **Creperiet** (☎ 154440; Karlsbergatan 4; crepes from Skr45), a cosy, candle-lit place serving sweet or savoury crepes in true Bretagne style, with occasional jazz evenings in summer.

The huge **Ankdammen** (☎ 181110; Maga-sin 1, Inre Hamn) is a popular summer drink-ing (and eating) spot with outdoor seating on a floating jetty at the harbour.

The **Hemköp supermarket** (Järnvägsgatan 3) is inside Åhléns and **Systembolaget** is across the street.

Getting There & Around
Karlstad is the major transport hub for west-central Sweden. **Swebus Express** (☎ 0200 218218; W www.swebusexpress.se) has daily services on a number of routes including the following: Gothenburg–Karlstad–Falun–Gävle; Stockholm–Örebro–Karlstad–Oslo; and Karlstad–Mariestad–Jönköping. The long-distance bus terminal at Drottninggatan 43, 600m west of the train station. **Svenska Buss** (☎ 0771-676767; W www.svenskabuss .se) runs four times weeklybetween Karlstad and Uppsala via Västerås and Örebro.

Intercity and X2000 trains between Stockholm and Oslo pass through Karlstad; Intercity trains to Stockholm take three hours and cost Skr390; to Oslo takes 2½ hours on the express trains and costs around Skr370. Several daily services also run to/from Gothenburg (Skr209, three hours).

Värmlandstrafik (☎ 020 225580) runs re-gional buses. Bus No 302 travels to Sunne (Skr60, two to seven daily) and Torsby (Skr75, two or four daily). Local trains also operate on this route; prices are the same as for buses.

Bikes to use for free are available from the Solacykeln booth on Stora Torget.

SUNNE
☎ 0565 • pop 13,500
Sunne is pleasantly located between two ribbon lakes and has several cultural attrac-tions in the vicinity. It's also the largest ski resort in southern Sweden.

The **tourist office** (☎ 16400; e turist@ sunne.se, W www.turist.sunne.se; open 9am-9.30pm daily early June-mid-August, 9am-5pm Mon-Fri rest of year) is at the reception building of the camping ground (see Places to Stay & Eat). The town has banks, super-markets and most other tourist facilities, which can primarily be found on Storgatan.

Things to See & Do
The most interesting place in the area is the house at **Mårbacka** (☎ 31027; adult/child Skr60/30; open 10am-4pm daily mid-May–Aug, 10am-5pm July, 11am-2pm Sat & Sun Sept), 9km southeast of Sunne, where the famous Swedish novelist Selma Lagerlöf was born in 1858. Many of Lagerlöf's tales are based in the local area and the house is popular with Swedish visitors, but it's a beautiful place and worth visiting for its own sake. The library and kitchen are par-ticularly good. Admission is by guided tours only (45 minutes), which leave on the hour; a tour in English is given daily at 2pm. Inquire at the tourist office about buses out here.

Sundsbergs Gård (☎ 10363; adult/child Skr50/free; open noon-4pm Tues-Thur & Sat-Sun late June–mid-Aug) opposite the tourist office), featured in Lagerlöf's *Gösta Berlings Saga* and now contains a new forestry museum, art exhibition, café and manor house with beautiful furnishings.

SVEALAND

Some 6km south of Sunne, the mansion and park at **Rottneros Park** (☎ 60295; bus No 302; adult/child Skr100/free; open daily mid-May–mid-Sept) has an excellent flower garden and arboretum. The grounds include an extensive area of sculptures, a children's zoo, restaurants and a climbing forest. In addition to being accessible by bus, Rottneros has its own train station.

The steamship **Freya af Fryken** (☎ 41590) sank in 1896 but was raised in 1994 and sails again along the lakes north and south of Sunne; departures are several times each week from late June to mid-August, and short trips cost from Skr80/40 per adult/child. Lunch and dinner cruises are also on the programme.

Places to Stay & Eat

Kolsnäs Camping (☎ 16400; e kolsnas@sunne.se; tent sites Skr130-160, 2-bed cabins Skr260-350, 4-bed cabins Skr310-440) is a large, family-oriented camping ground at the southern edge of town, with a pool, mini-golf, beach, kiosk, restaurant and assorted summer activities, plus bikes, boats and canoes for rent.

The pretty, well-equipped **STF Vandrarhem** (☎ 10788; Hembygdsvägen 7; dorm beds Skr130) is just north of the town centre at a homestead museum, with accommodation in wooden cabins. Breakfast is available for Skr50, and bikes and canoes can be rented for exploring the countryside.

The historic 'sheriff's house', **Länsmansgården** (☎ 14010; e info@lansman.com; singles/doubles from Skr645/820) is 2km north of the centre of Sunne, by road No 45. It features in *Gösta Berlings Saga* and is a picturesque place to stop for a fine lunch or restful evening. The lakeside gardens are lovely and the staff friendly. There's also an excellent **restaurant** (lunch Skr95, à la carte mains Skr135-240), with mains including salmon, beef, reindeer and lamb dishes.

Storgatan has the usual array of grill bars and supermarkets. Behind the **ICA supermarket** is a pleasant waterside park with good dining option. **Eurasia** (☎ 13383; Mejerigatan 2; meals Skr65-150) is a steakhouse and a Chinese restaurant, with an extensive menu of fish, meat, rice and noodle dishes, plus pasta, salads and vegetarian meals. Further into the park is the appealing **Strandcafeet** (☎ 10488; mains Skr65-130),

with outdoor seating over the water and live music on some summer evenings.

Getting There & Away

Regional trains to Torsby and Karlstad (one to three daily) are faster than (but cost the same as) bus No 302, which also runs to Torsby (Skr40, two or four daily) and Karlstad (Skr60, two to four daily).

TORSBY & AROUND

☎ 0560 • pop 13,500

Sleepy Torsby, deep in the forests of Värmland and at the northern end of the ribbon lake Övre Fryken, is only 38km from Norway. It's the home town of Sven-Goran Eriksson, coach of the English football (soccer) team.

The **tourist office** (☎ 10550; e turist@torsby.se, w www.torsby.se; open daily mid-June–mid-Aug, Mon-Fri rest of year) is by road No 45 on the western side of town. The town has all facilities in its small central area.

Things to See

Torsby Finnkulturcentrum (☎ 16293; admission Skr20; open 11am-4pm daily mid-June–mid-Aug; noon-4pm Tues-Fri rest of year) has displays describing the 17th-century Finnish settlement of the area, a library and information leaflets about local places of interest. The excellent, neighbouring **Fordonsmuseum** (☎ 71210; admission Skr30; open noon-5pm Mon-Fri May-Sept, also Sat & Sun May-Aug), near the Finnkulturcentrum, has a collection of vintage cars and motorcycles.

Hembygdsgård (☎ 71861; Levgrensvägen 36; open daily June-Aug), down beside the lake, has a number of old houses, museums and a cute café with a pretty outlook. Inquire about guided tours in English.

Ritamäki Finngård (☎ 50225; open 11am-6pm daily June-Aug), 25km west of Torsby and 5km from of Lekvattnet, is one of the best preserved 'Finnish homesteads' in the area and probably dates from the late 17th century or early 18th century. In the mid 16th-century, ethnic groups from eastern Finland, emigrated to the western parts of Sweden. These Finns didn't stay in the towns nor did they become agricultural labourers or tenants. Instead they made for the forests, where, with 'slash and burn' methods of agriculture, they began to settle new areas and build farms and villages. Ritamäki was inhabited until 1964, which

Exploring the Wilderness

Vildmark i Värmland (☎ 14040; e info@vild mark.se, W www.vildmark.se) is a local company that organises a number of outdoor activities in the pristine wilderness of Värmland in summer, including canoe trips (from half a day to two weeks), beaver-spotting canoe safaris, rock-climbing and rafting. The company also offers one of the most interesting options we know of for a real get-away-from-it-all, back-to-nature experience: a raft trip on the Klarälven river, but you have to build your own raft first! Under instruction, you build your raft from logs and rope (no nails) so it can be dismantled at the end of the trip and the logs re-used; each raft can accommodate five or six people

The trips can last from one day to a week; prices start at Skr390 for a day trip, Skr1070 for five days (four nights) or Skr2050 for eight days (seven nights). If you choose a longer option, you're free to sleep on board the moored raft or climb ashore and camp for the night (tent, stove, sleeping bags etc can be hired at additional cost). You can while away your days fishing, swimming, wildlife spotting and enjoying the serenity. Check out the website for more information.

makes it the last permanently inhabited Finnish homestead in Sweden. It now belongs to the local heritage society and has been listed as a historic building since 1967; it is surrounded by a nature reserve. Bus No 310 goes to Lekvattnet but there is no public transport to Ritamäki.

Activities

Finnskogleden is an easy, well-marked, long-distance path that roughly follows the Norwegian border for 240km from near Charlottenburg to Søre Osen (in Norway); it passes the old Finnish homestead Ritamäki Finngård. There's a guide book (available from tourist offices, Skr125) that has text in Swedish only but all the topographical maps you'll need. The best section, Øyermoen to Röjden (or vice-versa), requires one or two overnights. Bus No 311 runs from Torsby to near the border at Röjdåfors (twice daily on weekdays), and bus No 310 runs to Vittjärn (four times daily on weekdays), 6km from the border on road No 239.

There are a number of summer activities and tours in the area, including fishing, canoeing, white-water rafting, rock-climbing, mountain biking, and beaver or elk safaris. Contact the tourist office for information.

Skiing (☎ 31300; W www.hovfjallet.se) 20km north of Torsby, is possible from December to Easter. There are several ski lifts (up to 542m above sea level) and a variety of runs. A day pass starts at Skr195 and alpine **ski hire** (☎ 31255) costs Skr185 per day.

Places to Stay & Eat

Lakeside **Torsby Camping** (☎ 71095; e tors bycamping@swipnet.se; Bredviken; tent sites Skr100, cabins from Skr300; open May–mid-Sept), 4km south of town, is a large, well-equipped ground.

The **STF Vandrarhem** (☎ 12563; Järnvägsgatan 34; dorm beds Skr130; open mid-June–late July) offers good accommodation in very comfortable student lodgings during summer break. Most are single rooms; the kitchen and living areas are excellent.

The cosy **Hotell Örnen** (☎ 14664; e info@hotell-ornen.com; Östmarksvägen 4; dorm beds June-Aug Skr200, singles/doubles Skr610/725) is a pretty place set behind a white picket fence close to the centre of town. In summer there is an annex with hostel-style accommodation.

By far the most appealing eatery in Torsby is **Faktoriet**, down at the harbour (at the far end of Sjögatan). The view of the harbour is not at all attractive, but this is a cool place with a good menu of light meals (pasta, baked potatoes, fajitas) averaging Skr80, and is a popular drinking spot.

There is definitely not a shortage of fast-food places and pizzerias in the town. **Wienerkonditoriet** (☎ 10139; Järnvägsgatan) is a passable bakery-café.

Other good options are out of town, and if you have your own transport it's worth exploring the beautiful countryside. In summer there's a programme of live music and other entertainment at **Heidruns Book & Bildcafe** (☎ 42126), 10km north of Torsby on road No 45 at Fensbol. It's a charming place that's run by a local poet; you can buy books and artworks or sample excellent home-baked cakes in the pretty gardens.

Further north (20km from Torsby) by a stunning lakeside is **Vägsjöfors Herrgård**

SVEALAND

(☎ 31330; e info@vagsjoforsherrgard.com; lunch Skr65), a large manor house that serves lunch only. Accommodation is also available here – dorm beds from Skr170, B&B for Skr310 per person – and canoe rental.

Getting There & Away
See Getting There & Away in the previous section on Sunne. A few buses run north of Torsby, but generally on weekdays only.

Dalarna

FALUN
☎ 023 • pop 54,600

Falun, which is traditionally the main centre of Dalarna, is synonymous with mining. The **Falun Folkmusik festival** (w www.falufolk .com), which has an international flavour as well as airing regional traditions, is held over four days in mid-July.

Information
The **tourist office** (☎ 83050; e turist@visit falun.se, w www.visitfalun.se; Trotzgatan 10-12; open 9am-7pm Mon-Fri, 9am-6pm Sat, 10am-5pm Sun mid-June–mid-Aug; 9am-6pm Mon-Fri, 10am-2pm Sat rest of year) can help with visitor information.

Most services (banks, supermarkets etc) are found on or just off Stora Torget. There's Internet access available at the **public library** (Kristinegatan 15), or at **Billiard & IT Café** (Falugatan 4), a central cybercafé.

Falu Koppargruva
This copper mine was the world's most important by the 17th century and drove many of Sweden's international aspirations during that period. The first mention of this mine is in a document from 1288, when the Bishop of Västerås bought shares in the company; the mine closed in 1992, and these days it's on Unesco's World Heritage List. The mine provided, as a by-product, the red coatings that became the characteristic house paint of the 17th century. The minerals and vitriol in this paint protect wood and Falurödfarg paint is still practical and popular today. The huge hole in the ground was caused by a major collapse in the mine in the 17th century.

The **mine and museum** (☎ 711475; w www .kopparberget.com; bus No 709; adult/child

Skr40/free; open 10am-5pm daily May-Sept, 11am-4pm Sat & Sun Oct-Apr) are at the wes of town at the top end of Gruvgatan.

You can go on a one-hour tour of the bowels of the disused mine (adult/child Skr80/30, including museum entry; bring warm clothing); call in advance to find ou times of tours in English.

Carl Larssongården & Porträttsamling
Sundborn, 13km from Falun, is a pretty vil lage that's good for walking and exploring Here you'll find the beautiful early-20th century home (☎ 60053; open 10am-5pm daily May-Sept, Tues Oct-Apr) of the artis Carl Larsson and his wife Karin. Wel worth a visit, it's a bright, lively and airy place with superb colour schemes, decora tion and furniture. Tapestries and embroi dery that were made by Karin Larsson reveal she was as skilled an artist as her husband. Even today, the modern styles ir most of the house (especially the dining room) will inspire interior decorators. The **mine master's room** has a beautiful painted ceiling (from 1742) and there's a display of Larsson's collection of **Sami handicraft** ir the long passage.

Admission is by guided tour only. Tours run almost continuously (45 minutes, adult child Skr70/30), but call in advance for times of tours in English (alternatively you can follow a Swedish tour with an English handbook).

If you like Larsson's work, you can see more at the **Carl Larssons Porträttsamling** (☎ 60053; adult/child Skr250/free; open 10am-5pm daily mid-June–mid-Aug), where there are 12 portraits of local worthies.

Restaurang Hyttstugan (☎ 60271; lunch Skr74) is a pleasant café-restaurant by Carl Larssongården.

Bus No 64 (Skr30) runs from Falun to Sundborn village.

Other Attractions
Restored homes from the mine's heyday are grouped around Östanfors (north of the town centre), and Gamla Herrgården and Elsborg (west of the town centre).

There's more folk culture at **Dalarnas Museum** (☎ 765500; Stigaregatan; adult/child Skr40/20; open 10am-5pm Mon-Fri, noon-5pm Sat & Sun). This fine museum features local culture and art, and Selma Lagerlöf's study is preserved here.

Kristine Kyrka *(Stora Torget; open 10am-6pm daily June-Aug; 10am-4pm daily Sept-May)* was consecrated in 1655 and its baroque interiors show some of the riches that came into the town.

Don't miss the late-14th-century **Stora Kopparbergs Kyrka** *(open 10am-6pm daily June-Aug; 10am-4pm daily Sept-May)*, the oldest building in Falun, off Mariabacken and a bit north of the town centre; many of its ecclesiastical accoutrements date from the 15th century.

The Lugnet area in Falun and the Bjursås area to the northwest are both winter-sports centres with plenty of ski runs, nordic courses and toboggan runs. Also in Lugnet is the **Idrottsmuseum** *(☎ 13824; bus No 705 or 713; admission Skr10; open 10am-4pm Mon-Fri, noon-4pm Sat)*, showcasing local sports.

If you're feeling energetic, hike up to **Hopptornen** *(☎ 83561; open 10am-6pm daily mid-May–mid-Aug)*, the tower and ski jump in the hills behind the camping ground. You can take a lift to the top *(Skr20)* for a great view.

About 35km east of Falun, **Korså Bruk** *(☎ 70077; bus No 61 or 63; admission free; open 24hr)* is a delightful former industrial settlement in an excellent state of preservation; there's also a **museum** *(open June-Aug)*.

Svärdsjö Gammelgård *(☎ 10422)*, 28km northeast of Falun, is an interesting 18th-century homestead; you can wander around the grounds at all times. There are activities and entertainment scheduled here regularly in summer.

Stadigs Stuga *(☎ 50737; bus No 60 or 70; admission free; open 11am-5pm daily July–mid-Aug)*, in Bjursås (20km northwest of Falun), is decorated with typical 19th-century Dalarna paintings of Biblical scenes.

Vika Kyrka *(bus No 20; open 8am-6pm daily mid-May–Sept)*, about 15km south of Falun, has magnificent 16th-century wall paintings and medieval sculptures.

Places to Stay
Large, well-equipped **Lugnet Camping** *(☎ 83563; bus No 705 or 713; tent sites from Skr95, simple 2-bed huts from Skr150, cabins Skr550; open year-round)* is in the ski and sports area 2km northeast of the town centre.

The big, well-kept **STF Vandrarhem** *(☎ 10560; e stf.vandrarhem.falun@telia.com; Vandrarvägen 3; dorm beds from Skr130)* is 3km east of the town; take bus No 701 to Koppartorget, from where it's a 10-minute walk. There's a café on site, and bikes are available for rent *(Skr70 per day)*.

The friendly SVIF **Falu Fängelse Vandrarhem** *(☎ 795575; e info@falufangelse.se; Villavägen 17; dorm beds Skr180)* is a more central option, and accommodation is in the cells of an old prison, used for its original purposes up until the mid-1990s.

There are some good hotel choices right by the tourist office, including **Hotel Falun** *(☎ 29180; Trotzgatan 16; singles/doubles Skr540/740, discounted to Skr500/600)*, offering comfortable modern rooms with private toilet and shared shower (or you can pay extra for rooms with full private bathroom).

Hotel Winn *(☎ 701700; Bergskolegränd 7; singles/doubles from Skr1070/1330, discounted to Skr650/690)* is a fine place near the tourist office offering quality rooms and good service.

Scandic Hotel Falun *(☎ 669 2200; e fal un@scandic-hotels.com; Svärdsjögatan 51; singles/doubles Skr1201/1524, discounted to Skr660/760)* is a large, modern building just east of the town centre on road No 80, close to Lugnet. It has heaps of facilities, including a restaurant and bar, pool and even a bowling hall in the basement!

Places to Eat
There are a number of eateries on the main square and the adjoining pedestrian malls of Holmgatan and Åsgatan. **Banken Bar & Brasserie** *(☎ 71911; Åsgatan 41)* is a classy place with a grand interior. The menu includes a *gott & enkelt* (good and simple) category featuring the likes of burgers and pasta for Skr89 to Skr125, plus more upmarket options. **Två Rum & Kök** *(☎ 26025; Stadshusgränd 2; mains Skr190-235)* shares the same kitchen as Banken, just around the corner, but it's more exclusive and serves dinner only.

An excellent choice for lunch is **Café Kopparhattan** *(☎ 19169; Stigaregatan)*, attached to Dalarnas Museum. It serves sandwiches for around Skr40, soup for Skr52 and a vegetarian buffet for Skr65. Another excellent café is **Bryggcafeet** *(☎ 23330; cnr*

Östra Hamngatan & Kristinegatan), with a stylish interior, great coffee and cake selections, and seating over the river.

Harrys *(☎ 794887; Trotzgatan 9-11)* is entered off Åsgatan, and it has everything – pub, restaurant, outdoor area and disco.

Lilla Pizzerian *(☎ 28834; Slaggatan 10)* does takeaway and eat-in pizzas and kebabs, with nothing on the menu over Skr55.

Out at the copper mine, there are two good options: pretty **Gjuthuset** *(☎ 13212)* is a café in an 18th-century house on the edge of the Big Pit, where you can get coffee, sandwiches, cake etc. **Geschwornergården Värdshus** *(☎ 782616; lunch Skr68)* does excellent hot lunch specials.

For self-caterers, there's a central **ICA** supermarket *(Falugatan)* and **Systembolaget** *(Åsgatan 19)*.

Getting There & Away

Falun isn't on the main train lines – change at Borlänge when coming from Stockholm or Mora – but there are direct trains to/from Gävle (Skr95). **Swebus Express** *(☎ 0200 218218;* Ⓦ *www.swebusexpress.se)* has buses on the Gothenburg–Karlstad–Falun–Gävle route, and has connections to buses on the Stockholm–Uppsala–Borlänge–Mora route.

Regional transport is run by **Dalatrafik** *(☎ 020 232425)*, which covers all corners of the county of Dalarna. Tickets cost Skr15 for trips within a zone, and Skr15 extra for each new zone. A 31-day *länskort* costs Skr800 and allows you to travel throughout the county. Regional bus No 70 goes to Rättvik and Mora.

LAKE SILJAN REGION

This pretty, traditional area in the county of Dalarna is a popular summer tourist destination for both Swedes and foreigners, with numerous festivals and reasonable-sized towns offering good facilities and attractions. **Siljansleden**, an excellent walking and cycling path, extends for more than 300km around Lake Siljan; maps are available from tourist offices. Another way to enjoy the lake is by boat: in summer, **M/S Gustaf Wasa** has a complex range of lunch, dinner and sightseeing cruises from the main towns of Mora, Rättvik and Leksand. Inquire at any of the area's tourist offices for a schedule.

Check out the Siljan area website (Ⓦ www .siljan.se) for lots of good information. All the tourist offices in the area have brochures and maps for visitors, and all can help organise accommodation in the region.

Leksand
☎ 0247 • pop 15,300

If you're looking for traditional culture in Dalarna, Leksand is the place to go. Leksand's Midsummer Festival is the most popular in Sweden; up to 20,000 spectators watch the Midsummer pole being set up on the evening of the first Friday after 21 June.

The **tourist office** *(☎ 796130;* Ⓔ *leksand@ siljan.se; Stationsgatan 14; open 9am-7pm Mon-Fri, 10am-5pm Sat & Sun mid-June–mid-Aug, shorter hours Mon-Fri rest of year)* is at the train station. The town has all tourist facilities, including banks and supermarkets, primarily on Sparbankgatan. The **library** *(Kyrkallén)* has Internet access, as does Siljans Konditori (see Places to Stay & Eat).

Things to See & Do Beside Lake Siljan and just west of the centre, **Hildasholm** *(☎ 10062; admission Skr30)* is a sumptuously decorated early-20th-century mansion set in beautiful gardens. Guided tours in English are occasionally given – phone ahead to find out times. Tours run hourly from 11am to 5pm Monday to Saturday and 1pm to 5pm on Sunday, from June to mid-September (adult/child Skr60/30).

Kulturhuset *(☎ 80245; admission Skr10; open 11am-5pm Mon-Fri, 11am-4pm Sat, 1pm-4pm Sun mid-June–mid-Aug, closed Sun-Mon rest of year)* on Kyrkallén, houses the town library, as well as exhibitions of traditional clothing and local wall and furniture paintings.

Leksands Kyrka *(open 9.30am-8pm daily June–mid-Aug; 9.30am-3.30pm daily rest of year)* dates from the early 13th century but has been extensively renovated and enlarged. The church has extravagant baroque furnishings.

Äventyret Sommarland *(☎ 13939; bus No 58; admission Skr165; open 10am-5pm daily June-Aug, to 6pm in July)* is 2km north of Leksand, by the camping ground. It's a huge (and expensive) water- and fun park, with pools, slides, rides and other amusements.

The amazing **Tennfigurmuseum** *(☎ 61113; bus No 58; adult/child Skr25/10; open 10am-4pm daily mid-June–mid-Aug)*, at Hjortnäsgården (6km north on the lakeside road

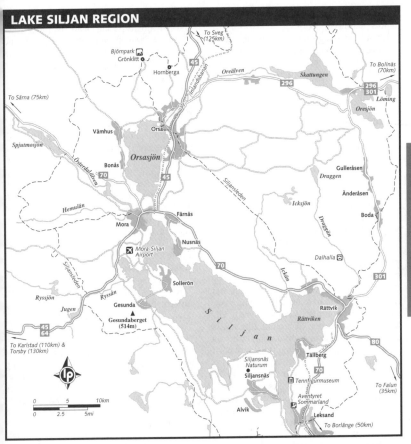

LAKE SILJAN REGION

to Tallberg) is an unusual collection of thousands of tiny tin figures in historical scenes.

Siljansnäs Naturum (☎ 23300; bus No 84 from Leksand; adult/child Skr40/20; open daily mid-May–Aug), 14km northwest of Leksand, has lots of interesting information about local geology, flora and fauna, as well as a collection of over 100 stuffed animals.

Places to Stay & Eat The huge, friendly, lakeside **Leksands Camping & Stugby** (☎ 80313; e leksands.camping.stugby@lek sand.se; bus No 58; tent sites low/high season Skr85/100, cabins & chalets from Skr260) is 2km north of town. It has all the facilities you could require, including restaurant and neighbouring waterpark. In high season it's

less crowded than the camping grounds at either Mora or Rättvik.

The **STF Vandrarhem** (☎ 15250; dorm beds Skr110) is a friendly, pleasant hostel, 2km south of town at Källberget. Bikes are available for rent.

Hotell Leksand (☎ 14570; e info@hotellek sand.com; Leksandsvägen 7; singles/doubles Skr690/890) is a new, modern small hotel right in the heart of town.

Bygatan 16 (☎ 15505; Bygatan 16; meals Skr69-192) is a classy establishment with a menu of light and main meals, including creative pasta, beef and fish dishes.

Nearby, **Siljans Konditori** (☎ 15070; Tor get; sandwiches Skr20-45) is a large and inviting bakery-café that has outdoor seating and serves good sandwiches. Downstairs you'll find an Internet café, with one hour online costing Skr30.

If you're craving some vitamins, **Jos-Juice** (☎ 80257) is a juice and salad bar at Kulturhus, and to undo your good work, opposite Kulturhus you'll find a **kiosk** serving sandwiches, hot dogs and tempting, freshly baked fruit pies (Skr15).

Getting There & Around Trains from Stockholm to Mora stop at Leksand up to six times daily. Bus No 58 regularly connects Leksand with Tällberg and Rättvik. The **OKQ8 petrol station** (☎ 10275; Hagagatan) has cars for hire, so you can explore the region independently, as does **Statoil** (☎ 34251; Leksandsvägen).

The **STF hostel** (see Places to Stay & Eat previously) hires bikes for Skr70 per day. For a taxi, call **Taxi Leksand** (☎ 14700).

Tällberg
☎ 0247

Tiny Tällberg, mid-way between Rättvik and Leksand, is a gem of a town, but if you visit, you certainly won't be alone. This pretty village has a population of around 200 and is home to no less than eight upmarket hotels (most with attached restaurants), a few posh galleries and boutiques, and little else (there's no tourist office). It's a lovely place to enjoy lunch and a wander (and possibly an overnight splurge), but you may prefer to stay in nearby Rättvik or Leksand and catch the bus here for an afternoon. See the town's website (W www.infotallberg.nu); it's in Swedish only but has links to all the hotels.

Klockargården (☎ 50260; e hotell@klockargarden.com; Siljansvägen 6; singles/doubles from Skr495/990) is a fine hotel in the homestead museum at Tällberg, a collection of old timber buildings set around a courtyard that's home to the **restaurant** and **bar**. The daily lunch buffet is Skr125; à la carte meals are around Skr200. Weekend, half-board and good-value last-minute packages are available.

Elegant **Åkerblads** (☎ 50800; e info@akerblads-tallberg.se; Sjögattu 2; singles/doubles Skr695/1290) is the oldest hotel in town. It's a beautiful collection of buildings, some of which date from the 15th century. The **restaurant** here is considered one of the region's finest, and has a lunch buffet for Skr145, plus à la carte main courses

nightly from Skr175 to Skr325. Weekend and half-board packages are available.

Bus No 58 between Rättvik and Leksand stops in the village regularly (two to six times daily). Tällberg is also on the train line that travels around Lake Siljan; the train station is about 2km from the village proper.

Rättvik
☎ 0248 • pop 10,900

Rättvik is a popular town on Lake Siljan, with sandy beaches for summer and ski slopes for winter. The **tourist office** (☎ 797210; e rattvik@siljan.se; Riksvägen 40; open 9am-7pm Mon-Fri, 10am-5pm Sat & Sun mid-June–mid-Aug, shorter hours Mon-Fri rest of year) is at the train station. The town has an almost weekly programme of special events, including a midsummer festival, **Musik vid Siljan** (W www.musikvidsiljan.se; early July), a **folklore festival** (W www.folklore.se; late July) and **Classic Car Week** (W www.classiccarweek.com; late July and/or early August).

Rättvik's facilities include banks and supermarkets on Storgatan, and a **library** (Storgatan 2) with Internet access.

Things to See & Do The 13th-century church, rebuilt in 1793, features 87 well-preserved **church stables**, the oldest dating from 1470. The pseudo-rune **memorial** beside the church and lake commemorates the 1520s rising of Gustav Vasa's band against the Danes – the rebellion that created modern Sweden.

About 500m further north is **Gammelgården** (☎ 51445; open noon-5pm daily mid-June–mid-Aug; admission free), an open-air museum with a good collection of furniture painted in the local style. Guided tours in summer at 1pm and 2.30pm cost Skr20; inquire about tours in English.

Central **Kulturhuset** (☎ 70195; Storgatan 2; adult/child Skr20/free; open daily), near Enån River, houses the library, art exhibitions, and displays on local flora and fauna. There's also a display describing the Siljansringen meteor impact 360 million years ago.

Views from surrounding hills and the easy **ski slopes** are excellent; there are four lifts and a day pass is Skr150. Visit **Vidablick Utsiktstorn** (adult/child Skr20/5; open daily mid-May–Aug), a viewing tower about 5km southeast of central Rättvik, for a great panorama of the lake region. There's also a good café up here, and a hostel (see Places to Stay).

Try the 725m-long **rodel run** (☎ 51300; one/three rides Skr30/70; open 11am-6pm or 7pm daily June-Aug), a sort of summer bob-sled chute that's lots of fun. Don't miss the longest wooden pier in Sweden, the 625m **Långbryggan** out over the lake.

Dalhalla (☎ 797950; W www.dalhalla.se), an old open-cut quarry 7km north of Rättvik, is used as an open-air theatre and concert venue in summer; the acoustics are incredible and the setting is stunning. It's well worth going along to see a performance; tickets usually start at Skr150. See the tourist office for a programme of concerts.

Places to Stay Near the train station, **Siljansbadets Camping** (☎ 51691; tent sites low/high season Skr90/135, 4-bed cabins from Skr280/390) is on the lake shore. **Rättviksparken** (☎ 56110; tent sites low/high season Skr90/120, double rooms Skr250, cabins from Skr275/400) is by the river off Centralgatan (1km from the train station). Both camping grounds are large, well-equipped and crowded in the high season; book ahead if you're planning to travel between mid-June and mid-August.

The well-appointed **STF Vandrarhem** (☎ 10566; e rattviksparken@rattviksparken .fh.se; Centralgatan; dorm beds Skr120; open year-round), by Rättviksparken, is really excellent. Also of good value is the mission-run **Jöns-Andersgården** (☎ 10735; Bygatan 4; bus No 74; dorm beds Skr120; open June-Aug), up on the hill (the view is superb), with beds in traditional wooden huts dating from the 15th century.

Vidablicks Vandrarhem (☎ 30250; dorm beds Skr125), up at the Vidablick lookout tower some 5km from town, offers simple, comfortable hostel accommodation and the view is excellent. But there's no transport here, and it wouldn't be much fun carting backpacks up the hill!

Pretty, church-run **Stiftsgården** (☎ 51020; Kyrkvägen 2; singles/doubles Skr375/530, with bath Skr485/720) is by the lake and near the church, away from the hustle and bustle of town but within walking distance.

Hotell Vidablick (☎ 30250; e vidablick@ hantverksbyn.se; Faluvägen; singles/doubles Skr500/795) is behind the OKQ8 petrol station on the road to Leksand about 3km

south of town. It's an excellent choice, offering rustic hotel accommodation in grass-roofed huts.

Places to Eat Behind the town hall, **Restaurang Anna** (☎ 12681; Vasagatan 3; dishes Skr95-190) is your best option for 'finer dining'. It's a good mid-range place serving Swedish and international dishes, including fish, lamb, pork and reindeer. You might want to head to Tällberg or Mora for other good choices; Rättvik doesn't excel in the restaurant department!

The cheapest eateries are opposite the train station. The old-style **Fricks Bageri** (☎ 13336; Torget; sandwiches from Skr30) has sandwiches, quiches, cakes and coffee. **Erkut Pizzeria** (☎ 51388; Torget) offers pizza from Skr40 and kebabs from Skr45. **Palm-bergs** (☎ 51528; Storgatan; lunch Skr65) has good coffee, fresh OJ and a range of sandwiches.

There is a **Systembolaget** and three **super-markets** on Storgatan.

Getting There & Away Buses depart from outside the train station. Dalatrafik's bus No 70 runs regularly between Falun, Rättvik and Mora. Direct trains from Stockholm and Mora stop up to eight times daily at Rättvik.

You can hire a bike from **Sörlins Sport** (☎ 10333; Storgatan 14) from Skr100/500 per day/week.

Mora
☎ 0250 • pop 20,000
The popular legend is that, in 1520, Gustav Vasa fled on skis from Mora after hiding from the Danes. Two good yeomen of Mora, after due consideration, chose to brave the winter and follow. Vasaloppet, the huge ski race which ends in Mora, commemorates Gustav's journey and involves 90km of gruelling Nordic skiing. Around 15,000 people take part on the first Sunday in March.

The **tourist office** (☎ 592020; e mora@sil jan.se; open 9am-7pm Mon-Fri, 10am-5pm Sat & Sun mid-June–mid-Aug, shorter hours Mon-Fri rest of year) is at the train station. There are banks, supermarkets and other facilities in town, primarily on Kyrkogatan. The **library** (Köpmangatan) has Internet access.

Things to See & Do The landmark **Mora Kyrka** *(open 8am-6pm daily in summer; 8am-4pm daily rest of year)*, dating from the 13th century, is an example of local style and has notable portraits inside.

Zornmuseet *(☎ 16560; Vasagatan 36; adult/child Skr35/2; open 9am-5pm Mon-Sat, 11am-5pm Sun mid-May–mid-Sept; noon-5pm Mon-Sat, 1pm-5pm Sun rest of year)* celebrates the works and private collections of the Mora painter Anders Zorn, who was one of the wealthiest Swedes until his death in 1920. Zorn's characteristic portraits and nudes have a great feeling of depth. Other artworks on display here include the odd traditional *dalmålningar* paintings and interesting statuettes.

The Zorn family house, **Zorngården** *(☎ 10004; Vasagatan 36; entry & tour adult/child Skr45/10; open 10am-4pm Mon-Sat, 11am-4pm Sun mid-May–mid-Sept; noon-3pm Mon-Sat, 1pm-4pm Sun rest of year)*, between the church and the museum, is an excellent example of a wealthy artist's house and reflects his National Romantic aspirations. The adjacent wooden studio is the second-oldest wooden building in Sweden (1292). Access to the house is by guided tour, every 30 minutes.

Zorns Gammelgård *(☎ 10454; adult/child Skr25/2; open noon-5pm daily June-Aug)*, Zorn's collection of local building traditions and textiles, is 1km south of the town centre.

The excellent **Vasaloppsmuseet** *(☎ 39225; Vasagatan; adult/child Skr30/20; 10am-5pm Mon-Fri, Sat & Sun also mid-June–mid-Sept)* has interesting displays on the largest skiing event in the world and has an exhibit of prizes. It also tells of the interesting history behind the race.

If you're after a souvenir of Dalarna, the best known painted wooden **Dala Horses** (Dalahästar) are made by **Nils Olsson Hemslöjd** *(☎ 37200; bus No 108; open daily mid-June–mid-August, closed Sunday rest of year)* at Nusnäs, 10km southeast of Mora. You can inspect the workshops and buy up big at the souvenir outlet; both are open daily in summer. Decide between a 3cm-high wooden horse for Skr50 or a 50cm-high one, costing Skr2154 (and there's lots of sizes in between).

Places to Stay In a great spot beside the river, 400m northwest of the church, busy **Moraparken** *(☎ 27600; tent sites from Skr75, 2-bed/4-bed cabins from Skr250/350)* has good facilities and is popular with families.

The **STF Vandrarhem** *(☎ 38196; ⓔ info@malkullann.se; Fredsgatan 6; dorm beds from Skr140)* is owned by Ann of the lovely **Målkull Ann's Pensionat** *(☎ 38190; Vasagatan 19; singles/doubles with shared facilities Skr450/600)*, who offers a good selection of accommodation in the centre of town.

Hotell Kung Gösta *(☎ 15070; Kristinebergsgatan 1; dorm beds from Skr120; hotel single/doubles Skr750/1090, discounted to Skr590/790)*, opposite the main train station and handy for travellers, has a hostel annexe in addition to its comfortable hotel rooms.

Vinäs Vandrarhem *(☎ 16344; bus No 107; dorm beds Skr150)* is about 5km south of Mora, in an atmospheric old schoolhouse. Breakfast is available for Skr50.

The classy **First Hotel Mora** *(☎ 592650; ⓔ mora@firsthotels.se; Strandgatan 12; singles/doubles from Skr1002/1252, discounted to Skr652/852)* is a good central, upmarket choice.

Places to Eat By Zornmuseet in the old part of town is the excellent **Claras Restaurang** *(☎ 15898; Vasagatan 38; lunch Skr75, meals Skr98-190)*, an elegant place with a good menu. Try the wonderful dessert of vanilla ice cream with warm cloudberries.

Målkull Ann's *(☎ 38190; Vasagatan)* is a pretty restaurant and café opposite Vasaloppsmuseet, with light meals around Skr70 and heartier selections for around Skr80 to Skr160.

Restaurang Verrazzano *(Vasagatan; meals Skr68-168)* is a pleasant Italian restaurant with a good selection of meals, including cheaper pasta, pizza and salads. Around the corner and in a converted warehouse, **Jérnet Bar & Matsal** *(☎ 15020; meals Skr85-220)* is a trendy restaurant and bar with an interesting menu – try the moose burger and fries (Skr118).

There are a few fast-food joints and supermarkets on Kyrkogatan, plus some old-style cafés. **Moras Kaffestuga** *(☎ 10082; Kyrkogatan 8; meals Skr35-50)* offers standard lunch fare – salads, quiches, baguettes and so on.

Getting There & Around The airport is 6km southwest of town on the Malung road. **Skyways** *(☎ 020 959500; ⓦ www.skyways.se)*

The Dala Horse

Bob Hope once received a **Dalahäst** (Dala Horse), as did Elvis Presley and members of the Supreme Soviet. Bill Clinton was given one by Prime Minister Göran Persson, and when the Swede Carl Bildt left his peace-making mission in Bosnia, he gave away 400 of them. The Dalahäst is a wooden horse painted in bright, cheerful colours, and to many people it represents the original, genuine symbol of Sweden, more powerful than the Swedish flag. The exact origin of these colourful wooden horses is uncertain, but they may have been around in some form as early as the 17th century, when the horses were carved out of a piece of wood in the evening firelight after the day's work in the forest. That it should be a horse was obvious – the horse was at the same time friend, workmate and a symbol of strength. The painted form that is so well known today made its international breakthrough at the World Exhibition in New York in 1939, and has been a favourite souvenir for travellers to Sweden ever since.

has three flights on weekdays between the **Mora-Siljan airport** and Stockholm Arlanda.

All Dalatrafik buses use the bus station at Moragatan 23. Bus No 70 runs to Rättvik and Falun, and bus Nos 103 and 104 runs to Orsa. Once or twice daily, bus No 170 goes to Älvdalen, Särna, Idre and Grövelsjön, near the Norwegian border.

Mora is an SJ terminus and the southern terminus of Inlandsbanan, which runs north to Gällivare (mid-June to mid-August). The main train station is about 1km east of town, by the lake. The more central Mora Strand is a platform station in town, but not all trains stop there so check the timetable.

When travelling to Östersund, you can choose between Inlandsbanan (Skr240, 6½ hours) or bus No 45 (Skr255, 5¼ hours), which runs twice daily. For more information on the Inlandsbanan (Inland Railway) see the boxed text in the Norrland chapter.

Hire a car in Mora to see the best of the region, especially northwest Dalarna; for smaller budget models try **Statoil** (☎ 10984; Brudtallsvägen 2). You can rent a bike for Skr100/500 per day/week at **Fliesbergs Sport & Fritid** (☎ 16001; Kaplandsgatan 1), a large

store selling all manner of outdoor and ski equipment.

Orsa
☎ 0250 • pop 7000

Orsa, only 16km north of Mora, isn't too exciting itself but the surrounding area has some attractions. There's a **tourist office** (☎ 552550; Dalagatan 1; open daily mid-June–mid-Aug; Mon-Fri only rest of year), and the nearby town centre has all tourist facilities.

Grönklitt Björnpark (☎ 46200; adult/child Skr75/40; open 10am-3pm daily mid-May–mid-Sept, until 6pm mid-June–mid-Aug, 10am-3pm Sat & Sun mid-Sept–mid-Oct), 15km from Orsa, is an excellent place where you can see bears, lynx, wolves and wolverines. The animals have a lot of space and fairly natural surroundings (apart from the fences). The bears are usually fed around noon, when you'll get a great view of them. Bus No 118 from Mora takes you to the park, via Orsa (twice daily weekdays, once on Sunday).

There's also a **ski area** (ski passes per day Skr150; open roughly Dec-Mar) out at Grönklitt, plus a **camping ground** (☎ 552300; tent sites from Skr95), an **STF Hostel** (☎ 46200; dorm beds Skr140), and a **wärdshus** (inn; ☎ 46055; lunch Skr75, dinner mains Skr65-125). Summer activities such as fishing, canoeing and elk or beaver safaris can be organised at the camping ground's information desk.

Bus Nos 103 and 104 run regularly between Mora and Orsa.

SÄLEN & AROUND
☎ 0280 • pop 400

For such a small village, Sälen's importance to Swedish tourism seems completely out of proportion: there are nearly 60,000 beds available for guests! The Transtrandsfällen area just west of the village is one of Sweden's premier winter resorts and snow is guaranteed from 15 November to April. In summer, there are beaver safaris and canoe trips, and fishing and horse riding is also available – inquire at the tourist office.

Head first to the Centrumhuset complex, where you'll find a bank, doctor, pharmacy, Systembolaget and most other facilities, including the **tourist office** (☎ 18700; e info@salen.se, w www.salen.se; open daily June-Aug

& Dec-Apr; Mon-Sat rest of year). Opposite the complex are supermarkets and stores where you can rent your ski gear in winter, and in-line skates, boats and canoes in summer.

The **ski areas**, with chalets, pubs and nightclubs, are strung out for 20km along the road running through the steep-flanked flat-topped mountains west of Sälen. There are dozens of lifts and pistes of all degrees of difficulty. Gustav Backen at Lindvallen is the busiest ski run in Europe; for skiing information visit W www.skistar.com.

There's also some good **hiking** in the area in summer, mainly north of the road. North of Sälen, cheaper and quieter skiing is available at **Näsfjället**.

Places to Stay & Eat

Winter visitors should contact their travel agent or the tourist office for accommodation, or get in contact with **Ski Star** *(☎ 88000; e bokning@salen.com, W www.skistar.com)* for packages.

The **STF Vandrarhem** *(☎ 82040; dorm beds Skr120-160)* is 27km north of Sälen, in a nature reserve at Grasheden (near Näsfjället). Kungsleden (see the 'Hiking' special section) passes 1.5km from the hostel. There's no public transport out this way.

Sälens Gästgiveri *(☎ 20185; e info@gastis .com; singles/doubles Skr450/550, with bath Skr550/650)*, in the village, has comfortable accommodation plus a restaurant and bar; the popular lunch buffet costs Skr79. Accommodation prices given here are for the summer season; winter prices are higher by Skr50 to Skr200 per room.

The excellent, friendly **Sju Rum & Kök** *(☎ 20020; e info@sjurum.com; Sälenvägen 29; B&B per person Skr300)* is a small, boutique-style ski lodge (also open in summer) with comfortable, good-value rooms, some with bathrooms. The **restaurant** here is the best in town, with mains from around Skr200.

Inside the Centrumhuset complex, you'll find a **delicatessen** selling fresh local produce, plus an excellent **bakery**, with sandwiches or hot meals priced around Skr50. Just outside the complex is **Bygrillan**, serving hamburgers, kebabs and salads.

Getting There & Around

Bus No 95 runs from the ski area to Mora via Sälen, once daily. A ski bus tours around the ski area in winter.

IDRE & GRÖVELSJÖN
☎ 0253

The small town of Idre lies close to some beautiful upland wilderness for hikers, and there's also very good skiing here. The friendly **tourist office** *(☎ 20000; e info@idre turism.se, W www.idreturism.se; Framgårdsvägen 1; open 10am-7pm Mon-Fri, noon-6pm Sat-Sun June-Aug; shorter hours rest of year)* has lots of brochures and hiking advice, plus free Internet access. Staff also can arrange a variety of activities, including dog-sledging, skiing, hiking, canyoning, rock-climbing, boat trips, elk safaris, beaver safaris by canoe, horse riding, rafting and canoeing. Staff can also book accommodation in the area. The town's website is in Swedish only.

Idre Fjäll ski centre *(☎ 41000; W www .idrefjall.se; open Nov-Apr)*, 9km east, has three chairlifts, 29 ski-tows and 37 downhill runs, including 11 black runs (day lift passes Skr200). There are also 60km of prepared cross-country tracks.

Grövelsjön, 38km northwest of Idre and close to the Norwegian border, lies on the edge of the wild 690 sq km **Långfjällets Nature Reserve**, which is noted for its lichen-covered heaths, moraine heaps and ancient forests. Reindeer from Sweden's southernmost Sami community near Idre wander throughout the area. **Boat trips** across Grövelsjön lake cost Skr60 (daily except Saturday in summer). The STF lodge is the starting point for many great hikes.

Places to Stay & Eat

Sörälvens Fiske Camping *(☎ 20117; tent sites Skr100, cabins Skr480)* is just out of Idre, 2.5km towards Grövelsjön. It offers rather shadeless camping areas but good cabins, and is popular with the fishing crowd.

The **STF Fjällstation** *(☎ 596880; e info@ grovelsjon.stfturist.se; dorm beds from Skr175, singles/doubles from Skr295/400; open Feb-Apr & mid-June–Sept)* is an excellent hostel and lodge in Grövelsjön, with a wide array of facilities, including kitchen, restaurant, day spa, shop and outdoor gear rental. The rather good **restaurant** here has breakfast for Skr68, lunch from Skr60, and dinner from Skr140. Half-board and full-board arrangements are available. This is a big and busy place, with a huge range of day tours and other activities available.

Ask the tourist office about **cabins** and **chalets** *(from Skr300/800 per day/week)*.

Älgen *(☎ 20411; Byvägen 30; dorm beds from Skr200)* has passable accommodation and a restaurant, which serves unremarkable grub, including some 70 different types of pizza for around Skr70.

A 2km walk out of town will take you to the local golf course, where there's a pleasant **café** *(☎ 20273)* in green surrounds and with good lunch options (wraps, salads, baked potatoes) from about Skr60.

Idre Grill *(☎ 20580)* is across the street from the Konsum supermarket, with good kebabs and pizzas from Skr45 and homestyle *pytt i panna* or schnitzel from Skr70.

Getting There & Away

Dalatrafik bus No 170 travels on a route between Mora, Idre and Grövelsjön (it's three hours from Mora to Idre, four to 4½ hours to Grövelsjön). There are two services to Grövelsjön on weekdays, and one or two on weekends.

Skåne

The county of Skåne, sometimes anglicised as Scania, lies in the extreme south of the country. It was part of Denmark until 1658 and still retains differences from the rest of Sweden. This is easily detected in the strong dialect and in the distinctive architecture. Natives of Skåne look more towards Copenhagen than Stockholm, and the new Öresund bridge has brought Copenhagen even closer.

Hiking and cycling trips are popular in the county, which has a gently rolling landscape with more farmland and less forest than most other areas in Sweden. There are more hostels here than in any other region of the country, and there are numerous attractions, including castles, stone ship settings, sandy beaches and some of Sweden's best coastal bird-watching.

Highlights

- Sipping a cup of coffee alfresco in cosmopolitan Malmö
- Travelling across the new Öresund bridge
- Wandering through the medieval streets of Lund
- Visiting one of the old Danish Scanian castles
- Hiking along the sandy beaches in Stenshuvud National Park
- Admiring the grand architecture of Kristianstad

Regional Tourist Offices

Tourist facilities are well organised in Skåne, and there are helpful tourist offices in all major towns. **Skånes Turistråd** *(☎ 046-350570; e info@skanetourist.com, w www.skanetourist.com; Bredgatan 25, SE-22221 Lund)* dispenses information about the entire region and publishes some very good brochures and maps (although we must admit to being a little stumped by their English advertising slogan: 'Not for the lagom people, more for the rest of us'!).

If you enter the region from Denmark via the bridge over the Öresund, there is a tourist office just off the highway a few kilometres into the country. This office, called **Skånegården** *(☎ 040-341201; Bunkeflov 40)* is open daily and can supply information on Malmö, Skåne and the whole of Sweden.

Many of the tourist offices in Skåne stock brochures and maps for Copenhagen as well as Denmark for those planning to cross the Öresund.

Getting Around

Public transport in Skåne is efficient and well managed; **Skånetrafiken** *(☎ 020-567567; w www.skanetrafiken.skane.se)* operates the local bus and train *(pågatågen)* networks, and there are regular connections to Denmark via the Öresund bridge or the Helsingborg–Helsingør ferry.

An integrated Öresundregionen transport system is now operational, with trains from Helsingborg via Malmö and Copenhagen to Helsingør. For a round tour of the Öresund or a visit to Copenhagen, the Öresund Runt card for Skr199 gives two days' free travel on ferries and local trains; this covers transport within Skåne and also along the coast north of Copenhagen.

Skånetrafiken sells a variety of value cards and passes. A summer card covering all buses and local trains in the region is available from 15 June to 15 August for Skr395 (valid any 25 days of the two months). Another card is valid for one month in Skåne on all trains and buses for Skr850. Check out the website, which includes a travel planner.

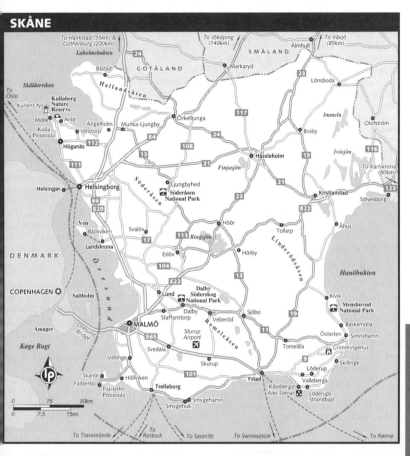

SKÅNE

To Halmstad (55km) &
Göthenburg (200km)

To Oslo

To Jököping (140km)

To Växjö (85km)

Laholmsbukten

24

Båstad

GOTÄLAND

Markaryd

SMÅLAND

Älmhult

Lönsboda

23

Skälderviken

Hallandsåsen

Kullaberg Nature Reserve

Kullens fyr

Orkelljunga

117

Immeln

Olofström

Molle Arild
Kulla Peninsula

Ängelholm Munka-Ljungby

24

Broby

116

Ivösjön

Jonstorp

E4

Höganäs

112

108

13

21

Hässleholm

19

111

Finjasjön

To Karlskrona (80km)

Söderåsen

Ljungbyhed

21

Helsingør **Helsingborg**

Söderåsen National Park

23

Kristianstad

123

E6

Höör

E22

Sölvesborg

Ven

E20

Svalöv

113 *Ringsjön*

Tollarp

Linderödsåsen

Åhus

Bäckviken

17

DENMARK

Landskrona

Eslöv

104

Hörby

Hanöbukten

Öresund

E22

13

COPENHAGEN Saltholm

Lund

Dalby Söderskog National Park

Sjöbo

19

Kivik

Stenshuvud National Park

Amager

Dalby
Staffanstorp

Veberöd

11

Romeleåsen

Baskemölla

Österlen Simrishamn

Köge Bugt

MALMÖ

Öresund Bridge

E65

Sturup Airport

Tomelilla

Glimmingehus

9

Vellinge

Svedala

Skurup

Löderup Skillinge

101

Valleberga

Skanör
Falsterbo

Höllviken

Ystad

Falsterbo
Peninsula

Trelleborg

Käseberga
Ales Stenar

Löderups
Strandbad

Smygehamn
Smygehuk

0   15   30km
0   7.5   15mi

To Travemünde

To Rostock

To Sassnitz

To Swinoujscie

To Rønne

BikeTour Sweden (☎ 0411-42000; W www .biketoursweden) offers self-guided or guided cycling tours in Skåne. See the Cycling section of the Activities chapter for more details.

MALMÖ
☎ 040 ● pop 262,400

Malmö, the most 'continental' of Sweden's cities, is a lively and vibrant place with an interesting history. The influence of Copenhagen across the Öresund is evident and the relatively large proportion of immigrants among the population – there are people from around 150 nations currently living in the city – adds a multicultural aspect. The 16km Öresund bridge and tunnel link, which includes Europe's longest bridge (7.8km), opened in summer 2000 and has brought Copenhagen and Malmö even closer together.

History
In the 13th century, Malmö consisted of little more than a few streets centred around Adelgatan, then on the shore of Öresund. With the arrival of the Hanseatic traders in the following century, grand houses were built for wealthy merchants and large churches were constructed. The first castle was built in 1434 and housed the Danish royal mint. The greatest medieval expansion of Malmö occurred under the auspices of Jörgen Kock, who became mayor in 1524. The town square, Stortorget, was laid out and many of the buildings from this period are still extant.

After the city capitulated to the Swedes in 1658, Malmö rose in importance as a commercial centre and the castle was strengthened to protect trade. In the 20th century, the city developed as a centre for heavy industry, including car and aircraft manufacture, and shipbuilding. The huge Kockums submarine and shipyard opened in 1909 and dominated shipbuilding worldwide for many years. However, as elsewhere in Europe, the heavy industries have disappeared and have been replaced by smaller companies, particularly in the service, financial and IT sectors. There has also been an upsurge in the number of students living in Malmö (currently around 18,000) with the opening of a new university campus here in the late 1990s.

Orientation

Gamla Staden (Old Town) is the city centre and is encircled by a canal. There are three principal squares here: Stortorget, Lilla Torg and Gustav Adolfs Torg. Malmöhus castle, in its park setting, guards the western end of Gamla Staden. Across the canal on the northern side you'll find the bus and train stations as well as the harbour. South of the city centre, there's a complex network of more modern streets with most interest focused on the square Möllevångstorget. The Öresund bridge is about 8km west of the city centre, served by a motorway which passes south and east of the city.

Information

Tourist Offices The **tourist office** (☎ 341200; e malmo.turism@malmo.se, w www.malmo .se; open 9am-8pm Mon-Fri, 10am-5pm Sat & Sun June-Aug; 9am-6pm Mon-Fri, 10am-1pm Sat & Sun May & Sept; 9am-5pm Mon-Fri, 10am-2pm Sat Oct-Apr) is inside Centralstationen (the central train station). Pick up a free map and the free official booklet, which is a very useful general guide for visitors.

Skånegården (open 8am-8pm daily June-Aug; 9am-5pm Mon-Fri, 10am-4pm Sat & Sun Sept-May) is a tourist office in a restored 19th-century farmhouse on the E20, 800m from the Öresund bridge tollgate. It's designed purely to give information to motorists entering the country from Denmark, and can provide details on Malmö, Skåne and the whole of Sweden.

Another excellent source of information on the city can be found on the Internet at w www.malmo.com.

Discount Cards The discount card Malmökortet covers free bus transport, free street parking, free entry to several museums and discounts at other attractions and on sightseeing tours. It's good value at Skr120/ 150/180 for one/two/three days – the price includes one adult and up to two children under 16. Buy it at the tourist office.

Money If you need to exchange money, **Forex** has counters by the tourist office inside Centralstationen (open 7am-9pm daily), and opposite the train station in Börshuset, and on Gustav Adolfs Torg. **X-Change** (Hamngatan 1; Mon-Sat) also has a central branch.

Banks and ATMs can be found along Södergatan.

Post The central **post office** (Skeppsbron 1; open 7am-7pm Mon-Fri) is behind the train station, but you can buy stamps and post letters from a number of shops and kiosks around town.

Email & Internet Access You can get online at **Cyberspace Café** (☎ 611 0116; Engelbrektsgatan 13; open 10am-midnight Mon-Fri, noon-midnight Sat & Sun); it's Skr22 for 30 minutes. **Surfers Paradise** (☎ 121520; Amiralsgatan 14), south of the centre, has the same hours as Cyberspace and similar prices. Coffee and snacks are available at both places.

The city library, **Malmö Stadsbibliotek** (☎ 660 8500; Regementsgatan; open 10am-7pm Mon-Thur, 10am-6pm Fri, noon-4pm Sat), has free Internet access.

Travel Agencies You'll find **Kilroy Travels** (☎ 0771-545769; Engelbrektsgatan 18) near the Hotel Temperance.

Bookshops The best place for general books and guidebooks is **Akademibokhandeln** (Södergatan 3). For newspapers and international magazines go to **Press Stop** (Södergatan 20), next door to Hotel Baltzar, or **Pressbyrån** in Centralstationen.

Laundry If needed, **Tvätt-Tjänst i Malmö** (☎ 611 7070; St Knuts Torg 5; open 8am-5pm Mon-Fri) can wash and dry your clothes.

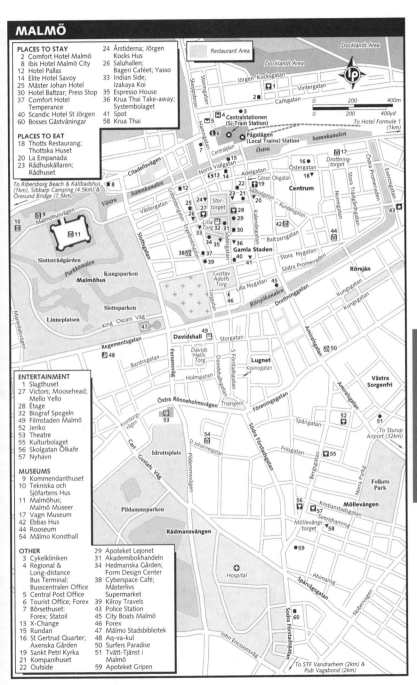

MALMÖ

PLACES TO STAY
2 Comfort Hotel Malmö
8 Ibis Hotel Malmö City
12 Hotel Pallas
14 Elite Hotel Savoy
25 Mäster Johan Hotel
30 Hotel Baltzar; Press Stop
37 Comfort Hotel
   Temperance
40 Scandic Hotel St Jörgen
60 Bosses Gästvåningar

PLACES TO EAT
18 Thotts Restaurang;
   Thottska Huset
20 La Empanada
23 Rådhuskällaren;
   Rådhuset

24 Årstiderna; Jörgen
   Kocks Hus
26 Saluhallen;
   Bageri Caféet; Yasso
33 Indian Side;
   Izakaya Koi
35 Espresso House
36 Krua Thai Take-away;
   Systembolaget
41 Spot
58 Krua Thai

*To Ribersborg Beach & Kallbadshus
(1km), Sibbarp Camping (4.5km) &
Öresund Bridge (7.5km)*

ENTERTAINMENT
1 Slagthuset
27 Victors; Moosehead;
   Mello Yello
28 Étage
32 Biograf Spegeln
49 Filmstaden Malmö
52 Jeriko
53 Theatre
55 Kulturbolaget
56 Skolgatan Ölkafe
57 Nyhavn

MUSEUMS
9 Kommendanthuset
10 Tekniska och
   Sjöfartens Hus
11 Malmöhus;
   Malmö Museer
17 Vagn Museum
42 Ebbas Hus
44 Rooseum
54 Malmö Konsthall

OTHER
3 Cykelkliniken
4 Regional &
   Long-distance
   Bus Terminal;
   Busscentralen Office
5 Central Post Office
6 Tourist Office; Forex
7 Börsethuset:
   Forex; Statoil
13 X-Change
15 Rundan
16 St Gertrud Quarter;
   Axenska Gården
19 Sankt Petri Kyrka
21 Kompanihuset
22 Outside

29 Apoteket Lejonet
31 Akademibokhandeln
34 Hedmanska Gården;
   Form Design Center
38 Cyberspace Café;
   Mästerlivs
   Supermarket
39 Kilroy Travels
43 Police Station
45 City Boats Malmö
46 Forex
47 Malmö Stadsbibliotek
48 Aq-va-kul
50 Surfers Paradise
51 Tvätt-Tjänst i
   Malmö
59 Apoteket Gripen

To Hotel Formule 1 (1km)

To Sturup Airport (32km)

To STF Vandrarhem (2km) & Pub Vagabond (2km)

SKÅNE

Left Luggage There are small/medium/large lockers by platform 4 in Centralstationen for Skr15/20/25 per 24 hours.

Camping & Outdoor Gear All your equipment needs can be met at **Outside** (☎ 300910; Kyrkogatan 3), at the northeastern corner of Stortorget.

Emergency & Medical Services For medical emergencies visit **Akutklinik** (☎ 333685; entrance 36, Södra Förstadsgatan 101), the emergency ward at the general hospital. You can call the dentist and doctor on duty on ☎ 676 9292. The duty pharmacy is **Apoteket Gripen** (☎ 192113; Bergsgatan 48; open 8am-midnight daily).

The main **police station** (☎ 201000; Porslinsgatan 6) is just east of the city centre.

Malmöhus

A castle on this site was built in 1434 by Erik of Pomerania to control the growing town of Malmö and shipping in Öresund. Most of the medieval town lay to the east and two of the walls met at the site, so only two further walls were required. A few years later the castle was named Myntergaarden when the Danish royal mint was moved here. Between 1534 and 1536 there was a popular uprising in Skåne and the castle was destroyed.

In the years immediately after the rebellion, King Christian III of Denmark ordered the castle to be rebuilt in rather forbidding, late-Gothic and early-Renaissance styles. The former has pointed niches and crow-stepped gables, while the latter has bay windows and tower stairs.

The most famous prisoner at Malmöhus (from 1567 to 1573) was James Hepburn, Earl of Bothwell. Hepburn married Mary Queen of Scots, but later it was revealed he had plotted the murder of her previous husband, Lord Darnley. He fled Scotland and turned up in Norway, but was detained by the Danes until his death in 1578.

After the Swedish takeover of Skåne in 1648, the Danes made a futile attempt to recapture the castle in 1677. With peace now restored between Denmark and Sweden, interest in the castle waned and most of it became derelict by the 19th century. Then a devastating fire in 1870 left only the main building and two gun towers intact and these sections were renovated in 1930.

Malmö Museer

Malmö Museer (☎ 344437; W www.museer.malmo.se; Malmöhusvägen; combined entry adult/child Skr40/10, free with Malmökortet; open 10am-4pm daily June-Aug, noon-4pm daily Sept-May) includes the four museums in and around Malmöhus castle. Some of them are housed in dismal-looking, red-brick, Functionalist buildings (dating from 1937), which don't blend in at all.

You can walk through the **royal apartments** with their 16th- and 17th-century furniture and portrait collections. The **Knight's Hall** has various late-medieval and Renaissance exhibits, such as the regalia of the order of St Knut. In the **Stadsmuseum** (City Museum) you'll find permanent local collections (mostly regarding the cultural history of Malmö and Skåne). The galleries of **Malmö Konstmuseum** contain the largest Swedish collection of 19th-century Nordic art and a substantial collection of Russian *fin de siècle* art.

The especially interesting **aquarium** is really a zoo and has a nocturnal hall, a rainforest vivarium, coral reefs, caves and brightly coloured tropical fish. There are also representatives of local species such as cod and pike. The aquarium is associated with the **Naturmuseum** (Natural History Museum), which has typical collections of rocks, stuffed animals and birds.

The old **Kommendanthuset** (Commandant's House) arsenal is just opposite the castle and you'll find the well-presented **Tekniska och Sjöfartens Hus** a short way to the west. This technology and maritime museum displays aircraft, motor vehicles, an 1863 stagecoach, a horse-drawn tram (1887) and steam engines. However, the finest exhibit is the 'U3' walk-in submarine, which lies just outside the main building; it was launched in Karlskrona in 1943 and decommissioned in 1967.

There's a restaurant here which serves lunch, coffee and snacks.

Sankt Petri Kyrka

This is the oldest church (Göran Olsgatan; open 8am-6pm Mon-Fri, 10am-6pm Sat & Sun) in the city and was completed before 1346. It consists of the original triple-aisled nave, with a transept and ambulatory, characteristic of Baltic Gothic style and based on St Mary's Church in Lübeck. The medieval

SKÅNE

frescoes were whitewashed by Protestant zealots in 1555 and removed entirely in the 1850s. However, there's a magnificent altarpiece dating from 1611. Much of the church has been rebuilt and the 96m tower was constructed in 1890. There's a votive ship in the south aisle, dedicated to all who died at sea in WWII.

The 14th-century **Krämarekapellet** is inside at the rear of Sankt Petri Kyrka and has original wall-paintings and a canopied font decorated with biblical baptism scenes.

Other Attractions

Around Malmö's oldest square, **Stortorget**, there are many old and impressive buildings. **Rådhuset**, the city hall, was originally built in 1546, but has been subsequently altered. The former Danish Trading Company building, **Kompanihuset**, dates from around 1520 and lies behind the *rådhuset*. At the southeastern corner of the square, **Apoteket Lejonet** was founded in 1571 – it's the city's oldest pharmacy and is still in business. The building dates from 1895 and its interior is set out as a 19th-century-style pharmacy, with a large collection of historical items. It's fine to go in and take a look.

When Gustav Vasa visited the city in 1524, he stayed with Mayor Jörgen Kock in the newly built **Jörgen Kocks Hus**, at the opposite corner of the square. There's a good restaurant in the atmospheric vaults underneath this house.

The cobbled streets and interesting buildings around **Lilla Torg** are restored parts of the late-medieval town – the oldest of the half-timbered houses here was built in 1597. The houses are now occupied by galleries, boutiques, cafés and restaurants. Just off Lilla Torg in **Hedmanska Gården**, a wonderful building from 1529, the **Form Design Center** (☎ 664 5150; admission free; open 11am-5pm Tues-Fri, 10am-4pm Sat, noon-4pm Sun) features temporary exhibitions on architecture, design and the arts.

The excellent **St Gertrud Quarter** is just off Östergatan and consists of 19 buildings featuring different styles from the 16th to 19th centuries. The oldest is now a café but was the home of Nils Kuntze, an early mayor of Malmö, and dates from 1530. **Axenska Gården** is a fine example of a 17th-century half-timbered house. Across the road, **Thottska Huset** is the oldest half-timbered house in

Malmö (1558). It has been turned into a restaurant, so you can take a look inside. It's also worth wandering around Drottningtorget to see more examples of old Malmö.

The historic horse-drawn carriages of the **Vagn Museum** (☎ 344459; Drottningtorget; adult/child Skr10/5; open 9am-4pm Fri) are housed in a former army riding school and are well worth a look. **Ebbas Hus** (☎ 344423; Snapperupsgatan 10; adult/child Skr10/5; open noon-4pm Wed only), is the smallest house in Malmö and it has been left as it was in 1970 when the last occupant departed. Both of these museums are free with Malmökortet.

Contemporary art exhibitions are held in **Rooseum** (☎ 121716; W www.rooseum.se; Gasverksgatan 22; adult/child Skr40/20, free with Malmökortet; open 2pm-8pm Wed-Fri, noon-6pm Sat & Sun), an extraordinary place which was the turbine hall of a power station. **Malmö Konsthall** (☎ 341294; St Johannesgatan 7; admission free; open 11am-5pm daily), south of the city centre, has a large display area for contemporary art and features temporary exhibitions by Swedish and foreign artists. Guided tours are at 2pm daily.

Activities

Ask at the tourist office for the free cycling map *Cykla i Malmö*, which includes routes to some destinations outside the city. See Getting Around later for information about renting a bike locally.

Aq-va-kul (☎ 300540; Regementsgatan 24; adult/child Skr65/40; open daily), near the library, is a water amusement park with heated indoor and outdoor pools, a sauna, solarium and even a Turkish bath. Between 9am and noon on weekdays the adult price for admission is reduced to Skr45.

Ribersborg is a long sandy beach backed by parkland and recreational areas about 2km west of the town centre. Out in Öresund, and reached by a 200m-long pier, is a naturist pool and sauna, **Riversborgs Kallbadshus** (☎ 260366; admission Skr35; open 8.30am-7pm Mon-Fri, 8.30am-4pm Sat & Sun), which dates from 1898. There is a cold, open-air saltwater pool and wood-fired sauna, and separate sections for men and women.

You can discover the canals of Malmö at your own pace in a pedal boat, which you can hire (Skr70/100 for 30/60 minutes; 50% discount with Malmökortet) from May to August. Head to **City Boats Malmö** (☎ 511381)

SKÅNE

at Amiralsbron on Södra Promenaden, not far east of Gustav Adolfs Torg.

Organised Tours
Sightseeing bus tours of the city centre and the Öresund bridge depart from outside the tourist office at noon daily from late May to the end of August (1½ hours). Information and tickets are available from the tourist office for Skr100/50 (half-price with Malmö-kortet). The guides speak Swedish, English and German.

Rundan (☎ 611 7488) has an office by the canal, opposite Centralstationen. Depending on the weather, 45-minute boat tours of the canals run regularly from late April until late September (from 11am to 7pm mid-June to mid-August). Commentary is in Swedish, German and English; the tours cost Skr70/40.

Special Events
The biggest annual event in the city is the week-long Malmö Festival, held in the second week of August. Events include theatre, art, singing, music, dance and dragonboat competitions, and most events are free. The opening night is celebrated with a fireworks display and there's a huge crayfish party on Friday in Stortorget. During the week you can get food at a great variety of international stalls. Make inquiries at the tourist office.

Places to Stay
Camping, Hostels & Private Rooms
About 5km southwest of the centre of town, **Sibbarp Camping** (☎ 155165; e sibbarps .camping@swipnet.se; Strandgatan 101; low/ high season tent sites Skr125/170, 2-bed cabins Skr260/390, 4-bed cabins Skr370/490; open year-round) is by the beach and has a great view of the Öresund bridge. Take bus No 12B or 12G from Gustav Adolfs Torg (Skr14).

Malmö is a bit short of hostel accommodation. The **STF Vandrarhem** (☎ 82220; e info@malmohostel.se; Backavägen 18; dorm beds Skr130; singles/doubles Skr285/ 350; open year-round) is 3.5km south of the city centre, near the E6. It's big, bright and well equipped, offering breakfast for Skr50 (take bus No 21 from Centralplan in front of Centralstationen).

Bosses Gästvåningar (☎ 326250; Södra Förstadsgatan 110B; singles/doubles from Skr275/325) is a central SVIF hostel, close

to Möllevångstorget and opposite the town hospital. Rooms are of a decent standard.

Private rooms or apartments from about Skr250 per person are available through **City Room** (☎ 79594; e cityroom@telia.com). The agency has no office address but is staffed on weekdays during office hours. Otherwise, contact the tourist office.

Hotels For help with hotel reservations in the city try **Malmö Tourism** (☎ 109210; e hotel@malmo.se).

Central **Hotel Pallas** (☎ 611 5077; Norra Vallgatan 74; singles/doubles from Skr355/ 395) is a recommended cheapish hotel near the train station; breakfast is an extra Skr30. You can pay a little extra to get one of the very spacious double rooms (Skr475).

The bargain-basement **Hotel Formule 1** (☎ 930580; Lundavägen 28; rooms Skr290) is 1.5km east of Stortorget. Smallish, functional rooms can sleep up to three people for a flat rate.

Ibis Hotel Malmö City (☎ 664 6250; Citadellsvägen 4; rooms Sun-Thur Skr540-680, Fri & Sat Skr540-575) is a good, reasonably priced central option, with rooms that are pleasant but nothing special.

All the better hotels offer good discounts on weekends and in summer. Try the modern **Comfort Hotel Malmö** (☎ 611 2511; e malmo@comfort.choicehotels.se; Carlsgat an 10C; singles/doubles Skr945/1095, discounted to Skr620/760), tucked out of the way in the business area north of the train station.

Hotel Baltzar (☎ 665 5700; e info@ baltzarhotel.se; Södergatan 20; singles/doubles from Skr980/1300, discounted to Skr700/850) is another good choice, in the heart of the action. It offers comfortable rooms, some furnished with antiques, in an imposing historical building. In a similar vein and offering similar standards of location and comfort is **Comfort Hotel Temperance** (☎ 71020; e temperance@comfort.choicehotels.se; Engelbrektsgatan 16; singles/doubles Skr1390/1690, discounted to Skr790/990).

Scandic Hotel St Jörgen (☎ 693 4600; e stjorgen@scandic-hotels.com; Stora Nygatan 35; singles/doubles from Skr1315/2028, discounted to Skr770/870) is on the corner of Gustav Adolfs Torg and has all the amenities you would expect from this upmarket chain. Better value is the **Elite Hotel Savoy** (☎ 664 4800; e info.savoy@elite.se; Norra Vallgatan

62; singles/doubles from Skr1390/1690, discounted to Skr900/950), a refined place with excellent service and a wonderful restaurant.

Top of the heap is **Mäster Johan Hotel** (☎ 664 6400; e reservation@masterjohan.se; Mäster Johansgatan 13; singles/doubles from Skr1545/1945, discounted to Skr1000/1250), arguably the best hotel in town (it's been awarded the 'Best Hotel in Sweden' award by Hotel Barometern a number of times in recent years). It has excellent rustic-style rooms and a glass-roofed courtyard where you can enjoy the breakfast buffet. Decor, service, facilities and location are all first-rate.

Places to Eat

Årstiderna (☎ 230910; Frans Suellsgatan 2B; mains Skr195-270) is among the most exclusive restaurants in the city, located in the vaulted cellar of Jörgen Kocks Hus, just off Stortorget. With lots of arches and alcoves and friendly staff, there's a great atmosphere in here – just the place for a romantic dinner.

Rådhuskällaren (☎ 79020; Stortorget; lunch special Skr75; à la carte mains Skr172-235) is in the 16th-century, barrel-vaulted cellar of the town hall. Rumour has it that two members of the Beatles were turned away here in 1967 because they weren't wearing neckties – thankfully things have relaxed a little since then! The food is excellent although the menu is quite small.

For a special treat and an atmospheric meal, try **Thotts Restaurang** (☎ 698 4800; Östergatan 10; mains Skr165-205), in a lovely half-timbered house dating from the 16th century. Well-prepared mains include the likes of grilled rack of wild boar with lingonberries, or you can choose a two-course set menu for Skr245. Enter via the SAS Radisson Hotel.

The central squares become quite a scene on summer evenings, with well over a dozen restaurants offering alfresco dining and drinking. Lilla Torg (the Little Square) is a picturesque cobbled square lined with restaurant-bars and is often heaving with people. Any of the three major bar-restaurants on the square here can really satisfy your hunger pains; you should check out their menus and see what takes your fancy.

For something different, try the new and sleek **Izakaya Koi** (☎ 75700; Lilla Torg 5; lunch Skr60-75, dinner mains Skr100-150), serving up quality Japanese cuisine, which includes

highly rated sushi, to Malmö's fashionable set. Next door is **Indian Side** (☎ 307744), with a wide selection of Indian dishes around the Skr100 mark.

For excellent lunchtime Italian sandwiches and salads, visit the stylish **Spot** (☎ 120203; Stora Nygatan 33); daily pasta and risotto dishes cost from Skr60. Another good spot for coffee and snacks is **Espresso House** (☎ 308048; Skomakaregatan), not far from Lilla Torg.

The area around Möllevångstorget reflects the city's interesting ethnic mix, and there's good, cheap food on offer from a mix of stalls, shops and student-frequented restaurants and bars. Also here is popular **Krua Thai** (☎ 122287; Möllevångstorget 14), a large, long-standing Thai restaurant with dishes around the Skr70 mark. The restaurant has also opened a more central **takeaway** venue, downstairs at Södergatan 22.

Guests at the STF hostel don't need to travel too far for a meal and drink – **Pub Vagabond** (☎ 191882; Jöns Risbergsgatan 8; meals Skr40-105) is next door. This simple neighbourhood krog serves light pub meals such as chicken wings and hamburgers, or big and hearty meat and fish main courses. Vegetarians will struggle.

The cheap and cheerful **La Empanada** (☎ 120262; Själbodgatan 10), opposite Sankt Petri Kyrka, is highly recommended for budget travellers. It has an extensive menu of mainly Mexican dishes served cafeteria-style; tacos, enchiladas and burritos cost Skr30 to Skr40. It's open 10am to 7pm Monday to Saturday.

For a light meal, or if you're on a budget, your best bet is to head to **Saluhallen**, the covered food market at one corner of Lilla Torg, with an excellent range of food stalls offering something to appeal to every taste, including fish, pasta, sushi, kebabs, Chinese dishes and baked potatoes. **Bageri Caféet** (☎ 305313), inside Saluhallen, does filled bagels, baguettes and ciabattas from Skr20. Nearby, **Yasso** (☎ 121272; Izak Slaktaregatan 6; dinner mains Skr100-150) serves up authentic Greek favourites like moussaka, souvlaki and calamari, plus lunch for Skr58 and a range of mezes (small appetiser dishes) from Skr30.

Self-caterers can buy supplies near Cyberspace Café at the central **Mästerlivs supermarket** (Engelbrektsgatan), opposite the Comfort Hotel Temperance and open

9am to 9pm daily. The best **produce market** is on Möllevångstorget, from Monday to Saturday. **Systembolaget** *(Södergatan 22)* sells beers, wines and spirits.

Entertainment

Malmö has an excellent array of nightlife venues – for up-to-date information pick up a local newspaper or listings mag *Dygnet Runt*, which covers venues in Lund as well as Malmö. It's all in Swedish but the club and cinema information should be easy to understand. Alternatively, take the train across to Copenhagen for a huge selection of capital-city delights; trains run every 20 minutes until around 11pm, then hourly until 5am.

Pubs & Clubs For evening diversions, head to Lilla Torg or Möllevångstorget and take your pick of bars. On Lilla Torg, **Victors** *(☎ 127670)*, **Moosehead** *(☎ 120423)* and **Mello Yello** *(☎ 304525)* stand side by side and compete for custom; all are popular and offer outdoor seating and meals.

Möllevångstorget and its surrounds probably appeal more to the arty and studenty crowd. **Nyhavn** *(☎ 128830)* is the drinking spot of choice, and offers reasonably priced meals to go along with the beer, but there are numerous other places located in the vicinity. **Skolgatans Ölkafe** *(☎ 301066; Södra Skolgatan 43; open until 1am daily)* has friendly staff, lots of beer choices and good snacks. It's a café by day and very popular evening drinking establishment. **Jeriko** *(☎ 103020; Spångatan 38)* is another good option, with regular performances of jazz, folk and world music.

Kulturbolaget *(☎ 302011; Bergsgatan 18)* continues to attract some big-name live-music acts, but it's still a good choice if there's no live music – there's a bar and nightclubs with DJs, as well as a highly regarded restaurant. Among other popular clubs are the central, more mainstream **Étage** *(☎ 302089; Stortorget 6; open Mon-Sat)*, with two dance floors (one of them playing classics and the other playing dance music) and four bars; plus the massive (8500 sq m) 'entertainment complex' **Slagthuset** *(☎ 71112; Jörgen Kocksgatan 7A)*, north of the train station. There are both restaurants and bars here, and a nightclub that is open from midnight to 5am on Friday and Saturday nights.

Note that minimum age requirements vary from venue to venue and depend also on the night of the week – it could be anything from 20 to 25, so bring ID. Entry usually costs between Skr50 and Skr100.

Cinema There are a number of cinemas located in the city centre, including **Filmstaden Malmö** *(☎ 660 2090; Storgatan 22)*, showing Hollywood movies, as well as **Biograf Spegeln** *(☎ 125978; Stortorget 29)*, hosting more alternative selections.

Getting There & Away

Air There are up to eight nonstop **SAS** *(☎ 020 727000)* flights to Stockholm Arlanda daily from **Sturup airport** *(☎ 613 1000)*, 33km southeast of the city. SAS also flies direct to Örebro and Västerås on weekdays. **Malmö Aviation** *(☎ 020 550010;* W *www.malmoaviation.se)* flies a number of times daily to Stockholm Bromma airport, and **GoodJet** *(☎ 031-708 9000;* W *www.goodjet.com)* offers a regular no-frills service to Stockholm Arlanda, as well as daily flights from Sturup to Paris.

The low-cost carrier **Ryanair** *(☎ 0870-156 9569;* W *www.ryanair.com)* flies to Sturup from the UK (London's Stansted airport). Trains run directly from Malmö to Copenhagen's main airport (Skr80), which has a much better international flight selection.

Bus The *länstrafik* operates in zones, with costs ranging from Skr14 within the city of Malmö to a maximum of Skr82 within the county. The local trains are your best bet for travel to/from the major towns in Skåne; buses are a good option for those towns and out-of-the-way areas not on the train lines. Bus No 146 is a useful service to the ferries departing Trelleborg; this service runs once or twice an hour. Another useful service is bus No 100 to Falsterbo.

Regional and long-distance buses depart from Stormgatan, opposite the central post office (behind the train station), and the **Busscentralen** *(☎ 431670)* office there handles inquiries and sells tickets. **Swebus Express** *(☎ 0200 218218;* W *www.swebusexpress.se)* runs two to four times daily to Stockholm (Skr435, 9¼ hours) via Jönköping (Skr250, 4½ hours) and five times daily to Gothenburg (Skr260, four hours). Three times daily there's a service to Oslo (Skr350, 7½ hours), via Gothenburg. **Svenska Buss** *(☎ 0771-676767;* W *www.svenskabuss.se)* services to

Bridging the Gap

For over 100 years, the people of Skåne wondered about a bridge to Denmark and the economic stimulation this could bring to the region. Recent advances in engineering made possible what seemed very unlikely not so long ago; construction on the Öresund bridge and tunnel began in October 1995 and the route opened to traffic in summer 2000. The new bridges and tunnels between the Danish islands and Jutland mean that you're now able to drive all the way from Sweden to Germany without using a ferry.

The Öresund bridge is the longest cable-stayed bridge in the world for both road and rail traffic and measures 7.8km from Lernacken (on the Swedish side, near Malmö) to the artificial island Peberholm, south of Saltholm. The artificial island is 4km long, then there's a 3km undersea tunnel which emerges just north of Copenhagen airport. This tunnel is the longest combined road/rail tunnel in the world. The bridge is a two-tier structure with a two-way railway on the lower deck and a four-lane motorway on the upper deck. At its highest, clearance above water level is 57m and the bridge has been designed not to obstruct the flow of water in Öresund.

While most of the local commuters pay tolls via an electronic transmitter, tolls for the rest of us are payable by credit card, debit card or in Danish and Swedish currency at the Lernacken toll booths. There has been some controversy over the high prices of the tolls and lower-than-expected traffic figures. The crossing certainly isn't cheap – for a motorcycle the price is Skr150, private vehicles (up to 6m) pay Skr275 and private vehicles with trailers, vans or minibuses cost Skr650. If you're travelling between Sweden and Denmark with your own transport, it might pay you to look at other options (such as ferries between Helsingborg and Helsingør).

Stockholm (Skr360, 10 hours) via Växjö (Skr190, three hours) depart four times weekly (only Friday and Saturday). Svenska Buss also runs a daily service to Gothenburg (Skr200, four hours) via Halmstad. Four times a week there is a coastal service to Stockholm via Kristianstad, Karlskrona, Kalmar and Oskarshamn.

There are a few buses heading across the Öresund bridge, but trains are obviously the best option for journeys to Copenhagen and beyond.

Train *Pågatågen* trains run to Helsingborg (Skr82), Lund (Skr34), Ystad (Skr70), Landskrona (Skr70), Simrishamn (Skr82) and other destinations in Skåne (bicycles are half-fare, but are not allowed during peak times, except during mid-June to mid-August). The platform is at the end of Centralstationen and you buy tickets from the machine. International rail passes are accepted.

SJ runs regularly to/from Gothenburg (Skr371, 3½ hours) via Lund. Direct X2000 trains run between Stockholm and Malmö (Skr946, 4½ hours); Intercity trains run much less frequently and take longer (6½ hours), but cost considerably less (Skr551).

There's a new and integrated Öresundregionen transport system which operates trains from Helsingborg via Malmö and Copenhagen to Helsingør. The Malmö to Copenhagen Kastrup airport or Copenhagen central station trips takes around 20 or 35 minutes, respectively (both journeys Skr80); trains leave every 20 minutes.

At Centralstationen you can shower for Skr20 and rest rooms cost Skr15 per hour (Skr25 per hour with shower included).

Car & Motorcycle The E6 motorway runs north-south through the eastern and southern suburbs of Malmö on its way from Gothenburg to Trelleborg. The E65 highway runs east to Ystad, the E22 runs northeast to Lund and Kristianstad, and the E20 goes west across the Öresund bridge to Copenhagen and north (with the E6) to Gothenburg.

Car hire is available at **Statoil** (*☎ 129950*), in Börsethuset directly opposite Centralstationen. You can also hire a car at Sturup airport; contact **Avis** (*☎ 500515*) for further details.

Boat The boats that once plied Öresund between Malmö and Copenhagen have all ceased to operate; the bridge and excellent train connections between the two cities have rendered them obsolete.

SKÅNE

Getting Around

The regular **Flygbuss** (☎ 020 567567) runs from Centralstationen to Sturup airport (Skr80), roughly hourly on weekdays and Sunday, less frequently on Saturday; a taxi should cost no more than Skr350.

Malmö Lokaltrafik (☎ 020 567567) offices are at Gustav Adolfs Torg and Värnhemstorget (at the eastern end of Kungsgatan). Local tickets are Skr14 for one hour's travel. The bus hubs are Centralplan (in front of Centralstationen), Gustav Adolfs Torg, Värnhemstorget and Triangeln. The Malmökortet card includes city bus travel.

Car parking in the city is expensive. Typically, multistorey parking houses charge around Skr12 per hour or Skr80 per day (24 hours). Most hotels also charge for parking.

Taxi companies (☎ 232323, ☎ 979797) in Malmö are known to rip off unsuspecting tourists and you're advised to avoid them if you can. Don't get into any taxi without arranging a fare with the driver in advance.

Bicycles can be rented for Skr120/600 per day/week from **Cykelkliniken** (☎ 611 6666; Carlsgatan), behind Centralstationen.

LUND

☎ 046 • pop 99,600

The second-oldest town in Sweden, Lund was founded by the Danes around 1000. Construction of the cathedral began about 1100 and Lund became the seat of the largest archbishopric in Europe. Much of the medieval town which surrounded the cathedral, with cobbled streets and quaint old houses, can still be seen. The university was founded in 1666, only eight years after Sweden took over Skåne. In 1676, invading Danes were routed at the Battle of Lund. Today, Lund retains its quiet yet airy campus feel and has a youthful population, including some 35,000 students. In summer, when the tourist buses visit, it's a much quieter place with the students on vacation.

Information

The friendly **tourist office** (☎ 355040; e tur istbyran@lund.se, w www.lund.se; Kyrkogatan 11; open 10am-6pm Mon-Fri, 10am-2pm Sat & Sun June-Aug; Mon-Sat May & Sept; Mon-Fri Oct-Apr) is opposite the cathedral.

There's a **Forex** (Bangatan 8; open Mon-Sat) in town and banks can be found along the main street (north of Stortorget this is

called Kyrkogatan, south of Stortorget it's Stora Södergatan). The large **public library** (Sankt Petri Kyrkogatan 6; open 10am-7pm Mon-Thur, 10am-6pm Fri, 10am-3pm Sat) has free Internet access, or you can try the nearby Internet café, **Nine** (☎ 700096; Lilla Gråbrödersgatan 2), charging around Skr50 for an hour online and open until at least 11pm nightly. **Press Stop** (Klostergatan 8) is the place to go for foreign magazines.

You can read about the **university** (W www.lu.se) online, and if you understand Swedish, W www.lund.cc is a good Internet site about the town.

Things to See

The magnificence of Lund's Romanesque cathedral, **Domkyrkan** (☎ 358700; open 8am-6pm Mon-Fri, 9.30am-5pm Sat, 9.30am-6pm Sun), with its impressive twin towers, is well known. However, for a real surprise, visit at noon or 3pm (1pm and 3pm on Sunday and holidays) when the astronomical clock strikes up In Dulci Jubilo and the figures of the three kings begin their journey to the child Jesus. Within the crypt, you can find Finn, the mythological giant who helped construct the cathedral.

The main university building, which faces Sandgatan, is worth a glance inside and Scanian **rune stones** are arranged in the park nearby.

The 8-hectare **Botanical Gardens** (Östra Vallgatan 20; admission free; open 6am-9.30pm mid-May–mid-Sept, 6am-8pm rest of year), east of the town centre, feature around 7000 species. Also on the site are tropical **greenhouses** (admission free; open noon-3pm daily).

Take a look in the charming old-style pharmacy, **Apoteket Svanen** (Kyrkogatan 5), not far from the tourist office.

Museums The excellent **Kulturen** (☎ 350 400; W www.kulturen.com; Tegnerplatsen; adult/child Skr50/free; open 11am-5pm daily mid-Apr–Sept; noon-4pm Tues-Sun Oct–Apr) claims to be the world's second oldest open-air museum (it opened in 1892). Its impressive collection of about 40 buildings fills two blocks and includes period homes from the 17th century and countless displays. Ask about guided tours in English. There's a popular outdoor restaurant here, and nearby **Hökeriet** (☎ 350404; cnr St Annegatan &

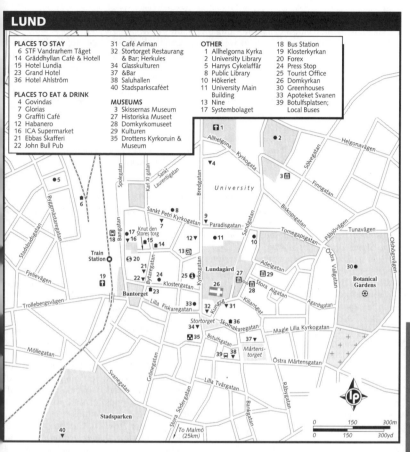

LUND

PLACES TO STAY
6 STF Vandrarhem Tåget
14 Gräddhyllan Café & Hotell
15 Hotel Lundia
23 Grand Hotel
36 Hotel Ahlström

PLACES TO EAT & DRINK
4 Govindas
7 Glorias
9 Graffiti Café
12 Habanero
16 ICA Supermarket
21 Ebbas Skafferi
22 John Bull Pub

31 Café Ariman
32 Stortorget Restaurang
& Bar; Herkules
34 Glasskulturen
37 &Bar
38 Saluhallen
40 Stadsparkscaféet

MUSEUMS
3 Skissernas Museum
27 Historiska Museet
28 Domkyrkomuseet
29 Kulturen
35 Drottens Kyrkoruin &
Museum

OTHER
1 Allhelgorna Kyrka
2 University Library
5 Harrys Cykelaffär
8 Public Library
10 Hökeriet
11 University Main
Building
13 Nine
17 Systembolaget

18 Bus Station
19 Klosterkyrkan
20 Forex
24 Press Stop
25 Tourist Office
26 Domkyrkan
30 Greenhouses
33 Apoteket Svanen
39 Botulfsplatsen;
Local Buses

Tomegapsgatan; open daily June-Aug, Mon-Sat Sept-May), an old-fashioned general store, is worth a look.

Just behind the cathedral you can find out all you need to know about the cathedral's history in **Domkyrkomuseet** *(☎ 222 7944; Kraftstorg)*. The attached **Historiska Museet** has a large collection of pre–Viking Age finds, including a 7000-year-old skeleton. Both museums are open 11am-4pm Tuesday to Friday (combined entry Skr20/free).

On Kattesund, you can see **Drottens Kyrkoruin**, 11th-century church ruins; the **underground museum** *(☎ 141328; Kattesund 6; adult/child Skr10/free; open 9am-4pm Tues-Fri, noon-4pm Sat & Sun)* here has models and exhibits that fill in the details of Lund's past.

There are a number of galleries, plus small, special-interest museums and archives in town, many attached to university departments. Inquire at the tourist office. The **Skissernas Museum** *(Sketch Museum; ☎ 222 7283; Finngatan 2)* has an extensive collection of sketches and designs of public decorative art in Sweden and abroad. It was closed for renovation and enlargement at the time of research and is due to reopen sometime in 2004.

Places to Stay

You could easily keep Lund as a base and take trains to nearby towns if you stay at the central **STF Vandrarhem Tåget** *(☎ 142820; e trainhostel@ebrevet.nu; beds Skr120)*, behind the station (connected by overpass).

You sleep in old railway carriages set in parkland, with three bunks to a room – quiet yet tiny and perhaps too familiar to weary train travellers.

Private rooms can be booked at the tourist office from Skr200 per person plus a Skr50 fee.

Book early for tiny **Gräddhyllan Café & Hotell** *(☎ 157230; e graddhyllans@swipnet .se; Bytaregatan 14; singles/doubles Skr495/ 795, discounted to Skr400/600)*, a lovely place offering all of four rooms above a café.

Hotel Ahlström *(☎ 211 0174; Skomakaregatan 3; singles/doubles from Skr575/725, discounted to Skr525/625)* is a comfortable, central, mid-range option, but it's closed from Midsummer to mid-August.

Hotel Lundia *(☎ 280 6500; e info@lundia .se; Knut den Stores torg 2; singles/doubles from Skr960/1550, discounted to Skr795/ 995)* is a newly renovated place offering sleekly modern rooms and a downstairs brasserie in the centre of town.

Grand Hotel *(☎ 280 6100; e einfo@grand ilund.se; Bantorget 1; singles/doubles from Skr1440/1795, discounted to Skr950/1295)* is a centrally placed and rather luxurious establishment that opened in 1899. It too has an upmarket restaurant on site.

Places to Eat & Drink

Lund has plenty of eating possibilities, ranging from fast-food eateries and library cafés to popular evening hang-outs.

Grand Hotel *(☎ 280 6100; Bantorget 1; lunch Skr89, dinner mains Skr170-320)* has a refined restaurant with well-prepared, classic menu items like roast venison, wild duck breast and fillets of sole with lobster sauce; the wine selection is equally impressive. The *husmanskost* (home-style) lunch special is well priced.

Still relatively upmarket but a little more affordable, the cool **&Bar** *(☎ 211 2288; Mårtenstorget 9)* is a fashionable but relaxed place; lunchtime meals of bagels, salads and various specials cost from Skr45 to Skr65, à la carte dinner mains are Skr90 to Skr180. DJs play here of an evening and the place becomes a popular nightspot.

On Stortorget, **Stortorget Restaurang & Bar** *(☎ 139290; meals Skr80-170)* and its neighbour, **Herkules**, are heaving on sunny summer afternoons and evenings. Nearby is **Glasskulturen**, a gourmet ice-cream shop

that has long queues of customers on warm summer days.

Ebbas Skafferi *(☎ 134156; Bytaregatan 5)* is a delightful courtyard café well worth seeking out; there's an excellent lunchtime selection from Skr50, including quiche, risotto and crepes.

Funky **Cafe Ariman** *(☎ 131263; Kungsgatan 2B)* is one of the best cafés in town, with a great view of the cathedral, strong coffee and a fine array of café fare along the lines of ciabatta, salads and burritos.

Stadsparkcafeet *(☎ 211 4447; Stadsparken)* is an excellent place to spend a few hours; there's food, drink, games, and sometimes live music (Sundays in summer).

For more good-value lunches, head to **Habanero** *(☎ 211 0632; Kyrkogatan 21)*, perfect for an el-cheapo Tex-Mex fill (lunch is Skr59). **Govindas** *(☎ 120413; Bredgatan 28)* is full of earnest student types enjoying the vegetarian deal for Skr55. Nearby **Graffiti Café** *(☎ 211 3032; cnr Paradisgatan & Bredgatan)* has baked potatoes, salads and baguettes from Skr30.

Saluhallen *(Mårtenstorget)* is the spot for a variety of reasonably priced food, from pasta to croissants, hamburgers and kebabs.

John Bull Pub *(☎ 140920; Bantorget 2; meals Skr50-250)* is an English-style pub popular with expats; you can get a range of international beers, snacks, light meals (pasta, baked spuds) or traditional English pub food like fish and chips or steak. Drawing a younger crowd is **Glorias** *(☎ 151985; St Petri Kyrkogatan 9; burgers from Skr90)*, an often-rowdy, American-style sports bar serving somewhat pricey food, and hosting occasional live music.

Those self-caterering can stock up at the **ICA supermarket** *(Bangatan)* opposite the train station. The **Systembolaget** *(Bangatan 10)* is nearby.

Getting There & Away

It's just 15 minutes from Lund to Malmö by train and there are frequent SJ and *pågatågen* (local train) departures (Skr34). Some trains continue to Copenhagen; the journey from Lund to Copenhagen takes just under an hour and costs Skr100. Other direct services run from Malmö to Kristianstad and Karlskrona via Lund. All long-distance trains from Stockholm or Gothenburg to Malmö stop in Lund.

The regular **Flygbuss** (☎ 020 567567) runs to Sturup airport (Skr80).

Buses leave from outside the train station. Most long-distance buses to/from Malmö (except buses to Trelleborg and Falsterbo) run via Lund. See Getting There & Away in the Malmö section earlier for details.

Getting Around

Stadstrafiken Lund (☎ 355300) operates town buses for Skr10 per ride; the terminal for local buses is on Botulfsplatsen, west of Mårtenstorget. There's also **Taxi Skåne** (☎ 330330) for getting around. To hire a bike, try **Harrys Cykelaffär** (☎ 211 6946; Banvaktsgatan 2), west of the train station.

FALSTERBO PENINSULA
☎ 040

The Falsterbo Peninsula, 31km south of Malmö by road, is significant for its nature reserve and bird life, and for its popular beaches.

The area's major **tourist office** (☎ 425454; e turisten@vellinge.se, w www.vellinge.se /turism; Östra Hamnplan 2; open 9am-6pm Mon-Fri, 10am-4pm Sat & Sun mid-June–mid-Aug; closed weekends rest of year) is in Hollviken, next to a canal that cuts through the peninsula. Hollviken is a reasonable-sized town with facilities like banks and supermarkets.

Bärnstensmuseum

Near the southern edge of Höllviken (and just off the coast road to Trelleborg), the Bärnstensmuseum (Amber Museum; ☎ 454504; w www.brost.se; Södra Mariavägen 4; adult/child Skr10/5; open 10am-6pm daily mid-May–Aug, 11am-5pm Sat & Sun rest of year) is one of the most unusual attractions in the area with intriguing displays of insects, some up to 250 million years old, trapped and perfectly preserved in amber. The museum owner advised the film-makers of Jurassic Park on the insects of the period. There's also lots of information on local natural history, geology and archaeology.

Foteviken

Within sight of the 21st-century Öresund bridge and about 700m north of Höllviken, Fotevikens Vikingacenter (☎ 456840; w www /foteviken.se; adult/child Skr50/25; open 10am-4pm Mon-Fri mid-May–August, 10am-4pm Sat & Sun mid-June–mid-Aug) is unique and well worth a visit. It's an excellent 'living' reconstruction of a late–Viking Age village by the site of the Battle of Foteviken (1134), and you'll learn more here about Vikings and their way of life than you could ever glean from a history book. Entry price includes a highly recommended one-hour guided tour (available in English, German and Swedish); these depart at 1.30am, 1pm and 2.30pm.

This Viking 'reserve' is an amazing place with authentic reconstructions of Viking Age houses with reed or turf roofs (there were 16 at the time of research, more are planned), including the houses of a fisherman, weaver and blacksmith, as well as a fish smokehouse and a tannery. There are also the houses of the town's jarl (commander of the armed forces), juror and scribe. The chieftain's house has wooden floorboards, fleeces and a Battle of Foteviken tapestry. There's even a great hall (the Thinghöll) and a reconstructed warship. The amazing thing is that this reserve is the home of a group of people who live as Vikings did, eschewing most modern conveniences and following the traditions and laws of these historic folk – even after the last tourist has left! These modern-day Vikings (and the men really do look exactly as you would imagine, bearded and wild!) lead visitors on the guided tours and provide an insightful and entertaining glimpse into Viking times.

If you visit in early June you can witness Viking warrior training and a re-enactment of the 1134 battle; Viking Week is held in late June, and culminates in a Viking market.

There's a reasonable **hostel** (dorm beds Skr125) just outside the reserve for visitors. People belonging to Viking societies live as Vikings here – the website has more details.

Falsterbo

Falsterbo Museum (☎ 470513; Sjögatan; adult/child Skr20/10; open 10am-7pm daily mid-June–mid-Aug), at the southern tip of the peninsula, has an interesting local history collection, including the remains of a 12th-century boat. Nearby is **Falsterbo Fågelstation** (☎ 470688; Sjögatan), which looks after the bird life in the nature reserve, with over 50 species including little terns, Kentish plovers (rare in Sweden) and avocets. The sandy hook-shaped island

SKÅNE

Måkläppen is a strange feature and is growing in a westerly direction; it's a nature reserve that's off-limits to the public from February to October on account of the bird life and seal population during this time.

Falsterbo has a long sandy beach that's popular with locals and holiday-makers from Malmö and other surrounding towns. Catering to the fashionable city set is the stylish **Kust Café** (☎ 473830; Storgatan 14), with excellent coffee and light meals.

Getting There & Away
Bus No 100 runs every 30 minutes (hourly on Sunday) from Malmö to Falsterbo Strandbad (about 600m east of the Fågelstation) via Skanör and Höllviken.

TRELLEBORG
☎ 0410 • pop 38,600
Trelleborg is the main southern gateway between Sweden and Germany. It's a pleasant enough place and the summer display of palm trees is indicative of its (relatively) balmy climate, but if you're arriving in Sweden here, there's no reason to linger in town long – better to move on to Malmö or Ystad.

The **tourist office** (☎ 53322; e turist@ trelleborg.se, W www.trelleborg.se; Hamngatan 9; open 9am-7pm Mon-Fri, 9am-6pm Sat, 10am-6pm Sun mid-June–mid-Aug, 9am-5pm Mon-Fri rest of year) is in a newly renovated harbour-side complex.

Forex (CB Friisgatan 1; open Mon-Sat) is opposite the tourist office; banks and ATMs can be found near Forex and on Algatan. There's an **Internet café** (☎ 13800; Östergatan 12), but you can also access the Internet at the **public library** (CB Friisgatan 17-19), near Stortorget.

Things to See
Trelleborg's few medieval remnants are complemented by a re-creation of a 9th-century Viking fortress, **Trelleborgen** (☎ 46077; admission free; open daily) off Bryggaregatan and just west of the town centre. There are free guided tours 11am and 1pm June to August. Special events such as battle re-enactments and handicraft workshops are held on occasion.

Trelleborgs Museum (☎ 53050; Östergatan 58; adult/child Skr20/free; open 11am-5pm Tues-Sun June–mid-Aug, 1pm-5pm Tues-Sun mid-Aug–May), just east of the town centre,

is housed in an old hospital and covers a wide range of themes. Admission prices include the gallery Axel Ebbe Konsthall.

Just off Stortorget, the 58m-high **water tower** dates from 1912 and has a pleasant ground-floor café. The adjacent town park has music events in summer. By the town park, the **Axel Ebbe Konsthall** (☎ 53056, Hesekillegatan 1; adult/child Skr20/free; open 1pm-4pm Tues-Sun) is a Functionalist building featuring mostly nude sculptures by the native Scanian Axel Ebbe (1868–1941).

Places to Stay & Eat
Dalabadets Camping (☎ 14905; Dalköpinge Strandväg 2; tent sites Skr140, 4-bed cabins from Skr350) is the nearest camping ground, over 3km east. It's a well-equipped place between road No 9 and the beach.

If you need a central place to stay, the simple but functional **Night Stop** (☎ 41070, Östergatan 59; singles/doubles Skr199/299) is diagonally opposite the town museum, about 500m from the tourist office. Breakfast is an additional Skr40.

Hotel Prinz (☎ 713239; Hamngatan 9, singles/doubles Skr795/995) is a newly appointed hotel with good facilities located in the harbour-front building that also houses the tourist office. Beautiful **Dannegården** (☎ 48180; e office@dannegarden.se; Strandgatan 32; singles/doubles from Skr1092/1428 discounted to Skr644/868), near Trelleborgen is the most luxurious hotel in town and was once a sea captain's villa. The gardens and restaurant are excellent.

The bustling **Restaurang & Pizzeria Istanbul** (☎ 44444; Algatan 30; meals Skr60-150, has a huge menu with loads of inexpensive choices (Skr60 to Skr75), including pasta pizza, salad and kebabs, plus more expensive fish and meat dishes. For surroundings with a bit more character, **Värdshus Två Lejon** (☎ 19700; Gamla Torg 4; lunch Skr60, main Skr60-200) is the oldest inn in Trelleborg and has a decent menu of classic dishes. **Kapten Morris Pub** is just behind the restaurant here; it's a cosy place with a nautical atmosphere. **Pad Thai** (☎ 17899; Östergatan 8; lunch from Skr55, dishes from Skr70) serves up excellent Thai cuisine.

Getting There & Away
Bus No 146 runs every half-hour or so between Malmö and Trelleborg's bus station

some 500m inland from the ferry terminals (behind the town park and library). See Ystad for further bus information.

For details of international trains from Malmö to Berlin via Trelleborg, see the Germany section in the introductory Getting There & Away chapter.

There are two ferry terminals, both behind the tourist office. **Scandlines** (☎ 042-816100; W www.scandlines.se) ferries connect Trelleborg to Sassnitz (five daily) and Rostock (two or three daily). **TT-Line** (☎ 56200; W www.ttline.com) ferries and catamarans shuttle between Trelleborg and Travemünde three to five times daily, and between Trelleborg and Rostock up to three times daily; its ticket office is inside the building housing the tourist office at Hamngatan 9. See the introductory Getting There & Away chapter for full details.

SMYGEHUK
☎ 0410

The most southerly point in Sweden (latitude 55°20'), Smygehuk has become something of a tourist centre with shops, museums and exhibitions.

You can walk along the coast here and enjoy the views and prolific bird life, or admire the view from the top of the now-defunct lighthouse (17m), dating from 1883, and visit the tiny maritime museum located in **Captain Brinck's Cabin** (admission free), which keeps erratic hours but should be open daily in summer. On the other side of the little harbour, **Köpmansmagasinet** is a renovated 19th-century warehouse with local exhibitions of handicrafts and art. There's also a summer **tourist office** (☎ 24053) in the building, and a café. Ask for details of summer activities here, including art exhibitions, music festivals and folk dancing. Near Köpmansmagasinet, there's a huge 19th-century **lime kiln**, evidence of the bygone lime industry; it closed in 1954.

STF Vandrarhem Smygehuk (☎ 24583; e info@smygehukhostel.com; dorm beds Skr130; open Feb-Nov) is a comfortable, well-equipped hostel in the old lighthouse keeper's residence, next to the lighthouse. You must book beforehand outside of the high season (mid-May to mid-September).

There are a few eating options at the harbour, including a kiosk serving fast food (burgers, kebabs) and waffles, and a fish

smokehouse. The closest food shops are about a kilometre away.

Smygehuk is between Ystad and Trelleborg on the pleasant coastal road No 9. The Trelleborg to Ystad bus service will take you to Smygehuk (see Ystad).

YSTAD
☎ 0411 • pop 26,200

Rambling cobbled streets and more than 300 half-timbered houses remain in this very picturesque medieval town, which was Sweden's window to Europe from 1658 to the mid-19th century. Many new ideas and inventions arrived here first, including the first car, bank and hotel. Now the town is a terminal for ferries to Bornholm and Poland and there's no shortage of interesting museums and sights in the town and surrounds, so it's worth staying for a day or two.

Orientation & Information

Ystad has a compact historical central area next to the ferry terminals. The bus and train stations are by the harbour, between the centre and the ferries.

The friendly **tourist office** (☎ 577681; e turistinfo@ystad.se, W www.visitystad.com; St Knuts Torg; open 9am-7pm Mon-Fri, 10am-7pm Sat, 11am-6pm Sun mid-June–mid-Aug; 9am-5pm Mon-Fri rest of year, & 11am-2pm Sat mid-May–mid-June & late Aug), just opposite the train station, provides a good town map and excellent free booklets covering the town and surrounds.

You can change money at **Forex** in both ferry terminals. Banks, ATMs and other services are along Hamngatan. The **town library** (Surbrunnsvägen 12), just north of the centre, has free Internet access.

Things to See

There are plenty of half-timbered houses around town, especially on Stora Östergatan. Most are from the latter half of the 18th century, but the facade of the beautiful **Änglahuset** on Stora Norregatan dates from around 1630.

Don't miss the **Sankta Maria Kyrka** (Stortorget; open 10am-6pm daily June-Aug, 10am-4pm daily Sept-May). Part of the church dates from the 13th century and it houses a baroque pulpit carved in the 1620s and an altarpiece completed in 1733. The church clock-tower has a little window

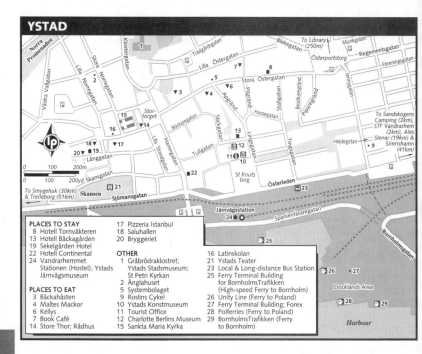

YSTAD

through which the night watchman traditionally has blown his horn (since around
1250) every 15 minutes from 9pm to 3am;
the watchman was traditionally beheaded if
he fell asleep! **Latinskolan**, next to the
Sankta Maria Kyrka, is a late-15th-century
brick building and is the oldest preserved
school in Scandinavia (it closed in 1841).

Ystads Stadsmuseum *(☎ 577286; St Petri
Kyrkoplan; adult/child Skr20/free; open noon-
5pm Mon-Fri, noon-4pm Sat & Sun)*, in the old
Franciscan monastery of **Gråbrödraklostret**,
features local textiles and silverware, and
there's a slide show. The monastery includes
St Petri Kyrkan, with a central nave from
1267 and around 80 gravestones from the
14th to 18th centuries.

Next door to the tourist office is the large
Ystads Konstmuseum *(☎ 577285; adult/
child Skr20/free; open noon-5pm Tues-Fri,
noon-4pm Sat & Sun)*, with a substantial collection of southern Swedish and Danish art.
The late-19th-century home and garden
Charlotte Berlins Museum *(☎ 18866; Dammgatan 23; adult/child Skr10/free; open noon-
5pm Tues-Fri, noon-4pm Sat & Sun June-Aug)*
is just behind Konstmuseum.

Any model railway enthusiasts will enjoy
Ystads Järnvägsmuseum *(☎ 10169; open
11am-7pm Mon-Fri, 1pm-5pm Sun mid-
June–mid-Aug; 11am-5pm Mon-Fri rest of
year)*, at the train station. It also features historic items from the local railway.

Places to Stay

Those with their own wheels can choose
between B&B and cabin options along the
scenic coastal roads on either side of Ystad.
The tourist office can arrange B&B from
Skr150 per person (plus a Skr30 to
Skr40 fee).

Sandskogens Camping *(☎ 19270; e sand
skogens.camping@telia.com; low/high season
tent sites Skr100/130, cabins from Skr330/
390; open mid-April–mid-Sept)* is a large
wooded ground 2km east of Ystad on road
No 9 to Simrishamn, across the road from
the beach and STF hostel. Bus No 572
drives past from town. The pleasant beachside **STF Vandrarhem** *(☎ 66566; Kantarellen;
dorm beds Skr135; open year-round)* has
good facilities for travellers, including bike
rental for covering the 2km into the town
centre.

The conveniently located **Vandrarhemmet Stationen** (☎ 0708-577995; e ystad.stationen@ home.se; dorm beds Skr180) is a central SVIF hostel in the old but renovated railway building at Ystad train station.

There are some really lovely accommodation options in town, with hotels and guesthouses full of history and character. **Hotell Bäckagården** (☎ 19848; Dammgatan 36; singles/doubles from Skr450/625) is a cosy guesthouse in a pretty 17th-century home one block behind the tourist office, and **Hotell Tornväkteren** (☎ 78480; Stora Östergatan 33), above a café on the main street, has similar prices.

Sekelgården Hotel (☎ 73900; e anno .1793.sekelgarden@swipnet.se; Långgatan 18; singles/doubles from Skr695/895) is a family-run hotel in a magnificent half-timbered house (1793) with a very nice courtyard and pleasantly decorated rooms.

Hotell Continental (☎ 13700; e info@ hotelcontinental-ystad.se; Hamngatan 13; singles/doubles from Skr840/940, discounted to Skr690/790) claims to be Sweden's oldest hotel (it opened in 1829). It's full of old-world charm, with a rather grand lobby dominated by chandeliers, leadlight and a marble staircase. Rooms are modern and comfortable.

Places to Eat

For an upmarket treat, classy **Store Thor** (☎ 18510; Stortorget; dinner mains Skr95-185) is an amazing place in the atmospheric arched cellar of the old rådhus (town hall; 1572). The cellar wasn't uncovered again until the 1930s, and it's the oldest licensed cellar in Sweden. The decor, food and service are excellent; there are light meals such as spicy chicken and fetta salad or a gourmet burger, or a selection of grilled meats with a variety of sauces and accompaniments.

Another good recommendation is the unique **Bryggeriet** (☎ 69999; Långgatan 20; lunch Skr65, mains Skr95-195), a relaxed restaurant and pub in an old brewery. The sunny courtyard is an excellent spot to linger over a well-prepared meal and Ysta Färsköl, a beer brewed on the premises.

Kellys (☎ 12370; Stora Östergatan 18; lunch Skr57, dinner mains Skr85-98) has an excellent international menu, main courses include fish, steaks and curries, with the added bonus of no dish over Skr100.

Pizzeria Istanbul (☎ 16515; Stortorget 15; pizzas around Skr60) has a good menu of pizzas and grilled dishes, plus a great position by the main square.

There are some lovely cafés in among Ystad's beautiful old buildings; **Bäckahästen** (☎ 14000; Lilla Östergatan 6) is an inviting place in a half-timbered house, with lots of garden seating. Food on offer includes sandwiches and baguettes for Skr40 to Skr50, and light meals like salads and pastas for Skr64 to Skr74. The charming **Book Café** (☎ 151712; Gåsegränd) is well worth seeking out: inside is an inviting living room full of mismatched old furniture and books to peruse; outside there's a delightful courtyard. There's good foccacia, pastries and coffee on offer.

Most budget eating places are on Stora Östergatan, the main pedestrian street. Busy **Maltes Mackor** (☎ 10130; Stora Östergatan 12) has a great range of sandwiches and rolls for Skr26 to Skr46.

The **Saluhallen** (Stora Västergatan; open 8am-9pm daily), behind the church, is a great central place to stock up on groceries. For alcohol, head to **Systembolaget** (Stora Östergatan 13).

Entertainment

The extraordinary **Ystads Teater** (☎ 577199; Skansgatan; tickets around Skr300) has remained virtually unchanged since opening in 1894 and unusual operas are performed here in late June and July, and also in September and October. Contact the tourist office for details.

Getting There & Away

Bus In Ystad, buses depart from outside the train station. To get to Trelleborg by bus, first take bus No 303 to Skateholm then transfer to bus No 183. The direct bus to Simrishamn via Löderup and Skillinge (No 572) runs three to nine times daily. Bus No 322 to Skillinge runs via Ales Stenar and Löderups Strandbad three times daily in summer; at other times take bus No 392, which runs twice daily Monday to Friday only.

SkåneExpressen bus No 6 runs hourly to Lund (infrequently on weekends) and bus No 4 runs three to nine times daily to Kristianstad. Local train is the best way to get to Malmö.

Train There are *pågatågen* trains running roughly every hour (fewer on weekends) to/from Malmö (Skr70), and some continue to Copenhagen (Skr120). Other local trains run up to six times daily to Simrishamn (Skr34).

Boat There are daily crossings between Ystad and Swinoujscie by **Unity Line** (☎ 556900; W *www.unityline.pl)* and **Polferries** (☎ 040-121700; W *www.polferries.se)*. The ferry terminal in Ystad is within walking distance of the train station (drivers must follow a more circuitous route).

There are frequent ferries and catamarans also running between Ystad and the Danish island of Bornholm; these are operated by **BornholmsTrafikken** (☎ 558700; W *www .bornholmferries.dk)*. Catamarans depart at and arrive from a new terminal directly behind the train station.

See the Getting There & Away chapter for more details on these ferry services.

Getting Around
There are a handful of local bus services and all depart from outside the tourist office (St Knuts Torg). Try **Taxi Ystad** (☎ 72000) for a taxi. For bike hire, contact **Roslins Cykel** (☎ 12315; *Jennygatan 11)*; prices start at Skr40/195 per day/week.

AROUND YSTAD
Ales Stenar
One of Skåne's most intriguing attractions is Ales Stenar, in the middle of a field and perched on a ridge 19km east of Ystad at Kåseberga. It's a mysterious stone ship setting, probably constructed in the Migration Period, around AD 500 or 600. The stones form an oval 67m along the long axis, with the largest stone (3.3m) at the stern. The ends of the oval point northwest (towards sunset in midsummer) and southeast (towards sunrise in midwinter).

The area can be very touristy in the middle of the day and it's best to avoid the chaotic car park at the Kåseberga harbour – drivers should use the car park just off the main road. Down at the harbour, there are several fish smokeries, including **Kåseberga Fisk**, serving bizarre herring burgers and eelburgers (yum!), plus lots of other fishy products.

Ales Stenar is always open and admission is free. Take bus No 322 from Ystad, which runs three times daily in summer; at

other times, this area is not particularly well served by public transport – bus No 392 runs twice daily on weekdays only.

Löderups Strandbad
☎ 0411
The Baltic resort of Löderups Strandbad, 4km east of Ales Stenar, with its long stretches of white sand beaches, is a decent place to hang out as long as the Swedish schools aren't on holiday.

Dag Hammarskjölds Hus (☎ 526611; *Backåkra; adult/child Skr30/free; open noon-5pm daily June-Aug)*, about 1km east of Löderups Strandbad, and previously a small farmhouse, was rebuilt in 1957 as the summer house for the secretary-general of the UN. Hammarskjöld was killed in a mysterious plane crash in Zambia in 1961 and many of his interesting and unusual belongings and souvenirs were subsequently moved here. The house is now a museum managed by STF.

Löderups Strandbads Camping (☎ 526311; *tent sites Skr130, cabins from Skr450; open Apr-Sept)*, on the edge of the Hagestad Nature Reserve, is a pleasant spot in a pine forest and next to the beach.

STF Vandrarhem Backåkra (☎ 526080; e *backakra.vandrarhem@swipnet.se; dorm beds Skr90-140; open June-Aug)*, beside the main road, is a well-equipped hostel that is popular with groups; it's worth phoning ahead to book.

Near the camping ground is **Löderups Srandbad Hotell** (☎ 526260; *singles/doubles Skr410/595, with bath Skr515/740)* is popular in summer, and also offers cabins sleeping up to six (Skr920 per night, or available weekly). There's a restaurant and pool here too.

The earlier Ystad section has bus details.

ÖSTERLEN
☎ 0414 • pop 19,400
Österlen is a part of Skåne unfortunately often overlooked by travellers. Artists appreciate the soft light of Österlen and have moved into the area en masse; the area is noted for apple orchards, good restaurants and its many art galleries and is well worth exploring if you want a taste of the Swedish countryside. If you don't have a car, the best base for the area is Simrishamn, although pretty Kivik also has a few good options.

Ales Stenar near Ystad, Skåne

Walpurgis bonfire, Skåne

Winter in Skåne: the relatively mild climate seldom allows the snow to stay for long

The Viking market, Skåne

An idyllic retreat in Skåne

Viking sculpture, Skåne

Scaling the heights at Kullaberg Nature Reserve, Skåne

Fishing off the rocks at sunset, Skåne

Rådhuset, the city hall, on Stortorget square, Malmö, Skåne

Dag Hammarskjöld

Dag Hammarskjöld (1905–61), one of Sweden's greatest statesmen, was secretary-general of the United Nations from 1953 to 1961 when he died in a plane crash. His nonconfrontational diplomatic style served the UN well and successful missions included Beijing (1955) and the Middle East (1956 and 1958). Hammarskjöld helped set up the UN emergency force that intervened in Egypt during the 1956 Suez crisis and the UN observation forces that were sent to Laos and Lebanon. Hammarskjöld was posthumously awarded the 1961 Nobel Peace Prize.

The son of Hjalmar Hammarskjöld, a former prime minister, Dag was educated at the universities of Uppsala and Stockholm and was awarded a PhD in 1934. Hammarskjöld entered government service in 1930 and served as chairman of the board of the Bank of Sweden (1941–48), performed many diplomatic missions and entered the Swedish cabinet as deputy foreign minister in 1951.

Always keen on mountaineering and the outdoor life, he was elected vice chairman of Svenska Turistföreningen (STF) in 1951 and held the position until his untimely death.

From 1951, Hammarskjöld also served in the Swedish delegation to the UN. In 1953, he was elected to the post of secretary-general and was re-elected four years later. Hammarskjöld greatly boosted the prestige of his position and the influence of the UN in general.

His close involvement with the UN's intervention in the Republic of the Congo (opposing the Soviet Union) proved unwise and he was killed when his plane crashed while on a mission in Northern Rhodesia (now Zambia) on 18 September 1961.

Simrishamn

This attractive small town has little of the bustle of Malmö, but the harbour can be busy. The rather quaint pastel-coloured houses on **Lilla Norregatan** are worth a look, as is the nearby **St Nikolai Kyrka**.

The **tourist office** (☎ 819800; e info@tur istbyra.simrishamn.se, w www.turistbyra.sim rishamn.se; Tullhusgatan 2; open 9am-8pm Mon-Fri, 10am-8pm Sat, 11am-8pm Sun June–mid-Aug; 9am-5pm Mon-Fri rest of year) has all the latest details on exhibitions at the local galleries and information about theatre and music performances in the region (daily during July). Ask at the tourist office for details of the many small local museums (none of them are particularly notable). Banks and other services are along Storgatan.

Places to Stay & Eat By the beach 2km north of the town centre, **Tobisviks Camping** (☎ 412778; tent sites Skr60-175, cabins Skr500-600) is open year-round (prices vary depending on season).

The brand-new **STF Vandrarhem** (☎ 10540; Christian Barnekowsgatan 10C; dorm beds Skr190; open year-round) is quite well-hidden, near the town hospital (pick up a map before setting off!). It's worth seeking out, however; it offers spotless, colourful, modern accommodation with excellent facilities, including bathroom facilities in each room. Breakfast is available for an additional Skr50.

Maritim Krog & Hotell (☎ 411360; e info@maritim.nu; Hamngatan 31; singles/ doubles from Skr850/950), the old blue building by the harbour, is a wonderful boutique hotel with very stylish decor (ask for the Herring Room, the pick of the rooms, which has a balcony and views of the harbour). Also on the premises is an excellent restaurant (lunch Skr75, dinner mains Skr150 to Skr210), not surprisingly specialising in creative and carefully prepared fish dishes.

There are a number of fast-food kiosks and eateries at the harbour-front, as well as bakeries and cafés on Storgatan. The hip **Hökarns Krog & Cafe** (☎ 14348; Storgatan 3; dinner mains Skr165-185) serves ecologically sound meals with French flair and occasionally has live jazz evenings.

Getting There & Around SkåneExpressen bus No 3 runs every hour or two on weekdays (infrequently on weekends) from Simrishamn (train station) to Kristianstad via Baskemölla and Kivik (but it doesn't stop at the Stenshuvud National Park access road). See also the section on Ystad.

Österlenfågeln is a minibus service that departs from the train station for local destinations (including Kivik, Glimmingehus and Skillinge) every hour or two between

SKÅNE

9am and midnight, in July only (Skr20 for a single trip, or Skr60 for a day pass).

Local trains run every two or three hours from Simrishamn to Ystad, with connections from Ystad on to Malmö, and farther to Lund and Copenhagen.

Try **Taxi Österlen** (☎ *17777*) for assistance in getting around the area. **Österlens Cykel & Motor** (☎ *17744; Stenbocksgatan*), by the train station, rents bikes from Skr50 per day. This area is ideal for exploration by bike.

Skillinge & Glimmingehus

South of Simrishamn is Skillinge, still a reasonably active fishing village and home to a tiny **marine museum**, but the main attraction in the area is the imposing, five-storey castle **Glimmingehus** (☎ *18620; adult/child Skr50/30; open 10am-6pm daily June–mid-Sept, 11am-5pm daily May & late Sept*), about 5km inland. The castle was completed in 1499 on the orders of a Danish admiral and is amazingly well preserved. It has a deep moat all around, a basement kitchen with a well, and 11 different ghosts! Thatched reconstructions of outhouses lie next to the castle. Guided tours in English are at 2pm daily from June to mid-September. There's a restaurant-café on the premises (the lunch special is Skr80). From mid-June to mid-August there's a programme of events here, including a medieval festival, guided ghost tours, musical performances and even overnight stays.

Pretty **Sjöbacka** (☎ *30166;* e *info@sjo backa.nu; doubles from Skr640*) is 700m west of Skillinge and offers B&B in a traditional Scanian farmhouse. There are two good restaurants in Skillinge, and a fish smokehouse.

For bus information see the sections on Ystad and Simrishamn.

Kivik

Small and sleepy Kivik, north of Simrishamn, is the heart of this apple-growing region and has a few attractions and good budget accommodation options.

Kivikgraven (☎ *70337; adult/child Skr10/5; open 10am-6pm mid-May–mid-Aug*) is an extraordinary low, shield-like cairn about 75m in diameter which is Sweden's most important Bronze Age site. It contained a burial cist from around 1000 BC and eight engraved slabs, but it was looted in 1748 (and later).

All but one slab have now been traced. Replicas are now in place in the tomb. An informative booklet is available for Skr25.

A few (signposted) kilometres down the road, **Kiviks Musteri** (☎ *71900;* w *www .kiviksmusteri.se; open daily Apr-Sept*) is quite unique – it's an apple orchard open to the public with a restaurant, well-stocked shop (selling the cider produced here, among other apple-related products) and cider tastings. It's also home to **Äpplets Hus**, a modern museum dedicated to all things apples.

Back in town, the **STF Vandrarhem** (☎ *71195; Tittutvägen; dorm beds Skr150-170; open year-round*) offers comfortable hostel accommodation and has bikes for rent; **Björkhagens Vandrarhem** (☎ *70119;* e *bjorkhagen-kivik@telia.com; dorm beds from Skr150*) is an SVIF hostel in an old farmhouse.

For bus information see the Getting There & Away entry under Simrishamn.

Stenshuvud National Park

Just south of Kivik is Stenshuvud National Park, which consists of woodland, marshes, sandy beaches and high headland. The flora, surveyed by Linnaeus in 1749, includes oak, hornbeam, ivy, orchids and hazel. Among the interesting fauna there are dormice, tree frogs and thrush nightingales. There are several fine walks in the area, including the hike to the 6th-century ruined hill fort on top of the 97m-high hill. The long-distance path Skåneleden goes through the park, along the coast; you can hike the best section from Vik to Kivik in two or three hours.

The **Naturum** (*visitors centre;* ☎ *70882; open 11am-6pm daily June-Aug, 11am-4pm Sept-May*) is 2.5km from the main road; parking costs Skr25. There's a slide show and an exhibition; guided tours (1½ hours, Skr25) of the park with knowledgeable rangers depart daily in summer at 10am (Sunday only in spring and autumn). Pretty **Kaffestugan Annorlunda** (☎ *24286*), on the road to the Naturum, serves meals and snacks daily from mid-May to August.

KRISTIANSTAD
☎ 044 • pop 74,500

Known as the most Danish town in Sweden, the construction of Kristianstad was ordered by the Danish King Christian IV in 1614 and then named after his humble self. The

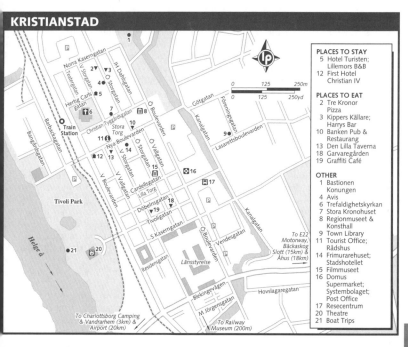

KRISTIANSTAD

PLACES TO STAY
5   Hotel Turisten;
     Lillemors B&B
12 First Hotel
     Christian IV

PLACES TO EAT
2   Tre Kronor
     Pizza
3   Kippers Källare;
     Harrys Bar
10 Banken Pub &
     Restaurang
13 Den Lilla Taverna
18 Garvaregården
19 Graffiti Café

OTHER
1   Bastionen
     Konungen
4   Avis
6   Trefaldighetskyrkan
7   Stora Kronohuset
8   Regionmuseet &
     Konsthall
9   Town Library
11 Tourist Office;
     Rådshus
14 Frimurarehuset;
     Stadshotellet
15 Filmmuseet
16 Domus
     Supermarket;
     Systembolaget;
     Post Office
17 Resecentrum
20 Theatre
21 Boat Trips

current rectangular street network in the town centre still follows the original town plan, but many of Kristianstad's beautiful buildings are actually from the 18th and 19th centuries. By the late 19th century, the wide boulevards in the town had earned Kristianstad the nickname 'Little Paris'.

Kristianstad is now one of the busiest towns in Skåne; surprisingly, the county government meets here, rather than in Malmö. It's also a major transport hub.

Information
The **tourist office** (☎ 121988; e touristinfo@ kristianstad.se, w www.kristianstad.se; Stora Torg; open 9am-7pm Mon-Fri, 9am-3pm Sat, 2pm-6pm Sun mid-June–mid-Aug; 10am-5pm Mon-Fri rest of year) can help with visitor inquiries.

Lilla Torg has banks and ATMs. The large Domus shopping centre on Östra Boulevarden, near the bus station is home to the post office, as well as a large supermarket. The own **library** (Föreningsgatan 4) has Internet access.

Kristianstadsdagarna, the annual, weekong town festival, is held in early July. The

events (in Tivoliparken) include music, dance and a jazz festival.

Things to See & Do
The most interesting architecture can be seen on Stora Torg, Västra Storgatan and Östra Storgatan. Narrow streets and alleys still exist around Lilla Torg.

The restored rampart **Bastionen Konungen**, with its earthworks and cannons, is by the canal which goes around the centre of the city. Just off Västra Boulevarden, and considered to be the finest Renaissance church in Scandinavia, **Trefaldighetskyrkan** (open 8am-5pm daily) was completed in 1628, before the Danes were kicked out of Skåne. It has seven spiralled gables and a well-appointed interior with many of the original fittings, including oak benches and an ornate marble and alabaster pulpit.

On a summer evening, pretty **Tivoli Park**, in the town's west, is a lively place – stroll around it or along the canal. Two-hour sightseeing **boat trips** (☎ 619840) leave from behind the striking Art Nouveau theatre. Tours operate daily from May to mid-September and cost Skr80/45 per adult/child.

SKÅNE

Next to the tourist office on Stora Torg, the **Rådshus** (town hall) was built in 1891, but imitates the Renaissance style. On the northern side of Stora Torg, **Stora Kronohuset** is a military building and an example of the Empire style (1841). The inscription 'Legibus et Armis' translates as 'For Laws and Arms'. Diagonally across the square is the impressive **Frimurarehuset**, opened by Oskar II in 1884 as the headquarters of Freemasonry in southern Sweden and presently houses the Stadshotellet.

The **Regionmuseet & Konsthall** (☎ 135800; Stora Torg; free admission; open 11am-5pm daily June-Aug, noon-5pm Tues-Sun Sept-May) is opposite the tourist office. Originally intended as a palace, the building became an arsenal but was converted to a museum in 1957. Exhibits cover local, county and military history, art, handicrafts and silverware.

Kristianstad has Sweden's only film museum, **Filmmuseet** (☎ 135729; Östra Storgatan 53; admission free; open 1pm-4pm Tues-Fri, noon-5pm Sun June-Aug), in the studios where Swedish film-making began. There's also a **railway museum** (☎ 135723; Hammarslundsvägen 4; admission free; open 1pm-4pm daily mid-June–mid-Aug, 1pm-4pm Sat & Sun mid-Aug–mid-Sept), just south of the town centre, with a collection of old locomotives, carriages and an operational steam train.

Places to Stay

Charlottsborgs Camping & Vandrarhem (☎ 210767; e charlottsborg@swipnet.se; Jacobs väg 34; tent sites & hostel beds Skr125, cabins from Skr250; open year-round) is about 3km southwest of the town centre, by the E22 motorway; take bus No 22 or 23 from Resecentrum. The camping area is fine but the hostel is a bit down at heel; especially if you have your own transport, you may be better heading to hostels out of town (such as Bäckaskog Slott, or see the following Åhus section).

Bäckaskog Slott (☎ 53020; e info@back askogslott.se; Kiaby; dorm beds Skr200-250, singles/doubles from Skr550/820, discounted to Skr500/720) is a charming castle set in lovely grounds between two lakes 15km northeast of Kristianstad. It was originally built as a monastery in the mid-13th century and is an impressive place – accommodation

is available in various wings and outhouses. All prices include breakfast. There's also a moderately priced restaurant here. The bus connections aren't great – there are two buses on weekdays from Kristianstad.

The tourist office keeps a list of **private rooms** and B&Bs – these cost from Skr150 per person.

Cosy **Lillemors B&B** (☎ 219525; Västra Storgatan 19; singles/doubles from Skr525/650, discounted to Skr400/550) is in a central location and offers good-value, homely accommodation.

Part of the Sweden Hotels chain, friendly **Hotel Turisten** (☎ 126150; e info.turisten@swedenhotels.se; Västra Storgatan 17; singles/doubles Skr750/995, discounted to Skr550/750) is next door to Lillemors and offers modern rooms with good facilities.

The rather grand **First Hotel Christian IV** (☎ 126300; Västra Boulevarden 15; singles/doubles from Skr999/1452, discounted to Skr652/799) is the nicest place in town, offering fine rooms in a turn-of-the-century building that once housed a bank. One of the former bank vaults now houses a wine cellar; there's also a restaurant here. Summer and weekend prices are reasonable.

Places to Eat

Kippers Källare (☎ 106200; Östra Storgatan 9; mains Skr180-250), an excellent basement restaurant, is the most atmospheric place in town, dating from 1615. Main courses include vegetarian options. The popular **Harrys Bar** is on the same premises.

The appealing **Garvaregården** (☎ 213500; Tivoligatan 9; meals Skr82-192) offers an interesting menu with cheaper pasta dishes or fancier meat and fish dishes, including a super-rich house speciality of lobster-stuffed steak with gorgonzola sauce and potatoes gratin. Enjoy your food in the great outdoor dining area.

Den Lilla Taverna (☎ 216304; Nya Boulevarden 6; dishes Skr69-99), opposite the tourist office, is a popular place, serving up excellent, authentic Greek dishes such as grilled swordfish, lamb, souvlaki, pastitsio and moussaka plus, in true Greek style, a great variety of starters.

By the museum, the cool **Banken Pub & Restaurang** (☎ 102023; Stora Torg; bar meals Skr25-95), in an old bank, has a wide selection of beers plus a bar menu with good snack options, including a club sandwich or Tex-Mex choices like nachos, burritos and fajitas.

Tre Kronor Pizza *(Östra Storgatan 6; meals Skr35-50)* offers cheap pizza and kebabs, to eat in or take away. A healthier option is **Graffiti Café** *(☎ 125990; Västra Storgatan; meals Skr25-55)*, with excellent budget meals, including salads, baguettes and baked spuds.

There is a large **supermarket** inside the Domus centre on Östra Boulevarden, and the **Systembolaget** is also here.

Getting There & Away

Kristianstad's **airport** *(☎ 238850)* is about 20km south of the town centre. **Air Lithuania** *(☎ 238820)* flies four times a week to Kaunas, and **SAS** *(☎ 020 727727)* flies daily direct to Stockholm.

Long distance buses depart from the Resecentrum on Östra Boulevarden. There are frequent SkåneExpressen buses to Lund and Malmö. Bus No 3 runs regularly to Simrishamn (less frequent services on weekends), bus No 4 runs regularly to Ystad. There are also two to six daily departures daily to Helsingborg on bus No 8. **Svenska Buss** *(☎ 0771-676767; W www.svenskabuss.se)* runs to Malmö, Karlskrona, Kalmar and Stockholm several times weekly.

Trains run daily to Lund (Skr82) and Malmö (Skr82), and many services continue on to Copenhagen (Skr150, two hours). Kustpilen trains run every hour or two to Malmö (with connections at Hässleholm for Helsingborg or Stockholm).

Getting Around

Airport buses (Skr60) depart from Stadshotellet on Stora Torg 50 minutes before domestic flight departures, 75 minutes before departures to Lithuania. Town and regional buses depart from the Resecentrum on Östra Boulevarden. **Taxi Kristianstad** *(☎ 246246)* can help you get around. There is central car hire available from **Avis** *(☎ 103020; Östra Storgatan 10)*.

ÅHUS
☎ 044

The small coastal town of Åhus, 18km southeast of Kristianstad, is a pleasant place to spend a relaxing afternoon, or longer. The town is a popular summer spot, due to its long sandy beach.

Åhus is the home town of **Absolut Vodka**, but sadly the distillery is not open to the public except on rare occasions in the summer, when tours are given. At the time of research there were tours once a week from mid to late June, and again in August. The 1½ hour tour costs Skr30; book through the **tourist office** *(☎ 240106; e touristinfo@kristianstad.se; Köpmannagatan 2)*.

All the facilities you'll need (bank, supermarket etc) are near the tourist office, and you can rent bikes here. Also in the neighbourhood is the very good **STF Vandrarhem** *(☎ 248535; Stavgatan 3; dorm beds Skr150, doubles Skr320-360; open year-round)*.

While you're here, be sure to try the local specialty – smoked eel – at restaurants around town. Many good dining possibilities are down by the harbour, including the relaxed and fun **Østermans** *(☎ 289106)*, where you buy your prawns by weight. It also has an adjacent grill bar, cleverly named the **Hard Räk Café** *(räk is Swedish for prawn)*, where you can get burgers and the like.

Bus No 551 runs two or three times an hour between Kristianstad and Åhus (Skr22); it drops you off at the tourist office.

HELSINGBORG
☎ 042 • pop 118,500

Helsingborg was always a strategic place, and a castle has perched on the edge of the plateau above the town since the 12th century. However, the 17th-century wars that occurred between Sweden and Denmark severely damaged the town. In 1709, the Danes invaded Skåne but they were finally defeated the following year in a battle just outside Helsingborg.

Too many travellers leave Helsingborg without seeing any more than the underground train station, but it's a relaxed and appealing town with quality budget accommodation, and it's worth taking some time to explore.

Orientation

Helsingborg is a busy port on the coastline of the Öresund and often experiences strong winds. There's a summer boulevard atmosphere in Stortorget and the older buildings in the winding streets blend well with the newer shops and restaurants. The seaside character is enhanced by the architectural pastiche of the high beachfront houses on

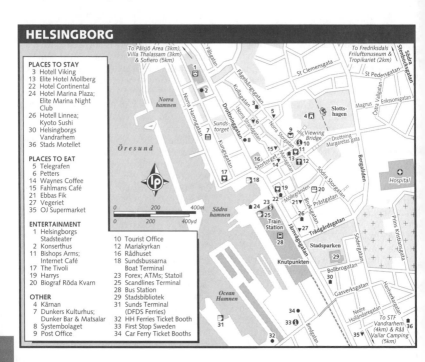

HELSINGBORG

PLACES TO STAY
3 Hotell Viking
13 Elite Hotel Mollberg
22 Hotel Continental
24 Hotel Marina Plaza;
   Elite Marina Night
   Club
26 Hotell Linnea;
   Kyoto Sushi
30 Helsingborgs
   Vandrarhem
36 Stads Motellet

PLACES TO EAT
5 Telegrafen
6 Petters
14 Waynes Coffee
15 Fahlmans Café
21 Ebbas Fik
27 Vegeriet
35 OJ Supermarket

ENTERTAINMENT
1 Helsingborgs
  Stadsteater
2 Konserthus
11 Bishops Arms;
   Internet Café
17 The Tivoli
19 Harrys
20 Biograf Röda Kvarn

OTHER
4 Kärnan
7 Dunkers Kulturhus;
  Dunker Bar & Matsalar
8 Systembolaget
9 Post Office

10 Tourist Office
12 Mariakyrkan
16 Rådhuset
18 Sundsbussarna
   Boat Terminal
23 Forex; ATMs; Statoil
25 Scandlines Terminal
28 Bus Station
29 Stadsbibliotek
31 Sunds Terminal
   (DFDS Ferries)
32 HH Ferries Ticket Booth
33 First Stop Sweden
34 Car Ferry Ticket Booths

the coastal roads out of town. Denmark is only 25 minutes away by ferry.

Information

The well-organised **tourist office** (☎ 104350; ℮ turistbyran@stad.helsingborg.se, ⊠ www .visit.helsingborg.se; Stortorget; open 9am-8pm Mon-Fri, 9am-5pm Sat & Sun June-Aug; 9am-6pm Mon-Fri, 10am-2pm Sat Sept-May, & 10am-2pm Sun in May) provides information as well as good, free brochures and maps. **First Stop Sweden** (☎ 104130; ⊠ www.firststopssweden.com; Bredgatan 2; open 9am-9pm daily June-Aug, 8am-5pm Mon-Fri Sept-May), near the car-ferry ticket booths, dispenses tourist information on the whole country.

Most other travel-related needs are met inside the vast Knutpunkten complex at the seafront, including **Forex** for currency exchange as well as banks and ATMs. There are also left-luggage lockers here. More banks are on Stortorget.

The **post office** (Stortorget) is near the tourist office. The large **public library** (Stadsbibliotek; Stadsparken), near Knutpunkten, offers Internet access, and there's a small **Internet café** (Mariatorget 17), by the church, where an hour online costs Skr40.

Things to See

You can access the square medieval tower **Kärnan** (☎ 105991; adult/child Skr15/5; open 11am-7pm daily June-Aug, closed Mon rest of year) from steps near the tourist office. The tower is all that remains of the late-14th-century castle, which looked out over the Öresund to the Danish heartland and upon struggles that finally delivered the fortress to Swedish hands; the tower was restored from dereliction in 1894, and the view from the top (34m) is excellent. The impressive steps and archways leading up from Stortorget are 20th century.

The eye-catching new **Dunkers Kulturhus** (☎ 107400; ⊠ www.dunkerskulturhus.com; Kungsgatan 11; admission free; open 11am-6pm daily, to 10pm Tues & Thur), in the area just north of the transport terminals, opened in 2002 and houses the very good **town museum** and **art museum** (combined admission adult/child Skr60/free), plus **concert hall**, **restaurant** and **café**. It was designed by Danish architect Kim Utzon, the son of Jørn

Utzon, the man who designed the Sydney Opera House. Take a stroll along the northern waterfront from here to admire the sleek and attractive apartment buildings and restaurant-bars, which are all part of a very successful harbour-redevelopment project.

The 15th-century, Gothic-style, triple-naved, brick church **Mariakyrkan** *(Mariatorget; open 8am-4pm Mon-Fri, 9am-4pm Sat & Sun)* has a magnificent interior, including a triptych from 1450 and an ornate pulpit from 1615. Choral and organ concerts are held here. The outrageous **rådhuset** *(town hall; Stortorget)* was completed in 1897 in neo-Gothic style and contains stained-glass scenes illustrating Helsingborg's history.

The pretty manor, gardens and museum village at **Fredriksdals Friluftsmuseum** *(☎ 104500; adult/child Skr40/free; open 10am-7.30pm daily June-Aug, shorter hours rest of year)* is off Hävertgatan, 2km northeast of the centre. It's a lovely place for a stroll; wildflowers of the area are grown in the botanic gardens. Highlights of the summer programme here include performances in the baroque open-air theatre.

Opposite the entrance to Frederiksdal, **Tropikariet** *(☎ 130035; Hävertgatan 21; adult/child Skr60/30; open 11am-4pm Tues-Sun)* has an interesting reptile house, aquarium and comical tiny monkeys, housed in environments that attempt to recreate their natural habitats.

North of the town, by Villa Thalassa hostel, the **Pålsjö area** contains a fine park, including the 16th-century Pålsjö Slott (closed to the public) and a nature reserve. About 5km north of the town centre, **Sofiero** *(☎ 137400; bus No 219; Sofierovägen; adult/child Skr60/free; open 10am-6pm daily April-Mar–mid-Sept)* is an impressive former royal summer residence and park with great rhododendrons (best when in full bloom in May and June). The tours of the manor cost Skr40.

Places to Stay

Camping & Hostels About 5km south of the city centre, by Öresund, **Råå Vallar Camping** *(☎ 107680; Kustgatan; low/high season tent sites Skr150/190, cabins Skr350/450; open March-Nov)* is a huge, well-equipped camping ground, with a shop, café and a heated swimming pool. Take bus No 1 from rådhuset to get there.

The SVIF hostel **Villa Thalassa** *(☎ 380660; Dag Hammarskjöldsväg; dorm beds from Skr160, singles/doubles from Skr275/400; open year-round)*, which is 3km north of the city centre in the Pålsjö area, is reached by walking 500m along a path from the bus stop at Pålsjöbaden (bus No 219). The early-20th-century villa and gardens are beautiful, but hostel accommodation is in huts. The better hotel-standard rooms are worth investigating if you can afford the extra money.

The **STF Vandrarhem** *(☎ 131130; boka@stfvandrarhem.helsingborg.nu; Planteringsvägen 69-71; dorm beds from Skr160)*, 4km south of town, offers very high quality accommodation in a newly fitted and stylishly decorated hostel. Take bus No 1.

Helsingborgs Vandrarhem *(☎ 145850; e info@hbgturist.com; Järnvägsgatan 39; dorm beds from Skr165)*, the most central hostel, is another excellent new place in a nondescript office building about 200m from Knutpunkten.

Private Rooms The tourist office can organise private rooms for as little as Skr150 per person (without breakfast), but charges a booking fee.

Hotels The exterior of **Stads Motellet** *(☎ 127955; Hantverkargatan 11; singles/doubles Skr695/795, discounted to Skr595/645)* is very dated, inside is a little better. Rooms are comfortable but nothing special, but they are among the cheapest in town.

You may be better off paying a little extra for a room at the charming, central **Hotell Linnea** *(☎ 214660; e linnea@hotell-linea.se; Prästgatan 4; singles/doubles Skr795/895, discounted to Skr620/720)*, with pretty Decor and friendly management. It's the pick of the town's mid-range offerings. Nearby, **Hotel Continental** *(☎ 120710; Järnvägsgatan 11; e hotelcontinental@telia.com; singles/doubles Skr795/945, discounted to Skr525/695)* is almost directly opposite Knutpunkten and offers reasonable accommodation in rooms that must be due for renovation soon.

Tucked away a little but still nicely central is the inviting **Hotell Viking** *(☎ 144420; e hotell.viking@helsingborg.se; Fågelsångsgatan 1; singles/doubles from Skr910/1245, discounted to Skr675/845)*, with smart modern decor.

More expensive hotels on Stortorget or near the harbour give good discounts at weekends and in summer. The square is dominated by **Elite Hotel Mollberg** (☎ 373700; e mollberg.helsingborg@elite.se; Stortorget 18; singles/doubles from Skr1090/1150, discounted to Skr650/750), a classy establishment with excellent facilities in the heart of town. Its sister establishment, **Elite Hotel Marina Plaza** (☎ 192100; e marinaplaza@ elite.se; Kungstorget 6; singles/doubles Skr1095/ 1450, discounted to Skr675/790) has modern, luxurious rooms right by the harbour, next to Knutpunkten, and with a number of restaurants and bars on the premises. You can pay a little extra for sea views.

Places to Eat

Pålsjö Krog (☎ 149730; Drottninggatan 151; mains Skr139-229), near Villa Thalassa hostel, is a great old seaside inn that has been renovated and turned into an elegant restaurant, with a lovely verandah and outdoor seating, plus good food choices. Closer to town, **Dunker Bar & Matsalar** (☎ 322995; Kungsgatan 11; lunch Skr65, light meals Skr50-120), at Dunkers Kulturhus, is an excellent option, with good views, a light, airy interior and tasty menu items. Wander north of here and you'll encounter some upmarket restaurant-bars at the base of some seriously stylish apartment blocks.

Telegrafen (☎ 181450; Norra Storgatan; dinner mains around Skr150) is an inviting pub-restaurant serving a good selection of pub grub (nachos, fish and chips, chicken drumsticks) for under Skr50, plus an à la carte menu of more substantial dishes.

Veggies will rejoice at **Vegeriet** (☎ 240303; Järnvägsgatan 25; lunch from Skr48, dinner from Skr65), an appealing vegie café-restaurant with dishes like curry, lasagne, tortilla and wok dishes.

The quickest snacks and a good variety of restaurants are found upstairs in the **Knutpunkten** complex, but don't miss out on the excellent offerings in the city centre. **Kyoto Sushi** (☎ 125713; Prästgatan 6), next to Hotell Linea, offers fresh sushi, including a good-value lunch special (Skr59) of nine pieces of sushi and miso soup. **Petters** (Kullgatan; meals from Skr29) has a variety of well-priced fast food, including hot dogs, baguettes and burgers, plus lots of outdoor seating.

Fahlmans Café (☎ 213060; Stortorget 11) is the most traditional of the town's cafés, serving sandwiches and pastries; in contrast is trendy **Waynes Coffee** (☎ 149696), opposite, serving the usual modern café fare (bagels, wraps, salads, muffins). Unique **Ebbas Fik** (☎ 281440; Bruksgatan 20) is styled in 1950s retro with superb results; there's an extensive café menu here too.

OJ (Carl Krooks gata) is the best central supermarket. There's also **Systembolaget** (Hästmöllegränd) off Drottninggatan.

Entertainment

There are lots of good pubs and bars around town, including **Harrys** (☎ 139191; Järnvägsgatan 7), and the **Bishops Arms** (☎ 373777; Södra Storgatan 2), both English-style pubs with a range of beers available as well as comprehensive food menus.

Down by the harbour, **Marina Night Club**, (☎ 192100; Marina Plaza Hotel, Kungstorget 6; admission Skr70) is a great waterside venue. Not far away, the **Tivoli** (☎ 187171; Kungsgatan 1) is popular with the younger crowd, and there's sometimes live music.

Helsingborgs Stadsteater (☎ 106810; Karl Johans gata 1) has regular drama performances, and its neighbour, the **Konserthus** (☎ 104350; Drottninggatan 19), regularly plays host to Helsingborg's Symphony Orchestra. Information and tickets are available from the tourist office.

Central **Biograf Röda Kvarn** (☎ 145090; Karlsgatan 7) is Helsingborg's oldest cinema. It's recently been renovated and now shows mostly independent films.

Getting There & Away

The main transport centre is the large, waterfront Knutpunkten complex.

Bus The bus terminal is at ground level in Knutpunkten. Regional Skånetrafiken buses dominate (see respective destinations for details), but long-distance services are offered by **Swebus Express** (☎ 0200 218218; W www.swebusexpress.se), **Svenska Buss** (☎ 0771-676767; W www.svenskabuss.se) and **Säfflebussen** (☎ 020 1600 600; W www .safflebussen.se). All three companies offer services north to Halmstad and Gothenburg (Swebus Express and Säfflebussen services continue to Oslo), and Swebus Express and Svenska Buss operate south to Malmö.

Swebus Express also runs services northeast to Stockholm via Jönköping. Peak fares to Stockholm cost around Skr380 (eight hours), to Gothenburg is Skr180 (three hours), and to Oslo is Skr315 (seven hours).

Train Underground platforms serve both SJ and *pågatågen* Kustpilen trains, which depart daily for Stockholm (Skr965, five hours), Gothenburg (Skr285, 2½ to three hours), Copenhagen, Oslo and nearby towns including Lund (Skr70), Malmö (Skr82), Kristianstad (Skr82) and Halmstad (Skr95).

Boat Knutpunkten is the terminal for the frequent **Scandlines** (☎ 186300) car ferry to Helsingør (Skr22, free with rail passes). Across the inner harbour, **Sundsbussarna** (☎ 216060) has a terminal with a passenger-only ferry to Helsingør every 15 to 20 minutes in summer (Skr20, rail passes valid). The frequent **HH-Ferries** (☎ 198000) service to Helsingør is the cheapest, both for cars (from Skr245, including up to five passengers) and individual passengers (from Skr9, rail passes not valid).

DFDS Seaways (☎ 241000; ⓦ www.dfds seaways.com) runs a ferry every evening to Oslo (low/high season from Skr675/975) from the Sunds terminal.

See the Getting There & Away chapter for more details.

Getting Around

Town buses cost Skr14 and run from rådhuset (town hall). Bike hire is available at the tourist office (Skr125 per day). Try **Taxi Helsingborg** (☎ 180200) for cabs. To hire a car, call **Statoil** (☎ 180350; Knutpunkten).

KULLA PENINSULA
☎ 042

The scenic Kulla Peninsula, 37km north of Helsingborg, juts out into the Kattegatt. Out at the point, there's **Kullens fyr** (lighthouse) and **Kullaberg Nature Reserve**, with 11 caves and lots of bird life. The diving is reputedly the best in Sweden, and there's good coastal fishing, several hiking trails

and rock climbing. You can go caving with **experienced guides** (☎ 347035), join a **rock-climbing course** (☎ 347725) or go on a **dive** (☎ 347714). There's a Skr30 road toll beyond Mölle; the toll booth has information leaflets about the area.

The village of **Mölle** is the main tourist centre within the area, but prettier **Arild**, 5km east, is a well-preserved fishing village with interesting old houses and coastal nature reserves.

Places to Stay & Eat

Accommodation in the area isn't cheap. For budget travellers, the best bet is **Möllehässle Camping** (☎ 347384; ⓔ mollehassle@ telia .com; low/high season tent sites Skr110/60, cabins & chalets from Skr310; open year-round), an excellent place 2km southeast of Mölle. It's a large, well-equipped ground, and you can rent bikes here for exploring the area (Skr60 per day).

Mölle Turisthotellet (☎ 347084; ⓔ info@ molleturisthotell.se; Kullabergsvägen 32; singles/doubles from Skr850/1050) in the village of Mölle is a classic hotel dating from 1872, with great sea views. The elegant **Strand Hotell** (☎ 346100; ⓔ strand.hotell@ swipnet.se; Stora Vägen 42; singles/doubles from Skr750/850) offers charming old-world accommodation in picture-perfect Arild.

Ransvik Cafe (☎ 347666; open Apr-Sept) is a traditional place overlooking a popular bathing spot about 1km beyond the toll booth. Here you can get sandwiches and baguettes from Skr30, or enjoy coffee, cake and a swim from the rocks. Signposted off the main road between Arild and Jonstorp is **Flickorna Lundgren** (☎ 346044; open late-Apr–early-Sept), a well-known café serving sandwiches, cakes and pastries in a gorgeous garden setting.

Getting There & Away

Bus Nos 219 and 220 run frequently from Helsingborg to Höganäs; from there, bus No 222 runs every hour or two to Mölle, and Nos 223 and 224 run to Arild.

Götaland

Although the medieval kingdom of Götaland joined Svealand and Norrland to become Sweden 1000 years ago, Danish influence remained strong in the west. After Gothenburg (Göteborg) was founded by Gustav II Adolf in 1621, Danish power in the region began to wane and, once the Swedes conquered Skåne in 1658, their influence in this part of the country was over.

Orientation & Information

Götaland consists of five different regions *(landskaps)*: Bohuslän, Dalsland and Västergötland in the west, Halland in the south, and Östergötland in the east. These regions are grouped into the three counties *(läns)* Västra Götalands Län (taking in Västergötland, Dalsland and Bohuslän), Hallands Län and Östergötlands Län. Götaland is influenced by the two largest lakes in Sweden – Vänern and Vättern. The latter divides Götaland into two distinct parts.

Tourists are drawn by the wide variety of attractions in the area. The beautiful Bohuslän coastline has myriad islands, wonderful fishing villages and Bronze Age rock carvings. Dalsland is characterised by its forests and lakes, such as the huge Vänern. Västergötland has more towns and includes the largest city in the west, Gothenburg, but this extensive landscape is also a historical and cultural treasure trove. Mostly of coastal interest, Halland has sandy beaches and historical seaside towns. In Östergötland, there's plenty of interesting history, from rune stones to convents, and two of Sweden's small industrial cities, Norrköping and Linköping, are also here.

Regional Tourist Offices

Each county has a regional tourist office. Visitors can contact the following agencies for more detailed information on the area:

HallandsTurist (☎ 035-109560,
ⓔ info@hallandsturist.se, ⓦ www.hallandsturist.se) Hamngatan 35, Box 68, SE-30103 Halmstad

Västsvenska Turistrådet (☎ 031-818300,
ⓔ infor@vastsvenskaturistradet.se, ⓦ www.vastsverige.com) Kungsportsavenyn 31-35, SE-41136 Gothenburg

Highlights

- Going wild on the rides in Liseberg fun park, Gothenburg
- Cruising down the river to see the Nya Älvsborg Fästning (fortress), Gothenburg
- Visiting the picturesque fishing villages of Bohuslän, particularly Smögen and Åstol
- Admiring the ancient works of the Bronze Age artists at Tanumshede, Bohuslän
- Marvelling at the fantastic castle, Läckö Slott
- Enjoying a relaxing tour on the Göta Canal, or just watching the boats pass through the locks at Bergs Slussar
- Ambling through the medieval streets of Vadstena

Östsvenska Turistrådet (☎ 011-155010,
ⓔ info@ostgotaporten.com, ⓦ www.ostgotaporten.com) SE-60181 Norrköping

Getting Around

The following companies provide regional transport links. If you're planning to spend a reasonable amount of time in any of these counties, it's worth inquiring about value or rebate cards, monthly passes or a *sommarkort*, offering discount travel in the peak summer period (ie, from Midsummer to mid-August). Check also the respective websites for routes, schedules, fares and passes; these sites don't always have information in English, but if you call the telephone numbers

GÖTALAND

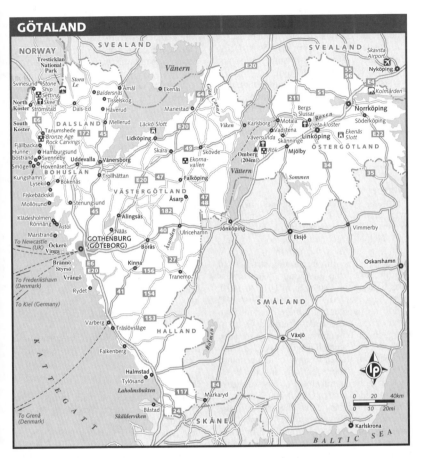

GÖTALAND

listed you'll usually reach someone who can help you in English.

Hallandstrafiken (☎ 0346-48600, 0771-331030,
  [W] www.hlt.se)
ÖstgötaTrafiken (☎ 0771-211010,
  [W] www.ostgotatrafiken.se)
Västtrafik (☎ 0771-414300,
  [W] www.vasttrafik.se)

The main railway lines in the west connect Gothenburg to Oslo, Karlstad, Stockholm and Malmö. In the east, the most important line runs from Stockholm via Norrköping and Linköping to Malmö. Express buses connect major towns on much the same routes.

One of the best ways of seeing the region is the long and unforgettable journey along the Göta Canal – from the rolling country of Östergötland, north of Linköping, into the great Lake Vättern, before continuing into the region of Västergötland on the other side and on to Gothenburg. See the introductory Getting Around chapter.

Gothenburg

☎ 031 • pop 471,300

Gothenburg (the Swedish name, Göteborg, sounds like 'yoo-te-bor'), on the river Göta älv, has a busy port that's the most important in Scandinavia, and most of Sweden's oil is imported through here. The city has a more continental outlook than Stockholm, but isn't quite as friendly as Malmö. Around the coast, there's a small archipelago with good transport links where you can escape the bustle. Despite being on a west-facing coast, the weather's surprisingly good and sunshine levels are quite high.

There's a lot more to Gothenburg than the showpiece Kungsportsavenyn boulevard and multitude of museums, not least its industrial and architectural heritage. The Liseberg fun park is the largest amusement park in Scandinavia and it's Sweden's most popular tourist attraction, with around 3.5 million visitors every year.

History

Surprisingly, Gothenburg has nothing in the way of medieval history. Although there were small towns in the area as long ago as the 11th century, the Älvsborg fortress standing guard at the mouth of the river Göta älv is the only remaining structure of significance from this period. The fortress was held by the Danes from 1612 to 1619, but they yielded the castle to Gustav II Adolf on payment of a huge ransom. Two years later the Swedes founded Gothenburg, about 3km upstream from the fortress.

Dutch and Scottish people played prominent parts in the early days of Gothenburg, with Dutch experts constructing the canal system in the central area. The city was heavily fortified in case of Danish attack and it resembled a military camp. Just south of the central area, the workers lived in what has now become Haga and around a fifth of the original Haga buildings are still standing. Most of the old wooden buildings went up in smoke – the city was devastated by no less than nine major fires between 1669 and 1804.

Once Sweden had annexed Skåne, Gothenburg expanded as a trading centre. By the 18th century, wealthy merchant companies, such as the Swedish East India Company, were making huge profits and many grandiose buildings were built during that boom period. In 1841, shipbuilding took on greater significance when the Scot James Keiller opened a large shipyard, and this industry formed a large part of the city's economy until its total collapse in the 1980s. Volvo's first car was wheeled out of here in 1927 and now it's one of Sweden's largest companies (although it was taken over by Ford in 1999). Today, Gothenburg is Sweden's most important industrial and commercial city.

Orientation

The kernel of the city within the remains of canal defences – a result of the 17th-century expansion and militarism of Gustav II Adolf and his successors – is now well-suited to sightseeing. A branch of the canals snakes its way to the Liseberg fun park, but many of the Dutch planners' original canals have been filled in.

From the centre of the city, Kungsportsavenyn crosses the canal and leads southeast up to Götaplatsen. The Avenyn is the heart of the city with boutiques, restaurants, galleries, theatres and street cafés. The huge Nordstan shopping centre lies just north of the canal system, opposite Centralstationen (the central train station).

The recently closed shipyards, and much of the heavy industry (including Volvo), are on the northern island of Hisingen, which is formed by bifurcation of the Göta älv. Hisingen is reached by road via the monumental bridge Älvsborgs bron, southwest of the city, by Götaälvbron (north of Centralstationen), and by the E6 Hwy tunnel, Tingstadstunneln, northeast of the city centre.

The main E6 motorway runs north-south, between Oslo and Malmö, just east of the city centre.

Information

Tourist Offices The main **tourist office** (☎ 612500; e turistinfo@gbg-co.se, W www.goteborg.com; Kungsportsplatsen 2; open 9am-6pm daily June-Aug; 9am-6pm Mon-Fri, 10am-2pm Sat Sept-May, & 10am-2pm Sun in May) is central and busy, and hands out good, free brochures and maps.

There is also a **branch office** (open 9.30am-6pm Mon-Fri, 10am-4pm Sat, noon-3pm Sun) at the Nordstan shopping complex.

If you can read Swedish, the website W www.alltomgoteborg.se is an excellent resource for information on the city.

Discount Cards The Göteborg Pass is a discount card giving free entry to Liseberg, free city sightseeing tours and entry to a number of city attractions, as well as free parking and free travel by public transport within the region. It costs Skr175/95 per adult/child for 24 hours, Skr295/190 for 48 hours. The card is available at tourist offices, hotels and numerous Pressbyrån newsagencies.

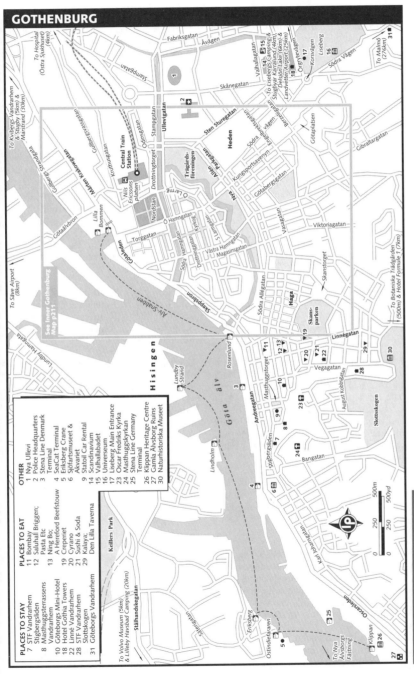

GOTHENBURG

PLACES TO STAY
7 STF Vandrarhem
   Stigbergsliden
8 Masthuggsterrassens
   Vandrarhem
10 Göteborgs Mini-Hotel
18 Hotel Gothia Towers
22 Linné Vandrarhem
28 STF Vandrarhem
   Slottsskogen
31 Göteborgs Vandrarhem

PLACES TO EAT
11 Bombay
12 Saluhall Briggen;
   Pasta Etc
13 Ning Bo;
   A Hereford Beefstouw
19 Creperiet
20 Cyrano
21 Sushi & Soda
29 Kalaya;
   Den Lilla Taverna

OTHER
1 Nya Ullevi
2 Police Headquarters
3 Stena Line Denmark
   Terminal
4 SeaCat Terminal
5 Eriksberg Crane
6 Sjöfartsmuseet &
   Akvariet
9 Statoil Car Rental
14 Scandinavium
15 Valhallabadet
16 Universeum
17 Liseberg Main Entrance
23 Oscar Fredriks Kyrka
24 Masthuggskyrkan
25 Stena Line Germany
   Terminal
26 Klippan Heritage Centre
27 Gamla Älvsborg Ruins
30 Naturhistoriska Museet

GÖTALAND

Göteborgspaketet (Gothenburg Package) is a package offered at various hotels with accommodation prices starting at Skr450 per person per night, and including the Göteborg Pass for the number of nights you stay. You can book in advance with a credit card via the Internet or telephone the tourist office on ☎ 615250. There is also the option of a more expensive 'show package', which includes a ticket to a theatre performance or musical show (opera, concert etc).

Money If you need them, **Forex** exchange offices are at Centralstationen *(open 7am-9pm daily)*, inside the Nordstan shopping complex, opposite the tourist office on Kungsportsplatsen, at Kungsportsavenyn 22 and at Landvetter airport.

Banks with ATMs can be found all over, including inside the Nordstan complex and along Kungsportsavenyn.

Post The **post office** inside the Nordstan complex has the longest hours *(9am-7pm Mon-Fri, 10am-3pm Sat, noon-3pm Sun)*. Many kiosks and newsagents also provide postal services – look for the blue-and-yellow postal symbol.

Email & Internet Access One cental Internet café is **Janemans IT Palats** *(☎ 133113; Viktoriagatan 14)*, charging Sk50 per hour. You can also try **Palatset** *(☎ 132480; Ekelundsgatan 9-11)*, a large bar and billiards hall open until at least midnight daily and offering Internet access for Skr39 per hour, or the city library (see the Libraries entry later in this section).

Travel Agencies Catering for youths and students is **Kilroy Travels** *(☎ 0771-545769; Vasagatan 7)*. If queues are too long here you can also try **Ticket** *(☎ 176860; Östra Hamngatan 35)*.

Bookshops The best bookshops are the central branches of **Akademibokhandeln**; one is located inside the Nordstan shopping complex, the other can be found in the **university** area at Vasagatan 26–30. You can also get English-language books at the **Pocketshop** *(Centralstationen)*.

For English-language newspapers and magazines, head to **Press Stop** *(Drottninggatan 58)* or **Pressbyrån** *(Centralstationen)*.

Libraries The city library, **Stadsbiblioteket** *(☎ 616500; Götaplatsen)*, has plenty of imported newspapers and magazines, books in English, a modern computer section (with free Internet access, but the wait can be long and the time limit is short), and a good café.

Universities Founded in 1954, **Gothenburg University** *(Ⓦ www.gu.se)* is now one of the largest and liveliest universities in the country. The main building is just off Vasagatan and some departments are nearby, but the rest are scattered around the city.

Laundry Try to use a hotel, hostel or camping ground laundry service if you can. Otherwise, there's **Wasatvätten** *(☎ 711 0911; Viktoriagatan 22; open 8am-6pm Mon-Fri)*, which charges Skr150 per machine load (up to 6kg) and you can usually collect the same day if you leave your washing before 11am.

Left Luggage Small/medium/large luggage lockers are available at Centralstationen and the Nils Ericsson Terminalen (long-distance bus terminal) for Skr15/20/25 for up to 24 hours.

Camping & Outdoor Gear A wide range of equipment is available at **Naturkompaniet** *(☎ 135160; Stora Nygatan 33; open Mon-Sat)*.

Emergency & Medical Services The hospital, **Östra Sjukhuset** *(☎ 343 4000)* is about 5km northeast of the centre, near tram terminus No 1. **Apoteket Vasan** *(☎ 804410)*, inside the Nordstan complex, is open 8am to 10pm daily. For emergency dental treatment, contact **Akuttandvården** *(☎ 807800; Stampgatan 2)*. Medical information is available around the clock on ☎ 703 1500.

Dial ☎ 112 for fire, police or ambulance in emergency situations only. The **police station** *(☎ 739 2000; Ernst Fontells Plats)* is off Skånegatan.

Dangers & Annoyances Gothenburg is a reasonably safe city by European standards, but travellers should be alert and take care in the Nordstan shopping complex late at night, which becomes a pretty unsavoury venue and is not a place that is likely to feel comfortable for solo women.

Liseberg

Liseberg fun park (☎ 400100; ⱳ www.lise berg.se; enter from Örgrytevägen; tram No 5; adult/child Skr50/free, with Göteborg Pass free; open to 10pm or 11pm most days May-Aug, & during Christmas period), southeast of the city centre, was founded in 1923 and is today dominated by its futuristic spaceport-like tower. The ride to the top, some 83m above the ground, climaxes in a spinning dance and a breathtaking view of the city. The other amusements and rides seem tame by comparison but there's no lack of variety. You can buy a pass for Skr235 that allows you to ride the attractions all day, otherwise individual rides cost between Skr10 and Skr40 each. There are often summer shows and concerts staged here. Opening hours are complex – it's best to check the website.

Museums

After Liseberg the museums are Gothenburg's strongest attractions and, if several take your fancy, use the Göteborg Pass.

Stadsmuseum Located in the former head-quarters of the Swedish East India Company (Östindiska huset), the Stadsmuseum (☎ 612770; Norra Hamngatan 12; adult/child Skr40/10; open 10am-5pm daily May-Aug; Tues-Sun rest of year) has archaeological, local and historical collections, including the Äskekärr Ship, Sweden's only original Viking ship. There's also an impressive collection of East Indian porcelain and a recon-struction of a tea and porcelain auction room.

Konstmuseet The main city art collection is at Konstmuseet (☎ 611000; Götaplatsen; adult/child Skr40/10; open 11am-6pm Tues-Thur, 11am-5pm Fri-Sun). This museum has impressive collections of Nordic and Euro-pean masters and is notable for works by the French impressionists, Rubens, Van Gogh, Rembrandt and Picasso. There's also a sculpture section behind the main hall, the **Hasselblad Center** photographic collection in the entrance hall and temporary exhibi-tions covering the latest in the Nordic art.

Konstmuseet also has a specialist art bookshop and an excellent café.

Röhsska Museet The excellent Röhsska Museet (☎ 613850; Vasagatan 37; adult/child Skr40/10; open noon-9pm Tues, noon-5pm Wed-Sun) is Sweden's only design and ap-plied art museum. There are lots of examples of ultramodern, 20th- and 21st-century Scandinavian design and decorative arts – furniture features strongly, but there's also some outrageous crockery. The more his-torical exhibits include baroque furniture and silverware, and a whole floor devoted to Chinese and Japanese sculpture, handi-crafts and ceramics. There are usually tem-porary exhibitions on the first floor.

Göteborgs Maritima Centrum Near the Operahouse north of the centre, Göteborgs Maritima Centrum (Gothenburg's Maritime Centre; ☎ 105950; Packhuskajen; adult/child Skr60/30; open 10am-4pm daily Mar-May & Sept-Nov, 10am-6pm daily June & Aug, 10am-7pm daily July) claims to be the largest float-ing ship museum in the world and usually displays 13 historical ships, but some can only be viewed from the outside. It's quite fascinating and there's a lot to see, so allow at least 1½ hours.

The highlight is the 69m-long submarine *Nordkaparen*, but you need to climb verti-cal ladders and pass through small holes to see it from the inside. The largest vessel is the 121m-long, 3344-tonne-displacement destroyer *Småland*, which saw service from 1952 to 1979. It's difficult not to get lost in here – the ship is a labyrinth. *Fladen* is the red-painted lightship, built in 1915 and de-commissioned in 1962.

Sjöfartsmuseet & Akvariet The main museum of maritime history is Sjöfarts-museet (☎ 612900; Karl Johansgatan 1; tram No 3, 9 or 11; adult/child Skr50/10; open 10am-5pm daily May-Aug; 10am-4pm Tues-Fri, 11am-5pm Sat & Sun Sept-Apr), by Stig-bergstorget about 2km west of the city centre. It includes model ships, cannons, a ship's medical room and a large collection of fig-ureheads, such as the vicious-looking *Vinthunden* from the frigate with the same name. The interesting attached aquarium (in-cluded in the entry fee) has a good selection of Nordic marine life and a tropical section with two alligators, piranhas and electric eels.

Nya Älvsborgs Fästning The 'new' island fortress at the mouth of the river Göta älv (also called Elfsborgs Fästning), about 8km downstream from Gothenburg, was built in the mid-17th century to defend the young city from Danish attack. It's an impressive place with thick stone walls and an interesting history – it proved particularly useful during the Great Nordic War in the early 18th century. Nowadays, visitors can see the church built for Karl XII's troops and the dungeons for when they stepped out-of-line. Boat trips and guided tours (adult/child Skr85/50) are run by Börjessons (see Organised Tours) daily from May to August and weekends in September, and most tours are free for holders of the Göteborg Pass (except for tours departing between 11.30am and 1pm). Tours depart from Lilla Bommen harbour, north of the train station.

Volvo Museum About 8km west of the city centre at Arendal, is the interesting Volvo Museum (☎ 664814; Hisingen; adult/child Skr30/10; open 10am-5pm Tues-Fri, 11am-4pm Sat & Sun June-Aug; noon-5pm Tues-Fri, 11am-4pm Sat Sept-May). A film describes the history of this world-famous motor-vehicle manufacturer from 1927 to the present. The exhibits include the first Volvo vehicle, many different prototypes and experimental cars, the first electric car, and various marine and aero engines – including the first jet engine used by the Swedish Air Force. Gothenburg's reliance on Volvo is immense – it's estimated that around 25% of the population depend on the company in some way.

Interestingly, you really need a car to get here! Otherwise, take tram No 2, 4 or 5 to Eketrägatan, then bus No 128 to Skrovtorget.

Other Museums Near Liseberg is the striking new **Universeum** (☎ 335 6450; Södra Vägen; admission summer & Sat & Sun Skr110, rest of year Skr80; open 10am-8pm June–mid-Aug; 11am-6pm Tues-Sun rest of year), a huge and impressive 'science discovery centre' featuring everything from rainforests to a shark tank. It's got lots of good displays and hands-on experiments, but it's not cheap.

Just off Linnégatan is in Slottsskogen park, **Naturhistoriska Museet** (Natural History Museum; ☎ 775 2400; adult/child Skr40/10; open 11am-5pm daily May-Aug; 9am-4pm Tues-Fri, 11am-5pm Sat & Sun Sept-Apr) has a collection of some 10 million specimens covering wildlife from around the world and the highlight is a stuffed blue whale. Take tram No 1 or 2 to Linnéplatsen.

South in the same park, **Tropikhuset** (☎ 414050; Slottsskogen; adult/child Skr60/30; open 11am-6pm daily July-Aug; 11am-4pm Mon-Fri, 11am-5pm Sat & Sun Sept-June) has a collection of snakes, spiders, crocodiles and bats. There's also **Barnens Zoo** (Children's Zoo; open daily May-early Sept) and **Djurgårdarna**, an animal park with farm animals, elk, deer and other Swedish animals and birds. Feeding time at the seal pond is 2pm daily.

Skansen Kronan (☎ 145000; Haga area; adult/child Skr30/10; tram No 2; open noon-2pm Tues & Wed, noon-3pm Sat & Sun Apr-Sept) is the last of the city's defensive towers in any state of repair, sitting on Skansberget about a kilometre southwest of the business district with, naturally, fine views. Uniforms and firearms dating from the 17th century are exhibited in the tower's **military museum**.

A cultural heritage centre depicting past waterfront life, the **Klippan precinct** includes 18th-century sailor's cottages, the Gamla Älvsborgs ruins, the remains of Gamla Älvsborgs slott (the fort ransomed from the Danes in 1619), the brewery opened by the Scot David Carnegie, (now a hotel) and St Birgittas kapell. Klippan is just off Oscarsleden, about 400m east of Älvsborgs bron – take bus No 19 or 64 from Brunnsparken, or the Älvsnabben ferry.

Near the **Eriksberg crane** (a leftover from the days of shipbuilding), the traditional wooden-built East Indiaman **Ostindiefararen** (☎ 779 3450; admission Skr60; open 11am-6pm Mon-Fri, 11am-4pm Sat & Sun) is the only ongoing shipbuilding in Gothenburg. The ship is due to be launched in 2004; the intention is to sail it to China. Until then you can see it being built (admission includes the guided tour). Take the Älvsnabben ferry to Eriksberg or Ostindiefararen. Eriksberg was once a shipyard, but is now undergoing redevelopment; it's home to a few good cafés and restaurants and is worth a visit.

Churches

Gothenburg's churches aren't very old but they reflect Swedish architecture more than Stockholm's Italian imitations.

The classical-style **Domkyrkan** (Gustavi Cathedral; Västra Hamngatan; open 8am-6pm Mon-Fri, 9am-4pm Sat, 10am-3pm Sun) was consecrated in 1815 – two previous cathedrals were destroyed by town fires. Many of the cathedral's contents are modern, but there's an 18th-century clock and reredos.

Hagakyrkan *(Haga Kyrkoplan)* was consecrated in 1859 and has a neo-baroque organ dating from 1992. The neo-Gothic **Oscar Fredriks kyrka** *(Oscar Fredriks Kyrkogatan)* is a remarkable building which was consecrated in 1893. One of the most impressive buildings in Gothenburg, **Masthuggskyrkan** *(Storebackegatan)* was completed in 1914 and its interior design is like an upturned boat. The church is also a great viewpoint for the western half of the city.

Parks

Laid out in 1842, the lovely **Trädgårds-föreningen** *(City Park; ☎ 611804; Nya Allén; adult/child Skr15/free; open 7am-9pm daily May-Aug, 7am-7.30pm daily Sept-Apr)* is a large protected area off Nya Allén. In the park, the impressive **Palmhuset** *(☎ 415773; adult/child Skr20/free; open 10am-5pm daily May-Aug, 10am-4pm daily Sept-Apr)*, opened in 1878, is a miniature version of Crystal Palace in London and has five halls with different climates ranging from cool and moist (with camellias) to hot and humid, where water lilies have leaves up to 2m across. The **Rosarium** *(free admission)* is Europe's largest and has around 2500 varieties. **Fjärilshuset** *(Butterfly House; ☎ 611911; adult/child Skr35/10; open 10am-5pm daily June-Aug; 10am-4pm Apr, May & Sept; 10am-3pm Oct-Mar)* is a tropical place with lots of free-flying butterflies. There are a number of cafés scattered through the park.

Slottsskogen *(admission free; open 24hr)* is great for a stroll and there are several attractions in the park (see the Other Museums section earlier), as well as cafés and theatres. **Botaniska Trädgården** *(admission free; open 9am-sunset daily)*, just across Dag Hammarskjöldsleden from Slottsskogen, is Sweden's largest botanic garden, with around 12,000 plant species.

The rocky heights of Ramberget (86m) in **Keillers Park** *(Hisingen)* give the best view of the city but, unless you take the city bus tour, you're in for a climb. Take bus No 21 from Centralstationen to Hjalmar Brantingsplatsen, then catch bus No 31 to the foot of Ramberget.

Other Attractions

Kronhuset, lying between Postgatan and Kronhusgatan, is the city's oldest secular building and was built in Dutch style between 1642 and 1654. It was here that Karl X held the disastrous *riksdag* (parliament) in 1660 – he died while it was in session. Kronhuset now has changing art exhibitions and occasional concerts. **Kronhusbodarna**, just across the courtyard from Kronhuset, consists of several workshops with handicraft boutiques making and selling pottery, silverware, glass and textiles.

Centralstationen was built in 1858 and renovated in the early 1990s – it's the oldest railway station in Sweden and it's now a listed building. Just downstream from Götaälvsbron, the **Barken Viking** is an attractive sailing ship, launched in Denmark in 1906 as a training vessel and now used as a hotel and restaurant (see Places to Stay later). The red-and-white 'skyscraper' **Götheborgs-Utkiken** *(☎ 609670; adult/child Skr30/15; open 11am-5pm daily May-Aug, 11am-5pm Sat & Sun Sept-Apr)*, using the archaic spelling of the city's name, gives great views of the harbour from its top-floor café.

On Rosenlundsgatan is **Feskekörka** *(open Mon-Sat June-Aug, Tues-Sat rest of year)*, also called the Fish Church due to its curious appearance, isn't a church at all – it's a seafood market.

At the head of Kungsportsavenyn, **Götaplatsen** is the main city square and it's dominated by the bronze **Poseidon fountain**, which was unveiled to public outcry in 1931. This 7m-high colossus also had colossal private parts and the good citizens of Gothenburg demanded some drastic reduction surgery!

The **Haga district** is Gothenburg's oldest suburb and dates back to 1648. In the 1980s and '90s, the area was thoroughly renovated but, although the mixture of old and new buildings looks good, some character seems to be missing.

Gothenburg has over 30 art galleries, all with art for sale, so admission is free. Ask the tourist office for the handy leaflet *Konst i Göteborg* which has a map showing locations for many of the galleries.

Activities

A day or week in Gothenburg doesn't have to mean only museums and crowds.

Bohusleden is an easy walking trail that runs for 360km through lovely Bohuslän from Lindome (south of Gothenburg) to Strömstad, passing just east of the city.

GÖTALAND

There's some good rock climbing around Gothenburg. Tram Nos 6, 7 and 11 go to Kviberg, close to some of the best climbing, at Utby. Contact **Göteborgs Klätterklub** (☎ 431386; W www.gbgkk.nu) for more information (the website is in Swedish only).

Cyclists should ask the tourist office for the map *Cykel Karta Göteborg* (Skr20) which shows the best routes in and around the city. See also Getting Around later for details of where to hire bikes.

Outdoor swimming is best in **Delsjön lake**, 6km east of the centre (take tram No 5 to Töpelsgatan). In the city, a swim and sauna at the indoor pool **Valhallabadet** (☎ 611956; *Valhallagatan 3*) costs Skr35, and there's also a relaxing Roman bath here (Skr90). The best indoor pool is the magnificent and exclusive **Hagabadet** (☎ 600600; *Södra Allégatan 3*), which first opened in 1876. For Skr320 you can swim all day and use the attached sauna, gym and aerobics facilities; between 7am and 9am, you can swim for Skr95. There's all manner of health and beauty treatments offered here too, if you're feeling weary after lots of travel.

Canoe hire (☎ 402237) is available at Delsjön lake. You can also fish for pike or perch here; ask the tourist office for details, as you'll need a permit.

For serious island hopping, take tram No 11 southwest to Saltholmen and you'll have at least 15 different islands to explore – see Around Gothenburg later.

Organised Tours

Five times daily from June to August, **Börjessons** (☎ 609660; W www.borjessons.com) operates one-hour bus tours of the city (adult/child Skr75/50), leaving from outside Stora Teatern, just south of the tourist office.

One of the most popular ways for tourists to pass time in Gothenburg is to take a boat cruise on the Göta älv, or farther afield to the sea. From late April to September **Paddan** (☎ 609670; W www.paddan.com) offers frequent 50-minute boat tours of the canals and harbour from Kungsportsbron, near the tourist office (adult/child Skr80/50).

Most Börjessons cruises from Lilla Bommen harbour (Lilla Bommens Hamn) to the island fortress Nya Älvsborg (see the earlier section on Nya Älvsborg) are free for holders of the Göteborg Pass (otherwise adult/child Skr85/50) and include a guided tour of the

fort. Between early May and late August, boats depart at least six times daily, and you can spend a good few hours on the island and catch a later boat back to town.

Börjessons also runs tours from Lilla Bommen to Marstrand (one-way/return Skr100/160, daily July to mid-Aug), Vinga (return Skr100, daily from July to mid-August) and around the island of Hisingen (Skr130, Tuesday to Sunday evenings from late June to mid-August). The company brochure details these and other tours.

Places to Stay

Gothenburg offers several good hostels near the city centre, and even hotel prices seem quite reasonable compared to those in other Swedish cities. Most hotels offer exceptionally good discounts at weekends and in summer.

Camping Camping in Gothenburg can be very expensive, with summer rates as high as Skr200 for a tent site.

The closest camping ground to town is the well-equipped **Lisebergs Camping & Stugbyar Karralund** (☎ 840200; e boende.lgab@liseberg.se; *Olbergsgatan 1; tram No 5 to Welandergatan; tent sites Skr100-200, hostel-standard doubles Skr275-475, cabins & chalets Skr450-1200*). It's owned and operated by the fun park, and is fully geared for families. It has a wide range of cabins, cottages and hostel rooms for rent. Prices for tent sites vary depending on the time of year.

Also part of the Liseberg 'empire', **Lilleby Havsbad Camping** (☎ 565066; *Lillebyvägen; tent sites Skr135-160; open May-Aug*) is by the sea, 20km west of the city centre in Torslanda. To get there take bus No 21 from Centralstationen to Torslanda, then change to bus No 23.

Hostels There are a number of good hostels, most clustered in the central southwest area, in apartment buildings that sometimes inspire little confidence from the outside, but inside offer accommodation of a very high standard. All are open year-round, and usually offer double rooms for not much more than the cost of two dorm beds.

The well-run **Masthuggsterrassens Vandrarhem** (☎ 424820; e masthuggsterrassen .vandrarhem@telia.com; *Masthuggsterrassen 8; dorm beds/doubles Skr150/380*) is very

INNER GOTHENBURG

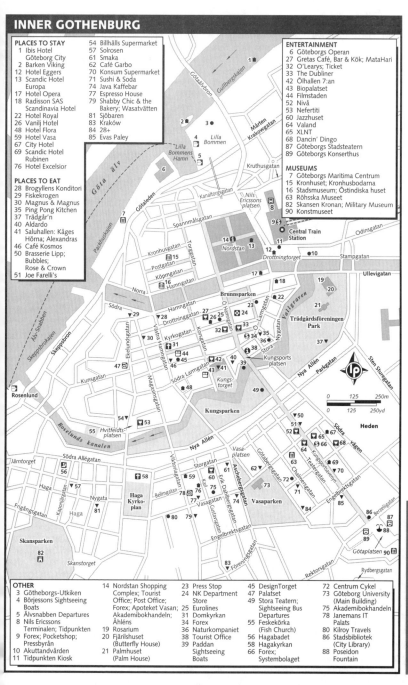

PLACES TO STAY
1 Ibis Hotel Göteborg City
2 Barken Viking
12 Hotel Eggers
13 Scandic Hotel Europa
17 Hotel Opera
18 Radisson SAS Scandinavia Hotel
22 Hotel Royal
26 Vanilj Hotel
48 Hotel Flora
59 Hotel Vasa
67 City Hotel
69 Scandic Hotel Rubinen
76 Hotel Excelsior

PLACES TO EAT
28 Brogyllens Konditori
29 Fiskekrogen
30 Magnus & Magnus
35 Ping Pong Kitchen
37 Trädgår'n
40 Aldardo
41 Saluhallen: Kåges Hörna; Alexandras
46 Café Kosmos
50 Brasserie Lipp; Bubbles; Rose & Crown
51 Joe Farelli's

54 Billhälls Supermarket
57 Solrosen
61 Smaka
62 Café Garbo
70 Konsum Supermarket
71 Sushi & Soda
74 Java Kaffebar
77 Espresso House
79 Shabby Chic & the Bakery; Wasatvätten
81 Sjöbaren
83 Kraków
84 28+
85 Evas Paley

ENTERTAINMENT
6 Göteborgs Operan
27 Gretas Café, Bar & Kök; MataHari
32 O'Learys; Ticket
33 The Dubliner
42 Ölhallen 7:an
43 Biopalatset
44 Filmstaden
52 Nivå
53 Nefertiti
60 Jazzhuset
64 Valand
65 XLNT
68 Dancin' Dingo
87 Göteborgs Stadsteatern
89 Göteborgs Konserthus

MUSEUMS
7 Göteborgs Maritima Centrum
15 Kronhuset; Kronhusbodarna
16 Stadsmuseum; Östindiska huset
63 Röhsska Museet
82 Skansen Kronan; Military Museum
90 Konstmuseet

OTHER
3 Götheborgs-Utkiken
4 Börjessons Sightseeing Boats
5 Älvsnabben Departures
8 Nils Ericssons Terminalen; Tidpunkten
9 Forex; Pocketshop; Pressbyrån
10 Akuttandvården
11 Tidpunkten Kiosk

14 Nordstan Shopping Complex; Tourist Office; Post Office; Forex; Apoteket Vasan; Akademibokhandeln; Åhléns
19 Rosarium
20 Fjärilshuset (Butterfly House)
21 Palmhuset (Palm House)

23 Press Stop
24 NK Department Store
25 Eurolines
31 Domkyrkan
34 Forex
36 Naturkompaniet
38 Tourist Office
39 Paddan Sightseeing Boats

45 DesignTorget
47 Palatset
49 Stora Teatern; Sightseeing Bus Departures
55 Feskekörka (Fish Church)
56 Hagabadet
58 Hagakyrkan
66 Forex; Systembolaget

72 Centrum Cykel
73 Göteborg University (Main Building)
75 Akademibokhandeln
78 Janemans IT Palats
80 Kilroy Travels
86 Stadsbibliotek (City Library)
88 Poseidon Fountain

GÖTALAND

clean, quiet and close to the ferries to Denmark. Take tram No 3, 4 or 9 to Masthuggstorget and follow the signs (upstairs behind the supermarket).

Nearby is the STF hostel **Stigbergsliden** (☎ 241620; ℮ vandrarhem.stigbergsliden@ swipnet.se; Stigbergsliden 10; tram No 3, 4 or 9 to Stigbergstorget; dorm beds Skr115, singles/doubles Skr240/280), in a renovated 19th-century seaman's house. Breakfast is Skr40, and there's a good kitchen, laundry, TV room and garden, plus old bikes for rent (Skr40 per day).

STF's second hostel in Gothenburg is **Slottsskogen** (☎ 426520; ℮ mail@slottssko genvh.se; Vegagatan 21; tram No 1 or 2 to Olivedalsgatan; dorm beds Skr100-115, singles/doubles Skr235/280), a friendly, appealing place with excellent facilities. There are two large, 12-bed dorms with beds for Skr100; beds in smaller rooms are more expensive.

Down the road is another good option, the SVIF hostel **Linné Vandrarhem** (☎ 121060; Vegagatan 22; dorm beds Skr160, doubles Skr360). Clean and inviting **Göteborgs Mini-Hotel** (☎ 241023; ℮ info@minihotel.se; Tredje Långgatan; dorm beds Skr130-150, doubles Skr360) is located in the same area, offering renovated rooms all with TV and fridge, and shared bathroom facilities.

Göteborgs Vandrarhem (☎ 401050; ℮ info@goteborgsvandrarhem.se; Mölndalsvägen 23; tram No 4 to Getebergsäng; dorm beds Skr150-160, singles/doubles Skr350/370) is just south of Liseberg and is yet another well-equipped hostel.

The very pleasant SVIF **Kvibergs Vandrarhem & Stugby** (☎ 435055; ℮ famlin@ algonet.se; Kvibergsvägen 5; dorm beds from Skr120, singles/doubles from Skr210/290, 5-bed cabins Skr600-895) has hostel accommodation as well as good self-contained cabins a few kilometres northeast of the city centre, reached by tram No 6, 7 or 11.

Private Rooms The tourist office can arrange **private rooms** from Skr175/225 for a single/double, plus a Skr60 booking fee.

Hotels Probably the best accommodation bargain in town, **Hotel Formule 1** (☎ 492400; Axel Adlersgata 2; tram No 1, 7 or 8; rooms Skr270) is in Västra Frölunda, about 7km south of the city centre. Functional but bland

rooms have shared facilities and can sleep up to three people. Breakfast is not included in the price.

Ibis Hotel Göteborg City (☎ 802560; Gullbergskajen 217; rooms Skr525-650) is a large floating hotel with comfortable, well-priced rooms (prices don't include breakfast). The down side is that it is in quite an isolated part of town. More upmarket and with a better location is another large boat hotel, **Barken Viking** (☎ 635800; ℮ barken.viking@lise berg.se; Gullbergskajen; singles/doubles in 'crew quarters' Skr600/800), built in 1906 and now moored near Lilla Bommen harbour. You can pay extra (from Skr800/1000) for a little more luxury and private facilities in an 'officer's cabin'.

City Hotel (☎ 708 4000; ℮ receptionen@ cityhotelgbg.se; Lorensbergsgatan 6; singles/ doubles Skr395/495) is in a fine location behind Kungsportsavenyn. For about Skr300 extra you can have a better standard of room with private facilities.

In a similar vein is **Hotel Flora** (☎ 138616; Grönsakstorget 2; singles/doubles Skr415/575, with bath Skr780/990, discounted to Skr650/850), not far from the tourist office. It also offers very comfortable rooms with private facilities in addition to its budget rooms.

Another agreeable option is **Vanilj Hotel** (☎ 711 6220; ℮ info@vaniljhotel.entersol.se; Kyrkogatan 38; singles/doubles Skr795/995, discounted to Skr545/795), a small, cosy and personal place above a lovely café, situated in the heart of town.

Hotel Vasa (☎ 173630; ℮ info@hotel vasa.se; Viktoriagatan 6; singles/doubles Skr845/995, discounted to Skr550/720) is an attractive, family-run place handy to the cafés of Vasagatan. Not far away is another decent mid-range option with lots of character, **Hotel Excelsior** (☎ 175435; ℮ info@ hotelexcelsior .nu; Karl Gustavsgatan 7; singles/doubles Skr930/1090, discounted to Skr575/760).

Central **Hotel Opera** (☎ 805080; ℮ info@ hotelopera.se; Norra Hamngatan 38; budget singles/doubles Skr725/875, standard singles/doubles Skr1095/1195, discounted to Skr695/795) is conveniently located close to the train station and bus terminal. Budget rooms are in an older part of the hotel and are quite small but adequate; all rooms have private facilities, TV and phone.

GÖTALAND

The elegant **Hotel Eggers** (☎ 806070; e hotel.eggers@telia.com; Drottningtorget; singles/doubles from Skr1310/1640, discounted to Skr695/950), located nearby, was founded as a railway hotel in 1859, but parts of the building date back to 1820. The very pleasant rooms with fine atmosphere are particularly good value on weekends and also during the summer.

Hotel Royal (☎ 700 1170; e info@hotel-royal.com; Drottninggatan 67; singles/doubles from Skr995/1295, discounted to Skr690/790) is the oldest hotel in Gothenburg (built in 1852) and has comfortable rooms and a rather grand entrance hall, compete with painted ceiling.

A very fine hotel, **Scandic Hotel Europa** (☎ 751 6500; e europa@scandic-hotels.com; Köpmansgatan 38; singles/doubles Skr1350/1650, discounted to Skr850/950) features a lovely pool and sauna area on the sixth floor, with views of the town. Part of the same chain of quality hotels and with similar prices, **Scandic Hotel Rubinen** (☎ 751 5400; e rubinen@scandic-hotels.com; Kungsportsavenyn 24) has well-appointed rooms in the heart of the Avenyn action, as well as an on-site restaurant and bar.

Radisson SAS Scandinavia Hotel (☎ 758 5000; Södra Hamngatan 59-65; singles/doubles from Skr1350/1610, discounted to Skr790/1090) is one of the most luxurious hotel in Gothenburg. It's an ultramodern place with indoor pool and health club, as well as a bright and appealing bar and restaurant in the atrium.

Top of the heap in Gothenburg is the 23-storey **Hotel Gothia Towers** (☎ 750 8800; e info@gothiatowers.com; Mässans Gata 24; tram No 5; singles/doubles from Skr1590/1990, discounted to Skr840/940), the largest hotel in Scandinavia. The decor here is very stylish and modern, and there are good restaurants and bars, including one on the top floor. Summer and weekend prices are very reasonable. The hotel is handily located opposite Liseberg and only a few minutes' walk to Kungsportsavenyn.

Places to Eat

Gothenburg is awash with sleek and fashionable restaurants, and you can sample almost every international cuisine here, but note that many restaurants are closed on Sunday.

Kungsportsavenyn, the 'Champs-Élysées of Gothenburg', is lined with all kinds of restaurants and alfresco dining is popular when the sun comes out. Vasagatan and Linnégatan are similar, with quite a few popular places.

Restaurants The award-winning and high-quality **28+** (☎ 202161; Götabergsgatan 28; à la carte mains Skr295-365) is a special occasion place. It's worth investigating if you feel like a real splurge – the seven-course degustation fish menu is Skr728 and includes exceptional dishes.

Magnus & Magnus (☎ 133000; Magasinsgatan 8; 2-course meal Skr335) is a stylish, modern restaurant with a relaxed atmosphere. There's a good à la carte menu, with well prepared fish and meat selections.

Fiskekrogen (☎ 101005; Lilla Torget 1; dinner mains Skr255-335) is a magnificent fish and seafood restaurant in former East India Company buildings. It has an impressive circular dining room called Blåskajsa, and an equally impressive wine list.

Trädgår'n (☎ 102080; Nya Allén; mains Skr145-285) is a spacious and modern restaurant, bar and nightclub facing the lovely Trädgårdsföreningen park. Lunch here is a good deal, with meal-deals for only Skr69 in the cheaper Backfickan section, or from Skr85 in the dining room.

You're spoilt for choice with the abundance of popular restaurants, bars and cafés lining Kungsportsavenyn, although prices along here can be higher than you might expect to pay in other parts of town. **Joe Farelli's** (☎ 105826; Kungsportsavenyn 12; dishes Skr100-250) is a casual restaurant-bar with an Italian-American kitchen pumping out pricey sandwiches, salads, pasta, burgers, steaks and the like. The classic, classier **Brasserie Lipp** (☎ 105830; Kungsportsavenyn 8; meals Skr90-220) has good light meals on its menu, including Caesar salad or a club sandwich, plus more substantial main courses.

New **Ping Pong Kitchen** (☎ 131600; Östra Larmgatan 20; lunch around Skr95, dinner meals Skr95-175), near the tourist office, is a sleek and trendy new restaurant serving Asian cuisine, with popular Thai and Japanese dishes (noodles, curry, soups, sushi) featuring heavily on the menu.

Smaka (☎ 132247; Vasaplatsen 3; mains Skr89-200) serves up wonderful, traditional

Swedish *husmanskost* (home cooking) and more adventurous local cuisine, including meatballs with mashed potato and lingonberries (Skr89), elk burgers, fish soup and lemon sole. Finish your meal with a delicious cloudberry souffle for dessert.

For something a little different, **Kraków** (☎ 203374; Karl Gustavsgatan 28; mains Skr72-150) serves filling Polish food at very reasonable prices and is popular with students. The 'snacks, starters, soups and salads' section of the menu has items costing Skr25 to Skr85, including a bowl of borsch served with a meat-filled pancake for only Skr49.

Near the hostels in the southwestern part of town, friendly and inviting **Cyrano** (☎ 143010; Prinsgatan 7; lunch Skr65, dinner mains around Skr180) is a highly regarded French bistro-style restaurant, where three-course set menus of an evening cost from as little as Skr135 (if your main course is a pizza), or Skr185 for fish or meat mains. There's also a selection of good French à la carte dishes, including duck and lamb, and simpler pizzas (Skr60-80).

Ning Bo (☎ 424090; Fjärde Långgatan 3; lunch buffet Skr57, dishes Skr69-105) has a cheap lunch buffet where you can load up on Asian dishes. The place looks rather dingy, but the food's pretty good.

If you're looking to up your iron intake, **A Hereford Beefstouw** (☎ 775 0441; Linnégatan 5; lunch Skr82, mains Skr110-325), around the corner from Ning Bo, is an upmarket steakhouse offering all manner of meat, including T-bone and rib-eye steaks, veal sirloin and rack of lamb. There are also fish selections, but vegetarians will struggle here.

If nonmeat dishes are more your style, better to head to vegetarian **Solrosen** (Karponjärgatan 4), a slightly grungy place with great buffets and dishes from Skr60.

Nearby is cosy **Sjöbaren** (☎ 711 9780; Haga Nygata 25; meals from Skr90), in the Haga district and offering excellent Swedish seafood; classic dishes like gravadlax (cured salmon) with potatoes, fish soup or seafood pasta cost around Skr95.

Bombay (☎ 120039; Andra Långgatan 8; meals from Skr70) does good-value Indian dishes to eat in or take away, with tempting tandoori and vegetarian selections.

Pasta Etc (☎ 247472; Plantagegatan 3; pasta Skr75-115) has a wonderful array of pasta dishes with a large selection of sauces,

including salmon and vodka, seafood, Parma ham and pesto, and sausage and peppers.

Cheap and popular **Kalaya** (☎ 123998; Olivedalsgatan 13; dishes from Skr55) has excellent Thai noodle and curry dishes. Its neighbour, **Den Lilla Taverna** (☎ 128805; Olivedalsgatan 17; mains under Skr100), is a charming spot with authentic, reasonably priced Greek dishes, including all the favourites, plus a great array of starters (Skr35 to Skr60) perfect for sharing.

Cafés There are numerous and invariably high-quality cafés in Gothenburg. **Café Garbo** (☎ 774 1925; Vasagatan 40) and the very trendy **Espresso House** (☎ 39750; Vasagatan 22) are two of several excellent places along the leafy Vasagatan boulevard, both offering large windows and good people-watching plus good coffee and fashionable café fare priced from Skr30 to Skr60.

Not far away is the wonderfully named **Shabby Chic & the Bakery** (☎ 711 4888; Viktoriagatan 20), comprising a café with a rustic interior serving lunch for Skr49, plus its neighbouring bakery, which exudes gorgeous aromas.

Java Kaffebar (Vasagatan 32) is a popular student haunt and has a slightly grungy feel. It offers cheap bagels and sandwiches (from Skr26) to its young, groovy crowd.

Brogyllens Konditori (☎ 138713; Västra Hamngatan 2) is a lovely traditional place selling great breads and pastries. Linger over coffee and cake under the grand chandeliers. Down the road and a world away in decor is **Café Kosmos** (☎ 131400; Västra Hamngatan 20), a slick, modern place attracting a young and funky crowd.

Evas Paley (☎ 163070; Kungsportsavenyn 39) is a huge, popular place open until late every evening and serving a wide range of good-value dishes including baked potatoes, wraps, pasta (always vegetarian options), salads and lots of fresh muffins in a variety of flavours (Skr20).

Fast Food & Snacks If you need something quick, the enormous Nordstan shopping complex houses many fast-food outlets.

Right near the tourist office, busy **Aldarde** (Kungstorget 12) is a great spot to pick up authentic Italian fast food – home-made pizza *al taglio* (by the slice) costs around Skr25 and pasta is from Skr35. In the middle of neighbouring **Saluhallen**, full of excellent budget eateries and food stalls, **Kåges Hörna** serves some of the best cheap food around – chicken salad, lasagne and the pasta special all only cost about Skr35. **Alexandras**, also in Saluhallen, is renowned for its excellent soups and stews – on a cold day, try the hearty lentil soup or fish soup (Skr30 to Skr40).

Not as busy as the central Saluhallen but also housing a good array of lunch stalls is **Saluhall Briggen** (Nordhemsgatan), not far from the hostel district.

Sushi & Soda (Kristinelundsgatan 3 • Prinsgatan 4) serves excellent Japanese takeaways, with lunch deals, including miso soup and 11 pieces of sushi, for around Skr60.

Those with a sweet tooth should head to the **Creperiet**, a takeaway van near the McDonald's branch on Linnégatan. It's open until late each night and offers sweet crepes from Skr15, savoury from Skr30.

Self-Catering Central **Saluhallen** is the perfect place to put together your picnic pack (or even have a sit-down meal). It's a classic old market hall on Kungstorget where a whole range of delicatessen foods is sold.

Billhälls supermarket (Hvitfeldtsplatsen) is a good, cheap, central supermarket, open daily. The **Konsum supermarket** (Kungsportsavenyn) is also handy.

Systembolaget (Kungsportsavenyn 18) is the most central place selling beer, wine and spirits.

Entertainment

Pubs & Clubs As authentic an Irish pub as you'll ever find on the continent, the **Dubliner** (☎ 139020; Östra Hamngatan 50B) has live Celtic music every weekend. Pints of Guinness and Kilkenny cost Skr49 and bar meals range from Skr59 to Skr98, including Emerald Isle staples such as fish and chips or beef-and-Guinness pie. Almost opposite is **O'Leary's** (☎ 711 5519; Östra Hamngatan 36), an American-style sports bar with lots of TV screens and a menu of good bar snacks.

The **Rose & Crown** (☎ 105827; Kungsportsavenyn 6) is an English-style pub popular with tourists and locals, and just in case there are any nationalities feeling left out of the pub scene, the **Dancin' Dingo** (☎ 811812; Kristinelundsgatan 16) is an entertaining Australian pub not far off Kungsportsavenyn.

One place that you should check out is **Ölhallen 7:an** (☎ 136079; Kungstorget 7), not far from the tourist office. This little gem is a well-worn Swedish beerhall that hasn't changed in about 100 years. There's no food, wine or pretension, just beer, and plenty of choices.

Swedish licensing laws mean that bars must have a restaurant section – in most cases, it's vice versa. Stroll down Kungsportsavenyn for a huge selection of restaurant-bars, and see what takes your fancy. Popular nightclubs include **Bubbles** at No 8; downstairs next to Brasserie Lipp and a favourite of the fashionable set, **Nivå** at No 9 with a few floors of action; and vintage **Valand**, on the corner of Vasagatan and drawing a mixed, party-hardy crowd. **XLNT** (Vasagatan 43B), east of Kungsportsavenyn, is hard to find but it's very trendy and draws punters in the 23-to-30 age group from Wednesday to Saturday.

Gretas Café, Bar & Kök (☎ 136949; Drottninggatan 35) is a café, bar and restaurant catering to the gay crowd, but not exclusively so. There's great kitschy decor, and usually a large after-work crowd. The nightclub here, **MataHari**, heats up on Friday and Saturday nights.

Cinema, Concerts & Theatre One of many cinemas around town, the 10-screen **Biopalatset** (☎ 174500; Kungstorget), behind Saluhallen, shows regular blockbuster films. **Filmstaden** (Kungsgatan 35), near the Domkyrka, is another central option.

Super-cool **Nefertiti** (☎ 711 1533; Hvitfeldtsplatsen 6), near the Fish Church, is a large and well-established venue for live jazz, blues and ethnic music; it also has a nightclub, restaurant and café.

Jazzhuset (☎ 133544; Erik Dahlbergsgatan 3) is an old jazz club drawing a more mature crowd to its live music sessions.

Facing each other near Konstmuseet are **Göteborgs Stadsteatern** (City Theatre; ☎ 615050; W www.stadsteatern.goteborg.se; Götaplatsen; tickets from Skr190), with a number of dramatic performances (usually in Swedish), and **Göteborgs Konserthus** (Concert Hall; ☎ 726 5300; Götaplatsen), home to the local symphony orchestra.

It's worth investigating what is on at the really modern **GöteborgsOperan** (☎ 131300; W www.opera.se; Christina Nilssons gata;

GÖTALAND

tickets Skr100-500), at Lilla Bommen harbour, which stages ballet, opera and assorted musical performances.

Nya Ullevi *(☎ 811020;* W *www.ullevi.se; Skånegatan)* is an outdoor stadium where pop and rock concerts are held, and nearby **Scandinavium** *(☎ 811020;* W *www.scandi navium.se; Valhallagatan 1)* is an indoor concert venue. Websites for these arenas are in Swedish only.

Check local events listings or with the tourist office for current schedules and prices.

Spectator Sports

Gothenburghers are avid sports fans, and the city has outdoor stadiums such as **Nya Ullevi**, hosting football matches, and the indoor **Scandinavium**, where ice hockey is played in front of an enthusiastic crowd. See earlier for contact details of these venues, which also regularly host pop and rock concerts.

Shopping

The large department stores, **Åhléns** *(Nordstan)* and **NK** *(Östra Hamngatan)*, stock a good range of quality souvenirs and prices are reasonable. The huge Nordstan shopping complex has some 150 stores and is open daily.

Visit **DesignTorget** *(Vallgatan 14)*, a great store showcasing the works (usually quite affordable) of both established and up-and-coming designers. Otherwise, pick up a brochure from the tourist office that outlines the galleries and designers around town. There are also good craft and handiwork stores in the area around Kronhuset (see Other Attractions, earlier).

Getting There & Away

Air Twenty-five kilometres east of the city **Landvetter airport** *(☎ 941000;* W *www.land vetter.lfv.se)* has frequent direct daily flights to/from Stockholm Arlanda and Bromma airports with SAS and Malmö Aviation (up to 30 daily), as well as weekday services to Borlänge, Västerås and Sundsvall (Skyways), daily services to Umeå (Malmö Aviation) and to Linköping (City Airline). See the introductory Getting There & Away chapter for contact details for these major airlines.

Many European cities have air links with Gothenburg, including Amsterdam (KLM), Brussels (SAS), Copenhagen (SAS), Dublin (Malmö Aviation, once or twice weekly from late May to late September), Frankfurt (Lufthansa and SAS), Helsinki (Finnair, Skyways and SAS), London (SAS and British Airways), Manchester (BA and City Airline), Munich (SAS), Oslo (SAS) and Paris (Air France and Goodjet).

Säve *(☎ 926060)* is a minor airport some 20 minutes north of the city, used by Ryanair for its direct flights to London's Stansted airport.

Bus The modern bus station, **Nils Ericssons Terminalen**, is next to the train station. There's a **Tidpunkten** office here, open daily, giving information and selling tickets for all city and regional public transport within the Göteborg, Bohuslän and Västergötland area.

Eurolines *(☎ 020 987377;* W *www.euro lines.com; Kyrkogatan 40)* has its main Swedish office in central Gothenburg. See the Getting There & Away chapter for details on international bus services offered by the company.

Swebus Express *(☎ 0200 218218;* W *www .swebusexpress.se)* has an office at the bus terminal and operates frequent buses to most major towns. Services to Stockholm (Skr350) take seven hours and run seven to 10 times daily. Other direct destinations include Copenhagen (Skr270), Falun (Skr360) Helsingborg (Skr220), Jönköping (Skr155) Oslo (Skr225), Malmö (Skr260), Strömstad (Skr250) and Örebro (Skr245), and closer destinations such as Uddevalla (Skr60) and Halmstad (Skr160).

Cheaper but less frequent is **Svenska Buss** *(☎ 0771-676767;* W *www.svenskabuss.se)* which runs buses to Halmstad (Skr140) Helsingborg (Skr180) and Malmö (Skr200) five times weekly. Twice-weekly buses depart for Kalmar and Oskarshamn (Skr260) departures for Stockholm (Skr320) via Jönköping are daily.

Säfflebussen *(☎ 020 1600 600;* W *www.sa flebussen.se)* runs services to Copenhagen (Skr260, six daily), Oslo (Skr210, six daily) and Stockholm (Skr290, once or twice daily)

Bear in mind that prices can be considerably lower than those quoted here for travel from Monday to Thursday, especially with **Swebus Express** and **Säfflebussen**.

Train Centralstationen serves SJ and regional trains, with direct trains to Copenhagen (Skr450, 4½ hours), Malmö (Skr409 3½ hours) and Oslo (Skr378, four hours), as

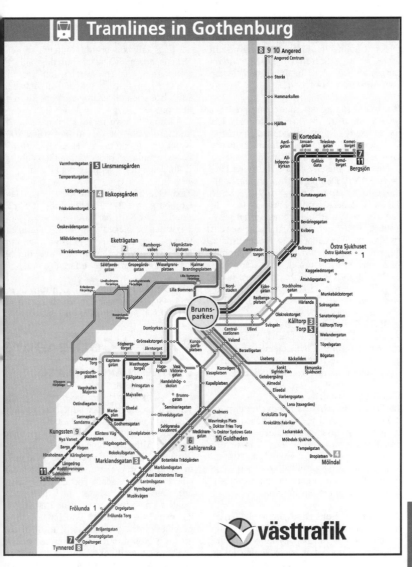

well as numerous other destinations in the southern half of Sweden. Direct Intercity trains to Stockholm depart approximately every two hours (Skr542, 5¼ hours), with quicker but more expensive X2000 trains (Skr1041, 3¼ hours) also every two hours. Booking your ticket at least a week in advance will bring decent reductions to the prices quoted here.

The overnight trains to the far north of Sweden (via Stockholm) are operated by Tågkompaniet.

Car & Motorcycle The E6 motorway runs north-south from Oslo to Malmö just east of the city centre and there's also a complex junction where the E20 motorway diverges east for Stockholm.

A number of the large, international car-hire companies (eg, Europcar, Avis) have desks at Landvetter airport. For car hire in town, contact **Statoil** (☎ 859780; Andra Långgatan 46), close to the hostels in the southwestern part of town.

Boat Gothenburg is a major entry point for ferries, and there are several terminals. For more details of ferry services to Denmark, Germany and the UK, see the introductory Getting There & Away chapter.

Nearest to the city centre, the **Stena Line** (☎ 704 0000) Denmark terminal near Masthuggstorget (tram No 3, 4 or 9) has up to 11 daily departures for Frederikshavn in summer, with a 50% discount for rail pass-holders. Faster and more expensive **SeaCat** (☎ 720 0800) catamarans to Frederikshavn depart up to three times daily in summer from near Sjöfartsmuseet. Take tram No 3 or 9 to Stigbergstorget. Farther west is the Stena Line terminal for the daily car ferry to Kiel (Germany). Take tram No 3 or 9 to Chapmans Torg.

DFDS Seaways (☎ 650650) sails twice weekly to Kristiansand (Norway) and Newcastle (UK) from Skandiahamnen on Hisingen (buses leave 1½ hours before departures from Nils Ericsson Terminalen; Skr50).

Getting Around

To/From the Airport Landvetter airport, 25km east of the city, can be reached by the frequent Flygbuss from Nils Ericssons Terminalen (Skr50, 30 minutes). A taxi from the city centre will cost around Skr310.

There are also buses to Säve airport some 90 minutes before flight departures (Skr30), departing from the bus terminal.

Bus, Tram & Boat Buses, trams and ferries run by **Vasttrafik** (☎ 0771-414300) make up the city public transport system; there are Tidpunkten information booths selling tickets and giving out timetables inside Nils Ericssons Terminalen, at Brunnsparken and on Drottningtorget, in front of the train station. An individual ticket on transport costs Skr16, but holders of the Göteborg Pass travel free. Cheaper and easy-to-use 'value cards' cost Skr100 (from Tidpunkten or Pressbyrån newsagencies) and reduce the cost considerably. A 24-hour Dagkort (day pass) for the whole city area costs Skr50.

The easiest way to cover lengthy distances in Gothenburg is by tram. There are 11 lines, all converging somewhere near Brunnsparken, one block from the train station. Also convenient and fun are the Älvsnabben ferries, which run between Lilla Bommen and Klippan every 30 minutes or so.

Västtrafik have regional passes for 24 hours (Skr190) or for 30 days (Skr1200) which give unlimited travel on all *länstrafik* buses, trains and boats within Gothenburg, Bohuslän and the Västergötland area.

Taxi One of the larger companies is **Taxi Göteborg** (☎ 650000), with rates of Skr27 flagfall and Skr9 per kilometre thereafter. Taxis can be picked up outside Centralstationen, at Kungsportsplatsen, and on Kungsportsavenyn. Women travelling by taxi at night can expect a fare discount.

Bicycle For bicycle rental, **Centrum Cykel** (☎ 184300; Chalmersgatan 19) charges from Skr100 per day; they also do repairs.

Around Gothenburg

SOUTHERN ARCHIPELAGO
☎ 031 • pop 4300

Just a short hop from the busy city, the southern archipelago is a popular residential area for wealthy commuters, but there are also several nature reserves and lots of open country. Although some islands, especially those with beaches, can become quite busy in summer, there are many quiet areas where you can escape the crowds. There are nine major islands and numerous smaller ones; the largest island is Styrsö, but even it's less than 3km long. Due to previous military restrictions, most of the area was closed to foreigners until 1997.

There's a really excellent 16-destination passenger-only ferry network running from Saltholmen (take tram No 11 from Gothenburg city centre) on the mainland, and you can hop from island to island too. A single ticket (Skr16) takes you all the way from central Gothenburg to Vrångö and the Göteborg Pass is valid; bikes cost an extra Skr10 (only if there is space available). Boats run frequently to Asperö, Brännö, Köpstadsö and Styrsö from around 5.30am to 1am less frequent at weekends), but services to the other islands (including Vrångö) run less often. For information, stop in at one of the Tidpunkten offices in Gothenburg (see Getting Around under Gothenburg, earlier).

Ask at the Gothenburg tourist office for information about the islands. The best information is contained in the detailed English-language booklet *Touring the Archipelago* (free), published by Västtrafik (the public transport authority).

Brännö
pop 650

The populated eastern half of this island is remarkably quiet – the only car is the local taxi – but the locals drive *lastmoped* – bizarre-looking mopeds with large trays. The main ferry terminal is Rödsten, in the northeast (20 minutes from Salthomen), but ferries also call less frequently at Husvik in the southwest, where there's a popular outdoor dance-floor. Once a week from mid-June to mid-August, **Börjessons** (☎ 609670) runs evening cruises out to this dance-floor, where passengers can enjoy live music and dancing for a couple of hours before returning to Gothenburg. The tour costs Skr120/60 per adult/child; dinner is available on board the boat at additional cost.

Brännö has a long history. In the 10th century, at a market on the island, an Irish king's daughter was sold as a slave to the Icelander Hoskuld Dalakollson for three silver marks. In 1676, the Danes sacked the island and looted everything that could be moved.

From the church in the centre of the island, follow the cycle track through the woods towards the west coast. A 15-minute walk from the end of the track leads to a stone causeway and the island **Galterö** – a strange treeless landscape of rock slabs, ponds, deserted sandy beaches and haunting bird calls. You can watch ships of all sizes and colours sail into or out of Gothenburg harbour.

You can get away from it all at the simple and cosy **Pensionat Bagge** (☎ 973880; e boka@baggebranno.se; singles/doubles low season Skr330/500, high season Skr390/660), a friendly place about a kilometre south of the ferry quay; it also offers bike hire. With the same owners, nearby **Brännö Värdshus** (☎ 970478, open daily in summer) has a restaurant, café and bakery and serves excellent meals; the local speciality, *rödspotta*

(catfish) is Skr149. There's a grocery shop near the church.

Other Islands

Just southeast of Brännö, **Köpstadsö** is a small island with a quaint village of white-painted houses and narrow streets. Transport on the island is even more basic than on Brännö: locals use individually named wheelbarrows, which you'll see neatly parked by the quay!

In the central part of the archipelago, **Styrsö** has two village centres (Bratten and Tången, both with ferry terminals), a mixture of old and modern houses, and a colourful history of smuggling. There is a café and pizzeria at Tången, and a supermarket. A bridge crosses from Styrsö to neighbouring densely populated **Donsö**, with its functioning fishing harbour.

The southern island of **Vrångö** has a good beach for swimming on the west coast, about 10 minutes' walk from the ferry. The northern and southern ends of the island are part of an extensive nature reserve.

Tiny **Vinga**, 8km west of Galterö, has impressive rock slabs and good swimming, and it has been home to a lighthouse since the 17th century. The writer, composer and painter, Evert Taube, was born on the island in 1890 – his father was the lighthouse-keeper. **Borjessons** (☎ 609660) runs full-day tours (adult/child Skr100/50) from Lilla Bommen (Gothenburg) to Vinga via Nya Älvsborg Fästning, daily from early July to mid-August (once weekly in June and late August).

MARSTRAND
☎ 0303 • pop 1300

Picturesque Marstrand, with its wooden buildings and island setting, conveys the essence of Bohuslän fishing villages and is almost free of cars. Like many other places along the coast, it has become an upmarket weekend destination for wealthy sailors. It's humming with people in summer but is well worth a day trip from Gothenburg, or even an overnight trip.

The **tourist office** (☎ 60087; Hamngatan; w www.kungalv.se/turism; open daily early June–mid-Aug) is a few minutes' walk from the ferry quay (turn left after disembarking). **Carlstens Fästning** (☎ 60265; adult/child Skr50/20; open noon-4pm June-Aug,

11am-6pm mid-June–mid-Aug) is a fortress constructed in the 1660s after the Swedish takeover of Bohuslän. It's an impressive structure with a round tower reaching 96m above sea level and it reflects a long martial and penal history. Admission includes the guided tour on the hour from noon to 3pm. The **town hall** is the oldest stone building in the area and the **Maria Kyrka**, just inland from the harbour, dates from the 13th century. You can walk around the island in about an hour; pick up the English-language *Discover Marstrand* brochure (Skr10) from the tourist office before setting off.

Most of the accommodation options on the island are upmarket and pricey, with the notable exception of **Båtellet** *(☎ 60010; dorm beds Skr155-235)*, a private hostel 400m from the ferry dock (turn right after disembarking and follow the waterfront). Prices vary depending on the season. There's a large indoor pool here too, and the attached **Restaurang Drott** serves lunch specials and à la carte selections, with a great view.

Hotell Nautic *(☎ 61030; e info@hotell nautic.com; Långgatan 6; B&B singles/doubles Skr760/960)* has bright and simple rooms decked out in blues and whites.

There are numerous eating options along the harbour, including cheap **fast-food stalls** (one sells fresh fish and chips for Skr45). You can follow your nose to **Bergs Konditori** *(☎ 60096; Hamngatan 9)*, selling fresh bread and pastries, plus sandwiches from Skr25 to Skr60. There are many more cafés and upmarket restaurants here.

From Gothenburg you can take bus No 312 to Arvidsvik (on Koön; Skr40) then cross to Marstrand by frequent passenger-only ferry (adult/child Skr13/8). The complete journey should take only about 40 minutes. Alternatively, in midsummer, catch the boat from Lilla Bommen at 9.30am (Skr100/160 one-way/return) for a pleasant three-hour journey to Marstrand.

BOHUS FÄSTNING
☎ 0303

The well-defended Bohus Fästning *(☎ 99200; adult/child Skr25/10; open 10am-7pm daily May, June & Aug; 10am-8pm daily July; 11am-4pm daily Sept)* is on an island in the Nordre älv near the modern industrial town of Kungälv. Construction of the fortress was ordered in 1308 by the Norwegian King Haakan

V Magnusson, to protect Norway's southern border. The building was enlarged and extended over the coming centuries and it fell into Swedish hands when Sweden gained Bohuslän at the Peace of Roskilde in 1658. Nowadays, substantial ruins remain, including a remarkable **round tower**. Tourist information for the area is available at the fortress.

Kungälvs Vandrarhem & Camping *(☎ 18900; Färjevägen 2, Kungälv; dorm beds & tent sites Skr120, cabins Skr450)* is a well-equipped place in a pleasant riverside setting directly across the road from the fortress. The hostel is open from mid-April to December, camping from May to mid-September. There's also a café here, and you can rent small boats.

Grön Express bus No 6A runs frequently from Gothenburg to Kungälv (Skr40); get off at the Fars Hatt stop and walk the remaining 750m.

Bohuslän

BOHUSLÄN COAST
This beautiful coastline contains some of the finest scenery in Sweden. Picturesque fishing villages, rock-slab shorelines, craggy islands and the soft western light help create a special kind of magic for photographers, artists, and anyone who cares to wander, watch and wonder.

Transport connections in the area are good: the E6 Hwy runs north from Gothenburg to Oslo via the larger towns of Stenungsund, Ljungskile, Herrestad (close to the regional centre of Uddevalla), Munkedal, Tanumshede and passing close to Strömstad before crossing the Norwegian border. There is a local train service that runs frequently from Gothenburg to Strömstad, via much the same towns as on the E6 route, and bus connections are also good from these towns to the outlying islands and coastal areas, although some routes don't run terribly frequently. This is an area that lends itself well to independent exploration – it may be worth hiring a car (or bike) in Gothenburg to see things at your own pace and enjoy the scenery.

If you're heading north from Gothenburg, it is worth stopping by the **tourist office** *(☎ 0303-83327; e info@bastkusten.se, w www.bastkusten.se; Kulturhuset Fregattan)* in

Stenungsund to pick up brochures and especially maps of the surrounding area.

Tjörn
☎ 0304

A large bridge crosses from Stenungsund on the Swedish mainland to the island of Tjörn (W www.tjorn.se), and there are a few places here worth checking out.

Skärhamn and **Rönnäng**, in the island's southwest, are the main settlements and have a few facilities. Skärhamn is worth a visit for the impressive new **Nordiska Akvarellmuseet** (Nordic Watercolour Museum; ☎ 600080; Södra Hamnen; adult/child Skr60/ 10; open 11am-6pm daily May-Aug, noon-5pm Tues-Sun Sept-Apr), a sleek and stylish new waterside building housing interesting changing exhibits. There's an adjacent café and restaurant, **Vattern** (☎ 670087), serving up good food. There are other eateries at the busy boating harbour here, and a supermarket in the village.

Klädesholmen, in the island's far south and connected by causeway, is among the finest of the west-coast fishing villages, although activity here is fairly subdued due to the departure of the herring (there are still a handful of locally owned herring factories, but there used to be 30). Klädesholmen is home to a **herring museum** (☎ 673361; Sillgränd; adult/child Skr10/5; open 3pm-7pm daily late June–mid-Aug), which tells the story of the industry from 1910 to 1960. The neighbouring **Salt & Sill** (☎ 673480; 3-course menu Skr355) restaurant has a good choice of main courses, and naturally herring features heavily on the menu.

Nearby **Åstol** is a very attractive place – almost the entire island is covered with houses perched on rocks; you can reach Åstol by ferry from Rönnäng, roughly hourly (Skr24), and there's a good SVIF hostel here, **Rönnängs Vandrarhem** (☎ 677198; Nybronvägen 5; dorm beds Skr165).

The Tjörnexpressen bus runs up to eight times on weekdays (twice on Saturday and Sunday) from Gothenburg's bus terminal to Tjörn, calling at Skärhamn, Klädesholmen and Rönnäng. Bus No 350 from Stenungsund also circles the island.

Orust
☎ 0304

A bridge connects Tjörn with its northern neighbour, Orust (W www.orust.se). There's

an outstanding STF hostel, **Tofta gård** (☎ 50380; e info@toftagard.se; dorm beds Skr140-160) near Stocken in the island's west and about 5km from the larger village of Ellös. The charming hostel is an old farmhouse and outbuildings in a delightful setting, with good walking, swimming and canoeing nearby. There's also a café here in peak season.

The village of **Mollösund**, in the island's southwest, is a great place on a sunny day and it's not overly touristy. **Mollösunds Hembygdsmuseum** (☎ 21469; admission free; open 11am-1pm & 5.30pm-7.30pm daily late-June–mid-Aug) is in an old fisher-folks house near the water and has exhibits about local life. **Morlanda Kyrka** is about 15km north and it's worth a look if you're passing.

Vandrarhem h'Emma (☎ 21175; e café .emma@cafeemma.com; dorm beds Skr200), on the harbour in Mollösund, is a small and welcoming café and hostel, and you can rent bikes here for further exploration of the area. The café serves excellent food, including salads, fish soup and baked potatoes, and exceptional ice cream.

Mollösunds Wärdshus (☎ 21108; doubles from Skr700) is an upmarket place with lunch from Skr75. The dinner menu has lots of seafood, and main courses start at Skr135. You will also find an **ICA supermarket** in Mollösund.

Bus No 375 stops in Stocken and Mollösund; it departs from Uddevalla and runs via Henån, the island's main settlement in the north. The Orustexpressen bus runs regularly from Gothenburg to Henån, via Stenungsund.

Lysekil & Around
☎ 0523 • pop14,800

Lysekil is a fairly large and windy place at the tip of the Stångenäs peninsula. The **tourist office** (☎ 13050; e turistinfo@ly sekil.se; Södra Hamngatan 6; open 9am-7pm daily mid-June–mid-Aug, 9am-5pm Mon-Fri rest of year) is helpful, and there are good facilities for travellers around town, including banks, supermarkets and also a cybercafe, **Bogart Video** (Rosvikstorg), which is really a video store with Internet access for Skr35 an hour.

Things to See & Do Off Strandvägen, **Havets Hus** (☎ 19671; adult/child Skr60/30; open 10am-4pm daily mid-Feb–Nov; to 6pm *mid-June–mid-Aug)* is an interesting aquarium. The architecture of the **Carl Curman villas** by the guest harbour is unique. Up on the hill, the **church** *(open 11am-7pm daily)* has superb paintings and stained glass. Right out at the point (just a kilometre from the town centre), there's the **Stångehuvud Nature Reserve**, with lots of coastal rock slab and a comical wooden hut perched above the water.

The recommended 4½-hour **boat trips** to the island of **Käringön** depart three times a week from mid-June to mid-August (adult/child Skr140/75). The two-hour **seal safaris** run three times daily from late June to mid-August (adult/child Skr90/45). Book these trips at the tourist office.

Passenger-only ferries cross the Gullmarn fjord roughly hourly (Skr24 one-way) to **Fiskebäckskil**, where there are lots of cobbled streets, wood-clad houses and a harbour full of boats and a few good restaurants. The interior of the excellent **church** is like an upturned boat; it has two votive ships and fine ceiling and wall paintings.

Places to Stay & Eat About 2km north of town, **Siviks Camping** *(☎ 611528; tent sites low/high season Skr110/150)* is a large beachside ground.

Friendly **Strand Vandrarhem & Kusthotell** *(☎ 79751; e strand@strandflickorna.se; Strandvägen 1; dorm beds Skr160, hostel singles/ doubles Skr195/390, hotel singles/doubles Skr765/965)* is not far from Havets Hus and offers a good range of accommodation in a large, newly renovated, late-19th-century house.

Near a pleasant park one block back from the bustling waterfront, **Stadshotellet** *(☎ 14030; Kungstorget; singles/doubles Skr690/850)*, dating from 1880, is today in need of a good coat of paint but offers pleasant, old-style rooms with character.

You cannot miss **Pråmen** *(☎ 14352; mains Skr140-230)*. It is an atmospheric floating restaurant and bar specialising, understandably, in both fish and seafood. **Sjökanten** *(☎ 15252; Södra Hamngatan 6; meals Skr75-230)* is upstairs with a terrace overlooking the water and an extensive menu, featuring light meals like pasta, pizza and salads. Downstairs, **Västkustens Grill** offers a wide range of kebabs, burgers and pizzas, priced from around Skr40. There are a few fast-food

places on and around Rosvikstorg and there's no shortage of other eateries along the main street.

Getting There & Away Bus Nos 840 and 841 run regularly from Gothenburg to Lysekil via Uddevalla.

Kungshamn & Smögen
☎ 0523

Kungshamn, at the tip of the Sotenäs peninsula, has good facilities and the **tourist office** *(☎ 665550; e info@sotenasturism.se; w www.sotenasturism.se; Hamngatan 6)* has details about attractions in the area, including the biggest drawcard, Smögen, a fishing village on an island (reached by a bridge) lying immediately west of Kungshamn. Unfortunately, the classic wooden boardwalk **Smögenbryggan** around the harbour is usually packed with tourists – to get peace and quiet here, go first thing in the morning or out of season. On weekdays at 8am (and Monday to Thursday at 5pm and 7pm) there's a **fish auction** in the Fiskhall at the harbour. Boats depart to the nature reserve on the nearby island **Hållö** up to 15 times daily from Smögen harbour (Skr45 return) in summer.

There are a number of camping grounds in the area. The nearest **STF Vandrarhem** *(☎ 37463; Solbacken; beds in 10-bed/4-bed dorms Skr75/100; open May-Sept)* is in Hovenäset, 4km northeast of Kungshamn.

Some good budget accommodation options in Smögen, including **Bryggens Gästhem** *(☎ 70391; Madenvägen 2; dorm beds Skr150-250)*, just up from the harbour.

Makrillvikens Vandrarhem *(☎ 31565; e info@makrillviken.se; Makrillgatan; dorm beds Skr170-220)* is an excellent choice – 500m from the boardwalk crowds, and with an old waterside sauna for guest use. Some rooms have en suite.

There are a few cafés and grill-bars along Smögenbryggan, but **Skärets Krog** *(☎ 32317; Hamnen 1; mains Skr175-240)*, near the Fiskhall, is the place to go for a quality seafood dinner in very pleasant surrounds. It's upstairs with a fine view, above **Skärets Konditori**, serving light meals and café fare.

Bus Nos 860 and 861 (the SmögenExpressen) runs regularly from Gothenburg to Smögen, via Uddevalla, Munkedal, Hunnebostrand (see following) and Kungshamn.

Kungshamn to Fjällbacka

On the coast, just 9km north of Kungshamn, is the small town of **Hunnebostrand**. The **STF Vandrarhem** (☎ 0523-58730; dorm beds Skr135; open June-Aug) here offers excellent accommodation in quaint surrounds, and you're not far from restaurants down near the harbour.

You can walk around **Nordens Ark** (☎ 0523-79590; adult/child Skr105/50; open 10am-7pm mid-June–mid-Aug, 10am-4pm or 5pm daily rest of year) safari park, which is at Åby säteri (6km east of Hunnebostrand), and experience the flora and fauna of all the Nordic countries, including some endangered species. Guided tours of the park are available daily in peak season and on weekends the rest of the year (included in entry price).

The old Romanesque church at **Svenneby** is early-12th-century and the bell on the cliff-top above is 13th-century. The most notable thing in **Hamburgsund** is the narrow strait separating the island **Hamburgö** from the mainland – at under 200m, this must be one of the shortest car ferries in Europe.

Fjällbacka, about 30km north of Kungshamn, is a very pretty place with brightly coloured houses and rocky hills; this is where Ingrid Bergman spent her summers, and the main square is named after her.

Get away from it all at the **STF Vandrarhem** (☎ 0525-31234; dorm beds Skr130; open May-Aug), on the offshore island of Valö; the manager will advise you about the boat service when you reserve a bed.

Back in the village, **Oscars II** (☎ 0525-32210; e info@oscar-2.com; Ingrid Bergmanstorg 2; low/high season doubles Skr650/850) is an excellent place – it's a cosy café, bar and brasserie, and it has pretty rooms for rent upstairs.

Also in Fjällbacka, the incredible **Stora Hotellet** (☎ 0525-31003; w www.storahotellet-fjallbacka.se; Galärbacken; rooms Skr800-1870) offers a trip 'around the world in 23 rooms'. The hotel was originally owned by a ship's captain who decorated the hotel with souvenirs and beautiful objects from around the world. Each room was named by the captain after his favourites – ports, explorers (and girls!) – and each tells its own story. Check out the website for more information.

Bus No 875 runs between Gothenburg and Strömstad via Hamburgsund and Fjällbacka.

UDDEVALLA

☎ 0522 • pop 49,300

Uddevalla, between Gothenburg and Tanumshede, is at the head of a fjord. You may find yourself spending some time here while awaiting transport connections but, although the town is Bohuslän's capital, it's mostly fairly modern and industrial and there's little reason to linger. The **tourist office** (☎ 99700; e info@uddevallaforum.se; w www.uddevalla forum.se; Kungstorget 4; open 9am-6pm Mon-Fri, 11am-4pm Sat June-Aug; 1am-6pm Mon-Fri Sept-May) can help with information.

Bohusläns Museum (☎ 656500; admission free; open 10am-8pm Mon-Thur, 10am-4pm Fri-Sun May-Aug, closed Mon Sept-Apr), near the bus station, has a local folk history exhibition covering the traditional stone, boat-building and fish-preserving industries.

In a wonderful waterside location at the old spa of Gustafsberg, the STF hostel, **Gustafsberg** (☎ 15200; e jan.gustafsberg@telia.com; dorm beds Skr135; open mid-June–mid-Aug) is 4km from the centre, and there are recreation areas and a café down this way too. The area can best be reached by boat (Skr16) six times daily from the jetty across the river from the museum, or by local bus.

Hotel Gyldenlöwe (☎ 14610; Lagerbergsgatan 8; singles/doubles from Skr825/925, discounted to Skr520/750) is centrally located and has reasonable rooms.

Kvarterskrogen (☎ 31333; Norra Drottninggatan 21; mains Skr92-190) is an atmospheric fish restaurant decorated with nets and lobster pots. The menu features pasta and lots of meat and fish dishes, plus Chilean specialities and Chilean wines.

Harrys (☎ 39599; Kålgårdsbergsgatan 8) is a good place for a casual pub meal or drink.

Regional trains run daily to Strömstad and Gothenburg, but the express buses are better and faster. **Swebus Express** (☎ 0200 218218; w www.swebusexpress.se) runs to Gothenburg (Skr60), Strömstad (Skr75) and Oslo (Skr185) up to six times daily, but buses drop off and pick up from the bus station on the E6 Hwy, rather than in the centre of town. There are also frequent services to Trollhättan, Lidköping and on to Örebro.

TANUMSHEDE

☎ 0525

The Bronze Age hällristningar rock carvings are well-represented in Bohuslän, but the best

GÖTALAND

are the Unesco World Heritage List ones at **Vitlycke**, 2.5km south of Tanumshede – there are around 30,000 carvings in the immediate area. The carvings themselves are in the open and free to view, but it's well worth visiting the excellent **Vitlycke Museum** (☎ 20950; W www.vitlycke.bohusmus.se; adult/child Skr50/30; open 10am-6pm daily Apr-Sept, 10am-4pm Tues-Sun Oct, closed Nov-Mar), which does a very good job explaining the rock art, with its focus on sexual imagery, animal hunts and ships. There's also a slide show, temporary exhibitions and even a reconstruction of a Bronze Age farm. There's a **restaurant** here that serves dagens rätt (daily specials) for Skr69.

Tanumshede itself is an unremarkable place and there's no reason to linger. The seasonal **tourist office** (☎ 29991; W www.tanum turist.se; open Mon-Fri June-Aug) is at the central bus station, and regional buses stop here regularly on the Gothenburg-Uddevalla-Strömstad route. If you catch a train and get off at the Tanumshede train station, you'll have to then walk or catch a connecting bus to the town (the train station is 2.5km southwest of town). There are no buses from the town centre to the Vitlycke area.

STRÖMSTAD
☎ 0526 • pop 11,200

Strömstad is an attractive fishing harbour and seaside resort near the Norwegian border, so it's usually packed with Norwegian tourists and drinkers, taking advantage of Sweden's cheaper prices. The town has good museums and some excellent attractions nearby, including the **sandy beaches** at Capri and Seläter. Boat trips run to the Koster islands, the most westerly in Sweden and popular for cycling.

The busy **tourist office** (☎ 62330; W www .stromstadtourist.se; Torget; open 9am-6pm Mon-Fri, 10am-6pm Sat & Sun June-Aug, shorter hours rest of year) is between the two harbours on the main square. Check your email at the **public library** (Karlsgatan 17), or down the road at **Data Service** (Karlsgatan 10).

Things to See & Do

Strömstad Museum (☎ 10275; Södra Hamngatan 26; adult/child Skr20/free; open 11am-4pm Mon-Fri, 11am-2pm Sat) has displays on the town's history and also on other local themes.

Blomsholm Manor, 6km northeast of Strömstad and on the other side of the E6, has 20 **Iron Age graves** and a magnificent **stone ship setting** (admission free; open 24hr), one of Sweden's largest at 41m long and with 49 stones. Stone ship settings are monuments associated with barrows, also called tumuli or grave mounds. In Sweden, most barrows contain the cremated remains of someone of great importance – usually a local chieftain. The purpose of the stone ship settings is clearly religious (ships were thought to provide transport to the afterlife), but some settings also have astronomical alignment (the normal alignment is with the sun). The stem and stern stones at Blomsholm Manor are over 3m high and the site has been dated to around AD 400 to 600. Ask at the tourist office or at the bus station for information on buses, or hire a bicycle (see Getting There & Around); alternatively, there's a lovely walking path from the north of town.

The Romanesque stone **Skee Kyrka** (open 8am-3pm Mon-Fri June-Aug) is about 6km east of Strömstad and has a 12th-century nave. There's also a painted wooden ceiling and an unusual 17th-century reredos with 24 sculptured figures around Christ on the cross. Nearby, there are **Iron Age graves**, a weird **bell tower** and a mid-Neolithic **passage tomb** (circa 3000 BC).

Boat trips run from the north harbour of Strömstad to the Koster islands roughly every two hours in summer (Skr90 return). **North Koster** is hilly and has good beaches, while **South Koster** is flatter and better for cycling. In summer there are also **seal safaris**; inquire at the tourist office for times and prices.

Places to Stay & Eat

Strömstads Camping (☎ 61121; low/high season tent sites Skr100/135, 2-bed cabins from Skr250/400) is a large, pleasant park at the southern edge of town. The central STF hostel, **Crusellska Hemmet** (☎ 10193; Norra Kyrkogatan 12; dorm beds July Skr160, rest of year Skr140; open Mar-Nov) is well-appointed and fills up early, so it's worth booking ahead.

Krabban Hotell (☎ 14200; e hotell.krab ban@swipnet.se; Bergsgatan 15; singles/doubles Skr590/690) is a very pretty, friendly place in the centre of town. Rooms with en suite cost Skr100 extra.

On Torget near the tourist office, **Lilla Blå** (☎ 60065; mains Skr125-210) is a very stylish

Patrons at an outdoor café in Gothenburg, Götaland

These ancient Tanumshede rock carvings, in Götaland, are World Heritage–listed

The changing autumn colours reflected in a lake in Halland, Götaland

Suburban Swedish house, Gothenburg, Götaland

Läckö Slott, Lidköping, Götaland

restaurant-bar with fresh seafood. Next door is **Laholmens Fisk** (☎ 10240; *Torget*), selling baguettes filled with yet more fresh seafood (from Skr40), along with fish fresh off the boats. There's a **Sibylla** burger outlet nearby, also on Torget.

Cosy and inviting **Göstases** (☎ 10812; *Strandpromenaden; meals Skr45-135*) has a nice nautical atmosphere and an excellent menu of light meals.

The **Konsum supermarket** (*Oslovägen 1*) is central, and **Systembolaget** (*Oslovägen 7*) is also nearby.

Getting There & Around
Buses and trains both use the train station near the southern harbour. The **Swebus Express** (☎ 0200 218218; W *www.swebusexpress.se*) service from Gothenburg to Oslo calls here up to six times daily and Strömstadsexpressen runs to Gothenburg (Skr120) up to five times daily. Strömstad is the northern terminus of the Bohuståg train system, with regular trains to/from Gothenburg.

Ferries run from Strömstad to Sandefjord in Norway (see the introductory Getting There & Away chapter).

For a taxi, call **Strömstads Taxi** (☎ 12200). Car hire is available from **Statoil** (☎ 12192; *Oslovägen 42*). Bike hire is available from **Cykelhandlarn** (☎ 60770; *Oslovägen 53*) from Skr70 per day.

Dalsland

DALS-ED
☎ 0534 • pop 5000
Scenically located between the lakes Stora Le and Lilla Le, sleepy Dals-Ed (also known as Ed) is a quiet place deep in the Dalsland forests and well off the tourist trail.

The seasonal **tourist office** (☎ 19022; e *tourist@dalsed.se; Strömstadsvägen 2; staffed 8am-4pm Mon-Fri June-Aug*) is in the large Mühlbocks complex, and is often open, unstaffed, for longer hours. Most facilities are available in the tiny town centre, on or around the main square.

The best website for the town and region is W www.dalsland.com.

Things to See & Do
Located Behind Torget, **Eds MC & Motormuseum** (☎ 10123; *adult/ child Skr40/free;*

open 11am-6pm daily June-Aug; 11am-4pm Tues-Sun mid-Apr–May & Sept–mid-Oct) has an impressive collection of motorcycles, boat engines and chainsaws – everything a backwoodsman would want! The wooden **church** at Gesäter, 16km southwest of Dals-Ed, has a 13th-century wooden sculpture of Madonna and other medieval items.

Canodal (☎ 61803; W *www.canodal.com; Gamla Edsvägen 4*) rents out two-person canoes from Skr160/800 per day/week; you can paddle along the narrow Stora Le all the way to Norway (38km) and enjoy the wilderness. The company can also supply equipment needed for wilderness camping.

Other popular activities include fishing, cycling and hiking; make inquiries at the tourist office. **Tresticklan National Park** lies 15km northwest of Ed and it protects around 3000 hectares of undisturbed ancient forest. There's a circular walking trail about 8km long. You'll need your own wheels to get here and there's no information centre, just a display board.

Places to Stay & Eat
Gröne Backe Camping (☎ 10144; e *grone backecamping@telia.com; low/high season tent sites Skr110/125, 4-bed cabins from Skr325/395*) is a large, excellent ground near Lilla Le, with lots of information about the area and also bikes, canoes and boats for hire. There's even a wood-fired sauna on a pontoon in the lake.

The cosy **STF Vandrarhem** (☎ 10191; *Strömstadsvägen 18; dorm beds Skr110-120; open mid-May–Aug*) is in a late-17th-century vicarage with an interesting history.

Hotell Carl XII (☎ 61155; e *info@carlxii .com; Storgatan 45; singles/doubles from Skr625/850*) is an old hotel full of character and with wonderful views of both lakes.

Eating options are very limited. Head to the **restaurant** at Hotell Carl XII, the **grill bar** on the main square or **Pizzeria Valencia** (☎ 61816; *Storgatan 18*), offering a wide range of pizza and kebabs (from around Skr50), as well as à la carte dishes.

Getting There & Around
Trains run two or three times daily to Oslo and Gothenburg. Bus No 706 runs a few times daily from the train station to Åmål. There are also daily bus connections to Uddevalla (bus No 719).

GÖTALAND

Head to the camping ground (see earlier) for bike hire (Skr95 per day).

HÅVERUD & AROUND
☎ 0530

The villages of Håverud and **Upperud** lie next to the scenic **Dalsland Canal**, which is only 10km long but links a series of narrow lakes between Vänern and Stora Le, providing a route 250km long. The most intriguing part of the canal is at Håverud, where an **aqueduct** crosses the river and a road bridge crosses above. The area around the aqueduct is a hive of activity, with a good **museum** telling the history of the canal, an **STF hostel** (☎ 30275; dorm beds Skr120) and pizzeria on one side, and an information centre, café-restaurant and delicatessen on the other. The information centre can book boat trips in the immediate area, but these usually only run from late June to mid-August.

About 3km south of the aqueduct in Upperud is the excellent **Dalslands Museum & Konsthall** (☎ 30098; adult/child Skr40/free; open 10am-6pm daily Apr-Dec) in a lovely location and with exhibitions of local art, furniture, ceramics, ironware and magnificent Åmål silverware. The grounds are worth a wander in to check out the interesting modern sculptures, and **Café Bonaparte** here is a good place to relax over coffee and a snack.

Another few kilometres south at Skållerud is a beautiful 17th-century wooden **church** (open 8am-6pm Mon-Sat, 9am-6pm Sun June-Aug), with many well-preserved paintings and sculptures depicting biblical scenes.

About 8km north of Håverud, **Högsbyn Nature Reserve**, near Tisselskog, has Bronze Age rock carvings on 40 slabs, featuring cup and ring marks, animals, boats, circles, labyrinths and hand and foot marks – follow the signs indicating 'Hällristningar'. There's a small **museum** (admission free; open daily June-Aug) here, and a **café**, reputedly haunted.

Baldersnäs Herrgård (☎ 0531-41244; admission free), 10km farther north past the village of Dals Långed, is a lovely manor house in beautiful grounds, complete with English garden, swimming spots, restaurant and café, handicraft stalls and a small Naturum detailing the local geology, flora, fauna and cultural history. Quality accommodation is offered here too, with single/double rooms costing Skr695/995.

Mellerud is on the main Gothenburg to Karlstad train line, and **Swebus Express** buses between Gothenburg and Karlstad stop here three times daily in either direction. Local bus No 720 runs from Mellerud to Håverud, via Skållerud and Upperud.

ÅMÅL
☎ 0532 • pop 12,800

Åmål, on Lake Vänern, is the main town in Dalsland, but most of it is relatively new and dates from after a fire in 1901. The town became infamous after the 1999 release of the Swedish-language film with the title *Fucking Åmål*, which was actually filmed in Trollhättan and was given the very boring title *Show Me Love* for its release to the English-speaking world.

The **tourist office** (☎ 17098; e amalturism@telia.com; w www.amal.se; open daily mid-June–mid-Aug; Mon-Fri rest of year) is near the guest harbour, where visiting yachts can berth. The town's compact centre on Kungsgatan has all services. There are a few diversions in the town, but there's no pressing reason to linger long – the real attractions are out in the surrounding waterways and forests. The Old Town, around the church **Gamla Kyrkan** (completed in 1669), survived the blaze and it's worth a quick look. **Åmåls Hembygdsmuseet** (☎ 15820; Hamngatan; adult/child Skr20/free; open 1pm-6pm daily mid-June–Aug; Sat & Sun mid-May–mid-June), near the tourist office, is a particularly interesting local museum.

Örnäs Camping (☎ 17097; tent sites from Skr90, cabins from Skr315) is a large lakeside ground south of the centre. The well-equipped **STF Vandrarhem** (☎ 10205; Gerdinsgatan 7; dorm beds Skr130) is just north of the town centre, and central, elegant **Åmåls Stadshotell** (☎ 61610; Kungsgatan 9; singles/doubles Skr750/1090, discounted to Skr650/890) has comfortable rooms and helpful staff, plus a good restaurant (the lunch buffet is Skr65).

Hamn Compagniet (☎ 10010; Hamngatan 3; lunch Skr65, meals Skr70-160) is a flash complex not far from the tourist office, with a restaurant, bar and disco, plus lots of outdoor seating by the lake.

Café Liljan (☎ 10808; Södra Ågatan 11), near the pretty Plantaget park, is an inviting café with good coffee, sandwiches and cakes. There are also a number of pizzerias and grill bars in the town centre.

SJ trains to Gothenburg (Skr152) or Karltad (Skr105) stop in Åmål up to four times daily. **Swebus Express** buses follow the same route and call three times daily. The train and bus stations are about a kilometre southwest of the town centre.

Västergötland

VÄNERSBORG
☎ 0521 • pop 36,800

Vänersborg, founded in 1644, is a pleasant but unremarkable town at the outlet of Vänern. The town got off to a bad start and it was burnt down by Danish invaders in 1645, and again in 1676, the same year the church bells were stolen – they're now in Copenhagen.

The **tourist office** (☎ 271400; e turist@vanersborg.se, w www.vanersborg.se; open daily mid-June–mid-Aug, closed Sat & Sun rest of year) is at the train station, and banks and other facilities are found mostly along Edsgatan.

Vänersborgs Museum (☎ 264100; Östra Plantaget; adult/child Skr20/free; open noon-4pm Tues-Thur, Sat & Sun) is one of the country's oldest museums and has a remarkable southwest African bird collection along with more local exhibits.

The two-part **Hunneberg & Hanneberg Nature Reserve**, 8km east of the town centre, covers two unusual forested plateaus which reach 155m. This area is popular with hunters (including the king) and is known for its elk; there are regular, three-hour **elk-spotting safaris** (adult/child Skr240/175) a few evenings a week from mid-June to mid-August. Tours depart from the train station; contact the tourist office for bookings. **Älgens Berg** (☎ 220280; adult/child Skr60/30; open 10am-6pm daily May-Sept, 10am-4pm Tues-Sun Oct-Apr), the new royal hunting museum, is out at Hunneberg and displays everything you could ever wish to know (and then some) about the elk. In summer bus No 665 heads out here.

Places to Stay & Eat
Hunnebergs Vandrarhem (☎ 220340; Berggårdsvägen 9, Vargön; tent sites Skr50, dorm beds Skr160) is a large, well-equipped SVIF hostel near the cliffs of Hunneberg, 7km east of the town centre. Take bus No 62 from Torget, the town square, to Vägporten,

then walk 500m. Camping is permitted in the grounds, and there are bikes for rent.

Hotell 46:an (☎ 711561; Kyrkogatan 46; singles/doubles Skr595/750, discounted to Skr550/650) is a small, family-run place offering simple but comfortable rooms.

Elegant **Ronnums Herrgård** (☎ 260000; e info@ronnum.softwarehotels.se; Vargön; singles/doubles Skr1140/1345, discounted to Skr895/1145) is a luxurious historic manor, with high-quality lodgings in a variety of buildings that are scattered throughout lovely grounds. The hotel **restaurant** is one of the best in the region (if you feel like treating yourself, a three-course set menu costs around Skr450).

Grab an excellent takeaway meal – a large salad, soup or sandwich costs from Skr35 – from **Kalasboden** (Kungsgatan 21) and have a picnic in the park opposite.

Ristorante Italia (☎ 61220; Edsgatan 7; meals from Skr55) is one of a number of popular eateries on the main street and serves a mixture of Italian and Swedish food, including reasonably priced pizza and pasta.

Getting There & Away
The **airport** (☎ 82500) is midway between Vänersborg and Trollhättan. Skyways flies direct daily except Saturday to/from Stockholm Arlanda. Taxis are your only option to get to or from the airport; expect to pay Skr85 from Trollhättan, and Skr115 from Vänersborg.

Local buses run from Torget and long-distance services stop at the train station. Bus Nos 600 and 605 run regularly between Vänersborg and Trollhättan, and No 600 continues to Gothenburg. **Säfflebussen** (☎ 020 1600 600; w www.safflebussen.se) runs once daily to Karlstad and Gothenburg; **Swebus Express** (☎ 0200 218218; w www.swebusexpress.se) runs three times daily to Gothenburg via Trollhättan, and also north to Karlstad and Falun, with one service daily continuing on to Gävle.

SJ trains to Uddevalla (Skr29) run every one/two hours. Trains to Trollhättan (Skr38) and Gothenburg (Skr91) run about every hour (some require a change at Oxnered).

TROLLHÄTTAN
☎ 0520 • pop 52,800
Trollhättan is an interesting industrial town just 10km south of Vänersborg. There are

Hooray for Trollywood

In recent years Trollhättan has become home to the Swedish film industry and has earned itself the inevitable nickname 'Trollywood'. A number of Swedish and Scandinavian films have been filmed in and around the town, including Danish producer Lars von Trier's award-winning *Dancer in the Dark*, and his new movie, *Dogville*, to be released in 2003 and starring Nicole Kidman and Swedish actor Stellan Skarsgaard.

Film i Väst (W *www.filmivast.se)* is the large film production company based in Trollhättan. Check its website for more information, and also ask at the tourist office if you want to know what film sets (and stars) you might stumble across as you wander around town.

many things worth seeing near the Göta älv (river) and the parallel **Trollhätte Canal**, which is part of the Göta Canal.

The **tourist office** (☎ 488472; e tourist@visittrollhattan.se; W www.visittrollhattan.se; Åkerssjövägen 10; open 10am-6pm daily June-Aug, 10am-4pm Mon-Fri Sept-May), near the Saab Bilmuseum and Innovatum, is about 1.5km south of the town centre. If you want to visit all the attractions, ask the tourist office for an **Innovatum Sommarkortet** (Skr100; available from early June to mid-August), which includes a return trip in the cable car, and entry to Innovatum, Kanal-museet and the Saab Bilmuseum.

Things to See

Saab Bilmuseum (☎ 84344; Åkerssjövägen 10; adult/child Skr30/20; open 10am-6pm daily mid-June-mid-Aug, 11am-4pm Tues-Fri rest of year) is well worth a visit. There are Saab car models from 1947 to present (including the first and the latest models), showcasing wonderful Swedish automobile design over the decades. There are also interesting videos showing rally cars in action, and details of car safety features. You can even organise to test drive one of the latest models. **Innovatum Kunskapens Hus** (☎ 488480; adult/child Skr50/30; open 10am-6pm daily mid-June-mid-Aug, 11am-4pm Tues-Sun rest of year), adjacent to the Saab Bilmuseum, is a science centre geared mainly to children, with experiments and interactive displays describing the history of technology.

In four minutes, the **Innovatum Linbana** (cable car; ☎ 488480; adult/child Skr40/20, operates 10am-6pm daily mid-June-mid-Aug, 11am-4pm Sat & Sun mid-April-mid-June & mid-Aug-Sept) will take you across the canal and over the locks and industrial area. The ride is impressive, and from the other side of the canal you can take a wander south to **Slussområde**, a pleasant waterside area of old locks and parkland. There are cafés here as well as **Kanalmuseet** (☎ 472206; Åkersberg; adult/child Skr10/free; open 11am-7pm daily June-Aug; noon-5pm Sat & Sun Apr, May & Sept), next to locks dating back to 1800. The museum describes the history of the canal and has over 50 model ships.

The spectacular **waterfall** near the Hojum power station runs at 3pm on weekends from May to August and also at 3pm on Wednesday in July and August (the water is normally diverted through the power stations). At 11pm on Friday evenings in July the falls are illuminated, creating a remarkable sight. There are also **canal tours** in summer; inquire at the tourist office for times and details.

Places to Stay & Eat

The friendly STF hostel **Gula Villan** (☎ 12960, e trollhattansvandrarhem@telia.com; Ting-vallavägen 12; dorm beds Skr130) is an excellent place about 200m from the train station in a pretty old yellow villa. You can rent bikes here, and breakfast is available.

Hotell Bele (☎ 12530; Kungsgatan 37, singles/doubles Skr690/790, discounted to Skr550/650) is a central, no-frills option with basic but comfortable accommodation. For more luxury, head to the upmarket **Scandic Hotel Swania** (☎ 89000; e swania@scandic-hotels.com; Storgatan 47; singles/doubles Skr1200/1525, discounted to Skr710/910), on the canal and with quality facilities including pool, restaurant and nightclub on site. The **Grand Café** (☎ 89009; meals Skr70-150, here has a good menu offering a range of food from light snacks to hearty steaks, and prices are more reasonable than the swish decor might have you expect. The bar here is a bustling after-work spot, and the outdoor area is popular in good weather.

One of the best – and busiest – places in town is trendy **Strandgatan** (☎ 83717, Strandgatan; lunch meals around Skr55), a classy café-bar offering dishes like bagels, quiche, salads and baked potatoes, plus great outdoor, canal-side seating.

Getting There & Around
See Vänersborg for transport details. To reach the attractions in Trollhättan from the train station or the Drottningtorget bus station, walk south along Drottninggatan, then turn right into Åkerssjövägen, or take town bus No 11 – it runs most of the way.

You can rent bikes from Innovatum Kunskapens Hus (Skr40/75 three hours/day).

LIDKÖPING
☎ 0510 • pop 36,800
The bright and cheery town of Lidköping on Lake Vänern has an interesting central area with several old buildings, but the finest attractions lie some way out of town. The main square, Nya Stadens Torg, is dominated by the old courthouse and its tower – it's actually a replica of the original structure which stood in the square until it burnt down in 1960. A previous fire, in 1849, destroyed most of the town but the 17th-century houses around Limtorget (300m from the train station) survived and are still there today.

The friendly tourist office (☎ 770500; e turist@lidkoping.se, w www.lidkoping.se /turist; Bangatan 3; open 9am-8pm Mon-Fri, 10am-8pm Sat, 1pm-6pm Sun mid-June–mid-Aug; 9am-5pm Mon-Fri rest of year) is at the train station. The public library (Nya Stadens Torg 5) has Internet access.

Läckö Slott
Situated near Vänern, 23km north of Lidköping, Läckö Slott (☎ 10320; w www.lacko slott.se; open May-Sept) is a fairy-tale castle and an extraordinary example of 17th-century Swedish baroque architecture, with cupolas, towers, paintings and ornate plasterwork. The first castle on the site was constructed in 1298, but it was improved enormously by Count Magnus Gabriel de la Gardie after he acquired it in 1615.

The castle now has 240 rooms and the finest one is the King's Hall, with 13 angels hanging from the ceiling and nine huge paintings describing the Thirty Years War.

From May to August, 45-minute guided tours of the castle run from 11am to 5pm daily (11am to 2pm daily in September); the cost is Skr70/15 per adult/child, and parking costs Skr10 extra. The castle restaurant, Fataburen, serves lunch for Skr95, and there's also a café here serving cheaper snacks. You can make a day out of this excursion and enjoy swimming nearby, or rent a kayak, canoe or boat for exploring the lake. The rental kiosk (☎ 10111) is not far from the castle. There's even a camping ground here.

Classical music and opera events are held in the courtyard several times a week in July (tickets around Skr265); inquire at the tourist office. Bus No 132 runs four to seven times daily from Lidköping to the castle.

Husaby Kyrka & St Sigfrids Well
In 1008, King Olof Skötkonung was converted to Christianity and baptised by the English missionary, Sigfrid. Tradition states this important event took place at St Sigfrid's Well, near the church Husaby Kyrka (open 8am-4pm daily Apr, 8am-8pm May-Sept), around 15km east of Lidköping. The well is a popular tourist attraction since many Swedish kings have carved their names into the rocks here. The church actually dates from the 12th century, but the base of the extraordinary three-steepled tower may well be that of an earlier wooden church. Inside the church, there's 13th-century furniture, 15th-century lime murals and carved floor slabs; an audio guide is available in English. There are several 12th-century burial monuments in the area and there's a rune stone in the churchyard.

Bus No 106 runs to Husaby. There's a small, seasonal tourist office (open daily June-Aug) near the church.

Other Attractions
Rörstrand Fabriksbod & Museum (☎ 82346; Fiskaregatan 4; open 10am-6pm Mon-Fri, 10am-2pm Sat, noon-4pm Sun), is the second-oldest porcelain factory (still in operation) in Europe. There is a museum here and a café, plus a shop where you can buy copies of the porcelain used at the Nobel banquets in Stockholm!

Vänermuseet (☎ 770065; Framnäsvägen 2; adult/child Skr20/free; open 10am-5pm Tues-Fri, noon-5pm Sat & Sun) has geological exhibits (including an ancient meteorite) and displays about Vänern (which is the third-largest lake in Europe at 5650 sq km). The most curious item is a 3m-long glass boat.

GÖTALAND

The hard-topped hill **Kinnekulle**, 18km northeast of Lidköping, rises to 306m and there's the good, 45km-long **Kinnekulle vandringsled** (walking trail) in the area – ask the tourist office for a map (Skr20). Local trains run to Källby, Råbäck and Hällekis, providing access to the trail.

Places to Stay & Eat
Krono Camping (☎ 26804; *tent sites Skr120-175, 2-person cabins Skr310-420*) is a huge, family-oriented lakeside camping ground, 1.5km northwest of the train station beside the road to Läckö.

The best accommodation options are in the attractive, older part of town, just south of the train station. The well-equipped **STF Vandrarhem** (☎ 66430; *Nicolaigatan 2; dorm beds Skr130*) is a good choice, in a pretty spot only a couple of minutes' walk from the train station.

Hotel Läckö (☎ 23000; *Gamla Stadens Torg 5; singles/doubles Skr690/890, discounted to Skr490/690*) offers good value in a comfortable, family-run hotel. The nearby **Hotel Stadt** (☎ 22085; *Gamla Stadens Torg 1; singles/doubles Skr945/1260, discounted to Skr610/760*) is the best hotel in town and offers a range of facilities, including a restaurant and nightclub.

Sleek **Café O Bar** (☎ 27027; *Nya Stadens Torg 4; lunch Skr59, meals Skr129-189*), on the main square, is a fashionable restaurant-bar with a good selection of interesting meals, including mushroom risotto or lamb racks with couscous.

Seek out **Cafe Limtorget** (*Mjölnagården*), a cute little old place with a rose-filled garden not far from Gamla Stadens Torg. It serves sandwiches and ciabatta from Skr30, plus pastries, waffles and other temptations. There are many more options around the square and surrounding streets – Källaregatan is fertile ground for cheap pizzerias and grill bars, while Grevgatan has some interesting old cafés.

Getting There & Around
Town and regional buses stop on Nya Stadens Torg. Local buses run regularly on weekdays (only twice on Saturday and Sunday) between Trollhättan, Lidköping and Skara.

Säfflebussen runs to Stockholm (via Örebro) and Gothenburg (via Vänersborg and Trollhättan) once daily. Länståg trains from Lidköping to Hallsberg or Herrljunga connect with Stockholm and Gothenburg services respectively.

Bicycle hire from **Krono Camping** (see Places to Stay & Eat) costs Skr50/350 per day/week.

KARLSBORG
☎ 0505
Karlsborgs Fästning, on Lake Vättern some 80km west of Lidköping, was one of Europe's largest construction projects. It's an enormous fortress that cost a fortune and took from 1820 to 1909 to complete; it was out of date even before it was finished, so it was mothballed immediately! The perimeter is around 5km and most of the 30-odd buildings inside are in original condition.

The **tourist office** (☎ 17350; e *info@karls borgsfastning.se; Ankarvägen 2; open 9am-6pm daily June-Aug, 9am-5pm Mon-Fri Sept-May*) is in an octagonal wooden house between the fort's main entrance and the lake.

There's a **military museum** (☎ 85470; *adult/child Skr35/10; open 10am-4pm or 6pm daily mid-May–Aug, 10am-3pm Mon-Fri rest of year*) and a **church**, which has an extraordinary candelabra constructed from 276 bayonets. The fortress area is always open and you're free to wander around, but **guided tours** (*adult/child Skr70/30*) run daily at 1pm from June to August (from Midsummer to early August, there are as many as 12 tours daily).

The **STF Vandrarhem** (☎ 44600; *dorm beds Skr130-140*) is right near here. A good option is to stay here and self-cater (there are supermarkets in the nearby town centre), although you'll find a few more accommodation and eating selections in town, especially beside the Göta Canal about 2km northwest of the fortress (follow the main road).

A reasonably frequent bus service runs to Skövde, connecting with SJ trains to Gothenburg or Stockholm.

Halland

HALMSTAD
☎ 035 • pop 85,700
Founded along the Nissan River, Halmstad was Danish until 1645. A previous Swedish attack on the town in 1563 was successfully

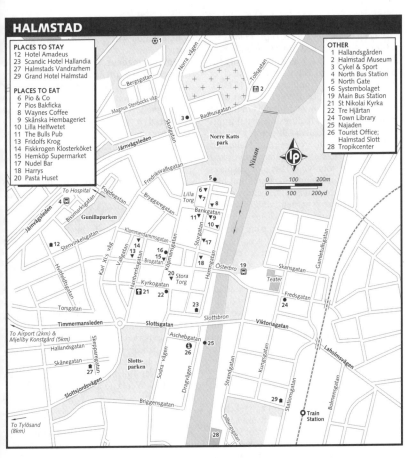

HALMSTAD

PLACES TO STAY
12 Hotel Amadeus
23 Scandic Hotel Hallandia
27 Halmstads Vandrarhem
29 Grand Hotel Halmstad

PLACES TO EAT
6 Pio & Co
7 Pios Bakficka
8 Waynes Coffee
9 Skånska Hembageriet
10 Lilla Helfwetet
11 The Bulls Pub
13 Fridolfs Krog
14 Fiskkrogen Klosterköket
15 Hemköp Supermarket
17 Nudel Bar
18 Harrys
20 Pasta Huset

OTHER
1 Hallandsgården
2 Halmstad Museum
3 Cykel & Sport
4 North Bus Station
5 North Gate
16 Systembolaget
19 Main Bus Station
21 St Nikolai Kyrka
22 Tre Hjärtan
24 Town Library
25 Najaden
26 Tourist Office;
   Halmstad Slott
28 Tropikcenter

repulsed and later the Danish King Christian IV awarded Halmstad a coat of arms with three crowns and three hearts. After the huge town fire of 1619, Christian IV laid out the modern street plan, with the familiar Stora Torg and Lilla Torg.

Nowadays, this lively town is especially popular in summer with a hip young crowd, who hang out at the bars and clubs at night, and roast themselves on **Tylösand** beach, 8km east of town, by day.

The **tourist office** (☎ 109345; ℮ info@ tourist.halmstad.se; ⋓ www.halmstad.se; open 9am-7pm Mon-Sat, 3pm-7pm Sun late June–mid-Aug, shorter hours rest of year) is inside Halmstads Slott (castle) and open variable hours outside the peak season. Stora Torg and Storgatan have most of the facilities

travellers will require, including banks and supermarkets. There's a **town library** (Fredsgatan 2) with Internet access not far from the bus station.

Things to See

Christian IV fortified the town and built **Halmstad Slott** and the town walls (the latter were demolished in the 18th century). The castle is open very irregularly to guided tours in summer (Skr30). Ask at the tourist office for details.

Other medieval attractions include the 14th-century church **St Nikolai Kyrka** (open 8.30am-6pm daily June-Aug, 8.30am-3pm daily Sept-May), which survived the 1619 fire, and the **Tre Hjärtan** (Three Hearts) building on Stora Torg, which also houses a café.

The museum ship **Najaden** *(admission free; open 5pm-7pm Tues & Thur, 11am-3pm Sat June-Aug)*, berthed just outside the castle and built in 1897, was a training ship for the Swedish Royal Navy. Across the river and downstream, **Tropikcenter** *(☎ 123333; adult/child Skr60/30; open 10am-6pm daily July, 10am-4pm daily Aug-June)* is in the old customs house and features the usual tropical life. Kids under 1m tall get in for free! To the north of the town centre, **Halmstad Museum** *(☎ 162300; Tollsgatan; adult/child Skr20/5; open noon-4pm Tues-Sun)* displays tapestries, ship carvings, local cultural history, photography and art. The nearby open-air annexe **Hallandsgården** *(admission free; open noon-6pm mid-June–mid-Aug)* consists of 10 buildings only; only some are open to casual visitors, but all can be seen on the guided tour (daily at 2pm). There's a café on site, open May to August.

Mjellby Konstgård *(☎ 31619; adult/child Skr40/free; open noon or 1pm-5pm Tues-Sun mid-Mar–late Sept; 1pm-5pm Wed, Sat & Sun rest of year)* is 5km from town, but worth a trip if you're into modern art – the museum here includes the permanent Halmstad Group exhibition of surrealist and cubist art, but all labels are in Swedish. Take irregular bus No 330 from the North Bus Station.

Places to Stay

Camping is very popular down at the beach. **Krono Camping** *(☎ 30510; e tylosand@kronocamping.se; Kungsvägen 3; tent sites Skr130-220, cabins from Skr525)*, off Kungsvägen at Tylösand, is a huge and bustling camping ground with lots of family-friendly facilities. Avoid holidays such as Midsummer, when the price goes stratospheric: a whopping Skr820 for three days!

Central hostel options aren't great: the SVIF **Halmstads Vandrarhem** *(☎ 120500; e halmstad@hallonstenturist.se; Skepparegatan 23; dorm beds from Skr140; open late June–mid-Aug)* is open in summer only. You're better off heading out of town: near the beach at Tylösand, the good **Tylebäck** *(☎ 32460; e info@tyleback.com; Kungsvägen 1; tent sites Skr150, dorm beds from Skr160, hotel single/doubles Skr645/890)* is in a rustic location and offers hostel, hotel and camping options in a pleasant green locale.

The tourist office can arrange **private rooms** from Skr120 per person, plus booking

fee (the lowest prices are for self-catering accommodation where you provide your own linen).

Hotel Amadeus *(☎ 109770; e info@amadeus.se; Hvitfeldtsgatan 20; singles/doubles Skr850/1050, discounted to Skr540/740)* has comfortable rooms in town, and train travellers may appreciate **Grand Hotel Halmstad** *(☎ 219040; e info@grandhotel.nu; Stationsgatan 22; singles/doubles Skr1095/1310, discounted to Skr690/850)*, directly opposite the station and with clean, spacious rooms.

Central **Scandic Hotel Hallandia** *(☎ 295 8600; e hallandia@scandic-hotels.com; Rådhusgatan 4; singles/doubles Skr1200/1526, discounted to Skr690/790)* is on the main square and offers high standard accommodation in bright and airy rooms, plus a good restaurant.

Hotel Tylösand *(☎ 30500; e info@tylosand.se; Tylöhusvägen; singles/doubles from Skr1195/1295)* is the place to try if you're into the beach, nightclubbing and/or Roxette (it's part-owned by Per Gessle, one half of the well-known Swedish pop duo). It's a large, upmarket complex on the beach, with lots of eating options and summer entertainment happenings; check out the glamorous foyer full of art, and Leifs Lounge nightclub. Weekend and summer packages are available.

Places to Eat

Halmstad is totally jam-packed with places to eat. **Fiskkrogen Klosterköket** *(☎ 124050; Klammerdammsgatan 21; mains Skr170-230)* is a pricey fish restaurant with a really great atmosphere. The best value can be had here during lunchtime, when the 'daily catch' is only Skr79.

Fridolfs Krog *(☎ 211666; Brogatan 26; meals Skr69-225)* is another pleasant place for a fine dinner. There are cheaper pasta options for under Skr100, or well-prepared meat and fish meals.

Pio & Co *(☎ 210669; Storgatan 37; mains Skr155-220)* is an upmarket brasserie-style restaurant with an extensive menu of quality dishes; behind it is **Pios Bakficka** *(Lilla Torg; meals under Skr100)*, literally 'Pio's Backpocket', a more casual spot with outdoor seating and a good bar menu.

Skånska Hembageriet *(☎ 212407; Storgatan 40)* is a good, old-fashioned bakery with sandwiches from Skr25 and lots of pastries to choose from. For those who like their cafés modern and sleek, **Waynes Coffee** (☎ 175800; Storgatan 42) is opposite, serving trendy café fare including bagels, wraps, salads and baked goods.

For quick, cheap sustenance, **Nudelbar** (Storgatan) is a small, hole-in-the-wall establishment serving takeaway noodle meals for Skr50 including drink; the **Pasta Huset** van on Stora Torg does cheap pasta (Skr29).

Among the popular restaurant-bars in the northern part of Storgatan and on nearby Lilla Torg are **Harrys** (☎ 105595; Storgatan 22) and the **Bulls Pub** (☎ 140921; Lilla Torg), in a former fire station. Both are English-style pubs serving up a good range of snacks and meals. **Lilla Helfwetet** (☎ 210420; cnr Hamngatan & Bastionsgatan) is a cool new restaurant, bar and cocktail lounge in a great converted warehouse near the river, one block from Storgatan. Alternatively, on summer nights head down to the venues at Tylösand.

There is a **Hemköp supermarket** and a **Systembolaget** just off Stora Torg.

Getting There & Away

The **airport** (☎ 128070) is only 2km west of the town centre. SAS and Skyways have regular connections to Stockholm's Arlanda and Bromma airports.

The train station is in the southeastern corner of the town centre, and the bus station is a few blocks away at Österbro. Both **Svenska Buss** (☎ 0771-676767; w www.svenskabuss.se) and **Swebus Express** (☎ 0200 218218; w www.swebusexpress.se) run regular buses to Malmö (Skr155), Helsingborg (Skr75) Gothenburg (Skr165) via Lund. Svenska Buss is slightly cheaper but runs less frequently (Swebus Express runs five times daily). Swebus Express also has a twice-weekly service to Jönköping (Skr155).

The regular trains between Gothenburg (Skr190) and Malmö (Skr200) stop in Halmstad, calling in at Helsingborg (Skr110) and Varberg (Skr95).

Getting Around

Local bus No 10 runs at least half-hourly to the clubs and beaches at Tylösand (Skr15).

Try **Taxi Halmstad** (☎ 218000) for assistance getting around. You can hire a bike from **Cykel & Sport** (☎ 212251; Norra vägen 11) for Skr60/100 per half/full day.

VARBERG

☎ 0340 ● pop 53,100

This popular and pleasant beach town boasts that its population triples in the summer. There's a beach near the centre, but the total length of sandy strand in the area is 60km.

The **tourist office** (☎ 43224; e turist@var berg.se, w www.turist.varberg.se; Brunnparken; open 9am-7pm Mon-Sat, 3pm-7pm Sun late June-early Aug; shorter hours rest of year; closed Sat & Sun Oct-Mar) is located in the centre of town, and most facilities are nearby.

Things to See

The **medieval fortress** (☎ 18520; adult/child Skr50/10; open 10am-6pm daily mid-June–mid-Aug; 10am-4pm Mon-Fri, noon-4pm Sat & Sun rest of year), with its superb museums, is the main attraction in Varberg. The most unusual exhibits are a 14th-century costume found on a body (perfectly preserved in a bog) at Åkulle in 1936, and the tools the poor fellow was carrying when he died.

You might also want to brave the brisk Nordic weather and swim in the striking **Kallbadhuset** (☎ 17396; adult/child Skr40/25; open daily summer), a bizarre Moorish-style outdoor bath-house built on stilts above the sea just north of the fort.

Getterön Nature Reserve is just 2km north of the town and has excellent bird life (mostly waders and geese). There's a **Naturum** (visitors centre; ☎ 87510; open 10am-4pm daily May-Aug; Fri, Sat & Sun Sept-Apr) with good exhibitions.

The old fishing village **Träslövsläge** is 7km south of Varberg and it's worth a visit (take bus No 1).

Places to Stay & Eat

Camping isn't really a particularly cheap option. The well-equipped **Getteröns Camping** (☎ 16885; low/high season tent sites Skr135/185, cabins & chalets from Skr365/440) on the Getterön peninsula has plenty of space but is busy in high season.

SVIF hostel **Vandrarhemmet Varbergs Fästning** (☎ 88788; e andrarhem@turist.var berg.se; dorm beds Skr165-185), within the fortress, is one of the finest hostels in Sweden. It offers singles in old prison cells or larger rooms in other buildings. Central **Varbergs Vandrarhem** (☎ 611640; Villagatan 13; dorm beds Skr160; open June-Aug) is another good option.

GÖTALAND

Friendly **Hotell Gästis** (☎ 18050; [e] gastis @algonet.se; Borgmästaregatan 1; singles/ doubles from Skr795/995, discounted to Skr595/795) is highly recommended and probably offers the best value in town in summer. Although it doesn't look like much from the outside, inside it's bright, clean, stylish and colourful, with lots of extras like a library and outdoor terraces, plus guests can rent bikes for Skr25 per day. All prices include breakfast and a dinner buffet.

When it comes to dining, upmarket **Lundquistska Huset** (☎ 14390; Brunnsparken; mains Skr120-180) is near the tourist office and offers excellent cuisine, including vegetarian options.

Most cheap restaurants are along the pedestrianised Kungsgatan; **Harrys** (Kungsgatan 18) is a popular pub-restaurant serving a range of meals (pub grub from Skr85). There are also some good cafés, including **Kafé Blå Dorren** (☎ 673440; Norrgatan 1), with baguettes, quiche and baked potatoes. However, **Café Fästnings Terrassen** (☎ 10581) at the fortress offers the best sea views in town.

Getting There & Around
Buses depart from outside the train station; local buses run to Falkenberg, but regular trains are your best bet for places like Halmstad, Gothenburg and Malmö.

Stena Line ferries operate between Varberg and the Danish town of Grenå (see the introductory Getting There & Away chapter); the ferry dock is next to the town centre.

Bike hire from **Erlan Cykel** (☎ 14455; Västra Vallgatan 41) costs Skr80 per day. For a taxi try **Varbergs Taxi** (☎ 16500).

Östergötland

NORRKÖPING
☎ 011 • pop 122,900
The industrial development of Norrköping began in the 17th century, but it really took off in the late 19th century when large textile mills and factories sprang up alongside the swift-flowing Motala ström. Today, the impressive industrial-revolution architecture, complete with canals, locks and waterfalls, is a fine example of inner-city regeneration and it's well worth stopping for a look. Although 70% of Sweden's textiles were once made in Norrköping, the last mill closed in the 1970s

and the city's heavy industries have now all been replaced with electronics, computing and microwave technology.

Many central attractions are free – most unusual for Sweden. Another key attraction is the animal park at Kolmården, some 30km to the northeast.

Information
The **tourist office** (☎ 155000; [e] info@ destination.norrkoping.se, [w] www.destination .norrkoping.se; Dalsgatan 16; open 9.30am-7pm Mon-Fri, 10am-5pm Sat & Sun late-June–July; 10am-6pm Mon-Fri, 10am-2pm Sat rest of year) can help with information.

You can change money at **Forex** (Drottninggatan 46) in town, and banks with ATMs can be found along the same street. The city's **library** (Stadsbiblioteket; Södra Promenaden 105) has free Internet access. There is also Internet access available at **Norrköpings Biljard och IT Café** (☎ 163400; Prästgatan 48, downstairs), for Skr29 per hour.

Things to See & Do
Industrilandskapet is the well-preserved industrial area near the river; pedestrian walkways and bridges lead past the magnificent former factory buildings and around the ingenious system of locks and canals. The most impressive waterfall is **Kungsfallet**, near the islet Laxholmen.

The industrial past is exhibited at the city museum, **Stadsmuseum** (☎ 152620; Holmbrogränd; admission free; open 10am-5pm Tues-Fri, 11am-5pm Sat & Sun); some of the factory equipment is still operational. More general is Sweden's only museum of work, the excellent **Arbetets Museum** (☎ 189800; Laxholmen; admission free; open 11am-5pm daily), just across the bridge from the Stadsmuseum. **Holmens Museum** (☎ 128992; admission free; open 9am-1pm Tues & Thur) describes the history of Louis de Geer's paper factory, founded in the early 17th century. A modern addition to the riverside scenery is the extraordinary 1300-seat **Louis de Geer Concert Hall** (☎ 122030; Gamla Torget), in a former paper mill and still containing the original balconies.

Norrköpings Konstmuseum (☎ 152600; Kristinaplatsen; adult/child Skr30/free; open noon-4pm Tues & Thur-Sun, noon-8pm Wed June-Aug; 11am-5pm Tues & Thur-Sun, 11am-8pm Wed Sept-May), the large art museum

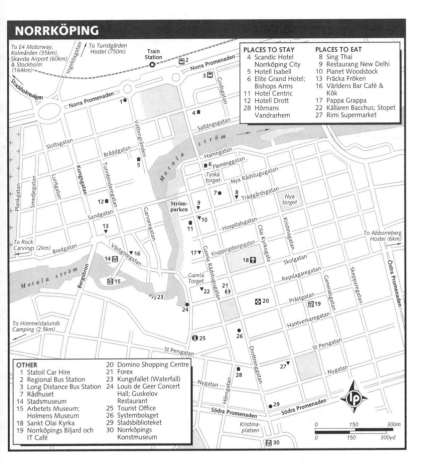

NORRKÖPING

To E4 Motorway,
Kolmården (35km),
Skavsta Airport (60km)
& Stockholm
(164km)

To Turistgården
Hostel (750m)

Train
Station

To Abborreberg
Hostel (6km)

To Rock
Carvings (2km)

To Himmelstalunds
Camping (2.5km)

PLACES TO STAY
4 Scandic Hotel
  Norrköping City
5 Hotell Isabell
6 Elite Grand Hotel;
  Bishops Arms
11 Hotel Centric
12 Hotell Drott
28 Hörnans
  Vandrarhem

PLACES TO EAT
8 Sing Thai
9 Restaurang New Delhi
10 Planet Woodstock
13 Fräcka Fröken
16 Världens Bar Café &
  Kök
17 Pappa Grappa
22 Källaren Bacchus; Stopet
27 Rimi Supermarket

OTHER
1 Statoil Car Hire
2 Regional Bus Station
3 Long Distance Bus Station
7 Rådhuset
14 Stadsmuseum
15 Arbetets Museum;
  Holmens Museum
18 Sankt Olai Kyrka
19 Norrköpings Biljard och
  IT Café
20 Domino Shopping Centre
21 Forex
23 Kungsfallet (Waterfall)
24 Louis de Geer Concert
  Hall; Guskelov
  Restaurant
25 Tourist Office
26 Systembolaget
29 Stadsbiblioteket
30 Norrköpings
  Konstmuseum

south of the centre, has important early-20th-century works, including examples of modernism and cubism. For a view of the city and out to the fjord Bråviken, climb the 68m-high **Rådhuset tower** *(Drottninggatan)*; you can visit at 3pm Monday to Friday from mid-June to mid-August (Skr25). **Sankt Olai Kyrka**, in a small central park, is one of the few noteworthy baroque churches in Sweden.

Two kilometres west of the city centre, near the river, are good examples of **Bronze Age rock carvings**, with an adjacent museum, **Hällristningsmuseet** *(☎ 165545; Himmelstalund; admission free; open daily May-Aug)*. Guided tours of the rock carvings take place at 2pm daily in July (adult/child Skr30/free). Take bus No 115 to Riksvägen, then walk the last 500m.

From early July to mid-August, the tiny vintage tram No 1 runs a short guided tour through the town centre. The tram leaves from outside the train station at 5pm Monday, Wednesday and Friday (Skr25).

Kolmården

Kolmården **zoo** *(☎ 249000; ⓦ www.kolmarden.com; open 10am-5pm daily May, 9am-6pm daily June-Aug, Sat & Sun Sept)* is billed as the largest in Europe and has about 1000 animals from all continents and climates of the world. The complex is divided into two areas: the main **Djurparken** (zoo) with its excellent dolphin show **Delfinarium** *(adult/child Skr195/95)*; and **Safariparken** *(adult/child Skr80/40)*, which you drive around (in a bus or your own transport). An excellent,

GÖTALAND

separate **Tropicarium** (☎ 395250; adult/child Skr70/45) opposite the entrance includes spiders, sharks, alligators and snakes and completes the attraction. A general 'maxi' ticket for the zoo and safari park costs Skr245/125. The cable car (Skr80/40) around the park gives a better view of the forest than of the animals.

You'll need all day to take the zoo in fully. Kolmården is 35km north of Norrköping, on the north shore of Bråviken (regular bus No 432 or 433 from Norrköping; Skr48).

Places to Stay
Camping Approximately 2.5km from the city, **Himmelstalunds Camping** (☎ 171190; Campingsvägen; camping per person Skr30, cabins from Skr450) is on the south bank of Motala Ström. The easiest way to get here by public transport is to take tram No 3 to Kneippen, then walk 1.5km along the river.

There is also a huge, well-equipped and very family-focused camping ground 5km from Kolmården and some 30km from town, **Kolmårdens Camping & Stugby** (☎ 398250; e info@kolmardenscamping.se; tent sites from Skr105, rooms/cabins from Skr395/495). Take bus No 432 or 433.

Hostels STF's **Turistgården** (☎ 101160; e info@turistgarden.se; Ingelstagatan 31; dorm beds Skr145) is about 800m north of the train station and offers good budget accommodation. The second STF hostel, **Abborreberg** (☎ 319344; e info@abborreberg.nu; dorm beds Skr125; open May-Sept) is beautifully situated in a coastal pine wood 6km east of town. Accommodation is in cottages scattered through the surrounding park. Take bus No 101 or 111 to Lindö; bikes and boats can also be rented here.

The third budget option is right in the heart of town: friendly **Hörnans Vandrarhem** (☎ 168271; e hornans.vandrarhem@telia.com; Hörngatan 1; dorm beds Skr160, singles/ doubles Skr265/320) is above a pub and has comfortable lodgings.

Hotels The best budget bet is the small, simple, family-run **Hotell Isabell** (☎ 169082; Vattengränden 7; singles/doubles Skr450/550, discounted to Skr350/450). Pleasant **Hotel Centric** (☎ 129030; e info@centrichotel.se; Gamla Rådstugugatan 18) and **Hotell Drott** (☎ 180060; Tunnbindaregatan 19) are a step

up, with unremarkable but comfortable rooms and private facilities. Both offer single/double rooms for Skr695/795, discounted on weekends and in summer to around Skr390/490.

Scandic Hotel Norrköping City (☎ 495 5200; e norrkopingcity@scandic-hotels.com; Slottsgatan 99; singles/doubles from Skr1200/ 1525, discounted to Skr630/830) is near the train station and offers upmarket lodgings in a light, modern environment.

Top choice in town is the classy **Elite Grand Hotel** (☎ 197100; e info@grandhotel .elite.se; Tyska torget 2; singles/doubles from Skr1125/1425, discounted to Skr690/890), where the stylish lobby area hints at the quality to be found in the hotel's rooms.

Places to Eat & Drink
There are plenty of eateries in the shopping district along Drottninggatan, including cheap fast-food outlets. Another good place for a wander when you're peckish is the student quarter around Kungsgatan.

Guskelov (☎ 134400; Dalsgatan 15; lunch special Skr65), at the concert hall, is a good choice for good-value lunches or upmarket evening dining. There's a good selection of tapas dishes (Skr30 to Skr50), plus à la carte mains (Skr120 to Skr225), or set menus (two courses for Skr280).

Pappa Grappa (☎ 180014; Gamla Råd-stugugatan 26) is a cosy, intimate place of-fering authentic Italian dishes from Skr95, and you can stop by for a drink at the bar, and take your pick from the grappa on offer (or a better indulgence is the tiramisu).

Popular **Källaren Bacchus** (☎ 100740; Gamla Torget 4) is a restaurant and pub with a great outdoor serving area. Lunch here is good value at Skr63 (dinner mains cost from Skr85).

Sing Thai (☎ 186188; Trädgårdsgatan 15; meals Skr95-170) has excellent service and a range of quite pricey Thai meals, including curries, satays, seafood and noodle dishes. The lunch deal is good value at Skr59.

Not so true to its heritage, **Restaurang New Delhi** (☎ 126828; Trädgårdsgatan 3; meals Skr50-140) offers an interesting mix of Swedish and Indian dishes, with every-thing from pepper steak to chicken tandoori and lamb curry, plus cheap bar meals like baked potatoes and pytt i panna (Swedish-style hash).

The kind of place that backpackers love, **Planet Woodstock** (☎ 188111; Gamla Rådstugugatan 11) is open until at least 11pm (until 5am Friday and Saturday) and has an extensive menu of bagels, baked potatoes and hot dishes like moussaka and lasagne, all for under Skr60.

There are some excellent options near the industrial area, including **Fräcka Fröken** (☎ 288823; Kungsgatan 43), a cool café offering good coffee, sandwiches, salads and cakes, and the funky, colourful **Världens Bar Café & Kök** (☎ 134510; Västgötegatan 15; meals Skr59-115), with great dishes – and music – from around the world. Menu items include Bombay Chicken, Trafalgar Square Fish & Chips and Khadaffis Felafel, but there are also standard burgers and baguettes.

Another popular drinking spot is **Stopet** (Gamla Torget), it is an atmospheric cellar pub that fills up after the locals have finished their work. The **Bishops Arms**, at the Grand Hotel, is a good English-style pub where you can while away an hour or two, sitting outside with a beer and a great view of the river.

For a supermarket, you should try **Rimi** (Spiralen centre). And for alcohol, go to **Systembolaget** (Drottninggatan 50B).

Getting There & Away

Sweden's third-largest airport (Nyköping Skavsta) is only 60km away – see the Getting There & Away chapter for details. To get there take the train to Nyköping, then catch a local bus.

The regional bus station is next to the train station and long-distance buses leave from a terminal across the road. **Swebus Express** (☎ 0200 218218; W www.swebusexpress.se) has frequent services to Stockholm (Skr175), Gothenburg (Skr265), Jönköping (Skr175) and Kalmar (Skr215), as does **Svenska Buss** (☎ 0771-676767; W www.svenskabuss.se). Norrköping is on the main north-south railway line, and SJ trains depart roughly hourly for Stockholm (Skr205) and Malmö (Skr504). Frequent regional trains run south to Tranås, via Linköping. Kustpilen SJ trains run roughly every two hours, northwards to Nyköping and southwards to Linköping and Kalmar.

Statoil (☎ 138400; Norra Promenaden 117) can organise car hire.

Getting Around

Norrköping's urban transport is based on länstrafiken, the regional netework, and the minimum fare is Skr16. Trams cover the city and are quickest for short hops, especially along Drottninggatan from the train station.

For a taxi, ring **Taxi Norrköping** (☎ 100100). Bicycle hire is available at the STF **Abborreberg hostel** (see Places to Stay earlier) for Skr25 per day.

SÖDERKÖPING

☎ 0121 • pop 13,900

Located 17km southeast of Norrköping, near the Göta Canal and near its eastern outlet, Söderköping is a delightful place to spend a few hours. There's a **tourist office** (☎ 18160; e turistbyran@soderkoping.se; W www.turism.soderkoping.se; Margaretagatan 19; open daily late June–early-Aug; shorter hours rest of year; closed Sat & Sun Sept-Apr) near the E22 Hwy (the main road through the town). Staff can help with information on how best to explore and enjoy the Göta Canal, including cycling or walking along part of it, or cruising some or all of its length.

Söderköping is known for its tiny wooden houses, reminiscent of Toytown; the quaintest area is **Drothemskvarteren**. There you'll find the two medieval churches **St Laurentii Kyrkan** (13th-century Gothic, with an 11th-century rune stone) and **Drothems Kyrka** (14th-century, with an older sacristy and a huge votive ship).

Stadsmuseum (☎ 21484; Gamla Skolgatan 6; admission free; open 11am-5pm daily June-Aug; 9am-noon Mon-Thur rest of year) has historical collections relating to the town. Cross the canal from Slussgränd and climb the steps right to the top of 78m-high **Ramundberget** for a great view. The town boasts the world's oldest existing **dry dock**, by the canal.

Korskullens Camping (☎ 21630; tent sites Skr110, cabins & chalets from Skr300) has a pretty set-up just off the E22 Hwy southeast of the centre, with green areas, a windmill and a café. Bike hire is also available. Next door to the camping ground is the STF hostel **Mangelgården** (☎ 10213; Skönbergagatan 48; dorm beds Skr130; open May-Sept), in a lovely 18th-century wooden building. You need to book in advance.

Söderköpings Brunn (☎ 10900; e info@soderkopingsbrunn.se; Skönbergagatan 35;

GÖTALAND

The Göta Canal

The Göta Canal, a passage through Sweden joining the North Sea with the Baltic Sea and linking the great lakes Vättern and Vänern, is one of the country's biggest attractions as well as its greatest civil engineering feat. Its total length of 190km comprises 103km of natural lakes and rivers and 87km of man-made waterways, built between 1802 and 1832 by a team of some 60,000 soldiers. When the canal finally opened it provided a hugely valuable transport and trade link between Sweden's east and west coasts.

There are two sections to the canal: the western section from Sjötorp, on the shores of Vänern, to Karlsborg on Vättern; and the eastern section from Motala, north of Vadstena on Vättern, to Mem, southeast of Norrköping. Along these stretches of the canal are towpaths, used in earlier times by horses and ox pulling barges, and nowadays these paths are utilised by walkers and cyclists, and the occasional canalside youth hostel breaks the journey.

Visitors to the region can see and experience the canal in a number of ways, and boat trips are obviously a favourite drawcard for this area. You can go on a four- or six-day cruise of the entire length of the canal, travelling from Stockholm to Gothenburg (or vice versa) and stopping to enjoy the attractions along the way; see the introductory Getting Around chapter for more information on this option. Alternatively, there are a number of shorter, cheaper boat trips on various sections of the canal – any tourist office in the area should be able to advise you. Tourist office staff should also be able to inform you of other options, such as canoeing, cycling or even horse-riding along certain sections.

A good website for information about the canal and the various activities and packages for travellers can be found at W www.gotakanal.se.

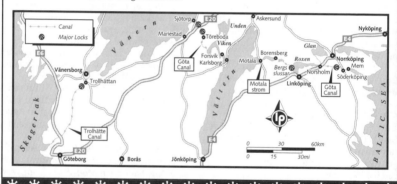

singles/doubles from Skr1100/1600, discounted to Skr745/1300) is a large, luxurious spa dating from the 1770s and full of old-world class. It offers quality accommodation, pretty grounds and an excellent restaurant.

There are some good restaurants around town, including the interesting **La Uva** *(☎ 10338; Rådhustoget; dinner mains Skr160-195)*, with a Spanish theme and good tapas selections, but the pick of the crop for location alone has to be **Göta Källare** *(☎ 15655; Bergsvägen 3; meals Skr60-185)*, a pub and restaurant with seating right by the canal and a range of light or more substantial meals on offer.

The bus stop is near the tourist office, on the E22. Regular local buses run to Norrköping, and **Swebus Express** runs twice daily, north to Stockholm and south along the coast to Västervik, Oskarahamn and Kalmar.

LINKÖPING
☎ 013 • pop 134,000

Linköping's history stretches right back to medieval times and the city is known for its fine medieval cathedral. In 1598, the Battle of Stångebro was fought between the Catholic forces of King Sigismund and the Protestant army of Duke Karl just east of the present city centre. The Catholics were defeated and some of Sigismund's advisors were later executed in the 'bloodbath of Linköping', leaving the Protestants in full control of Sweden.

Nowadays, Saab (Swedish Aeroplane Akti Bolaget) is the major employer, with a workforce of around 6000 making aircraft. Linköping is both a modern, industrial city and a preserver of traditions in its numerous museums.

Information
The **tourist office** (☎ 206835; e turism@ekoxen.se; W www.linkoping.se; Klostergatan 68) is inside Quality Hotel Ekoxen. It's open 24 hours, with plenty of brochures and such, but is usually staffed only during office hours.

There are banks and other services around Stora Torget. The striking city **library**, near the cathedral, has been rebuilt after a fire and offers Internet access. There's also **SITE cybercafe** (Bantorget 1), not far from the long-distance bus station and charging Skr25 for an hour online.

Gamla Linköping & Valla Fritidsområde
The town's best attractions are just outside the centre. Some 2km west of the city is Gamla Linköping (☎ 121110; bus No 202 or 214; admission free; open daily), one of the biggest living-museum villages in Sweden. It consists of six streets and a central square and, among the roughly 90 quaint, 19th-century houses there are about a dozen theme museums, many shops and a small chocolate factory. The museums all have different opening times (some are open daily in summer) and are free. You can wander among the 19th-century buildings at will.

Just 300m through the forest from Gamla Linköping is **Valla Fritidsområde**, a recreation area with domestic animals, a children's playground, mini-golf, a few small museums and many old houses.

Kinda Canal
Most visitors to Sweden know about the engineering marvel of the Göta Canal, but Linköping boasts its own canal system, the 90km **Kinda Canal**, which opened in 1871. There are 15 locks, including the deepest one in Sweden. A variety of cruises runs from early May to the end of September along the canal. The trip on **M/S Kind** (☎ 0141-233370) leaves the Tullbron dock on Wednesday and

Thursday for Rimforsa and costs Skr235 (return by bus or train included).

Other Attractions
The enormous **Domkyrka** (open 9am-6pm daily), with its 107m spire, is the landmark of Linköping and one of Sweden's oldest and largest churches (its foundations were laid around 1250). There are numerous gravestones, a large crucifix, two altar-pieces and other medieval treasures dating back to the 14th century. The nearby castle houses the **Slott & Domkyrkomuseum** (☎ 122380; adult/child Skr40/free; open 11am-4pm Tues-Fri, noon-4pm Sat & Sun Apr-Sept), with exhibits of the history of the cathedral, and the surrounding parks and streets (including Hunnebergsgatan and Storgatan) contain old houses that are worth seeing.

Just north of the cathedral, **Östergötlands Länsmuseum** (☎ 230230; Vasavägen; adult/child Skr20/10; open 10am-5pm Tues-Fri, 11am-4pm Sat & Sun) houses an extensive collection by various European painters, including Cranach's view of Eden, Original Sin, and Swedish art dating to the Middle Ages.

The concrete floor of **Sankt Lars Kyrka** (Storgatan; open 11am-4pm Mon-Thur, 11am-3pm Fri, 11am-1pm Sat) was built in 1802 above the previous medieval church crypt. Downstairs, you can see 11th-century gravestones and skeletons.

Approximately 7km west of the centre is **Flygvapenmuseum** (☎ 283567; Carl Cederströms gatan; bus No 213; adult/child Skr30/free; open 10am-5pm daily June-Aug, Tues-Sun rest of year), with exhibits on airforce history, including 60 aircraft.

Ekenäs Slott (☎ 77146; tours Skr70; guided tours on the hour 1pm-3pm Sat & Sun May-June & Aug; 1pm-3pm Tues-Sun July), built between 1630 and 1644, is the best-preserved Renaissance castle in Sweden. It has three spectacular towers, and a moat. The furniture and fittings are from the 17th to 19th centuries. At Whitsun, there's a medieval tournament at the castle – knights in armour etc. The castle is 20km east of Linköping and you'll need your own transport to get there.

Places to Stay
Camping The huge **Glyttinge Camping** (☎ 174928; e glyttinge@swipnet.se; Berggårdsvägen; tent sites, cabins from Skr375) is 4km west of the city centre.

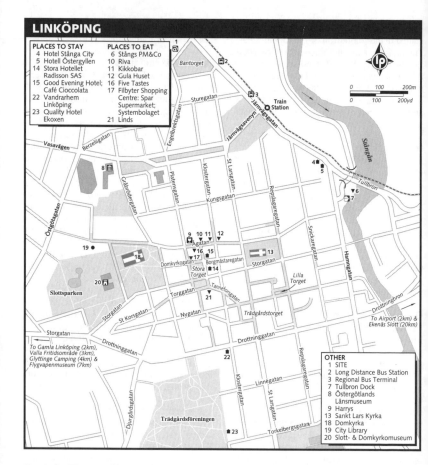

LINKÖPING

PLACES TO STAY
4 Hotel Stånga City
5 Hotell Östergyllen
14 Stora Hotellet
    Radisson SAS
15 Good Evening Hotel;
    Café Cioccolata
22 Vandrarhem
    Linköping
23 Quality Hotel
    Ekoxen

PLACES TO EAT
6 Stångs PM&Co
10 Riva
11 Kikkobar
12 Gula Huset
16 Five Tastes
17 Filbyter Shopping
    Centre: Spar
    Supermarket;
    Systembolaget
21 Linds

OTHER
1 SITE
2 Long Distance Bus Station
3 Regional Bus Terminal
7 Tullbron Dock
8 Östergötlands
    Länsmuseum
9 Harrys
13 Sankt Lars Kyrka
18 Domkyrka
19 City Library
20 Slott- & Domkyrkomuseum

Hostels The excellent and central STF **Vandrarhem Linköping** (☎ 149090; e lkpg vandrarhem@swipnet.se; Klostergatan 52A; dorm beds from Skr180, single/double hotel rooms Skr595/680, discounted weekends to Skr455/550) has dorm beds and a few hotel-style rooms, most with kitchenette.

In the centre of Valla Fritidsområde is **Mjellerumsgårdens Vandrarhem** (☎ 122730; dorm beds Skr160), in a great setting and with a small café and breakfast on offer, but with no guest kitchen.

Hotels Not far from the train station is **Hotell Östergyllen** (☎ 102075; Hamngatan 2B; singles/doubles from Skr350/500) and its neighbour, **Hotel Stångå City** (☎ 311275; singles/doubles Skr745/890, discounted to Skr445/595), both reasonable mid-range choices.

The very central **Good Evening Hotel** (☎ 129000; Hantverkaregatan 1; singles/doubles Skr795/895, discounted to Skr475/575) is another OK option, that has decent rooms and aircraft-themed decor, as well as friendly staff.

The large **Quality Hotel Ekoxen** (☎ 252600; e info.ekoxen@quality.choice hotels.se; Klostergatan 68; singles/doubles Skr1290/1590, discounted to Skr690/790) has very well-appointed rooms and good facilities, including a spa and massage centre and acclaimed restaurant – there's even a fully equipped hospital on the premises!

Located in the heart of town, **Stora Hotellet Radisson SAS** (☎ 103190; Stora Torget 9;

singles/doubles from Skr1380/1525, discounted to Skr700/800) is similarly upmarket and also has excellent, modern rooms as well as excellent facilities (minus the hospital, of course).

Places to Eat

Most places to eat (and drink) are on the main square or nearby streets, especially along buzzing Ågatan. Down near the Kinda Canal docks, off Hamngatan in the town's east, **Stångs PM&Co** (☎ 312000; Södra Stånggatan 1; lunch Skr72, mains Skr189-265) is a highly rated restaurant in a great location. The dinner menu is very impressive – with prices to match – and the lunchtime fare is great value.

Kikkobar (☎ 131310; Klostergatan 26; mains Skr118-220) is a cool place offering an international menu where 'East meets West'. There are Western dishes like steak and salmon, but there's also a heavy Japanese influence, with plenty of sushi, rice and noodle dishes. For simpler fare or an evening beverage, head to popular **Harrys** (☎ 133390; Ågatan 43), one of the ubiquitous Swedish restaurant-pub chain. Here you can get good beer-drinking food like spareribs, burgers and burritos.

The new and trendy **Riva** (☎ 144515; Ågatan 43; meals Skr90-260) has gourmet pizzas to fit the decor, plus other pricey Italian dishes, including lots of pasta options and even osso bucco. The more traditional **Gula Huset** (☎ 138838; Ågatan; lunch Skr60, dinner mains Skr80-200) offers a good-value lunch plus an extensive menu featuring pasta, favourite Swedish meals, and seafood, meat and vegetarian dishes.

Around Stora Torget, **Linds** (☎ 100065) has a Skr59 lunch buffet, à la carte meals from Skr45 (including nachos and pasta) and a courtyard area that's popular for after-work drinks.

Café Cioccolata (Hantverkaregatan 1), near the Good Evening Hotel, is a stylish café offering a wide range of coffees and filled panini or ciabatta (Skr35).

For a quick, cheap meal, **Five Tastes** (☎ 105544; Ågatan 32), opposite the cinema, offers a decent selection of pizza and kebab meals for around Skr50.

The **Filbyter** shopping centre on Stora Torget is home to both a Spar supermarket and small Systembolaget store.

Getting There & Away

The **airport** (☎ 181030) is only 2km east of town. **SAS** (☎ 020 727727; ⓦ www.scandinavian.net) and **Skyways** (☎ 020 959500; ⓦ www.skyways.se) fly daily direct to Stockholm and Copenhagen. There's no airport bus, but **Taxi Linköping** (☎ 146000) charges around Skr100 for the ride.

Regional and local buses, run by **Östgöta-Trafiken** (☎ 0771-211010), have their terminal and platforms adjacent to Centralstationen (the train station); route maps and timetables are available at the information office here. Journeys cost from Skr16; the 24-hour dygnskort (Skr100) is valid on all buses and local trains within the region. To get to Vadstena, take the train to Mjölby, then bus No 661.

Long-distance buses depart from a terminal 500m northwest of the train station. **Swebus Express** buses run seven or eight times daily, south to Jönköping (Skr135) and Gothenburg (Skr240), and north to Norrköping (Skr50) and Stockholm (Skr205).

Linköping is on the main north-south railway line and SJ trains between Stockholm and Malmö stop here roughly every hour. Frequent regional trains run south to Tranås and north to Norrköping. Kustpilen SJ trains run roughly every two hours, northwards to Norrköping and Nyköping (Skr115), and southwards to Kalmar (Skr165).

Getting Around

Most city buses (Skr16 minimum fare) depart from Centralstationen. For a taxi, ring **Taxi Linköping** (☎ 146000). Bicycle hire is available at **Bertil Anderssons Cykel & Motor** (☎ 314646; Plantensgatan 27), in the northern part of town.

BERGS SLUSSAR
☎ 013

Bergs Slussar, 12km northwest of Linköping, is one of the most scenic sections of the Göta Canal – there are seven locks and the height gain is 19m. The nearby ruin **Vreta kloster**, Sweden's oldest monastery, was founded by Benedictine monks in 1120. It's worth a look but the adjacent well-preserved 13th-century **abbey church** is much more interesting.

There is a good **STF Vandrarhem** (☎ 60330; ⓔ info@wardshuset.com; dorm beds Skr165; open May-Aug) in a lovely location near the locks, with a café, mini-golf and bikes for rent. There are a couple of cafés and a few restaurants out this way, including **Kanalkrogen** (☎ 60076; meals Skr135-192), with a great range of meals and a **Bakfiken** selling pizzas from Skr45.

Bus Nos 521 and 522 run regularly from Linköping.

VADSTENA
☎ 0143 • pop 7600

Beautiful Vadstena on Vättern lake is a legacy of both church and state power and now the abbey and castle compete for the visitor's interest. The dominant historical figure was St Birgitta, who lived in Rome but established the abbey and her Order of the Most Holy Saviour here in 1370. The atmosphere in the old town (between Storgatan and the abbey), with its wonderful cobbled streets and wooden buildings, makes Vadstena one of the most pleasant spots in Sweden, if you don't meet up with one of the many local ghosts.

Information
The **tourist office** (☎ 31570; Ⓔ info@tourist.vadstena.se; ⓦ www.vadstena.se/turism; open daily mid-May–mid-Sept, Mon-Fri rest of year) is inside the castle. Ask for details about the town walking tours and local boat tours. You'll find various facilities (bank, post etc) east of the castle, on Storgatan and around Stora Torget.

Things to See
Located near the lake, the Renaissance castle **Vadstena Slott** (☎ 31570; Slottsvägen; adult/child Skr50/10; open same hours as tourist office, guided tours mid-May–mid-Sept) was the mighty family project of the early Vasa kings and in the upper apartments there are some items of period furniture and paintings.

The superb **Klosterkyrkan** (abbey church; admission free; open daily May-Sept), consecrated in 1430, has a combination of Gothic and some Renaissance features. Inside are the accumulated relics of St Birgitta (her bones are in the reliquary) and medieval sculptures, including the saint depicted during revelation. The carved floor slabs are particularly interesting.

Near the church is the **Klostermuseet** (☎ 76807; Lasarettsgatan; adult/child Sk35/free; open 11am-4pm daily mid-May–Aug). It's housed in Bjälboättens Palats, which dates from 1250 and was originally a royal residence but became the convent after consecration in 1384.

The old courthouse **rådhus**, on the town square, and **Rödtornet** (Sånggatan) also date from late medieval times.

Rökstenen
Sweden has many historical regions but the area around Vadstena is certainly one that deserves a closer look. Cycling is an option as the scenic flatlands around Vättern lend themselves to the pedal. A whole series of ancient legends is connected with Rökstenen, Sweden's most impressive and famous rune stone, near the church at Rök, just off the E4 on the road to Heda and Alvastra. In ancient intricate verse using short-twig and cryptic runes, the sections we understand refer to the Ostrogothic hero-king Theodoric, who conquered Rome in the 6th century, but the stone is dated to the 9th century. There's a small, seasonal tourist office on the site. The outdoor exhibition (covered), and the stone, are open at all times.

Bus No 664 runs to Rök one to three times daily from the main line train station at Mjölby.

Väversunda
The 12th-century limestone-built Romanesque **Väversunda kyrka**, situated 15km southwest of Vadstena, is a bizarre-looking church containing restored wall paintings that date back to the 13th century. The adjacent **Tåkern Nature Reserve** is popular with bird-watchers as it attracts many different species. There's a bird-watcher's tower near the church.

Bus No 610 runs through this area to Vadstena and Motala, several times daily.

Places to Stay & Eat
The large **Vätterviksbadet** (☎ 12730; tent sites Skr150, simple rooms & cabins from Skr300; open May–mid-Sept) is near the lake 2km north of the town. There's a pool, kiosk and café, and other good facilities.

The central **STF Vandrarhem** (☎ 10302; Skänningegatan 20; dorm beds Skr145) is open year-round, but from late August to early June it is essential to book in advance. A far more appealing option is the recommended, lakeside **STF Vandrarhem Borghamn** (☎ 20368; Ⓔ info@borghamnsvandrarhem.nu;

dorm beds Skr135), a friendly place in a lovely, quiet setting 15km southwest of Vadstena. Take bus No 610, and it's about a 750m walk from the bus stop at Borghamn; you can rent a bike here to explore further.

The small, central **27:ans Nattlogi** *(☎ 13447; Storgatan 27; singles/doubles from Skr500/600)* has five rooms (some with private facilities, some shared) and breakfast is included in the price. **Pensionat Solgården** *(☎ 14350; Strågatan 3; singles/doubles from Skr440/590)* is another pleasant guesthouse, with a range of unique rooms.

Vadstena Klosterhotel *(☎ 31530;* e *hotell@klosterhotel.se; singles/doubles from Skr995/1295)*, next to Klosterkyrkan, is a luxurious place with great lake views. The excellent restaurant here serves a fine buffet lunch for Skr85.

Pizzas costing around Skr50 are available at **Pizzeria Venezia** *(☎ 13345; Klostergatan 2).*

For filled baguettes from Skr40 and other light meals, you could visit the open-air café **Hamnpaviljongen**, in the park in front of the castle.

The pleasant cellar restaurant **Rådhuskällaren** *(☎ 12170; Rådhustorget)* is under the old courthouse, and has dinner mains from Sk70 to Skr180. Opposite the courthouse is a central **supermarket** *(Rådhustorget)* for self-caterers.

Getting There & Around

See Linköping for regional transport information. Only buses run to Vadstena – take bus No 610 to Motala (for trains to Örebro), or bus No 661 to Mjölby (for trains to Linköping and Stockholm). **Swebus Express** runs once daily from Jönköping to Örebro via Vadstena.

Sport Hörnan *(☎ 10362; Storgatan 26)* has bikes for rent.

Småland

Until 1658, the densely forested region of Småland served as a buffer zone between the Swedes and Danes. In the 19th century, rural poverty in this underdeveloped part of Sweden caused mass emigration, mainly to the USA. Nowadays, the population density is still fairly low but there are some reasonably large towns, both on the coastal strip and inland. Småland has become famous for glass production at its numerous factories, many of which are open to visitors. In the factory shops of what has become known as Glasriket (the 'Kingdom of Crystal') you can buy beautiful glass art.

Orientation & Information

Småland consists of three Swedish *landskaps* (regions): Småland itself, Blekinge in the south and the unique and virtually treeless island Öland, in the east. There are four *(läns)* counties, namely Jönköpings, Kronobergs, Blekinge and Kalmar (which includes Öland). For ease of reference, Öland is discussed in a separate section.

Most of Småland is dominated by forest, with many small to medium-sized lakes. The west has lots of marshland and the north, known as Höglandet (the Highlands), is fairly hilly, reaching 377m just east of Eksjö. Blekinge has forest and good fishing rivers and lakes, and there's also a scenic archipelago off the southern coast. Öland, the long, thin island just off the east coast of Sweden, has unique geology, flora and cultural history.

Regional Tourist Offices

Visitors can contact the following agencies for more detailed information on the area:

Blekinge Turism (☎ 0454-307120, Ⓔ info@blekingeturism.com, Ⓦ www.blekinge turism.com) Tullgatan 5, SE-37435 Karlshamn
Smålands Turism (☎ 036-351270, Ⓔ info@visit-smaland.com, Ⓦ www.visit -smaland.com) Västra Storgatan 18A, Box 1027, SE-55111 Jönköping
Turism i Kalmar Län (☎ 0480-448336, Ⓔ info@kalmar.regionforbund.se, Ⓦ www.kalmar.regionforbund.se/turism) Nygatan 34, Box 762, SE-39127 Kalmar
Turism i Kronoberg (☎ 0470-742570, Ⓔ turism.kronoberg@kommun.vaxjo.se) Stationen, Norra Järnvägsgatan, SE-35230 Växjö

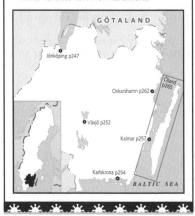

Ölands Turist (☎ 0485-560600; Ⓔ info@olands turist.se, Ⓦ www.olandsturist.se) Turistvägen, Box 74, SE-38621 Färjestaden

Getting Around

Express buses mainly travel along the coast (to Västervik, Oskarshamn, Kalmar and Karlskrona), follow the E4 via Jönköping, or cruise along highway No 33 from Jönköping to Västervik (via Eksjö and Vimmerby). A few express services go through the region's interior, mainly operated by **Svenska Buss** (☎ *0771-676767;* Ⓦ *www.svenskabuss.se).* **Swebus Express** (☎ *0200 218218;* Ⓦ *www .swebusexpress.se)* also operates in the region.

The main Malmö to Stockholm railway runs through the region, but you'll have to change to local trains to reach places of most interest. SJ trains run west from Karlskrona to Kristianstad or north from Karlskrona to

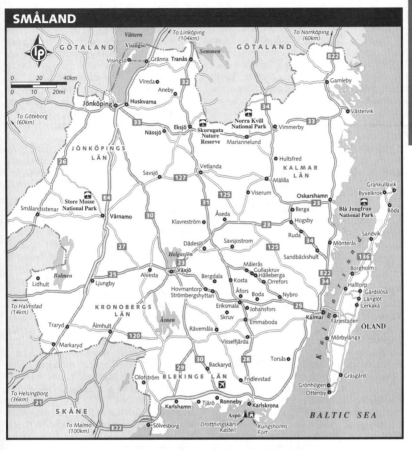

Kalmar. There are also SJ services from Kalmar to Linköping, and inland routes from Oskarshamn to Nässjö and Kalmar to Gothenburg. The Nässjö to Jönköping and Falköping trains are run by **Vättertåg** (☎ 0380-554402).

The following companies provide regional transport links. If you're planning to spend a reasonable amount of time in any of these *län*, it's worth inquiring about monthly passes or a *sommarkort*, offering discount travel in the peak summer period (ie, from Midsummer to mid-August). Check also the respective websites for routes, schedules, fares and passes; these sites don't always have information in English, but if you call the telephone numbers listed you'll usually reach someone who can help you in English.

BlekingeTrafiken (☎ 0455-56900, Ⓦ www.blekingetrafiken.se)
Jönköpings Länstrafik (☎ 0771-444333, 036-199550, Ⓦ www.jlt.se)
Kalmar Läns Trafik (☎ 0491-761200, Ⓦ www.klt.se)
Länstrafiken Kronoberg (☎ 020 767076, 0470-727551; Ⓦ www.lanstrafikenkron.se)

Jönköpings Län

JÖNKÖPING
☎ 036 • pop 117,900
Pleasantly located at the southern end of Vättern lake, Jönköping is a popular summer spot and the proud home of the safety match (the local radio station is even called Radio

Match). In more recent times, ABBA's Agnetha Fältskog was born in the town.

Jönköping is the main centre of an urban strip stretching eastwards around the lakeshore to include Huskvarna, known for its sewing machines and motorcycles. There are several good museums, especially in the restored match-factory area, and there's a pleasant wooded park by the river.

Information

The **tourist office** (☎ 105050; e turist@stk.jon koping.se, w www.jonkoping.se; open 8am-7pm Mon-Fri, 10am-2pm Sat year-round & 10am-1pm Sun June-Aug) is in the Juneporten complex, in the overpass connected to the train station (or accessed from Västra Storgatan).

Banks can be found along Östra Storgatan. The large **public library** (Dag Hammarskjölds plats), with Internet access and café, is adjacent to the länsmuseum.

Things to See

The museum of the history of matches, **Tändsticksmuseet** (☎ 105543; Tändsticksgränd 27; adult/child Skr30/free; open 10am-5pm Mon-Fri, 10am-3pm Sat & Sun June-Aug; noon-3pm Tues-Sat Sept-May), in an old match factory, deals with this Swedish innovation that is much taken for granted, and it's more interesting than it sounds! Ask for the English-language brochure to guide you around and explain the exhibits.

Near the Tändsticksmuseet is the **Radio Museum** (☎ 713959; admission Skr20; open 10am-5pm Mon-Fri, 10am-1pm Sat, 11am-3pm Sun June–mid-Aug; closed Sun & Mon mid-Aug–May) with a collection of over 1000 radio sets and related memorabilia – a playground for technical buffs.

In the old town square of Hovrättstorget are the 17th-century buildings of **Göta Hovrätt** and the red **Gamla Rådhuset** (old town hall), which has displays on the history and practice of Swedish jurisprudence. The neoclassical **Kristine kyrka** (Östra Storgatan) is in a restored part of the old town.

Jönköpings Länsmuseum (☎ 301800; Dag Hammarskjölds plats; adult/child Skr40/free; open 11am-5pm Tues-Sun, 11am-8pm Wed) has collections covering local history and contemporary culture, including Stone Age flint axes and modern plastic egg cups. Do not miss the childlike, yet strangely haunting

fantasy works of the artist John Bauer, who was inspired by the local countryside.

Above the town to the west is the expanse of **Stadsparken** and its curiosities, including the 1458 mounted ornithological taxidermic masterpieces of **Fågelmuseet** (☎ 129983; admission free; open 11am-5pm daily May-Aug), and the little baroque church **Bäckaby kyrka**, part of which dates back to the 1580s. The **Solberga bell tower** dominates a fine lookout over Vättern lake.

About 2km east of the town centre (near the E4) at the A6 Center is **Tropikhuset** (☎ 168975; Kompanigatan 8; adult/child Skr50/30; open 10am-5pm daily June-Aug, 10am-4pm daily Sept-May), which is full of snakes, crocodiles, primates and tropical birds. Also at the A6 Center, there's the **Försvarshistoriska Museum** (☎ 190412; adult/child Skr30/15; open 10am-5pm daily), which will appeal if you're interested in military history.

In Huskvarna (7km east of Jönköping), the **Husqvarna fabriksmuseum** (☎ 146162; Hakarpsvägen 1; adult/child Skr30/free; open 10am-5pm Mon-Fri, 1pm-4pm Sat & Sun May-Sept, 10am-3pm Tues-Fri Oct-Apr) covers the manufacturing and technical history of the Husqvarna factory, which started as a small arms factory but has since produced chainsaws, sewing machines and motorcycles.

From April to September, visitors can enjoy **cruises** (☎ 070 637 1700) on Vättern lake on board the MS Nya Skärgården. Evening trips usually include a buffet dinner and cost around Skr350. The boat departs from Hamnpiren.

Places to Stay

Rosenlunds Camping (☎ 122863; e villabjork hagen@swipnet.se; tent sites Skr160, cabins & rooms from Skr490) is on the lakeshore off Huskvarnavägen approximately 3km east of the town centre. It is a well-equipped place that's open year-round and offers a range of accommodation.

East of the town centre, **Huskvarna Vandrarhem** (☎ 148870; e 148870@telia.com; Odengatan 10, Huskvarna; dorm beds Skr150; singles/doubles Skr495/550) is a year-round STF hostel. It's a good choice, with bright, pleasant rooms – all with TV and private toilets (showers in the hall). There are also bicycles for rent, and breakfast is available (Skr40). Take bus No 1.

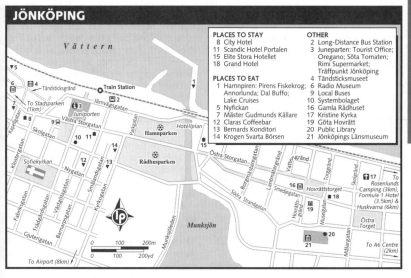

JÖNKÖPING

Vättern

Train Station

Tändsticksgränd

To Stadsparken (1km)

Juniporten

Västra Storgatan

Skolgatan

Hamnparken

Hotellplan

Kapellgatan

Klostergatan

Sofiekyrkan

Nygatan

Kyrkogatan

Rådhusparken

Östra Storgatan

Fabriksgatan

Västergatan

Trädgårdsgatan

Smålandsgatan

Barnarpsgatan

Borgmästaregatan

Lantmätargränd

Vättergränd

Smedjegatan

Hovrättstorget

Hovrätts-gränd

Södra Strandgatan

Torggränd

Skolgränd

To Rosenlunds Camping (3km), Formule 1 Hotel (3.5km) & Huskvarna (6km)

Gjuterigatan

Munksjöleden

Munksjön

Munksjögatan

Östra Torget

Mälargatan

To A6 Centre (2km)

To Airport (8km)

0   100   200m
0   100   200yd

PLACES TO STAY
8 City Hotel
11 Scandic Hotel Portalen
15 Elite Stora Hotellet
18 Grand Hotel

PLACES TO EAT
1 Hamnpiren: Pirens Fiskekrog;
     Annorlunda; Dal Buffo;
     Lake Cruises
5 Nyfickan
7 Mäster Gudmunds Källare
12 Claras Coffeebar
13 Bernards Konditori
14 Krogen Svarta Börsen

OTHER
2 Long-Distance Bus Station
3 Junparten: Tourist Office;
     Oregano; Sôta Tomaten;
     Rimi Supermarket;
     Träffpunkt Jönköping
4 Tändsticksmuseet
6 Radio Museum
9 Local Buses
10 Systembolaget
16 Gamla Rådhuset
17 Kristine Kyrka
19 Göta Hovrätt
20 Public Library
21 Jönköpings Länsmuseum

Hotel Formule 1 (☎ *302565; Huskvarnavägen 76; 3-person rooms Skr270*) is another budget option, which offers bland but functional rooms with TV and shared facilities (there's no kitchen for self-catering). It's a few kilometres from the centre of town (take bus No 1).

Grand Hotel (☎ *719600;* ℮ *info@grandhotel jonkoping.se; Hövrättstorget; singles/doubles from Skr690/840, discounted to Skr490/550*) is probably the cheapest option right in town, with budget, standard and superior rooms available; **City Hotel** (☎ *719280;* ℮ *hotel@city hotel.nu; Västra Storgatan 25; singles/doubles from Skr895/995, discounted to Skr495/595*) has similar discounted prices but is a slight step up with regard to quality. Both hotels offer comfortable accommodation in the central area.

Two upmarket central choices are the stylish **Scandic Hotel Portalen** (☎ *585 4200;* ℮ *portalen@scandic-hotels.com; Barnapsgatan 6; singles/doubles Skr1200/1340, discounted to Skr590/720*), not far from the train station, and the rather grand **Elite Stora Hotellet** (☎ *100000;* ℮ *info@jonkoping.elite.se; Hotellplan; singles/doubles from Skr1260/1460, discounted to Skr590/690*), with a better location near the river and opposite the harbour restaurants. Both have restaurants and bars, and discounted summer and weekend prices offer excellent value.

Places to Eat

Classy **Krogen Svarta Börsen** (☎ *712222; Kyrkogatan 4; mains Skr295-335*) is the best dining establishment in town, with great atmosphere, fine food and superb service to justify the high prices. **Mäster Gudmunds Källare** (☎ *100640; Kapellgatan 2; dinner mains Skr99-179*) is a cellar restaurant with an appealing medieval atmosphere and weekday lunch specials for Skr60. Main courses include vegetarian options in addition to well-prepared fish and meat choices.

Head down to popular Hamnpiren, the central harbour area, to find a multitude of restaurants and good lunch specials (usually Skr60 to Skr70), or crowds enjoying al fresco dining on a summer evening. Popular **Pirens Fiskekrog** (☎ *150096; dinner mains Skr98-169*) offers a wide range of fish dishes; next door is **Annorlunda** (☎ *719450; mains Skr115-135*), with Thai and Chinese cuisine on its menu; and **Dal Buffo** (☎ *168406; mains Skr69-179*) has a selection of Italian meals, including pizza and pasta.

Bernards Konditori (☎ *711121; Kyrkogatan 12*) opened in the 1910s and serves tasty cakes and good coffee. Near the Tändsticksmuseet, **Nyfickan** (☎ *190686*) is an excellent café with a studenty feel; sandwiches cost Skr35, lunch is Skr50. **Claras Coffeebar** (☎ *300115; Barnarpsgatan 18*) offers gourmet *panini* and coffee in very stylish surrounds.

Most cheap eateries are on the pedestrian streets in the eastern part of the town centre. Near the tourist office in Juneporten there are a few good-value options, including **Oregano**, with kebabs, pizza and grill dishes, and **Söta Tomaten**, with lunchtime pasta dishes for Skr50.

Self-caterers should head straight for the **Rimi supermarket** in the Juneporten complex. There's a nearby **Systembolaget** *(cnr Skolgatan & Trädgårdsgatan)*.

Getting There & Away
Jönköping's **airport** *(☎ 311100)* is about 8km southwest of the town centre. **Skyways** *(☎ 020 959500)* has one to three flights daily to/from Stockholm Arlanda, and **SAS** *(☎ 020 727727)* operates direct daily flights to/from Copenhagen. Bus No 18 serves the airport.

Länstrafiken information and tickets can be obtained at the Träffpunkt Jönköping office in Juneporten, near the tourist office. Long-distance buses depart from next to the train station; most local buses use the station opposite Juneporten, on Västra Storgatan. All local traffic is run by **Jönköpings Länstrafik** *(☎ 199550, 0771-444333;* **W** *www.jlt.se)*, including bus No 1, which runs regularly to Huskvarna (Skr16).

Swebus Express bus services include Nos 830 and 831 to Gothenburg (Skr150, two to three hours, up to 15 daily), No 831 to Stockholm (Skr265, five hours, up to 10 daily), No 833 to Helsingborg (Skr210) and Malmö (Skr245), No 839 to Karlstad (Skr230) and No 857 to Västervik (Skr180). Buy tickets at the office in the train station. Svenska Buss runs to Eksjö, Gothenburg, Kalmar, Oskarshamn and Stockholm.

Jönköping is not on the main train lines. From the central train station Vättertåg trains run roughly hourly to connect with SJ services on the main lines (in Nässjö and Falköping), and require no seat reservation nor supplement for rail-pass holders. Länståg trains run to Värnamo.

Taxi Jönköping *(☎ 344000)* is the local taxi firm.

GRÄNNA & VISINGSÖ
☎ 0390

Gränna is a busy, touristy place with some tacky gift shops, but the location (beneath rocky cliffs and on Vättern lake) is pleasant. The town is known for its peppermint rock candy *(polkagris)* – there are about a dozen factories in the area and free visits can be made. The peaceful 14km-long island of Visingsö, 6km west and connected by frequent ferries, is a great place for cyclists, and for those wishing to get off the beaten track.

There's a **tourist office** *(☎ 41010;* **e** *turist@grm.se,* **W** *www.turist.grm.se; Brahegatan 38; open 10am-7pm daily May-Aug, 10am-5pm daily Sept-Oct, noon-5pm daily Nov-Apr)* in central Gränna, and also one at the harbour in Visingsö *(☎ 40193;* **e** *visingsotur ist@grm.se,* **W** *www.visingso.net; open 10am-7pm mid-June–Aug, 10am-5pm daily May-early June & late Aug, 8am-2pm Mon-Fri Sept-early May)*.

The main street of Gränna, Brahegatan, has most services travellers may require.

Things to See
At the tourist office (and with the same opening hours), the fascinating **Andréemuseet** *(adult/child Skr40/20)* describes the disastrous attempt of Salomon August Andrée (who hailed from Gränna), and two friends, to reach the North Pole from Svalbard by balloon in 1897 (see the boxed text). Don't be put off by Andrée's ballooning misfortune: you can take a one-hour scenic **hot-air balloon trip** *(☎ 30525)* over the area for Skr1550 per person.

Directly across from the tourist office is **Gränna Polkagriskokeri** *(Brahegatan 39)*, one of the places where you can see the famous red-and-white candy being made according to a 19th-century recipe.

Visingsö has a 17th-century **church**, a ruined **castle** and an **aromatic herb garden**. An extensive network of footpaths and bicycle trails lead through oak woods. You can hire bikes at the harbour (Skr40 for three hours, Skr60 for a day).

In June and July there are daily **boat tours** *(☎ 51050; adult/child Skr140/70)* of lakes Bunn and Ören, southeast of Gränna. The lakes and forests of this beautiful area inspired the trolls and fairies painted by local artist John Bauer nearly 100 years ago; you can see his wonderful works in Jönköpings Länsmuseum (see earlier in this chapter).

Places to Stay & Eat
Gränna The tourist office arranges **private rooms** from Skr150 per person per night (plus Skr50 booking fee).

Up, Up & Away

One of Sweden's most famous explorers was Salomon August Andrée, who was born in Gränna in 1854. Andrée's interest in ballooning began in 1876 when he visited the USA and, in 1882, he took part in a Swedish scientific expedition to Svalbard.

By 1893, Andrée was able to purchase his first balloon and he made atmospheric observations that were published in scientific journals. These flights brought him to the attention of the newspapers and the public. Two years later, Andrée announced to the Swedish Academy of Sciences that he wished to fly over the North Pole and needed Skr130,000 for the project. Initial scepticism was quashed by the great explorer Adolf Erik Nordenskiöld (the discoverer of the Northeast Passage). Other supporters included Alfred Nobel and King Oskar.

Despite failing to take off in 1896, the crew tried again in 1897 and *The Eagle*, with Andrée and two other passengers, took off on 11 July 1897 from Danskøya, a bleak offshore island near the northwest tip of Svalbard. Apart from sporadic contact during the first few days, nothing further was heard. The balloon disappeared and its fate wasn't known until 33 years later.

Three days into its flight, the balloon crashed on the frozen Arctic Ocean. The explorers salvaged what they could and headed south towards Kvitøya, in appalling ice conditions. They soon discovered they could carry very little across the ice and they lost even more when an ice floe they were camping on broke up. However, after three months, they reached Kvitøya but perished, one by one, over the next few days.

In 1930, the crew of a Norwegian ship discovered the explorers' bodies on Kvitøya, more than 300km east of Danskøya. They were shipped (with the equipment and all film intact) back to Stockholm. Thousands of people attended the funeral as a mark of respect to the end of the most tragic of Swedish expeditions.

Grännastrandens Camping (☎ 10706; ⓔ info@grannacamping.se; Hamnen; tent sites/dorm beds Skr150/140, 4-bed cabins from Skr400) is a well-equipped place down by the harbour, offering camping (from May to September), a café, shop, minigolf, boat hire and a hostel that's open year-round.

Västanå Slott (☎ 10700; doubles from Skr850; open May-Sept), about 6km south of town, is a beautiful 18th-century castle with period decor. Also south of town is the imposing **Gyllene Uttern** (☎ 10800; ⓔ info@gylleneuttern.se; singles/doubles from Skr1095/1330, discounted to Skr795/1050), a classy, romantic hotel off the E4. The views from the quality restaurant here are excellent.

If you're looking for a place to eat in Gränna, check out the offerings along the main street, Brahegatan, where you'll find fast-food places and a supermarket. The pick of the eateries here is charming **Fiket**, a bakery-café with kitsch 1950s decor. You could also head to the harbour for a bite; here you'll find **Pir Kro**, a pub-restaurant with a comprehensive menu, and **Lax Stugan**, a small building serving a range of salmon products (eg, quiche, salad, pâté).

Visingsö The small **STF Vandrarhem Visingsö** (☎ 40191; ⓔ t_hansen@algonet.se; dorm beds from Skr140, pension doubles from Skr500; open May-Aug) is 2km from the ferry pier in a wooded setting. Reception is nearby at **Visingsö Pensionat** (same contact details; double/4-bed rooms from Skr750/950; open year-round), which offers rooms with private facilities; there is no kitchen, but breakfast is included. Prices are higher from mid-June to mid-August (double/four-bed rooms from Skr900/1200); there are discounts year-round for staying more than one night.

There are a few eateries on the island, including **cafés** and **kiosks** at the harbour. Not far from the ferry dock are two good restaurants; both are open May to August. **Visingsö Värdshus** (☎ 40496; meals around Skr70) offers a wide range of meals, including fish, pasta and vegetarian selections, in a rustic setting. **Restaurant Solbacken** (☎ 40029; mains Skr50-150) is a lively restaurant, pub and pizzeria with a large deck overlooking the water.

Getting There & Around

Local bus No 121 runs regularly from Jönköping to Gränna (Skr49). Bus No 120 runs from Gränna to the mainline train station in Tranås (Skr49). Daily Swebus Express destinations include Gothenburg, Jönköping, Linköping, Norrköping and Stockholm.

A daily **ferry** (☎ 41025) runs hourly between Gränna and Visingsö; return tickets are Skr40/20 for adult/child passengers (Skr25 for a bicycle and Skr150 for a car and driver).

EKSJÖ
☎ 0381 • pop 16,800

Eksjö was granted city rights in 1403, but the town was burnt down during fighting in 1568 to prevent the Danish army from sheltering and looting. Parts of Eksjö date back to the reconstruction after 1568; many of the original buildings and part of the medieval street plan have been preserved, making Eksjö one of the best-preserved wooden towns in Sweden. A disastrous fire in 1856 destroyed 50 buildings in the area south of Stora Torget, but this area was reconstructed over the following 20 years.

The **tourist office** (☎ 36170; e turis@eksjo.se, W www.eksjo.se; Norra Sorgatan 29; open 8am-8pm daily mid-June–mid-Aug; 10am-4pm Mon-Fri, 10am-2pm Sat mid-Aug–mid-June) is on the main street. You can rent bicycles here (Skr60 per day) for touring the local area.

The city is celebrating its 600th 'birthday' in 2003, and there are a few festivities planned to mark the occasion; be sure to inquire at the tourist office if you're planning a visit during this time.

Things to See

Stroll through the delightful streets and courtyards of Eksjö, especially those north of Stora Torget. You'll see excellent old buildings at **Fornminnesgårdens Museum** (☎ 36170; Arendt Byggmästares gatan; adult/child Skr10/free; open noon-4pm daily mid-June–mid-Aug) – some were built in the 1620s. Exhibits chart the history of the area from the Stone Age to modern times. The museum opens outside of official opening hours by arrangement (check with the tourist office).

Eksjö Museum (☎ 36170; Österlånggatan 31; adult/child Skr20/free; open 10am-6pm Tues-Fri, 11am-4pm Sat & Sun mid-June–mid-Aug; 1pm-5pm Tues-Fri, 11am-4pm Sat & Sun mid-Aug–mid-June), adjacent to Fornminnesgårdens Museum, charts the town's history

from the 15th century to the present day and includes displays featuring Albert Engström, a famous local writer, artist and caricaturist. In the same building as Eksjö Museum, **Husarmuséet** (adult/child Skr10/free) covers the history of the town garrison. It's open variable hours or by arrangement. Under construction at the time of research, and due for opening in 2004, is **Smålands Miltärhistoriska Museum**, which details the military history of the region itself.

Aschanska gården (☎ 36170; Norra Storgatan 18) is an interesting 1890s-style house with guided tours at 1pm and 3pm daily mid-June to mid-August (Skr40).

Make inquiries at the tourist office regarding guided **tours** of the town (Skr20), held in summer; these can occasionally be arranged in English.

The rural surroundings of Eksjö are also worthy of a visit. Hikers and cyclists should ask at the tourist office for details of the Höglandsleden track and the Höglandstrampen cycle route (booklets in English, Skr60). The **Skurugata Nature Reserve** lies 13km northeast of Eksjö and includes a strange gorge that is around 800m long and has vertical walls 56m high; the Höglandsleden track passes through the reserve. From the top of the nearby hill **Skuruhatt** (320m), there are great views of the forests. You'll need your own transport to get here.

Places to Stay & Eat

Eksjö Camping (☎ 10945; e info@eksjo camping.nu; tent sites low/high season Skr75/100, 4-bed cabins Skr320/380) is a friendly place with a picturesque location by Husnäsen lake, about a kilometre east of the town centre. There's a restaurant and café here, plus minigolf and good swimming opportunities. Also here is a pleasant **SVIF hostel** (low/high season dorm beds Skr145/175), with good kitchen facilities.

The small, central **STF hostel** (☎ 36180; e vandrarhem@eksjo.se; Österlånggatan 31; dorm beds from Skr120; open year-round) is five minutes' walk from the train station in a quaint wooden building by the town museum; reception is at the tourist office.

Stadshotell (☎ 13020; e info@eksjostads hotell.se; Stora Torget; singles/doubles Skr795/980, discounted to Skr495/690) is an impressive place right in the centre of things, offering the flashest accommodation in town, with comfortable rooms and a fine **restaurant-bar** *(lunch Skr60, dinner mains Skr125-210)*.

Lennarts Konditori *(☎ 611390; Stora Torget)* is also in the heart of town and sells bread, cakes, sandwiches and quiche. **Balkan Restaurang** *(☎ 10020; Norra Storgatan 23; lunch from Skr58, pizzas Skr60, à la carte dishes Skr90-130)* has a surprising menu of Chinese, Swedish and pizza dishes. Opposite is a popular modern **café** serving baguettes from Skr25 and the usual café fare.

There's a central **Hemköp supermarket** *(Österlånggatan)* and a **Systembolaget** *(Södra Storgatan 4)*.

Getting There & Around

Take the tiny *länståg* (regional train; up to seven runs daily, all rail passes accepted), or the frequent bus No 320, from the mainline station at Nässjö (Skr23). Some *länståg* trains continue to Oskarshamn. The bus station is by the train station in the southern part of town. Local buses also run to Vimmerby (Skr75) and Jönköping (Skr62).

Swebus Express has daily services operating between Jönköping, Eksjö, Vimmerby and Västervik. Svenska Buss runs between Eksjö and Gothenburg, Kalmar, Malmö, Oskarshamn and Stockholm.

Kronobergs Län

VÄXJÖ

☎ 0470 • pop 74,100

Växjö (pronounced **vak**-choo, with the 'ch' sound as in the Scottish loch; it's quite unpronounceable for non-Swedes – ask a local to demonstrate!) was one of the Catholic centres in medieval Sweden. By 1050, a wooden church established by the missionary, St Sigfrid, was already in the place where the imposing 15th-century cathedral now stands. Växjö was sacked and burned by the Danes in 1612 and accidental fires devastated the town in 1838 and 1843. In more recent times, Mats Wilander, the former tennis player, was born in Växjö.

Karl Oscar Days is a festival to commemorate the mass 19th-century emigration from the area; it's named after the protagonist of Vilhelm Moberg's books about the subject. The festival takes place on a weekend in mid-August; the Swedish-American of the year is chosen at this time.

Information

At the train station, you'll find the **tourist office** *(☎ 41410; Norra Järnvägsgatan,* **e** *turistbyran @kommun.vaxjo.se,* **w** *www.turism.vaxjo.se; open 9am-6pm Mon-Fri, 10am-2pm Sat & Sun mid-June–mid-Aug; closed weekends rest of year)*. Storgatan is the main pedestrian mall and you'll find banks and other services along here. There is a large **library** (Biblioteksgatan) offering Internet access.

Things to See

The impressive twin-spired **Domkyrkan** *(Cathedral; open 9am-5pm daily)* has been struck by lightning and repeatedly ravaged by fire – the latest renovation was in 1995. Inside, there's a fine 15th-century altar and displays of local artwork (in glass, wood and iron). You'll also find a Viking rune stone in the eastern wall.

Millions of Americans have their roots in Sweden, many of them in Småland. Those who return to Sweden should not miss **Utvandrarnas Hus** *(Emigrant House; ☎ 20120; Södra Järnvägsgatan; adult/child Skr40/5; open 9am-4pm Mon-Fri, to 6pm June-Aug, 11am-4pm Sat & Sun year-round)*, which has archives, information and historical exhibitions on the beckoning America. It includes a replica of Vilhelm Moberg's office and original manuscripts of his famous novels. The house is just behind the central train and bus station, and close to **Smålands Museum** *(☎ 704200; Södra Järnvägsgatan 2; adult/child Skr40/free; open 10am-5pm Mon-Fri, 11am-5pm Sat & Sun June-Aug; closed Mon rest of year)*, which has an excellent collection of glass from Glasriket and a great café.

To experience hands-on science and illusions (especially good for kids) at **Xperiment Huset** *(☎ 10125; adult/child Skr60/45; open 10am-4pm Mon-Fri, 11am-4pm Sat & Sun June-Aug, closed Mon rest of year)*, turn left off Storgatan (heading west) and follow the Regimentsgatan.

In 1542, the Småland rebel Nils Dacke spent Christmas in **Kronobergs Slott**, now a ruin. The 14th-century castle is on a small island (reached by footbridge) in Helgasjön lake, about 8km north of the town. This is a lovely, picturesque area with an excellent summer café; take bus No 1B from town.

Inquire at the tourist office about guided **walking tours** of the town, held from mid-June to mid-August, and also about two-hour

SMÅLAND

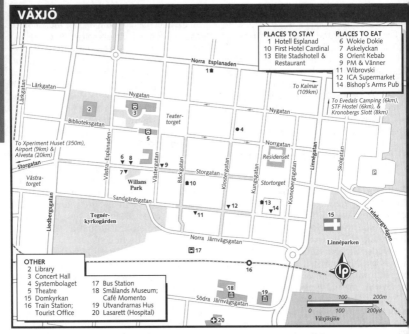

VÄXJÖ

PLACES TO STAY
1 Hotell Esplanad
10 First Hotel Cardinal
13 Elite Stadshotell &
   Restaurant

PLACES TO EAT
6 Wokie Dokie
7 Askelyckan
8 Orient Kebab
9 PM & Vänner
11 Wibrovski
12 ICA Supermarket
14 Bishop's Arms Pub

OTHER
2 Library
3 Concert Hall
4 Systembolaget
5 Theatre
15 Domkyrkan
16 Train Station;
   Tourist Office

17 Bus Station
18 Smålands Museum;
   Café Momento
19 Utvandrarnas Hus
20 Lasarett (Hospital)

sightseeing tours (☎ 81684; adult/child Skr55/30) in a red double-decker London bus, conducted a couple of times a week from Midsummer to mid-August.

Places to Stay

Evedals Camping (☎ 63034; e evedals.camp ing@telia.com; Evedalsvägen; tent sites Skr135, cabins from Skr500) is 6km north of the centre, in a pleasant lakeside recreational area where you can enjoy swimming, canoeing, boating and minigolf. The friendly **STF hostel** (☎ 63070; dorm beds from Skr110) is also out here, in a former spa hotel dating from the late 18th century. Take bus No 1C from town.

The cheapest hotel is **Hotell Esplanad** (☎ 22580; Norra Esplanaden 21A; singles/ doubles Skr650/750, discounted to Skr400/ 570), with adequate, central accommodation.

To step up in quality, **First Hotel Cardinal** (☎ 722800; e cardinalhotel@jesab.se; Bäck gatan 10; singles/doubles from Skr795/ 1195, discounted to Skr595/695) has a variety of rooms in a central location, including both 'budget-style' and more luxurious.

The grand-looking **Elite Stadshotellet** (☎ 13400; e info@vaxjo.elite.se; Kungsgatan 6; singles/doubles Skr1150/1360, discounted to Skr650/775) offers a distinctly upmarket experience. There's a popular restaurant and bar here too.

Places to Eat

For sustenance, **Wibrovski** (☎ 740410; Sand gärdsgatan 19; mains Skr145-195) is a classy restaurant in an old timber house, with well-prepared mains of fish, lamb and chicken and a three-course summer menu of Skr295. Stylish **PM & Vänner** (☎ 700444; Storgatan 22) is the favourite spot in town for fashionable locals, with a bar (occasional live music and DJs) and bar menu (meals Skr65 to Skr150), plus finer à-la-carte dining (mains Skr135 to Skr250).

Head to Storgatan for a good selection of eateries. **Askelyckan** (☎ 12311; Storgatan 23, is a bakery-café with sandwiches, baguettes great pastries and a large shady courtyard **Café Momento** (☎ 39129) at Smålands Museum is another great lunch spot, with an excellent selection of gourmet sandwiches salads and cakes, and a pretty courtyard.

The **terrace restaurant** at Elite Stadshotel is a popular spot; also attached to the hotel is the **Bishop's Arms** (☎ 27666; entry from Sandgärdsgatan), an English-style pub serving a good range of food and international beers.

Orient Kebab (☎ 12032; Storgatan 28) has the usual run of kebabs, burgers and pizzas for around Skr40. The nearby **Wokie Dokie** (☎ 777555; Storgatan; dishes Skr25-75) has takeaway Asian food, with good vegetarian selections.

There's an **ICA supermarket** (cnr Klostergatan & Sandgärdsgatan), and for alcohol visit **Systembolaget** (Klostergatan 14).

Getting There & Away

Växjö's **airport** (☎ 758210) is 9km northwest of town. **SAS** (☎ 020 727727) has direct flights to Stockholm, and **Skyways** (☎ 020 959500) flies daily to Copenhagen. The airport bus No 50 connects with flights (Skr50), otherwise take a **taxi** (☎ 13500) from the town centre.

Länstrafiken Kronoberg (☎ 020 767076) runs the regional bus network, with buses to Halmstad, Kosta and Karlshamn, among others. Long-distance buses depart from next to the train station. Svenska Buss runs daily north to Eksjö, Linköping (Skr220) and Stockholm (Skr310), and south to Lund (Skr200) and Malmö (Skr200).

Växjö is served by SJ trains that run roughly hourly between Alvesta (on the main north-south line) and Kalmar (Skr124). Some trains run directly to Karlskrona (Skr124), Malmö (Skr262) and Gothenburg (Skr252).

Blekinge Län

KARLSKRONA

☎ 0455 • pop 60,600

In 1998 the entire town of Karlskrona was added to the Unesco World Heritage List due to its well-preserved 17th- and 18th-century naval architecture. The town was founded on the small island of Trossö in 1680, after the failed Danish invasion of Skåne in 1679, to provide a southern naval base for Swedish forces. A fire in 1790 destroyed much of the town centre, but it was rebuilt and many of the grand, baroque buildings from that period remain today.

Information

The **tourist office** (☎ 303490; e turistbyran@ karlskrona.se, w www.karlskrona.se/turism; Stortorget 2; open 9am-7pm Mon-Fri, 9am-4pm Sat & Sun mid-June–mid-Aug; 10am-5pm Mon-Fri, 10am-1pm Sat rest of year) can help visitors.

You'll find ATMs and the post office in the Wachtmeister shopping centre on Borgmästeregatan. The **library** (Stortorget 15-17) has free Internet access. Internet access (Skr25 per hour) is also available at the **video shop** at Admiraltetsgatan 4, near the park. The **Scandia cinema** (☎ 10636) is on Ronnebygatan.

Things to See & Do

Karlskrona can keep you active for a while. The finest attraction is the extraordinary off-shore **Kungsholms Fort**, with its curious circular harbour, established in 1680 to defend the town. Four-hour boat tours to the fort depart at 10am (from Fisktorget) on Tuesday, Thursday, Saturday and Sunday from Midsummer to mid-August and are Skr140/free for adults/under-12s; book at the tourist office. Another option is the boat operated by **Skärgårdstrafiken** (☎ 78330), which runs from Fisktorget to the fort at 10am daily from mid-June to mid-August, returning at 1pm (Skr60/30 adult/child return); you must inform the tourist office of your visit in advance if you take this second option.

The tower **Drottningkärs kastell** on the island of Aspö, which Admiral Nelson of the British Royal Navy described as 'impregnable', can also be visited on a Skärgårdstrafiken boat (Skr70/30 adult/child return), departing from the end of Östra Köpmansgatan. You'll pass the strangely named **Fyren Godnatt** (Goodnight Lighthouse) on the way.

The striking **Marinmuseum** (☎ 53900; Stumholmen; adult/child Skr50/25; open 10am-6pm daily June-Aug, closed Mon rest of year) is the national naval museum and it includes a wreck, minesweeper, sailing ship and submarine, as well as a history of the Swedish Navy. Near the Marinmuseum, the **Konsthall** (☎ 303422; Bastionsgatan 8; admission free; open noon-4pm Tues-Fri, to 7pm Wed, noon-5pm Sat & Sun), once a seamen's barracks, is now a modern art and handicraft museum.

The quite extensive **Blekinge Museum** (☎ 304960; Fisktorget 2; adult/child Skr20/ free; open 10am-6pm daily mid-June–mid-Aug, closed Mon rest of year) features fishing, boat

SMÅLAND

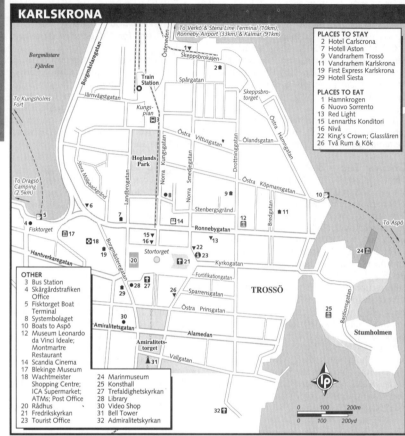

KARLSKRONA

PLACES TO STAY
2   Hotel Carlscrona
7   Hotell Aston
9   Vandrarhem Trossö
11 Vandrarhem Karlskrona
19 First Express Karlskrona
29 Hotell Siesta

PLACES TO EAT
1   Hamnkrogen
6   Nuovo Sorrento
13 Red Light
15 Lennarths Konditori
16 Nivå
22 King's Crown; Glasslären
26 Två Rum & Kök

OTHER
3   Bus Station
4   Skärgårdstrafiken Office
5   Fisktorget Boat Terminal
8   Systembolaget
10 Boats to Aspö
12 Museum Leonardo da Vinci Ideale; Montmartre Restaurant
14 Scandia Cinema
17 Blekinge Museum
18 Wachtmeister Shopping Centre; ICA Supermarket; ATMs; Post Office
20 Rådhus
21 Fredrikskyrkan
23 Tourist Office
24 Marinmuseum
25 Konsthall
27 Trefaldighetskyrkan
28 Library
30 Video Shop
31 Bell Tower
32 Admiralitetskyrkan

building, the local shipping trade, quarrying, a baroque garden, a pleasant café and a host of other things.

A pleasant way to spend a sunny summer afternoon is to tour around Karlskrona's **archipelago**. A three-hour tour taking in the eastern islands costs Skr110/50 per adult/child; contact the Skärgårdstrafiken office at Fisktorget for timetables and information. Alternatively, inquire at the tourist office about two-hour **guided walks** of the city *(adult/child Skr60/20)*, held a few times a week in peak season.

The surprising **Museum Leonardo da Vinci Ideale** *(☎ 25573; Drottninggatan 28; adult/child Skr20/10; open 11am-7pm Wed-Sun)* exhibits a private collection of art, from the Renaissance to modern works.

On huge Stortorget, the baroque church **Fredrikskyrkan** was consecrated in 1744 and re-roofed after the town fire of 1790. Just across the square, **Trefaldighetskyrkan** (Trinity Church) looks more like an opera house than a church.

Places to Stay

Dragsö Camping *(☎ 15354;* e *info@dragso camping.nu; Dragsövägen; tent sites Skr140, cabins from Skr250, hostel-style doubles Skr260; open late Apr-late Oct)*, 2.5km northwest of the town centre, is a large, well-equipped ground on a scenic bay. There are lots of good facilities, including boat and bicycle hire. Take bus No 7 (Skr13) from the town centre, which stops about a kilometre from the camping ground.

STF has two good hostels located in the town centre: **Vandrarhem Trossö** (☎ 10020; e trosso.vandrarhem@telia.com; Drottninggatan 39; dorm beds Skr115; open year-round), and **Vandrarhem Karlskrona** (same contact details; Bredgatan 16; beds from Skr130; open mid-June–mid-Aug); reception for both is at Vandrarhem Trossö.

Newly renovated **Hotell Siesta** (☎ 80180; e siesta.hotell@telia.com; Borgmästaregatan 5; singles/doubles from Skr615/715, discounted to Skr495/615) is a decent mid-range option, right near Stortorget. **Hotell Aston** (☎ 19470; Landbrogatan 1; singles/doubles Skr845/945, discounted to Skr595/695) is another smart place located in the centre of town.

For a little more luxury, **First Express Karlskrona** (☎ 27000; Borgmästaregatan 13; singles/doubles Skr1152/1402, discounted to Skr752/905) offers comfortable, tastefully decorated rooms. Better value is the prominent **Hotel Carlscrona** (☎ 361500; e info@carlscrona.softwarehotels.se; Skeppsbrokajen; singles/doubles Skr1195/1285, discounted to Skr695/895), with attractive, nautical-themed decor. The hotel is close to the train station in the northern part of town.

Places to Eat

Nivå (☎ 10371; Stortorget 14; menu items Skr39-225) is a cool bar and steakhouse with an excellent menu of light, well-priced dishes (nachos, burgers, baguettes, salads, baked potatoes), plus more hearty offerings from the grill (eg, steak, fish, barbecue ribs). Another good choice for an evening is classy **Två Rum & Kök** (☎ 10422; Södra Smedjegatan 3; fondue Skr98-216), which is known for its magnificent fondue (minimum two persons per fondue); chocolate fondue with fresh fruit is Skr98.

In the northern part of town, busy **Hamnkrogen** (☎ 80336; Skeppsbrokajen 18; lunch Skr60, dinner mains Skr79-190) has a pleasant view of moored boats, plus it offers pizzas and meat and fish courses.

Nuovo Sorrento (☎ 81101; Borgmästaregatan 24; meals Skr60-160) is a popular place with a menu featuring good-value pizzas (from Skr60) and pasta dishes for around Skr90. More upmarket is **Montmartre** (☎ 311833; Drottninggatan 28; meals Skr60-140), a typical Florentine restaurant near Museum Leonardo da Vinci Ideale, complete with art gallery, and serving excellent pizza for around Skr70.

King's Crown (☎ 10088; Stortorget), by the tourist office, is an English-style pub with good bar meals, such as nachos and burgers, all for under Skr100. Next door is **Glasslären**, an extremely popular ice-cream café (open summer only).

The northern side of the huge Stortorget and the street behind it (Ronnebygatan) are home to a good choice of eateries. **Red Light** (☎ 17503; Ronnebygatan 21) has the usual fast-food selections (kebabs, pizzas etc) for around Skr50. **Lennarths Konditori** (☎ 310332; Norra Kungsgatan 3) is an old-fashioned bakery-café good for coffee and snacks.

The **ICA supermarket** is in the Wachtmeister shopping centre and there's a central **Systembolaget** (Norra Kungsgatan 10).

Getting There & Away

The **airport** (☎ 0457-659010) is 33km west of Karlskrona, at Ronneby; SAS flies to Stockholm daily. Local bus No 9 runs to the airport (Skr75).

Local buses in the region are operated by **BlekingeTrafiken** (☎ 0455-56900). Regular 'Kustbussen' (coast buses) operate between Kalmar, Karlskrona, Karlshamn and Kristianstad. The fare to between Karlskrona and Karlshamn is Skr65.

The bus and train stations are just north of the town centre. Svenska Buss runs four times a week: north to Kalmar and on to Stockholm (Skr350) via Västervik and Norrköping, or west to Karlshamn and Kristianstad. Train connections are better: direct trains run to Copenhagen via Karlshamn (Skr91), Kristianstad (Skr143), Lund (Skr214) and Malmö (Skr214) up to 10 times daily. Regular trains also run to Emmaboda, and from there to Kalmar or Växjö (Skr124) and on to Gothenburg (Skr376).

Stena Line ferries to Gdynia (Poland) depart from Verkö, 10km (by road) east of Karlskrona (take bus No 6). See the introductory Getting There & Away chapter for details.

The tourist office has basic bicycles for hire for a bargain Skr30 per day. For a taxi, call **Karlskrona Taxi** (☎ 19100).

KARLSHAMN
☎ 0454 • pop 30,650

This pleasant town, with some cobbled streets and old wooden houses, received its town charter 10 years after Denmark ceded Blekinge to Sweden. Karlshamn was rebuilt after being burnt down in 1763. The town was a major producer of alcoholic drinks in the 19th century. The **tourist office** (☎ 81203; e turistbyran@karlshamn.se, w www.karlshamn.se; Ronnebygatan 1; open daily June-Aug, closed Sept-May) can help with information. Drottninggatan is where you'll find most services.

The **utvandrar-monumentet** stands in a park by the harbour commemorating all the emigrants who left Sweden from that harbour. The figures on the monument are Karl Oscar and Kristina, the characters from Vilhelm Möberg's classic work *The Emigrants*. Nearby, You'll find a 300-year-old **fishing cottage** (open in summer).

Also worth a look are the museums in **Karlshamns Kulturkvarter** (Vinkelgatan; open noon-5pm Tues-Sun June-Aug, 1pm-4pm Tues-Fri Sept-May), the town's 'culture quarter'. Here you'll find the town museum, an art gallery and **Skottsbergska Gården**, an 18th-century merchant's house.

Places to Stay & Eat

STF hostel (☎ 14040; e stfturistkhamn@hotmail.com; Surbrunnsvägen 1C; beds Skr145) is on the eastern side of the town grid near the train station and offers good rooms, all with private bathroom.

Tjärö STF Turiststation (☎ 60063; e info@tjaro.stfturist.se; beds Skr195, camping per person Skr50; open early May-early Sept) lies on an idyllic island nature reserve, 11km due east of Karlshamn, and is a highly recommended summer hostel. Boats run from Karlshamn a few times daily (Skr65); it's a good idea to call ahead to arrange times. Breakfast is available and there's also a café and fully licensed restaurant, plus boat and canoe hire.

Just opposite the tourist office, **First Hotel Carlshamn** (☎ 89000; e carlshamn@firsthotels.se; Varvsgatan 1; singles/doubles Skr1102/1352, discounted to Skr602/752) offers high-quality accommodation.

Stroll along Drottninggatan for the best dining options. **Gourmet Grön** (☎ 87038) at No 61 is an acclaimed restaurant with wonderful lunch-time and evening buffets, with an emphasis on vegetarian food, but not exclusively so. **Köpmannagården** (☎ 31787) at No 88 is a pleasant restaurant and pizzeria with a lovely courtyard.

Getting There & Away

The bus station is next to the train station in the northeastern part of town. For bus and train information, see the previous section on Karlskrona.

Lisco Line sails daily between Karlshamn and Klaipéda in Lithuania; see the Getting There & Away chapter for details.

Kalmar Län

KALMAR
☎ 0480 • pop 59,800

The port of Kalmar was long the key to Baltic power and was once the third-largest town in Sweden. The short-lived Kalmar Union of 1397, when the crowns of Sweden, Denmark and Norway became one, was agreed to at the town's grand castle. The castle was rebuilt as a Renaissance palace by the Vasa kings in the 16th century. Kalmar was still vital to Swedish interests in the 17th century, when a new town was built on Kvarnholmen; this area, with its cobbled streets and impressive edifices, retains a strong historical flavour.

Information

Visit the **tourist office** (☎ 15350; e info@turistbyra.kalmar.se, w www.kalmar.se/turism; Larmgatan 6; open 9am-8pm Mon-Fri, 10am-5pm Sat & Sun mid-Jun-mid-Aug; Mon-Sat May & Sept; Mon-Fri Oct-Apr) for information. The **public library** (Tullslätten 4), with free Internet access, is just to the west of the city grid.

Storgatan is the main street and you'll find banks and other services here. The **Biostaden** (☎ 12244) cinema is in the Baronen shopping centre on Skeppsbrogatan.

Things to See & Do

The once powerful Renaissance castle **Kalmar Slott** (☎ 451490; adult/child Skr70/20; open 10am-4pm daily Apr-May & Sept, 10am-5pm June & Aug, 10am-6pm July), by the sea south of the railway, was the key to Sweden before lands to the south were claimed from Denmark. The panelled **King Erik chamber** is the interior highlight, while another chamber exhibits punishment methods used on women in crueller times. Throughout the castle, you'll see beautiful coffered ceilings and superb stonework and

Renaissance-era Kalmar Slott, Småland

Wooden windmills, Öland, Småland

Elk hunter's watchtower, Småland

Eketorp Fort, Öland, Småland

Limestone formations *(raukar)* at Langhammarshammaren, Fårö, Gotland

The medieval port town of Visby, Gotland

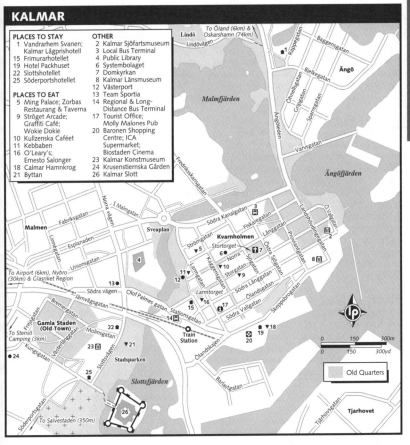

KALMAR

PLACES TO STAY
1 Vandrarhem Svanen;
  Kalmar Lågprishotell
15 Frimurarhotellet
19 Hotel Packhuset
22 Slottshotellet
25 Söderportshotellet

PLACES TO EAT
5 Ming Palace; Zorbas
  Restaurang & Taverna
9 Ströget Arcade;
  Graffiti Café;
  Wokie Dokie
10 Kullzenska Caféet
11 Kebbaben
16 O'Leary's;
  Ernesto Salonger
18 Calmar Hamnkrog
21 Byttan

OTHER
2 Kalmar Sjöfartsmuseum
3 Local Bus Terminal
4 Public Library
6 Systembolaget
7 Domkyrkan
8 Kalmar Länsmuseum
12 Västerport
13 Team Sportia
14 Regional & Long-
  Distance Bus Terminal
17 Tourist Office;
  Molly Malones Pub
20 Baronen Shopping
  Centre; ICA
  Supermarket;
  Biostaden Cinema
23 Kalmar Konstmuseum
24 Krusenstiernska Gården
26 Kalmar Slott

frescoes. From October to March, the castle is only open from 11am to 3.30pm on the second weekend of each month.

The tourist office sells an English-language brochure called *Walk in Kalmar* (Skr30), which details a self-guided **walk** throughout the town.

Kalmar Konstmuseum (☎ 426282; Slottsvägen 1D; adult/child Skr40/free; open 11am-5pm daily), in the Old Town not far from the castle, displays works by well-known Swedish artists.

Kalmar Länsmuseum (☎ 451300; Skeppsbrogatan; adult/child Skr50/free; open 10am-6pm daily mid-June–mid-Aug, closed Mon rest of year) is in the old steam mill by the harbour. The highlight is the exhibition of finds from the flagship *Kronan*, which sank

controversially off Öland during a battle in 1676 – a disaster to match the sinking of the *Wasa*, now on show in Stockholm. Aft and slightly to port is **Kalmar Sjöfartsmuseum** (☎ 15875; Södra Långgatan 81; admission Skr30; open 11am-4pm Mon-Fri, noon-4pm Sat & Sun mid-June–mid-Sept; noon-4pm Sun only rest of year), a delightfully eccentric little maritime-history museum.

A few blocks away is the landmark baroque **Domkyrkan** (Cathedral; Stortorget; open daily). It was designed by Tessin, who was the leading 17th-century architect working for the Swedish crown.

Krusenstiernska Gården (☎ 411552; Stora Dammgatan 11; adult/child Skr15/7; open 1pm-5pm Mon-Fri, 1pm-4pm Sat & Sun June-Aug) is a fully furnished, 19th-century middle-class home, 200m from the castle entrance, off Kungsgatan. Entry to the pretty gardens surrounding the museum is free; they're open May to September.

Västerport was the original point of entry into the city. Nowadays you can watch glass-blowing and pottery-making at the studios here, and buy the results.

Special Events
Historical Kalmar is noted for its wide variety of festivals and events, largely centred just around the castle. **Renässansdagarna** (☎ 67266), or Renaissance Days, is a two-day festival with people in 16th-century dress (held in late June or early July, at the castle, tickets Skr80 per day). The **Medeltidsfestival & Marknad** is a medieval festival and market, including jousting, music, handicrafts, food and drink; it's held on a weekend in late July, in Salvestaden (about 500m south of the castle in Kalmarsundsparken) and entry costs Skr75 per day.

Places to Stay
Stensö Camping (☎ 88803; Stensövägen; tent sites/cabins Skr135/400; open Apr-Sept) is on the island of Stensö, 3km southwest of town. It's got the usual family-friendly facilities: swimming; boat, canoe and bicycle rental; a restaurant; and minigolf. Take bus No 412.

Vandrarhem Svanen (☎ 12928; e info@ hotellsvanen.se; Rappegatan 1; dorm beds Skr160) is a well-equipped STF hostel attached to **Kalmar Lågprishotell** (☎ 25560), on the island of Ängö (take bus No 402) adjacent to the city centre. Comfortable singles/ doubles at the 'low-price hotel' cost from Skr465/595. There is a kitchen for guests and the breakfast buffet – open to hotel and hostel guests – is fair value at Skr55.

Söderportshotellet (☎ 12501, Slottsvägen 1; singles/doubles Skr350/530; open mid-June–mid-Aug) is right outside the castle and offers good summertime accommodation in student digs.

There are plenty of quality hotels in the city, but not much for those on a budget. Try the older-style **Frimurarhotellet** (☎ 15230; Larmtorget 2; singles/doubles Skr875/1085, discounted to Skr625/795), in the heart of the action. More interesting options are the elegant **Slottshotellet** (☎ 88260; e romantikho tel@slottshotellet.se; Slottsvägen 7; singles/ doubles from Skr995/1325, discounted to Skr675/825), in a gorgeous green setting not that far from the castle, and modern **Hotel Packhuset** (☎ 57000, fax 86642; Skeppsbro-gatan 26; singles/doubles Skr1250/1500, discounted to Skr745/950), in a converted 18th-century waterfront warehouse.

Places to Eat
A good area for upmarket dining is the harbour, although the view is somewhat industrial. Stylish **Calmar Hamnkrog** (☎ 411020; Skeppsbron; mains Skr182-229) serves excellent meals. Looking more expensive than it actually is, **Byttan** (☎ 16360; Stadsparken; lunch Skr65, dinner mains Skr155-175) is a classy restaurant in the park by the castle, offering wonderful views of Kalmar's major attraction.

Fiskaregatan is home to a few restaurants, including **Ming Palace** (☎ 16686; Fiskaregatan 7; lunch Skr54, dishes from Skr129), with primarily Chinese cuisine but also some Thai and Indonesian dishes on offer. Next door is **Zorbas Restaurang & Taverna** (☎ 411744; light meals Skr40-75, mains Skr85-198), rustling up really good Greek grub.

Molly Malones (☎ 411344; Lärmgatan 6; meals Skr30-120), next to the tourist office, is a cosy Irish pub, which serves bar snacks as well as authentic Irish meals (eg, steak-and-Guinness pie, fish and chips). Nearby, Larmtorget is home to **O'Leary's** (☎ 440970), an American-style sports bar, and **Ernesto Salonger** (☎ 20050), an Italian restaurant, nightclub and bar.

The pick of the town's cafés is **Kullzenska Caféet** (☎ 28882; upstairs, Kaggensgatan 26), a gorgeous place with 19th-century atmosphere and a range of sandwiches (from around Skr30) and cakes (try the great fruit crumbles).

Ströget arcade (Storgatan 24) houses a small food hall with a good selection of eateries, including **Graffiti Café**, which offers salad, baguettes and baked potatoes for Skr40 to Skr50, and **Wokie Dokie**, which provides Asian noodle and stir-fry dishes. **Kebabben** (Lärmagattan 11) is another fast-food option, with burger and kebab meals for around Skr50.

There's an **ICA supermarket** in the Baronen shopping centre. For alcohol, take a visit to **Systembolaget** (Norra Långgatan 23).

Getting There & Around

The **airport** (☎ 58700) is 6km west of town. **SAS** (☎ 020 727727) flies several times daily to Stockholm and on weekdays to Copenhagen. Town bus No 20 runs to and from the airport (Skr30).

All regional buses are run by **Kalmar Länstrafik** (☎ 0491-761200), including the Rasken long-distance services and buses to Öland. All regional and long-distance buses depart from the train station; local town buses have their own station on Östra Sjögatan. Daily Swebus Express services run to Västervik (Skr125), Norrköping (Skr215) and Stockholm (Skr305). Svenska Buss has four services a week, going north to Stockholm (Skr310), and south to Karlskrona and Kristianstad.

SJ trains run every hour or two between Kalmar and Alvesta (with connections to the main Stockholm–Malmö line) and also to Gothenburg (Skr376). There are trains running to Linköping up to five times daily (Skr266), and most continue from there to Stockholm (Skr471).

For bicycle hire, contact **Team Sportia** (☎ 21244; Södravägen 2), which will charge around Skr50/200 per day/week. **Taxi Kalmar** (☎ 444444) can help you get around town.

GLASRIKET

With dense forests and quaint red houses, Glasriket (ⓦ www.glasriket.se) is very popular among tourists – it's the most visited area in Sweden outside Stockholm and Gothenburg. The 'Kingdom of Crystal' has at least 15 glass factories (look for *glasbruk* signs) scattered around the wilderness, and its roots go back a long way: Kosta was founded in 1742, and by the end of the 19th century 10 factories were in full swing. Factory outlets have substantial discounts on seconds (around 30% to 40% off), but don't just come for glass and crystal since there are also ceramics, wood, leather and handicrafts for sale in the area. Not everything is cheap, but you pay for the quality and design. The expert designers produce some extraordinary avant-garde styles and there's often a good deal of typically Swedish humour involved, too. The larger factories can arrange shipping of purchased goods.

The immense popularity of this region is not only with bus loads of northern Europeans – lots of Americans tour the country,

tracing their roots. Many people emigrated from this area around the end of the 19th century because they couldn't find work locally. Even now, Glasriket is still fairly isolated. Part of the region is in Kronobergs Län, but most is in Kalmar Län, and all parts are included in this section.

Getting There & Around

Apart from the main routes, bus services around the area are pretty much nonexistent, and so the easiest way to explore is with your own transport (drivers should beware of elk in this area). Bicycle tours on the unsurfaced country roads are excellent; there are plenty of hostels, and you can camp almost anywhere except near the military area on the Kosta–Orrefors road.

Kalmar Länstrafik's bus No 139 runs from mid-June to mid-August only and calls at a few of the glass factories. The service operates three times a day on weekdays, once only on Saturday (no services Sunday) and it runs between Kalmar, Nybro, Orrefors, Gullaskruv, Målerås and Kosta. Year-round bus services connect Nybro and Orrefors (regular on weekdays, infrequent on weekends), and Kosta is served by regular bus No 218 from Växjö (three to four daily). Buses and trains run from Emmaboda to Nybro and Kalmar (roughly hourly); trains also run to Karlskrona, Växjö and Alvesta, with daily direct services to Gothenburg and Stockholm.

Nybro

☎ 0481 • pop 19,800

Of the two glass factories in the eastern part of Glasriket, traditional **Pukeberg** (☎ 80029; ⓦ www.pukeberg.se) is worth a look for its quaint setting and high-quality wares. It also has displays of modern furniture and light fittings. Nybro's **tourist office** (☎ 45085; ⓦ www.nybro.se; Stadshusplan) is inside the town hall and can help with visitor inquiries for the town and the region.

About 2.5km west of the town centre is the 200m-long *kyrkstallarna* building, old church stables that now house the excellent museum **Madesjö Hembygdsgård** (☎ 17935; adult/child Skr25/5; open 10am-5pm Mon-Fri, 11am-5pm Sat & Sun June-Aug), with local cultural history displays.

The local STF hostel, **Nybro Lågprishotell & Vandrarhem** (☎ 10932; Vasagatan 22; dorm beds Skr130 or Skr170, singles/doubles

Skr490/690), south of the centre near Puke-berg, is , and you can rent bicycles here. It's clean and comfortable and has a kitchen on each floor; more expensive beds are in smaller rooms with showers and toilets. The other option in town is the **Stora Hotellet** (☎ *51935; Mellangatan 11; singles/doubles Skr790/895, discounted to Skr600/650)*, a dated but reasonable hotel on Stadhusplan, by the tourist office. The hotel is home to a restaurant that offers your best choice in town for a meal (pizzas from Skr55).

There's also a couple of **fast-food places** and **pizzerias** scattered around town, and **supermarkets**.

SJ trains between Alvesta and Kalmar stop here every hour or two. Regional bus No 131 runs to/from Kalmar.

Orrefors
☎ 0481

Founded in 1898, Orrefors (☎ *34195;* W *www .orrefors.se)* is perhaps the most famous of Sweden's glassworks. The factory is open daily year-round and has a museum, an impressive gallery, glass-blowing demonstrations and a shipping service in the large shop.

Aside from the glassworks, there is little else to the village. If you need to stay overnight, you'll find an excellent **STF hostel** (☎ *30020; dorm beds from Skr110; open May-Aug)*, conveniently located near the factory area; breakfast is available.

Orrefors Värdshus (☎ *30059)*, in the factory grounds, offers good meals (priced around Skr100) during the day, and there's also a kiosk in the glassworks area selling cheap snacks such as hotdogs or ice cream. These eateries close by around 6pm, after which there's little choice except for **Pizzeria Alexandra**, offering takeaway pizzas from Skr45 (eat in from Skr59) and other options such as kebabs. There's a **supermarket** in town as well.

Hälleberga & Målerås
☎ 0481

Hälleberga, a small village 5km northwest of Orrefors, has several preserved old houses around the modern church. **Veras Vandrarhem** (☎ *32021; beds from Skr150)*, at the south end of the village, has comfortable hostel accommodation in a rustic setting.

In **Gullaskruv**, about 1.5km from Hälle-berga, Uruguayan-born glassmaker Carlos

Herring à la Glassworks

In days gone by, glassworks were more than just a workplace – they acted as a focal point for the people of a community, an after-hours meeting place for workers, hunters and vagrants. They were the place to go to keep warm on long winters evenings, tell stories, make music and enjoy the company of others. Naturally, good food and drink were a vital part of these gatherings – strong aquavit (a potent, vodka-like spirit) was shared and food was cooked using the furnaces and cooling ovens. Today visitors to Glasriket can partake in *hyttsill* parties, where food is prepared using some of these traditional methods, participants sit at long tables and the practice of socialising and entertainment at the glassworks is continued.

The menu at *hyttsill* parties includes salted herring, smoked sausage, bacon and baked potatoes, as well as the regional specialty *ostkaka* (cheesecake). The cost to join a *hyttsill* party is Skr260/95 per adult/child, and the price includes beer, soft drinks and coffee (aquavit is available for an additional cost). Parties are held almost daily from May to August at the larger glassworks of Bergdala, Kosta, Målerås, Orrefors or Johansfors, and only occasionally outside these months. Contact the regional tourist offices or the glassworks themselves for more information or to make a reservation.

Pebaqué has one glass oven and makes extraordinary vases, and there's also an interesting ceramics gallery.

Målerås, 8km farther northwest, has the large and popular **Mats Jonasson factory** (☎ *31401;* W *www.matsjonasson.com)*, which produces engraved glass animal designs from around Skr200. There are also leather goods for sale in town and there's a **restaurant** plus a good **bakery-café**.

Kosta
☎ 0478

Kosta is where Glasriket started in 1742. At times it looks like the biggest tourist trap in southern Sweden but it's easier to appreciate if you concentrate on the finesse and quality of the local craftsmanship and not on the tourist buses and tacky discount stores. Your time is best spent at the two museums and admiring the glass-blowing and the old factory quarters of **Kosta Boda** (☎ 50300; W www.kostaboda.se).

Grönåsens Älgpark (☎ 50770; open daily Apr-Nov) is an elk park 3km´west of town towards Orrefors. The well-stocked and amusing shop here sells all manner of elk souvenirs (from elk sausage to elk droppings) – be sure to visit the display in the building behind the shop for the shock of your life (an astounding re-creation of a crash scene involving elk and car!). Otherwise, you can pay Skr25 to take a 1.3km walk in the forested enclosure here in the hope of seeing one of these huge beasts.

Across the road from the factory, **Kosta Värdshus** (☎ 50006; singles/doubles Skr400/650) offers simple, comfortable accommodation and serves inexpensive lunches. There's also a small **camping ground** in the village (☎ 50517; tent sites Skr90, dorm beds from Skr160).

For other eating options, try the cheery **Café Kosta**, inside the factory's outlet store, with lunch for around Skr50 and good coffee and cake, or the quaint **Lill Stugan** (☎ 50750), with a range of meals including home-cooked Swedish smörgåsbord and even roast elk.

Boda
☎ 0481
This is a quaint little village with a large factory outlet and several other shops, including the modern Boda Nova shop and café at the southern end. The **glass factory** (☎ 42410), founded in 1864, is now part of the Kosta Boda company and sells much the same range as that available at Kosta.

The **STF Hostel** (☎ 24230; e boda.van drarhem@telia.com; dorm beds Skr120; open May–mid-Sept) is an old school building and offers good accommodation not far from the factory. There's little else to this sleepy village!

OSKARSHAMN
☎ 0491 • pop 26,200
Quiet Oskarshamn has a pleasant central area with cobbled streets and a large central park, but there's little here to detain travellers for long. The town is primarily useful for its regular boat connections with Gotland.

The **tourist office** (☎ 88188; e turism@os karshamn.se, W www.oskarshamn.se; Hant-verksgatan 18; open 9am-6pm Mon-Fri,

10am-3pm Sat, 11am-4pm Sun early June–mid-Aug; 9am-4.30pm Mon-Fri mid-Aug–early June) is in Kulturhuset, near the bus station (Resecentrum). The train station is on the other side of the town centre, close to the ferry terminal.

Also in Kulturhuset you will find the **town library**, with free Internet access, and two museums: **Sjöfartsmuséet** (☎ 88045), with local maritime exhibits, and **Döderhultarmuséet** (☎ 88040), well worth a visit for the brilliant 20th-century woodcarvings by an acclaimed local artist, Döderhultaren. The museums are both open 9am to 6pm weekdays and 11am to 4pm weekends from early June to around mid-August, and noon to 4pm Tuesday to Friday, 11am to 3pm Saturday and noon to 4pm Sunday the rest of the year. The admission price of Skr30 covers entry to both museums.

Blå Jungfrun National Park
Blå Jungfrun (the Blue Maiden), a granite island rising 86m above sea level and only 1150m long, was long known as the 'Mountain of Witches' by sailors, and a curious stone maze, **Trojeborg**, remains. The island is noted for its fantastic scenery, smooth granite rocks, and gnarled trees.

Between mid-June and late August a local launch departs several times weekly from Brädholmskajen, the quay at the head of the harbour in Oskarshamn, allowing passengers 3¼ hours to explore the island (Skr160/80 per adult/child). Contact the tourist office for information and bookings.

Places to Stay & Eat
Gunnarsö Camping (☎ 13298; Östersjövä gen; tent sites low/high season Skr100/120; open May–mid-Sept), located 3km southeast of town, has seaside sites but poor transport connections. Without your own vehicle, you're better off at the hostel in town: the **STF Hostel** (☎ 88198, fax 81045; e vandrar hemmet@oskarshamn.se; Åsavägen 8; dorm beds Skr80-130; open year-round) is a pleasant, well-equipped place. It's conveniently placed for travellers, just 300m from the train station and not far from the Gotland ferry terminal.

Sjöfartshotellet (☎ 768300; e sjofarts hotel@telia.com; Sjöfartsgatan 13; singles/doubles Skr795/895, discounted to Skr545/645) is probably the cheapest hotel in town. It offers comfortable if smallish rooms by the harbour. A step up in price and location

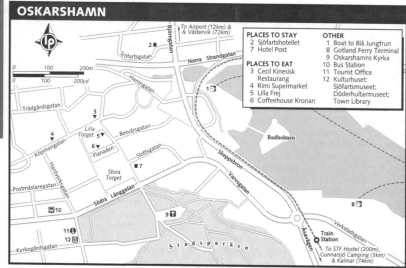

OSKARSHAMN

PLACES TO STAY
2 Sjöfartshotellet
7 Hotel Post

PLACES TO EAT
3 Cecil Kinesisk
   Restaurang
4 Rimi Supermarket
5 Lilla Frej
6 Coffeehouse Kronan

OTHER
1 Boat to Blå Jungfrun
8 Gotland Ferry Terminal
9 Oskarshamns Kyrka
10 Bus Station
11 Tourist Office
12 Kulturhuset:
   Sjöfartsmuseet;
   Döderhultarmuseet;
   Town Library

is offered at **Hotel Post** (☎ *16060; Stora Torget; singles/doubles Skr1245/1445, discounted to Skr765/850*), an upmarket hotel on the main square. All prices include an evening buffet; making the summer and weekends prices particularly good value.

Cecil Kinesisk Restaurang (☎ *18750; Lilla Torget; dishes Skr89-149*), offers Chinese cuisine as well as Swedish and even French dishes. There are lunch specials for Skr59 and an extensive menu of chicken, vegetarian, rice and noodle dishes. **Lilla Frej** (☎ *84300; Lilla Torget; lunch Skr65, meals Skr70-145*) is a pleasant place just across the square from Cecil Kinesisk, which has modern decor and a good menu offering lighter dishes such as pizza, pasta and salads, or more filling mains including fish and steak dishes.

Coffeehouse Kronan (☎ *14380, Flanaden 6*) is a great lunch spot, with filled baguettes and panini from Skr38, plus tasty cakes and good coffee. **Rimi supermarket** (*Köpmangatan*) is cheap and central.

Getting There & Away

Oskarshamn airport (☎ *33200*) is 12km north of town and **SAS** (☎ *020 727727*) flies once each weekday to Stockholm.

Regional bus services run up to six times daily from Oskarshamn to Kalmar (Skr69) and Västervik (Skr61). Swebus Express has two daily buses between Stockholm and Kalmar that call in at Oskarshamn. Svenska Buss operates a service from Stockholm to Malmö via Oskarshamn, Kalmar and Karlskrona four times a week. Long-distance bus services stop at the bus station, but some also stop at the train station (local buses run frequently between the bus and train stations). Regional trains run from Linköping and Nässjö.

Boats to Visby depart from the ferry terminal near the train station daily in winter and two or three times daily in summer (see the Gotland chapter).

VÄSTERVIK

☎ 0490 • pop 37,000

Västervik is a popular summer resort on the Baltic Sea. Accommodation may be impossible to find at short notice in July, but the nightlife's good and there are several things to see. The pleasant central area has cobbled streets, there are sandy beaches at Gränsö just east of town, and there's an extensive local archipelago of 5000 islands.

The town was burnt twice by the Danes (in the 15th and 17th centuries); between the 17th and 19th centuries it was a major shipbuilding centre. In more recent times, former tennis player, Stefan Edberg, was born here and Björn Ulvaeus from Abba grew up in the town too.

In a striking 1910 Art Nouveau builing, the **tourist office** (☎ 88900; ⒠ tyristbyran@ vastervik.se, ⒲ www.vastervik.se; Strömsholmen; open 10am-7pm daily mid-June–mid-Aug, Mon-Sat May–mid-June & late Aug, Mon-Fri only Sept-Apr) is located on an islet linked by road to the town centre (the building was formerly a heated bathhouse). There's also a **public library** (Spötorget) with Internet access.

Things to See & Do

Ask the tourist office for the very good brochure (Skr5) in English detailing a self-guided walking tour through town, taking in the sights of Västervik. **St Gertruds Kyrkan** (Västra Kyrkogatan) dates from 1433 and has a quite intriguing octagonal clock tower. **Aspagården**, next to the church, is the oldest wooden house in town (dating from the 17th century). Other old houses from the 1740s can be seen at picture-perfect **Båtmansstugorna** (Båtmansgatan) – as the name suggests, they are former ferrymen's cottages. There is a quaint café located in among the cottages.

Displays at the **Kulbackens Museum** (☎ 21177; adult/child Skr30/free; open 11am-6pm daily June-Aug, short hours rest of year), just north of the tourist office, cover the history of the town and its industries.

Two-hour **archipelago tours** (adult/child Skr110/50) with MS Freden depart from next to the tourist office daily from Midsummer to the end of August. Make inquiries and reservations at the tourist office.

Places to Stay & Eat

Lysingsbadets (☎ 88920; ⒠ lysingsbadet@ vastervik.se; camping Skr120-190, dorm beds Skr125-140, singles/doubles low season Skr300/450, high season Skr495/495, cabins & chalets Skr190-1350) is a huge, five-star 'holiday village' by the sea, 2.5km southeast of the centre, with a great range of facilities (eg, restaurant, golf, swimming pool, beaches, boats, bicycles and kayaks for hire). The hostel here is only open June to August; cabins and hotel rooms are available year-round. Take local bus No 2 or 8 (Skr12).

Båtmansstugor (☎ 31767 or 19403; Strömsgatan 42; cottages per person Skr200) is a collection of delightful 18th-century fishermen's cottages for rent in an atmospheric old part of town. Most cottages sleep four and have their own kitchen, but bathrooms are shared.

Västerviks Stadshotell (☎ 82000; ⒠ info@ stadshotellet.nu; Storgatan 3; singles/doubles Skr1045/1400, discounted to Skr760/1000) is a fine, central hotel with a restaurant and popular nightclub.

Tucked down an alley off Strandägen is the charming **Restaurang Smugglaren** (☎ 21322; Smugglaregränd 1; mains Skr160-220), which offers quality food in a cosy setting, complete with model ships and paraffin lamps.

Waterside Fiskaretorget is a hive of activity; there are a number of restaurant-bars located here, and all have outdoor terraces that are especially popular on long summer evenings. **Harry's** (☎ 17300) and **The Brig** (☎ 34200) are on the square; both offer a pub menu of simple bar food, plus an à la carte menu for finer dining, and are good spots just to relax over a drink. Also on Fiskaretorget is **Kebab Mästeren**, the 'master' of fast-food meals priced around Skr50.

Getting There & Away

Trains run between Västervik and Linköping up to five times daily (Skr125), but buses are better to/from Norrköping (Skr180). Regular daily bus services run to Vimmerby (Skr53), Jönköping (Skr175), Oskarshamn (Skr61) and Kalmar (Skr117). Svenska Buss runs to Stockholm, Kalmar, Karlskrona and Malmö four times a week, and Swebus Express services run to Vimmerby, Eksjö and Jönköping a few times daily. Long-distance buses stop outside the train station, at the eastern edge of the town centre.

V-V Line (☎ 258080; ⒲ www.vvlines.com) has ferries connecting Västervik with Paldiski in Estonia a few times a week. See the Getting There & Away chapter for more details.

VIMMERBY
☎ 0492 • pop 15,650

All young children and Pippi Longstocking fans should head for **Astrid Lindgrens Värld** (☎ 79800; ⒲ www.alv.se; open 10am-6pm daily mid-June–mid-Aug, 10am-5pm daily mid-May–mid-June & mid-late Aug), a theme park on the northern edge of town (only a 10-minute walk from the train station). It's one of Sweden's top visitor attractions. Prices vary according to time of year: an adult/child/family ticket costs Skr110/95/360 from mid-May to early June, Skr180/135/560 mid-June to mid-August, and Skr140/105/440 in the second half of August; family tickets are for

Astrid & Pippi

Astrid Lindgren was born in 1907. When she left school she went to Stockholm and trained to be a secretary, got a job in an office, married and had two children. In 1941, when Lindgren's daughter Karin was ill, she wanted to be told a story. Astrid asked her if she'd like to hear about a little girl called Pippi Longstocking. Pippi was a hit with Karin and her friends and the story was told over and over again.

In 1944, Lindgren sprained her ankle and to pass the time she started writing down the Pippi stories in shorthand. She sent a copy to a publisher but it was rejected. However, she had written a second book, which she sent to another publisher and this won second prize in a girls' story competition. The next year the same publisher organised a children's book competition and Lindgren entered a revised Pippi manuscript, which won first prize. In 1946, her publisher announced a new competition for detective stories for young people and she entered *Bill Bergson Master Detective*, and this won a shared first prize.

This was just the beginning of a prolific career. Lindgren's impressive output included picture books, plays and songs, and her books have been translated into more than 50 languages. She worked in radio, television and films, was head of the Children's Book Department at her publishers for four years and has received numerous honours and awards from around the world. Astrid died in early 2002.

two adults and up to three children; two-day tickets are also available. In peak season there are more activities and performances, hence the higher prices.

There are different settings from various books and around 100 buildings; plus you'll see actresses dressed as Pippi (with bizarre outfits and gravity-defying pigtails), singing and dancing. The Swedish kids love it! Older visitors have the chance to learn of the deeper themes in Lindgren's books, such as her anti-war and pro-animal-rights stance, especially at **Astrid Lindgren Gården** (☎ 79800; *adult/child Skr50/25 or free with admission to theme park; closed Mon & Tues Sept–May)*, an excellent museum of her life and work (it's adjacent to the theme park and is open year-round). There's a reasonably priced **restaurant**, with a buffet for Skr99/59 per adult/child, and a **fast-food joint** (burger meals from Skr39) in the park, and if you're a dedicated fan, you can even stay at the on-site **camping ground** *(tent sites low/high season Skr130/160, 4-bed cabins from Skr390/595)*.

Vimmerby has a helpful **tourist office** (☎ 31010; e turistbyra@vimmerby.se, w www .turism.vimmerby.se; *Västra Tullportsgatan 3; open daily mid-June–mid-Aug, Mon-Sat in May & late Aug, Mon-Fri Sept–May)*. In the town centre, look out for the old houses on Storgatan and the pleasant cobbled square, Stora Torget.

There's lots of accommodation in town, including **Vimmerby Vandrarhem** (☎ 10020; e info@vimmerbyvandrarhem.nu; *Järnvägsallén*

2; *dorm beds from Skr150)*, a new hostel right near the train station. **Vimmerby Stadshotell** (☎ 12100; e info@vimmerbystads hotell.se; *Sevedegatan 39; singles/doubles from Skr960/ 1095, discounted to Skr640/740)* is well located – it's the pretty pink building near the town square – and offers pleasant rooms with good facilities.

Buses depart from the Resecentrum (at the train station), and town buses run to Astrid Lindgrens Wärld (Skr15). Swebus Express runs two to four times daily to Eksjö, Jönköping and Västervik. Svenska Buss operates daily between Stockholm, Linköping, Vimmerby and Kalmar, sometimes continuing on to Oskarshamn. *Kustpilen* trains run several times daily south to Kalmar, or north to Linköping and Stockholm.

ÖLAND
☎ 0485 • pop 25,000

More windmills than Holland? There are 400 on Öland today, but there were once around 2000. Most are the characteristic wooden huts on a rotating base. Also prominent are the lighthouses at the northern and southern tips of the island. Öland's flora was fascinating for Linnaeus (see the boxed text 'Carl von Linné' in the Svealand chapter) and he spent two months here in 1742. The island stretches 137km, and is reached from Kalmar via the 6km Ölandsbron (bridge), the longest in Europe when it was opened in 1973.

Öland is a popular summer destination for Swedes and the island gets nearly two million visitors annually (mostly in July); around 90% stick to the beaches in the northern half of the island. The southern two-thirds is probably of greater interest to the active traveller. There are plenty of budget accommodation options – some 25 camping grounds and at least a dozen hostels. Note that camping in the northern half of the island is expensive in peak season (Midsummer to mid-August) and can cost up to Skr200 for a tent site. The island has also developed a reputation as a foodie's delight, with many quality restaurants.

Information

From Kalmar, the bridge lands you on the island just north of Färjestaden, where there is a large and well-stocked **tourist office** (☎ 560600; e info@olandsturist.se, w www .olandsturist.com; open daily May-Aug, Mon-Sat Sept, Mon-Fri Oct-Apr) at the Träffpunkt Öland centre. Staff here can book accommodation for you throughout the island, including cottages and cabins (for a fee). Within the tourist office, the **Historium** (adult/child Skr40/25) is worth a visit if you are touring the island's ancient sites; there is also a **Naturum** (free) in the same building.

There is also a smaller tourist office in Borgholm (see that entry later).

Getting There & Around

There are no bicycle lanes on the bridge between Öland and Kalmar, so cyclists take their lives into their own hands! Cyclists aren't allowed on the bridge in summer, however, but there is a free 'Cykelbuss' service that will carry cyclists and their bikes in summer (inquire at the tourist office in Kalmar).

Buses connect all main towns on the island from Kalmar – buses to Borgholm (Skr45) are roughly hourly, but buses to Mörbylånga (Skr29) run every hour or two. Buses to Byxelkrok and Grankullavik (both Skr85), both in the far north, run every two or three hours. Services to quieter parts in the south are fairly poor, with some improvement in the summer period (May to August).

Silver Linjen (☎ 26111) operates direct express buses daily between Stockholm, Kalmar and Öland year-round; (Skr250 one-way, six to seven hours).

From mid-June to mid-August, MS *Solsund* (☎ 0499-44920) sails twice daily

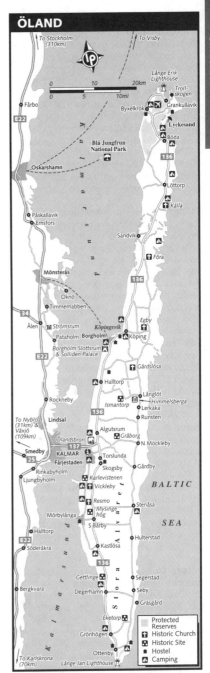

ÖLAND

To Stockholm (310km)
To Visby

Långe Erik Lighthouse
Fårbo
Byxelkrok
Troll-skogen
Grankullavik
Lyckesand
Böda
Blå Jungfrun National Park
Oskarshamn
Löttorp
Källa
Påskallavik
Emsfors
Sandvik
Föra
Mönsterås
Oknö
Timmernabben
Egby
Ålen
Strömsrum
Köpingsvik
Patahom
Borgholm
Köping
Borgholm Slottsruin & Solliden Palace
Gärdslösa
Halltorp
Rockneby
Långlöt
Himmelsberga
Ismantorp
Lerkaka
To Nybro (31km) & Växjö (109km)
Lindsal
Algutsrum
Gråborg
Runsten
N Möckleby
Ölandsbron
Smedby
KALMAR
Färjestaden
Torslunda
Skogsby
Gårdby
Rinkabyholm
Karlevistenen
BALTIC
Ljungbyholm
Vickleby
Resmo
Stenåsa
Mörbylånga
Mysinge hög
SEA
Hålltorp
S Bårby
Söderåkra
Kastlösa
Hulterstad
Gettlinge
Segerstad
Bergkvara
Degerhamn
Seby
Gräsgård
Eketorp
Grönhögen
Ottenby
To Karlskrona (70km)
Långe Jan Lighthouse

Protected Reserves
Historic Church
Historic Site
Hostel
Camping

between Borgholm and Mönsterås on the mainland (some 40km north of Kalmar). Tickets cost Skr100/60 per adult/child one way, and it's possible to take cars (Skr270) and bicycles (Skr25) on the ferry.

Borgholm & Around

The most happening town on Öland is Borgholm, the 'capital' of the island and a pleasant, small place with shops, cafés and an enormous ruined castle on its outskirts.

The **tourist office** (☎ 89000; Sandgatan 25; open daily mid-June–mid-Aug, 9am-3.45pm Mon-Fri rest of year) is at the bus station. There are banks and other services on Storgatan.

Things to See The town is dominated from the hill to the south by **Borgholm Slottsruin** (☎ 12333; adult/child Skr50/20; open 10am-6pm daily May-Aug, 10am-4pm Apr & Sept), northern Europe's largest ruined castle. It was finally burned and abandoned early in the 18th century after being used as a dye works. There's an excellent museum inside and a nature reserve nearby. The ruins are often used as a venue for summer concerts.

Sweden's most famous 'summer house', **Solliden Palace** (☎ 15355; adult/child Skr50/free; open 10am-6pm daily mid-May–Sept), 2.5km south of the town centre, and not far south of Slottsruin, is used by the royal family. Its beautiful parks and the pavilion exhibitions are open to the public.

VIDA Museum (☎ 77440; open 10am-7pm daily June-Aug, to 5pm May & Sept, Sat & Sun only Apr & Oct-Dec; adult/child Skr30/free) is a strikingly modern museum and art gallery in Halltorp, about 8km south of Borgholm.

On the east coast, about 13km southeast of Borgholm, there's **Gärdslösa kyrka** (open 8am-7pm daily mid-May–mid-Sept), the best preserved medieval church on Öland. It was consecrated in 1138, has an ornate wooden pulpit and reasonably well-preserved wall and ceiling paintings.

Places to Stay & Eat Beachside **Kapelludden Camping & Stugor** (☎ 560770; Sandgatan; e info@kapelludden.se; tent sites low/high season Skr145/175; 6-bed cabins Skr860-1385 depending on season) is the handiest camping ground in town, just north of the bus station. It's a huge place (some 450 sites) and has five-star, family-oriented facilities, including a swimming pool.

Coastal **Grönhags Camping** (☎ 72116; tent sites low/high season Skr100/150) is one of half a dozen large, neighbouring camping grounds in Köping (about 4km north of Borgholm). Most are open from late April to mid-September, and prices increase from Midsummer to mid-August.

Just east of town is the **STF hostel** (☎ 10756; dorm beds Skr110-160; open mid-May–Aug), in Rosenfors Manor, set in a pretty garden. **Olssons rumsuthyrning** (☎ 77939; Tullgatan 12A; doubles winter/summer from Skr400/600) has some simple doubles; prices exclude breakfast but there is a kitchen guests can use.

Guntorps Herrgård (☎ 13000; e ulf@guntorp.oland.com; Guntorpsgatan; singles/doubles from Skr695/895) is a delightful old farmhouse east of town, near the STF hostel. There's excellent accommodation on offer, plus the drawcard of a huge, good-value smörgåsbord (Skr155 per person) offering a great variety of local dishes from 6pm every evening.

Stylish **Hotel Borgholm** (☎ 77060; e info@hotellborgholm.com; Trädgårdsgatan 15; singles/doubles Skr890/990), in the centre of town, has been transformed into a colourful boutique hotel. The owner is Karin Fransson, one of Sweden's best-known chefs – the restaurant here is, naturally, very highly regarded. A two-course set menu starts from around Skr330.

The main square in town has the usual collection of **fast-food stalls** and **ice-cream kiosks**, and there are a few reasonable dining options nearby. **Nya Conditoriet** (☎ 10011; Storgatan 28) is a nice old-fashioned bakery-café serving good sandwiches and pastries. **Pubben** (Storgatan 18) is a classic English-style pub serving up snacks and light meals costing from Skr40, which you can wash down with a choice of fine beers.

There are **supermarkets** on Storgatan, and a central **Systembolaget** (Östra Kyrkogatan 19).

Northern Öland

Bus No 106 goes to the north from Borgholm. At Sandvik on the west coast, about 30km north of Borgholm, **Sandvikskvarn** (☎ 26172; open daily May-Aug) is a more familiar 'Dutch-style' windmill (it may be the largest in the world). In summer, you can climb its six storeys for good views across to the mainland.

There's also a **museum** *(adult/child Skr15/7)* and a **restaurant**, where the seats are old barrels; try the local speciality, *lufsa* (baked pork and potato; Skr54). The adjacent **pizzeria** is as quirky as the restaurant (pizzas start at Skr64).

The remains of the medieval fortified church **Källa ödekyrka**, at a little harbour 36km northeast of Borgholm off road 136, are fascinating, as it and other churches actually supplanted the mighty stone fortresses as defensive works. The broken **rune stone** inside shows the Christian Cross growing from the pagan tree of life.

Grankullavik, in the far north, has sandy beaches and dense summer crowds, and **Lyckesand** is one of the island's best beaches. The natural attractions (including strangely twisted trees) in the nearby **Trollskogen** nature reserve are worth a visit.

Northern Öland has plenty of camping grounds, and on the beachfront is the SVIF **Grankullaviks Vandrarhem** *(☎ 24040; dorm beds from Skr100; open June-Sept)* has a kitchen, restaurant and bakery. The well-equipped **STF hostel** *(☎ 22038; dorm beds Skr100-165; open May-Aug)* is in Böda.

Lammet & Grisen *(☎ 20350; Löttorp)*, 10km south of Böda, is a popular restaurant where of an evening you can eat as much spit-roasted lamb and pork as you like for Skr225.

Färjestaden & Around

Färjestaden (Ferry Town) has a pre-bridge name, and the old jetty area is still the centre of summer activities. The town itself has little of interest, but just north of the bridge and not far from the island's major tourist office (see Information earlier) is **Ölands Djurpark** *(☎ 30873; admission Skr160-180; open daily mid-May–Sept)*, which is a zoo, amusement park and water park popular with families. Kids under 1m high get in for free!

The vast **Ismantorp fortress**, with its remains of 88 houses and nine mysterious gates, is deep in the woods 5km west of the Himmelsberga museum (see later). It's an undisturbed fortress ruin, clearly showing how the village and its tiny huts were encircled by the outer wall (Eketorp, see Southern Öland following, is an imaginative reconstruction of similar remains). The area, just south of the Ekerum–Långlöt road, can be freely visited at any time.

On the middle of the east coast at Långlöt, **Himmelsberga** *(☎ 561022; adult/child Skr50/free; open 10am-6pm daily May-Aug)* is a farm village from a bygone age. This isn't the only one on Öland, but here the quaint cottages have been repainted and fully furnished as a museum.

The largest Iron Age ring fort on the island, **Gråborg** has a diameter of 200m and was built during the Migration Period (AD 400 to 500), but was also used around 1200, when the adjacent **St Knuts chapel** (now a ruin) was built. The arched entrance to the fortress is a reconstruction; much of the stonework from the fort has been plundered for building purposes. A 16km hiking trail leads from Gråborg to Ismantorp fortress. The Gråborg complex is about 8km east of Färjestaden, just off the Norra Möckleby road, and can be reached by the infrequent bus No 102.

The charming STF hostel **Ölands Skogsby** *(☎ 38395; e info@vandrarhskogsby.se; dorm beds Skr100-130; open mid-Apr–Sept)* claims to be Sweden's oldest hostel (it dates from 1934) and is 3km southeast of Färjestaden (bus No 103). There are a few good eateries at the old jetty area in Färjestaden, including pleasant **Café Restaurang Bojen** *(☎ 31037)*, with fresh fish on the menu and lots of outdoor seating.

Southern Öland

The southern half of the island is chiefly a haven for nature and the relics of humankind's settlements and conflicts, attested to by the Iron Age fortresses and graveyards of all periods. Most of the area is a treeless landscape, and it's now on Unesco's World Heritage List, recognised for its long cultural history and diverse landscapes.

The unusual limestone plain at **Stora Alvaret**, is of interest to naturalists, especially those keen on birdlife, insects and flora. The expanse takes up most of the inland southern half of Öland and can be crossed by road from Mörbylånga or Degerhamn. Late April to early June are usually good for venturing out, particularly if you're going bird-watching.

The ancient grave fields of **Mysinge** and **Gettlinge**, stretching out several kilometres on the ridge along the main Mörbylånga-Degerhamn road, include burials and standing stones from the Stone Age to the late Iron Age, but the biggest single monument is the

Bronze Age tomb **Mysinge hög**, 4km east of Mörbylånga.

The most southerly of the big ring forts, **Eketorp**, 6km northeast of Grönhögen, was used in three distinct periods, including as late as 1240. The fort has been partly reconstructed as a museum to show what the fortified villages, which went in and out of use over the centuries, must have been like in early medieval times. Excavations turned up 26,000 artefacts and three tonnes of human bones, including five Viking Age skeletons. The impressive fort can be viewed from the outside at any time, but inside is the **museum** (☎ 560607; adult/child Skr50/20; open 10am-5pm daily May-Aug), with many interesting displays. There are tours in English at 1pm daily from Midsummer to the end of August. Take bus No 114 from Mörbylånga.

On the east coast, about 5km north of Eketorp, **Gräsgårds Fiskehamn** is a delightful little fishing harbour. A little farther north, there's an 11th-century **rune stone** at Seby and, in Segerstad, there are **standing stones**, **stone circles** and over 200 graves.

At **Öland's southernmost point** (a curious place with the sea almost all around), there's an expensive car park (Skr50), nature reserve

and a **Naturum** (free) with bird displays. **Länge Jan lighthouse**, completed in 1785, is Scandinavia's highest at 42m.

Places to Stay & Eat In the small village of Mörbylånga, **Mörby Vandrarhem & Lågprishotell** (☎ 49393; Bruksgatan; dorm beds from Skr150, singles/doubles Skr300/500; open May-Aug) offers good accommodation. Another good option here is **Kajutan Hotell & Vandrarhem** (☎ 40810; e info@hotelkajutan .com; hostel beds from Skr120, hotel singles/doubles Skr685/790), down by the harbour; there's a restaurant and pub here.

Gammalsbygårdens Gästgiveri (☎ 663051; singles/doubles Skr450/600, with en suite Skr550/750) is a fine country house on the east coast, 5km north of Eketorp. The food here is also very good, with main courses for around Skr150.

Near Ottenby and Öland's southernmost , the **STF hostel** (☎ 662062; tent sites from Skr100, dorm beds Skr120; open year-round) is 7km south of Eketorp.

Fågel Blå (☎ 661201), near the lighthouse in the far south, offers cheap lunch-time meals. There are **supermarkets** in Mörbylånga, and also a **Systembolaget**.

Gotland

☎ 0498 • pop 57,400

Gotland, the largest of the Baltic islands, is also one of the most historical regions in Sweden, with almost 100 medieval churches and an untold number of prehistoric sites. Other attractions include the odd *raukar* (limestone formations that are fossilised remains of 400-million-year-old sea-creatures and corals), and the walled, medieval trading town of Visby.

Gotland was a significant trading centre in pre-Viking times and, during the Viking Age, it was a useful stepping-stone for expeditions across the Baltic Sea. Visby rose to the heights of its power in the 12th and 13th centuries with the success of the Hanseatic merchants making it one of the most important trade centres of medieval Europe. Gotland was devastated by periodic warfare from the mid-14th century. In 1361, the Danish king Waldemar captured Visby after a bloody battle outside the town walls which killed 2000 local men. The Swedes regained the island from the Danes in 1645.

Gotland is among the top budget travel destinations in Sweden; bicycle travel on the quiet roads is by far the best option, free camping in forests is easy and legal, many attractions are free and there are more than 30 hostels around the island. You could easily pass a week here seeing the highlights. Bear in mind that the island is also a favourite destination for locals, so it's recommended that you book your accommodation well in advance. The island is jam-packed with holidaying Swedes in June, July and August, and is *the* summer party spot for young Swedes, who come not for the history but for beaches and booze.

Orientation & Information

Gotland lies nearly halfway between Sweden and Latvia, in the middle of the Baltic Sea, roughly equidistant from the mainland ports of Nynäshamn and Oskarshamn. Gotland is both a region *(landskap)* and a county *(län)*. The island is basically flat (the highest point is only 81m) and forested, there are no rivers of any great size and there are only a few small lakes, mostly in the north. Visby is the only town, but there are several large and many small villages.

Highlights

- Walking around the 13th-century wall of pretty Visby
- Joining the summer crowds in early August for the annual Medieval Week festival
- Cycling the quiet back roads of the island
- Marvelling at the picture stones in the Gotlands Fornsal and in Bungemuseet
- Admiring the medieval heritage in some of Gotland's fine churches
- Watching the sun set behind the *raukar* (limestone formations) at Langhammarshammaren, Fårö

The large island Fårö lies off Gotland's northeastern tip and the island of Gotska Sandön National Park lies 38km further north. Stora Karlsö and Lilla Karlsö are two small islets just off the western coast.

The regional tourist office is **Gotlands Turistföreningen** *(☎ 201700; e info@gotlandinfo.com, w www.gotland.com; Box 1403, Hamngatan 4, SE-62125, Visby)*. **Gotland City** *(☎ 08-406 1500; e info@gotlandcity.se, w www.gotlandcity.se; Kungsgatan 57)* is a central travel agency in Stockholm, useful if you're planning your trip from the capital.

Other good information about Gotland is available on the Internet at w www.gotland.net and w www.guteinfo.com.

269

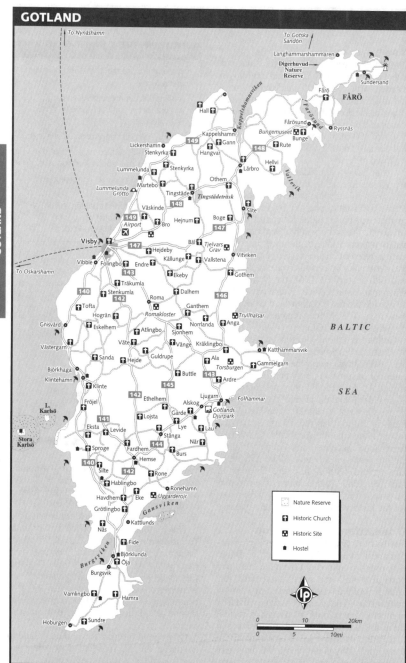

GOTLAND

To Nynäshamn

To Gotska Sandön

Langhammarshammaren

Digerhuvud Nature Reserve

Fårö

FÅRÖ

Sundersand

Ryssnäs

Hall

Kappelshamn

Lickershamn

Gann

Hangvar

Bungemuseet

Bunge

Fårösund

Rute

148

Stenkyrka

Stenkyrka

Othem

149

Lärbro

Hellvi

Lummelunda

Martebo

Tingstäde

Tingstädeträsk

Slite

Lummelunda Grotto

Väskinde

148

Boge

147

Visby

Hejnum

147

Bro

Bäl

149

Airport

Hejdeby

Tjelvars Grav

Vibble

Folingbo

Källunge

Vallstena

Vitviken

Endre

143

Gothem

Ekeby

To Oskarshamn

Träkumla

Dalhem

140

Stenkumla

Roma

142

Ganthem

146

Tofta

Romakloster

Hogrän

Eskelhem

Norrlanda

Anga

Trullhalsar

Gnisvärd

Atlingbo

Sjonhem

BALTIC

Västergarn

Väte

Vänge

Kräklingbo

Björkhaga

Sanda

Hejde

Guldrupe

Ala

Katthammarsvik

Klintehamn

Klinte

Buttle

Torsburgen

Gammelgarn

L. Karlsö

Fröjel

145

Ethelhem

143

Ardre

SEA

Ljugarn

Folhammar

Stora Karlsö

Eksta

141

Levide

Lojsta

Alskog

Garde

Gotlands Djurpark

Sproge

Fardhem

142

Lye

Lau

Silte

Hemse

Stånga

När

144

140

142

Rone

Burs

Hablingbo

Havdhem

Eke

Ronehamn

Grötlingbo

Uggarderojr

Näs

Kattlunds

Gansviken

Fide

Björklunda

Öja

Burgsvik

Vamlingbo

Hamra

Burgsviken

Hoburgen

Sundre

	Nature Reserve
	Historic Church
	Historic Site
	Hostel

0   10   20km

0   5   10mi

Prehistoric Sites
There are hundreds, perhaps thousands of sites around the island, many of them sign-posted, including stone ship settings, burial mounds and remains of hill-top fortresses. Keep your eyes open for the information boards along roadsides. You can visit these sites, as well as the numerous nature reserves, any time, free of charge.

Churches
Nowhere else in northern Europe are there so many medieval churches in such a small area. There are 92 of them in villages outside Visby; over 70 of them have medieval frescos and a few also have very rare medieval stained glass. Visby has a dozen church ruins and a magnificent cathedral.

A church was built in most villages during prosperous times from the early 12th century to mid-14th century. After 1350, the money ran out (mainly due to war), and the tradition ended. Lack of funds helped to keep the island in an ecclesiastical time-warp; the old churches weren't demolished, and new ones were never built (until 1960). Each church is still in use, and all those medieval villages still exist as entities.

Most churches are open 9am to 6pm daily from mid-May to late August. Some churches have the old key in the door even before 15 May, or sometimes the key is hidden above the door.

The Key to the Churches in the Diocese of Visby is a very useful English-language brochure, which is available free from tourist offices.

Getting There & Away
Air There are regular **Skyways** (☎ 020-959500; W www.skyways.se) flights between Visby and three mainland airports: Stockholm Arlanda, Stockholm Bromma (up to 10 times daily for each airport) and Norrköping (three flights daily on weekdays only). Prices between Stockholm and Visby generally cost from Skr600 to Skr800, but good deals are occasionally available.

The cheaper local airline is **Gotlands Flyg** (☎ 222222; W www.gotlandsflyg.se), with regular flights between Visby and Stockholm Bromma (one to six times daily). Prices start from Skr495 one way; book early for discounts, and inquire after stand-by fares (from Skr300).

The island's **airport** (☎ 263100) is 4km northeast of Visby and is served by buses.

Boat Year-round car ferries between Visby and both Nynäshamn and Oskarshamn are operated by **Destination Gotland** (☎ 201020; W www.destinationgotland.se). Departures from Nynäshamn are from one to five times daily (about five hours, or three by high-speed catamaran). From Oskarshamn, there are one or two daily departures (except Saturday from early November until mid-March) in either direction (four to five hours).

Regular one-way adult tickets for the ferry/catamaran cost Skr174/276, but from mid-June to mid-August there is a more complicated fare system, with prices ranging from Skr152 to Skr258 for the ferry trip and Skr236 to Skr474 for the catamaran sailing (some overnight, evening and early-morning sailings in the middle of the week have the cheaper fares).

If you want to transport a bicycle on the ferry/catamaran it will cost Skr35/62; a car usually costs Skr274/408, although again in the peak summer season a tiered system operates. Between mid-June to mid-August the price of taking a car on the ferry is from Skr236 to Skr384; and on the catamaran the charge is between Skr408 and Skr608.

Getting Around
There are over 1200km of roads in Gotland, typically running from village to village through the pretty landscape. Cycling on the quiet roads is highly recommended, and bikes can be hired from a number of places in Visby. The forested belt south and east of Visby is useful if you bring a tent and want to take advantage of the liberal camping laws.

Many travel agents and bike-rental places on the island rent out camping equipment. In Visby, you can hire bikes for from Skr60/300 per day/week from behind Saluhall (on the harbour) or at Österport (down by the outside of the wall). **Gotlands Cykeluthyrning** (☎ 214133), behind Saluhall, also rents tents (Skr75/250 per day/week), or for Skr200/1000 you can hire the 'camping package' – two bikes, a tent, camping stove and two sleeping mats. **Gotlands Resor** offers similar packages (see Places to Stay in the Visby section for contact details).

A few companies and service stations offer car hire. A central office in Visby is **Avis**

(☎ 219810; ⓔ godman@gotlandica.se; Donners plats 2), where you can rent a small car from Skr530/2945 per day/week. At the **guest harbour** (☎ 215190) you can also rent cars, motorbikes and mopeds.

Kollektiv Trafiken (☎ 214112) runs buses via most villages to all of the corners of the island. The most useful routes, that have connections up to seven times daily, operate between Visby and Burgsvik in the far south, Visby and Fårösund in the north (also with bus connections on Fårö), and Visby and Klintehamn. A one-way ticket will not cost you more than Skr59 (if you take a bike on board it will cost an additional Skr40), but enthusiasts will find a monthly ticket good value at Skr590.

VISBY
☎ 0498 • pop 21,400

The narrow cobbled streets and impressive town walls of the medieval port of Visby, a living relic with more than 40 proud towers and the ruins of great churches, attest to the town's former Hanseatic glories. Today it's a Unesco World Heritage-listed town that leaves few tourists disappointed.

The place is heaving with holiday-makers in the summer, and from mid-May to mid-August cars are banned in the old town. The highlight of the season is the costumes, performances, crafts, markets and re-enactments of **Medeltidsveckan** (Medieval Week; ⓦ www .medeltidsveckan.com), during the first or second week of August, when it is almost impossible to get any sort of accommodation unless you have thought to book well in advance.

Information
The tourist office, **Gotlands Turistförening** (☎ 201700; ⓔ info@gotlandinfo.com, ⓦ www .gotland.com; Hamngatan 4; open 8am-noon & 12.30pm-4pm Mon-Fri Oct-Apr; 8am-5pm Mon-Fri May-Sept; 8am-7pm Mon-Fri 8am-6pm Sat & Sun mid-June–mid-Aug; 10am-4pm Sat & Sun May–mid-June & late August; 11am-2pm Sat & Sun Sept) is down near the harbour.

There's a **bank** and ATM on Adelsgatan. The **ICA supermarket** on Stora Torget sells stamps, as does the tourist office. The public **library** (Cramérgatan) is good for free Internet access. For rainy days, there's the **Röda Kvarn cinema** (☎ 210181; Mellangatan 17).

Things to See
The town is a noble sight, with its **13th-century wall** of 40 towers; be sure to take a few hours and walk around the perimeter (3.5km). Also set aside time to stroll around the Botanic Gardens and the narrow roads and pretty lanes just south of the gardens. Pick up a copy of the booklet entitled Visby on Your Own (Skr35), which will guide you around the town and give you good snippets of local history. In summer the tourist office also organises two-hour guided walking tours of the town (Skr80), with English-language walks up to four times a week.

The ruins of 10 medieval churches, all within the town walls, include **St Nicolai Kyrka**, built in 1230 by Dominican monks. The monastery was burned down when Lübeckers attacked Visby in 1525. The **Helge And Kyrka** ruin is the only stone-built octagonal church in Sweden and it was built in 1200, possibly by the Bishop of Riga. The roof collapsed after a fire in 1611. On Stora Torget, **St Karins Kyrka** has a beautiful Gothic interior and was founded by Franciscans in 1233. The church was extended in the early 14th century, but the monastery was closed by the Reformation and the church fell into disrepair.

The ruins contrast with the old but sound **Cathedral of St Maria** (open 8am-5pm Mon-Fri, 8am-6.30pm Sat, 9am-5pm & 6pm-8pm Sunday summer, shorter hours rest of year). This is an impressive building, with stained-glass windows, carved floor slabs, an ornate carved reredos and wall plaques.

Gotlands Fornsal (☎ 292700; Strandgatan 14; adult/child Skr50/free; open 10am-5pm daily May–mid-Sept, noon-4pm Tues-Sun mid-Sept–Apr) is one of the largest and best regional museums in Sweden – allow a few hours if you want to appreciate it. Amazing 8th-century, pre-Viking picture stones, human skeletons from chambered tombs, silver treasures and medieval wooden sculptures are highlights. **Konstmuseum** (☎ 292775; Sankt Hansgatan 21; adult/child Skr30/free; open 10am-5pm daily May–mid-Sept, noon-4pm Tues-Sun mid-Sept–Apr), nearby, is an art museum featuring exhibitions by local, national and international artists.

Places to Stay
The closest camping ground is **Norderstrands Camping** (☎ 212157; low/high season tent

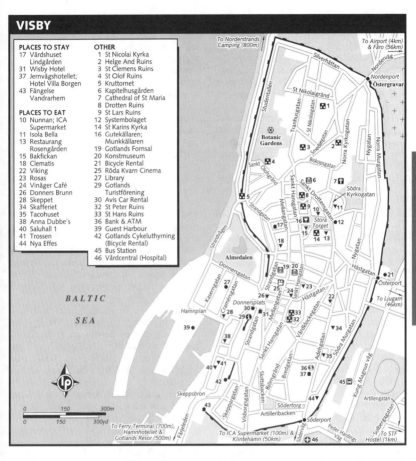

VISBY

PLACES TO STAY
17 Värdshuset Lindgården
31 Wisby Hotel
37 Jernvägshotellet; Hotel Villa Borgen
43 Fängelse Vandrarhem

PLACES TO EAT
10 Nunnan; ICA Supermarket
11 Isola Bella
13 Restaurang Rosengården
15 Bakfickan
18 Clematis
22 Viking
23 Rosas
24 Vinäger Café
26 Donners Brunn
28 Skeppet
34 Skafferiet
35 Tacohuset
38 Anna Dubbe's
40 Saluhall 1
41 Trossen
44 Nya Effes

OTHER
1 St Nikolai Kyrka
2 Helge And Ruins
3 St Clemens Ruins
4 St Olof Ruins
5 Kruttornet
6 Kapitelhusgården
7 Cathedral of St Maria
8 Drotten Ruins
9 St Lars Ruins
12 Systembolaget
14 St Karins Kyrka
16 Gutekällaren; Munkkällaren
19 Gotlands Fornsal
20 Konstmuseum
21 Bicycle Rental
25 Röda Kvarn Cinema
27 Library
29 Gotlands Turistförening
30 Avis Car Rental
32 St Peter Ruins
33 St Hans Ruins
36 Bank & ATM
39 Guest Harbour
42 Gotlands Cykeluthyrning (Bicycle Rental)
45 Bus Station
46 Vårdcentral (Hospital)

GOTLAND

---

sites *Skr85/145, cabins from Skr350/550; open late-Apr–mid-Sept),* by the sea 800m north of Visby's ring wall (well connected by a walking and cycling path).

The **STF hostel** *(☎ 269842;* e *carl.tholin@ tjelvar.org; dorm beds from Skr115; open mid-June–mid-Aug)* is southeast of the town centre off Lännavägen, in a school residence and therefore only open in peak season.

Fängelse Vandrarhem *(☎ 206050; Skeppsbron 1; dorm beds from Skr150),* in a good location between the ferry dock and the harbour restaurants, offers beds year-round in the small converted cells of an old prison.

You will have to call ahead to book at **Jernvägshotellet** *(☎ 271707;* e *staff@visby jernvagshotell.com; Adelsgatan 9; beds from*

Skr170; open year-round), a small, comfortable and very central hostel.

Gotlands Resor *(☎ 201260;* e *info@got landsresor.se; Färjeleden 3),* at Hamnhotellet, is a travel agency that books private rooms in Visby – singles/doubles cost around Skr285/425 inside the town walls, or Skr240/380 outside. This agency can also organise cabin rental, provide bike hire and rent camping equipment.

Hamnhotellet *(☎ 201250; Färjeleden 3; singles/doubles low season Skr560/600, high season Skr640/760)* is not far from the ferry terminal and offers uninspiring but cheap (for Visby) hotel rooms.

Värdshuset Lindgården *(☎ 218700;* e *lind garden.vardshuset@telia.com; Strandgatan 26; singles/doubles low season Skr595/745, high* season Skr750/945) is a good, central option, with rooms set in a pretty garden beside a quality restaurant.

Hotel Villa Borgen (☎ 279900; e hotell.vil laborgen@telia.com; Adelsgatan 11; singles/ doubles low season Skr860/970, high season Skr910/1070) also has pleasant rooms set around a pretty, quiet courtyard.

Top of the heap in Visby is the luxurious, landmark **Wisby Hotel** (☎ 204000; e info@ wisbyhotell.se; Strandgatan 6; singles/doubles low season from Skr865/1240, high season Skr1535/1870), with pillars and vaulted ceilings creating a lovely medieval atmosphere.

Places to Eat & Drink

Most restaurants and bars are around the Old Town squares, on Adelsgatan or at the harbour. Good places around buzzing Stora Torget include **Restaurang Rosengården** (☎ 218190), in the shadow of the ruins and offering weekday lunches for Skr62, plus evening à la carte dishes from Skr105 to Skr215.

Nunnan (☎ 212894), with a menu featuring Greek dishes (meals from Skr80 to Skr180), is another appealing option. The neighbouring cellar restaurant-bars of **Gutekällaren** (☎ 210043) and **Munkkälleren** (☎ 2271400) are both home to nightclubs popular with the summer crowd.

The menu at the highly rated **Bakfickan** (☎ 271807; mains Skr118-218) features well-prepared fish and seafood.

Between Stora Torget and the cathedral is **Isola Bella** (☎ 218787; Södra Kyrkogatan 20; mains Skr75-185), serving authentic Italian cuisine.

Donners Brunn (☎ 271090; Donners plats; mains Skr95-235) is among the finest restaurants in town – brunn means 'well' and you'll see it just inside the door. The Swedish and international menu is adventurous and tempting, and there are cheaper vegetarian and husmanskost (home-style fare). This restaurant is deservedly popular; it's wise to book ahead.

In summer, visit atmospheric **Clematis** (☎ 210288; Strandgatan 20; open Midsummer–mid-Aug), a medieval restaurant serving food cooked according to medieval recipes, accompanied by music and entertainers, including the occasional fire-eater.

Be sure to also check out **Nya Effes** (☎ 210622; snacks & meals Skr80-180), just off Adelsgatan. Full of character, it's a pub-bar

built into the town wall and is a good place for a meal or drink; there's a simple bar menu, an outdoor courtyard, pool tables and regular live music here in summer.

Skeppet (☎ 210710; Hamnplan 5), down by the water, is an upmarket restaurant by day and a nightclub by night. Other hangouts around the harbour are popular on warm summer days and evenings, including the restaurants **Anna Dubbe's** and **Trossen**, and the cheap stalls selling ice cream, sandwiches and pizza at **Saluhall 1**.

Rosas (☎ 213514; St Hansgatan 22), a pretty half-timbered house with a sunny courtyard, is an excellent lunch spot, serving baguettes, filled crepes, baked potatoes and the island speciality, saffron pancakes (all around Skr30 to Skr50). **Skafferiet** (☎ 214597; Adelsgatan 38) is similarly inviting.

Vinäger Café (☎ 211160; Hästgatan 3) is a stylish place where you'll find a fashionable crowd enjoying the usual café fare – but at slightly inflated prices to pay for the sleek furnishings.

There are a few cheap fast-food type places on Adelsgatan, including **Viking** at No 37 serving pizzas, kebabs etc from Skr49. Nearby **Tacohuset** (☎ 249822) at No 22 has pizzas, pasta and salads from Skr42, plus Mexican dishes such as tacos and nachos from Skr65.

There is a central **ICA supermarket** (Stora Torget) for self-caterers, or a much larger one on Söderväg, which is south of Söderport. **Systembolaget** (Stora Torget) is central.

AROUND VISBY

There's not much of interest until you're at least 10km from Visby. If you're heading northeast, visit the remarkable **Bro church**, which has several 5th-century picture stones in the south wall of the oratory, excellent sculptures, and interior lime paintings.

Heading southeast on road No 143, on your way to Ljugarn, check out the 12th-century Cistercian monastery ruin **Romakloster** (☎ 50123; adult/child Skr20/free; open 10am-6pm daily June-Aug, & weekends May & Sept), a kilometre from the main road. Summer theatre performances here cost around Skr250 (tickets from Visby tourist office). The 18th-century manor house is also impressive.

Dalhem, 6km northeast of the Cistercian monastery, has a large church with 14th-century stained glass (the oldest in Gotland)

and magnificent (albeit restored) wall and ceiling paintings – take note of the scales of good and evil. The **steam railway** (☎ 38043; adult/child Skr25/15) here operates on Wednesday, Saturday and Sunday in summer.

There's a good range of services in the reasonable-sized town of **Klintehamn**. From here, you can catch a passenger-only boat to the island nature reserve **Stora Karlsö** (W www.storakarlso.com) one to three times daily from May to August (Skr200 return, 30 minutes). You can visit the island as a day trip (with five or six hours ashore), or stay overnight at the hostel (see following). The extensive birdlife here includes thousands of guillemots and razorbills, and there are impressive cliffs by the lighthouse.

Places to Stay & Eat

In Klintehamn, **Pensionat Warfsholm** (☎ 240010; e warsholm@telia.com; tent sites Skr85, dorm beds from Skr100, rooms per person from Skr250) is in a pretty waterside spot and has a restaurant.

If you want to get away from it all, you can stay on Stora Karlsö at the simple **STF hostel** (☎ 240500; boka@storakarlso.com; dorm beds Skr150). There's a nature exhibit, restaurant and café on the island.

EASTERN GOTLAND

Ancient monuments include the Bronze Age ship setting **Tjelvars grav**, 1.5km west of road No 146 (level with Visby), and its surrounding landscape of standing stones, almost all linked with the Gutasaga legends. **Gothem church** is one of the most impressive in Gotland; the nave is decorated with friezes dating from 1300. **Torsburgen**, 9km north of Ljugarn, is a partly walled hill fort (the largest in Scandinavia) measuring 5km around its irregular perimeter.

Ljugarn is a small seaside resort, and there are impressive *raukar* formations at **Folhammar** nature reserve 2km north. Southwest of Ljugarn in the village of Alskog, **Gotlands Djurpark** (☎ 493500; adult/child Skr85/50; open 10am-6pm daily mid May-Aug) is a small zoo, home to around 40 types of animals, including kangaroos, ostriches and zebras. Southwest of here, the impressive **Garde church** has four extraordinary medieval lych gates and an upside-down medieval key in the door; the original 12th-century roof can still be seen.

Places to Stay & Eat

The **STF hostel** (☎ 493184; dorm beds from Skr115; open mid-May–August) has a fine spot at the eastern end of the Ljugarn village (down by the water). In Garde is another **STF hostel** (☎ 491391; e gardavh@sverige.nu; dorm beds Skr115; open Feb-Dec).

Frejs Magasin (☎ 493011; e info@lju garn.com; singles/doubles Skr450/650, with private facilities Skr700/800) is a large, central pension in Ljugarn. Prices quoted here are for high season; off-peak the rooms are Skr100 to Skr200 cheaper. There are also good-value three- and four-bed rooms, plus apartments and cabins available by the week.

There's a **Konsum supermarket** in Ljugarn, and good (summer-only) dining options. **Restaurang Kråkan** (☎ 493371; mains Skr150-200), just off the main road through town, is quite an upmarket place, and nearby **Bruna Dörren** (☎ 493289; Strandvägen 5) is a more casual restaurant and pizzeria with a large outdoor courtyard. **Espegards Konditori** (☎ 493040) offers tasty baked goods and sandwiches.

NORTHERN GOTLAND & FÅRÖ

Worthwhile is a visit to the **Bungemuseet** (☎ 221018; adult/child Skr60/free; open 10am-4pm daily mid-May–Aug, 10am-6pm July–mid-Aug), an open-air museum with 17th-century houses and picture stones dating from 800. It's near the northeastern tip, not far from where the ferry connects to Fårö.

The **grotto** (☎ 273050; adult/child Skr60/35; open daily May–mid-Sept) south of Lummelunda is the largest in Gotland. The temperature in the grotto is a cool 8°C, so bring warm clothing. The impressive *raukar* formations at nearby **Lickershamn** are up to 12m high.

The frequent car ferry to Fårö is free. This island has magnificent *raukar* formations; watch the sunset at **Langhammarshammaren** if you can. There are lots of fossils in the rocks by **Fårö lighthouse**, at the eastern tip of the island. British troops who fought in the Crimean war are buried at **Ryssnäs**, in the extreme south.

Places to Stay & Eat

There are good **STF hostels** in Fårö (☎ 223639; dorm beds from Skr85) 17km northeast of the ferry, near the small settlement of Sudersand, and in Lärbro (☎ 225033;

dorm beds Skr125), on road No 148 between Visby and Fårösund. Both are open from mid-May to the end of August. There is a beachside **SVIF hostel** *(☎ 273043; dorm beds from Skr130)* in Lummelunda, signposted from the main road.

Café Valnöten in Fårösund, near the ferry dock, serves up simple café-style fare, and neighbouring **Fårösunds Grill** has the usual fast-food offerings. There's an **ICA supermarket** (with an ATM) in Fårösund and another one on Fårö, 1.5km from the hostel.

GOTSKA SANDÖN NATIONAL PARK

Isolated, triangular-shaped Gotska Sandön (W *www.gotskasandon.com)*, with an area of 37 sq km, is an unusual island, with 30km of beaches, sand dunes, pine forest, a church, and lighthouses at its three corners. There is a really good network of trails right around the island. The website is in Swedish only.

Camping *(sites per person Skr50, beds in basic huts Skr110, cabins from Skr450)* near the northern tip is possible; there are basic facilities but you must bring all supplies with you.

Boats *(☎ 240450; operating early May-early Sept)* run from Fårösund and Nynäshamn three to four times weekly (Skr675/875 return from Fårösund/Nynäshamn, Skr100 for bikes).

SOUTHERN GOTLAND

Hemse is a commercial centre, with good services (supermarkets, banks, bakery), and the smaller village of **Burgsvik**, farther south, is similar.

Öja church dates from 1232 and has Gotland's highest church tower (67m). It has a magnificent cross and the wall and ceiling paintings are very detailed. Look for the inscribed stone slabs under the covered shelter just outside the churchyard. **Hablingbo church** has three lavishly carved doorways, a votive ship, carved floor slabs and rune stones.

Lojsta has the deepest lakes in Gotland, remains of an early medieval fortress and a fine church. On the eastern coast near Ronehamn, **Uggarderojr** is a huge, late–Bronze Age cairn with nearby traces of settlement. The cairn, probably a navigation marker, is now a long way inland due to post-glacial uplift.

Places to Stay & Eat

The Hablingbo **STF hostel** *(☎ 487070; ⓔ van drarhem@gutevin.se; beds Skr150; open May-Sept)* is next to **Gute Vin**, a good restaurant and commercial vineyard.

In Björklunda, 2km north of Burgsvik, friendly **Värdshuset Björklunda** *(☎ 497190; dorm beds Skr165, singles/doubles Skr590/790)* is a delightful place reminiscent of a Greek villa, with pretty whitewashed buildings. Meals at the restaurant here are good and reasonably priced.

Norrland

The northern half of Sweden, Norrland, has always been considered separate from the rest of the country. It's associated with forest, lake and river, and with the pioneers' struggle to produce the timber and iron ore necessary in the construction of the railways that opened up the region. The development of the Swedish working class here was decisive and far-left politics are still topical today.

The sustainable extraction of timber continues, but most heavy mining has moved north to Kiruna and Malmberget.

Areas along the Norwegian border, all the way to the Arctic Circle and beyond, are known for their great natural beauty and attract walkers, skiers and canoeists.

Orientation

There are six regions *(landskaps)* along the Bothnian coast and three along the Norwegian border. In northern areas, the region and county *(län)* boundaries don't relate at all.

From north to south, the regions of Gästrikland and Hälsingland make up Gävleborgs Län, and Medelpad and most of Ångermanland form Västernorrlands Län. Västerbotten and the southern third of Lappland create Västerbottens Län, and Norrbotten combines with the rest of Lappland to make Norrbottens Län. In the southwest, Härjedalen and Jämtland form Jämtlands Län.

Almost all of the population live in the major towns and cities on the Bothnian coast, with another concentration in central Jämtland as well as around the Storsjön lake. The scenery here is dominated by coniferous forest, but the western mountains rise well above the tree line and there are also many small glaciers, especially north of the Arctic Circle. Large tracts of Lappland are protected with either nature reserve or national park status. The rivers tend to be large and slow-moving, with long narrow lakes a common feature away from the coast. Coastal islands tend to be small though they are often located in substantial archipelagos. In summer, sandy beaches, long hours of sunshine and reasonably high water temperatures attract crowds of tourists. The far north has the legendary midnight sun during summer and the extraordinary northern lights (aurora borealis) during the winter.

Highlights

- Admiring the wonderful scenery of Höga Kusten

- Scouring the surface of Storsjön for a glimpse of the monster

- Visiting the super-cool Ice Hotel in Jukkasjärvi

- Hiking, skiing, rafting and dog sledging in the mountains and rivers of Jämtland

- Strolling around Gammelstad church village in Luleå

- Climbing Kebnekaise, Sweden's highest peak

- Trekking part of Kungsleden, Sweden's premier hiking trail

- Visiting the remote Sarek National Park to see the wildest mountains and largest elk in the country

Regional Tourist Offices

Visitors can contact the following agencies for more detailed information on the area:

Gästrikland Turism (☎ 026-147437, e gastrikland@gavletourism.se, w www.gastrike.com) Box 1175, SE-80135 Gävle. This is one of two regional tourist offices in Gävleborgs Län.

Hälsingetur (☎ 0270-76660, e info@halsingetur.com, w www.halsingland.com) Box 130, SE-82623 Söderhamn. This organisation is the second office within Gävleborgs Län.

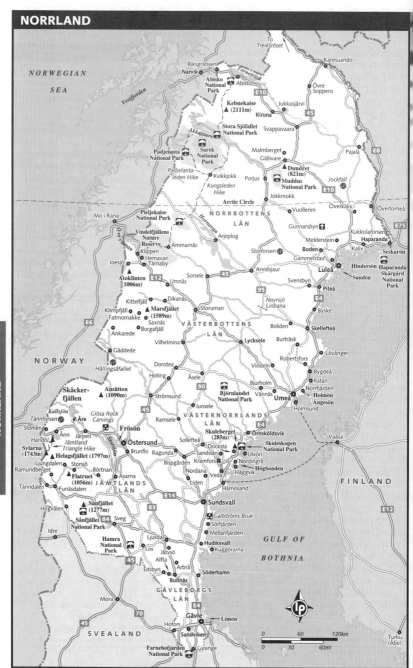

NORRLAND

Jämtland Härjedalen Turism (☎ 063-144022,
E info@jht.se, W www.jamtland.info)
Rådhusgatan 44, SE-83182 Östersund. This
office covers Jämtlands Län.
Mitt Sverige Turism (☎ 0611-557750, E info@
mittsverigeturism.se, W www.mittsverigeturism
.se) Norra Kyrkogatan 15, SE-87132 Härnösand.
This office covers Västernorrlands Län.
Turism i Norrbotten/Lappland (☎ 0920-293500,
E turism@itnorrbotten.se, W turism
.norrbotten.se)
VästerbottensTurism (☎ 090-785 7176,
E kansli@vasterbotten.net, W www.vaster
botten.net) Köksvägen 11, SE-90189 Umeå

Getting Around

Bus You'll probably find yourself relying
more on buses than trains if you're spending
any length of time in Norrland. The following companies provide regional transport
links, and if you're planning to spend a reasonable amount of time in any of these
counties, it's worth inquiring about monthly
passes or a *sommarkort*, offering discount
travel in the peak summer period (ie, from
Midsummer to mid-August). Check also the
respective websites for routes, schedules,
fares and passes; these sites don't always
have information in English, but if you call
the telephone numbers listed you'll usually
reach someone who can help you in English.

Länstrafiken i Jämtlands Län (☎ 063-168400,
W www.lanstrafiken-z.se)

Länstrafiken i Norrbotten (☎ 020 470047,
W www.ltnbd.se)
Länstrafiken i Västernorrland (☎ 020 511513,
W www.dintur.se). Also commonly known as
Din Tur.
Länstrafiken i Västerbotten (☎ 020 910019,
0950-10357, W www.lanstrafikeniac.se)
X-Trafik i Gävleborgs Län (☎ 020 910109,
W www.x-trafik.se)

Ybuss *(☎ 0200 334444; W www.ybuss.se)*
runs express buses daily between Stockholm
and Sundsvall, Östersund and Umeå. Other
handy regional services include **Länstrafiken
i Västerbotten** bus No 100, which runs several times daily between Sundsvall and Luleå
via the major towns along the E4; bus No 45,
which runs daily between Östersund and
Gällivare; and bus No 31, which once daily
connects Umeå and Mo i Rana (Norway), via
Storuman and Tärnaby.

Länstrafiken i Jämtlands Län bus No 45
runs twice daily between Mora (Dalarna)
and Östersund. **Länstrafiken i Norrbotten**
runs two daily buses connecting Luleå and
Kiruna – its bus network covers 100,000 sq
km (one-quarter of Sweden), and it will carry
bikes for Skr50.

Train A historic railway, **Inlandsbanan**
(☎ 063-104409; W www.inlandsbanan.se) runs
for 1067km through Sweden's interior from
Mora to Gällivare via Östersund, Storuman,

Inlandsbanan

Until the early 20th century Norrland's rich natural resources had been left largely unexploited. The
Inlandsbanan, or Inland Railway, was intended to change this by opening up the northern forests
and mountains for colonisation and development.

Digging ditches, excavating gravel, blasting mountains and laying sleepers and rails in an area
where there were no roads was no mean feat. For over 30 years, the sleepers continued their inex-
orable progress northwards, from Kristinehamn in the south to Gällivare in the north – a distance of
over 1300km. The Inlandsbanan was the last major undertaking of the Swedish navvies; construction began in 1907 and the project was completed in 1937.

However, by the time the Inlandsbanan was inaugurated, a serious competitor to the train, the
car, was already making an impact on Sweden and soon railway lines were closed in many parts of
the country. When it was proposed that even larger stretches of the Inlandsbanan should be closed
down, strong protests were heard not only from the regions directly affected, but from all over Sweden. The Inlandsbanan north of Mora is still operating today largely as a result of the wide popular
support it received in the face of closure.

If you'd like to know more about the history of the Inlandsbanan and the people who made it
happen, visit the Navvy Museum in Moskosel and the Inlandsbanan Museum in Sorsele. A new railway museum with links to the Inland Railway has also been inaugurated in Jamtli in Östersund.

NORRLAND

Arvidsjaur and Jokkmokk (see the boxed text in this chapter). Today it can be covered in either direction by a combination of *rälsbuss* (railcar) and – with some planning – steam train. The journey is popular with tourists and can be done only from late June (just after Midsummer) to early August. Travel on the line is slow (a speed of 50km/h is usual) and it takes seven hours from Mora to Östersund (Skr240) and 15 hours from Östersund to Gällivare (Skr485), but you can break your journey in any of the small towns en route. You can buy tickets for certain legs of the journey, or a special card that will allow you two weeks' unlimited travel on the route for Skr950; ScanRail card-holders get a 25% discount on this ticket, but not on individual tickets, and Interrail pass-holders under 26 can ride on the Inlandsbanan for free.

Getting to the far north from Gävle by train is a night exercise only and Ånge is the usual change for Östersund. SJ (☎ 0771-757575; W www.sj.se) trains run as far north as Härnösand; beyond there, you'll need to use trains operated by a different company, **Tågkompaniet** (☎ 020 444111; W www.tag kompaniet.se).

The new, 190km **Botnia Banan** (W www .botniabanan.se) railway line from Kramfors to Umeå via Örnsköldsvik should be completed by 2005.

Gästrikland

GÄVLE
☎ 026 • pop 91,200

Gävle was granted its town charter in 1446 and it is the gateway to Norrland. It is probably the most pleasant of the northern cities to walk in because of its architecture and its parks; you should note the contrast between the wooden residences of Villastaden and Gamla Gefle.

Information

The helpful **tourist office** (☎ 147430; e tur istbyran@gavletourism.se, W www.gavle.se /turism; Drottninggatan 37; open 9am-6pm Mon-Fri, 9am-2pm Sat, 11am-4pm Sun June-Aug; 9am-5pm Mon-Fri Sept-May) is not far from the train station.

There are banks and other services on Drottninggatan and on or around the large

Stortorget. The public **library** (Slottstorget 1), near the castle, offers free Internet access. For English-language newspapers and magazines go to **Internationell Press** (Södra Kungsgatan 11).

Things to See & Do

The wooden old town of **Gamla Gefle**, south of the city centre, shows what Gävle was like before it was almost completely destroyed by fire in 1869. One of the houses, **Joe Hill-gården** (☎ 613425; Nedre Bergsgatan 28; admission free; open 11am-3pm Tues-Sat June-Aug), was the birthplace of the US union organiser who was executed for a murder he didn't commit in Utah, 1915. Some of his poetry forms part of the memorial here.

Berggrenska gården (Kyrkogatan) is the only remaining early-19th-century commercial courtyard in Gävle and it was lucky to survive the 1869 fire. The nearby **rådhus** (town hall) wasn't so lucky – its present appearance is post-1869, but a town hall has stood on the site since 1628.

The regional **Länsmuseum** (☎ 655600; Södra Strandgatan 20; adult/child Skr30/free; open noon-4pm Tues-Sun) has an excellent art collection from the 17th century to today, displays of local silver and glassware, and historical exhibitions.

The **Silvanum Skog Museum** (☎ 538360; Kungsbäcksvägen 32; adult/child Skr20/free; open 10am-4pm Tues-Fri, noon-4pm Sat & Sun), situated by the river, features aspects of forestry and conservation, and across the footbridges you'll find a practical demonstration around the parks of **Stadsträdgården** and **Boulognerskogen** (used for open-air music and summer theatre).

The oldest of the churches in Gävle is the **Heliga Trefaldighets kyrka** at the western end of Drottninggatan; it has an 11th-century **rune stone** inside. The buildings of the **castle** on the southern bank of Gävleån are now in administrative use, but there are temporary **art exhibitions** here and a small **prison museum** (open for tours noon to 2pm Sunday).

From June to August daily **boat tours** (Skr30 each way) run from Södra Skeppsbron to the island of **Limön**, which is part of an archipelago. The island has a **nature trail**, a **mass grave** and a **memorial** to the sailors of a ship that was here lost in the early 1800s.

Bönan, 13km northeast of town, is a pretty waterside settlement that's also worth a look;

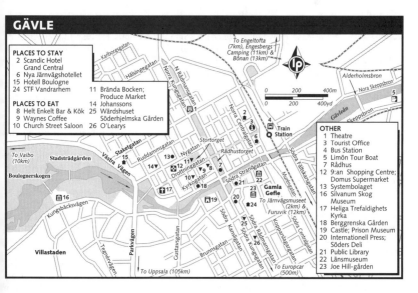

GÄVLE

PLACES TO STAY
2 Scandic Hotel
  Grand Central
6 Nya Järnvägshotellet
15 Hotell Boulogne
24 STF Vandrarhem

PLACES TO EAT
8 Helt Enkelt Bar & Kök
9 Waynes Coffee
10 Church Street Saloon

11 Brända Bocken;
   Produce Market
14 Johanssons
25 Wärdshuset
   Söderhjelmska Gården
26 O'Learys

To Engeltofta
(7km), Engesbergs
Camping (11km) &
Bönan (13km)

Alderholmsbron

Nora Skeppsbron

0   200   400m
0   200   400yd

OTHER
1 Theatre
3 Tourist Office
4 Bus Station
5 Limön Tour Boat
7 Rådhus
12 9:an Shopping Centre;
   Domus Supermarket
13 Systembolaget
16 Silvanum Skog
   Museum
17 Heliga Trefaldighets
   Kyrka
18 Berggrenska Gården
19 Castle; Prison Museum
20 Internationell Press;
   Söders Deli
21 Public Library
22 Länsmuseum
23 Joe Hill-gården

Train Station

Gamla
Gefle

To Järnvägsmuseet
(2km) &
Furuvik (12km)

To Valbo
(10km)   Stadsträdgården

Boulognerskogen

Villastaden

To Uppsala (105km)

To Europcar
(500m)

there's a popular restaurant and a fish smoke-house. Bus No 95 runs out here.

Railway buffs will enjoy the preserved steam locomotives and carriages of the **Järnvägsmuseet** (☎ 144615; Rälsgatan; adult/child Skr40/free; open 10am-4pm daily June-Aug, Tues-Sun rest of year), the national rail museum, 2km south of the town centre, off Österbågen.

The leisure park and zoo named **Furuvik** (☎ 177300; adult/child Skr95/75; open daily mid-May–Aug), about 12km southeast of Gävle, aims to provide a little of everything; you can behave like a monkey on the amusement rides and then see the real thing at the ape enclosure. Tickets for rides cost from Skr10 to Skr40; a day pass for unlimited rides costs Skr130. From the train station, take frequent bus No 838.

One of the more unusual attractions in the area is **Mackmyra Svensk Whisky** (☎ 132979; Bruksgatan 4, Valbo), established in 1999 as the first Scandinavian malt whisky distillery. It's about 10km west of Gävle and offers regular tours (Skr120) of the distillery from late June to August (once a week outside of peak time). Inquire at the tourist office for details.

Places to Stay

Engesbergs Camping (☎ 99025; e info@engesbergscamping.se; bus No 95; low/high season tent sites Skr75/100, cabins Skr350/

350; open May-Sept) has good facilities and is in a pretty setting by the sea about 11km northeast of town.

The central **STF Vandrarhem** (☎ 621745; e stf.vandrarhem@telia.com; Södra Rådmansgatan 1; dorm beds from Skr120) is clean and quiet and set around a pleasant courtyard in the old part of town. Bike hire is available, as is breakfast, and there's a good kitchen. Another STF hostel, **Engeltofta** (☎ 96160; e engeltofta@swipnet.se; Bönavägen 118; bus No 95; dorm beds Skr140; open June-Aug) is about 7km northeast of the city.

Just opposite the train station, the simple **Nya Järnvägshotellet** (☎ 120990; singles/doubles Skr395/525, discounted to Skr300/450) is the cheapest hotel in town. The reception and a pub are on the ground floor.

The small and friendly **Hotell Boulogne** (☎ 126352; Byggmästargatan 1; singles/doubles from Skr395/545, discounted to Skr375/495) is another decent mid-range option, although it doesn't look like much from the outside. Some bathroom facilities are shared.

A sizeable step up is the classy **Scandic Hotel Grand Central** (☎ 495 8400; e grand.central@scandic-hotels.com; Nygatan 45; singles/doubles from Skr1030/1524, discounted to Skr610/760), near the station and with well-priced summer rooms and excellent facilities.

Places to Eat

Johanssons (☎ *100734; Nygatan 7; lunch Skr75, mains Skr75-175)* is rated among the best restaurants in town and offers an excellent menu of quality dishes like veal, beef fillet or sole, plus a vegetarian dish and a *husmanskost* (home-style) meal for under Skr100.

Fashionable **Brända Bocken** (☎ *124545; Stortorget; meals Skr64-149)* is right in the heart of the action on the main square. Its outdoor area is a good spot to enjoy a drink, light meal and a spot of people-watching. Sleek **Waynes Coffee** (☎ *660866; Drottninggatan 16)* is not far away, serving its usual good coffee and modern café fare.

Church Street Saloon (☎ *126211; Kyrkogatan 11; meals from Skr70)* is an incongruous restaurant-bar with a 'wild west' theme and lots of Tex-Mex items on its huge menu.

Helt Enkelt Bar & Kök (☎ *120604; Norra Kungsgatan 3; snacks Skr30-65, meals Skr65-150)* is a favourite with the locals for its good atmosphere, friendly service and well-priced, unpretentious fare. It has sleek decor but not the prices to match – all but one dish on the menu is under Skr100.

Excellent, tiny **Söders Deli** (*Södra Kungsgatan 11),* near Internationell Press, serves good coffee and authentic Italian ciabatta or pasta (Skr40 to Skr75). Nearby **Wärdshuset Söderhjelmska Gården** (☎ *613393; Södra Kungsgatan 2B)* offers fine food in a great setting – a wooden house dating from 1773 with lots of outdoor seating; lunch is Skr68, à la carte meals range from snacks to traditional Swedish dishes and cost from Skr38 to Skr154.

There are popular pub-restaurants around town, with a few to be found along the eastern parts of Drottninggatan, and along Södra Kungsgatan, including **O'Leary's** (*Södra Kungsgatan 31).*

There's a daily **produce market** held on Stortorget. You'll find a **Domus supermarket** in the 9:an shopping centre (between Nygatan and Drottninggatan) and nearby there is a **Systembolaget** (*Nygatan 13).*

Getting There & Away

There are numerous long-distance bus services, leaving from behind the train station (connected by underpass). **Ybuss** runs daily to Sundsvall (Skr170), Umeå (Skr280) and Östersund (Skr210). **SGS Bussen** (☎ *133030)* has two to four daily services to Stockholm (Skr110). **Swebus Express** runs to Uppsala (Skr120) and Stockholm (Skr165) once or twice daily.

SJ trains run to Stockholm via Uppsala, and northwards to Sundsvall and beyond; there are up to six X2000 services and several slower trains daily. Other useful direct trains include Gävle to Falun and Örebro.

Local buses leave mainly from around Rådhustorget. **Europcar** (*Södra Kungsgatan 62)* has car rental. Ask the tourist office about bicycle hire.

GYSINGE
☎ 0291

Gysinge, 55km south of Gävle and on the border with Uppland, is known for the fine **Gysinge Bruk** ironworks that operated from 1668 to the early 20th century and it's a pleasant place for a wander. There's a small **tourist office** (☎ *21000;* e *turist.gysinge@ sandviken.se; Granövägen 6; open 10am-5pm daily May-Sept, 10am-5pm Mon-Fri Oct-Apr)* in town; you can rent boats and canoes here.

You can try your hand at forging at **Krokiga Smedjan** (*Crooked Forge; admission free; open 10am-6pm daily June-Aug; noon-5pm Tues-Sun rest of year),* which began operations in 1764; there's also a high-quality **handicraft exhibition.** Traditional **Bagarstugan** still bakes unleavened bread and is a good place for a coffee and a sandwich. In **Smedsbostaden** (*Smith's Cottage; admission free; open noon-5pm daily May-Sept)* you can experience what local living conditions were like in the late-19th-century. **Dalälvarnas Flottningsmuseum** (*Museum of River Driving; adult/child Skr20/10; open noon-5pm daily mid-June–mid-Aug)* covers the once crucial but now defunct occupation of guiding logs downstream to the sawmills.

Gysinge Wärdshus (☎ *21200;* e *ysinge@ swipnet.se; singles/doubles Skr950/1100, discounted to Skr600/750),* in the middle of the ironworks area at Gysinge, has very comfortable accommodation plus an excellent **restaurant** (*à la carte meals from Skr70).*

Bus No 49 runs four to six times daily from Gävle to Gysinge.

FÄRNEBOFJÄRDEN NATIONAL PARK

The mighty river Dalälven flows through the area and is central to Färnebofjärden National

Park, a 100-sq-km park south of Gysinge that's half-land, half-water and is a bird-watcher's paradise, with ospreys, sea eagles, seven types of woodpecker, Ural owls and capercaillie. Lynxes have also been observed. Fishing on the river and in the lakes is also extremely good. There are wonderful sandy beaches, especially on the island **Sandön**.

Östa Stugby (☎ 0292-43004; e osta@ stugby.com; open year-round) is in beautiful wilderness near the national park some 30km south of Gysinge. It offers excellent, self-contained six-bed chalets from Skr500 to Skr675 per night, depending on season. It also hires canoes and boats.

There's no public transport to the park. Västmanlands Lokaltrafik bus No 71 runs one to six times daily from Heby (connections from Sala) to Tärnsjö (8km from Östa.

Hälsingland

SÖDERHAMN & AROUND
☎ 0270 • pop 27,500

Known as the town of parks, Söderhamn, founded in 1620 by Gustav II Adolf, is a pleasant coastal town with a few things to see. The **tourist office** (☎ 75353; e info@tur ism.soderhamn.se; open year-round) is at the train station, just off the E4 Hwy and 1.5km west of the town centre. The town centre has all facilities including banks and supermarkets, mostly along Köpmangatan.

Things to See
The history of the town is covered by **Söderhamns Museum** (☎ 15791; Oxtorgsgatan 5; adult/child Skr20/free; open noon-5pm Tues-Sun mid-June–mid-Aug). The hill Östra Berget lies south of the town centre and has the odd 23m-high tower **Oscarsborg** (admission free; open 10am-6pm daily), with a café, on top. **Ulrika Eleonora Kyrka** (open 8am-4pm Mon-Fri), just north of the town hall, was designed by Nicodemus Tessin the Younger (completed in 1693). **Söderhamns F15 Flygmuseum** (☎ 14284; adult/child Skr30/15; bus No 59; open 10am-5pm daily June-Aug, 11am-3pm Sun Sept-May), located by the airfield, 5km southeast of town, has a collection of old military aircraft.

About 15km northwest of town, **Trönö Gamla Kyrka** (open daily May-Sept) is a well-preserved church that dates from the 12th century. Take bus No 67 (two to 11 daily).

Bergviks Industrimuseum (☎ 423280; admission free; open Tues-Sun), around 16km west of Söderhamn, is a pretty spot with an outdoor café as well as displays about the history of the world's first sulphate factory, opened in 1874. Bus No 64 runs to Bergvik every two hours or so.

Skärså, an ideal cycling destination about 12km north of Söderhamn, is one of the most beautiful fishing villages in the area. The picturesque red-painted buildings include old boat sheds, houses, summer houses, a restaurant, museum and café. There's also a fish shop. Take bus No 65 (weekdays only).

Places to Stay & Eat
Lakeside **Mohed Natura Camping** (☎ 425233; e mohed@natura-invest.se; Mohedsvägen 59; camping per person from Skr100, dorm beds Skr120, cabins from Skr250), 11km west of Söderhamn, is a well-equipped camping ground that is also shares home with an **STF Vandrarhem**, open June to August. You can rent bikes and boats here. Bus Nos 63 and 100 run to Mohed from Söderhamn.

Flygstaden (☎ 73840; bus No 59; hostel beds Skr120, hotel singles/doubles Skr500/700, discounted to Skr350/550) is a decent hostel and hotel at Söderhamn airfield, 5km southeast of town.

Scandic Hotel Söderhamn (☎ 265200; e soderhamn@scandic-hotels.com; Montörsbacken 4; singles/doubles Skr1128/1451, discounted to Skr600/700) is only 300m from the train station and offers good discounted rates as well as its usual high standards of accommodation.

Mousquet (☎ 19897; Köpmangatan 2; lunch Skr60, meals from Skr90) serves something for everyone, with cheap pub snacks, lots of pizza choices, and seafood, meat and chicken meals. Opposite is a **Sibylla** fast-food outlet, for a quick refuel.

The atmospheric **Albertina** (☎ 32010; mains Skr70-150), perched above the water in Skärså, is the nicest place to eat in the area. There's an assortment of fish on the menu, including lots of herring and salmon, plus meals for non-fish-lovers too.

Getting There & Away
Skyways flies from the airfield to Stockholm once or twice on weekdays.

NORRLAND

All buses and trains leave from the Resecentrum, at the train station. **Ybuss** runs daily to Östersund (Skr180), Stockholm (Skr190), Umeå (Skr230) and Uppsala (Skr190). SJ trains run daily to Hudiksvall, Sundsvall, Härnösand, Gävle and Stockholm.

JÄRVSÖ & AROUND
☎ 0651 • pop 2000

Järvsö is a pleasant, sleepy village in the hilly interior of Hälsingland and at the northern end of a string of lakes that extends all the way from the Bothnian coast at Ljusne, just south of Söderhamn. The final event of the **Hälsinge Hambon** (W *www.halsingeham bon.x.se*), an annual folk dancing event (with up to 1000 competitors), takes place in Järvsö in early July and it's quite a spectacle, with a festival atmosphere. There's a statue of dancers by the train station.

There's a **tourist office** (☎ 40306; *Turistvägen 29; open daily mid-June–mid-Aug, shorter hours rest of year*) on the main road through town, as well as banks and supermarkets.

Things to See

The main attraction is **Järvzoo** (☎ 41125; *adult/child high season Skr95/60, low season Skr80/50; open daily*), where you can follow 3km of easy wooden walkways through the forest and observe bears, lynxes, honey buzzards, snowy owls and aggressive wolverines in fairly natural surroundings. It's open a complex set of hours, but is generally open from 10am or 11am until 4pm or 5pm June to August, 11am until 2pm or 3pm the rest of the year.

Completed in 1838, **Järvsö Kyrka** (*open 9am-4pm or 5pm daily*) is one of the largest rural churches in Sweden and it has an impressive location on an island in the river. Most of the island is a wooded nature reserve.

The hill **Öjeberget**, just west of the village, gives great views – there's a restaurant on top and you can ski down in winter. Just across the bridge from the church (on the eastern bank of the river), **Stenegård** (☎ 767300; *open daily Mat-Sept, Sat & Sun rest of year*) is an old manor and farm with good handicraft stalls, a café, restaurant and a theatre in an old barn.

Places to Stay & Eat

Järvsö Camping (☎ 40339; *tent sites Skr80, cabins from Skr220*) is on the main road through the town and offers good facilities.

The small and homey **Gästgivars** (☎ 41690; *Jon Persvägen 7; dorm beds/singles Skr165/ 215*) is near the bridge (follow the signs) and offers very inviting hostel accommodation, plus breakfast for an additional Skr35.

Friendly **Järvsöbaden** (☎ 40400; e *info@ jarvsobaden.se; singles/doubles from Skr550/ 720*), founded as a health farm in 1905, is the best place to stay in town. It's a charming old place set in pretty grounds that include a nine-hole golf course, and it has a variety of rooms (some with shared facilities). The restaurant here has a superb lunch smörgåsbord that has to be seen to be believed – it costs Skr150/ 230 on weekdays/weekends. There are good half-board packages available.

Öje (☎ 40340; *Turistvägen 39; pizzas Skr40-65*) offers cheaper meals than Järvsöbadens; it's adjacent to the rather grim-looking OKQ8 petrol station, but the food is good. **Järvsö Café & Konditori** (☎ 41111) is a basic little café down by the train station.

Getting There & Away

Bus No 51 runs regularly between Bollnäs and Ljusdal via Arbrå and Järvsö. Trains run north from Järvsö to Östersund and south to Gävle and Stockholm.

HUDIKSVALL & AROUND
☎ 0650 • pop 37,300

Hudiksvall has some interesting architecture, a few diversions and a well-placed town centre, sandwiched between a small lake and a fjord. The **tourist office** (☎ 19100; e *turist@ hudiksvall.se,* W *www.hudiksvall.se; open daily mid-June–mid-Aug, Mon-Sat rest of year*) is at Möljen, by the harbour. In town, you'll find banks and other services on Storgatan and Drottninggatan. The **library** (*Storgatan*) has free Internet access; the local **museum** also has computers for Skr15 per half-hour (see following for address).

Things to See & Do

The good **Hälsinglands Museum** (☎ 19600; *Storgatan 31; adult/child Skr20/ 10; open variable hours daily mid-June–mid-Aug, Mon-Sat rest of year*) covers local history, culture and art, including the **Malsta Stone** with unusual runic inscriptions. Just southwest of the centre, **Jakobs kyrka** dates from 1672. Parts of **Hälsingtuna Church**, 4km north, were built around 1150 but more extraordinary is the 15th-century **Bergöns Kapell**, 18km due northeast, the oldest fishermen's church in the district.

Attractive **Kuggörarna** is about 30km east of Hudiksvall and is an excellent example of a fishing village (take bus No 37, twice daily). The coast shows **raised beaches** caused by post-glacial uplift (still continuing) – the forests are growing in boulder-fields. **Mellanfjärden**, 30km north of Hudiksvall, isn't the most photogenic village, but there is a gallery with displays of local crafts, a summer theatre, a good restaurant and several nature reserves. **Sörfjärden**, 10km north of Mellanfjärden, has an unusual harbour in the river Gnarpsån, and a good sandy beach nearby.

There is an attractive route between the two lakes **Norrdellen** and **Sördellen**, just west of Hudiksvall. Around the neoclassical **Norrbo Kyrka** there are nine Iron Age graves, church stables from the 1920s and also a mid-18th-century bell tower. **Avholmberget**, just north of Friggesund, is the best viewpoint – you can drive or cycle up.

Places to Stay & Eat

Malnbadens Camping (☎ 13260; ⓔ info@ malnbadenscamping.com; camping from Skr80, dorm beds Skr120, cabins from Skr350), 4km east of the centre of Hudiksvall, is a large wooded camping ground that's also home to the pleasant **STF Vandrarhem**, open year-round. Bus No 5 runs out here in summer.

The small, family-run **Hotell Temperance** (☎ 31107; Håstgatan 16; dorm beds Skr150, singles/doubles from Skr550/700, discounted to Skr450/600) is between the train station and Jakobs Kyrka and offers simple, comfortable accommodation at reasonable prices.

First Hotell Statt (☎ 15060; Storgatan 36; singles/doubles from Skr1152/1402, discounted to Skr702/852) is the pick of the town's hotels, with central, upmarket lodgings and facilities, including an indoor swimming pool. **Stadt Nöje**, attached to the hotel, is a stylish and popular restaurant-bar with good-value lunches (Skr59) plus many appealing à la carte offerings.

Nearby, **Dackås Konditori** (☎ 12329; Storgatan 34) is a kitsch bakery that hasn't changed since the 1950s. It has an upstairs café, sandwiches from Skr30 and cakes and pastries to satisfy sugar cravings. Another budget option is **Möljens Gatukök**, in an old warehouse by the harbour (between the train

station and information office) – it sells burgers, hot dogs and ice creams, and has outdoor seating.

Down on the water behind the tourist office is **Gretas Krog** (☎ 96600; lunch Skr59, meals Skr130-200), offering good Swedish dishes, a broad seafood selection and a large, bustling outdoor deck.

Getting There & Away

The bus station is next to the central train station, by the harbour. **Ybuss** travels daily to Gävle, Östersund, Stockholm and Umeå. SJ trains run north to Sundsvall and south to Gävle, Söderhamn and Stockholm.

Medelpad

SUNDSVALL
☎ 060 • pop 93,100

Much of Sundsvall was reduced to ashes by the great fire of 1888, but the town centre was rebuilt in grand style over the next 10 years and has fine examples of neo-Gothic, neo-Renaissance and neobaroque architecture. It's a pleasant place to spend a day or two, admiring the impressive buildings and enjoying the good restaurant scene. Things heat up considerably in the first week of July, when Sundsvall hosts one of Sweden's largest street festivals (attended by up to 100,000 people), which includes a large musical concert in the centre of town.

Information

There's a helpful, central **tourist office** (☎ 610450; ⓔ info@sundsvallturism.com, ⓦ www.sundsvallturism.com; Stora Torget; open 10am-6pm Mon-Fri, 10am-2pm Sat year-round) to assist with traveller inquiries. Staff can give you information on activities in the area plus summer boat tours, and can supply maps detailing galleries in town, or a self-guided pub crawl for those who aren't such culture-vultures!

You can exchange money at **Forex** (Köpmangatan 1). Storgatan is the main street, with banks, supermarkets and most facilities. The **public library** is in the Kultur Magasinet (see following) and offers Internet access.

Things to See

Kultur Magasinet, on Sjögatan down near the harbour, is a magnificent restoration of

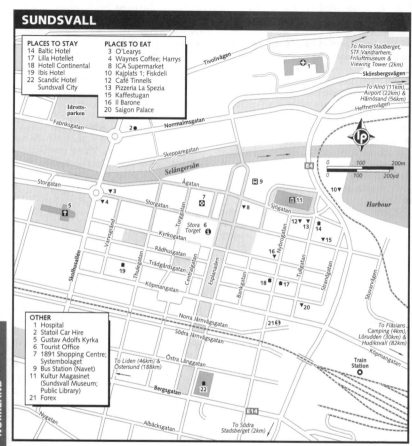

SUNDSVALL

PLACES TO STAY
14 Baltic Hotel
17 Lilla Hotellet
18 Hotell Continental
19 Ibis Hotel
22 Scandic Hotel
   Sundsvall City

PLACES TO EAT
3 O'Learys
4 Waynes Coffee; Harrys
8 ICA Supermarket
10 Kajplats 1; Fiskdeli
12 Café Tinnells
13 Pizzeria La Spezia
15 Kaffestugan
16 Il Barone
20 Saigon Palace

OTHER
1 Hospital
2 Statoil Car Hire
5 Gustav Adolfs Kyrka
6 Tourist Office
7 1891 Shopping Centre;
  Systembolaget
9 Bus Station (Navet)
11 Kultur Magasinet
   (Sundsvall Museum;
   Public Library)
21 Forex

old warehouses. The buildings now contain the town library and **Sundsvall Museum** (☎ 191803; admission Skr20/free; open 11am-7pm Mon-Thur, 10am-6pm Fri, 11am-4pm Sat & Sun), which has exhibits of local and natural history, local Iron Age archaeology and geology.

The central church, **Gustav Adolfs kyrka** (open daily), is worth a look. There's music here every Wednesday evening in summer.

Up on the hill **Norra Stadsberget** (150m), there is a **viewing tower** as well as a typical **friluftsmuseum** (outdoor museum; admission free; open daily), a collection of local houses. The southern hill, **Södra Stadsberget** (250m), has an extensive plateau that's good for hiking, with trails up to 12km long. There's also free fishing on the **Sidsjön** lake and several

downhill ski runs (nordic skiing is also popular). Buses run to either hill once every two hours in summer.

The large island **Alnö**, just east of Sundsvall, has the magnificent **Alnö Gamla Kyrka** (admission free; open noon-7pm daily mid-June–mid-Aug), 2km north of the bridge (at Vi). The old church, below the road, is a mixture of 12th- and 15th-century styles. The lower parts of the wall paintings were badly damaged by whitewashing in the 18th century, but the upper wall and ceiling paintings are in perfect condition (apart from removal of certain faces by Protestant vandals) and show various biblical scenes. The painting was probably done by one of Albertus Pictor's pupils. Even better is the late 11th-century carved wooden **font** in the new church, across the road; the upper part combines Christian and Viking symbolism, while the lower part shows beasts, the embodiment of evil. Take bus No 1 to Vi (two or three hourly), then take a Plus bus to the churches (every one or two hours).

For a pleasant excursion, head to **Lörudden**, a picturesque fishing village about 30km southeast of town, with restaurants and fish smokehouses. Take bus No 20 south to Njurundabommen, then change to bus No 126.

Liden, by the ribbon lake on Indalsälven, is about 46km northwest of Sundsvall on road No 86. **Liden Gamla Kyrka**, completed in 1510, has a lovely location and contains excellent medieval **sculptures** from the 13th, 15th and 16th centuries. There are rather faded wall paintings from 1561 and also a 13th-century crucifix. The view from the **Vättberget**, reached by a 3km unsurfaced road from Liden, is one of the finest in Sweden and shows the ribbon lake to its best advantage. To reach Liden, take bus No 30.

Places to Stay

Fläsians Camping (☎ 554475; *Norrstigen 15; tent sites Skr95, cabins from Skr250*) is near the E4, 4km south of Sundsvall. It's a large, well-equipped and pleasant ground despite all the industry between here and the city centre. Take bus No 2 or 52.

The very good **STF Vandrarhem** (☎ 612119; e *stf.vandrarhem.sundsvall@telia.com; Gafelbyvägen; dorm beds Skr140-195*) is above the town on Norra Stadsberget, and has both older rooms and more expensive modern rooms with en suite. The walk to the hostel is pleasant but not much fun with heavy bags – a bus runs up here in summer.

Lilla Hotellet (☎ 613587; e *lillahotellet@ swipnet.se; Rådhusgatan 15; singles/doubles from Skr450/650, discounted to Skr350/595*) is small and rather basic but reasonable value and central. In a similar vein is nearby **Hotell Continental** (☎ 150060; e *hotell.continen tal@spray.se; Rådhusgatan 13; singles/doubles Skr580/750, discounted to Skr405/545*).

A good deal is offered by central **Ibis Hotel** (☎ 641750; *Trädgårdsgatan 31; rooms Skr600, discounted to Skr450*), with somewhat bland but comfortable rooms that can sleep up to three people for a reasonable flat rate. Breakfast isn't included in the price.

Towards the upper end of the scale is the **Baltic Hotel** (☎ 140440; e *info.baltic@sweden*

hotels.se; Sjögatan 5; singles/doubles from Skr1025/1130, discounted to Skr535/715), near Kultur Magasinet. It has excellent discounted rates for its bright, modern rooms.

The large and upmarket **Scandic Hotel Sundsvall City** (☎ 785 6200; e *sundsvallcity@ scandic-hotels.com; Esplanaden 29; singles/ doubles Skr1200/1525, discounted to Skr798/ 898*), has very comfortable rooms, plus lots of facilities on the premises, including a cinema, restaurant and popular pub.

Places to Eat

Classy **Il Barone** (☎ 176604; *Kyrkogatan 14; mains Skr120-220*) is a highly regarded restaurant serving up authentic Italian cuisine, with risotto and pasta dishes at the lower end of the price scale (Skr120 to Skr150), plus well-prepared meat and fish meals.

Kajplats 1 (☎ 156006; *Hamnplan 1; meals Skr89-225*) has a hotchpotch of interior styles (nautical meets opulent Oriental) but it all comes together in a great harbour restaurant-bar, where the emphasis is on fresh fish. Soups and salads are offered for under Skr100, plus there's a selection of tapas plates (around Skr50). Or you might wish to pick up some seafood from the adjacent **Fiskdeli**.

Tucked away a little, **Saigon Palace** (☎ 173091; *Trädgårdsgatan 5; lunch Skr65, dishes Skr70-125*) has an extensive menu of Chinese, Vietnamese and even Japanese dishes, plus a cheap lunch buffet.

Slick café fare in modern surroundings is offered by **Café Tinells** (☎ 56149; *Sjögatan 7; meals Skr40-65*), a funky, colourful place with excellent food, including ciabatta, salads, baked potatoes, quiche and tempting sugary treats. At the other end of town is **Waynes Coffee** (☎ 121943; *Storgatan 33*), with more of their winning formula – light meals in stylish surrounds.

Pizzeria La Spezia (☎ 611223; *Sjögatan 6*) offers very cheap pizza and kebab deals for around Skr35. Not far away is **Kaffestugan** (☎ 613807; *Storgatan 6*), the oldest café in town, dating from 1905 and in a beautiful old building. Sandwiches cost around Skr35.

There are lots of pubs around town, including **Harrys** (☎ 175533; *Storgatan 33*) and **O'Learys** (☎ 124144; *Storgatan 40*) opposite each other on Storgatan. Both attract a mixed crowd, and both offer a range of pub food and fine alcoholic beverages.

NORRLAND

There's a central **ICA supermarket** *(Esplanaden 5)*. **Systembolaget** is in the 1891 shopping centre on Storgatan.

Getting There & Away

The **airport** *(☎ 197600)* is 22km north of Sundsvall and buses run from the Scandic Hotel and the bus station three to nine times daily (Skr65) to connect with SAS and Skyways flights to Gothenburg, Luleå and Stockholm.

All buses depart from the Sundsvall bus station, known as Navet, in the northern part of town near Kultur Magasinet. **Ybuss** runs daily to Östersund (Skr120), Gävle (Skr170) and Stockholm (Skr200). Länstrafiken Västerbotten bus No 100 runs several times daily to Umeå and Luleå and most other coastal towns.

Trains run west to Östersund (Skr180) and south to Söderhamn (Skr120), Gävle (Skr195) and Stockholm (Skr465). The station is just east of the centre, on Köpmangatan.

Statoil *(☎ 152070; Norrmalmsgatan 1)* has car hire. **Taxi Sundsvall** *(☎ 199000)* can help you get around.

Ångermanland

HÄRNÖSAND
☎ 0611 • pop 25,200

Härnösand, on a narrow strait between the island Härnön and the mainland, was sacked by the Russians in 1721. It's not a particularly interesting town, but it is useful for transport connections, including a ferry service to Vassa in Finland.

There's a **tourist office** *(☎ 88140;* e *trist info@harnosand.se,* w *www.mittsverigeturism .se; Järnvägsgatan 2; open daily in summer, Mon-Fri rest of year)* outside the town centre, just off the E4, and it has bike rental available. From here you need to cross Nybron (bridge) to get to the town centre, with the regular facilities (banks, supermarkets etc) in town.

The good **Länsmuseet Västernorrland** *(☎ 88600; admission free; open 11am-5pm daily)*, at Murberget (1km north of the tourist office), is Sweden's newest regional museum and covers the culture and history of the region. It costs Skr20 for a tape and headset, in English. The open-air museum, **Friluftsmuseet Murberget** *(admission free; open noon-4pm daily mid-June–mid-Aug)*, adjacent to Länsmuseet Västernorrland, includes a shop, church and school.

There are interesting boat trips available in summer, taking in the impressive coastal scenery and journeying up to the dramatic Höga Kusten bridge – inquire at the tourist office for details.

Summer-only **STF Vandrarhem** *(☎ 10446;* e *vhemmet@harnosandshus.se; Volontären 14; dorm beds Skr120; open mid-June–mid-Aug)* is 2km east of the train station and offers good amenities.

Hotel City *(☎ 27700;* e *hotelcity@kajutan .com; Storgatan 28; singles/doubles Skr790/ 990, discounted to Skr520/670)* is in the heart of town and has comfortable rooms plus a popular adjacent restaurant-bar-club, **Kajutan** *(☎ 18300; meals Skr75-250)*, offering lunch for Skr65 and a comprehensive menu of snacks, pasta, meat, fish and vegetarian dishes.

The classy restaurant-bar **Apotequet** *(☎ 511717; Nybrogatan 3)* is a unique place with its bar area in an old pharmacy.

Länstrafiken Västerbotten bus No 100 runs several times daily to Sundsvall, Luleå and points in-between. **Ybuss** runs daily to Gävle and Stockholm. Local buses connect to Sundsvall for train connections to Gävle and Stockholm.

There are regular ferry services from the harbour to Vaasa in Finland, operated by **Botnia Link** *(☎ 550555;* w *www.botnialink .se)*. See the Getting There & Away chapter for details.

HÖGA KUSTEN
☎ 0613

One of the most attractive parts of Sweden's coastline, Höga Kusten (meaning the High Coast) is a hilly area with many lakes, fjords and offshore islands. Although the scenery is not quite as dramatic as the name suggests, the region was recently listed as a Unesco World Heritage Site, recognised as a unique area largely shaped by the combined processes of glaciation, glacial retreat and the emergence of new land from the sea (which continues today at a rate of 0.9m per century).

Höga Kusten stretches from north of Härnösand to Örnsöldsvik, both pleasant but unremarkable towns. Tourist offices in both these towns should be able to help you with information on exploring the region. There is also a **tourist office** *(☎ 50480;* w *www .hogakusten.com; open daily)* serving the area;

Enjoying the view in Norrland

Snowboarding at Riksgränsen, Norrland

Happy skiiers, Riksgränsen, Norrland

Dog sledging in reverse, Norrland

Practical ski wear, Norrland

Ski around the clock in Norrland

Chill out at the Ice Hotel near Kiruna, Norrland

White-water rafting, Norrland

it's located inside Hotell Höga Kusten, just north of the spectacular E4 suspension bridge over Storfjärden. Here you can pick up information on attractions and accommodation options in the tiny villages along the coast. The information area is crowded with brochures, but the desk is staffed only from 10am to 6pm June to August. There's also useful information on the Internet at w www .turistinfo.kramfors.se.

Unfortunately, however, there's little public transport in the area (buses cruise along the E4 Hwy but don't make it into the villages). Hence, this area is virtually impossible to explore without your own set of wheels – unless, of course, you wish to walk the Höga Kustenleden, a 127km hiking trail stretching from Veda in the south, through Kramfors, and finishing near Örnsköldsvik, with shelters and cabins situated along its length. Ask the tourist office for the map and guide book (Skr80).

As well as the striking landscapes, the other major attractions of the region are the many well-preserved fishing villages, the pick of them being Barsta, Bönhamn and Norrfällsviken, and the lovely off-shore islands, especially Högbonden (accessed by boat from Barsta and Bönhamn) and Ulvön (boats from Ullanger, Docksta and Mjällomslandet). Ulvön is worth a day visit for the view from the hill Lotsberget (100m) but the charm of the main village is somewhat spoiled by the large tour groups who have to take it in turns to see the tiny, 17th-century chapel. Also worth checking out are Hembygdsgården, a 19th-century house and furnishings, and Sandviken, a 17th-century village at the northern end of the island.

Back on the mainland, be sure also to visit Mannaminne (☎ 20290; admission Skr20; open daily June-Sept; Sat & Sun Oct-Nov & Apr-May) near Häggvik an eccentric collection of just about everything from subjects as diverse as farming, emigration and technology, plus a café and handicraft stalls. Walk up the steep hill behind the museum for the best view in the area (35 minutes return).

Friendly Skuleberget Naturum (☎ 40171; admission free; open daily June-Aug, shorter hours rest of year), by the E4 just north of Docksta, has exhibitions and lots of information on the area. The steep mountain Skuleberget (285m) soars above the Naturum; ask about hiking routes, the chairlift

(Skr50/30) on the other side, and rock-climbing routes (grades II to III).

Skuleskogen National Park, a few kilometres northeast, consists of varied and magnificent scenery, including Slåtterdalskrevan, a 200m-deep canyon. The park is signposted from the E4, and the Höga Kustenleden walking trail passes through it.

Places to Stay & Eat

You can stay at the Hotell Höga Kusten (☎ 722270; singles/doubles Skr845/1095, discounted to Skr500/750), the large hotel just off the E4, by the bridge and with excellent views. There's also a café here serving coffee as well as snacks, and a restaurant called Bridge Brasserie & Bar, with meals from Skr80 to Skr170, including burgers, salads and pasta dishes.

Mannaminne (☎ 20290; e info@man naminne.se), near tiny Häggvik, offers B&B accommodation (singles/doubles Skr250/450) as well as cottages from Skr300, and there's a café here too.

Delightful Norrfällsviken has a very good camping ground (☎ 21382; tent sites Skr110, cabins from Skr320), and also a popular fish restaurant and pub, Fiskarfänget (☎ 21117; most meals under Skr100), with seating on a large deck over the water.

Kustgårdens Vandrarhem (☎ 21255; dorm beds Skr120) is also in Norrfällsviken – it's operated by the nearby Brittas Restaurang (☎ 21255; low/high season cabins from Skr790/ 910), a popular summer complex consisting of a restaurant, pub, pool plus self-contained cabins.

Vandrarhem Högbonden (☎ 23005, 42049; dorm beds from Skr195; open May-Oct) is a relaxing getaway on the island of Högbonden, reached by boat from Bönhamn and Barsta (Skr70). You'll need to book well in advance. There's a kitchen here, and a café open in summer.

The area surrounding the Naturum at Skuleberget is well set up for outdoor enthusiasts, with a camping ground (☎ 13064; tent sites Skr90, cabins from Skr295), restaurant and shops selling outdoor gear.

There's an STF Vandrarhem (☎ 13064; e kustlada@telia.com; tent sites Skr100, dorm beds/cabins from Skr100/250; open year-round), at Skoved, 3km south of Docksta. It has good facilities, including a pool, restaurant and outdoor stage for summer concerts.

NORRLAND

There are **supermarkets** in Ullanger, Nordingrå, Docksta and Mjällom.

Getting There & Around
Bus No 217 runs one to six times daily between Nordingrå, the bridge and Kramfors. Other than that, you'll need to walk, cycle or drive yourself around the area. Länstrafiken Västerbotten bus No 100 runs along the E4.

ÖRNSKÖLDSVIK
☎ 0660 • pop 55,400
Örnsköldsvik, founded in 1894, is the largest town in Ångermanland and is situated between small hills and the sea, but there's not a great deal to warrant a lengthy stay.

There's a helpful **tourist office** (☎ 88100; ℮ turism@ornskoldsvik.se, ⓦ www.ornskolds vik.se; Nygatan 18; open daily mid-June–mid-Aug, Mon-Fri rest of year) in the centre of town. There are banks around Stora torget, and the **library** (Lasarettsgatan 5) has Internet facilities.

Walk up **Varvsberget** (around 80m high) for a good view of the town. It's south of the centre – some 275 steps lead up from Modovägen.

Örnsköldsviks Museum (☎ 88601; Läroverksgatan 1; adult/child Skr20/free; open noon-4pm daily mid-June–mid-Aug, Tues-Sun rest of year) covers 9000 years of local history and includes a section on the Sami. The impressive-looking **Rådhuset Konsthall** (☎ 88608; Rådhusgatan 1; adult/child Skr20/ free; open noon-4pm Tues-Sun) features local art exhibitions.

Gene Fornby (☎ 53710; adult/child Skr55/ 30; open noon-5pm daily July–mid-Aug), 5km south of the centre, is an interesting reconstruction of an Iron Age farm complete with actors and a wide range of activities, from baking to iron working. Guided tours run at 12.30pm, 2pm and 3.30pm. Take bus No 21 to Geneåsvägen, then walk to the farm, or ask at the tourist office about the regular direct bus service from town.

Places to Stay & Eat
The **STF Vandrarhem** (☎ 70244; dorm beds/ cabins from Skr110/150; open year-round), is in a lovely setting 9km west of town, just off the E4. Take bus No 40 or 412.

In the town centre, **Strand City Hotell** (☎ 10610; Nygatan 2; singles/doubles from Skr595/850, discounted to Skr450/550) offers good mid-range accommodation, and **First Hotel Statt** (☎ 265590; Lasarettsgatan 2; singles/doubles from Skr152/1402, discounted to Skr702/852) is a more upmarket option, with facilities typical of a high-end chain hotel.

Café Galleri M (☎ 16860; Storgatan 8; lunch Skr59) is a pleasant little café and a good spot for lunch, with a small adjacent art gallery. Nearby **Mamma Mia** (☎ 14700; Storgatan 6; meals Skr60-200) has an extensive menu of Italian food, including pizza and pasta dishes under Skr100.

Restaurang Varvberget (☎ 84480; lunch Skr65), on top of Varvberget, does typically Swedish food with a good weekday lunch special, which you can enjoy along with great views. The best area for dining, however, is down by the inner harbour, especially on a sunny day. Down here you'll find some good options, including the excellent **Fina Fisken** (☎ 15005; meals Skr85-170), serving local fish dishes in a fine atmosphere, and **Harrys** (☎ 85590), one of a nationwide chain of popular restaurant-pubs.

Getting There & Away
Länstrafiken Västerbotten runs bus No 100 along the E4 several times daily – south to Sundsvall, north to Umeå and Luleå.

Västerbotten

UMEÅ
☎ 090 • pop 105,000
Umeå, known as the city of birches, contains a large university and a port with ferry connections to Finland. It is one of the fastest-growing towns in Sweden and has some 22,000 students, making it an agreeable place to just hang out for a spell.

The central **tourist office** (☎ 161616; ℮ ume turist@umea.se, ⓦ www.umea.se/turism; Renmarkstorget 15; open 8am-7pm Mon-Fri, 10am-4pm Sat, noon-4pm Sun mid-June–mid-Aug; Mon-Fri rest of year) can help you with visitor inquiries.

To change money, **Forex** is on Renmarkstorget near the tourist office, and banks can be found in the vicinity, along Kungsgatan. There's a **public library** (Rådhusesplanaden 6A) with Internet access available, or you can try **Spixel** (Skolgatan 44), an Internet café not far from the STF hostel.

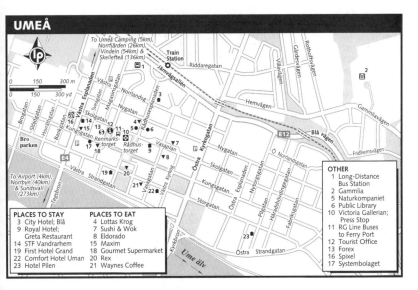

UMEÅ

To Umeå Camping (5km),
Norrfjärden (26km),
Vindeln (54km) &
Skellefteå (136km)

Train Station

Riddaregatan

To Airport (4km),
Norrbyn (40km)
& Sundsvall
(273km)

Ume älv
Östra Strandgatan

PLACES TO STAY
3 City Hotel; Blå
9 Royal Hotel;
   Greta Restaurant
14 STF Vandrarhem
19 First Hotel Grand
22 Comfort Hotel Uman
23 Hotel Pilen

PLACES TO EAT
4 Lottas Krog
7 Sushi & Wok
8 Eldorado
15 Maxim
18 Gourmet Supermarket
20 Rex
21 Waynes Coffee

OTHER
1 Long-Distance
   Bus Station
2 Gammlia
5 Naturkompaniet
6 Public Library
10 Victoria Gallerian;
   Press Stop
11 RG Line Buses
   to Ferry Port
12 Tourist Office
13 Forex
16 Spixel
17 Systembolaget

There are international magazines available at **Press Stop**, inside the Victoria Gallerian shopping centre, and outdoor gear is sold by **Naturkompaniet** (Rådhusesplanaden 7).

Things to See & Do
Gammlia, 1km east of the town centre, has several museums and shouldn't be missed. It includes the cultural-history and Sami collections of the regional **Västerbottens Museum** (☎ 171800; adult/child Skr20/free), the modern art museum **Bildmuseet** and the **Maritime Museum**. The surrounding **Friluftsmuseet**, with old houses and staff wearing period clothes, is also worth a look. The museums are open daily June to August (closed Monday rest of the year; only the regional museum has an admission charge).

Holmön, pitched as the sunniest place in Sweden, is a 15km-long offshore island with a **boat museum** (adult/child Skr20/free; open daily June-Aug) and a collection of traditional craft, plus a good quayside restaurant and swimming beaches. In July there's a rowboat race to Finland, which is only 36km away. Free ferries depart two or four times daily from Norrfjärden, 26km northeast of Umeå (bus No 118 or 119, Skr32).

The island of **Norrbyskär**, 40km south of Umeå, is another interesting destination. It has an interesting history – a sawmill community was built up here from nothing in

less than 10 years, only to disappear just as suddenly 10 years later. There is a museum here and other attractions; buses run to from Umeå to Norrbyn to connect with ferries – inquire at the tourist office for times.

There are a number of **activities** in the surrounding area, especially at Vindeln, 54km northwest of Umeå. Activities on offer include fishing, white-water rafting, jet-boating and canoeing on the local rivers, plus horse riding and a variety of walking trails (from two hours to three days). The tourist office can help organise these. Bus No 16 connects Vindeln and Umeå.

Places to Stay
Well-equipped **Umeå Camping** (☎ 702600; e umea.camping@umea.se; tent sites Skr125, basic huts from Skr200, cabins & chalets from Skr265) is 5km northeast of the town centre and just off the E4; take bus No 2, 6 or 3 (Skr16).

The busy and well-run **STF Vandrarhem** (☎ 771650; e info@vandrarhemmet.se; Västra Esplanaden 10; dorm beds from Skr115) is clean and central.

City Hotel (☎ 702341; e mail@cityhotel .umea.com; Rådhusesplanaden 14; singles/doubles Skr395/595) is a good, central option, right beside Blå restaurant-bar.

Hotel Pilen (☎ 141460; Pilgatan 5; singles/doubles Skr550/750, discounted to Skr450/550) is a family-run place, dated but comfortable, and is located in a quiet area some 600m from the town centre.

Royal Hotel (☎ *100730;* [e] *hotelroyal@ telia .com; Skolgatan 62; singles/doubles Skr850/ 1020, discounted to Skr550/720)* offers good accommodation in the heart of town and with an excellent restaurant. Of a similar high standard is **Comfort Hotel Uman** (☎ *127220; Storgatan 52; singles/doubles Skr1155/1355, discounted to Skr655/755)*, which is in a quieter location.

Storgatan is home to a few more upmarket hotels, including the **First Hotel Grand** (☎ *778870;* [e] *umea.grand@firsthotels.se; Storgatan 46; singles/doubles Skr855/1055, discounted to Skr550/650)*, which is the oldest hotel in Umeå and has good service and friendly staff.

Places to Eat

Upmarket, stylish **Greta** (☎ *100735; Skolgatan 62; mains Skr130-250)* at the Royal Hotel offers well-prepared Swedish and international dishes, with good fish and seafood options.

Rex (☎ *126050; Rådhustorget; mains Skr100-200)* is at the back of the town hall and offers an excellent cocktail list and a menu of favourites in bright and breezy surrounds.

Sushi & Wok (☎ *141900; Vasaplan; lunch Skr65, meals Skr90-150)* is a cool new restaurant and bar serving up good Asian dishes, with appealing sushi options.

Lottas Krog (☎ *129551; Nygatan 22; mains Skr89-218)* is a friendly pub-restaurant with an extensive menu with something for everyone, from fish and chips or a vegie burger through to chicken tandoori or fillet of wild boar. Nearby is **Blå** (☎ *132300; Rådhuses-planaden 14; meals Skr72-128)*, a large, shiny, trendy place with a nightly all-can-eat Thai buffet (Skr99, not available in summer) or regular menu of fashionable fare like risotto, gnocchi and baked salmon. Blå turns into a nightclub as the evening progresses.

You'll find lots of kiosks selling burgers, pizzas and kebabs on busy Rådhustorget.

Eldorado (*Vasagatan 10)* serves felafel, pasta, kebabs and salads for around about Skr50, and **Maxim** (☎ *138283; Kungsgatan 47)*, which is handily located by the STF hostel, has a similar menu and prices. **Waynes Coffee** (☎ *701700; Storgatan 50; meals Skr30-60)* offers coffee, cake, salads and sandwiches in stylish surrounds, plus there is an outdoor area for soaking up the long daylight hours.

Self-caterers should go to the **Gourmet supermarket** (*Renmarkstorget 5A)* and drinkers should head for **Systembolaget** (*Kungsgatan 50A)*.

Getting There & Away

Air The airport (☎ *716100)* is 4km south of the city centre. SAS and Malmö Aviation each fly to Stockholm up to seven times daily; there are also direct flights to Luleå, Kiruna and Östersund.

Bus The long-distance bus station is directly opposite the train station. **Ybuss** runs daily south to Gävle (Skr280) and Stockholm (Skr320), via the coastal towns of Sundsvall, Örnsköldsvik, Härnösand, Hudiksvall and Söderhamn.

Umeå is the main centre for **Länstrafiken i Västerbotten** (☎ *020 910019)*, the regional bus network that covers over 55,000 sq km. Direct buses to Mo i Rana in Norway (Skr210) run once daily, but buses as far as Tärnaby run up to four times daily. Other daily destinations include Östersund, Skellefteå and Luleå.

Train Tågkompaniet trains leave daily from Umeå to connect at Vännäs with the north-south trains between Stockholm and Boden and Luleå; from Boden there are connections to Kiruna and Narvik (Norway).

Boat There are two companies operating ferries between Umeå and Vaasa in Finland; see the Getting There & Away chapter for details. RG Line is more passenger-oriented than Botnia Link, which is used primarily by freight trucks. A bus to the port leaves from near the tourist office an hour before RG Line's departures.

Getting Around

Local buses leave from Vasaplan on Skolgatan. The No 80 **Flybuss** (☎ *141190)* departs regularly from Vasaplan (Skr30) or call **Umeå Taxi** (☎ *770000)* – it's about Skr100 to the airport.

SKELLEFTEÅ & AROUND
☎ 0910 • pop 72,000

One of the most agreeable coastal towns in northern Sweden, Skellefteå also has some attractions in the surrounding area and it's not a bad place to break your journey. The biggest festival here is Skellefteå Festi-valen, on the first weekend in July.

The **tourist office** (☎ 736020; e turist byra@komuun.skelleftea.se, w turistinfo.skel leftea.se; Trädgårdsgatan 7; open daily mid-June–mid-Aug, Mon-Fri rest of year) is in the town centre, just off Torget, the main square. There are banks along Nygatan, and there's Internet access at the **library** (Vikto-riaplatsen), in the eastern part of the town centre (follow Kanalgatan east).

Things to See & Do

All the town attractions are in the parks along the river, west of the town centre. A pleasant walk takes you to the **Nordanå park**, which includes the cultural-history collec-tions of the **Skellefteå Museum** (☎ 735510; adult/child Skr20/free; open daily) and several old houses, some of which contain handicraft shops.

West of Nordanå is **Bonnstan**, a unique housing precinct with 392 preserved 17th-century wooden houses – many of them are still inhabited in summer. Farther west, there is the small island of Kyrkholmen (which has an excellent café) and an early-16th-century **church**. You'll find a 13th-century wooden **Madonna** inside as well as an adjacent store-house for tithes (from 1674). Cross the river on **Lejonströmsbron**, Sweden's longest wooden bridge, built during the year 1737.

The recommended gold-mine museum, **Bergrum Boliden** (☎ 580060; bus No 204 or 205; adult/child Skr20/10; open 10am-5pm daily June-Aug), 35km west of Skellefteå, has interesting multimedia displays cover-ing geology and mining.

The tiny settlement of Örträsk, around 80km west of Skellefteå (north of Norsjö), has **Norsjö Linbana** (☎ 0918-21025; adult/child Skr220/90; tours at 1pm daily Midsummer–mid-Aug), the world's longest cable-car ride (13km), previously used for iron-ore trans-port, on which you can glide silently over the woods and marshes. At the time of research there was no public transport out to the area, but it's worth asking at the tourist office. Call ahead to check departure times.

Lövånger, 50km south of town and by the E4, has a medieval **church** and a well-preserved **church village**. Some houses have doors big enough to admit a horse and carriage, as well as the church-goers. Buses

run roughly hourly from Skellefteå, and there's an STF hostel here.

Places to Stay & Eat

Skellefteå Camping & Stugby (☎ 18855; low/high season tent sites Skr90/130, doubles Skr245/270, cabins from Skr280) is a large camping ground with excellent, family-friendly facilities off the E4 1km just north of town.

Just behind the old church on Brännavä-gen, the idyllic, church-run **Stiftsgården** (☎ 725700; e stiftsgarden.skelleftea@sven skakyrkan.se) is home to both the **STF hostel** (dorm beds Skr200) and also a **guesthouse** (singles/doubles Skr650/1000, discounted to Skr460/625) offering bright, comfortable, hotel-standard rooms.

Near the tourist office, **Hotel & Café Vik-toria** (☎ 17470; Trädgårdsgatan 8; singles/doubles Skr660/850, discounted to Skr400/580) offers simple but more than adequate rooms in a small hotel above a café. Around the corner and a step up in standard is the **First Hotel Statt** (☎ 14140; Statonsgatan 8; singles/doubles Skr1002/1252, discounted to Skr452/652), with good service and upmar-ket amenities.

Kriti (☎ 779535; Kanalgatan 51; lunch Skr75, meals Skr80-210) is an excellent choice for a hearty meal, with authentic Greek dishes on offer – lots of meat and fish, plus pasta, pizza and moussaka.

Monaco (☎ 17710; Nygatan 31; meals Skr65-150) offers good pizza and pasta dishes, and the pretty, nearby **Café Lilla Mari** (☎ 39192; Nygatan 33) offers sand-wiches from Skr25, hot lunches for Skr60 and an array of sweet temptations served in a small, leafy courtyard.

You can get the usual fast food on the main square in town. **Mr Greek** is a pub next door to Kriti with a casual setting and bar food offered. **O'Learys** (☎ 739308; Kanal-gatan 31), down the road from Kriti, is a popular watering hole offering pub food.

Getting There & Away

Bus No 100 runs every two hours on the Sundsvall–Umeå–Skellefteå–Luleå route (some buses continue as far north as Ha-paranda). Länstrafiken i Norrbotten has a daily bus from Skellefteå to Bodø (Skr400, nine hours) in Norway, via Arvidsjaur. Skellefteå's nearest train station is Bastuträsk and bus No 27 connects there three times daily (Skr45).

Norrbotten

PITEÅ
☎ 0911 • pop 40,500

Piteå is the main beach resort in northern Sweden and it attracts thousands of sun-seeking Norwegians in summer, when the water gets surprisingly warm. Piteå has all facilities and a **tourist office** (☎ 93390; e *pitea.turistbyra@pitea.se*, w *www.pitea.se; Sundsgatan 41; open 8am-8pm daily mid-June–mid-Aug, 8am-5pm Mon-Fri rest of year)*, at the busy, central bus station. You can rent bikes here for Skr30 per day.

Aside from the summer attractions of sun, sand and nightclubs, in nearby Öje-byn, 5km north of town, there's an interesting early-15th-century **church**, a **church village** with many houses perched on rocks, and a **museum** *(open daily June-Aug)*. The 16th-century **church**, off Sundsgatan in central Piteå, is one of the oldest wooden churches in Norrland. It escaped being burned by the Russians in 1721 because they were using it as their headquarters. There are several interesting wooden buildings on Storgatan, including a **rådhuset** (town hall), which now houses the **Piteå Museum** (☎ 12615; admission free; open Mon-Sat in summer).

The beachside **Pite Havsbadet** (☎ 32700; e *info@pite-havsbad.se)* area, about 8km south of Piteå itself and connected by frequent bus No 1, is the summer destination of choice for many holiday-makers – it's huge and has an expensive **camping** area *(tent sites Skr175)*, lots of **cabins** *(from Skr400)*, an ugly **hotel** *(summer singles/doubles from Skr790/ 990)* and conference centre, restaurant, café, pool, mini-golf, Imax theatre and some other family-focused activities, plus summer concerts and events.

If that doesn't sound like your cup of tea, you may be better off in town at the central **STF Vandrarhem** (☎ 15880; Storgatan 3; dorm beds Skr140)*, in an old hospital set in a pretty park, or the more upmarket **Piteå Stadshotell** (☎ 19700; e *info@piteastads hotell.com; Olof Palmesgata 1; singles/doubles from Skr1165/ 1395, discounted to Skr750/950)*, an elegant old hotel with lots of good facilities.

At the Stadshotell, you'll find **Restaurang Röda Rummet** *(mains Skr165-250)*, probably the finest restaurant in town (how does gin-flambéed reindeer fillet sound?), and **Cockney Pub**, with a more casual atmosphere and menu to match (pasta, baked potatoes etc under Skr100).

Bus No 100 runs between Umeå and Luleå via Piteå every one to three hours.

LULEÅ
☎ 0920 • pop 72,000

One of Sweden's busiest airports lies just outside Luleå, the capital of Norrbotten. Luleå was granted its charter in 1621, but the town was moved to its present location in 1649 because of the falling sea level (9mm per year, which is due to post-glacial uplift of the land). You will find an extensive off-shore archipelago of some 1700 large and small islands.

Storgatan is the main pedestrian mall; it has the main **tourist office** (☎ 293500; e *tur istbyra@lulea.se*, w *www.lulea.se; Storgatan 42; open daily mid-June–mid-Aug, Mon-Sat rest of year)*, which can help with inquiries (there is also a small office at Gammelstad – see Things to See & Do following). **Forex** *(Storgatan 46)* can exchange currency, and banks and most other services are also found along Storgatan. The **library** *(Kyrkogatan)* has Internet access, as does **LuLan** *(Kungs-gatan 14)*, a central cybercafé charging Skr40 per hour online.

For both newspapers and magazines, go to **Interpress** *(Storgatan 17)*. **Naturkompaniet** *(Kungsgatan 17)* sells all sorts of outdoor equipment.

Things to See & Do
Norrbottens Museum (☎ 243500; Storgatan 2; admission free; open Tues-Sun) is worth a visit just for the Sami section, but there are also exhibits about the Swedish settlers. **Konstens Hus** (☎ 294080; Smedjegatan 2; admission free; open Tues-Sun) is a modern art gallery. The neo-Gothic **Domkyrka** *(open Mon-Fri summer)* dates from 1893 and has an unusual altar-piece.

Teknikens Hus (☎ 492201; adult/child Skr50/30; open daily mid-June–Aug, Tues-Sun rest of year)*, within the university campus 4km north, is a museum with hands-on exhibitions of technological phenomena (take bus No 17 or 35).

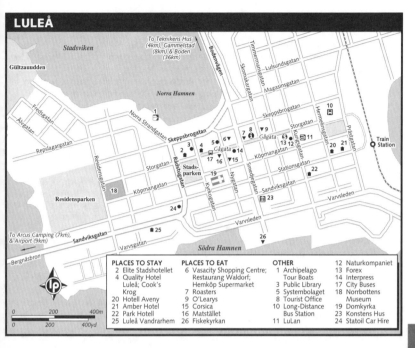

LULEÅ

PLACES TO STAY
2 Elite Stadshotellet
4 Quality Hotel
  Luleå; Cook's
  Krog
20 Hotell Aveny
21 Amber Hotel
22 Park Hotell
25 Luleå Vandrarhem

PLACES TO EAT
6 Vasacity Shopping Centre;
  Restaurang Waldorf;
  Hemköp Supermarket
7 Roasters
9 O'Learys
15 Corsica
16 Matstället
26 Fiskekyrkan

OTHER
1 Archipelago
  Tour Boats
3 Public Library
5 Systembolaget
8 Tourist Office
10 Long-Distance
  Bus Station
11 LuLan

12 Naturkompaniet
13 Forex
14 Interpress
17 City Buses
18 Norrbottens
  Museum
19 Domkyrka
23 Konstens Hus
24 Statoil Car Hire

0   200   400m
0   200   400yd

The most famous sight in Luleå is the Unesco World Heritage-listed **Gammelstad**, or 'Old Town', which was the medieval centre of northern Sweden. The stone church (from 1492), 424 wooden houses (where the pioneers stayed overnight on their weekend pilgrimages) and six church stables remain. Many of the buildings are still in use, but some are open to the public. Guided tours (Skr30) of the site leave from the Gammelstad **tourist office** (☎ 254310; ⓔ worldheritage.gammelstad@lulea.se; open 9am-6pm daily mid-June–mid-Aug, 10am-4pm Tues-Thur rest of year) frequently between 10am and 4pm, mid-June to mid-August. The open-air museum **Hägnan**, the old shop **Lanthandeln** and a nature reserve are nearby, and there are craft shops and a number of cafés in the area to rest weary sightseeing legs. Take hourly bus No 32 from Luleå to the area (Skr22).

A programme of **boat tours** of the archipelago with M/S *Laponia* and M/S *Favourite* depart from Norra Hamnen daily between June and August; typical prices are around Skr150. Evening cruises are also popular; inquire at the tourist office.

Places to Stay

Arcus Camping (☎ 435400; ⓔ camping@lulea.se; low/high season tent sites Skr110/140, chalets from Skr480/540) is 7km west of town, in a wooded, waterside setting not far from the E4 (take bus No 6).

There's no STF hostel in town. The SVIF **Luleå Vandrarhem** (☎ 222660; Sandviksgatan 26; dorm beds Skr150) doesn't look like much from the outside, but inside it's clean and comfortable. The large dorms are not so great (tri-level bunks) – better are the twin rooms, for only a little extra (Skr175 per person).

There are a number of mid-range options near the train station: **Park Hotell** (☎ 211149; ⓔ hotellet@parkhotell.se; Kungsgatan 10; singles/doubles from Skr490/690, discounted to Skr390/550) offers pleasant rooms (some have private bathroom and cost a little extra). A step up, **Amber Hotel** (☎ 10200; ⓔ hotel.amber@telia.com; Stationsgatan 67; singles/doubles Skr790/950, discounted to Skr440/590) has rooms in a pretty, wooden guesthouse. **Hotell Aveny** (☎ 221820; Hermelinsgatan 10) offers comfortable rooms at the same price as Amber Hotell.

NORRLAND

Gammelstad

During the 13th century the Pope increased the number of fast days, during which only fish could be eaten. This resulted in the rich Gulf of Bothnia fishing grounds becoming of great interest to the rest of Europe, and meant profit for whoever controlled the area.

With the northern border between Sweden and Russia insecure after the Treaty of Nöteborg in 1323, the Swedish crown secured control of northern Bothnia by handing over its river valleys as fiefs to noblemen from central Sweden. In 1327, Luleå was named for the first time in connection with such an enfeoffment and, in the 1340s, the region became a parish of its own, with separate chapels in Piteå and Torneå.

By the end of the 14th century, Luleå Old Town (today's Gammelstad) was the centre of a parish stretching from the coast to the mountains along the Lule and Råne rivers. The Luleå farmers prospered during the economic boom of the Middle Ages and a stone church was built in the 15th century.

In 1621, Luleå was granted a town charter but its development progressed very slowly. This proved to be rather fortunate because by 1649 the previously navigable channel from the archipelago had become too shallow and it was necessary to move the whole city to a better harbour, namely the present northern harbour of the current Luleå City. The church, the church village and the surrounding buildings became Luleå Old Town (Gammelstad).

Gammelstad church is the largest medieval church in Norrland and the only one with a reredos worthy of a cathedral and choir stalls for a whole consistory.

The church village developed because parishioners had to travel considerable distances to attend church and required overnight accommodation. Today, Gammelstad is the largest church village in Sweden.

There are two historical walks around Gammelstad – the church walk and town walk – each can be done in approximately one hour.

The town's two finest hotels are neighbours at the eastern end of Storgatan – both have upmarket facilities, restaurants, bars as well as nightclubs, and prices are identical: singles/ doubles Skr1195/1395, discounted to Skr590/790. **Elite Stadshotellet** (☎ 67000; ℮ stadhotellet@lulea.elite.se; Storgatan 15) has more old-world charm and elegance than the more modern **Quality Hotel Luleå** (☎ 201000; ℮ lulea@quality.choicehotels.se; Storgatan 17), which also has a pool.

Places to Eat

Cook's Krog (☎ 211800; Storgatan 17; meals Skr80-250), at the Quality Hotel, is a cosy place specialising in steaks and other meat and fish from the charcoal grill.

Restaurang Waldorf (☎ 222616; Storgatan; lunch Skr65, meals Skr85-175), inside the Vasacity shopping centre, is a busy place, especially at lunchtime. It has a bizarre menu featuring almost every known cuisine, from Italian to Chinese, including Japanese and Swedish.

In an old warehouse at the south harbour, atmospheric **Fiskekyrkan** (☎ 220201; Södra Hamn; meals Skr50-170) is a favourite with the locals, and its not hard to see why – there's live music Wednesday to Saturday, plus an affordable lunch buffet (Skr69) and a range of meals on offer, from fast-food cheapies (kebabs and pizzas) to more 'gourmet' offerings. This is also a popular drinking spot.

Friendly **Corsica** (☎ 15840; Nygatan 14; meals under Skr100), nearby, has an extensive menu of good-value meals (eg, salads, pasta, souvlaki, fish).

Bright, modern **Matstället** (cnr Nygatan & Storgatan; meals Skr40-60) is a cut above most fast-food outlets, with an appealing interior and a great selection of food (pizzas, kebabs, burgers, pasta, Tex-Mex and Asian dishes) at kiosk prices.

There is a very good **café** on either side of the tourist office, including pricier **Roasters** (☎ 88840; Storgatan 43; lunch Skr62), with great coffee, an interesting menu of trendy café fare (eg, grilled focaccia and ciabatta) and excellent cakes.

Central **O'Learys** (☎ 16616; Skomakargatan 22) is another appealing pub serving up a good range of food.

There's a **Hemköp supermarket** in the Vasacity shopping centre on Storgatan; to purchase alcohol, visit nearby **Systembolaget** (Storgatan 25).

Getting There & Around

Air The airport (☎ 244900) is 9km southwest of the town centre. SAS/Skyways fly regularly to Stockholm, Sundsvall and Umeå, and Malmö Aviation flies daily to Stockholm. Other airlines serve smaller destinations, including Gällivare and Kiruna. Take the airport bus (Skr40) outside the Elite and Comfort Hotels on Storgatan.

Bus Bus No 100 is one of the most useful for travellers – it runs between Haparanda, Luleå, Skellefteå, Umeå and Sundsvall at least four times daily. Bus No 28 runs frequently to Boden, bus No 21 goes to Arvidsjaur (via Boden and Älvsbyn), and bus No 44 to Jokkmokk and on to Gällivare (via Boden and Vuollerim).

Train Direct Tågkompaniet trains from Stockholm and Gothenburg run at night only. Most trains from Narvik and Kiruna via Boden terminate at Luleå.

Car & Taxi For car rental you should call **Statoil** (☎ 18622; Stationsgatan 30). If you need a cab, call **Luleå Taxi** (☎ 10000).

BODEN
☎ 0921 • pop 28,400

Boden is Sweden's largest military town and it's surrounded by forts built between 1901 and 1998 to defend the country from the Russians. The town was closed to foreigners but there are few restrictions now. Boden has all facilities, including a friendly **tourist office** (☎ 62410; e info@upplevboden.nu, w www .upplevboden.nu; Kungsgatan 40; open daily June-Aug, Mon-Sat rest of year), in the middle of the town centre and surrounded by the usual facilities.

Rödbergsfortet (☎ 483060; tours adult/ child Skr75/35; open daily late-June–mid-Aug), south of the town centre, is the only fort remaining from Boden's old defences. It's open to guided tours only – these run every half-hour from 10am to 4pm. **Pansarmuseet** (☎ 68156; adult/child Skr20/free; open 11am-4pm Mon-Fri, noon-4pm Sat & Sun mid-July–mid-Aug), 3km towards Jokkmokk, is a museum of tanks and armoured cars. On the southwestern edge of town, **Garnisonsmuséet**

(☎ 68399; Sveavägen; admission free; open 11am-4pm Mon-Fri, noon-4pm Sat & Sun mid-July–mid-Aug) faithfully re-creates living conditions for the troops in the past.

Western Farm (☎ 15100; Buddbyvägen 6; adult/child Skr75/50; open daily July–mid-Aug), 3km north of the station, is an unexpected find in this part of the world – it's a small Wild West town with staff dressed up as native Americans, cowboys, etc, with regular events and entertainment.

Luleå has a better selection of places to stay and eat, but there's a good **STF Vandrarhem** (☎ 13335; Fabriksgatan 6; dorm beds from Skr120) opposite the train station. In the heart of town is **Quality Hotel Bodensia** (☎ 17710; Kungsgatan 47; singles/doubles Skr895/1130, discounted to Skr595/790), with comfortable, well-equipped rooms and good discounted rates. There's no shortage of pizzerias, grill bars and other eateries in town. **Hanssons** (☎ 54484; Drottninggatan 9) is a pleasant café with a good selection of lunchtime snacks.

The Viking-style train station is a kilometre east of the town centre. See the previous Luleå section for bus and train details.

HAPARANDA
☎ 0922 • pop 10,400

Haparanda was founded in 1821 as a trading town to replace Sweden's loss of Tornio to Russia (now in Finland). These days the two border towns almost function as one entity (both the krona and euro are accepted at most places in both towns; Tornio is an hour ahead of Haparanda).

Haparanda's **tourist office** (☎ 12010; e info.turism@haparanda.se, w www.hapar anda.se/turism; Torget 7) is in Stadshotellet. There is another, joint, Haparanda-Tornio tourist office located on the 'green line'.

There are few sights in Haparanda and the ugly church looks exactly like a grain silo, but one noteworthy attraction is the unique golf course. The **Green Zone Golf Course** (☎ 10660) is right on the border of the two countries; during a full round of golf the border is crossed exactly four times. The cost to play 18 holes is €22 and club hire is an additional €10. You will need to book in advance if you want to play under the midnight sun.

Full-day **boat tours** (☎ 13395) of the archipelago sail on Wednesday and Thursday in

July (adult/child Skr450/350), and include a visit to **Sandskär**, the largest island in Haparanda Skärgård National Park. Inquire at the tourist office about **white-water rafting** trips on the Kukkolaforsen rapids; two hours on the river costs around €50.

The scenic **Kukkolaforsen** rapids, on the Torne älv 15km north of Haparanda, run at three million litres per second and you can watch **fishing** for whitefish using medieval dip nets in summer. There's an excellent tourist village here that includes a **camping ground and cabins** (☎ 31000; tent sites Skr140, 4-bed cabins from Skr480), restaurant, café, fish smokehouse, saunas and a museum, and it's well worth a visit.

The excellent **STF Vandrarhem** (☎ 61171; e info@haparandavandrarhem.com; Strandgatan 26; dorm beds from Skr110; open year-round) is not far from the town centre. There's a kitchen and meals are available in the attached café. Farther up the road, **Resandehem** (☎ 12068; Storgatan 65B; singles/doubles Skr150/250) is a simple guesthouse offering basic but comfortable accommodation. The large, once-grand **Stadshotellet** (☎ 61490; Torget 7; singles/ doubles Skr1090/1390, discounted to Skr610/810; summer budget beds Skr195) is the focus of the town, and its pub-restaurant, the **Gulasch Baronen** offers a great range of reasonably priced meals (from Skr65 to Skr110).

Tapanis Buss (☎ 12955) runs express coaches from Tornio to Stockholm three or four times a week (Skr500). Regular buses connect Haparanda and Tornio (Skr10). There are regional buses from Luleå (Skr110) and towns farther south, and daily bus No 53 travels north along the border via the scenic Kukkolaforsen rapids, Övertorneå and Pajala, then continues west to Kiruna (Skr250).

THE INTERIOR

Northern parts of Norrbotten are dominated by forest and wandering reindeer, and there are numerous small towns to use as pit stops for further exploration.

The first major town you'll encounter if you head north from Haparanda, following the Torneälven river that marks the border with Finland, is the dull **Övertorneå**; there's a bridge across the river to Finland, and a tourist office by the bridge.

West of Övertorneå is **Överkalix**, a much better option – it's located at a scenic river

junction on the Kalixälv and has little hills nearby. The area is popular with anglers; ask for permits at the **tourist office** (☎ 0926-10392; w www.overkalix.se; Storgatan 27). There's a road to the top of the nearby hill **Brännaberget**, where there's a fine view. **Sirillus**, about a kilometre from the northern end of the bridge, is a beautiful Russian Orthodox church with an octagonal tower. **Martingården**, 5km north on road No 392, is a 17th-century **farm museum** with 'Överkalix paintings' on a cupboard and bed. There are a couple of eateries in the town, mostly grill bars.

There's a sign to commemorate the crossing of the Arctic Circle on road No 392, and about 12km north of here is **Jockfall**, an impressive waterfall with a nearby **camping ground** (☎ 0926-60033; tent sites from Skr60, cabins from Skr500), shop and **café-restaurant** (meals Skr38-98) serving locally caught salmon. This scenic area is a paradise for fishing folk.

Pressing on farther north, **Pajala** (population 7300) has the **world's largest circular sundial** and a helpful **tourist office** (☎ 0978-10015; w www.pajalaturism.bd.se) located at the bus station. Other things worth a look are **Laestadius pörtet**, the mid-19th-century home of Lars Levi Laestadius, local vicar and founder of a religious movement, and **Kengis Järnbruk**, a 17th-century iron foundry.

Bykrogen (☎ 0978-71200; Soukolovägen 2; singles/doubles Skr650/850) offers comfortable, newly renovated hotel rooms in Pajala, plus there's a wide range of meals on offer at its attached restaurant, **Linkan** (meals Skr60-200), a surprisingly modern, attractive dining room. There are a couple of other eateries in town, as well as a camping ground, cabins and two more hotels. At the camping ground you can rent bikes, canoes and boats.

Bus No 55 runs from Luleå to Pajala via Överkalix, while bus No 53 runs between Haparanda and Kiruna via Övertorneå and Pajala. From Pajala, you can press on southwest to Gällivare (bus No 46), or northwest to Vittangi (bus No 51 or 53), and from Vittangi you can journey through the wilderness north to Karesuando (bus No 50), west to Kiruna (bus No 53).

See the Getting There & Away chapter for details of bus links with Finland over this northern border.

Lappland

KARESUANDO (GÁRRASAVVON)
☎ 0981 • pop 350

This remote place is the northernmost village in Sweden and lies across the bridge from the Finnish town of Kaaresuvanto. From 26 May to 17 July, there's a 90% chance of observing the midnight sun, but in winter temperatures drop to -50°C.

There's a seasonal **tourist office** (☎ 20205; Ⓦ www.karesuando.com; open May-Sept), near the bridge across to Finland. Inside there's regional information, souvenirs and a café serving drinks and cakes. There are no banks in the town, but there are grocery shops and service stations; eating options are very limited.

Items of interest in Karesuando are an **octagonal school** (1993); **Vita Huset**, a folk museum with mainly Norwegian items from WWII; and **Sámiid Viessu**, a Sami art and handicraft exhibition and museum.

Treriksröset, about 100km northwest of the village, is the point where Norway, Sweden and Finland meet; ask the tourist office for details of boats leaving from Kilpisjärvi (on the Finnish side of the border) to visit this hard-to-access area.

There's a small **STF Vandrarhem** (☎ 20000; dorm beds Skr125; open mid-May–mid-Sept) way up here, about a kilometre before you reach the bridge and tourist office, and across the road from the hostel is **Hotel Karuesando** (☎ 20330; singles/doubles Skr550/650), with a restaurant serving good, simple meals.

Motell Arctic (☎ 20370; doubles with shared facilities Skr450) is 1km towards Kiruna and also has a restaurant serving mostly fast-food and grill items, for around Skr60.

See Kiruna for transport details.

KIRUNA (GIRON)
☎ 0980 • pop 23,900

Kiruna is the northernmost town in Sweden and, at 19,446 sq km, its district is the largest in the country. The area includes Sweden's highest peak, **Kebnekaise** (2111m) and several fine national parks and hiking routes; see the previous Abisko section and the Hiking special section for details. This far north, the midnight sun lasts from 31 May to 14 July, and there's a bluish darkness throughout December and New Year. Many people speak Finnish and Samis are

a small minority. It's worth making the effort to get up here!

The helpful and efficient **tourist office** (☎ 18880; Ⓔ lappland@kiruna.se, Ⓦ www.kiruna.se, Ⓦ www.lappland.se; Lars Janssonsgatan 17; open 8.30am-9pm Mon-Fri, 8.30am-6pm Sat & Sun June-Aug, Mon-Sat rest of year) is next to the Scandic Hotel and has loads of excellent brochures. Staff can arrange various activities including rafting, dog sledging and snow scooter trips, but they can be quite expensive.

Banks and other facilities can be found on Lars Janssonsgatan, and the **library**, behind the bus station, offers Internet access.

Things to See & Do

A visit to the depths of the **LKAB iron-ore mine**, 540m underground, is recommended – many of the facts about this place are mindboggling. English-language tours depart from the tourist office regularly from mid-June to mid-August (Skr140/50, 2½ hours); make bookings through the tourist office.

Kiruna kyrka (Gruvvägen; open 10am-9pm daily summer) looks like a huge Sami kåta (hut), and it's particularly pretty against a snowy backdrop. Another landmark, the very ugly **Stadshus** (town hall; ☎ 70521; Hjalmar Lundbohmsvägen; open 9am-6pm daily), is actually very nice inside and has a free slide show on the hour and free guided tours.

Hjalmar Lundbohms-gården (☎ 70110; Ingenjörsgatan 1; adult/child Skr30/10; open 8am or 10am-6pm Mon-Fri summer) is the former home of the first LKAB director and is now a museum. **Samegården** (☎ 17029; Brytaregatan 14; adult/child Skr20/free; open 10am-5pm Mon-Fri summer) has displays about Sami culture and an expensive handicrafts shop.

As well as the famous Ice Hotel, tiny **Jukkasjärvi**, 18km east of Kiruna, is home to a **church** (open 8am-10pm daily summer), which has a modern Sami painting behind the altar. Near the church is **Gárdi** (adult/child Skr60/30; tours 1pm-4pm Mon-Fri mid-June–mid-Aug), a reindeer yard that you can tour with a Sami guide to learn about reindeer farming and Sami culture. Also in this area is the **Hembygdsgård**, an open-air homestead museum. Regular bus No 501 runs between Kiruna and Jukkasjärvi (Skr23).

Some 27km farther out is the space base **Esrange**, which researches the northern lights

NORRLAND

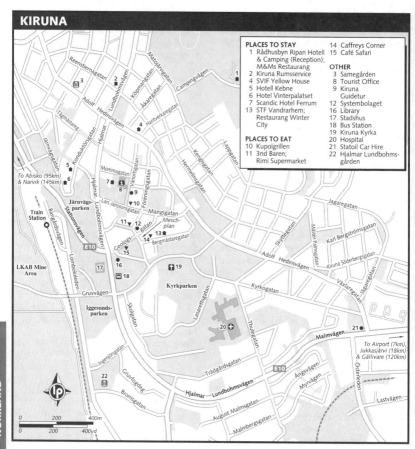

KIRUNA

PLACES TO STAY
1 Rådhusbyn Ripan Hotell & Camping (Reception); M&Ms Restaurang
2 Kiruna Rumsservice
4 SVIF Yellow House
5 Hotell Kebne
6 Hotel Vinterpalatset
7 Scandic Hotel Ferrum
13 STF Vandrarhem; Restaurang Winter City

PLACES TO EAT
10 Kupolgrillen
11 3nd Baren; Rimi Supermarket

14 Caffreys Corner
15 Café Safari

OTHER
3 Samegården
8 Tourist Office
9 Kiruna Guidetur
12 Systembolaget
16 Library
17 Stadshus
18 Bus Station
19 Kiruna Kyrka
20 Hospital
21 Statoil Car Hire
22 Hjalmar Lundbohms-gården

(norrsken) – see the boxed text 'Arctic Phenomena' in this chapter. Detailed four-hour tours (Skr290) of the facility are offered to enthusiasts in summer; inquire at the tourist office.

Places to Stay

In the northern part of town, **Rådhusbyn Ripan Hotell & Camping** (☎ 63000; e ripan@kiruna.se; Campingvägen 5; tent sites Skr100, hotel singles/doubles Skr650/750, 4-bed cabins Skr650) is a large and well-equipped ground. It has hotel-standard chalets in addition to its caravan and tent sites, and there's a pool in summer and a very good restaurant on site.

The central **STF Vandrarhem** (☎ 17195; Bergmästaregatan 7; dorm beds Skr130, singles/doubles Skr245/310; open year-round) has good facilities and also an adjacent Chinese restaurant. SVIF **Yellow House** (☎ 13750; e yellowhouse@mbox301.swipnet.se; Hantverkaregatan 25; dorm beds Skr120, singles/doubles Skr300/400) also has excellent facilities, including a sauna, kitchen and laundry, and a TV in each room.

A good option is the **Kiruna Rumsservice** (☎ 19560; e krs@kiruna.se; Hjalmar Lundbohmsvägen 53; doubles from Skr350), especially for small groups. It offers rooms and apartments with a varying number of beds. Breakfast is additional (Skr45). Or try **Hotell Kebne** (☎ 68180; e info@hotellkebne; Konduktörsgatan 7; singles/doubles Skr945/1125, discounted to Skr595), with comfortable rooms and good summer rates.

Arctic Phenomena

Aurora Borealis

There are few sights as mesmerising as an undulating aurora. Although these appear in many forms – pillars, streaks, wisps and haloes of vibrating light – they're most memorable when they take the form of pale curtains, apparently wafting on a gentle breeze. Most often, the Arctic aurora appears as faint green, light yellow or rose, but in periods of extreme activity it can change to bright yellow or crimson.

The visible aurora borealis, or northern lights *(norrsken)*, are caused by streams of charged particles from the sun and the solar winds, which are diverted by the earth's magnetic field towards the polar regions. Because the field curves downward in a halo surrounding the magnetic poles, the charged particles are drawn earthward here. Their interaction with atoms in the upper atmosphere (about 160km above the surface) releases the energy creating the visible aurora. (In the southern hemisphere, the corresponding phenomenon is called the aurora australis.) During periods of high activity, a single auroral storm can produce a trillion watts of electricity with a current of one million amps.

Although science dismisses it as imagination, most people report that the aurora is often accompanied by a crackling or whirring sound. Don't feel unbalanced if you hear it – that's the sort of sound you'd expect to hear from such a dramatic display, and if it's an illusion, it's a very convincing one.

The best time of year to catch the northern lights in Sweden is from October to March, although you may well see them as early as August in the far north.

Midnight Sun & Polar Night

Because the earth is tilted on its axis, the polar regions are constantly facing the sun at their respective summer solstices and are tilted away from it in the winter. The Arctic and Antarctic Circles, at 66°32' north and south latitude respectively, are the southern and northern limits of constant daylight on the longest day of the year.

The northern one-seventh of Sweden lies north of the Arctic Circle but, even in central Sweden, the summer sun is never far below the horizon. Between late May and mid-August, nowhere north of Stockholm experiences true darkness and in Umeå, for example, the first stars aren't visible until mid-August. Although many visitors initially find it difficult to sleep while the sun is shining brightly outside, most people get used to it.

Conversely, winters in the far north are dark and bitterly cold, with only a few hours of twilight to break the long polar nights. During this period, some people suffer from SAD (seasonal affective disorder) syndrome, which occurs when they're deprived of the vitamin D provided by sunlight. Its effects may be minimised by taking supplements of vitamin D (as found in cod liver oil) or with special solar spectrum light bulbs.

NORRLAND

The pretty **Hotel Vinterpalatset** (☎ 67770; e vinterp@kiruna.se; Järnvägsgatan 18; singles/doubles from Skr725/890, discounted to Skr490/590) is near Hotel Kebne and has pleasant upmarket rooms, plus good-value accommodation in a cheaper annexe.

Scandic Hotel Ferrum (☎ 398600; e ferrum@scandic-hotels.com; Lars Janssonsgatan 15; singles/doubles Skr1212/1410, discounted to Skr690/840), near the tourist office, is a town landmark. It offers the finest rooms in town and has excellent facilities, including a café, restaurant and nightclub on the premises.

Places to Eat

Kiruna is not particularly well endowed with great eateries, but the **M&Ms Restaurang** (Campingvägen; meals Skr95-225), at the camping ground (of all places) is an excellent restaurant with an interesting, creative menu, including tortillas, beef fillets, reindeer, salmon, vegie dishes and burgers. The lunch buffet is Skr75, dinner is Skr130.

3nd Baren (Föreningsgatan 11; meals Skr85-240) is a popular, moderately priced restaurant and lively drinking spot of an evening; you can try local specialities like reindeer or arctic char, and there are also vegetarian selections.

Caffreys Corner (☎ 61111; Bergmästaregatan; meals Skr75-185) is an unremarkable restaurant with a comprehensive menu, but the cosy bar is an inviting place, and there's an outdoor terrace where you can take advantage of good weather.

The Ice Hotel

The absolute highlight of a trip this far north is a visit to the fabulous **Ice Hotel** (**W** *www.iceho tel.com*), truly a unique and super-cool experience, if you'll pardon the pun.

Every winter at Jukkasjärvi, 18km east of Kiruna, an amazing structure is built from hundreds of tonnes of ice taken from the frozen local river. This custom-built 'igloo' has a chapel (popular for weddings – giving new meaning to the expression 'cold feet'!), plus a bar – you can enjoy a drink (preferably vodka) from a glass made purely of ice – and exhibitions of beautiful ice sculpture by international artists. It also has 50 'hotel rooms' where guests can stay, on beds covered with reindeer skins and inside sleeping bags guaranteed to keep you warm despite the -5°C temperatures (and in winter that's nothing – outside the hotel it can be as low as -30°C!).

There are numerous activities for guests to pursue here, and staff can arrange an afternoon snowmobile safari, skiing, ice-fishing, dog sledging etc. And if cultural pursuits are more your cup of tea, for the winter of 2002–3, there were plans to construct a replica of Shakespeare's Globe Theatre from ice near the hotel, and Sami theatre groups were to perform *Hamlet* in their language (tickets were expected to cost around Skr500, and it's hoped that this will become an annual winter event).

All this can be quite pricey for a budget traveller, but anyone can visit the hotel on a day visit (adult/child Skr100/50), and it's highly recommended. If you do visit, ask the bartender where the stereo is being kept – chances are it's in the fridge, as it's warmer there!

In summer, after the Ice Hotel has melted away, visitors can still experience a little of the magic. Inside a giant freezer warehouse (called the **Ice Hotel Art Center**), at a temperature of -5°C, there are a few of the Ice Hotel features: a bar, ice sculptures and even small igloos where guests can stay overnight. Day visitors are welcome (entry fee is the same as in winter; warm clothing is supplied; open daily).

Rooms inside the hotel in winter cost from Skr1960 for two, igloos in summer cost from Skr1000. There are also stylish new hotel rooms (heated – and *not* made of ice; Skr1095/645 per person in winter/summer), three-bed cabins with skylights enabling you to watch the northern lights in winter (Skr775 to Skr1045 per person in winter, Skr900 per cabin in summer), and chalets with kitchen sleeping up to four (from Skr535 per person in winter, Skr700 per chalet in summer). These are all available year-round – summer prices are quite reasonable. See the website for more details, plus a list of seasonal rates.

Restaurang Winter City (☎ 10900; Bergmästaregatan 7; lunch Skr65, meals Skr55-140) is at the STF hostel, offering a lunch special, plus a range of pizzas as well as classic Chinese and other Asian dishes.

Kupolgrillen (*Vänortsgatan 2*) is a decent central spot for burgers and kebabs. The nicest café in town is **Café Safari** (☎ 17460; Geologsgatan 4), with good coffee, cakes and light meals like sandwiches, quiche and baked potatoes.

Jukkasjärvi Wärdshus is opposite the Ice Hotel in Jukkasjärvi and was closed for renovations at the time of research, so we were unable to determine prices. Given that the restaurant is under the same management as the Ice Hotel, however, you can expect high standards and prices to match.

The **Rimi supermarket** is on Föreningsgatan near 3nd Baren and **Systembolaget** (*Geologsgatan 7*) is also central.

Getting There & Around

The small **airport** (☎ 68000), 7km east of the town, has two to three daily nonstop flights to Stockholm with SAS, and to Umeå (weekdays only) with Skyways. The **airport bus** (☎ 15690) connects with most flights (Skr40).

Regional buses to/from the bus station, on Hjalmar Lundbohmsvägen, opposite the Stadshus, serve all major settlements around Norrbotten. Bus No 10 runs twice daily to Gällivare (Skr110) and Luleå (Skr230), and No 92 goes two to four times daily to Nikkaluokta (Skr64) for the Kebnekaise trail head. To reach Karesuando (Skr146) and Finland, take bus No 50 (not Saturday). Bus No 91 runs two or three times daily to Riksgränsen (Skr110) via Abisko (Skr87).

Trains connect Kiruna with Luleå (Skr215), Stockholm (Skr350) and Narvik (Norway; Skr168). Trains to Narvik call at Abisko (Skr70) and Riksgränsen (Skr95).

Contact **Statoil** *(☎ 14365; Växlaregatan 20)* for car hire.

Standard bicycles are available for hire from **Kiruna Guidetur** *(☎ 81110; Vänortsgatan)* for Skr75/295 per day/hour. Mountain bikes are also available (Skr125/495).

ABISKO (ABESKOVVU)

☎ 0980 • pop 180

The 75-sq-km **Abisko National Park**, on the southern shore of scenic Lake Torneträsk, is well served by trains, buses and the scenic mountain highway between Kiruna to Narvik. It's the soft option of the northern parks – less rugged and more accessible. Abisko is the driest place in Sweden, with only 300mm of rainfall per year. One of the most renowned mountain profiles in Lappland, **Lapporten**, can be seen from Abisko.

The popular **Kungsleden** trail follows the Abiskojåkka valley and day trips of 10km or 20km are no problem from Abisko village. Kungsleden extends 450km south from Abisko to Hemavan, but STF huts and lodges don't serve the whole route; see the Hiking special section for more details. Other fine hikes include the overnight trip to the STF hut at **Kårsavagge** (west of Abisko, 15km each way), the four-hour return trip to the rock formations at **Kärkevagge** with **Rissájávrre** the 'Sulphur Lake', and the four-hour return hike to **Paddus**, a former Sami sacrificial site, 4km south of Abisko Östra station,. There's also a short route around **Abisko canyon** and the 39km-long **Navvy Trail** to Riksgränsen, alongside the railway line. Use the map Fjällkartan BD6 (available at the STF lodge).

The **Naturum** *(☎ 40177; open daily July–mid-Sept)*, next to the STF lodge in Abisko, provides good information. The **Linbana** chair lift (one-way/return from Skr70/95) takes you to 900m on **Njulla** (1169m), where there's a **café** *(open 9.30am-3pm)*. In Björkliden, 8km northwest of Abisko, **Hotell Fjället** *(☎ 64100; W www.bjorkliden.com)* offers various summer and winter activities, including a half-day cave tour for Skr195. There are tours that are also organised by STF at Abisko Turiststation; and both places offer outdoor gear that is for hire.

Places to Stay & Eat

Abisko Fjällturer *(☎ 40103; e info@abisko.net; camping/dorm beds per person Skr60/125)*, just behind the town, is a backpackers delight. The small hostel has basic comfortable accommodation and a wonderful wooden sauna, but the treat is in the reasonably priced activities on offer, especially in winter. Owner Tomas and his father keep a large team of sledge dogs, and for Skr500 in winter you get a night's hostel accommodation plus the chance to drive your own sledge, pulled by dogs, for about 10km. There are also very popular week-long sledge trips for Skr7900, which include all of your meals and accommodation – you will need to book very early for these. During summer you can take mountain walks with the dogs. Read more on W www.abisko.net.

Abisko Fjällstation *(☎ 40200; e info@abisko.stfturist.se; dorm beds from Skr170)* is another excellent option, kept to the usual high STF standards. Trekking gear can be hired here, there's a variety of guided tours, a shop with basic groceries, and breakfast/lunch/dinner costs Skr70/70/155. There's an **ICA supermarket** in Abisko village for self-caterers, and a restaurant nearby.

Hotell Fjället *(☎ 64100; e info@bkorkliden.com; tent sites from Skr70, cabins from Skr595, singles/doubles from Skr640/980)* is a well-equipped resort about 8km northwest of Abisko in Björkliden and offering camping and cabin accommodation as well as a large hotel. There are loads of facilities, including restaurant, bar, equipment rental (ski gear, or bicycles, golf, fishing and hiking gear in summer), organised activities, and even a nine-hole golf course. Prices listed here are for summer, and these increase significantly in the peak skiing months. See the website for more details of rates.

Låktatjåkko *(☎ 64100; dorm beds from Skr410)*, 9km farther west of Hotell Fjället, is the highest place to stay in Sweden, at 1228m, and you'll have to hike into the hills to reach it. It has good facilities for weary hikers, including sauna and restaurant, and breakfast is included in the tariff.

Self-service **STF huts** along Kungsleden are spread at 10km to 20km intervals between Abisko and Kvikkjokk; you'll need a sleeping bag. A bed costs from Skr160 to Skr220 (non-STF members pay an additional Skr50). Day visitors/campers are charged Skr25/45. See Accommodation in the Facts for the Visitor chapter and the 'Hiking' special section.

The really excellent 100km trek from Abisko to Nikkaluokta runs via the STF lodge

Kebnekaise Fjällstation (☎ 0980-55000; ⓔ info@kebnekaise.stfturist.se; dorm beds from Skr260; open Mar-Apr & mid-June–mid-Sept). Meals are available here, and guided tours to the summit of Kebnekaise are offered.

Getting There & Away
In addition to trains (stations at Abisko Östra and Abisko Turiststation) between Luleå and Narvik, bus No 91 runs from Kiruna to Abisko.

RIKSGRÄNSEN
☎ 0980 • pop 50
The best midnight (or daytime) skiing in June in Scandinavia awaits you at this rugged frontier area (Riksgränsen translates as 'National Border'). You can briefly visit Norway at full speed on downhill skis! Rental of downhill gear costs from Skr210 per day, and a day lift pass is Skr250.

There's not much to the tiny settlement here, but you can visit Sven Hörnell's **wilderness photography exhibition** at his own gallery (☎ 43111; open daily Feb-Sept). The exhibition itself is free, and there's an excellent audiovisual show daily at 3pm June to August (Skr60). The commentary is in Swedish, but you don't have to understand to appreciate the stunning photography.

The historical Navvy Trail walkway that follows the railway line takes you to Abisko (39km) or Rombaksbotn in Norway (15km).

Katterjåkk Turiststation (☎ 43108; ⓔ kat terjakk@kiruna.frilufts.se; summer dorm beds from Skr170; open Feb-Sept) is a well-run hostel 2km east of Riksgränsen.

Riksgränsen (☎ 40080; ⓔ info@riksgransen .nu; summer/winter accommodation from Skr405/715 per person) is a large resort popular with skiers in winter and offering an 'alpine spa' retreat in summer, plus lots of organised wilderness activities in both seasons (also open to nonguests). There's a café and restaurant here, and you can rent outdoor gear including mountain bikes and canoes.

Getting There & Away
From Kiruna, bus No 91 (two or three daily) goes to Riksgränsen (Skr110), via Abisko. Riksgränsen is the last train station in Sweden before the train rushes through tunnels and mountain scenery back to sea level at Narvik in Norway; three daily trains run on the Luleå-Kiruna-Narvik route.

GÄLLIVARE (VÁHTJER)
☎ 0970 • pop 19,700
Gällivare and its northern twin, Malmberget, are surrounded by forest and dwarfed by the bald Dundret hill. After Kiruna, Malmberget is the second largest iron-ore mine in Sweden.

The helpful **tourist office** (☎ 16660; ⓔ tur istinfo@gellivare.se, ⓦ www.gellivare.se; Storgatan 16; open daily mid-June–mid-Aug; Mon-Fri rest of year) is near the church in the town's centre, and staff can organise a number of activities and wilderness excursions. The town has all main facilities, primarily on Storgatan, and including banks and supermarkets. The **library** (Hantverkaregatan) has Internet access.

Stora Sjöfallet National Park
This wild area of mountains and lakes lies over 115km west of Gällivare, but transport links are good. At the eastern end of the park, you can cross the Stora Lulevatten lake on the STF ferry to Saltoluokta lodge and climb **Lulep Gierkav** (1139m) for the best views.

There's an interesting **Sami church** and inexpensive **handicraft outlet** at Saltoluokta, and the **Kungsleden trail** runs north and south from here. **Stora Sjöfallet** is now dry due to the hydroelectric schemes, and many of the local lakes have artificial shorelines. Take the bus to the end of the road at the Sami village **Ritsem**, where there's an STF lodge, and you can cross by ferry to the northern end of the **Padjelantaleden trail**. See the Hiking special section for details.

Other Attractions
The **Hembygdsmuseum** (admission free; open 11am-3.30pm daily mid-June–mid-Aug, Mon-Fri rest of year), above the tourist office, is a cute collection of local artefacts. The 1882 **church** (open daily summer) is also worth a look. The old church near the train station dates from 1755.

The **hembygdsområde** (open daily summer), by the camping ground, has pioneer and Sami huts in a small open-air museum in a pretty setting.

Dundret (821m) is a nature reserve with excellent views; you can see the midnight sun here from 2 June to 12 July. In winter there are four nordic courses and 10 ski runs of varying difficulty, and the mountain-top resort (see Places to Stay) rents out gear and organises numerous activities.

In Malmberget, 5km north of Gällivare, **Kåkstan** *(admission free; open daily)* is a historical 'shanty town' museum village dating from the 1888 iron-ore rush. Contact the Gällivare tourist office for details of the **LKAB iron-ore mine tour** *(Skr150; mid-July–late-Aug)*. Also of interest is the **Gruvmuseum** *(open 2pm-5pm Tues-Thur mid-July–late-Aug)*, covering 250 years of mining. Bus No 1 to Malmberget departs from directly opposite the Gällivare church.

The Gällivare tourist office also runs tours of the **Aitik copper mine** on weekdays from late June to early August for Skr150/75 per adult/child, if there is enough of a demand for it.

Places to Stay & Eat

Gällivare Camping *(☎ 10010; Hembygdsområdet; tent sites Skr100, 2-bed cabins Skr300; open June-early Sept)* is in a lovely spot beside the river. The **STF Vandrarhem** *(☎ 14380; Barnhemsvägen 2; dorm beds Skr120; closed May & Oct)* is just across the footbridges from the train station; and you will be able to hire bikes here.

Quality Hotel Gällivare *(☎ 55020;* e *gal livare@quality.choicehotels.se; Lasarettsgatan 1; singles/doubles Skr1090/1450, discounted Skr690/890)* is a central place opposite the train station. It has comfortable rooms and a good restaurant.

Dundret *(☎ 14560;* e *info@dundret.se; summer singles/doubles Skr750/895, cabins from Skr510)*, at the top of Dundret hill, is a large resort offering hotel and cabin accommodation, as well as a restaurant, outdoor gear rental and lots of activities, especially in winter. Prices are considerably higher in winter (singles/doubles Skr1080/1390, cabins from Skr690).

Your dining choices are pretty limited. Your best bet for anything other than fast food is the **Vassara Pub** *(Lasarettsgatan 1; lunch Skr68, meals Skr70-220)* which is located at the Quality Hotel, offering good-value lunch and a decent selection of à la carte dishes.

The eastern part of Storgatan is home to two reasonable restaurants: at No 17, **New Delhi** *(☎ 16960)* serves a range of Indian meals; **Restaurang Peking** *(☎ 17685)* at No 21 has Chinese and Thai dishes on offer. Both places have good lunch deals, priced around Skr65.

Getting There & Away

Regional buses depart from the train station. Bus No 45 runs daily to Östersund via Jokkmokk and Arvidsjaur, bus No 93 serves Ritsem and Kungsleden in Stora Sjöfallet National Park (mid-June to mid-September only), bus Nos 10 and 52 go to Kiruna and bus No 44 runs to Jokkmokk and Luleå.

Tågkompaniet trains come from Luleå and Stockholm (sometimes changing at Boden), and from Narvik in Norway. More exotic is Inlandsbanan, which terminates at Gällivare; the train journey from Östersund costs Skr485.

JOKKMOKK (DÁLVADDIS)
☎ 0971 • pop 5900

The village of Jokkmokk, which can be reached by Inlandsbanan, is just north of the Arctic Circle and started as a Sami market and mission. Since 1605, the **Sami winter fair** has taken place here; the three-day event attracts some 30,000 people and starts on the first Thursday in February, when you can shop seriously for Sami *duodji* (handicraft).

The **tourist office** *(☎ 12140;* e *turist@ jokkmokk.se,* w *www.turism.jokkmokk.se; Stortorget 4; open daily mid-June–mid-Aug, Mon-Fri rest of year)* can help with information, and has Internet access. There are banks and other facilities in the small town centre.

Things to See & Do

The **Ájtte museum** *(☎ 17070; Kyrkogatan 3; adult/child Skr50/free; open 9am-6pm daily mid-June–mid-Aug, 10am-4pm Mon-Fri rest of year)* is the highlight of a visit to Jokkmokk; it gives the most thorough introduction to Sami culture anywhere in Sweden, including Sami dress, silverware and an interesting display of 400-year-old shamans drums. It has extensive notes in English. The museum offers exhaustive information on Lappland's mountain areas, with a full set of maps, slides, videos and a library. A visit is recommended for planning wilderness trips.

Naturfoto *(☎ 55765; open daily June-Aug)*, at the main Klockartorget intersection, exhibits and sells work by local wilderness photographer, Edvin Nilsson. The beautiful **wooden church** *(Storgatan; open daily June-Aug)*, near Naturfoto, should be seen; the 'old' octagonal church on Hantverkargatan has been rebuilt, as the original was burned down in 1972.

Sami Culture & Traditions

Sami life was originally based on hunting and fishing but, sometime during the 16th century, the majority of reindeer were domesticated and the hunting economy transformed into a nomadic herding economy. While reindeer still figure prominently in Sami life, only about 16% of the Sami people are still directly involved in reindeer herding and transport by reindeer sledge, and only a handful of traditionalists continue to lead a truly nomadic lifestyle.

A major identifying element of Sami culture includes the *joik* (or *yoik*), a rhythmic poem composed for a specific person to describe their innate nature and is considered to be owned by the person it describes (see Sami under Population & People in the Facts about Sweden chapter). Other traditional elements include the use of folk medicine, Shamanism, artistic pursuits (especially woodcarving and silver smithing) and striving for ecological harmony.

The Sami national dress is the only genuine folk dress that's still in casual use in Sweden, and you'll readily see it on the streets of Jokkmokk, especially during the winter fair. Each district has its own distinct features, but all include a highly decorated and embroidered combination of red and blue felt shirts or frocks, trousers or skirts, and boots and hats. On special occasions, the women's dress is topped off with a crown of pearls and a garland of silk hair ribbons.

NORRLAND

Jokkmokks Fjällträdgård *(adult/child Skr25/free)*, by the lake, introduces mountain trees and other local flora. Just across the road, you'll find a **homestead museum**. **Jokkmokks Stencenter**, with lapidary and mineral exhibits, is reached from Borgargatan. These attractions are all open daily in summer, but keep irregular hours the rest of the year; check with the tourist office for details.

About 7km south of Jokkmokk you will cross the **Arctic Circle**; on road No 45 there is a café and campsite at the site; the café gives certificates for those interested in having proof that they have travelled this far north!

Hiking

Kvikkjokk (Huhttán), around 100km west of Jokkmokk, is on the **Kungsleden** and **Padjelantaleden** trails – see the Hiking special section. There are several great day walks from the village, including climbs to **Sjnjerak** (809m, three hours return), a steeper ascent of **Prinskullen** (749m, three hours return), and **Nammatj** (662m, two hours, but this requires taking a boat to the quay on the southern side of Tarraänto).

The best hiking of all is in **Sarek National Park** (☎ 0920-96200); ask a tourist office for advice on transport from Tjåmotis to Aktse/Rapadalen via Sitoälvsbron. The trail along the Laitaure lake is very poor and it's advisable to go by boat (once or twice daily from midsummer to August).

Places to Stay & Eat

Jokkmokks Camping Center (☎ 12370; ✉ campingcenter@jokkmokk.com; *tent sites Skr120, double hostel-style rooms Skr300, cabins from Skr510*) is 3km southeast of town and is popular in summer.

Gula Villan (☎ 55026; *Stationsgatan; singles/doubles Skr125/200*) is the yellow guesthouse with the sign advertising 'rum' as you exit the train station; rooms are simple but adequate. The STF hostel **Åsgård** (☎ 55977; ✉ asgard@jokkmokkhostel.com; *Åsgatan 20; dorm beds from Skr110; open year-round*) is a clean, comfortable place behind the tourist office.

Of good value is **Hotell Gästis** (☎ 10012; *Herrevägen 1; singles/doubles Skr700/900, discounted to Skr600/700*), it has very pleasant rooms, although it doesn't look too promising from the outside! There's also a good restaurant here, with lunch specials and à la carte dinners.

There is an unexpected surprise at the park located near the tourist office; here you will find a caravan where you can actually buy authentic takeaway **Laotian food** *(Skr55 for lunch)*. If you go to the Ájtte museum **restaurant** you can try local fish or perhaps a sandwich with reindeer meat (lunch specials Skr60).

Café Piano (☎ 10400; *Porjusvägen 4*) is another good choice – with a grand piano inside, a large garden outside and an extensive menu, including pasta and wok meals priced around Skr60.

There's a **Konsum supermarket** (Storgatan) in town.

Getting There & Away

Buses arrive and leave from the bus station on Klockarvägen. Bus Nos 44 and 45 run daily to/from Gällivare (Skr87), and bus No 45 to/from Arvidsjaur once daily (Skr133). Bus No 94 runs to Kvikkjokk (Skr110, twice daily).

Inlandsbanan trains stop in Jokkmokk. For main-line trains, take bus No 94 to Murjek via Vuollerim (up to six times daily) or bus No 44 bus to Boden (Skr118) and Luleå (Skr139). Another alternative is bus No 36 to Älvsbyn via Bredsel, where you can visit the spectacular 82m Storforsen, Europe's greatest cataract-falls (best in May/June).

ARVIDSJAUR

☎ 0960 • pop 7100

The small settlement of Arvidsjaur, on Inlandsbanan, was an early Sami market. The **tourist office** (☎ 17500; e info@arvidsjaurturism.se, w www.arvidsjaurturism.se; Garvaregatan 4; open daily mid-June–mid-Aug, Mon-Fri rest of year) is behind the park by the main square and can help provide useful information. There are facilities such as banks and supermarkets on Storgatan, the main road through town.

Lappstaden (admission free; open 24hr), a well-preserved Sami church village, contains almost 100 buildings as well as forestry and reindeer-breeding concerns. Guided tours cost Skr25 (July only). From early July to early August an old **steam train** makes return evening trips to Slagnäs on Friday and Moskosel on Saturday (Skr140/free). Also in summer is the opportunity for **white-water rafting** (adult/child Skr330/165) on the nearby Piteälven.

Arvidsjaur is bustling in winter, when test drivers from around Europe put their cars through their paces in the tough weather conditions, and there are excellent cold-weather activities available, including dog sledging. Inquire at the tourist office for more details of all activities.

Friendly, cosy **Lappugglans Turistviste** (☎ 12413; Västra Skolgatan 9) and the small, stylish **Rallaren** (☎ 070 682 3284; Stationsgatan 4; open summer only), both near the train station, have excellent hostel accommodation for Skr130 per person. **Kaffestugan**

(☎ 12600; Storgatan 21) is a popular café by the main square, with good daily lunch specials (Skr60), plus an assortment of cakes, sandwiches and light meals. There's also **Athena** (☎ 10595; Storgatan 10) offering pastas, salads and grill dishes for under Skr100.

The daily bus between Gällivare and Östersund (No 45) stops at the bus station on Storgatan. Bus No 200 runs daily between Skellefteå and Bodø (Norway) via Arvidsjaur. The Inlandsbanan train can take you north to Gällivare via Jokkmokk, or south to Mora via Östersund.

SORSELE

☎ 0952 • pop 3100

Sleepy Sorsele, on Inlandsbanan, has the **Inlandsbanemuseet** (adult/child Skr20/free; open daily summer) at the train station – a must for train enthusiasts. The **tourist office** (☎ 14090; e turist@vindelalven.se), at the Inlandsbanemuseet, has details of local activities, including fishing (very popular) and canoe tours. Sorsele has all facilities, including a bank, supermarket and public library (with Internet).

The local **Hembygdsgård** (open daily June-Aug) has a good café with home-made food. Also out this way is the STF **Vandrarhem** (☎ 10048; dorm beds Skr110, cabins per person Skr140), 500m west of the train station. Reception is at the nearby **camping ground** (☎ 10124; tent sites Skr75, 4-bed cabins from Skr295), with a swimming pool, plus bikes and canoes for hire.

NORRLAND

The Inlandsbanan train stops here and bus No 45 runs daily on the Gällivare–Jokkmokk–Arvidsjaur–Sorsele–Storuman–Östersund route.

TÄRNABY & AROUND
☎ 0954

In the Swedish lake district, Tärnaby, 125km northwest of Storuman on the E12, has most facilities and a **tourist office** (☎ 10450; w www.tarnaby.se; open daily mid-June–mid-Aug, Mon-Fri rest of year). The tourist office organises various local talks and tours in summer, including Sami culture evenings, fishing, hiking, cave tours and glacier tours. Mountain biking is a warm-weather activity growing in popularity in the region. There's a very popular winter **ski area** here, and many of Sweden's champion skiers hail from the area – ask at the tourist office if the planned museum dedicated to them and their achievements has opened. Take the time to hike to the top of **Laxfjället** (820m) for great views of the lakes.

Samegården (☎ 10440; Tärnafors; adult/child Skr30/15; open Mon-Fri summer), 5km east of the tourist office, has exhibits about the Sami and their lifestyle.

Hemavan, 18km north of Tärnaby, has a larger **ski area** and a summer **chairlift** (adult/child return Skr60/45), plus basic facilities. The southern entry to **Kungsleden**, Sweden's finest hiking route, is here, but most people do this section starting in Ammarnäs (see the Hiking special section).

The **STF Vandrarhem** (☎ 30002; dorm beds from Skr130; open Mar-May & mid-June–Sept) is a well-equipped place with good-value accommodation and meals available.

Friendly **Hotell Sånninggården** (☎ 33000; e bjarne@sanningarden.com; B&B/full board per person from Skr325/595), 6km north of Hemavan, is an excellent place with good-value, cosy accommodation and an acclaimed **restaurant** (lunch buffet Skr99, dinner mains Skr130-260). If you're out this way, it's well worth stopping in for a unique meal – the extensive menu includes well-prepared elk or reindeer fillet, game birds like grouse and capercaille, Arctic char, and even the occasional bear dish! There are vegetarian options for those uncomfortable with consuming the local wildlife, and the magnificent desserts will please everyone – try the delectable arctic raspberry and cloudberry parfait.

See the Storuman section for information on transport.

UMNÄS
☎ 0951

Umnäs Skoterhotellet (☎ 52020; e frihet.i.lapland@telia.com; dorm beds Skr150, singles/doubles Skr650/850) is a friendly place, about 6km off the scenic E12 road (also known as the Blå Vägen, or Blue Hwy), 64km northwest of Storuman. This is a great out-of-the-way tourist 'village' of sorts – there's a hotel with bar and restaurant (meals Skr35 to Skr185), hostel and self-contained cabins available, plus the opportunity for some great activities in the vicinity, including guided or self-guided snowmobile safaris (February to April is best). You will also find a really unique **snow scooter museum** (admission Skr40; open daily) on the premises here, which contains some 70 vehicles from the 1960s right up to the present, as well as a separate **museum** (admission Skr20) of local history.

The **Silent Way** (☎ 52043; w www.silent-way.com) is also based in Umnäs, near the hotel (and run by another family member). This company offers excellent guided **dog-sledging tours**, from December to May, with trips possible from a half-day excursion (US$90) to a 16-day safari. Appropriate cold-weather gear can be rented, and food and accommodation in cabins is included in the cost. These trips are extremely popular, so book well ahead. The website has comprehensive information, as well as options, schedules and prices.

Buses between Storuman and Tärnaby stop at Slussfors on the E12, about 8km from Umnäs.

STORUMAN
☎ 0951 • pop 6800

Storuman, on Inlandsbanan, has an interesting location at the southern end of the 56km-long lake with the same name. The very scenic road **Strandvägen** links the centre with a series of islands including **Luspholmen**, with a small outdoor museum. Follow the road Utsiktsvägen (across the E12 from the train station) for 1.5km to the viewpoint **Utsikten**; sunsets over the lake are magnificent. Sweden's largest **wooden church** is at **Stensele**, about 3km from Storuman towards Umeå on the E12.

NORRLAND

The **tourist office** (☎ 33370; ℯ entrelapp land@swipnet.se; Järnvägsgatan 13; open daily June-Aug, Mon-Fri rest of year) is at Hotell Luspen, near the station, and the town has most facilities.

Hotell Luspen (☎ 33380; ℯ luspenhotell@swipnet.se; hostel singles/doubles Skr200/300, hotel singles/doubles Skr600/720, discounted to Skr480/580) is a friendly place by the train station, offering accommodation to suit most budgets. The helpful tourist office is also here, and you can rent bikes for exploration for Skr60 per day.

There are a couple of eating options in the centre of the village, but the pick is **Nya Grill 79** (☎ 77000; meals Skr35-115), 1.5km towards Tärnaby on the E12 in a not-too-aesthetic locale (between two petrol stations). It offers an extensive menu (burgers, salads, Mexican dishes, souvlaki, vegetarian options) and excellent value.

Bus No 45 runs every day on the Gällivare–Jokkmokk–Arvidsjaur–Sorsele–Storuman–Östersund route. Buses between Mo i Rana in Norway and Umeå also run daily, via Storuman and Tärnaby and the **Lapplandspilen** (☎ 33370) buses run overnight three times weekly from Hemavan to Stockholm via Storuman. In summer, Inlandsbanan trains stop here.

FATMOMAKKE & AROUND

The southern areas of Lappland have some of the finest mountain scenery in Sweden, particularly around the mountain **Marsfjället** (1560m); you can hike up and back from Fatmomakke, but it's a long day (28km, 10 hours). The trek through the mountains to the village **Kittelfjäll** (where the scenery is even more impressive), via the wilderness cabin **Blerikstugan**, is best over two days (32km).

The late-18th-century **Sami church village** at Fatmomakke has an exhibition, *kåtas* (huts) and other old buildings. Silver shamanistic Sami jewellery was found here in 1981. The end of the public road is a tourist trap, but there are cheap, basic **camp site** (sites Skr30).

Klimpfjäll is about 20km west, and **Saxnäs**, a small village set in a scenic spot between lakes and considered a paradise for fishing folk, is about 25km east.

The journey south from Fatmomakke into Jämtland, close to the Norwegian border, offers some stunning scenery (mountains, plateaus, small lakeside settlements) and is highly recommended, although it's only possible with your own transport.

Jämtland

ÖSTERSUND
☎ 063 • pop 58,400

This pleasant town by Storsjön lake, in whose chill waters lurks a rarely sighted monster (the Storsjöodjuret), has very good budget accommodation and is worth a visit for a couple of days. Many of the attractions lie on the adjacent island of Frösön, where there's a winter-sports centre.

Jämtland used to be Norwegian; many of the locals still maintain an independent spirit and Östersund is the start of the St Olavsleden pilgrim route to Trondheim in Norway.

The huge four-day music festival, Storsjöyran, is usually around the last weekend in July and the town centre gets sealed off in the evenings. Some 50,000 people attend, but it's very expensive with admission costing up to Skr350 per evening. Accommodation prices also shoot up at this time.

Information

The **tourist office** (☎ 144001; ℯ turisbyran@ostersund.se, ☑ www.turist.ostersund.se; Rådhusgatan 44; open daily mid-June– Aug, 9am-5pm Mon-Fri rest of year) is opposite the town hall. The good-value Östersund Card (adult/child Skr120/55), valid for nine days between June and mid-August, gives discounts or free entry to many local attractions.

The large **public library** opposite the bus station has free Internet access. The town has all facilities, including banks, supermarkets and shops selling outdoor gear, primarily on Prästgatan.

Things to See & Do

Don't miss **Jamtli** (☎ 150100; adult/child June-Aug Skr90/free, rest of year Skr60/free; open daily June-Aug, Tues-Sun rest of year), a kilometre north of the town centre. This museum is the highlight of Östersund, combining the lively exhibitions of the regional museum and a large museum village with staff wearing period clothing in summer. The regional museum exhibits the curious **Överhogdal Tapestry**, a Christian Viking relic from around 1100 which features lots of animals, people, ships and also buildings

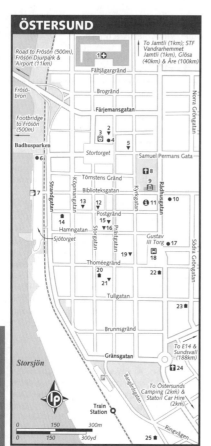

ÖSTERSUND

PLACES TO STAY
14 Östersunds Vandrarhem
20 Pensionat Svea
22 First Hotel Gamla Teatern
23 STF Vandrarhem
25 Vandrarhemmet Rallaren

PLACES TO EAT
2 Bistro Artist; Radisson Hotel; Café Artist
5 News
12 Kebab City
13 Brunkullans
15 Volos
16 Captain Cook
19 Domus Supermarket
21 Paviljong Thai

OTHER
1 Hospital
3 Theatre
4 Systembolaget
6 Badhusparken Uthyrningscenter
7 S/S (Thomée) Boat Departures
8 Gamla Kyrkan
9 Stadsmuseum
10 Rådhus
11 Tourist Office
17 Public Library
18 Bus Station
24 Stora Kyrkan

weekly from June to August. Book any of these at the tourist office. Canoes and fishing gear can be rented from **Badhusparkens Uthyrningscenter** (☎ 133838; Sjötorget).

Frösön This island is reached by road or footbridge from the middle of Östersund (the footbridge is from the pleasant Badhusparken – nearby you can rent bikes, inline skates and canoes). Just across the footbridge, outside Landstingshuset and near the Konsum supermarket, there's Sweden's northernmost **rune stone** which commemorates the arrival of Christianity in 1050.

Also featured on the island are the animals at **Frösöns Djurpark** (☎ 514743; bus No 5; adult/child Skr100/50; open daily mid-June–mid-Aug) as well as the restored, late-12th-century **Frösöns kyrka** (bus No 3; open 8am-8pm daily in summer, Mon-Fri rest of year), with its characteristic separate bell tower. If you are a skier there are both slalom and nordic runs on the island at Östberget, where there is a **viewing tower** (Skr10/5; open daily mid-May–mid-Sept) giving you fine views.

(including churches). It's one of the oldest of its kind in Europe and may even predate the famous Bayeux tapestry.

The **Stadsmuseum** (☎ 121324; adult/child Skr30/free; open daily June-Aug, Tues-Sun rest of year), across the street from the tourist office, contains items of local historical, cultural and topographical interest. The adjacent **Gamla Kyrkan** is the old town church, completed in 1846. The impressive brick building with cupola and the tiled roof is the **rådhus** (town hall).

Lake cruises on the old S/S Thomée steamship from June to early September cost from Skr65 to Skr95. There are also **sightseeing coach trips** (adult/child Skr90/30), **town walks** (Skr65/30) as well as the **elkspotting safaris** (Skr185/95) at least once

Glösa Rock Carvings Glösa, 40km north-west of Östersund and by the Alsensjön lake, has some of the finest **Stone Age rock carvings** *(admission free; open 24hr)* in Sweden. The carvings, on rock slabs beside a stream, feature large numbers of elk and date from 4000 BC. There's also an excellent reconstruction of a **Stone Age hut** and replicas of skis, snowshoes, a sledge and an elk-skin boat.

Nearby, there are some displays about elk-hunting using traps (prohibited since 1864) and more modern methods. There are roughly 13,000 *fängstgropar* (pit traps) in Jämtland, set in lines across migration routes; a short walk through the woods (follow the sign 'Fornminne') will take you to four of them.

Take bus No 533 from Östersund (two or three daily), then follow the sign from the public road (500m walk).

Places to Stay
The large and well-equipped **Östersunds Camping** *(☎ 144615; e ostersundcamping@ostersund.se; bus No 2, 6 or 9; tent sites from Skr100, hostel doubles from Skr280, cabins from Skr300)*, off Krondikesvägen, is 2km southeast of the town centre and right beside a large adventure swimming pool.

You can live among Östersund's big attraction: the quaint STF **Vandrarhemmet Jamtli** *(☎ 122060; dorm beds Skr140-160)* is inside the Jamtli museum precinct. A second, summer-only **STF Vandrarhem** *(☎ 139100; Södra Gröngatan 36; dorm beds from Skr95; open late June-early Aug)* is clean and central.

Östersunds Vandrarhem *(☎ 101027; Postgränd 4; dorm beds Skr145)* is in the centre, and **Vandrarhemmet Rallaren** *(☎ 132232; Bangårdsgatan 6; dorm beds Skr140)* is conveniently located next to the train station. **Frösötornets Härbäge** *(☎ 515767; Utsiktsvägen 10; dorm beds from Skr130; open May-Oct)* has hostel beds in wonderful turf-roofed huts at the viewing tower on Frösön.

Pensionat Svea *(☎ 512901; e pensionat svea@spray.se; Storgatan 49; singles/doubles Skr440/540)* is a cosy place close to the heart of town; prices include breakfast.

Elegant **First Hotel Gamla Teatern** *(☎ 511600; e bokning@gamlateatern.se; Thoméegränd 20; budget singles/doubles Skr902/1152, discounted to Skr502/652)* is in an old theatre. The budget rooms are OK and the summer prices are reasonable; better standard rooms cost Skr200 to Skr250 more.

Places to Eat
Bistro Artist *(☎ 556010; Prästgatan 16; mains Skr100-215)*, at the Radisson hotel, is a lovely restaurant offering predominantly Italian fare, including pasta dishes priced from Skr100 to Skr140. The adjacent **Café Artist** is a more casual place with light meals and the usual café fare for under Skr100.

Popular, classy **Brunkullans** *(☎ 101454; Postgränd 5; mains Skr100-200)* has a great late-19th-century atmosphere and an appealing menu, with gourmet pasta dishes, fish, steak and other classic dishes on offer, which can be enjoyed in the outdoor courtyard. The lunch buffet is excellent value at Skr65.

News *(☎ 101131; Samuel Permans gata 9; mains Skr110-280)* is a slick and somewhat pricey – new bar and bistro frequented by the fashionable set, who don't mind paying around Skr120 for a salad! There's trendy decor, good service and a pleasant outdoor terrace. Mains include, burgers, steak and rack of lamb, plus vegetarian options. Lunch is a better option, with filled bagels and ciabatta from Skr45.

Paviljong Thai *(☎ 130099; Prästgatan 50B; lunch from Skr60, dishes Skr60-150)* serves good-sized portions of great Thai cuisine, with all the favourite noodle, curry and seafood dishes on the menu.

Captain Cook *(☎ 126090; Hamngatan 9; meals Skr50-150)* is an Australian-themed pub with a good menu of pub food, ranging from light snacks to more hearty fare, with a selection of imported and local beer to wash it down.

Kebab City *(☎ 137022; Storgatan 31)* serves burger, kebab and falafel meals for around Skr50.

Most restaurants are on Prästgatan, the main pedestrian street, including **Volos** *(☎ 516689; meals Skr60-170)* at No 38, with something for everyone's tastes – pizzas, pasta, nachos, salads, kebabs, Greek dishes and more.

The **Domus supermarket** *(Kyrkgatan)* is just behind the bus station and **Systembolaget** *(Stortorget)* is a few blocks north.

Getting There & Around
The **airport** *(☎ 193000)* is on Frösön, 11km west of the town centre, and SAS flies several

NORRLAND

times daily to Stockholm. The airport bus leaves regularly from the bus terminal (Skr50).

The train station is a short walk south from the town centre, but the main regional bus station is central on Gustav III Torg; local buses usually run to both. Local bus Nos 1, 3, 4, 5 and 9 go to Frösön (Skr15, or free with the Östersund Card).

Bus No 45 runs south to Mora twice a day; in summer the Inlandsbanan train runs once daily to Gällivare (Skr485) or Mora (Skr240). Bus No 156 runs west to Åre; bus No 63 runs twice daily northeast to Umeå.

Direct trains run from Stockholm via Gävle, and some continue to Storlien (from where you can catch trains to Norway). You can also catch a train east to Sundsvall.

For car hire, contact **Statoil** (☎ 123975; *Krondikesvägen 97*). Bikes can be hired from **Badhusparkens Uthyrningscenter** (☎ 133838; *Sjötorget*), beside Badhusparken, for Skr50/200 per day/week; you can also get in-line skates here. There are also **taxis** (☎ 517200).

ÅRE & AROUND
☎ 0647 • pop 9600

Arguably Sweden's top mountain-sports destination, the Åre area (**w** *www.skistar.com /are*) has 45 ski lifts that serve some 100 pistes and 1000 vertical metres of skiable slopes, including a superb 6.5km downhill run (day pass Skr270). The skiing season is from November to mid-May, but conditions are best from February, when daylight hours increase, and Easter is a hugely busy time. Unfortunately, Åre gets far too busy in winter and you can hardly move, let alone park your car. **Duved** is quieter.

The Åre **tourist office** (☎ 17720; *open daily*) is in the train station. Most facilities are around the main square, which you reach by walking through the park opposite the station.

There are also excellent cross-country tracks in the area, and winter activities such as dog-sledging, snowmobile safaris and sleigh rides (which are horse- or reindeer-drawn!) are available. Åre also offers great summer outdoor recreation, including hiking, kayaking, rafting, fishing as well as mountain biking. The area west of Åre is popular among fell-walkers: there's a network of STF wilderness huts and lodges here for enthusiasts.

Places to Stay & Eat

In winter it's best to book accommodation and skiing packages via **Åre Resor** (☎ 17700; **e** *reservations@areresort.se*).

Åre Camping (☎ 50054; *tent sites from Skr130*) is a good summer option. **Park Villan** (☎ 17733; *Parkvägen 6; dorm beds Skr170*), the yellow house in the park opposite the train station, offers good backpacker accommodation outside of the ski season. The **STF Vandrarhem** (☎ 30138; **e** *brattlandsgarden@user .bip.net; dorm beds Skr120*) is 8km east of Åre. Not all hotels stay open in summer, but those that do offer great bargains. The huge ski lodge and resort **Åre Fjällby** (☎ 13600; **e** *reception@arefjallby.com; summer self-contained apartments from Skr520*), for example, had an offer at the time of research whereby you paid for two nights and received a third night free.

Like the hotels, the majority of restaurants are closed in summer, but there are still some very good choices, primarily centred on the main square. Typical Swedish fast food is available at **Åre Kiosk & Grill**, but nearby **Liten Krog** and **Werséns** (both with dishes from around Skr70) have more style. **Villa Tottebo**, opposite the train station, is a classy establishment open year-round. Evening main courses are Skr145 to Skr220, and there's an inviting bar upstairs. There's a **Konsum supermarket** on the square.

Getting There & Away

Regional bus No 156 runs from Östersund and connects Åre to the nearby winter-sports centre of Duved (much quieter and more family-oriented than Åre). Regular trains between Stockholm and Storlien, via Östersund, stop at Åre. Storlien is the terminus for SJ trains; change here for Norwegian trains to Hell and Trondheim.

STORLIEN & AROUND
☎ 0647

The area west of Åre is justly popular among fell-walkers, and Sylarna is one of the finest mountains in Sweden. The main track in the area forms the Jämtland Triangle just north of Sylarna; see the Hiking special section for details. There's a very good network of **STF wilderness huts and lodges** and meals are available in most lodges. Reservations aren't possible, but you're guaranteed a sleeping spot (possibly the floor).

Storlien, near the Norwegian border, has a fairly popular downhill skiing area (even the Swedish king has a winter chalet here), a supermarket, and a **tourist office** (☎ 70570; ⓔ *info@storlienfjallen.com*, Ⓦ *www.storlienfjallen.com*) at the train station.

There is an excellent **STF Vandrarhem** (☎ 70050; *dorm beds Skr100-120*) at Storvallen, 600m off the E14, about 5km east of Storlien, offering quality accommodation, good meals, friendly service and good hiking advice. **Le Ski**, in the village at Hotel Storlien, has a daily buffet (Skr89) plus a good menu of reasonably priced meals like pizza, meatballs, salmon and steak (mains Skr50 to Skr150).

See Getting There & Away under Åre & Around for transport information.

Härjedalen

pop 11,300

The least populated of Sweden's counties, Härjedalen could easily earn the epithet Empty Quarter. It's a wilderness of forest, lake and mountain in the west, and forest, lake and marsh in the east. The scenery in the far northwest is spectacular. Only one of the handful of small towns in the region is of any interest.

FUNÄSDALEN & AROUND
☎ 0684

Dominated by the impressive peak **Funäsdalsberget**, Funäsdalen and the surrounding area is of interest to outdoor sports enthusiasts.

The town has a **tourist office** (☎ 16410; ⓔ *info@funasdalsfjall.se*, Ⓦ *www.funasdalsfjall.se*; *Rörosvägen 30; open daily mid-June–mid-Aug, Mon-Fri rest of year*) is at the Fjällmuseum, and all the main tourist facilities are on Rörosvägen, the main road through town.

Things to See & Do

Härjedalens Fjällmuseum (☎ 16410; *adult/child Skr60/free; open daily*) has displays covering the Sami, local farmers and miners and includes the **Fornminnesparken** outdoor section. A **golf course**, one of Sweden's finest, can be found in Ljusnedal, just east of town.

Rogens Naturum (☎ 24200; *adult/child Skr30/free; open daily June-Aug & Dec-Apr*), located 15km south at Tännäs Fiskecentrum,

has information on the **Rogen Nature Reserve**, including the moraine ridges and the local musk ox. There's excellent hiking in the reserve, but it's better accessed from Grövelsjön in Dalarna. **Högvålen**, about 30km south of Tännäs on road No 311, is Sweden's highest village (830m).

Ramundberget, over 20km north of Funäsdalen, and **Tänndalen** (12km west), have excellent downhill and nordic **ski areas**. There are 24 ski lifts and 75 runs, and the 300km of cross-country trails constitute the longest ski system in the world. The profile of the mountain **Stor-Mittåkläppen** (1212m), as seen from Hågnvallen (4km east of Ramundberget), is most impressive.

Ljungdalen, about 40km north of Funäsdalen, is close to **Helagsfjället** (1797m), the highest peak in the area. There's good hiking and skiing here; the 12km one-way hike from Kläppen (north of Ljungdalen) to the STF cabin at Helags goes via some old **summer farms** and it's reasonably easy. There is also a small **ski area** as well as a **tourist office** (☎ 0687-20079).

Places to Stay & Eat

There are a few **STF hostels** in the area, including at Ljungdalen (☎ 0687-20285; *Dunsjögården; dorm beds Skr110*) and Tännäs (☎ 0684-22111; *Skavruets Fjällhotell; dorm beds Skr115-135*). Both are open year-round.

Off the main road in Funäsdalen is **Hotel Funäsdalen** (☎ 21430; ⓔ *info@hotell-funasdalen.se; summer hostel beds Skr175, singles/doubles Skr520/790*) is a large, well-equipped hotel with a range of accommodation options plus a good restaurant.

Wärdshuset Gyllene Bocken (☎ 21090; ⓔ *info@gyllenebocken.se; summer singles/doubles from Skr415/650*) is a lovely old inn opposite the fine golf course in Ljusnedal, with a good restaurant attached. Rooms with private facilities are also available. The staff can organise golf for guests, plus other activities in the area.

Veras Stekhus & Pub (☎ 21530; *lunch Skr89, mains Skr145-215*) in the heart of Funäsdalen, near the tourist office, is a relatively upmarket steakhouse with a great view from its outdoor terrace and a comprehensive menu of steak, reindeer and other meats (not much to please vegetarians). Not far away is **Café Loftet** (☎ 29149), with good café fare such as baguettes, quiche and salads from

NORRLAND

Skr30, plus more of that scenic panorama from its veranda.

Getting There & Away

Härjedalingen runs buses between Stockholm and Funäsdalen (Skr360) via Gävle and Järvsö several days weekly; on Saturday buses also connect with Tänndalen and Ramundberget. Contact the tourist office for information and bookings.

Local bus Nos 622 and 623 run from Funäsdalen to Ramundberget and Tänndalen, respectively; there are also daily ski buses during winter. There is not a direct connection with Ljungdalen; you should take the once-daily bus No 613 from Åsarna (which has an Inlandsbanan train station), about 100km east. Bus No 164 runs from Funäsdalen via Åsarna to Östersund once or twice daily.

Language

SWEDISH

Swedish is a Germanic language, belonging to the Nordic branch, and is spoken throughout Sweden and in parts of Finland. Swedes, Danes and Norwegians can make themselves mutually understood. Most Swedes speak English as a second language.

Since they share common roots, and the Old Norse language left sprinklings of words in Anglo-Saxon, you'll find many similarities between English and Swedish. The pronunciations differ, however, and there are sounds in Swedish that aren't found in English: try repeating the correct pronunciation of 'Växjö'. There are three extra letters at the end of the Swedish alphabet, namely **å**, **ä** and **ö**.

Swedish verbs are the same regardless of person or number: 'I am, you are' etc are, in Swedish, *Jag är, du är* and so on. There are two genders in Swedish, common (non-neuter) and neuter. They are reflected in the articles *en* and *ett* (a/an). The definite article (the) is added to the ends of nouns, eg, *ett hus* 'a house', *huset* 'the house'. There are no set rules for determining gender – it's something that has to be learnt word by word.

Pronunciation

Sweden is a large country and there's considerable dialectal variety. There are sounds in Swedish that don't exist in English, so in the following pronunciation guide we've tried to give the closest possible English equivalents.

Vowels

Vowels are long except when followed by double consonants, in which case they're short. Sometimes the distinction between the vowels **o/å** and **e/ä** can be blurred. There are, however, not as many exceptions to the rules of pronunciation as there are in English.

a	short, as the 'u' in 'cut' or long, as in 'father'
e	short, as in 'bet' or long, as in 'beer'
i	short, as in 'it' or long, as in 'marine'
o	short, as in 'pot' or long, as in 'pool'
u	short, as in 'pull' or long, as in 'ooze'
y	as the 'ee' in 'feet' but with pursed lips
å	short, as the 'o' in 'pot' or long, as the 'oo' in 'poor'
ä	as the 'e' in 'bet' or as the 'a' in 'act'
ö	similar to the 'er' in 'fern'

Consonants

Most consonants have similar pronunciation to their English counterparts. The following letter combinations and sounds are specific to Swedish:

c	as the 's' in 'sit'
ck	like a 'k'; shortens preceding vowels
dj	as the 'y' in 'yes'
g	as in 'go'; sometimes as the 'y' in 'yes' before certain vowels and after **r**
sj, ch	similar to the 'ch' in Scottish *loch*
tj, rs	as the 'sh' in 'ship'

Basics

Hello.	*Hej.*
Goodbye.	*Adjö/Hej då.*
Yes.	*Ja.*
No.	*Nej.*
Please.	*Snälla/Vänligen.*
Thank you.	*Tack.*
That's fine.	*Det är bra.*
You're welcome.	*Varsågod.*
Excuse me.	*Ursäkta mig.*
I'm sorry. (forgive me)	*Förlåt.*
May I/Do you mind?	*Får jag/Gör det något?*

Language Difficulties

Do you speak English?	*Talar du engelska?*
Does anyone here speak English?	*Finns det någon här som talar engelska?*
I understand.	*Jag förstår (inte).*
I don't understand.	*Jag förstår (inte).*
Could you speak more slowly, please?	*Kan du vara snäll och tala lite långsammare?*

Small Talk

What's your name?	*Vad heter du?*
My name is ...	*Jag heter ...*
Where are you from?	*Varifrån kommer du?*
I'm from ...	*Jag kommer från ...*
How old are you?	*Hur gammal är du?*
I'm ... years old.	*Jag är ... år gammal.*

Getting Around

Where is the ...?	Var är ...?
bus stop	busshållplatsen
train station	tågstationen
tramstop	spårvagns-hållplatsen

What time does the ... leave/arrive?	När avgår/kommer ...?
boat	båten
bus (city)	stadsbussen
bus (intercity)	landsortsbussen
tram	spårvagnen
train	tåget

I'd like ...	Jag skulle vilja ha ...
a one-way ticket	en enkelbiljett
a return ticket	en returbiljett

1st class	första klass
2nd class	andra klass
left luggage	effektförvaring
timetable	tidtabell

Where can I hire a car/bicycle?	Var kan jag hyra en bil/cykel?

Directions

Where is ...?	Var är ...?
Can you show me on the map?	Kan du visa mig på kartan?
Go straight ahead.	Gå rakt fram.
Turn left.	Sväng till vänster.
Turn right.	Sväng till höger.
near	nära
far	långt

Around Town

I'm looking for ...	Jag letar efter ...
a bank	en bank
the city centre	centrum
the ... embassy	... ambassaden
my hotel	mitt hotell
the market	marknaden
the museum	muséet
the post office	posten
a public telephone	en offentlig telefon
a public toilet	en toalettkiosk
the tourist office	turistinformationen

beach	strand
castle	slott
cathedral	domkyrka
church	kyrka
main square	huvudtorg

Signs

Ingång	Entrance
Utgång	Exit
Fullt	No Vacancies
Information	Information
Öppen	Open
Stängd	Closed
Förbjuden	Prohibited
Polisstation	Police Station
Lediga Rum	Rooms Available
Toalett	Toilets
Herrer	Men
Damer	Women

monastery	kloster
old city	gamla stad
palace	palats

What time does it open/close?	Hur dags öppnar/stänger de?

Accommodation

hotel	hotell
guesthouse	gästhus
youth hostel	vandrarhem
camping ground	campingplats

Where is a cheap/good hotel?	Var är ett billigt/bra hotell?
What's the address?	Vilken adress är det?
Could you write the address, please?	Kan du skriva ner adressen?
Do you have any rooms available?	Finns det några lediga rum?

I'd like ...	Jag skulle vilja ...
a single room	ha ett enkelrum
a double room	ha ett dubbelrum
a room with a bathroom	ha ett rum med bad
to share a dorm	bo i sovsal

How much is it per person/night?	Hur mycket kostar det per person/natt?
for one night	en natt
for two nights	två nätter

Does it include breakfast?	Inkluderas frukost?
May I see it?	Kan jag får se rummet?
Where is the bathroom?	Var är badrummet?

Shopping

Could I please have ...?	*Kan jag få ...?*
How much is it?	*Hur mycket kostar den?*
bookshop	*bokhandel*
camera shop	*fotoaffär*
clothing store	*modebutik*
delicatessen	*delikatessaffär*
laundry	*tvätt*
newsagency	*pressbyrå/tabaksaffär*
souvenir shop	*souveniraffär*
stationers	*pappershandel*

Health

Where is the ...?	*Var är ...?*
chemist/ pharmacy	*apoteket*
dentist	*tandläkaren*
doctor	*läkaren*
hospital	*sjukhus*
I'm ill.	*Jag är sjuk.*
My friend is ill.	*Min vän/väninna är sjuk.* (m/f)
I'm ...	*Jag är ...*
asthmatic	*astmatiker*
diabetic	*diabetiker*
epileptic	*epileptiker*
I'm allergic to antibiotics/ penicillin.	*Jag är allergisk mot antibiotika/ penicillin.*
I need medication for ...	*Jag behöver ett medel mot ...*
I have a toothache.	*Jag har tandvärk.*
I'm pregnant.	*Jag är gravid.*
antiseptic	*antiseptisk*
aspirin	*magnecyl*
condoms	*kondomer*
diarrhoea	*diarré*
medicine	*medicin*
nausea	*illamående*
stomachache	*ont i magen*
sanitary napkins	*dambindor*
syringe	*spruta*
tampons	*tamponger*

Time & Days

What time is it?	*Vad är klockan?*
today	*idag*
tonight	*i kväll*
tomorrow	*imorgon*
yesterday	*igår*

Emergencies

Help!	*Hjälp!*
Call a doctor!	*Ring efter en doktor!*
Call the police!	*Ring polisen!*
Call an ambulance!	*Ring efter en ambulans!*
Go away!	*Försvinn!*
I'm lost.	*Jag år vilse.*

morning	*morgonen*
afternoon	*efter middagen*
night	*natt*
Monday	*måndag*
Tuesday	*tisdag*
Wednesday	*onsdag*
Thursday	*torsdag*
Friday	*fredag*
Saturday	*lördag*
Sunday	*söndag*
January	*januari*
February	*februari*
March	*mars*
April	*april*
May	*maj*
June	*juni*
July	*juli*
August	*augusti*
September	*september*
October	*oktober*
November	*november*
December	*december*

Numbers

0	*noll*
1	*ett*
2	*två*
3	*tre*
4	*fyra*
5	*fem*
6	*sex*
7	*sju*
8	*åtta*
9	*nio*
10	*tio*
11	*elva*
12	*tolv*
13	*tretton*
14	*fjorton*
15	*femton*
16	*sexton*

17	*sjutton*	pie/quiche	*paj*
18	*arton*	rice	*ris*
19	*nitton*	salt	*salt*
20	*tjugo*	sandwich	*smörgås*
21	*tjugoett*	sauce	*sås*
30	*trettio*	soup	*soppa*
40	*fyrtio*	sugar	*socker*
50	*femtio*	tomato sauce	*ketchup*
60	*sextio*	yogurt	*yoghurt*
70	*sjuttio*		
80	*åttio*		
90	*nittio*		
100	*ett hundra*		
1000	*ett tusen*		

Grönsaker & Örtkryddor (Vegetables & Herbs)

one million	*en miljon*

ärter	peas
blomkål	cauliflower
bönor	beans
champinjoner	button mushrooms
dil	dill
gräslök	chives
gurka	cucumber
haricots verts	green beans
kryddor	spices
lök	onion
majs	corn
morot	carrot
mos	mashed potatoes
paprika	capsicum
persilja	parsley
potatis	potato
purjolök	leek
rödbetor	beetroot
rödkål	red cabbage
sallad	lettuce
sparris	asparagus
spenat	spinach
svamp	mushrooms
tomat	tomato
vitkål	white cabbage
vitlök	garlic

FOOD

Could I see the menu, please?	*Kan jag får se menyn?*
Is service included in the bill?	*Är serveringsavgiften inräknad?*
I'm a vegetarian.	*Jag är vegetarian.*
I don't eat meat.	*Jag äter inte kött.*

breakfast	*frukost*
lunch	*lunch*
dinner	*middag*
menu	*meny*
children's menu	*barnmeny*
wine list	*vinlista*
first courses/entrees	*förrattter*
main course	*huvudrätter/varmrätter*
daily special (usually only at lunchtime)	*dagens rätt*
takeaway	*avhämtning*

Frukt (Fruit)

ananas	pineapple
appelsin	orange
äpple	apple
aprikos	apricot
banan	banana
blåbär	blueberries
citron	lemon
hallon	raspberries
hjortron	cloudberries
jordgubbar	strawberries
lingon	lingonberries
päron	pear
persika	peach
smultron	strawberries
vindruvor	grapes

Basics

bread	*bröd*
butter	*smör*
cheese	*ost*
chips/french fries	*pommes frites*
chocolate	*choklad*
cooking oil	*matolja*
cream	*grädde*
crispbread	*knackebröd*
eggs	*ägg*
honey	*honung*
jam/marmalade	*sylt/marmelad*
mustard	*senap*
pasta	*pasta*
noodles	*nudlar*
pepper	*peppar*

Kött (Meat)

älg	elk
and	wild duck
anka	duck
biff	beef/steak
bröst	breast
entrecote	steak
filé	fillet
fläsk/griskött	pork
gryta	casserole
kalkon	turkey
kalvkött	veal
korv	sausage
kotlett	chop/cutlet
köttbullar	meatballs
köttfars	minced beef
kyckling	chicken
lammkött	lamb
lammstek	roast lamb
leverpastej	liver paté
nötkött	beef
oxfilé	fillet of beef
oxstek	roast beef
rådjur	venison
renstek	reindeer
rostbiff	roast beef
skinka	ham

Fisk & Skaldjur (Fish & Seafood)

abborre	perch
ål	eel
forell	trout
gädde	pike
hälleflundra/ helgeflundra	halibut
hummer	lobster
kaviar	caviar
krabba	crab
kräftor	crayfish
lax	salmon
makrill	mackerel
musslor	mussels
ostron	oysters
räkor	shrimps/prawns
rödspätta	plaice
sill	herring
sjötunga	sole
strömming	Baltic herring
torsk	cod
vitling	whiting

Desserter/Efterrätter (Desserts)

äppelpaj	apple pie
glass	ice cream
kaka	cake
ostkaka	cheesecake
pannkakor	pancakes
småkakor	sweet biscuits/cookies
tårta	filled cake
våffla	waffle

Cooking Styles

bakad	roasted/baked
friterad	deep fried
gravad	cured
grillad	grilled
halstrad	grilled
kokt	boiled
marinerad	marinated
rökt	smoked
stekt	fried
ugnstekt	roasted/baked

Drinks (Drycker)

beer	*öl*
coffee	*kaffe*
cordial	*saft*
hot chocolate	*varm chokolad*
milk	*mjölk*
mulled wine	*glögg*
orange juice	*apelsinjuice*
red wine	*rödvin*
soft drink (carbonated)	*läsk*
tea	*te*
water	*vatten*
white wine	*vitt vin*
wine	*vin*

SAMI LANGUAGES

Sami languages are related to Finnish and other Finno-Ugric languages. Five of the nine main dialects of the Sami language are spoken in Sweden, with speakers of each varying in number from 500 to 5000.

Most Sami speakers can communicate in Swedish, but relatively few speak English. Knowing some Sami words and phrases will give you a chance to access the unique Sami culture.

Fell (Northern) Sami

The most common of the Sami languages, Fell Sami is considered the standard variety of the language. It's spoken in Sweden's far north around Karesuando and Jukkasjärvi.

Although written Fell Sami includes several accented letters, it still doesn't accurately represent the spoken language – even some Sami people find the written language difficult to learn. For example, *giitu* (thanks) is pronounced '**geech**-too', but the strongly aspirated 'h' isn't written.

We've included here a few Sami phrases. To learn the correct pronunciation, it's best to ask a local to read the words aloud.

Hello.	*Buorre beaivi.*
Hello. (reply)	*Ipmel atti.*
Goodbye.	*Mana dearvan.*
	(to person leaving)
	Báze dearvan.
	(to person staying)
Thank you.	*Giitu.*
You're welcome.	*Leage buorre.*

Yes.	*De lea.*
No.	*Li.*
How are you?	*Mot manna?*
I'm fine.	*Buorre dat manna.*

1	*okta*
2	*guokte*
3	*golbma*
4	*njeallje*
5	*vihta*
6	*guhta*
7	*cieza*
8	*gávcci*
9	*ovcci*
10	*logi*

Glossary

You may encounter some of the following terms and abbreviations during your travels in Sweden. See also the Language chapter and the food section in the Facts for the Visitor chapter.

Note that the letters å, ä, and ö fall at the end of the Swedish alphabet, and the letters v and w are often used interchangeably (you will see the small town of Vaxholm also referred to as Waxholm, and an inn can be known as a *värdshus* or *wärdshus*). In directories such as atlases and telephone books they fall under one category (eg, *wa* is listed before *vu*).

akti bolaget (AB) – company
allemansrätt – literally 'every man's right'; a tradition allowing universal access to private property (with some restrictions), public land and wilderness areas
apotek – pharmacy
atelje – gallery
avgift – payment, fee (seen on parking signs)
avhämtning – takeaways

bad – swimming pool, bathing place, or bathroom
bakfickan – literally 'back pocket', an ordinary, low-profile eatery usually associated with a gourmet restaurant
bankautomat – cash machine, ATM
barn – child
bastu – sauna
bensin – petrol, gas
berg – mountain
bibliotek – library
bil – car
billjet – ticket
billjetautomat – automatic ticket machines for street parking
biluthyrning – car hire
bio, biograf – cinema
björn – bear
bokhandel – bookshop
bro – bridge
bruk – factory
bryggeri – brewery
buss – bus
busshållplats – bus stop
butik – shop
båt – boat

campingplats – camping ground
centrum – town centre
cykel – bicycle

dag – day
dagens rätt – daily special, usually only on lunchtime menus
dal – valley
diskotek – discotheque
domkyrka – cathedral
drottning – queen
dubbelrum – double room
dusch – shower
dygn – a 24-hour period
dygnet runt – around the clock
dygnskort – a daily transport pass, valid for 24 hours

ej – not
enkelrum – single room
etage – floor, storey
expedition – office

fabrik – factory
fall – waterfall
fest – party, festival
fjäll – mountain
fjällstation – mountain lodge
fjällstugor – mountain huts
fjärd – fjord, drowned glacial valley
flod – large river
flyg – aeroplane
flygbuss – airport bus
flygplats – airport
folkdräkt – folk dress
folkhemmet – welfare state
friluft – open-air
frukost – breakfast
fyr – lighthouse
fågel – bird
färja – ferry
färjeläge – ferry quay
fästning – fort, fortress
förbjuden – forbidden, prohibited
förbund – organisation, association
förening – club, association
förlag – company

galleri, galleria – shopping mall
gamla – old
gamla staden, gamla sta'n – the 'old town', the historical part of a city or town

321

gatan – street (often abbreviated to just **g**)
gatukök – literally 'street kitchen'; street kiosk/stall/grill selling fast food
glaciär – glacier
grotta – grotto, cave
grundskolan – comprehensive school
gruva – mine
gränsen – border
gymnasieskolan – upper secondary school
gård – farm
gästgiveri – guesthouse
gästhamn – 'guest harbour', where visiting yachts can berth; cooking and washing facilities usually available
gästhem, gästhus – guesthouse

hamn – harbour
hav – sea
hembygdsgård – open-air museum, usually old farmhouse buildings
hemslöjd – handicraft
hiss – lift, elevator
hittegods – lost property
hotell – hotel
hund – dog
hus – house, sometimes meaning castle
husmanskost – homely Swedish fare, what you would expect cooked at home when you were a (Swedish) kid
hytt – cabin on a boat
hällristningar – rock carvings
hälsocentral – health clinic
höst – autumn

i – in
i morgon – tomorrow
idrottsplats – sports venue, stadium
inte – not
is – ice
ishall – ice hockey stadium

joik – see *yoik*
jul – Christmas
järnvägsstation – train station

kaj – quay
kanot – canoe
kanotuthyrning – canoe hire
kart – map
Kartförlaget – State Mapping Agency (sales division)
klockan – o'clock, the time
klocktorn – bell tower
kloster – monastery
kommun – municipality

konditori – baker and confectioner (often with an attached café)
konst – art
kontor – office
kort – card
kreditkort – credit card
krog – pub, restaurant (or both)
krona (sg), kronor (pl) – the Swedish currency unit
kulle (sg), kullar (pl) – hill
kung – king
kust – coast
kväll – evening
kyrka – church
kyrkogård – graveyard
kåta – tepee-shaped Sami hut
källare – cellar, vault
kök – kitchen

lagom – sufficient, just right
landskap – region, province, landscape
lasarett – hospital
lavin – avalanche
lilla – lesser, little
linbana – chairlift
lo – lynx
loppis – second-hand goods (usually junk)
län – county
länstrafiken – public transport network of a *län*

magasin – store (usually a department store)
mat – food
medlem – member
Midsommar – Midsummer; first Saturday after 21 June (Midsummer Eve is when the real celebrations take place)
miljö – environment, atmosphere
morgon – morning (but *i morgon* means tomorrow)
museet – museum
mynt – coins
mynt tvätt – coin-operated laundry (rare in Sweden)
målning – painting, artwork

natt – night
nattklubb – nightclub
naturcamping – camping site with a pleasant environment
naturistcamping – nudist colony
naturreservat – nature reserve
Naturum – national park or nature reserve visitor centre

Naturvårdsverket – Swedish Environmental Protection Agency (National Parks Authority)
nedre – lower
norr – north
norrsken – aurora borealis (northern lights)
ny – new
nyheter – news
näs – headland

och – and

palats – palace
pendeltåg – local train
pensionat – pension, guesthouse
P-hus – multistorey car park
polarcirkeln – Arctic Circle, latitude 66°32' N
polis – police
post – post office
pris, prislista – price, pricelist
på – on, in
pågatåg – local train
påsk – Easter

raukar – limestone formations
resebyrå – travel agent
restaurang – restaurant
riksdag – parliament
rum – room
rådhus – town hall
rökning förbjuden – no smoking

simhall – swimming pool
sjukhus – hospital
självbetjäning – self-service
sjö – lake, sea
skog – forest
skål! – cheers!
skärgård – archipelago
slott – castle, manor house
smörgås – sandwich
smörgåsbord – Swedish cold table (buffet)
snabbtvätt – quick wash (at laundrette)
snö – snow
sommar – summer
sovsal – dormitory
spark – kicksledge
spårvagn – tram
stark – strong
statsminister – prime minister
stor, stora – big, large
stortorget – main square
strand – beach

stuga (sg), stugor/na – hut, chale
stugby – chalet park; a little village of chalets for tourists
städning – room cleaning
sund – sound
Sverige – Sweden
svensk – Swedish
Systembolaget – a state-owned liquor store
säng – bed
söder – south

tandläkare – dentist
teater – theatre
telefon kort – telephone card
tid – time
tidtabell – timetable
toalett – toilet
torg, torget – town square
torn – tower
trappe – stairs
trädgård – garden open to the public
tull – customs
tunnelbana, T-bana – underground railway, metro
turistbyrå – tourist office
tåg – train
tågplus – combined train and bus ticket
tält – tent

uteservering – outdoor eating area
uthyrningsfirma – hire company

vandrarhem – hostel
vattenfall – waterfall
vecka – week
vik – bay, inlet
vinter – winter
vuxen – adult
vår – spring
vårdcentral – hospital
väg – road
vänthall, väntrum, väntsal – waiting room
värdekort – value card; a travel pass that can be topped up at any time
värdshus – inn
väst – west (abbreviated to **v**)
västra – western
växel – switchboard, money exchange

wärdshus – inn

yoik – Sami 'Song of the Plains' (also referred to as *joik*)

å – stream, creek river
år – year

älg – elk
älv – river

ö – island
öl – beer
öppettider – opening hours
öst – east (abbreviated to ö)
östra – eastern
övre – upper

Abbreviations
AB – aktie bolaget (company)
ank – arrives, arrivals
avg – departs, departures
exkl – excluded

fr o m – from and including (on timetables)
Gbg – Gothenburg
inkl – included
MOMS – value added tax (sales tax)
M/S – motorised sailing vessel
obs! – take note, important
RFSL – Riksförbundet för Sexuellt Lika-berättigande (national gay organisation)
SAS – Scandinavian Airlines Systems
SJ – Statens Järnväg (Swedish Railways)
STF – Svenska Turistföreningen (Swedish Touring Association)
Sthlm – Stockholm
t o m – until and including

Date abbreviations:
e.Kr. – efter Kristus (AD)
f.Kr. – före Kristus (BC)

Thanks

Many thanks to the travellers who used the last edition and wrote to us with helpful hints, useful advice and interesting anecdotes:

Florian Allwein, Monica Andersson, Jeffry Angermann, Glenn Ashenden, Andrei Avram, Ray Baker, Paul Bakker, Christian Bertell, Irja Bjaringtoft, Tracy Bowman, Michael Brant, Chris Burin, Eric Carlson, Steve Carter, Claire Chambers, Sener Chatterjee, Sutapa Choudhury, Martin Conradsson, Karen Cooper, Ron Deacon, Chris Detmar, Sara Dupressoir, Robert Edmunds, Paul Eng, Stephanie Euler, Eva Fairnell, Megan Felton, Marcelo Gameiro de Moura, Jakob Gawlik, Sophie Goodrick, Phyllis Grant, Emm Hamilton, Lars Hoglund, Goran Hult, Darcy Hurford, Linus Ingulfson, Max Kamenetsky, Silke Kampowski, Erki Kurrikoff, Kurtis Kurt, Jane Liljedahl, Bjoern Lindroth, Johan Martens, John McKenzie, Brian Meegan, Matt Moore, Sofia Nilsson, Annica Nordlund, Mark Nutall, Andre Odeblom, Tuija Paukkunen, Jeff Philliskirk, Ramu Pyreddy, Frank Renold, Nat Robbins, Carl & Michelle Roe, Guy Ron, David Rutter, Sanjiv Sachdev, Stefan Samuelsson, Salvador Sanchez, Will Sanders, Barry and Birgitta Shay, Jason Shumate, Christian Sitta, David Slater, Mary-Louise Sloan, Kathleen Smith, Andy Stock, Jerker Svantesson, Martin Torres, Peter J Towey, Naylora Troster, Adrian Tschaeppeler, Fredrik Tukk, Marianne Undberg, Stefan vanwildemeersch, Martin von Bromssen, Henrik Waldenstrom, Tanja Walinschus

LONELY PLANET

Guides by Region

L onely Planet is known worldwide for publishing practical, reliable and no-nonsense travel information in our guides and on our Web site. The Lonely Planet list covers just about every accessible part of the world. Currently there are 16 series: Travel guides, Shoestring guides, Condensed guides, Phrasebooks, Read This First, Healthy Travel, Walking guides, Cycling guides, Watching Wildlife guides, Pisces Diving & Snorkeling guides, City Maps, Road Atlases, Out to Eat, World Food, Journeys travel literature and Pictorials.

AFRICA Africa on a shoestring • Botswana • Cairo • Cairo City Map • Cape Town • Cape Town City Map • East Africa • Egypt • Egyptian Arabic phrasebook • Ethiopia, Eritrea & Djibouti • Ethiopian Amharic phrasebook • The Gambia & Senegal • Healthy Travel Africa • Kenya • Malawi • Morocco • Moroccan Arabic phrasebook • Mozambique • Namibia • Read This First: Africa • South Africa, Lesotho & Swaziland • Southern Africa • Southern Africa Road Atlas • Swahili phrasebook • Tanzania, Zanzibar & Pemba • Trekking in East Africa • Tunisia • Watching Wildlife East Africa • Watching Wildlife Southern Africa • West Africa • World Food Morocco • Zambia • Zimbabwe, Botswana & Namibia
Travel Literature: Mali Blues: Traveling to an African Beat • The Rainbird: A Central African Journey • Songs to an African Sunset: A Zimbabwean Story

AUSTRALIA & THE PACIFIC Aboriginal Australia & the Torres Strait Islands •Auckland • Australia • Australian phrasebook • Australia Road Atlas • Cycling Australia • Cycling New Zealand • Fiji • Fijian phrasebook • Healthy Travel Australia, NZ & the Pacific • Islands of Australia's Great Barrier Reef • Melbourne • Melbourne City Map • Micronesia • New Caledonia • New South Wales • New Zealand • Northern Territory • Outback Australia • Out to Eat – Melbourne • Out to Eat – Sydney • Papua New Guinea • Pidgin phrasebook • Queensland • Rarotonga & the Cook Islands • Samoa • Solomon Islands • South Australia • South Pacific • South Pacific phrasebook • Sydney • Sydney City Map • Sydney Condensed • Tahiti & French Polynesia • Tasmania • Tonga • Tramping in New Zealand • Vanuatu • Victoria • Walking in Australia • Watching Wildlife Australia • Western Australia
Travel Literature: Islands in the Clouds: Travels in the Highlands of New Guinea • Kiwi Tracks: A New Zealand Journey • Sean & David's Long Drive

CENTRAL AMERICA & THE CARIBBEAN Bahamas, Turks & Caicos • Baja California • Belize, Guatemala & Yucatán • Bermuda • Central America on a shoestring • Costa Rica • Costa Rica Spanish phrasebook • Cuba • Cycling Cuba • Dominican Republic & Haiti • Eastern Caribbean • Guatemala • Havana • Healthy Travel Central & South America • Jamaica • Mexico • Mexico City • Panama • Puerto Rico • Read This First: Central & South America • Virgin Islands • World Food Caribbean • World Food Mexico • Yucatán
Travel Literature: Green Dreams: Travels in Central America

EUROPE Amsterdam • Amsterdam City Map • Amsterdam Condensed • Andalucía • Athens • Austria • Baltic States phrasebook • Barcelona • Barcelona City Map • Belgium & Luxembourg • Berlin • Berlin City Map • Britain • British phrasebook • Brussels, Bruges & Antwerp • Brussels City Map • Budapest • Budapest City Map • Canary Islands • Catalunya & the Costa Brava • Central Europe • Central Europe phrasebook • Copenhagen • Corfu & the Ionians • Corsica • Crete • Crete Condensed • Croatia • Cycling Britain • Cycling France • Cyprus • Czech & Slovak Republics • Czech phrasebook • Denmark • Dublin • Dublin City Map • Dublin Condensed • Eastern Europe • Eastern Europe phrasebook • Edinburgh • Edinburgh City Map • England • Estonia, Latvia & Lithuania • Europe on a shoestring • Europe phrasebook • Finland • Florence • Florence City Map • France • Frankfurt City Map • Frankfurt Condensed • French phrasebook • Georgia, Armenia & Azerbaijan • Germany • German phrasebook • Greece • Greek Islands • Greek phrasebook • Hungary • Iceland, Greenland & the Faroe Islands • Ireland • Italian phrasebook • Italy • Kraków • Lisbon • The Loire • London • London City Map • London Condensed • Madrid • Madrid City Map • Malta • Mediterranean Europe • Milan, Turin & Genoa • Moscow • Munich • Netherlands • Normandy • Norway • Out to Eat – London • Out to Eat – Paris • Paris • Paris City Map • Paris Condensed • Poland • Polish phrasebook • Portugal • Portuguese phrasebook • Prague • Prague City Map • Provence & the Côte d'Azur • Read This First: Europe • Rhodes & the Dodecanese • Romania & Moldova • Rome • Rome City Map • Rome Condensed • Russia, Ukraine & Belarus • Russian phrasebook • Scandinavian & Baltic Europe • Scandinavian phrasebook • Scotland • Sicily • Slovenia • South-West France • Spain • Spanish phrasebook • Stockholm • St Petersburg • St Petersburg City Map • Sweden • Switzerland • Tuscany • Ukrainian phrasebook • Venice • Vienna • Wales • Walking in Britain • Walking in France • Walking in Ireland • Walking in Italy • Walking in Scotland • Walking in Spain • Walking in Switzerland • Western Europe • World Food France • World Food Greece • World Food Ireland • World Food Italy • World Food Spain **Travel Literature:** After Yugoslavia • Love and War in the Apennines • The Olive Grove: Travels in Greece • On the Shores of the Mediterranean • Round Ireland in Low Gear • A Small Place in Italy

LONELY PLANET

Mail Order

Lonely Planet products are distributed worldwide.They are also available by mail order from Lonely Planet, so if you have difficulty finding a title please write to us. North and South American residents should write to 150 Linden St, Oakland, CA 94607, USA; European and African residents should write to 10a Spring Place, London NW5 3BH, UK; and residents of other countries to Locked Bag 1, Footscray, Victoria 3011, Australia.

INDIAN SUBCONTINENT & THE INDIAN OCEAN Bangladesh • Bengali phrasebook • Bhutan • Delhi • Goa • Healthy Travel Asia & India • Hindi & Urdu phrasebook • India • India & Bangladesh City Map • Indian Himalaya • Karakoram Highway • Kathmandu City Map • Kerala • Madagascar • Maldives • Mauritius, Réunion & Seychelles • Mumbai (Bombay) • Nepal • Nepali phrasebook • North India • Pakistan • Rajasthan • Read This First: Asia & India • South India • Sri Lanka • Sri Lanka phrasebook • Tibet • Tibetan phrasebook • Trekking in the Indian Himalaya • Trekking in the Karakoram & Hindukush • Trekking in the Nepal Himalaya • World Food India **Travel Literature**: The Age of Kali: Indian Travels and Encounters • Hello Goodnight: A Life of Goa • In Rajasthan • Maverick in Madagascar • A Season in Heaven: True Tales from the Road to Kathmandu • Shopping for Buddhas • A Short Walk in the Hindu Kush • Slowly Down the Ganges

MIDDLE EAST & CENTRAL ASIA Bahrain, Kuwait & Qatar • Central Asia • Central Asia phrasebook • Dubai • Farsi (Persian) phrasebook • Hebrew phrasebook • Iran • Israel & the Palestinian Territories • Istanbul • Istanbul City Map • Istanbul to Cairo • Istanbul to Kathmandu • Jerusalem • Jerusalem City Map • Jordan • Lebanon • Middle East • Oman & the United Arab Emirates • Syria • Turkey • Turkish phrasebook • World Food Turkey • Yemen **Travel Literature**: Black on Black: Iran Revisited • Breaking Ranks: Turbulent Travels in the Promised Land • The Gates of Damascus • Kingdom of the Film Stars: Journey into Jordan

NORTH AMERICA Alaska • Boston • Boston City Map • Boston Condensed • British Columbia • California & Nevada • California Condensed • Canada • Chicago • Chicago City Map • Chicago Condensed • Florida • Georgia & the Carolinas • Great Lakes • Hawaii • Hiking in Alaska • Hiking in the USA • Honolulu & Oahu City Map • Las Vegas • Los Angeles • Los Angeles City Map • Louisiana & the Deep South • Miami • Miami City Map • Montreal • New England • New Orleans • New Orleans City Map • New York City • New York City City Map • New York City Condensed • New York, New Jersey & Pennsylvania • Oahu • Out to Eat – San Francisco • Pacific Northwest • Rocky Mountains • San Diego & Tijuana • San Francisco • San Francisco City Map • Seattle • Seattle City Map • Southwest • Texas • Toronto • USA • USA phrasebook • Vancouver • Vancouver City Map • Virginia & the Capital Region • Washington, DC • Washington, DC City Map • World Food New Orleans **Travel Literature**: Caught Inside: A Surfer's Year on the California Coast • Drive Thru America

NORTH-EAST ASIA Beijing • Beijing City Map • Cantonese phrasebook • China • Hiking in Japan • Hong Kong & Macau • Hong Kong City Map • Hong Kong Condensed • Japan • Japanese phrasebook • Korea • Korean phrasebook • Kyoto • Mandarin phrasebook • Mongolia • Mongolian phrasebook • Seoul • Shanghai • South-West China • Taiwan • Tokyo • Tokyo Condensed • World Food Hong Kong • World Food Japan **Travel Literature**: In Xanadu: A Quest • Lost Japan

SOUTH AMERICA Argentina, Uruguay & Paraguay • Bolivia • Brazil • Brazilian phrasebook • Buenos Aires • Buenos Aires City Map • Chile & Easter Island • Colombia • Ecuador & the Galapagos Islands • Healthy Travel Central & South America • Latin American Spanish phrasebook • Peru • Quechua phrasebook • Read This First: Central & South America • Rio de Janeiro • Rio de Janeiro City Map • Santiago de Chile • South America on a shoestring • Trekking in the Patagonian Andes • Venezuela **Travel Literature**: Full Circle: A South American Journey

SOUTH-EAST ASIA Bali & Lombok • Bangkok • Bangkok City Map • Burmese phrasebook • Cambodia • Cycling Vietnam, Laos & Cambodia • East Timor phrasebook • Hanoi • Healthy Travel Asia & India • Hill Tribes phrasebook • Ho Chi Minh City (Saigon) • Indonesia • Indonesian phrasebook • Indonesia's Eastern Islands • Java • Lao phrasebook • Laos • Malay phrasebook • Malaysia, Singapore & Brunei • Myanmar (Burma) • Philippines • Pilipino (Tagalog) phrasebook • Read This First: Asia & India • Singapore • Singapore City Map • South-East Asia on a shoestring • South-East Asia phrasebook • Thailand • Thailand's Islands & Beaches • Thailand, Vietnam, Laos & Cambodia Road Atlas • Thai phrasebook • Vietnam • Vietnamese phrasebook • World Food Indonesia • World Food Thailand • World Food Vietnam

ALSO AVAILABLE: Antarctica • The Arctic • The Blue Man: Tales of Travel, Love and Coffee • Brief Encounters: Stories of Love, Sex & Travel • Buddhist Stupas in Asia: The Shape of Perfection • Chasing Rickshaws • The Last Grain Race • Lonely Planet ... On the Edge: Adventurous Escapades from Around the World • Lonely Planet Unpacked • Lonely Planet Unpacked Again • Not the Only Planet: Science Fiction Travel Stories • Ports of Call: A Journey by Sea • Sacred India • Travel Photography: A Guide to Taking Better Pictures • Travel with Children • Tuvalu: Portrait of an Island Nation

LONELY PLANET

You already know that Lonely Planet produces more than this one guidebook, but you might not be aware of the other products we have on this region. Here is a selection of titles that you may want to check out as well:

Stockholm
ISBN 1 74059 011 2
US$14.99 • UK£8.99

Scandinavian Phrasebook
ISBN 1 86450 225 8
US$7.99 • UK£4.50

**Summer Light:
A Walk Across Norway**
ISBN 1 86450 347 5
US$12.99 • UK£6.99

Copenhagen
ISBN 1 86450 203 7
US$14.99 • UK£8.99

Denmark
ISBN 1 74059 075 9
US$17.99 • UK£12.99

**Iceland Greenland & the
Faroe Islands**
ISBN 0 86442 686 0
US$19.99 • UK£12.99

Norway
ISBN 1 74059 200 X
US$19.99 • UK£11.99

Europe on a Shoestring
ISBN 1 74059 314 6
US$24.99 • UK£14.99

Scandinavian Europe
ISBN 1 74059 318 9
US$24.99 • UK£14.99

Finland
ISBN 1 74059 076 7
US$21.99 • UK£13.99

**Available wherever books
are sold**

Index

Text

Note: the letters å, ä and ö fall at the end of the Swedish alphabet, and the letters v and w are often used interchangeably.

Bold indicates maps.

Note: the letters å, ä and ö fall at the end of the Swedish alphabet, and the letters v and w are often used interchangeably.

Bold indicates maps.

Boxed Text

MAP LEGEND

CITY ROUTES

Freeway .... Freeway
Highway .... Primary Road
Road .... Secondary Road
Street .... Street
Lane .... Lane
.... On/Off Ramp
===== .... Unsealed Road
.... One Way Street
.... Pedestrian Street
.... Stepped Street
)=== .... Tunnel
.... Footbridge

HYDROGRAPHY

.... River, Creek
.... Canal
.... Lake
.... Flow direction
.... Spring; Rapids
.... Waterfalls

REGIONAL ROUTES

.... Tollway, Freeway
.... Primary Road
.... Secondary Road
.... Minor Road

TRANSPORT ROUTES & STATIONS

.......O... .... Train
.... Underground Train
.......M... .... Metro
.... Tramway
Cable Car, Chairlift

----□ .... Ferry
.... Walking Tour
----- .... Walking Trail
---- .... Cycling Trail
.... Path

BOUNDARIES

.... International
.... State
.... Disputed
.... Fortified Wall

AREA FEATURES

.... Building
.... Park, Gardens
.... Market
.... Sports Ground
.... Beach
.... Cemetery
.... Campus
.... Plaza

POPULATION SYMBOLS

○ **CAPITAL** .... National Capital
◉ **CAPITAL** .... State Capital
● **CITY** .... City
● **Town** .... Town
● Village .... Village
.... Urban Area

MAP SYMBOLS

▪ .... Place to Stay
▼ .... Place to Eat
● .... Point of Interest

✈ .... Airport	⊞ ⊡ .... Church	⚲ .... Monument	⊡ .... Pub or Bar
▣ .... Archaelogical Site	⊞ .... Cinema	▲ .... Mountain	⊠ ... Shopping Centre
⊖ .... Bank	⊡ .... Embassy	🏛 .... Museum	⚡ .... Ski Field
⊡⊡ .. Bus Stop; Terminal	⚓ .... Fountain	⊡ .... National Park	⊠ ...... Swimming Pool
⊡ .... Camping Ground	⊕ .... Hospital	⊡ .... Parking	⊡ .... Theatre
⊡ .... Castle	⊡ .... Internet Cafe	⊡ .... Police Station	❶ .. Tourist Information
⌂ .... Cave	⚱ .... Lighthouse	⊡ .... Post Office	🔲 .... Zoo

Note: not all symbols displayed above appear in this book

LONELY PLANET OFFICES

Australia
Locked Bag 1, Footscray, Victoria 3011
☎ 03 8379 8000 fax 03 8379 8111
email: talk2us@lonelyplanet.com.au

USA
150 Linden St, Oakland, CA 94607
☎ 510 893 8555 TOLL FREE: 800 275 8555
fax 510 893 8572
email: info@lonelyplanet.com

UK
10a Spring Place, London NW5 3BH
☎ 020 7428 4800 fax 020 7428 4828
email: go@lonelyplanet.co.uk

France
1 rue du Dahomey, 75011 Paris
☎ 01 55 25 33 00 fax 01 55 25 33 01
email: bip@lonelyplanet.fr
www.lonelyplanet.fr

World Wide Web: www.lonelyplanet.com *or* AOL keyword: lp
Lonely Planet Images: www.lonelyplanetimages.com